Modern India
1885–1947

Modern India
1885–1947

SUMIT SARKAR

Pearson

Associate Editor–Acquisitions: Moutushi Mukherjee
Editor–Production: Nikhil Rakshit

Copyright © 2014 Dorling Kindersley (India) Pvt. Ltd.

This book is sold subject to the condition that it shall not, by way of trade or otherwise, be lent, resold, hired out, or otherwise circulated without the publisher's prior written consent in any form of binding or cover other than that in which it is published and without a similar condition including this condition being imposed on the subsequent purchaser and without limiting the rights under copyright reserved above, no part of this publication may be reproduced, stored in or introduced into a retrieval system, or transmitted in any form or by any means (electronic, mechanical, photocopying, recording or otherwise), without the prior written permission of both the copyright owner and the above-mentioned publisher of this book.

Although the author and publisher have made every effort to ensure that the information in this book was correct at the time of editing and printing, the author and publisher do not assume and hereby disclaim any liability to any party for any loss or damage arising out of the use of this book caused by errors or omissions, whether such errors or omissions result from negligence, accident or any other cause. Further, names, pictures, images, characters, businesses, places, events and incidents are either the products of the author's imagination or used in a fictitious manner. Any resemblance to actual persons, living or dead or actual events is purely coincidental and do not intend to hurt sentiments of any individual, community, sect or religion.

In case of binding mistake, misprints or missing pages etc., the publisher's entire liability and your exclusive remedy is replacement of this book within reasonable time of purchase by similar edition/reprint of the book.

ISBN: 978-93-325-3574-9

First Impression, 2014
Thireenth Impression, 2021
Fiffteenth Impression, 2022

Published by Pearson India Education Services Pvt. Ltd, CIN: U72200TN2005PTC057128.

Head Office: 15th Floor, Tower-B, World Trade Tower, Plot No. 1, Block-C, Sector 16, Noida 201 301, Uttar Pradesh, India.
Registered Office: 7th Floor, SDB2, ODC 7, 8 & 9, Survey No.01 ELCOT IT/ ITES SEZ, Sholinganallur, Chennai – 600119, Tamil Nadu, India.
Website: in.pearson.com, Email: companysecretary.india@pearson.com

Compositor: Content Management Team India
Printed in India at Saurabh Printers Pvt. Ltd.

To Tanika

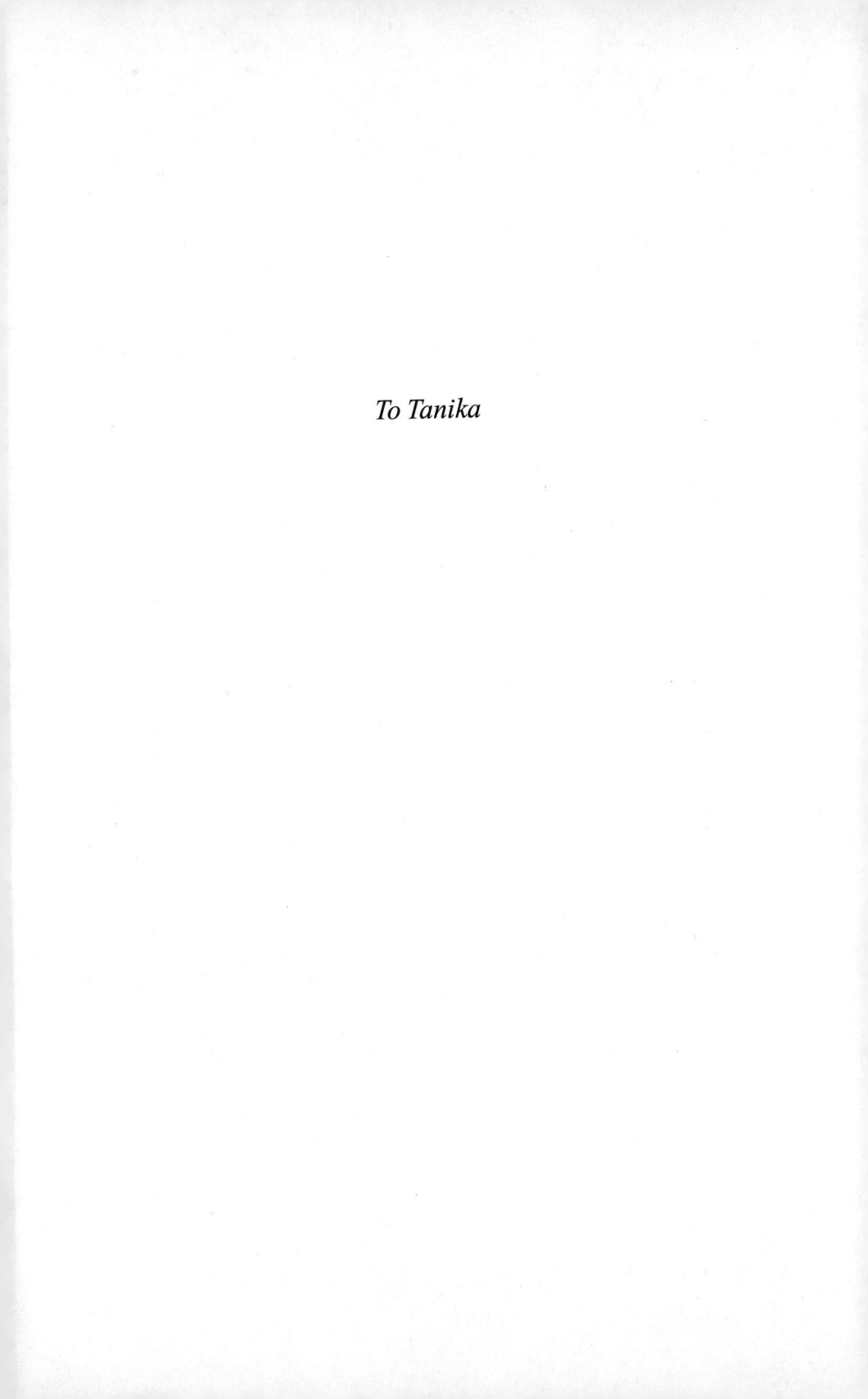

CONTENTS

Preface　*xiii*

Abbreviations　*xv*

CHAPTER 1　**Introduction**　1
　　Change and Continuity
　　Old and New Approaches　4

CHAPTER 2　**Political and Economic Structure: 1885–1905**　11
　　Imperial Structure and Policies　11
　　　Viceregal Attitudes　12
　　　Foreign Policy　13
　　　Army　14
　　　Financial and Administrative Pressures　15
　　　Local Self-Government and Council Reform　17
　　　Divide and Rule　18
　　　White Racism　19
　　The Colonial Economy　21
　　　Drain of Wealth　22
　　　Deindustrialization　25
　　　Commercialization of Agriculture　27
　　　Land Relations　29
　　　Agricultural Production　31
　　　Foreign Capital　32
　　　Indian Capitalist Development　33

CHAPTER 3　**Social and Political Movements: 1885–1905**　37
　　Towards a 'History from Below'　37
　　　Tribal Movements　38
　　　Phadke　41
　　　Moplahs　42
　　　Deccan Riots　43
　　　Pabna　44
　　　No-Revenue Movements　45
　　　Caste Consciousness　47
　　　Communal Consciousness　50
　　　Labour　52

	Business Groups and Upper Classes	54
	Princes and Zamindars	55
	'Middle-Class' Consciousness and Politics	56
	Social Roots of the Intelligentsia	56
	Hindu Reform and Revival	60
	Trends in Indian Islam	65
	Patriotism in Literature	70
	Nationalist Economic Theory	73
	Foundations of the Congress	75
	The Moderate Congress: Objectives and Methods	76
	Phases of Moderate Politics	79
	Roots of Extremism	82
CHAPTER 4	**Political and Social Movements: 1905–1917**	**87**
	The Viceroyalty of Curzon	87
	Foreign Policy	87
	Administrative Reforms	88
	Curzon and Nationalists	90
	Partition of Bengal	91
	The Swadeshi Movement in Bengal: 1905–1908	96
	Trends	97
	Boycott and Swadeshi	99
	National Education	101
	Labour Unrest	101
	Samitis	103
	Hindu-Muslim Relations	104
	The Shift to Terrorism	106
	Extremism in other Provinces: 1905–1908	107
	Punjab	109
	Madras	111
	Marashatrja	113
	The Congress Split	116
	Repression, Conciliation, and Divide and Rule: 1909–1914	118
	Morley and Minto	118
	Simla Deputation and Muslim League	120
	Revolutionary Terrorism	124
	War and Indian Politics	126
	Revolutionary Activities	126
	Unity at Lucknow	128
	Home Rule Agitation	129
	Movements from Below: 1905–1917	131
	Tribal Revolts	131
	Peasant Movements	133

Communalism	134
Caste Movements	135
Regional Sentiments and Languages	139

Chapter 5 Mass Nationalism: Emergence and Problems: 1917–1927 — 143

War, Reforms and Society	143
The Montford Reforms	143
Impact of the War	146
Mahatma Gandhi	154
The Appeal of Gandhi	154
The Role of Rumour	157
Champaran, Kheda, Ahmedabad	158
Rowlatt Satyagraha	162
1919–1920: Leaders and Masses	168
Gandhi, Khilafat and the Congress	168
Pressures from Below	171
1921–1922: Non-Cooperation and Khilafat	176
The All-India Movement	176
Social Composition	178
Regional Variations	181
Chauri-Chaura	193
1922–1927: Decline and Fragmentation	195
No-Changers and Swarajists	195
Nagpur, Borsad and Vaikom	196
Constructive Work	197
Swarajist Politics	199
Communalism	201
Emergence of New Forces: 1922–1927	204
Political and Economic Tensions	204
Tribal and Peasant Movements	206
Caste Movements	208
Labour	210
Emergence of the Communists	212
Revolutionary Terrorism	215
Subhas and Jawaharlal	217

Chapter 6 Nationalist Advance and Economic Depression: 1927–1937 — 219

An Overview	219
Cross-Currents in Politics	219
Depression and India	222
1928–1929: Simon Boycott and Labour Upsurge	225

Simon Commission and Nehru Report	225
Youth Movements	229
The H.S.R.A.	230
Labour Upsurge and the Communists	232
Peasant Movements and Bardoli	236
Business Attitudes	240
From Dominion Status to *Purna Swaraj*	242
1930–1931: Civil Disobedience	244
Towards Salt *Satyagraha*	244
Chittagong, Peshawar, Sholapur	246
Phases of Civil Disobedience	248
Regional Studies	255
The Round Table Conference	264
Gandhi–Irwin Pact	266
March–December 1931: Uneasy Truce	267
Ambiguities	267
Pressures from Below	270
Official Attitudes	273
1932–1934: Second Civil Disobedience Movement	275
Repression and Resistance	275
Business Realignments	279
Harijan Campaign	281
Return to Council Politics	283
The Left Alternative	284
1935–1937: The Constitution and The Congress	288
The 1935 Act	288
Labour and *Kisan* Movements	290
Leftism in Literature	293
Lucknow and Faizpur	294
Right Consolidation and Business Pressures	295

Chapter 7   Political Movements and War: 1937–1945   299

1937–1939: The Congress-Ministries	299
Elections and Ministry-Making	299
Congress and Bureaucracy	301
The Communal Problem	302
Gandhian Reforms	306
Capitalists and Congress	306
Congress and Labour	309
Congress and *Kisans*	310
States Peoples Movement	313
The Left in the Congress	316
The Tripuri Crisis	318
1939–1942: War and Indian Politics—	
The First Phase	321

Bureaucratic Counter-Offensive	321
League and Pakistan	323
Trends within the Congress	325
Economic Consequences	328
The New Phase of the War	328
Cripps Mission	329
1942–1945: Quit India, Famine, and the Last Phase of War	332
Roots of Rebellion	332
The All-India Pattern	337
Social Composition	339
Regional Variations	341
Aftermath of Revolt	345
The War and the Indian Economy: Famine and Super-Profits	346
The Advance of the League	349
Azad Hind	350
Communists and People's War	351

CHAPTER 8 Freedom and Partition: 1945–1947 — 355

1945–1946: 'The Edge of A Volcano'	355
Prelude to Negotiations	355
Simla Conference	357
I.N.A. Trials	358
R.I.N. Mutiny	363
1946 (March–August): The Cabinet Mission	365
Elections	365
Cabinet Mission	367
1946–1947: Communal Holocaust and Peasant Rebellion	370
Calcutta, Noakhali, Bihar, Punjab	370
The Mahatma's Finest Hour	374
Tebhaga	376
Punnapra-Vayalar	378
Telengana	379
1947: Freedom and Partition	382
The Mountbatten Plan	383
Integration of States	385
The Fifteenth of August	388

Further Readings List	391
Index	419

PREFACE

Modern India: 1885–1947 was planned some years back as part of a collective attempt to write the history of India in six volumes. Its publication now as an independent work requires a brief justification of its starting point. While 1885 was chosen mainly for convenience, it can be argued that what is recognizably 'modern' India began not with the Mughal break-up or with Plassey, but during the latter half of the nineteenth century. It was during these decades that colonial political and economic domination attained its finished apparently stable form, while its counterpoints had also started developing alike at the level of autonomous popular movements and of 'middle class' or intelligentsia based all-India nationalism. The period with which I deal relates to the subsequent unfolding of these contradictions down to the achievement of independence.

The present work has a twofold aim. It attempts a synthesis of the massive data unearthed in recent years by the flood of monographs on specific problems in political, social and economic history. At the same time it explores, in the light of my own research interests, the possibilities of a 'history from below' as distinct from the usual tendency in the historiography of Indian nationalism to concentrate on the activities, ideals, or factional maneuvers of leaders.

This book would have been inconceivable without the massive research output in modern Indian history during recent years. The format did not permit the usual acknowledgements through footnotes except in the case of direct quotations, but I have tried to honour my debts by lists of Further Readings which appear at the end of the book, arranged chapterwise.

I would like to acknowledge my gratitude to the students of my modern Indian history classes, on whom I have been testing many of the ideas, set out here, for years. Their questions and criticisms have been indispensable in sorting out my formulations.

I am grateful to Barun De, Asok Sen, Amiya Bagchi and Gyan Pandey, for going through the manuscript in whole or in part and offering extremely helpful comments and criticism. I remember with particular gratitude and pleasure a nightlong discussion with Ranajit Guha in Brighton in 1977 which modified many of my ideas at a time when I had just started collecting material for this book. The *Subaltern Studies* series which he was editing unfortunately reached me only after my manuscript went to press.

My father followed the writing of this book with unfailing interest, and it must always remain a matter of deep sorrow to me that I could not show him the finished work. Tanika as always was the source of undiminished criticism and sustenance. Aditya provided a delightful distraction.

I would like to thank my publishers, for prodding a lazy author into completing his manuscript and for indispensable typing and editorial assistance.

The responsibility for errors remains mine alone.

SUMIT SARKAR
Delhi University
October 1982

ABBREVIATIONS

I.O.L.	India Office Library, London
N.A.I.	National Archives of India, New Delhi
N.M.M.L.	Nehru Memorial Museum and Library, New Delhi
W.B.S.A.	West Bengal State Archives
Home Public FN / Home Political FN	Government of India Home Public/Home Political Files (N.A.I.)
A.I.C.C. F.N.	All India Congress Committee Files (N.M.M.L.)
E.P.W.	Economic and Political Weekly
I.E S.H.R.	Indian Economic and Social History Review
I.H.R.	Indian Historical Review
M.A.S.	Modern Asian Studies

CHAPTER 1

INTRODUCTION

CHANGE AND CONTINUITY

The sixty years or so that lie between the foundation of the Indian National Congress in 1885 and the achievement of independence in August 1947 witnessed perhaps the greatest transition in our country's long history. A transition, however, which in many ways remained grievously incomplete, and it is with this central ambiguity that it seems most convenient to begin our survey.

The illusion of permanence held powerful sway over the minds of the British in India in 1885, eight years after the Empire had been proclaimed at a grandiose Durbar held in the midst of famine. An ideology of paternalistic benevolence, occasionally combined with talk of trusteeship and training towards self-government, thinly veiled the realities of a Raj uncompromisingly white and despotic. Political decision-making and administration at higher levels were entirely the privilege of the Europeans, who in the early 1880s manned all but 16 of the 900-odd posts in the Indian Civil Service. The inclusion in 1861 of a handful of nominated 'natives' in Provincial and Supreme Councils had been accompanied by a reduction in the powers of the latter. Even the local self-government introduced with much fanfare by Ripon was essentially no more than a measure of necessary financial decentralization. 'We shall not subvert the British Empire by allowing the Bengali Baboo to discuss his own schools and drains', was the eminently appropriate comment of Finance Member Evelyn Baring. Even the fig-leaf was absent in really vital things like the army, where no Indian would be permitted till 1947 to rise above the rank of a Brigadier.

Indian collaborators were obviously indispensable for the day-to-day running of a huge country. What contributed greatly to British self-confidence was the ease with which such dependent allies seemed obtainable. The post-1857 years had seen the renewal and consolidation of links with princes, *zamindars* and a variety of urban and rural notables, and the 662 Indian native rulers in particular were to remain the most loyal of bulwarks till the very end. Macaulay's vision of an English-educated intelligentsia brown in colour but white in thought and tastes was, it is true, beginning to turn a bit sour by the 1880s. Yet the 'middle class' ambitions which went into the making of provincial associations in Calcutta, Bombay, Poona and Madras and eventually found expression through the Congress were still little more than an irritant. Hume's alarmist pleas for official patronage for Congress as a 'safety valve' to prevent another Mutiny could be dismissed by Dufferin with lofty aristocratic disdain: 'He [Hume] is clever and gentlemanlike, but seems to have got a bee in his bonnet.' (Dufferin to Reay, 17 May 1885)

In 1888, the Viceroy proclaimed Congress to represent no more than a 'microscopic minority' and Sir John Strachey assured Cambridge undergraduates: 'there is not, and never was an India, or even any country of India... no Indian nation, no "people of India" of which we hear so much... that men of the Punjab, Bengal, the North-West Provinces and Madras, should ever feel that they belong to one great Indian nation, is impossible. (*India,* London, 1888) The evident element of propaganda and wishful thinking has to be discounted, but such estimates and predictions did not seem too unrealistic in the 1880s. All-India connections were as yet largely confined to a thin upper crust of English-educated professional groups. Congress demands, put forward in the form of gentlemanly resolutions at staid annual sessions which still eagerly asserted their basic loyalism, could find as yet no resonance amidst the peasant millions, and despite the fairly clear-cut formulation of a perspective of independent capitalist development (which represented by far the greatest contribution of Moderate intellectuals to our nationalism), response from the emerging Indian bourgeoisie was also fairly minimal. Lower-class discontent was inevitably endemic in what had become by the nineteenth century certainly one of the poorest countries in the world, and the ten years or so before 1885 had seen powerful agrarian leagues in east Bengal against *zamindari* excesses, anti-moneylender riots in the Maharashtra Deccan, and a formidable tribal rising in the 'Rampa' region of Andhra. But the edge of such movements tended to be directed against the immediate oppressor rather than the distant British overlord, as when the Pabna peasants in 1873 wanted to become *raiyats* of 'Maharani Victoria' alone. There were ample objective foundations here for divide-and-rule policies, with divisions between communities often interlocking with class tensions: Muslim peasants and Hindu gentry in east Bengal, Moplah Muslim cultivators and Nambudri or Nair caste Hindu landlords in Malabar, Muslim *talukdars* and Hindu tenants in parts of the United Provinces, or Hindu moneylender-merchants and Muslim or Sikh peasants in the Punjab.

Yet the national movement did eventually go far beyond its original elite-intellectual confines. By 1936 the Congress President could legitimately claim that Congress had now 'become the largest organization of the common people drawn very largely from the village population and counting amongst its members lakhs of peasants and cultivators and a sprinkling of industrial and field workers.' The movement expanded in both geographical and social terms in a succession of waves and troughs, the obvious high-points being

1905–1908, 1919–1922, 1928–1934, 1942 and 1945–1946. The focus shifted from Bengal, Maharashtra and Punjab in the Extremist phase to new areas like Gujarat, Bihar, U.P., Central Provinces, and Andhra in the Gandhian, and from city intellectuals to small-town lower middle classes, large sections of the peasantry, and influential bourgeois groups. There was a corresponding evolution of new forms: *swadeshi,* boycott, and passive resistance, Gandhian *satyagraha* and constructive village work, as well as methods often frowned upon by the leaders, yet surely of considerable importance at times—revolutionary terrorism, strikes, outbursts of urban, peasant or tribal violence. By the 1930s, Kisan Sabhas and trade unions were fast becoming a real force in many parts of the country, and popular movements were also emerging in many of the princely states. Despite all the slide-backs, limitations and contradictions, what all this amounted to was the irreversible historical fact of the entry of the masses into active political life. A changed international situation and mass pressure combined to bring about the withdrawal of 1947, barely five years after a British Prime Minister had declared that he had not come to occupy his high post to preside over the liquidation of the Empire. This was followed by the quick elimination of the princely states, the abolition of *zamindari* and the establishment over the major part of the subcontinent of parliamentary democracy based on universal franchise. The underlying social changes had also been considerable, most notably the emergence of a number of rich peasant groups and the consolidation of a bourgeoisie weak and vacillating by the standards of classic capitalist development, yet of considerable strength and maturity if compared to most other countries of the Third World.

But the pattern evidently has been one full of paradoxes, of continuities as much as change. The Congress fought against the Raj, but it was also progressively becoming the Raj, eventually taking over without major change the entire bureaucratic and army structure, the 'heaven-born' civil service and all, merely substituting the brown for the white. Independence Day was replete with contradictions: unforgettable scenes of mass rejoicing, the swearing-in as Prime Minister of a flaming radical of the 1930s by Lord Mountbatten amidst all the pageantry of Empire, and a 'Father of the Nation' who said that he had run dry of messages and who was to spend the last months of his life in a lonely and desperate struggle against communal violence. Riots and Partition represented the most obvious of the failures from the point of view of the ideals of the Indian national movement. Perhaps even more fundamental was the fact that so very many of the aspirations aroused in the course of the national struggle remained unfulfilled—the Gandhian dream of the peasant coming into his own in *Ram-rajya,* as much as Left ideals of social revolution. And as the history of independent India and Pakistan (and Bangladesh) was to repeatedly reveal, even the problems of a complete bourgeois transformation and successful capitalist development were not fully solved by the transfer of power of 1947.

Our major theme must necessarily be the search for the roots of this profoundly ambiguous and contradictory pattern, and the central focus will be provided by the complex and conflicting history of anti-imperialist movements in modern India. As a preliminary, however, a brief glance at the existing state of historical literature on our subject seems called for.

OLD AND NEW APPROACHES

Writing a general history of the last sixty years of British rule has become today both more exciting and far more difficult than ever before, in view of the veritable flood of recent detailed studies particularly on the national movement.[1] Till about a decade back, the available literature consisted of a few studies of Viceroys, works on constitutional developments, a number of biographies of Indian leaders along with their own writings, and some general all-India surveys of the development of nationalism. Published secondary sources formed the basis for the bulk of such writings, as access to official archives was severely limited for recent periods and little systematic search had been made yet for private papers. Despite the obvious differences of approach between Chirol, Sitaramayya, Tarachand or R.C. Majumdar (to mention only a few notable examples), a certain rough consensus seemed to exist here. The basic pattern was of an English-educated 'middle class' reared by British rule, engaging in various renaissance activities, and eventually turning against their masters and so giving birth to modern nationalism—out of frustrated selfish ambitions, ideals of patriotism and democracy derived from Western culture, or natural revulsion against foreign rule, the imputed motive in each case depending on the viewpoint of the scholar. Scholars with imperialist affiliations tended to focus on the continued divisions within Indian society, the limited and sharply fluctuating appeal of even the Gandhian Congress, the Muslim breakaway and Partition. To nationalist historians, on the other hand, the ultimate breakthrough to the masses seemed both impressive and only natural, since potentially the interests of all Indians were surely always opposed to alien domination, and only a charismatic leader had been lacking. It has to be added that as a historiographical trend, nationalist writing on the freedom movement has been on the whole more than a little inadequate. Professional Indian scholars tended to keep away from such themes till the 1950s (preferring to express

---

1. For bibliographical details, see end of book.

their patriotism through the vicarious but safe medium of allegedly national Rajput or Maratha movements against Mughal rule) and regional and communal distortions have been all too obvious at times. In R.C. Majumdar's well-known volumes on the freedom movement, for instance, a veritable cult of the educated Bengali Hindu is combined with a frank acceptance of the two-nation approach. As in some writings on medieval India, Hindus and Muslims are assumed to have been always homogeneous entities naturally opposed to each other—a clear example of the reading back into the past of present-day communal prejudices. But even in more genuinely nationalist history-writing an abstract cult of the people or nation often did not prevent a basically elitist and sometimes quite uncritical glorification of a few great leaders. As for the socio-economic roots and dimensions of the national movement, it was natural for imperialist scholars to fight shy of such themes, but nationalist historians have not been very much better—since with a few exceptions they have seldom tried to integrate into their interpretations of modern Indian history even the findings of nationalist economists of the Naoroji–Dutt generation. Charges of elitism and neglect of the colonial framework certainly cannot be brought against the handful of serious early Marxist works on our period—R.P. Dutt above all, but also M.N. Roy, A.R. Desai and some Soviet scholars. But on the whole these failed to offer a fully satisfactory alternative, being usually over-general and sometimes rather mechanistic in their use of class-analysis.

That our subject wears a new look today (though often in appearance rather than essence, for we shall see many old assumptions lingering on) is due in part to the much greater use of archival material, private papers, as well as of local sources unearthed through field studies. Government archives are now open to scholars for the entire colonial period, rich collections of private papers have been built up in places like New Delhi's Nehru Memorial Museum and Library, and historians are becoming increasingly aware of the value of field studies and interviews. But even more important is the role of new hypotheses, always controversial and at times positively dubious, but still extremely stimulating—and in this field the so-called Cambridge school has been particularly prolific. Anil Seal on early Indian nationalism, the American historian Broomfield on Bengal, and to some extent Judith Brown on the rise of Gandhi, set the fashion of interpreting nationalism in terms of uneven development and competition of provincial, generally caste-based, elites—Bengali *bhadralok,* Chitpavan Brahman, the 'sub-elites' of the Hindi belt or Andhra. The further assumption that patriotism was no more than a rationalization of extremely narrow and selfish material motives like job-frustration created a picture not too different really from that drawn by numerous spokesmen of the Raj and blatant imperialists like Valentine Chirol.

In 1973, however, the Cambridge school announced with some fanfare that the elite approach had fallen down the 'trapdoor of historiography' and that from province and elite one must shift to locality and faction. (Gallagher, Johnson, Seal, eds., *Locality, Province and Nation*) A combination of administrative pressures and opportunities, as the British imposed new burdens and simultaneously sought new collaborators through constitutional reforms, would then allegedly explain the occasional coalescence of local patron-client groups into provincial or even national platforms. As applied most notably by Washbrook and Baker to south India, Bayly to Allahabad, Gordon Johnson to Bombay Moderates and Extremists, and Robinson to U.P. Muslims, this approach has certainly proved quite fruitful in terms of new data.

Yet certain continuities persist between the early and the modified Cambridge approach. With the exception of Bayly, perhaps, the tendency is still to play down the role of ideology and patriotic motivation. Such cynicism is at times a healthy corrective to the hero-worship typical of much nationalist history-writing Yet a logical distinction has to be made between the significance of a set of ideas and the possibly selfish motives which might have led particular individuals to formulate or accept them. Job-frustration may or may not have produced Bankimchandra's patriotic novels; their total impact remains an important historical fact. More significant is the slurring-over of the economic and racist dimensions of the colonial situation. The south Indian 'rural-local bosses' analysed by Washbrook were surely a dependent product of the colonial economy and polity. The statement that the Madras 'Governor and his minions…were distributing among themselves the scraps of the political system' contrasts oddly with the fact that in the early twentieth century the Viceroy had 700 servants and a salary double that of the British Prime Minister. Even in the 1930s, as Gandhi would remind Irwin on the eve of his Dandi March, the Viceroy's salary was 5000 times that of the average Indian, while a white junior Jail Governor of Bengal could afford a round the world trip on a holiday taken soon after shooting down political prisoners at Hijli. (Baker Papers, Cambridge South Asia Study Centre) The new patron-client model seems more than a little over-extended when it is used to describe both Malaviya's connections with the Tandon business group in Allahabad and the relations between Hindu *zamindars* and Muslim peasants of east Bengal. In their equation of politics with factionalism, the Cambridge scholars are modelling themselves on Namier's studies of mid-eighteenth century England. Illuminating for periods of oligarchical politics and bereft of fundamental tensions, such an approach becomes progressively less so when it is a question of analysing major conflicts involving large masses. Namierism tends in fact to by-pass periods of big movements: thus Bayly's otherwise valuable study of Allahabad ends abruptly in 1920. Above all, elitism may persist even when shifted down into the locality: 'The leaders of the movement, that is to say the people who created it, require a careful analysis, for in their ambitions must lie its causes.' (Washbrook, *Emergence of Provincial Politics,* p. 279) Very recently, however, historians like Bayly, Washbrook and Baker seem to be moving away from the study of patrons and factions towards straightforward economic history of considerable value.

It would be very unfortunate if the fame, at times amounting to notoriety, of the 'Cambridge School' is allowed to obscure the considerable work over the last decade of a large number of other historians, both Indian and foreign. Sussex and Canberra–based scholars associated with D.A. Low have been perhaps less prolific or systematic about hypotheses, but considerably more open in their ideas. The collections on the Rowlatt *Satyagraha* and the more recent *Congress and the Raj* have also been refreshingly free of inhibitions concerning the study of periods of mass upsurge. Peasant movements in contrast are often being given pride of place, though the generalization made at times about the role of dominant village groups or rich peasants may or may not be fully acceptable. Imperial policy-making is currently not a very fashionable field, but one must mention here the works of P.S. Gupta on British Labour attitudes to imperialism, R.J. Moore on the vicissitudes of the federal experiment and Peter Robb on the making of dyarchy. American contributions include studies of the Arya Samaj and nationalism in the Punjab, caste politics in south India, peasant movements in Bihar, and recently an excellent study of the early Congress by J.R. McLane. Among the numerous works on social and political trends among Muslims, mention may be made of Aziz Ahmed on Islamic modernism, Ziya-ul Hasan Faruki on Deoband, Peter Hardy's useful general analysis and the recent books of Rafiuddin Ahmed, Mushirul Hasan and Gail Minault. Indian Marxist historians have occasionally reacted to the Cambridge denigration of anti-imperialist movements by taking up a stance rather difficult to distinguish from conventional nationalism. 'Sectarian' and unduly negative estimates of the national leadership, characteristic of R.P. Dutt and some earlier Soviet writings, have been replaced at times by virtual hero-worship of Tilak, Gandhi or Nehru, in an unfortunate oscillation in which one extreme feeds the other. But Marxists have also produced detailed studies of Moderate economic ideology and of political movements in Bengal and Assam, as well as a considerable literature on Left movements. And both Marxist and non-Marxist scholars have been increasingly shifting to real grass-roots studies based on village level data, with historians like David Hardiman, Majid Siddiqi, Kapil Kumar, Gyan Pandey, Stephen Henningham and Hitesh Sanyal exploring Gujarat *patidars,* U.P. *kisans,* Bihar peasants and the rural Gandhian movements of parts of Bengal. What is emerging through such studies is a new emphasis on 'a history from below', distinct from all variations of elite approaches.

Such field-work has the additional advantage of bringing the historian into closer touch with the disciplines of sociology and social-anthropology and, hopefully, stimulating an interaction almost absent in our country so far. Indian anthropology for long was virtually identified with the study of tribal life in isolation; then from the 1950s came the new fashion of studies of caste structures, movements and associations. The modern Indian historian cannot afford to neglect the valuable data collected through such research, though he would be well-advised also to keep in mind Andre Beteille's warning that caste mobility might often represent no more than the upthrust of small groups of notables. 'A sociologist might certainly wonder why we have so many detailed studies of caste associations and so few of peasant organizations', Beteille added in a review of the Rudolphs' influential *Modernity of Tradition. (Indian Economic and Social History Review,* September, 1970)

Social history unfortunately still remains a very neglected subject in India, often being virtually equated with the study of social reform endeavours. Work on the formation of classes and class consciousness is only just beginning, and while the development of vernacular literatures is obviously one of the really crucial features of modern Indian history, there is little sign as yet of such things becoming the subject of scientific historical or sociological research. Written literature in a largely illiterate country, however, can be a guide to the ideas and values only of a minority. A recent French historian has emphasized the need to study also the 'songs, dances, proverbs, tales and pictures of the country folk to win an entry into the peasant mind' (Eugene Weber, *Peasants into Frenchmen*); such methods still await application in India.

Historians of modern India, finally, require major sustenance from economists, though here a problem is created by the ill-concealed contempt for economic history displayed at times by the more formalist and mathematically-minded contemporary practitioners of the latter discipline. For an understanding of the over-all working of the colonial economy, we often still have to turn to the nationalist economists of the turn of the century (supplemented in the 1930s by Buchanan and D.R. Gadgil and in the 1940s by R.P. Dutt), even though their work, path-breaking for their own time, appear more than a little dated and unsophisticated today. Historians for their part have done considerable work on eighteenth and nineteenth century trade, finance, revenue policies and agrarian relations, but relatively less on the post-1900 period, where some amount of technical training in economics becomes increasingly useful in the face of mounting complexities and statistical data. How valuable the contribution of economists can be has been amply indicated by the essays of the Thorners, George Blyn's study of agricultural productivity, Amiya Bagchi's analysis of colonial constraints on indigenous private investment in India, as well as by numerous research papers in the pages of the *Economic and Political Weekly* and the *Indian Economic and Social History Review*.

The sudden expansion of research on modern India over the last decade has made existing textbooks and general studies seriously out-of-date. Something like a synthesis, however, provisional or incomplete, of this wealth of new material has become essential, and that is the main purpose of this volume. While based in the main on available published books and papers, I have at times attempted to fill some of the gaps in data or methods through independent research. No historian can be free of bias, and unstated or unconscious bias is the most dangerous of all; it is best therefore to baldly state at this point my principal assumptions. First, I consider colonial exploitation and the struggle against it to be the central theme of the years I am trying to survey. At the same time, I feel that it would be quite inaccurate and misleading to ignore, as nationalist historiography has often tried to do, the many internal tensions within Indian society. Thirdly, while factional squabbles certainly form a part of our story, underlying class-tensions tended to be much more decisive in the long run—though class and class-consciousness are analytical tools which have to be used more skillfully and flexibly than has sometimes been the case. Finally, and above all, my basic quarrel with conventional nationalist, communalist, Cambridge, and even some Marxist historiography is that despite all their obvious mutual opposition, they have tended to share a common elitist approach. But anti-imperialism in our country, I believe, had both a relatively elite and a more populist level, and a historian must not ignore the second simply because the first is so much easier to study. It was through the complex interaction of these levels that there emerged ultimately the pattern of continuity through change that I consider dominant for this period.

In 1890, when Moderate Congress politics of 'mendicancy' seemed to be the only kind of nationalism that existed or could exist, this is what a Bombay Governor was writing confidentially to the Viceroy: 'The Forest policy, the Abkari (excise) policy, the Salt duty, the screwing up of land revenue by revision settlements, all make us odious.... We know pretty well what the educated natives want, but what the feelings are of the uneducated, I admit I don't know.' (*Reay to Lansdowne*, 20 February 1890) A vivid awareness surely of fires underground and forty years later Mahatma Gandhi would forge an all-India movement precisely around the issues of salt and land revenue, excise and forest rights. There are depths and continuities here waiting to be explored.

Chapter 2
POLITICAL AND ECONOMIC STRUCTURE: 1885–1905

IMPERIAL STRUCTURE AND POLICIES

Till well into the twentieth century, British Government in India was basically an autocracy of hierarchically organized officials headed by the Viceroy and the Secretary of State, while the ultimate Parliamentary control was spasmodic and largely theoretical. Developments after 1858 had in fact considerably enhanced the personal role of the Viceroy-Secretary of State combine, while bringing them into much closer contact with each other through the communications revolution symbolized by the submarine cable and the Suez Canal (1865–69). The East India Company's affairs had been live political and economic issues in England, and renewals of Charter Acts had provoked intense debates in Parliament. After 1858, the routine annual presentation of Indian financial statements and 'Moral and Material Progress Reports' usually quickly emptied the Commons. The Court of Directors had remained influential through its patronage functions; the Council of India set up by Lord Stanley's Act as a check on the Secretary of State never acquired much importance, as it could be overruled on most matters and by-passed through 'urgent communications' or 'secret orders' to the Viceroy. In India, too, the railway and the telegraph brought local governments closer to Calcutta, while Coupland reminds us that there was no trace of the federal idea' before 1919. (*Constitutional Problem*) The Indian Councils Act of 1861 had also strengthened the Viceroy's authority over his Executive Council by substituting a 'portfolio' or departmental system for corporate functioning. The imperial and local Legislative Councils enlarged or set up by the same Act included a few non-official Indians but were essentially decorative. Being entirely nominated bodies till 1892, they even lacked, before the reforms of that year, any statutory powers of discussing budgets or putting questions. The political structure thus concentrated enormous powers in the hands of the Viceroy and the Secretary of State, and so some consideration of their personal attitudes and political affiliations remains relevant—even though the habit of dividing British Indian history into neat Viceregal periods has fortunately died out.

Viceregal Attitudes

Politically conscious Indians in 1885 were certainly very much aware of differences between Viceroys, and above all, between what they considered to be the almost black-and-white contrast of Lytton with Ripon. They also tended to relate the change directly to the conflict between Tories and Liberals in British politics. Writing a history *of Indian National Evolution* in 1915, the Moderate Congress leader Ambikacharan Mazumdar counterposed 'the gathering clouds' under Lytton to 'the clouds lifted' and 'the dawning light' under Ripon and Dufferin, and even a much more recent and sophisticated scholar has contrasted the 'Conservative Adventure' of 1869–80 to the 'Liberal Experiment' of 1880–88. (S. Gopal, *British Policy in India*)

Rhetoric apart, the really significant difference lay in a shortlived attempt in the early 1880s to expand the circle of Indian collaborators from princes and *zamindars* to English educated 'middle-class' groups. Lytton had dismissed the latter as 'Babus, whom we have educated to write semi-seditious articles in the Native Press'; Ripon in contrast liked to talk about 'the hourly increasing... necessity of making the educated natives the friends, instead of the enemies, of our rule.' (Anil Seal, *Emergence of Indian Nationalism,* pp. 134, 149) The unexpected fury of the Anglo-Indian reaction to the Ilbert Bill in 1883 quickly ended that experiment, even while investing Ripon in educated Indian eyes with a largely unjustified near-martyr's halo.

Under Dufferin (1884–88), Lansdowne (1888–93) and Elgin (1893–98), the differences between Tory and Liberal attitudes towards India became steadily less evident. Dufferin uneasily and ineffectively sought to have the best of all possible worlds, surrendering to white commercial pressure in the annexation of Upper Burma, introducing pro-landlord modifications in Bengal and Oudh tenancy bills, briefly flirting with Hume, but then violently attacking the Congress in the St. Andrews' Dinner speech just before departure. In the end he managed to please no one, an Dinshaw Wacha pointed out to Dadabhai Naoroji in a private letter—the former in December 1888 went so far as to say that he could 'tolerate a Lytton but not a Dufferin'. (R.P. Patwardhan, ed., *Dadabhai Naoroji Correspondence,* Vol II, p. 137) How irrelevant British party divisions were becoming in the Indian context was revealed by the promptness with which Lansdowne, appointed by the Tory Salisbury ministry, took up Dufferin's private pleas for some elective element in provincial councils, both arguing in almost identical terms that such a move would 'take the wind out of the sails' of the Congress. Concessions to Lancashire in the form of countervailing excise duties on

Indian cottons were made under Elgin, a Viceroy appointed by Gladstone's last administration, and the 'Grand Old Man' himself badly let down his Indian admirers in 1892 by refusing to support an amendment to the Lord Cross Bill, wanting explicit introduction of elections, and again in 1893 when he allowed Kimberley and Lansdowne to ignore a Commons resolution wanting simultaneous ICS examinations.

The irrelevance of party divisions may have had something to do with the political confusion in England after the mid-1880s when the Liberals split over Gladstone's Irish Home Rule. The Liberal tradition in any case had always been somewhat ambiguous, including Whig admirers of aristocratic leadership, Radical advocates of greater democracy, Liberal-imperialists difficult to distinguish from Conservatives in foreign policy as well as 'Little-England-ers' genuinely opposed to military expansion (though not to the considerable material gains of free trade). More important than political ideologies, however, were certain consequences following from the over-all logic of the colonial situation, and it is to these more long-term trends that we must now turn.

Foreign Policy

In British Indian foreign policy, while there was no return before Curzon's time to the flamboyant imperialism of Lytton, attitudes on the the whole remained considerably more aggressive than in the days of 'masterly inactivity' of the 1860s. This becomes understandable in the context of the over-sharpening imperialist rivalries with Russia advancing towards Afghanistan and Persia and France establishing control over Indo-China. Liberals in opposition had violently denounced Lytton's Afghan adventure, yet Ripon's policy in the end hardly marked a total break. The plan for breaking up Afghanistan was abandoned, as well as the insistence on a British Agent at Kabul. But Abdur Rahman (Lytton's eventual choice) was allowed to remain as Amir with controls on foreign policy imposed in return for a subsidy, while the British retained Pishin and Sibi and turned them into British Baluchistan in 1887.

In Dufferin's time, the Russian seizure of the Afghan border-post of Panjdeh (March, 1885) led to acute tension, but eventually the issue was submitted to arbitration by the King of Denmark. An agreement concerning the Afghan frontier was reached with Russia in July 1887. With the militarist Lord Roberts as commander-in-chief from 1887–92, a forward policy was, however, followed on the north-west frontier involving numerous expensive expeditions against tribes, the construction of strategic railways, the imposition in 1893 of the Durand agreement demarcating the

Indo-Afghan border, and the seizure and eventual retention (despite Liberal qualms) of Chitral.

Dufferin's adminstration was also marked by the last really major extension of British Indian territory: the annexation of Upper Burma in January, 1886. A combination of political and commercial reasons help to explain the decision to march in British troops in November, 1885. The British were suspicious of French influence over Burma spilling over from neighbouring Indo-China, particularly after a trade treaty signed by King Thibaw in January, 1885 and a railway agreement with a French company in July. The British Chamber of Commerce in Rangoon was also eager for annexation, particularly after King Thibaw had imposed a heavy fine on a British timber trading company, for fraudulent practices in August, 1885. Randolph Churchill had assured Dufferin that in Britain, too, 'the large commercial interests', particularly Manchester, would 'warmly support annexation'. Upper Burma appeared attractive both in itself and as a possible gateway to Yunnan and S.W. China. The Salisbury ministry had enthusiastically supported Dufferin; the Gladstone cabinet that was in power when annexation was formalized had a few qualms of conscience, but then agreed 'with great reluctance'—a difference which just about sums up the distinction between Tories and Liberals in this period. The effete Mandalay court predictably collapsed almost without a fight, but it took five years and 40,000 troops to crush popular guerrilla resistance.

Army

All such adventures meant heavier outlays on the army, to which we must add the employment of Indian troops abroad mainly at the cost of the Indian exchequer in Egypt in 1882 by Gladstone, despite Ripon's protests, in Sudan against the Mahdi movement in 1885–86 and again in 1896 in China against the Boxers in 1900. The Panjdeh war-scare was the occasion for an increase in the strength of the army by 30,000, and military expenditure accounted for 41.9% of the Indian Government's budget in 1881–82 and 45.4% ten years later. By 1904–05, under Curzon, it had gone up to 51.9%. Military policy in fact provides numerous insights into the real nature of colonial rule. The predominant influence was still the memory of 1857—the British, Dufferin commented in December 1888, 'should always remember the lessons which were learnt with such terrible experience 30 years ago.' The Commissions of 1859 and 1879 insisted on the principles of a one-third white army (as against 14% before 1857), strict European monopoly over the artillery (even the rifles given to Indians were of an inferior quality till 1900!) and what Sir John Strachey once described as the 'policy of water-tight compartments...to prevent the growth of any dangerous identity of feeling from community of race, religion, caste or local sympathies.' (*India,* p. 63) The divide-and-rule principle in fact was stated with enviable clarity by Wood in 1862: 'I wish to have a different and rival spirit in different regiments, so that Sikh might fire into Hindoo, Goorkha into either, without any scruple in case of need.' The 1879 Army Commission reiterated the point: 'Next to the grand counterpoise of a sufficient European force comes the counterpoise of natives against natives.' (quotations from Hiralal Singh, *Problems and Policies of British in India 1885–1898,* pp. 140, 142) An ideology of 'martial races', which assumed that good soldiers could come only from some specific communities developed particularly from the late-1880s under Lord Roberts. It was used to justify a recruitment policy mainly directed towards Sikhs and Gurkhas—relatively marginal religious and ethnic groups, and therefore less likely to be affected by nationalism. There was of course no question of racial equality or Indianization of command. Even after a slight rise in salaries, an Indian infantry private got ₹9 a month in 1895, his British counterpart almost ₹24 plus a number of allowances. As late as 1926, the Indian Sandhurst Committee was visualizing a 50%, Indianized officer cadre—for 1952!

Financial and Administrative Pressures

Foreign adventures and army expansion inevitably meant financial strains. From 1873 onwards the burden on the Indian exchequer was greatly enhanced by the rapid depreciation of the silver rupee in terms of gold. A big part of Indian expenses had to be paid in sterling (pensions of British civilians and army officers, costs of the Secretary of State's establishment, interest on the India Debt and other items going into the so-called Home Charges), yet the rupee which stood at 2s in 1872 was worth little more than 1s 2d by 1893–94. The 'financial foundations of the Raj' have been explored in detail by Sabyasachi Bhattacharji in recent years, while Cambridge historians have made a significant contribution towards illuminating the connections between such financial problems, administrative pressures combined with devolution, and nationalist movements. 'The administrative grid', in Anil Seal's words, had to be 'pressed down more firmly by the heavier intervention of the Raj in local matters'. *Locality, Province and Nation,* p. 10) In more concrete terms, this involved attempts to extend old forms of taxation and explore new ones—a process itself fraught with many problems as the government was faced with a number of contradictory pulls.

Land revenue remained the single biggest source of income. Here, talk of an extension of the Permanent Settlement quite common in the immediate aftermath of the Mutiny, when loyal dependent landlords were being looked for, was naturally forgotten. Receipts increased from ₹19.67 crores in 1881–82 to ₹23.99 crores in 1901–02 despite the devastating famines of the late 1890s, thus providing, as we shall see, a major and standing nationalist grievance. Yet too much enhancement of the land tax was now increasingly felt to be both politically dangerous and economically unwise, as the British also urgently wanted to develop the export trade in raw cotton, sugar, jute, wheat and other agricultural commodities. The proportion of land revenue to the total state income was in fact gradually decreasing (the net revenue for the years cited above being ₹46.86 crores and ₹60.79 crores respectively). Import duties would have greatly helped budget-making and also pleased politically-conscious Indians, but here, as is well known, Lancashire repeatedly dictated otherwise. Cotton duties were bitterly attacked from the mid-1870s by the Manchester lobby backed by Salisbury as allegedly protecting the new Bombay industry. Lytton reduced these duties in 1878–79 despite the Afghan war, Ripon abolished them altogether in 1882, and when a restoration became inevitable in the 1890s in face of massive deficits, the notorious countervailing excise on Indian cloth was imposed together with the revived duty in 1894 and 1896. From James Wilson in 1860 onwards, British Indian Finance Members of the Viceroy's Council had been toying with the idea of income tax, despite protests from whites and influential Indians alike. In 1886, after, Panjdeh and Burma, Dufferin gave it a systematic and permanent shape. Two years later the heavily regressive sales tax was sharply enhanced.

Bayly's study of Allahabad together with Washbrook's of south India emphasize the role of this mid-1880s spurt in taxation in providing unusually wide support for the Congress sessions in Madras (1887) and Allahabad (1888). Washbrook also provides some interesting data on long-term trends at the provincial level. Thus in Madras land revenue provided 57% of the total in 1880 but only 28% in 1920. Excise duties on the liquor industry, in contrast, went up from ₹60 lakhs in 1882–83 to ₹5.4 crores in 1920. There was also an expansion of forest revenues, which meant restrictions on age-old rights to pasture and fuel of tribals and poor peasants as well the occasional curbing of more prosperous rural interests. Provincial associations were already protesting against Forest Laws and grazing restrictions in Madras in the 1880s and Assam in the 1890s, and the issue was repeatedly raised, as we shall see, in early Congress sessions.

Frykenburg's book on public administration in Guntur in the early 19th century (*Guntur District, 1788 to 1848,* Oxford, 1965) has revealed a picture cf considerable independence and financial benefits being enjoyed by subordinate Indian officials, who were closely connected with local notables in the relatively loosely organized company administration. Post-1858 developments associated with financial pressures naturally reduced such autonomy—a process analysed in detail for Madras by Washbrook, but confirmed interestingly for the Sylhet region of east Bengal by Bipin Pal's account of the gradual curbing of *zamindar* 'natural leaders' as centralized administration penetrated deeper into the localities. (*Memories of My Life and Times,* pp. 11–16)

Local Self-Government and Council Reform

But if financial pressures and administrative tightening-up were not to prove politically dangerous, they had to be combined with a search for more Indian collaborators. 'Systems of nomination, representation and election were all means of enlisting Indians to work for imperial ends', as Anil Seal has emphasized. (*Locality, Province and Nation,* p. 10) The financial and political aspects were neatly combined in the development of local self-government. The process really began under the Conservative Mayo and not the Liberal Ripon. The major motive was to tackle financial difficulties by shifting charges for local requirements on to new local taxes. But Mayo too felt that 'We must gradually associate with ourselves in the Government of this country more of the native element', and the second, political strand was prominently displayed in Ripon's famous May 1882 resolution promising elected majorities and chairmen in local bodies—a promise, however, implemented only slowly and incompletely, in face of resistance from most provincial bureaucrats. How important the financial aspect remained throughout in the process of devolution may be indicated by a much later example: the setting-up of Union Boards in Bengal in 1919–20 immediately implied a 50% hike in the *chaukidari* (village watchmen), tax and provoked a massive and successful nationalist protest in Midnapur.

From the late-1880s onwards, the rise of the Congress meant that collaboration at higher levels would have to be sought mainly through successive doses of Legislative Council reform. Lord Cross' Indian Councils Act of 1892 enlarged the non-official element, (to constitute 10 out of 16 members in the Imperial Council), for instance. Though not conceding elections explicitly, it did empower the Indian authorities to consult local bodies, university senates, chambers of commerce and landlord associations in nominating members. The Councillors obtained the right to discuss the budget and put questions, though not the power to move amendments, vote on the budget, or ask supplementaries.

The process of so-called 'constitutional reform' was associated throughout with two other major strands of official policy: periodic attempts to 'rally the moderates' (the formula was Minto's, but the attempt had been there long before him) and skilful use of divide-and-rule techniques. Local self-government despite Ripon's high hopes was not particularly successful in achieving the first objective, since municipalities and district boards were given little real power or financial resources. Nationalists entered such bodies, made some use of their patronage possibilities, but in general refused to confine their energies to the improvement of drains. The 1892 reforms possibly did help to reduce the tempo of Congress agitation for a few years, with a number of prominent leaders finding their way into provincial and Imperial Councils (*e.g.*, Lalmohan Ghosh, W.C. Bonnarji and Surendranath in Bengal, Pherozeshah Mehta, Gokhale and even for some time Tilak in Bombay, Mehta followed by Gokhale in the Imperial Council). General demands for Council reform were not very prominent in the agenda of Congress sessions between 1894 and 1900. The effect was quite shortlived, however the same years saw the first stirrings of Extremism, and by 1904 the Congress as a whole was again demanding a further big dose of legislative reform.

Divide and Rule

Much more significant ultimately was the encouragement of divisions within Indian elite-groups, along lines predominantly religious, but also sometimes caste and regional. Such divisions often had deep roots and no doubt nationalists tended to exaggerate the element of direct and conscious British responsibility. But, as we shall see, conflicts over scarce resources in education, administrative jobs, and later political spoils lay in the very logic of colonial underdevelopment, even apart from deliberate official policies. Political reforms consistently extended and sharpened such rivalries right through our period. Hunter's *Indian Musalmans* rapidly set the fashion in official circles of talking and thinking of Muslims as a homogeneous 'backward' community. Dufferin in 1888 described them as 'a nation of 50 millions' allegedly uniform in religious and social customs and sharing a 'remembrance of the days when, enthroned at Delhi, they reigned supreme from the Himalayas to Cape Comorin'. (*Dufferin to Cross*, 11 November, 1888) These were a set of assumptions as historically false as they proved politically useful to our foreign rulers. Recent studies of the United Provinces by Francis Robinson and of the Punjab by N.G. Barrier vividly reveal how the introduction of elected municipalities immediately sharpened Hindu-Muslim tensions in both provinces. By 1886, the Punjab Government of Lyall was already introducing separate electorates in towns like Hoshiarpur, Lahore and Multan. The original motive might have been, as Barrier argues, the reduction of an already-existing conflict; yet it remains an undeniable fact that separate electorates inevitably hardened the lines of division by encouraging and even forcing community leaders to cultivate their own religious followings alone. At the level of Council reforms too, Lansdowne was insisting in March, 1893 that representation had to be of 'types and classes rather than areas or numbers': the acceptance of demands for separate electorates lay not too far ahead in the future. Communal tensions beyond a certain point of course also posed serious law and order problems. Yet Secretary of State Hamilton's confidential letter to Elgin on 7 May, 1897 perhaps best typifies the most usual British thinking on the subject: 'I am sorry to hear of the increasing friction between Hindus and Mohammedans in the North West and the Punjab. One hardly knows what to wish for; unity of ideas and action would be very dangerous politically divergence of ideas and coliision are administratively troublesome. Of the two the latter is the least risky, though it throws anxiety and responsibility upon those on the spot where the friction exists.'

So far we have been considering only the logic of the British Indian political machinery and it is here that the Cambridge school is at its best. But it is surely a curious myopia that tries to treat administration and politics as a world or end in itself, and that can blithely assert, as Seal does in his 1973 article, that 'The argument that the rule of strangers in India goaded their subjects into organizing against it is not our concern.' (*Locality, Province and Nation,* pp. 5–6) Two other dimensions, vital for the understanding both of the national movement and of modern Indian history in general, tend to be missed out in much of the Cambridge analysis. The British Raj had a deeply racist aspect, and it ultimately existed to protect colonial exploitation.

White Racism

The British in India were quite conscious of being a master-race, as the tallest in 'native' society often learnt to his cost when he blundered into reserved compartments in railways or steamers or faced discrimination and barriers to promotion in his job or profession. The Ilbert Bill storm was the most extreme but by no means isolated expression of white racism. In 1878, for instance, the appointment of Muthusamy Iyer as High Court judge in Madras was opposed by the *Madras Mail* (organ of white businessmen) on the ground that 'native officials should not draw the same rate of pay as Europeans in similar circumstances'. (R. Suntharalingam, *Politics and*

Nationalist Awakening in South India, 1852–91, pp. 151–2) The uproar led directly to the foundation of the famous nationalist journal *Hindu*. For the less fortunate, racism took cruder forms of kicks and blows and shooting 'accidents' as the 'sahib' disciplined his *punkha* coolie or bagged a native by mistake while out on *shikar*. No less than 81 shooting 'accidents' were recorded in the years between 1880 and 1900. White dominated courts regularly awarded ridiculously light sentences for such incidents, and a glance at contemporary Indian journals or private papers immediately reveal how important such things were for the rise of nationalism. Thus Wacha complained to Naoroji on 30 October, 1891 that 'European murders of Natives are daily on the increase. Soldiers chiefly are the brutal offenders... [they are] always acquitted on some plea or another.' (R.P. Patwardhan, p. 265) The treatment of coolies on Assam tea plantations figured prominently in the work of the Indian Association in the late 1880s. Racial discrimination and brutality were indeed issues which could occasionally unite the highest in 'native' society with the lowest in a common sense of deprivation and injustice.

The more humane or far-sighted of British Indian statesmen certainly tried to restrain at times the grosser crudities of racism, and not only Ripon, but Curzon, too, acquired some unpopularity among their fellow-whites on this score. Curzon took disciplinary action against British soldiers in two notorious cases—one of collective rape of a Burmese woman, the other of the murder of an Indian cook for refusing to act as a procurer. The regiment involved in the second case was incidentally given a hero's reception by Europeans at the Delhi Durbar of 1903. But it has to be emphasized that excesses apart, a certain amount of white racism had a functional and necessary role in the political and economic structure of colonial India. It was not irrational, after all, from the British point of view, to exclude Indians from the really senior and key posts in the military and administrative cadre as much as possible. So an apparently trivial demand like the holding of simultaneous ICS examinations in India was bitterly opposed for fifty years. Elgin argued in a letter to Roseberry in July 1895 that 'we could only govern by maintaining the fact that we are the dominant race—though Indians in services should be encouraged, there is a point at which we must reserve the control to ourselves, if we are to remain at all.'

Even more crucial were the economic dimensions of racism, emphasized recently by Amiya Bagchi. Colour played an important role in preserving the unity of white businessmen in India against possible Indian competitors. The functioning of the various white Chambers of Commerce, Trade Associations and organizations of jute, tea and mining interests reveal that 'European traders and businessmen were great believers in reasonable compromise and mutual accommodation among themselves, however much they might believe in the virtues of competition for others.' (Bagchi, *Private Investment in India*, p. 170) Despite a few conflicts and a certain aristocratic disdain for trade affected by some bureaucrats, there always existed innumerable personal and 'club-life' ties between the white businessman and the white official in India. Lord Curzon in a speech to British mine-owners at Barakar in 1903 neatly summed up the essence of the relationship between government and business: 'My work lies in administration, yours in exploitation: but both are aspects of the same question and of the same duty.' (quoted in J.R. McLane, *Indian Nationalism and the Early Congress*, p. 37). As late as 1944, an Indian manufacturers' body was complaining about 'the silent sympathy from the mystic bond of racial affinity with the rulers of the land, which procures them [European businessmen] invisible, but not the less effective, advantages in their competition with their indigenous rivals.' (Bagchi, p. 166)

Racism thus helped to consolidate what Bagchi has termed the 'collective monopoly' of European businessmen which was such a striking feature of the industrial and commercial life of particularly the eastern part of India. It is to a study of the changing forms and consequences of this economic stranglehold that we must now turn.

THE COLONIAL ECONOMY

R.P. Dutt's *India Today*, which still remains in some ways the best over-all analysis of the Indian colonial economy nearly forty years after its first publication, developed some of the insights and stray comments of Marx into a theory of three successive phases of British exploitation of our country. The first, 'mercantilist' phase, from 1757 up to 1813, was marked by direct plunder and the East India Company's monopoly trade, functioning through the 'investment' of surplus revenues in the purchase, often at arbitrarily low prices, of Indian (primarily Bengal) finished goods for export to England and Europe. The Industrial Revolution in England dramatically changed the whole pattern of trade, and the years from 1813 to 1858 saw the classic age of free-trader industrial capitalist exploitation, converting India rapidly into a market for Manchester textiles and a source for raw materials, uprooting her traditional handicrafts—a period when 'the home-land of cotton was inundated with cotton'. (Marx) From the latter half of the nineteenth century onwards, finance-imperialism began to entrench itself in India through some export of capital and a massive chain of British-controlled banks, export-import firms and managing agency houses.

As R.P. Dutt himself occasionally indicates, the periodization here is somewhat arbitrary and over-schematic. It seems in fact much more realistic and helpful to operate with a concept of over-lapping phases, with old forms of exploitation never entirely dying out but getting integrated into newer patterns. This becomes clear from a brief look at what from the 1870s onwards soon became the dominant perennial theme of nationalist complaints—the 'drain of wealth'.

Drain of Wealth

Down to 1757, European traders had been obliged to bring bullion into India in the teeth of much criticism at home, as Indian cotton and silk goods had a flourishing market in the West while Indian demand for Western products (like British woollens) was usually negligible. The problem was solved dramatically by Plassey. Now the plunder from Bengal, profits made from duty-free inland trade, and the 'surplus' from *Diwani* revenues sufficed for what the Company euphemistically went on calling its 'investments' in India—a blatantly obvious process of drain, as the profits of military conquest in Bengal were being used to buy goods for export from Bengal. The decline of the traditional exports of cotton and silk manufactures in the face of Manchester competition raised acute remittance problems for the Company, its servants, and private traders alike. The remittance problem was initially tackled through the development of indigo and the export of opium to China for purchasing tea, and then on a more successful basis after the 1850s through the rapid expansion of new types of exports from India—western Indian raw cotton, Punjab wheat, Bengal jute, Assam tea, south Indian oilseeds and hides and skins, etc. The need for a unilateral transfer of funds to Britain was a constant factor and in fact progressively increased over time. The burden of the East India Company's London establishment and of dividends to its shareholders was replaced after 1858 by the costs of the Secretary of State's India Office, while the India Debt in England, already considerable thanks to the Company's military adventures and the expenses for suppressing the Mutiny, was sharply enhanced in that year when compensation to Company shareholders was added to its account. The Home Charges also included pensions to British Indian officials and army officers, military and other stores purchased in England, costs of army training, transport and campaigns outside India but charged on Indian finances, and the guaranteed interest on railways. In 1901–02, for instance, Home Charges came to £17.3 million, the major items in that year being railway interest, £6.4 million; interest on India Debt, £3 million; army expenses, £4.3 million; stores purchase, £1.9 million; and pensions, £1.3 million. To this official account must be added the remittances made by British officials in India and the transfer of profits made in India by British private investments. The real burden of Home Charges and private remittances alike increased sharply from the 1870s, as the silver rupee depreciated in terms of the gold-standard sterling (£).

In his 1888 lectures, Sir John Strachey explained the mechanism of drain with clarity and frankness. 'The Secretary of State draws bills on the Government treasury in India, and it is mainly through these bills, which are paid in India out of the public revenues, that the merchant obtains the money that he requires in India, and the Secretary of State the money that he requires in England.' (*India*, p. 115) In other words, would-be British purchasers of Indian exports bought Council Bills from the Secretary of State in return for sterling (which was used to meet the Home Charges). The Council Bills were then exchanged for rupees from the Government of India's revenues, and the rupees used to buy Indian goods for export. Conversely, British officials and businessmen in India bought Sterling Bills in return for their profits in rupees from British-owned Exchange Banks; the London branches of these banks paid in pounds for such bills with the money coming from Indian exports, purchased through the rupees obtained through sale of Sterling Bills. The diagram below may be helpful here.

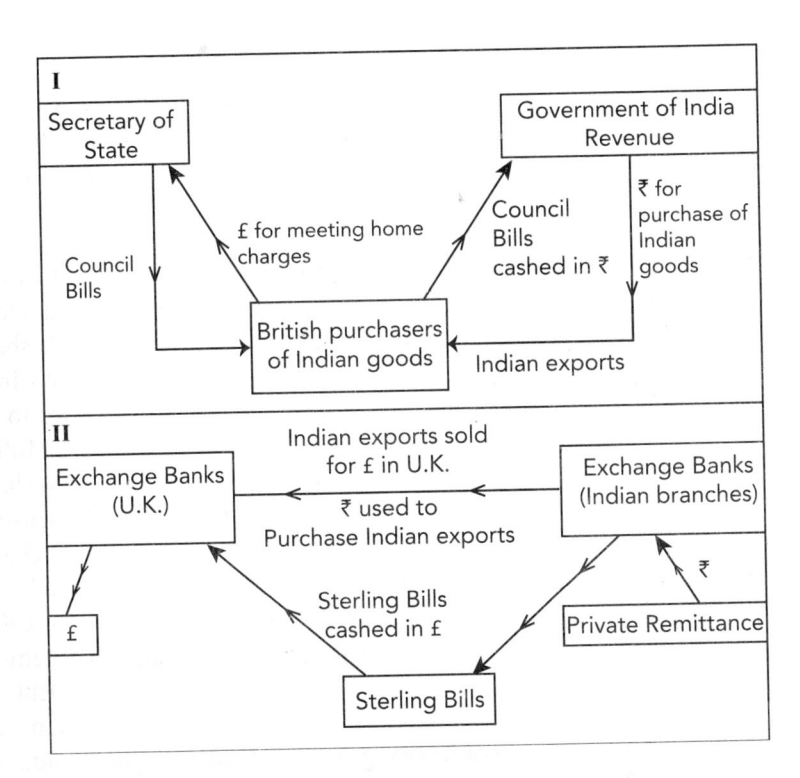

Both Home Charges and private remittances were thus funnelled through Indian exports, and so the drain of wealth, as nationalist economists repeatedly pointed out from Naoroji onwards, found its visible expression though India's growing export surplus. The originally mercantilist drain had therefore become closely associated both with the processes of exploitation through free trade and with the structure of British Indian finance capitalism.

India's export surplus had become absolutely vital for the whole complex mechanism of the United Kingdom's balance of payments by the end of the nineteenth century. With the rise of tariff walls around the other developing capitalist economies in Western Europe and America, Britain was running into major problems of deficits, as she still required heavy imports of agricultural products while her manufactures found markets difficult to obtain in an increasingly protectionist world. India proved vital in two ways. The forcible maintenance in India of what Strachey described as 'a nearer approach to complete freedom of trade...than in almost any other country' (*Ibid.*, p. 101) meant in practice the preservation of a captive market for Lancashire textiles. Secondly, India's constant export-surplus with countries other than Britain through massive outflows of agricultural products and raw materials counterbalanced British deficits elsewhere. Apart from military and strategic advantages, these were the solid gains from the Indian Empire for Britain as a whole.

The drain theory had its severe critics right from the beginning, and certainly some nationalist formulations of it appear crude and exaggerated today. The drain, it has been argued, was greatly exaggerated by nationalists, since foreign trade and export surplus could amount to only a small part of India's national income. But surely Naoroji had a point here when he argued (before the Welby Commission in 1895) that the amount being drained away represented a potential surplus which might have raised Indian income considerably if invested properly inside the country. The standard imperialist defence, however, was that outlined by Strachey: 'England receives nothing from India except in return for English services rendered or English capital expended.' (*Ibid*, p. 115) The first part of the argument clearly refers to the alleged benefits of good government, law and order, etc., brought in by the British, and deserves little discussion. The more 'economic' aspects of the drain have been defended on the ground that stores were being purchased in England, and loans raised in the London money market, at rates lower than would have been possible in nineteenth century India. One might still argue, as the nationalist economists did, that the probably higher payments (if the loans and purchases had been made within India) would have remained inside the country. The crucial point, however, remains that indicated by

Strachey in his phrase 'English capital expended'. Remittance of profits on British capital invested in railways, plantations, mines or mills has been sought to be defended on the ground that such things after all were 'developing' or 'modernizing' India. The basic issue is the precise pattern of development, and here the assumption once fairly common that British rule was bringing about a slower but still genuine modernization on bourgeois lines, roughly similar to that which had been achieved in the West, has come under increasing attack in recent times.

Deindustrialization

British officials and publicists tended to accept the decline of traditional Indian artisan production as a fact, sad but inevitable. Handicraft must go down before the machine in India just as in the West as part of the price of modernization. In England, however, the suffering caused by the decline of handicrafts was counterbalanced fairly soon by the much greater employment and income-generating effect of factory industries. In the Indian colonial case, the artisans were made to shoulder the burden of progress being achieved in a country six thousand miles away, since the growth of Indian factories was non-existent before the 1850s and 1860s and painfully slow even afterwards. It was left to a recent U.S. scholar, Morris D. Morris, however, to argue that deindustrialization itself was a myth. Precise statistical proof of the decline of handicrafts is admittedly difficult to find, both for the pre-Census period and even afterwards, as the 1881-1931 census series, often quoted by nationalists, was shown by Daniel Thorner to be based on a confusion of categories and therefore not a clear indicator of a decline in the proportion of population dependent on industries. Nationalists relied heavily on statistics of external trade indicating a collapse in traditional Indian textile exports, and a rapid increase in Lancashire imports, but these do not constitute a definite proof of decline in aggregate internal production. Nor was the collapse of handicrafts the single, uniform and cataclysmic process assumed in popular nationalist literature. One must distinguish between types of artisan products, regions and varying time-periods. Urban luxury manufactures like the high quality silks and cottons of Dacca or Murshidabad must have been hit first, by the almost simultaneous collapse of indigenous court demand and the external market on which these had largely depended. Village crafts in the interior, and particularly, in regions other than eastern India where British penetration was earliest and deepest, probably survived much longer, coming to be seriously affected only with the spread of railways. Enough remained of the *jajmani* system (the village artisans supplying traditionally fixed quantities of their products to peasant families in return for shares in the harvest) for it to become a subject of research by sociologists like Weiser and Beidelmann since the 1930s. A novel like Tarashankar Bandopadhyay's *Ganadevata,* describing village life in an interior district of West Bengal in the 1920s and 1930s, portrayed the decline of the *jajmani* system as a relatively novel thing.

Yet the arguments of Morris seeking to refute the whole theory of deindustrialization are in fact more conjectural and dubious then those usually offered by the much-abused nationalists. Indigenous textile production, Morris argues, could have remained constant or even increased despite the big rise in imports from Lancashire, because of an allegedly massive upswing in Indian demand sufficient to cover both—but no data at all is given to prove this upswing. The argument that indigenous weavers benefited from the lower price of imported yarn ignores both the ruin of Indian spinners as well as the problems caused by the fall in the price of woven goods, due to cost-reducing technological innovations in England but not in India. Lancashire manufacturers benefited from cost reductions in both spinning and weaving. Indian weavers gained from the use of cheaper imported yarn, but there was no decline in weaving costs, and yet they had to compete with the lower prices of imported cloth—and so, as Toru Matsui pointed out in his very effective rejoinder to Morris, their conditions could hardly have improved. (*Indian Economic and Social History Review,* 1968)

Deindustrialization was assumed to have been a fact, and a lot of scattered data was given about it, in a large number of unimpeachable official sources like Census and Famine Reports and regional industrial surveys. Surveys of Bengal manufactures, by Collin in 1890 and Cummings in 1908, might be cited here. The latter also makes the interesting point that the *Swadeshi* movement of 1905 had come as a saviour for many indigenous crafts by suddenly boosting demand on patriotic grounds. Amiya Bagchi has recently attempted a careful statistical comparison of Buchanan-Hamilton's survey of a number of Bihar districts in the early nineteenth century with the 1901 census data. His major findings are a decline in the percentage of population dependent on industries from 18% to 8%, and a massive fall in the number of cotton spinners and weavers. Nationalist economists seem to have been not so wrong after all ('Deindustrialization in Gangetic Bihar, 1809–1901' in *Essays in Honour of S.C Sarkar*). The sufferings of artisans have to be kept in mind as a significant factor in the understanding of many movements of our period: both in the way in which deindustrialization stimulated patriotic sentiments among intellectuals alike in the Moderate, Extremist and Gandhian eras, as well as more directly, in occasional urban and rural explosions of various types.

Commercialization of Agriculture

The inter-related processes of railway construction (only 432 miles in 1859, over 5000 miles just ten years later, nearly 25,000 miles by the end of the century), rising exports (particularly noticeable during the 'cotton boom' of the 1860s when the American Civil War made Lancashire turn to Deccan raw cotton for a few years, and again in the 1880s and early '90s) and commercialization of agriculture have been sometimes hailed as signs of 'modernization'. Orthodox economics tends to associate commercialization with the development of agricultural surpluses and rural prosperity; one might also expect tendencies towards capitalist farming through a differentiation among the peasantry which would certainly mean suffering for the poorer sections, but also growth in productivity. Yet here, as elsewhere, colonialism had a twisted logic of its own, for commercialization emerges on analysis to have been often an artificial and forced process which led to differentiation without genuine growth.

The precise pattern of commercialization naturally varied from crop to crop. Thus tea, an innovation in a region with little population pressure, required plantations directly managed by whites and using labour recruited from afar through an indenture system which came very close to slavery. Indigo in central Bengal was mainly cultivated by peasants themselves, but only through considerable coercion by very unpopular sahib planters forcing their advances on the *raiyats,* for profits were low and uncertain and the crop upset the harvest cycle. No direct coercion, however, was needed for jute in east Bengal, which was more profitable than rice. But despite such variations, certain common features stand out.

By the second half of the nineteenth century, British business houses were in virtual total control of the overseas trade, shipping and insurance of the country. So the bulk of the profits from the export boom was appropriated by foreign firms and went out of the country as 'foreign leakages'. A secondary but still substantial share went to Indian traders and *mahajans,* the middlemen who provided the necessary advances to the cultivators and thus established control over production. The need for such advances was again often connected with the burden of rent, and thus, as a recent microstudy of sugar-cane cultivation in Gorakhpur district has emphasized, capitalist penetration helped to consolidate the already established structure of landlord and moneylender exploitation (with sugar-mills engaging local *zamindars* and *mahajans* as contractors to collect cane from peasants). A small rich peasant upper stratum was also emerging in certain areas, as for instance in the Deccan cotton belt, the Godavari-Krishna and, Kaveri deltas in Andhra and Tamilnadu, and the Punjab lands opened up by large scale irrigation works at the end of the century. But the central fact was the built-in tendency of the entire system against significant advances in productive technology and organization. Made totally dependent on a very distant and unknown foreign market with which his only link was through a formidable chain of intermediaries, the Indian peasant was also repeatedly made to bear the burden of wildly-fluctuating prices. Thus the cotton boom of the 1860s collapsed as dramatically as it had appeared (the price of a pound of raw cotton in Bombay was 2 annas 7p in 1859, 11 annas 5p in 1864, and only 6 annas 2p in 1866). The prosperity of the Deccan cotton belt of the 1860s consequently turned into the heavy indebtedness, famine and agrarian riots of the mid-70s. The decline in world agricultural prices from the 1870s to the 1890s (due to the vastly increased supplies coming from North America, Argentina and Australia) affected Indian wheat and raw cotton. In the twentieth century, as we shall see, the adverse impact of an artificially high rupee-sterling ratio was to be followed by the major disaster of the 1930s depression.

The big export firms and skillful Indian traders and moneylenders could profit from low prices as well as high, but productive investment or innovation remained a very risky business. A peasant who had managed to accumulate some funds would therefore have every incentive to turn towards trade, usury, or renting-out of land to sub-tenants or sharecroppers, thus parasitically shifting the whole burden of production risks instead of going in for real capitalist farming. As for the vast majority of poorer peasants, commercialization was often a forced process, as money was needed to meet the growing burden of revenues and rents in cash. Coimbatore peasants once told a British Collector that they were growing cotton simply because they could not eat it; the grain they might have cultivated would have been consumed by themselves, whereas now they went half-fed, but at least had the money with which to meet revenue demands. The changeover to commercial crops and higher-priced foodgrains like wheat due to revenue and rent pressures meant a shift away from poor men's foodcrops like *jowar*, *bajra* or pulses, which often caused disaster in famine years. Growing dependence on moneylenders was another inevitable consequence, as commercial crops usually required higher inputs and therefore more advances. Thus commercialization did contribute to differentiation within the peasantry, but hardly (except perhaps in a few pockets) to real growth. One is tempted to apply to colonial India. Clifford Geertz's comment on what he has called 'agricultural involution' in Dutch-ruled Java: the point is not that so many peasants suffered (they would have suffered under capitalist modernization, too), but that they suffered for nothing.

Land Relations

The specific results of commercialization are obviously bound up with the structure of land relations established or consolidated by British revenue and tenancy policies. The evolution of the *zamindari* and *raiyatwari* systems falls outside the scope of the present volume; here we need only note a few long-term trends. British agrarian policies were moulded basically by a combination (in changing and sometimes conflicting proportions) of greed for more revenues (producing recurrent tendencies towards over-assessment) and desire to encourage certain types of agricultural production for export; while the need to win or retain political allies, administrative convenience, and changing ideological assumptions also played a certain role at times. A recurrent pattern of reversal of intentions is clearly noticeable. Thus the belief of the makers of the Permanent Settlement that 'the magic touch of property...would set a certain productive principle in operation' was never realized, as Bengal *zamindars* never developed into improving landlords of the eighteenth century British type. Left virtually free to extort as much rent as they liked while revenue remained perpetually fixed (and therefore became progressively less of a burden despite initial problems of over-assessment), they naturally preferred feudal and usurious exploitation to risky investments in capitalist farming. Enhancement of rent was easy. Since population recovered after the 1770 Famine—and by 1815 Moira was talking of a 'redundancy of the cultivating class'. What developed in fact were not self-managed large estates, but frequently partitioned and fragmented *zamindaris* (by the late nineteenth century 88.5% of the 110,456 permanently settled estates of Bengal and Bihar were less than 500 acres in size) with a mass of intermediate tenures below them providing the major economic basis for the Bengali *bhadralok*. Petty *zamindars* and tenure-holders were by no means always particularly rich people. By the turn of the century they were being hit hard by rising prices, diminishing employment opportunities in government services or professions, and some restrictions on rent-enhancement. But their landed income remained parasitic in nature. This helped to create a curious amalgam of radicalism and social inhibitions which we shall see to be basic for the understanding of nationalism in Bengal.

As for peasants in the areas of the Permanent Settlement, British policies after the 1850s did occasionally try to administer into existence a class of enterprising *raiyats* on the model of English yeomen farmers. Once again the colonial situation led to a paradoxical outcome. The privileged minority of 'occupancy *raiyats*', given legal protection in 1859 and 1885 from arbitrary eviction or rent-enhancement, seldom were, or remained, the actual cultivators, as the same pattern of shifting the burden and risks to groups below them (under-tenants or sharecroppers) soon asserted itself. Thus the direct producer was too oppressed to go in for improvements, while above him had developed a hierarchy of rentiers with no need to go in for entrepreneurial risks and consequently no capacity for innovation.

The ultimate pattern in the *raiyatwari* areas turned out to be not too dissimilar. Despite the theory of direct settlements with cultivators, the Madras *raiyat* became often, in Dharma Kumar's words, 'in effect a landlord who hired his land out' particularly after the 1850s as the burden of over-assessment (which had earlier appeared to necessitate even the use of torture by revenue officials) was gradually somewhat reduced (*Land and Caste in South India,* p. 85). *Raiyatwari* tenants became a growing category whose woes were enhanced by the fact they were unknown to and therefore unprotected by the law. Recent detailed studies have revealed significant regional variations here: Tanjore with its powerful *raiyatwari* landholders employing agricultural labourers; the less numerous and more scattered tiny elite of rich peasants in the interior dry zone of Tamil Nadu and Rayalseema, dominating the mass of cultivators through usury and trade; and the significantly different broad 'middle peasant' development of the Andhra delta. Soil and water supply conditions thus contributed to important variations in peasant differentiation. In Bengal, to take another example, where river flows have been shifting eastwards for centuries, there was a contrast between the western districts (the 'moribund delta') where peasants were splitting up into rich farmers or *jotedars* and share-croppers (*bar-gadars*), and the more prosperous 'active delta' of East Bengal where favourable ecology and profits from jute enabled the survival of a mass of independent small and middle peasant cultivators. Such differences were to have important political consequences.

Below the level of landholding peasants and tenants were a large mass of agricultural labourers, mostly coming from tribals or the lowest castes, and their number (along with their dependents) has been estimated at 52.4 millions in 1901, or almost one-fifth of the total population. Recent research indicates that landless labour was not a creation of the colonial period, as had been argued sometimes by nationalists postulating an idealized version of an egalitarian village community broken up by deindustrialization and consequent over-pressure on land, though the processes associated with colonialism might well have increased the number of the rural proletariat and worsened its conditions. South India, for instance, had from pre-colonial times a sizeable number of farmers with holdings too large for family labour, and often with upper-caste taboos against working with their hands, while there is ample evidence also of the existence of servile untouchable castes of field labourers, like the Cherumans of Malabar or the Tamil Paraiyans (Dharma Kumar, *Land and Caste,* Chapters III and XI). Caste has played a crucial role here, blocking some groups from access to landholding even in a land-surplus situation, and enabling upper-caste farmers to control various forms of semi-slave or 'bonded' labour, particularly at times of seasonal labour-shortage during harvesting, through a combination of social pressure and usury. As Jan Breman has shown in his field-study of the Dubla debt-serfs (*hali*) of Anavil Brahmans in Surat, exploitation in the traditional system was 'complicated and mitigated by a relationship of patronage', with the Dubla looking up to the master as *dhaniamo,* he who gives riches and protects. Colonial (and post-colonial) modernization has tended to reduce this element of patronage, making exploitation more blatant and converting the relationship 'to a labour agreement based on a condition of debt'. (Jan Breman, *Patronage and Exploitation,* pp. 21, 189)

'In no other period of Indian history', Daniel Thorner has pointed out, 'can we find so large, so well-established, and so secure a group of wealthy landholders as that which grew up and flourished between the 1790s and the 1940s.' (*Land and Labour in India,* p. 109) Zamindars and rich peasants often became considerably involved with the processes of commercialization, but what remained largely absent was any structural need to invest in direct agricultural production. Sub-letting of land, usury and trade were much more secure and profitable than direct capitalist farming. Even where agricultural labourers were employed by large farmers, there was little incentive to technical innovation given the existence of a numerous rural proletariat rendered abjectly dependent by a combination of caste pressures and indebtedness. Not modernity, but a consolidation of semi-feudal relations, was therefore the hallmark of the colonial impact on our agrarian scene.

Agricultural Production

Direct government efforts at agricultural improvement remained almost non-existent for a very long time, except for a few experimental farms and some paltry *taccavi* loans from the 1870s. The single major exception was large-scale canal irrigation in the Punjab, western U.P. and parts of Madras. It is interesting that investment in irrigation was conspicuously absent in permanently-settled eastern India, no doubt because there the government could not hope to benefit very much from improvements in cultivation. Irrigation was accepted as a limited but real benefit by nationalist historians, but the recent work of Elizabeth Whitcombe on the United Provinces has thrown considerable doubt on even this aspect of British rule. British canals, it seems, were often less suited to local conditions than traditional *kaccha* wells, and sometimes caused swamps and excessive salinity. In addition, the benefits went entirely to the minority of better-off cultivators, since canal rates were pretty high, while the encouragement through irrigation of crops like sugar, cotton and wheat led to a decline in the production of millets and pulses, the poor man's food. At the same time, there were some positive gains in areas like the Punjab, where virgin lands were put under cultivation through canals constructed by the British.

The colonial structure as a whole, to quote Daniel Thorner again, constituted a 'built-in depressor' for India's agrarian economy. The most obvious indication of this lay in the series of disastrous famines, in the 1870s and again in the late-1890s, the latter wave coinciding with the ravages of plague—while twenty years later even influenza managed to kill off millions. Till 1921, population increased very slowly or not at all (282 million in 1891, 285 million in 1901, 303 million in 1911, 306 million in 1921); whatever Indian poverty might have been due to, it was not caused by overpopulation, though already some apologists had offered that argument.

At a more long-term level, the researches of George Blyn on agricultural statistics from 1893 to 1946 have revealed a truly staggering picture of stagnation or even decline. Taking 1893–96 as the base period, the decennial average of crop output for 1936–46 was 93 for food-crops, 185 for commercial crops, and 110 for agricultural production as a whole. With the post-1921 demographic change, per capita output started to actually decline, becoming 80 for all crops and 68 for food crops by 1936–46. The supplementary calculations of Amiya Bagchi reveal a similar pattern for productivity per acre for the period 1900–05 to 1935–40. The value of commercial crops per acre went up very slightly from ₹36.7 to ₹37.9, while that of food crops declined from ₹25.4 to ₹22.7, and of all crops from ₹27.6 to ₹26.3 (A.K. Bagchi, *Private Investment in India,* p. 95). Equally significant is the contrast between the very sharp decline in Blyn's 'Greater Bengal' area and some advance in Punjab and Madras. The regional backwardness of eastern India which remains a central contemporary problem was already a well-established fact by the last decades of British rule.

Foreign Capital

The claim that British rule was an agency of 'modernization' rests ultimately on facts like railway construction, the development of plantations, mines and factories through British capital, and the introduction of capitalist production relations and modern methods of banking and industrial management by whites. The British did build in India an impressive railway network—the fifth largest in the world by 1900—but in estimating its total impact Marx's comment in a 1881 letter that the railways were 'useless to the Hindus' needs to be remembered more than his much-quoted prediction of 1853, when the first lines were being laid, about the railway system being 'the forerunner of modern industry'. Though railways comprised the single biggest item in British capital investment in India, much of the burden was shifted to the Indian tax-payer through the guaranteed interest system, by which the government paid a minimum dividend even if profits were non-existent. This had involved the payment of more than £50 million by 1900. The whole peculiar system of 'private investment at public risk' inevitably involved wasteful construction and operation—a standard and quite justified nationalist complaint. The network was entirely geared to British commercial and strategic needs, and Indian businessmen often complained of discriminatory freight charges. Above all, the normal 'multiplier' effects of railway investment were largely absent in colonial India. The bulk of railway equipment was imported from England, and the development of ancillary engineering industries consequently remained very inadequate—only about 700 locomotives, for instance, were indigenously produced in the entire pre-independence period. As late as 1921, only 10% of the superior posts in the railways were manned by Indians, so the diffusion of new skills remained limited while a substantial part of the income generated through railway investment leaked out abroad.

Plantations and mines, jute mills, banking, insurance, shipping and export-import concerns—promoted through a system of interlocking managing agency firms which usually combined financial, commercial and industrial activities—all undoubtedly implied significant innovations. How far they contributed to the progress of India is quite another matter, since the tendency was at best towards creating capitalist enclaves under foreign control which really inhibited the development of the rest of the economy. 'Export of capital' takes on a rather special meaning in the Indian context when we remember that in the 1870s, for instance, interest payments abroad regularly exceeded annual capital inflows. Above all, some recent studies of regional variations have revealed the ways in which British control over the decisive sectors of the economy inhibited indigenous capitalist growth throughout our period.

Indian Capitalist Development

The obvious contrast between Indian capitalist development in Bombay and Gujarat and its virtual absence in Bengal has often been sought to be explained by the alleged aversion of the Bengali *bhadralok* towards trade and industry, as well as by the Permanent Settlement attracting indigenous capital to land. But till the 1840s there had been considerable upper caste Bengali involvement in business, while throughout the nineteenth century newspapers and periodicals in Bengal repeatedly urged upon their readers the benefits and virtues of independent enterprise. Parsi business success has been attributed to the existence among them of something like a 'Protestant ethic', but modernistic cultural values were hardly conspicuous among the equally or more successful Gujarati Vanias and Marwaris, while modernism did not help the Bengali Brahmos in economic enterprise. As for land relations, we have already seen that the ultimate impact of the *zamindari* and *raiyatwari* systems was not all that different, while recent research on the land market has thrown doubt on the traditional thesis of the Permanent Settlement immediately attracting urban capital to land. On the whole, as Amiya Bagchi has argued, the easier explanation is in terms of the different degrees of alien imperialist domination over the economy.

The British presence inhibited indigenous capitalism not just through occasional grossly discriminatory tariff and excise policies directed against the Bombay industry, but through a whole variety of structural constraints. The multifarious social connections between white businessmen and white officials have been mentioned already. Behind a facade of *laissez-faire,* government policies often actively promoted European enterprise (railways under the guarantee system, and the allotment of vast tracts of land to Assam tea planters at nominal prices, would be two obvious examples) while discriminating against Indians. The railway network and freight-rates encouraged traffic with ports as against that between inland centres. The organized money-market was largely under white control, the only two major Indian banks before 1914 being the Punjab National Bank and the Bank of India. Most significant of all perhaps was the fact that nineteenth-century Indian economic growth was largely geared to export needs, and the British controlled the bulk of the external trade of the country through their Exchange Banks, export-import firms and shipping concerns.

The white 'collective monopoly' came earliest and remained most pronounced in eastern India. Indian merchants (particularly but not solely Parsis) of western India, in contrast, had always retained a 'toe-hold' on overseas commerce with China and elsewhere, largely because British political control came much later there (necessitating a greater dependence on Indian collaborators) and was somewhat less pervasive. 'Native' political power in western India was formidable till the collapse of the Marathas in 1818, and the patchwork of native states which survived even afterwards contrasts sharply with the map of Bengal. The Bombay hinterland was difficult to penetrate before the construction of railways, and had no indigo, tea or coal—the early targets of British interest.

Traditional Indian business communities did survive and even flourish, but mainly as moneylenders battening on the development of commercial agriculture or dependent traders serving as agents of British export-import firms in the interior The second half of the nineteenth century was in fact marked by an acceleration of the process of Marwari expansion over much of northern, eastern and central India, as well as by the movement of south Indian Chettiar traders and moneylenders into Burma and other parts of South East Asia as dependent collaborators of the British. Timberg's recent study has documented the essentially dependent role of Marwari family firms till the First World War. Thus the 'great firm' of Tarachand Ghanshyamdas which he has examined in detail acted as *banias* of Shaw Wallace, and similar relations of dependent collaboration existed between the Goenkas and Ralli Brothers, Jhunjhunwalla and Grahams, Jatia and Andrew Yule.

It was only in western India, initially in Bombay and a little later in Ahmedabad, that capital accumulated through compradore trade (in Bombay mainly trade with China) found a fruitful outlet in a genuinely capitalist indigenous textile industry. Raw cotton was readily available from a Deccan opened up by railways constructed during the short-lived cotton boom of the 1860s, while the British showed little interest in investing in a textile industry which would compete with Manchester.

The rise of Bombay was already causing acute alarm in Lancashire by the mid-1870s, and the unfair tariff and excise policies periodically adopted under Home pressure formed one of the major stimuli, accentuating growth of patriotic consciousness among the Indian intelligentsia. The relation between Bombay and Lancashire, however, was never one of simple or total conflict. The interlocking between finance, trade and industry characteristic of the managing agency system meant that many textile firms also had connections with the trade in imported yarn or piecegoods. Bombay mills depended heavily on European technical expertise and entirely on imported machinery. Above all, direct clashes between Bombay and Manchester were not very common before the early decades of the twentieth century due to a number of technical reasons. Down to the 1890s, Bombay concentrated on cotton twist and yarn rather than piecegoods, and much of the former was exported to the Far East or used to supply Indian handlooms. The bulk of Indian mill yarn, again, consisted of counts below 24, whereas only about 18% of the yarn imported into Bombay fell into this range in 1893–94. Piece-goods competition in the Indian home market was mainly limited to the 'coarse, medium' variety; for higher quality cloth Indian mill competition was quite ineffective till after 1905. At the turn of the century, war in China and plague in Bombay brought about the first sharp fall in the export of twist and yarn to the Far East followed by a steady decline in face of

Japanese competition. The consequent shift in emphasis from spinning to weaving was most noticeable in Ahmedabad, which had always catered more to the domestic market than Bombay and also used relatively higher-count yarn, and which therefore had to confront Lancashire much more directly. The greater involvement of Ahmedabad with the national movement once that movement seemed capable of delivering the goods with the rise of Gandhi thus had fairly clear economic roots.

Together with the industrial bourgeoisie, the working class constituted the second new element in the late nineteenth century Indian situation. Its growth remained fairly slow, with the number' of persons employed in organized industry estimated in 1911 at only 2.1 million (including 8 lakhs in plantations) in a population of 303 million. But, as in many other countries, concentration in big cities like Bombay and Calcutta would give the proletariat (from the 1920s onwards) an occasional striking power much in excess of its numbers. In British and Indian-owned enterprises alike, the horrors characteristic of early capitalist industrialization were compounded by numerous 'pre-capitalist' survivals. Coolies for Assam tea-plantations, as well as migrant Indian labour for Fiji, Mauritius, Natal and the West Indies, Were recruited through an indenture system which resembled slavery much more than wage-labour. Here, as elsewhere, imperialism was fostering pre-capitalist forms. Recruitment in mines, railways and factories was technically free, but carried on by intermediary jobbers or contractors whose demands for perquisites added to the burdens on the workers. East U.P., Bihar and Madras Presidency constituted the main catchment areas for the flow of labour to eastern Indian plantations, mines and factories, and the working class of the Calcutta industrial area thus became predominantly non-Bengali. Ahmedabad and Bombay in contrast drew their labour supply from nearby areas, the first from Gujarat villages and the second from the Maharashtra hinterland (particularly Ratnagiri district in Konkan)—a difference which would have some trade union and political consequences later on.

Despite such signs of growth in the 'modern' sector, the dominant fact in the economy of colonial India remained that of abject mass poverty. Early estimates of per capita annual national income involved a lot of sheer guess-work, and were also very much a part of the ongoing political debate between nationalists and defenders of British rule. They range pretty widely, therefore, from the Indophile Digby's figure of ₹18 for 1899 to Atkinson's ₹39.5 for 1895 in current prices. Yet even Atkinson's estimate came to only £2–13s-0d, whereas a generally accepted figure for Britain in 1901 is £52. The poverty of the masses would remain the permanent backdrop to all social, political and cultural trends in the life of modern India.

CHAPTER 3
SOCIAL AND POLITICAL MOVEMENTS 1885–1905

TOWARDS A 'HISTORY FROM BELOW'

Our survey so far of the structure of colonial political and economic domination has indicated the roots of numerous conflicts—between imperialism and most sections of the Indian people, as well as between various groups or classes within Indian society itself. What must be explored now are the ways in which these contradictions surfaced in the life and thought and activities of our people, and here the already-mentioned major lag in social history in the proper sense of that term immediately creates a major problem. A good deal has been written about the Western-educated intelligentsia, a group undoubtedly crucial but still quantitatively minute, and there exists considerable anthropological and sociological literature in the form of studies of particular tribes, villages and castes. But there is very little so far in the way of rounded general studies of major social groups at even a regional level, no real history of *zamindars* or peasants, agricultural labourers or artisans, industrial workers or bourgeois elements, analysing the changes both in their conditions of living and in their consciousness. This crucial gap leaves the history of political movements and particularly of nationalism in something like a vacuum, and tends to make such history essentially a study from the top downwards. A 'history from below', in which the tribal rebellion of Birsa Munda might find mention before the quarrels of Moderates and Extremists, is bound at present to remain extremely sketchy and provisional, yet perhaps an occasional attempt in that direction would not be out of place.

Over the last twenty years, research on so-called 'civil disturbances' has revealed *Pax Britannica* to have been largely a myth for at least a century after Plassey, broken as it was repeatedly in most parts of the country by revolts that were led by traditionalist elements (dispossessed local chiefs, *zamindars* or religious figures) but were predominantly lower-class in social composition. The anthropologist Kathleen Gough has recently compiled a list of 77 peasant uprisings involving violence for the entire British period, and classified them under five types—'restorative', religious, social banditry, terrorist vengeance, and armed insurrection. 1857 might be regarded as the culmination of the older type of anti-British resistance, led by dispossessed chiefs and with 'restorative' aims. We do get a general impression of a relative decline in such outbursts towards the close of the century—a decline explicable in terms of the consolidation of British links with princes and *zamindars* in the post-Mutiny era, the development of communications and of a more efficient military and administrative structure, and perhaps also the exhaustion caused by the repeated famines of the 1870s and 1890s. Yet sporadic plebian outbursts were by no means entirely absent, and at times they involved some interesting changes in forms.

Tribal Movements

As in earlier or later periods, the most militant outbreaks tended to be of tribal communities, which, in the words of a recent scholar, 'revolted more often and far more violently than any other community including peasants in India'. (K. Suresh Singh) The term 'tribe' is used to distinguish people so socially organized from 'caste' and should not convey a sense of complete isolation from the mainstream of Indian life. Actually, apart from some isolated and really primitive food-gatherers, the tribals were and are very much a part of Indian society as the lowest stratum of the peasantry subsisting through shifting cultivation, agricultural labourers, and increasingly, coolies recruited for work in distant plantations, mines and factories. British rule and its accompanying commercialization strengthened already present tendencies towards penetration of tribal areas by outsiders from the plains—moneylenders, traders, land-grabbers and contractors, the *dikus* so hated by the Santhals. British legal conceptions of absolute private property eroded traditions of joint ownership (like the *khuntkatti* tenure in Chota Nagpur) and sharpened tensions within tribal society. Christian missions were active in many tribal areas (particularly in Bihar and the Assam hills), bringing education and some promise of social ascent, but often provoking an interesting variety of reactions which included hostility as well as attempts to use some Christian tenets in anti- foreign ways. A new but increasingly important factor from the 1870s and '80s was the tightening of control by the colonial state over forest zones for revenue purposes. Shifting cultivation—which required no plough animals and therefore was often essential for the survival of the poorest in rural society—was banned or restricted in the 'reserved' forests from 1867 onwards, and attempts were made to monopolize forest wealth through curbs on use of timber and grazing facilities.

The tribal response included, as before, occasional violent outbursts, but also movements of internal religious and socio-cultural reform. Such movements of 'revitalization', borrowing elements from Christianity or Hinduism and promising a sudden miraculous entry into a golden age, became increasingly typical in the period 1860–1920, generally following in the wake of defeated uprisings under traditional chiefs. Thus the Santhal rebellion (1855) was followed by the Kherwar or Sapha Har movement of the 1870s, which preached monotheism and internal social reform at first but had begun to turn into a campaign against revenue settlement operations just before it was suppressed. Millenarianism (belief in an imminent golden age) could also take more violent forms, as when the Naikda forest tribe in Gujarat attacked police stations in 1868 in a bid to establish a *dharma-raj,* or the Kacha Nagas of Cachar in 1882 attacked the whites under a miracle-worker named Sambhudan who claimed that his magic had made his followers immune to bullets. Old District Gazetteers and anthropological surveys contain in fact numerous references to such things, and are at times strangely moving. In Vizagapatam Agency, for instance, in 1900 a Konda Dora named Korra Mallaya 'pretended that he was inspired…gathered round him a camp of 4–5000 people…gave out that he was a reincarnation of one of the five Pandava brothers; that his infant son was the god Krishna; that he would drive out the English and rule the country himself, and that, to effect this, he would arm his followers with bamboos, which should be turned by magic into guns, and would change the weapons of the authorities into water.' The result was predictable: the police shot dead 11 of the 'rioters' and put 60 on trial, of whom two were hanged. (Thurston and Rangachari, *Castes and Tribes of Southern India,* Vol. III, Madras 1909, p. 353)

The hills of the neighbouring Godavari Agency had been the scene of a much more formidable rebellion in 1879–80. Its heart lay in the 'Rampa' country of Chodavaram, whose tribal Koya and Konda Dora hill chiefs (*muttadars*) had risen against their overlord (a *mansabdar* family which had come to an understanding with the British in 1813) in 1840, 1845, 1858, 1861 and 1862. The major revolt of March, 1879 was rooted in the *mansabdar's* efforts to enhance taxes on timber and grazing, while police exactions, new excise regulations restricting domestic preparation of toddy, exploitation by low-country traders and moneylenders, and restrictions on shifting cultivation (*podu*) in forests provided additional grievances. The rebellion at its height affected no less than 5000 square miles, and it could be suppressed by November, 1880 only with the use of six regiments of Madras infantry. In another uprising in the same area in 1886, the rebels called themselves *Rama Dandu* (Rama's army), and Rajana Anantayya, one of their leaders, made an interesting 'proto-nationalistic' appeal to the Maharaja of Jeypore: 'Is it good, if the English be in our country?… We… should wage war with the English. The Russians are also troubling the

English. If the assistance of men end arms are supplied to me, I will play Rama's part.' (David Arnold, 'Dacoity and Rural Crime in Madras, 1860–1940', in *Journal of Peasant Studies,* January 1979) A use of the *Ramayana* legend rather different from Gandhi's later concept of *Ram-rajya*!

The best-known of the tribal rebellions of this period, however, is the *Ulgulan* (Great Tumult) of Birsa Munda in the region south of Ranchi in 1899–1900, the subject of a fine recent study by the anthropologist and historian K. Suresh Singh. The Mundas in course of the nineteenth century had seen their traditional *khuntkatti* land system (joint holdings by *khunts* or tribal lineages) being eroded by *jagirdars* and *thikadars* coming from the northern plains as merchants and moneylenders. The area had also become a happy hunting ground for contractors recruiting indentured labour. A succession of Lutheran, Anglican and Catholic missions appeared to promise some help, but eventually did nothing about the basic land problem. In the early 1890s, the tribal chiefs (*Sardars*) attempted to fight the alien landlords and the imposition of *beth begari* (forced labour) in the courts, through a Calcutta-based Anglo-Indian lawyer who seems to have cheated them. A missionary reported the *Sardars* as complaining: 'We have appealed to the Sarkar for redress and got nothing. We have turned to the Missions and they too have not saved us from the Dikus. Now there is nothing left us but to look to one of our own men.'

The Munda saviour came in the shape of Birsa (*c.* 1874–1900), son of a sharecropper who had received some education from the missionaries and had then come under Vaishnava influence, and who in 1893–94 had participated in a movement to prevent village waste lands being taken over by the Forest Department. In 1895 young Birsa is said to have seen a vision of a supreme God, after which he claimed to be a prophet with miraculous healing powers. Thousands began flocking to Chalked to hear the 'new word' of Birsa with its prophecy of an imminent deluge, while the *Sardars* started introducing an agrarian and political note into the initially religious movement. Birsa was jailed for two years in 1895 by the British who feared a conspiracy, but he returned much more of a firebrand. A series of night meetings were held in the forest during 1898–99, where Birsa allegedly urged the 'killing of Thikadars and Jagirdars and Rajas and Hakims and Christians' and promised 'that the guns and bullets would turn to water'. Effigies of the British Raj were solemnly burnt, and the Mundas responded enthusiastically to passionate hymns of hate:

> *Katong Baba Katong*
> *Saheb Katong Katong, Rari Katong Katong . . .*
> (O father, kill the Europeans, kill the other castes O kill, kill...).

On Christmas eve, 1899, the Birsaites (who had already won over large numbers of Christian Mundas to their new faith in a single god whose prophet was Birsa Bhagawan) shot arrows and tried to burn down churches over an area covering six police stations in the districts of Ranchi and Singbhum. The police themselves became the main targets in January 1900, leading to a veritable panic in Ranchi. On January 9, however, the rebels were defeated at Sail Rakab hill, and Birsa was captured three weeks later and died in jail. Nearly 350 Mundas were put on trial, three were hanged and 44 transported for life. The survey and settlement operations of 1902–10 and the Chotanagpur Tenancy Act of 1908, however, did provide some very belated recognition to *khuntkatti* rights and banned *beth begari*. Chotanagpur tribals won a degree of legal protection for their land rights, a generation in advance of the bulk of the Bihar peasantry: violent movements do not always fail. And Birsa Munda remains a living memory, both as the apostle of a small religious sect and more generally through some extraordinarily moving folk songs, which Suresh Singh has recorded in his field work. Not unexpectedly, perhaps, he is revered for different and sometimes quite contradictory reasons—as a full-fledged nationalist, a prophet of a separatist Jharkhand, or a hero of the extreme Left. Seeking a conscious all-India nationalist in Birsa is obviously futile. His vision could not have embraced anything broader than a heroic defence of his tribal homeland against all intruders—from which it does not follow, however, that a certain primitive but basic anti-imperialist content be necessarily denied to his movement.

Phadke

In the rising of Vasudeo Balvant Phadke in Maharashtra (1879) a short-lived concord, all but unique in its time, was achieved between conscious intelligentsia nationalism and plebian militancy. Phadke, a Chitpavan Brahman and a Commissariat Department clerk who had some English education, seems to have been influenced by Ranade's lectures on drain of wealth, the experience of the Deccan famine of 1876–77, and the growing Hindu revivalist mood among Poona Brahman intellectuals. In an autobiographical fragment written while hiding from the police in a temple, Phadke later recalled how he had thought of reestablishing a Hindu Raj by collecting together a secret band, raising money through dacoities, and instigating an armed revolt through disrupting communications. 'There is much ill-feeling among the people and now if a few make a beginning those who are hungry will join.' Much of this clearly anticipates later revolutionary terrorism. What is remarkable, however, is that Phadke's band of forty included a few

Brahman youths and many more low caste Ramoshis and Dhangars. The outcome was a type of social banditry, with the dacoits given shelter by the peasants. After Phadke's capture and life sentence, a Ramoshi dacoit band under Daulata Ramoshi remained active till 1883, while we also hear of a tribal Koli group committing 28 dacoities in seven months before being smashed. The Kolis in this region were being ousted from their ancestral lands, like their brethren in so many other parts of the country.

Moplahs

The turbulent history of the Moplahs of Malabar reveals yet another facet of the complexities of the Indian situation—the way in which religious 'fanaticism' has served as the outward form for the expression of anti-landlord and anti-foreign discontent. A bitter anti-white temper had developed among sections of the Malabar Muslims ever since the Portuguese had come in 1498 to capture the spice trade and seek to extend Christianity by fire and sword—a spirit reflected in Zayn al-Din's, *Tuhfat al-Mujahidin* of the 1580s and ballads like the *Kothupali Mala,* still popular today, honouring the martyrs or *shahids* of the holy war. British rule with its insistence on landlord rights had reestablished and vastly enhanced the position of the Hindu upper caste Namboodri and Nair *jenmis* (many of whom had been driven out by Tipu Sultan), and correspondingly worsened the condition of the largely Muslim leaseholders (*kanamdars*) and cultivators (*verumpattam-dars*)*,* locally known as Moplahs. An immediate consequence was a strengthening of communal solidarity, with the number of mosques in Malabar going up from 637 in 1831 to 1058 by 1851, and with the Tangals of Mambram near Tirurangadi (Sayyid Alawi followed by his son Sayyid Fadl who was exiled by the British in 1852) becoming increasingly prominent as the religious cum-political heads of Moplah society. There was also large-scale conversion of untouchable Cherumars to a religion which promised a degree of equality and some social ascent. Revolt became practically endemic in the Ernad and Walluvanad *talukas* of south Malabar, with 22 recorded between 1836 and 1854, and more risings in 1882–85 and again in 1896. It took the form of attacks on *jenmi* property and desecration of temples, by small bands of Moplahs who then committed what was practically a kind of collective suicide in the face of police bullets, courting death in the firm belief that as *shahids* they would go straight to heaven. The number of activists was rather small, 349 in all in the 28 outbreaks recorded between 1836 and 1919, for collective mass resistance was difficult in south Malabar with its poor communications and scattered homesteads. The Moplah outbreaks were thus 'a peculiar form of rural terrorism which...

was probably the most effective means of curbing the enhanced power of the *jenmi,* for the earthly benefit of Moplahs who themselves did not become participants'. 62 out of 82 victims of Moplah attacks down to 1919 were high-caste Hindus (22 Namboodri and 34 Nair), while of the 70 whose class background can be traced, 58 were *jenmis* and/or moneylenders. (Conrad Wood, 'Peasant Revolt: An Interpretation of Moplah Violence in the 19th and 20th Centuries', in Dewey and Hopkins, *ed., The Imperial Impact: Studies in the Economic History of Africa and India,* London, 1978) Most Moplah martyrs were poor peasants or landless labourers, but they usually got the sympathy of the better-off *kanamdars* and petty traders. One hears also of a widespread belief that a ship was coming with arms for the Moplahs—a myth startlingly similar to the 'cargo-cults' of Melanesia in the Pacific under colonial rule, which have been studied by anthropologists like Peter Worsley. The roots of Moplah discontent were clearly agrarian— there was a 244% increase in rent suits and a 441% increase in eviction decrees between 1862 and 1880 in the *talukas* of south Malabar. Hindu peasants also suffered, but the form of resistance differed. Large numbers of Hindu robber bands are reported to have been active in the Malabar villages in the 1860s and 1870s. In the absence of a millenarian ideology such as Islam could offer, Hindu peasant disaffection could not rise above the level of social banditry.

Deccan Riots

So far we have been considering outbreaks aiming at something like a total change, often with strong religious and millenarian overtones (natural in the absence of any secular modern ideology of social transformation), and rooted in the lowest depths of Indian society—tribals and poor peasantry. But there was also a tradition of another type of rural protest, sparked off by particular grievances and with specific and limited objectives, and deriving its leadership and much of its support from relatively better-off sections of the peasantry. In the Maharashtra Deccan, for instance, the rich peasant development brought about by the cotton boom of the 1860s had been abruptly cut short by the fall in prices in the next decade—a fall which coincided with sharp upward hikes in land revenue from 1867 onwards. The result was widespread indebtedness, and the immigrant Marwari moneylender became an obvious target of popular anger. The anti-*sowkar* Deccan riots of May-September 1875 affected 33 places in 6 *talukas* of Poona and Ahmednagar districts, and took the form of forcible seizure of debt bonds by enraged villagers led by their traditional headmen (*patels*). Riots were significantly uncommon in areas where the moneylenders were not outsiders but local petty-landholders or rich peasant elements turning to usury and trade (like the *khots* in Ratnagiri). Four years after the disturbances, the Deccan Agriculturists' Relief Act of 1879 provided some limited protection to better-off peasants through strengthening judicial procedures and remedies.

Pabna

Anti-moneylender riots were rare also in Bengal (except in tribal pockets), for here too the *mahajan* was often the local rich peasant or *jotedar* whose credit in any case was quite indispensable for production. The *zamindar* in contrast had virtually no productive role, and claims to 'high landlordism' led to widespread resistance by substantial *raiyats* in large parts of east Bengal in the 1870s and early '80s. The storm-centre was Pabna, a relatively prosperous district with a lot of double-cropping and a flourishing trade in jute, where more than 50% of the cultivators had managed to win occupancy rights (giving immunity from eviction and some restraints on rent-enhancement) under Act X of 1859. Yet *zamindari* rents had increased seven-fold since 1793 by 1872, and the landlords had launched a concerted drive in the 1860s and early '70s to enhance rent through a variety of *abwabs* (cesses), the use of arbitrarily short standards of measurement which automatically multiplied the cultivated area, and sheer physical coercion—moves which amounted to an attack on the new security won by the occupant *raiyats*. In 1873 peasants of Yusufshahi *pargana* of Pabna organized an agrarian league which raised funds to meet litigation expenses, held mass meetings to which villagers were called by the sounding of buffalo horns, drums and night cries passing from hamlet to hamlet, and also occasionally withheld rent. Similar movements were reported during the next decade from a number of neighbouring east Bengal districts (Dacca, Mymensingh, Tripura, Backergunj, Faridpur, Bogura and Rajshahi). Despite much panic-stricken talk, in Calcutta *zamindar* circles, of peasant violence and revolt, *raiyat* resistance was in fact eminently legalistic and peaceful apart from a few sporadic incidents in Pabna. The aims of the movement were also quite limited, for the withholding of rents was no more than a method for winning specific demands like a change in the measurement standard, abolition of illegal cesses, and some reduction in rents. Nor was the Pabna agitation consciously anti-British: the most extreme demand raised in fact was that the *raiyats* wanted 'to be the ryots of Her Majesty the Queen and of Her only'. Such appeals to the distant overlord as against the immediate oppressor are of course not uncommon in peasant movements, and the Pabna *raiyats* had been encouraged in fact by certain apparently pro-peasant moves by officials like Lt. Governor Campbell's proclamation in July 1873 which accepted peasant combinations as lawful even while condemning violence.

The Pabna league and similar movements in other districts evoked sharply varied reactions among the Bengali intelligentsia. The *zamindars*-dominated British Indian Association was bitterly hostile, and its organ *Hindoo Patriot* tried to portray the Pabna movement as a communal agitation of Muslim peasants against Hindu landlords. Actually, though the bulk of the peasants in Pabna happened to be Muslim and their *zamindars* mostly Hindus, the communal element was as yet virtually absent (in sharp contrast to what was to happen often in the twentieth century) the three principal leaders of the agrarian league being the petty landholder Ishan Chandra Roy, the village headman Shambhu Pal (both caste Hindus), and the Muslim *jotedar* Khoodi Mollah. Incidentally, one of the *zamindars* principally affected was Dwijendranath Tagore, elder brother of the poet Rabindranath, who urged the government to take drastic action 'for the restoration of order and tranquillity' in July 1873. Professional groups with less connections with big *zamindari*, however, took a more sympathetic attitude, as evidenced in R.C. Dutt's *Peasantry of Bengal* (1874) and a little later in the Indian Association campaign in defence of tenant rights (which even involved the organization of a number of *raiyat* meetings) on the eve of the Tenancy Act of 1885. Occupancy rights were preserved and somewhat extended by the latter Act, yet what is at least as significant is the total absence of concern whether in the Pabna movement, the later Indian Association agitation or in Government legislation, for peasants without occupancy claims, sharecroppers or agricultural labourers. Occupancy *raiyats* were in fact already often subletting their land to *korfa raiyats* who were left completely unprotected, and no emphasis was ever placed on linking up occupancy rights with actual cultivation. The ultimate effect of this entire period of agrarian unrest and tenancy legislation in Bengal was to foster the growth of *jotedar* groups who have proved as exploitative and parasitic as the *zamindars*, whom they were to gradually replace.

No-Revenue Movements

British attempts to hike up land revenue in temporarily-settled *raiyatwari* areas occasionally provoked yet another type of rural protest, marked by a high degree of unanimity, leadership by local notables, and much more unequivocal support from the intelligentsia. In the Kamrup and Darrang districts of Assam, for instance, a new revenue settlement in 1893–94 which enhanced rates by 50 to 70 per cent was met by the organization of *raijmels*, mass assemblies of villagers led by the rural elite (Brahmans, Gossains and Dolois) which enforced non-payment of revenue through the weapons of social boycott or ostracism of those who broke the popular consensus by submitting to the government. Thus a traditional instrument of caste authority was being used against the rulers, anticipating by more than a decade methods which middle-claas nationalism would begin to use only after 1905. There was also some looting of bazars, and two cases of police firing, at Rangiya and Patharughat, in January 1894. The demand for revenue reduction was supported by the Jorhat Sarvajanik Sabha, and the issue was raised at the Imperial Legislative Council by the Moderate Congress leader of Bengal, Rash-behari Ghosh; eventually some concessions were obtained. But, at the other end of the social scale, folk memory has also preserved the names of some plebian militants, like Pusparam Kanhar, the bell-metal artisan of Sarukhetri.

In the Maharashtra Deccan in 1896–97, famine conditions led to looting of grain-shops and demand for revenue-remissions under the Famine Code—a demand which the government rejected. The Poona Sarvajanik Sabha, which had been recently captured by Tilak, sent agents out into the countryside between October 1896 and April 1897 to popularize the legal rights of *raiyats* in a famine situation. The government was seriously alarmed, and talked of nationalists taking over the methods of Irish agitators. Actually Tilak's movement was largely confined to the holding of meetings and circulation of pamphlets, though some short-lived no-revenue combinations were started in districts like Thana, Kolaba and Ratnagiri. Popular pressure, in conjunction with some middle-class initiative, was here once again anticipating what was to become standard nationalist technique under Gandhi. As in Phadke's movement, popular resistance continued even after the nationalist agitators had withdrawn. In the central division of Bombay Presidency (the Maharashtra heartland around Poona), the number of the cases of distraint of moveable property for non-payment of revenue went up from an annual average of 26 during 1892–97 to 194 in 1897–98 and 2269 in 1898–99. After the famine of 1899–1900, no-revenue combinations allegedly led by rich peasants and moneylenders were reported from Surat, Nasik, Kheda and Ahmedabad districts, though the Poona Sarvajanik Sabha had by then become quite inactive.

Modern Indian history would have been very much simpler, however, if all important conflicts had been of the type we have been studying so far— fairly direct movements of resistance to exploitation by *dikus,* moneylenders, *zamindars,* or the colonial state. But the vast majority of Indians were accustomed to thinking in terms of caste and religious units which often cut across or blurred class differences, and despite the claims often made for it to have been a modernizing force, colonialism in practice strengthened such traditional loyalties in a variety of ways.

Caste Consciousness

Recent sociological work on caste has increasingly emphasized that the meaningful units here are not the somewhat abstract *varnas* (the theoretical all-India hierarchy as described in Sanskrit texts) but the mass of diverse local *jatis,* united by a varying degree of occupational identity, common rites and customs, and taboos on marriages or eating outside the group. The old assumption of an absolutely rigid and unchanging hierarchy of castes has also been rejected, and numerous instances are being discovered, in the recent and not-so-recent past, of what M.N. Srinivas called 'Sanskritizing' tendencies—*jatis* asserting a higher status for themselves through borrowing customs, manners and taboos from groups traditionally superior to them. In pre-British India, caste mobility had been facilitated by a fluid political system and a land-surplus permitting easy migration. The Sadgops of medieval Bengal, for instance, rose as farmers and traders from out of the originally pastoral Gop community, migrated into virgin lands along the Bengal-Bihar border, and sometimes also carved out local principalities. The colonial period closed or reduced some of these avenues, but opened up others. Carving out new kingdoms was now impossible, and virgin land was increasingly scarce. But improved communications made wider combinations possible, English education increasingly provided a new ladder to social promotion for small but growing minorities, and colonial exploitation did involve (as we have seen) a process of differentiation which benefited some Indian groups at the expense of others. From the 1901 Census onwards, the British also made a direct contribution by trying every ten years to classify castes on the basis of 'social precedence as recognized by native public opinion'—an attempt which immediately encouraged a flood of claims and counter-claims as *jati* leaders jostled for pre-eminence, organized caste associations, and invented mythological caste 'histories'. Caste solidarity one might add, was encouraged in at least two ways by the new situation. Successful leading members of a *jati* found it useful to mobilize support from caste-brethren in their usually quite parochial and selfish struggle for social recognition, jobs, and political favours—a process greatly encouraged by the gradual introduction of electoral politics from the 1880s onwards. As for the poorer members of a *jati,* links of patronage with more successful fellow-members seemed often the only means of survival in a harsh and increasingly alien world.

The net result has often been the expression of socio-economic tensions through a kind of false-consciousness of caste solidarity, caste rivalry, and movements for Sanskritization. Bernard Cohn's study of a Jaunpur village (eastern U.P.), for instance, reveals the way in which the Chamars (mostly small peasants or landless labourers, subjected to the power of Rajput Thakur landowners) have found solace in the doctrines of the Siva-Narayana sect and have tried to elevate their social status by imitating Brahmanical forms (like the taboo on beef). At the other end of the country, the untouchable Ezhavas of Kerala were inspired by Nanu Asan (Sri Narayana Guru, *c.* 1854–1928) from the early twentieth century to attack Brahman domination, demand entry into temples, and also to 'Sanskritize' some of their own customs. Ezhavas incidentally later became the firmest supporters of Communists in Kerala, and E.M.S. Namboodripad has gone so far as to state that caste associations at times were 'the first form in which the peasants masses rose in struggle against feudalism', though he hastens to add that 'the grip of these caste organizations on the peasantry has to be broken if they are to be organized as a class'. (*National Question in Kerala,* Bombay, 1952, p. 102)

In south Tamilnadu, Hardgrave's detailed study of the rise of the Nadars reveals how the untouchable caste of toddy tappers and agricultural labourers, originally called Shanans, developed a mercantile upper stratum which claimed Kshatriya status in the 1901 census and began calling itself Nadar (a term previously confined to the Shanan owners of land and palmyra trees). Its assertion of temple-entry rights led to serious riots at Tirunelveli in 1899. The Pallis of northern Tamilnadu similarly claimed Kshatriya origin from 1871, began to call themselves Vanniya Kula Kshatriya, and started imitating Brahmanical mores like the taboo on widow-remarriage. The Mahars of Maharashtra, later the backbone of Ambedkar's movement, were beginning to organize themselves under an ex-serviceman, Gopal Baba Walangkar, by the end of the nineteenth century. An 1894 petition drafted by Walangkar claimed Kshatriya origins and more jobs in the army and services for this untouchable caste of inferior village servants (watchmen, local arbitrators, messengers, sweepers, etc.), some of whose traditional occupations had been threatened under British rule but which had also for a time obtained new opportunities through military service. The new emphasis on north Indian 'martial races' in army recruitment provided the immediate provocation for the beginning of Mahar organization.

On the whole, however, the more effective caste movements in our present period tended to be connected with intermediate ranks, below the twice-born and above the untouchables, and usually included considerable landed or rich peasant elements with the capacity to produce urban educated groups.

In Maharashtra and Madras, clear-cut Brahman domination over the services and general cultural life was already leading to anti-Brahrnanical movements by the end of the century. The anti-Brahman tocsin was first sounded in Maharashtra in the 1870s by Jyotiba Phule with his book, *Ghulam-giri* (1872) and his organization, the Satyashodhak Samaj (1873), which proclaimed the need to save the 'lower castes from the hypocritical Brahmans and their opportunistic scriptures'. Started by an urban-educated member of the lowly *mali* (gardening) caste, this movement later struck some roots among the predominantly peasant Maratha caste-cluster. Gail Omvedt's valuable recent study (*Cultural Revolt in a Colonial Society: The Non Brahman Movement in Western India, 1873–1930*) has emphasized a dualism within the Satyashodhak movement, which contained 'both an elite-based conservative trend and a more genuine mass-based radicalism'. The first developed along moderate 'Sanskritizing' lines, occasionally claimed a Kshatriya origin for the Marathas, and from the 1890s received the patronage of the Maharaja of Kolhapur. It was openly loyalist and politically divisive, for the British were egging on Kolhapur against Tilak, and Bhaskarrao Jadav's non-Brahman party after 1919 was strongly anti-Congress. But there was also a second trend, working in villages rather than towns (unlike most other 19th century social reform movements) and using the Marathi vernacular rather than English, which attacked the caste system rather than merely claiming a higher status within it, and claimed to speak for the *bahujan samaj* against the *shetji-bhatji* (moneylenders and Brahmans). It would inspire peasant risings in Satara in 1919–21, and later help to revitalize the Gandhian Congress in rural Maharashtra. A somewhat similar pattern can be seen a little later in Madras, as the undoubted Brahman predominance in education and services (Brahmans accounted for 3.2% of the Presidency population, but about 70% of Madras University graduates between 1870 and 1918) came to be challenged by educated Tamil Vellalas, Telegu Reddis and Kammas, and Malayali Nairs. The sub-elite character of this challenge was clearly indicated by the frequent references in the non-Brahman Manifesto of December 1916 to the non-Brahmans as forming 'the bulk of the tax payers, including a large majority of the *zamindars*, landholders, and agriculturists...'. Irshchik's study provides ample evidence of British encouragement of what eventually became a kind of 'Dravidian' or Tamil separatism. This was to be quite obvious with the Justice Party of the 1920s and '30s, but as early as 1886, a convocation address by the Governor of Madras makes interesting reading: 'You are a pure Dravidian race. I should like to see the pre-Sanskrit element amongst you asserting itself rather more.... You have less to do with Sanskrit than we English have. Ruffianly Europeans have sometimes been known to speak of natives of India as "Niggers", but they did not, like the proud speakers or writers of Sanskrit, speak of the people of the South as legions of monkeys.' As with many other types of internal tensions (whether caste, religious, regional, or class), imperialists here made skilful use of real grievances to foster sectional consciousness. At the same time, as in Maharashtra, certain socially radical possibilities were not entirely absent in Tamilnadu, as seen by the emergence of the militant, and often atheistic, Self-Respect movement in the 1920s. The 'Sanskritization' label is thus not really appropriate for all 'caste movements', some of which have at times challenged the very basis of caste.

Brahman domination was less clear-cut in northern and eastern India, with other high-caste groups serving as buffers, (like Rajputs and Kayasthas in U.P. and Bihar, and Kayasthas and Vaidyas in Bengal). Mobilization along caste lines came somewhat later here, though it is important enough today. However, the Kayasthas by virtue of their inter-provincial professional connections were already starting an all-India association and newspaper (the Allahabad-based *Kayastha Samachar*) by 1900. In Bengal, lower-caste associations started getting important from the first decade of the twentieth century. Better-off Kaivartas of Midnapur, led by some local *zamindars* and a few Calcutta-based lawyers and traders, began calling themselves Mahishyas and started a Jati Nirdharani Sabha in 1897 and a Central Mahishya Samiti during the 1901 Census. Midnapur Mahishyas later played a prominent part in the national movement. British divide-and-rule tactics were much more successful, however, among the Namasudras of Faridpur, who started developing associations after 1901 at the initiative of a tiny elite of educated men and some missionary encouragement. The contrast may perhaps be partly explained by the fact that the Mahishyas of Midnapur were a locally dominant caste which included petty landlords and substantial peasants as well as the poor, while the Namasudras were untouchable poor peasants who felt upper-caste gentry exploitation to be a nearer enemy than the distant British overlord.

Communal Consciousness

The second major type of sectional consciousness bred and often directly fostered by colonialism was religious division—Hindu and Muslim 'communalism'. Clear thinking on this very complex subject has been hindered considerably by the development in the twentieth century of two opposite stereotypes—the communalist assumption of Hindus and Muslims as homogeneous and inevitably hostile entities, two 'nations' ever since medieval times; and the nationalist countermyth of a golden age of perfect amity broken solely by British divide-and-rule. Both stereotypes assume kinds of country-wide integration and uniformity almost certainly impossible prior to the development of communications and economic connections in the second half of the nineteenth century. Indian nationalism and Hindu and Muslim communalism are in fact both essentially modern phenomena. Instances of local conflicts between Hindus and Muslims may certainly be found occasionally in past centuries, just as there are numerous instances of Shia-Sunni clashes and caste quarrels. But communal riots do seem to have been significantly rare down to the 1880s. Thus in 1944 Coupland, a scholar with clear imperialist affiliations who surely had no reason to underplay the issue (he even declared that the Hindu-Muslim problem was 'the cause of the continuance of British rule'), found one major instance at Benares in 1809 (where Hindus are said to have destroyed 50 mosques), and the next big outbreak only in 1871-72, followed by a series of riots from 1885 onwards. (R. Coupland, *Constitutional Problem in India*, p. 29)

That communalism in a large measure sprang from elite conflicts over jobs and political favours has long been a truism, and scholars have generally concentrated on this level alone. Thus Francis Robinson's very detailed work on U.P. Muslims frankly excludes mass riots from its purview through its focus on 'elite groups concerned in making polities'. (*Separatism among Indian Muslims,* p. 6) The roots of elite communalism will be studied in the next section along with its historical contemporary, intelligentsia or 'middle-class' nationalism. But the tragic fact has to be admitted that communalism also acquired a mass dimension from an early date—though a dimension obviously not unconnected with the activities of elite groups. While the potentially communal dimensions of the Pabna riots or the Moplah out-breaks were not developed in our period—perhaps because of the absence as yet of a separatist intelligentsia leadership in Bengal or Malabar— Hindu and Muslim elites were much more evenly balanced in the United Provinces and the Punjab, and it was in this region that riots were becoming increasingly common from the 1880s onwards. Socio-economic tensions might have been ultimately responsible in part. Thus Hindu peasants faced Muslim *talukdars* and landlords in large parts of Avadh and the Aligarh-Bulandshahr region, urban Muslim concentrations in U.P. towns mainly consisted of artisans, shopkeepers and petty traders while most big merchants and bankers were Hindus, while in the Punjab Hindu traders and money-lenders easily became unpopular among Muslim peasants.

But the riots themselves usually occurred over issues quite far removed from economic grievances. In a movement only just beginning to be explored, a rash of rioting over cow-slaughter spread over much of northern India. Gerald Barrier mentions 15 major riots of this type in the Punjab between

1883 and 1891, and such disturbances reached their climax in eastern U.P. and Bihar between 1888 and 1893, the districts worst affected being Ballia, Benares, Azamgarh, Gorakhpur, Arrah, Saran, Gaya and Patna. Serious riots occurred also in Bombay city and a number of Maharashtrian towns between 1893 and 1895. A Gujarati mill-owner had organized a cow-protection society in Bombay in 1893, while an additional aggravating factor was Tilak's reorganization of the Ganapati festival on a *sarvajanik* or community basis. Songs written for Ganapati Utsavas urged Hindus to boycott the Muharram, in which they had freely participated before (the reformist journal *Sudharak* even commented in 1898 that Muharram had been much more of a national festival than Ganapati), and some of them were openly inflammatory: 'What boon has Allah conferred upon you/That you have become Mussalmans today? Do not be friendly to a religion which is alien.... The cow is our mother, do not forget her.' (R. Cashman, *The Myth of the Lokamanya,* p. 78) In the industrial suburbs of Calcutta, the first recorded riot took place in May 1891, followed by disturbances at Titagarh and Garden Reach during Bakr-Id in 1896 and the large-scale Talla riot in north Calcutta in 1897.

Labour

Dipesh Chakrabarti has recently used the Calcutta jute mill riots of the mid-1890s as a point of entry into a subject almost entirely unexplored in our country so far—the emergence of early labour consciousness. Sizeable proletarian concentrations had developed around the Bombay cotton and Calcutta jute mills by the 1890s, living and working in conditions every bit as appalling, if not worse, as those witnessed in similar phases of early industrial capitalism in other parts of the world. Even the paltry restrictions on the employment of children and women theoretically imposed by the Factory Acts of 1881 and 1891 (mainly at the instance of a Lancashire jealous of the Bombay Indian textile industry) were seldom observed, and a working day of 15, 16, sometimes even 18 hours remained extremely common. In Bombay, where a predominantly Marathi labour force facilitated some degree of social contact across class lines, middle-class philanthropic efforts to improve labour conditions began fairly early with N.M. Lokhande (an associate of Phule) starting the weekly *Dinabandhu* in 1880, organizing labour meetings to demand shorter hours in 1884, and even starting a Bombay Mill-hands' Association in 1890. This, however, was not a trade union, it merely involved Lokhande setting up an office to give free advice to mill-hands who came to him. Similar activities were started by the Brahmo social reformer Sasipada Banerji among the Bengali jute mill-workers of Baranagore, a Calcutta suburb—night schools, clubs, temperance societies, a journal named *Bharat Sramajeebi* (1874), all trying to inculcate a middle class Victorian morality of thrift, sobriety and self-help among labourers. European mill-managers declared 'that those of their hands who attended Sasi Babu's schools were the very people that were found to be most careful and painstaking in their work', and the manager of the Baranagore Jute Mills, W. Alexander of the Borneo Jute Company, was in fact one of Banerji's principal patrons. Even this kind of middle-class philanthrophy died away in Calcutta in the 1890s as up-country immigrant labour from eastern U.P. and Bihar increasingly displaced Bengalis in the jute mills. The coolies in the mines of Bihar and Bengal and tea gardens of Assam were also immigrants, wrenched hundreds of miles away from their homes amidst all the horrors of the indenture system, and living utterly isolated lives in their new environment. Bengali intelligentsia leaders like Dwarkanath Ganguli did launch a memorable campaign in the 1880s against the slave labour conditions in the tea plantations, but no one as yet made the attempt to organize the coolies themselves.

Workers did occasionally fight back in their own way, through assaults on overseers, sporadic riots and spontaneous short-lived strikes. Twenty-five important strikes have been recorded in Bombay and Madras between 1882 and 1890, several big strikes in Bombay in 1892–93 and 1901, and a new note of militancy was evident among Calcutta jute workers in the mid-1890s, leading the Indian Jute Mills' Association to ask the Bengal Government for 'additional police supervision' to curb 'riotous combinations' of mill-hands in April 1895. But the important point made by Chakrabarti is the way in which embryonic labour protest could often take the form of a kind of 'community-consciousness' rather than a clear recognition of class. Muslim workers demanded holidays for Id or Muharram, Hindus for Rathjatra, and at times fought each other bitterly over issues like cow-slaughter or the construction of places of worship on disputed land, as in the riots in and around Calcutta in 1896–97. There was evidently a carryover here of attitudes evolved in the labour catchment areas of east U.P. and Bihar, from where so many jute mill-workers were coming in the 1890s, and which were also the main centres of the cow-protection riots. If, as E.P. Thompson has shown so brilliantly, the making of the English working class was enormously helped by the rich tradition of artisan radicalism which had preserved and extended the more democratic aspects of the English bourgeois revolution of the seventeenth century, the impoverished Indian peasant or ruined artisan being sucked into factories tended to fall back upon sectional ties of region, caste, kinship or religion. The new urban environment in fact often strengthened such old loyalties, as the new immigrant found himself in an intensely competitive surplus labour market where unskilled hands fought each other for jobs—and jobs could usually be secured only through *sardars* who were likely to favour their own community or kin, and who could also at times act as carriers of the separatist ideology of their social superiors. Chakrabarti's paper shows contacts being established by 1896 between some Muslim jute mill-workers of Rishra through their local *imam* with a prominent up-country Muslim merchant of Calcutta, Haji Nur Muhammad Zakaria, himself already active in pan-Islamist agitation. It is also significant that the first relatively stable labour organization that we hear of in the Calcutta industrial area was Muhammedan Association of Kankinara, founded in 1895. which raised funds to improve mosques and provide alms and sickness benefits for its members.

Thus the sharpening economic tensions in the Calcutta jute mills in the mid-1890s—caused by a sudden influx of up-country labour, near-famine food prices, and the introduction of electric lights which immediately prolonged the working day—led to outbursts against employers but also fratricidal riots; though Chakrabarti's argument that there were perhaps more of the latter than the former has been questioned in a later detailed study by Ranjit Das Gupta. Such fluidity would remain a significant feature of twentieth century Indian history, with communal, class, and national consciousness interpenetrating and passing over into each other. Agrarian disturbances would often turn into communal riots, and cow-protection enthusiasts or pan-Islamist agitators could also alternate as labour or peasant leaders. Perhaps this is not so strange or unique after all—one might recall George Rude's comments on the pre-industrial crowd, where one type of militancy could easily turn into another, or John Foster's study of class struggle in the English industrial revolution, where 'sectional consciousness' could trigger off class consciousness or vice versa.

BUSINESS GROUPS AND UPPER CLASSES

If the new Indian proletariat was thus quite far from being an unequivocal bearer of any 'modern' ideology, the same comment seems to apply even more to the emerging Indian capitalist class. Of the major business communities, only the Parsis of Bombay early acquired a 'Westernizing' reputation, though even here the lead was usually taken by Elphinstone College graduates rather than the big business magnates (*shetias*). Gujarati Vanias and Marwaris remained in contrast almost proverbially orthodox in social and religious matters. A social reform movement developed among Calcutta Marwaris only in the twentieth century, at least two generations after their Bengali fellow-citizens. Historians like Timberg have in fact emphasized the positive role of traditional institutions like the joint family and close caste ties as a possible explanation for the Marwari success-story. The characteristic business unit remained the family-firm, while the Marwari immigrant was assured of a welcome wherever he went from *basas* maintained by his caste-brethren. It is also significant that of the numerous nineteenth-century socio-religious reform movements, only the highly ambivalent Arya Samaj managed to win some support among business groups. Again, despite the long-term objective contradictions between a 'national bourgeois' development and the colonial political and economic structure which seems clear today on hindsight, Indian business groups remained overwhelmingly loyalist till the 1920s—often for sound economic reasons, as we have already seen.

Princes and Zamindars

A positive leadership was clearly still less to be expected from the world of the 'native' princes and *zamindars*. Post-1857 British policy was fairly consistently geared towards an alliance with such 'feudal' elements— 'breakwaters in the storm', Canning had already described many of them to be even during the Mutiny itself. The new policy involved forgetting about the doctrine of lapse, returning Mysore to its Hindu ruling family after fifty years in 1881, Durbar pageantry under Lytton and an Imperial Service Corps under Dufferin, and public school-type education for the sons of princes at Mayo College in Ajmer and for Avadh *talukdars* at Colvin College in Lucknow. 'British paramountcy' was always firmly maintained in theory and enforced whenever necessary in practice through British Residents, but under this overall umbrella feudal paraphernalia and autocracy were encouraged to flourish in the one-third of India theoretically under 'native' rule—a reminder, once again, as to how little colonialism had to do with any genuine modernization. A few states did evolve administrative standards on par with, if not in some respects better than, British India. Thus Mysore and Baroda were quite active in social reform (marriage legislation in the latter state remained ahead of British India till independence), Travancore achieved a unusually high literacy rate, and Baroda even cultivated some contact with nationalists through employing, at various times, Naoroji, R.C. Dutt and Aurobindo Ghosh. Princely and *zamindari* patronage might have also helped to preserve some valuable aspects of traditional Indian culture—the rich heritage of classical music, for instance. But for the most part the princely states remained social, cultural and political backwaters, petty despotisms which did not have to bother about the legal forms and civic rights which had been developed with much fanfare in British India. It was only the development of the States Peoples' Movement from the 1930s which united these artificially secluded islands with the sub-continental mainstream, and thus the British claim to have been the unifiers of India is also more than a little dubious. As for the *zamindars,* landlord-dominated bodies like the British Indian Association of Calcutta had anticipated many of the later demands of the Moderate Congress in the 1850s, but with the rise of 'middle class' associations from the 1870s these rapidly degenerated into ultra-loyalist and largely inactive coteries.

Analysing the social composition of the delegates to the Calcutta session of 1886, the *Report of the Indian National Congress* noted 'the entire absence of the old aristocracy, the so-called natural leaders of the people'. It also admitted that 'the ryots and cultivating classes were insufficiently represented', while 'petty moneylenders and shopkeepers were conspicuous by their absence'. Though the *Report* claimed that 'the higher commercial classes, bankers, merchants' were fairly well represented, and that 'about 130 of the delegates were... landed proprietors of one kind or another', what distinguished at least the leadership of the early Congresses was clearly its identification with what historians have variously described as the 'educated middle class', 'English-educated elite', or 'intelligentsia'. No less than 455 of the 1200-odd delegates at the Allahabad Congress (1888), for instance, declared themselves to be lawyers, while there were 59 teachers and 73 journalists. It is to the social roots, ideology, and political activities of this intelligentsia that we must now turn.

'MIDDLE-CLASS' CONSCIOUSNESS AND POLITICS

Social Roots of the Intelligentsia

By the 1880s, the total number of English-educated Indians was approaching the 50,000 mark, if the number of matriculates may be taken as a rough indicator (only 5000 as yet had B.A. degrees). The number of those studying English went up fairly rapidly from 298,000 in 1887 to 505,000 in 1907, while the circulation of English-language newspapers climbed from 90,000 in 1885 to 276,000 in 1905. (J.R. McLane, *Indian Nationalism and the Early Congress,* p. 4) A 'microscopic minority', as the British never tired of pointing out (the literacy figures even in 1911 were only 1 per cent for English and 6 per cent for the vernaculars), this emerging social group enjoyed an importance far in excess of its size. English education gave its beneficiaries a unique capacity to establish contacts on a country-wide scale. English-educated government employees, lawyers, teachers, journalists or doctors worked fairly often outside their home regions. Already in the 1870s, for instance the, existence of colonies of educated Bengalis in many north Indian towns enabled Surendranath Banerji to make several successful political tours and the Indian Association to set up a large number of branches outside Bengal. Above all, Western education did bring with it an awareness of world currents and ideologies, without which it would have been difficult to formulate conscious theories of nationalism. At the same time, the alienating and divisive effects of education through a foreign medium were evident enough from the beginning, and have persisted right up to the present day. In 1883–84, only 9 per cent of college students in Bengal came from families with annual incomes of less than ₹200—which was but to be expected, as the tuition fees in the Calcutta Hindu College had already been ₹5 per month in the 1820s. Sharp regional disparities posed another problem, causing provincial tensions as English education increasingly became the sole path to good jobs. The Public Service Commission report of 1886–87 found 18,390 'educated natives' in Madras, 16,639 in Bengal, 7196 in Bombay—but only 3200 in the United Provinces, 1944 in Punjab, 608 in the Central Provinces, and 274 in Assam.

The early research of Anil Seal and John Broomfield made it very fashionable for a time to consider the English-educated as 'elite-groups' defined basically by their upper-caste status. It is certainly true that the traditional 'literary' castes tended to take more easily to the new education. Thus 84.7 per cent of Hindu College students in Bengal came from the three *bhadralok* castes of Brahman, Kayastha, or Vaidya in 1883–84. Brahman students predominated in Madras, Bombay or Poona, Kayasthas were prominent in U.P. But the value of this whole approach has come under serious questioning today. As Seal admitted in 1973 in a moment of self-criticism, the 'truisms of the Raj' had 'become the dogmas of historians'—official categories had been accepted a little too uncritically. Not all Bengali Brahmans were accepted as *bhadralok* by any means (e.g., the Brahman cooks, or even sometimes the *purohit*, custodian of family ritual), while in Bombay city in 1864 the allegedly 'dominant elite' of Chitpavan and Saraswat Brahmans included 10,000 beggars and 1880 domestic servants. The very use of the term 'elite' is dubious in this context, as the one genuine and truly exclusive elite in colonial India consisted of the whites. The ideology of the English-educated was seldom one of conscious defence or restriction of its privileges, whether educational or caste—which is what one would have expected of a true elite, and what one sees with the Englishmen in India. Rather, some of them made considerable personal sacrifices in social reform movements often aimed directly or indirectly against upper-caste privileges, and many more did their best to extend education through starting private schools and colleges in their home towns or villages. With the cutting-down of government aid to higher education following the recommendations of the Hunter Commission (1882), this was in fact the principal way in which education spread in India. The number of private unaided colleges went up from 11 to 53 between 1881–82 and 1901–02. It should also be remembered that the first bill to make primary education compulsory (and free for families earning less than ₹10 a month) was moved in the Imperial Council by G.K. Gokhale in 1911, and was rejected by the official majority. The Bombay Governor in a private letter to the Viceroy stated the real reason: nationalist 'power to stir up discontent would be immensely increased if every cultivator could read'. (B.R. Nanda, *Gokhale,* p. 392)

A more fruitful way of studying the intelligentsia is through a simultaneous analysis of its ideas and its socio-economic roots. This immediately reveals a significant contrast between broadly bourgeois ideals derived from a growing awareness of contemporary developments in the West, and a predominantly non-bourgeois social base. The contrast was perhaps clearest in Bengal. Here the nineteenth-century intelligentsia diligently cultivated the self-image of a 'middle class' (*madhyabitta-sreni*), below the *zamindars* but above the toilers. It searched for its model in the European 'middle class', which, as it learnt through Western education, had brought about the great transformation from medieval to modern times through movements like the Renaissance, the Reformation, the Enlightenment, and democratic revolution or reform. Yet its own social roots lay not in industry or trade, increasingly controlled by British managing agency firms and their Marwari subordinates, but in government service or the professions of law, education, journalism or medicine—with which was very often combined some connection with land in the shape of the intermediate tenures which were rapidly proliferating in Permanent Settlement Bengal. The *Amrita Bazar Patrika* of 9 December 1869 vividly expressed this dualism: 'Middle-class ("madhyabitta") people are always considered the most useful group in any society. Our country's welfare depends to a large extent on this class. If there is ever to be a social or any other revolution in this country, it will be by the middle class. All the beneficial institutions or activities that we see in our country today have been started by this class… The livelihood of middle-class people comes from landed property and the services…. Middle-class people are often, '**gantidars**'. (A form of intermediate tenure common in the Jessore-Nadia region, from which the *Amrita Bazar Patrika* was then being published)

It must be added that the Bengali intelligentsia's aloofness from business did not really come from any *bhadralok* aversion to trade, for 'middle-class' journals throughout the nineteenth century never tired of urging their readers to take to independent industry or trade. The link with a semi-feudal land system did not prevent bourgeois aspirations, but it did inhibit, as we shall have to repeatedly note, radical thought and action on agrarian issues—a limitation of ultimately momentous consequence for Bengal, with its large Muslim peasant population.

A broadly similar pattern can be seen in other provinces, though with some interesting regional variations. Thus in Madras Suntharalingam talks of an early prominence of a 'commercial elite', with merchants like Lakshmanarasu Chetti important in the Madras Native Association of the 1850s giving place to 'administrative' and 'professional elites' for reasons which he unfortunately fails to analyze. The Western-educated groups were once again often connected with petty landholding, though Washbrook has recently emphasized the behind the scenes role in the activities of the Madras Mahajana Sabha of the 1880s and the Congress run by it, of financial patrons coming from prosperous business groups like the Chettis of Madras town or the Komati merchants of the Andhra delta, as well as some big *zamindars*.

In Maharashtra the Poona intelligentsia, based on a town with virtually no industrial or commercial importance, could have little connection with business except through *swadeshi* aspiration. Tilak's journal *Mahratta*, however, noted an interesting and important paradox here in its issue of 6 September 1891, while commenting on the initiative taken by Poona in starting an annual Industrial Conference. 'Poona is, we freely admit, not a manufacturing or commercial centre. It is rich...in political traditions.... Bombay is richer than Poona, but the attention as well as the time of our Bombay commercial men, is entirely taken up by their pursuits, and in consequence the work of formulating a scheme of commercial revival must be done by other hands.' A link with land was once again often present in the form of petty rent-collecting *khoti* rights particularly in a district like Ratnagiri which supplied a disproportionately large number of Maharashtrian intellectuals (both Tilak and Gokhale came from families with *khoti* rights in Ratnagiri). As in Bengal, the social basis did not mechanically determine the ideology, but it did fix some limits. A Bombay Government move to restrain transfer of peasant lands to moneylenders in 1901 was bitterly opposed by Tilak as well as Gokhale, and the father of Extremism once even made the following revealing comments: 'Just as the government has no right to rob the 'sowcar' (moneylender) and distribute his wealth among the poor, in the same way the government has no right to deprive the khot of his rightful income and distribute the money to the peasant. This is a question of rights and not of humanity.' (quoted in Bhagwat and Pradhan, *Lokamanya Tilak*, p. 134)

Bourgeois connections were naturally somewhat more prominent in Bombay city. Though relations between *shetia* merchant-princes and 'Young Bombay' intellectuals had been rather uncertain and at times quite hostile, more stable links were forged between the new Bombay intelligentsia leadership of the 1880s and '90s (headed by the lawyer-triumvirate of Pherozeshah Mehta, K.T. Telang and Badruddin Tyabji) and the mill-owners through agitation over issues like abolition of import duties on Lancashire cottons and imposition of the countervailing excise. The connection was symbolized by the career of Dinshaw Wacha—principal contact of Naoroji in Bombay, secretary of the Bombay Presidency Association (1885–1915). general secretary of the Congress (1896–1913), member for 38 years of the Bombay Millowners' Association executive committee, and managing agent of several textile mills. And yet Wacha's letters to Naoroji are full of complaints about the parsimony of Bombay businessmen—it was quite a job to obtain the paltry sum of ₹500 from J.N. Tata for the Congress, for instance, in 1889. Indian capitalists were to unloosen their purse-strings for the nationalists only a generation later, after the First World War and with the rise of Gandhi.

In northern India, Bayly's micro-study of Allahabad brings out once again the connections between professional groups and small landlordism. He emphasizes more, however, the link between politicians like Madan Mohan Malaviya and Khattri and Agarwal banking and trading families (themselves, it should be noted, often also landlords—12 of the 24 major Allahabad commercial families listed by Bayly owned *zamindaris*)—a link mediated primarily through Arya Samajist and Hindu-revivalist cultural and religious activities.

Two general statements are commonly made about the pattern of thought and activity of the intelligentsia in the last quarter of the nineteenth century. Social and religious reform movements, so prominent down to the 1870s, were being swamped, we are told, by a rising tide of revivalism, and the latter again was intimately bound up with the emergence of more extreme varieties of nationalism. Like many generalizations, both these statements require some qualifications.

Hindu Reform and Revival

That reform movements were past their peak in Bengal was obvious enough after the 1870s, with the Brahmos torn by internal quarrels and losing influence, and Iswarchandra Vidyasagar retiring into tragic isolation. The pattern was by no means so unambiguous in western India, where M.G. Ranade remained a commanding influence in the intellectual world till his death in 1901. Along with his friend K.T. Telang (Prarthana Samajist and reformer as well as one of the pillars of the early Congress), Ranade followed a cautious policy of pursuing social reform 'along the lines of least resistance'—a caution which by the late 1890s was being attacked by men like R.G. Bhandarkar and N.C. Chandavarkar. A reform group had also emerged in the south, where Virasalingam of the Telegu-speaking country founded the Rajahmundri Social Reform Association in 1878 with promotion of widow remarriage as its principal objective, and K.N. Natarajan started the influential *Indian Social Reformer* in 1890. A Hindu Social Reform Association was also started in Madras in 1892 by the 'young Madras party' associated with that journal. For the first time, too, something like an all-India social reform movement had been launched with Ranade from 1887 organizing an annual National Social Conference which met in the Congress *pandal* till Tilak drove it out at Poona in 1895. Behramji Malabari's *Notes* on infant marriage and enforced widowhood in 1884 started a countrywide debate among intellectuals, and his sustained campaign (directed, it is true, as much if not more towards public opinion in England and British officials as to winning over Indians) did pressurize the government to pass the first major social reform legislation since the legalization of widow remarriage in 1856—the Age of Consent Act of 1891.

The short-lived but intense storm aroused over the Age of Consent issue, however, revealed how much the climate of educated opinion had changed since 1860, when sexual intercourse with a girl below the age of ten had been declared to be rape without much protest from anyone. The relatively minor reform raising this age from ten to twelve, which was all that the government eventually accepted of Malabari's far more wide-ranging proposals directed against child-marriage, now provoked massive opposition, particularly in Bengal and Maharashtra. Frankly conservative and obscurantist sentiments mingled here with the nationalist argument, put forward most notably by Tilak, that foreign rulers had no right to interfere with religious and social customs. The latter argument, it must be added, was slightly specious, since Hindu orthodox groups in the same period seldom hesitated to plead for legislation against cow-slaughter. Such legislation would surely also have been an interference with the religious and social customs of a big part of Indian society—the Muslims. The Bengal movement spearheaded by the newspaper *Bangabasi* (which attained a circulation of 20,000 as against 4000 of the pro-reform Brahmo journal *Sanjibani*, and against which a sedition case was launched) briefly anticipated some *swadeshi* moods and methods, with huge meetings at the Calcutta Maidan, a great *puja* at Kalighat, and even calls for boycott and a few efforts at organizing indigenous enterprises.

In Bengal, the intellectual mood had been changing under a variety of influences from the 1870s. Defence of Hindu traditions became more respectable as scholars like Max Müller rediscovered the glories of ancient Aryans, and as a romantic cult of the exotic Orient developed in the West, bearing strange and more than a little dubious fruit in the Theosophical movement of Olcott and Blavatsky. A small but influential group headed in the 1880s and '90s by Jogendrochandra Ghosh used Comte's Positivism to formulate a *via media* for intellectuals who had lost their traditional faith but still wanted social conformity. Sophisticated and intellectualized revivalism was best represented by the Bankimchandra of the 1880s, reinterpreting Krishna as ideal man, culture-hero and nation builder. At a more obscurantist level revivalism was represented by Sasadhar Tarkachudamani and Krishnaprasanna Sen, who claimed *shastric* precedents for all the discoveries of modern western science. But revivalism was most effective when it sought to appeal to emotions rather than to the intellect: through the neo-Vaishnavism of the *Amrita Bazar Patrika,* seeking inspiration in Chaitanya rather than the Krishna of the epics whom Bankim had sought to idealize, and above all through Ramakrishna Paramhansa, the saintly Dakshineswar priest who cast a spell over Calcutta's sophisticated intellectuals precisely through his eclecticism and rustic simplicity. In the 1890s, his disciple Vivekananda leapt to fame after a memorable appearance at the Chicago Congress of Religions. Vivekananda was very far from being an obscurantist or revivalist in any crude sense. One major effect of his work still was to weaken social reform further by condemning it (no doubt with considerable justice) as elitist and inspired by alien models and replacing it by the ideal of social service, and the Ramakrishna Mission founded by him in 1897 has proved an efficient philanthropic organization with no claims to social radicalism. Yet Vivekananda himself had combined passionate evocation of the glories of the Aryan tradition and Hinduism (particularly before Western audiences) with bitter attacks on present-day degeneration: 'Our religion is in the kitchen. Our God is the cooking pot.' 'As if religion consisted in making a girl a mother at the age of twelve or thirteen', was his private comment on the Age of Consent furore, and Vivekananda's remark about the cult of the cow—'like mother, like son', deserves to be recalled. He preached a this-worldly type of religion, emphasizing self-help and the building-up of manly strength: 'What our country now wants are muscles of iron and nerves of steel.' Equally remarkable was Vivekananda's concern for the plight of the 'Daridra-narayana', the Shudra and the untouchable, his occasional vague predictions about their gaining 'supremacy in every society... Socialism, Anarchism, Nihilism and other like sects are the vanguard of the social revolution that is to follow'—as well as his famous appeal to 'forget not that the lower classes, the ignorant, the poor, the illiterate, the cobbler, the sweeper, are thy flesh and blood, thy brothers'. Such rhetoric, however, was combined with a near-total lack of clarity about concrete socio-economic programmes, methods of mass contact, or even political objectives. Yet in eclecticism precisely lay the strength of Vivekananda's appeal, and his mixture of patriotism with the cult of manly virtues, vague populism, and evocation of Hindu glory was to prove heady wine indeed for young men in the coming *Swadeshi* period.

In Maharashtra, revivalism had its centre at Poona, and took on a more narrowly Brahmanical character than in Bengal. Connected initially with the declining position of the traditional literati of *shastris* who saw their *dakshinas* or stipends gradually drying up under British rule, the evocation of lost Hindu, Brahman and Maratha glory began finding increasing support from the English-educated, through the influence of Vishnu Krishna Chiplunkar's. *Nibandhmala* essays (1874–81). Tilak's alliance with the Poona revivalists in the 1890s, forged through opposition to the Age of Consent bill, the starting of the Ganapati Utsava, and the refusal to permit Ranade to hold his National Social Conference at the Congress *pandal* in 1895, may be best regarded perhaps as political utilization of an already existing reality—for personally he was hardly an obscurantist. He had even sponsored with Ranade, as late as 1890, a circular letter advocating women's education and raising of the age of marriage. In south India, where indigenous movements of reform or revival were relatively weak, the Theosophical Society founded at Adyar in 1882 acquired considerable influence among the English-educated, particularly after the arrival in 1893 of Annie Besant. In the 1890s, Mrs Besant repeatedly attacked social reformers and extolled the virtues of traditional Hinduism, though her views on this as well as on many other subjects were to change dramatically later on.

The one 'reform' movement, however, that was making spectacular advances in the 1880s and '90s was the Arya Samaj, founded by the wandering *sanyasi* from Kathiawar, Dayanand Saraswati (1824–83) but acquiring its principal base in northern India (Punjab and parts of western U.P.). The message of Dayanand attained success perhaps through its very ambiguity, for it combined sharp criticism of many existing Hindu practices (idolatry and polytheism, child marriage, the taboos on widow remarriage and foreign travel, Brahman predominance and the multiplicity of castes based on birth alone) with an extremely aggressive assertion of the superiority over all other faiths, Christianity, Islam or Sikhism, of purified Hinduism based on Vedic infallibility. The specific goals of the social reformers were thus absorbed into a dominant pan-Hindu revivalist framework. The Arya Samaj soon overshadowed the Brahmos in the contest for the loyalties of reform-minded educated young men of northern India, offering as it did a doctrine at once safer, less alienating, and unconnected with an increasingly unpopular Bengali immigrant community, which had initially occupied an undue portion of administrative and professional jobs due to its early lead in English education. The Arya Samajists also struck deep roots among the trading castes. The principal early Punjab leaders, Guru Dutt, Lala Hans Raj, Lala Lajpat Rai, and Lala Munshi Ram (Swami Shraddhanand), all came from Khatri, Arora or Aggarwal families. Kenneth Jones relates the four principal bases of the Samaj in the Punjab (Peshawar-Rawalpindi, Multan, Rohtak-Hissar, and the Jullundur Doab) partly to local business support. From 1900 onwards, they also went in for largescale *shuddhi* or mass purification and conversion of lower castes—Rahtias, Odhs, Meghs and Jats. With them as with trading groups, the Arya Samaj had thus become something like a channel for 'Sanskritizing' processes. Membership consequently rose in a spectacular manner: 40,000 in 1891, 92,000 in 1901, half a million by 1921 (the Brahmos in sharp contrast never numbered more than a few thousands in the census figures).

In 1893, the Arya Samaj split on the two issues of meat-eating *vs* vegetarianism and Anglicized *vs* Sanskrit-based education. The moderate 'College' faction led by Hans Raj and Lajpat Rai hence forward concentrated on building up a chain of 'Dayanand Anglo-Vedic' colleges, and also developed a somewhat sporadic interest in Congress politics as well as a more sustained involvement in *swadeshi* enterprise. The more openly revivalist and militant 'Gurukul faction founded by Lekh Ram and Munshi Ram started the Hardwar Gurukul in 1902 (unaffiliated to the official educational system, unlike the D.A.V. and based on principles of *brahmacharya* and Vedic training). They emphasized proselytization through paid preachers and *shuddhi*. Within both groups, however, the general trend was towards a shift 'from Arya Dharm to Hindu consciousness' (Kenneth Jones)—and a consciousness quite often openly communal and anti-Muslim. Lekh Ram's bitter polemics with the Ahmediya Muslim sect led to his assassination in 1897, while in February 1909 Lajpat's associate Lala Lal Chand clearly anticipated much of later Hindu Mahasabha and RSS ideology in his *Panjabee* article, 'Self-Abnegation in Politics'. Lal Chand bitterly attacked the Congress for ignoring the specific problems and demands of the Hindus. 'The consciousness must arise in the mind of each Hindu that he is a Hindu, and not merely an Indian'—and hence there was need for 'the substitution of Hindu Sabhas for Congress Committees, of a Hindu Press for the Congress Press, organization of a Hindu Defence Fund with regular office and machinery for collecting information and seeking redress by self-help... '. Thus despite much initial hostility (which had even included some plots against Dayanand's life), the Arya Samaj in practice was coming fairly close to the postures of orthodox Hinduism—an orthodoxy which was also trying to organize itself by the late nineteenth century through Hari Sabhas and Sanatan Dharma Sabhas, conferences at Kumbha Melas, and a big conference at Delhi in 1900 which started a Bharat Dharma Mahamandal—organizational efforts which have not drawn sufficient interest yet from historians.

'Revivalism' thus obviously contributed to the assertion of an aggressive Hindu identity. But one has to add that the difference here with the 'reform' movements was of degree rather than kind. Not only had 'modernistic' trends like the Brahmo or Prarthana Samajas or the more secular movements of Young Bengal or Vidyasagar been entirely Hindu in composition; with few exceptions, they too had operated with a conception of 'Muslim tyranny' or a 'medieval' dark age (an assumption we meet with in Rammohun and among Derozians almost as much as in Bankimchandra) from which British-rule with its accompanying alleged 'renaissance' or 'awakening' had been a deliverance. This was not a theory which could ever hope to appeal to Muslim intellectuals, while the attempts to purge Hindu religion and society of 'medieval' crudities and superstitions in the name of ancient standards and an emerging code of middle-class respectability also at times involved attacks on syncretist popular customs, like the worship in common of Hindu and Muslim holy men or shrines. As similar movements were developing at about the same time within Indian Islam too (e.g., the attack on Sufi eclecticism from the standpoint of a return to the purity and rigour of early Islam), the two communities tended to drift apart both at the level of the elite (where the unifying bond of a common Urdu-based culture was under severe strain in northern India) and of the peasant masses. District Gazetteers and biographical literature written in Bengal at about the turn of the century, for instance, frequently recall common participation in festivals like Durga Puja or Muharram and a variety of syncretist popular cults as important, but diminishing phenomena.

Trends in Indian Islam

A pattern of clear-cut reformist-revivalist conflict with the first tending to be loyalist and the second, anti-British, seems at first to be evident in late-nineteenth century Indian Islam, the two poles being represented by Sir Sayyid Ahmed Khan's Aligarh movement and the Deoband Dar-ul-Ulum or seminary founded in 1867 by two Mutiny veterans, Muhammad Qasim Nanawtawi and Rashid Ahmed Gangohi. Sayyid Ahmed tried to convert upper-class Muslims of western U.P. to the virtues and benefits of English education through a Scientific Society (1864), a modernistic Urdu journal *Tahzib al-akhlaq* (1870), and the Aligarh Anglo-Muhammadan Oriental College (1875). His interpretation of Islam emphasized the validity of free enquiry (*ijtihad*) and the alleged similarities between Koranic revelation and the laws of nature discovered by modern science. Yet the theology classes in Aligarh were directed by orthodox *mullahs,* and the modernistic elements in the Aligarh movement came to be considerably toned down over time, particularly under Muhsin al-Mulk. What is more important, Sayyid Ahmed had always stressed the need to import Western education to upper-class Muslims as Muslims, and to thus foster in them a sense of corporate unity. His programme dovetailed neatly with the aims of the new British policy as formulated by Hunter's *Indian Mussalmans,* commissioned by Mayo in 1871: the British should help to 'develop a rising generation of Muhammedans...tinctured with the sober and genial knowledge of the West. At the same time they would have a sufficient acquaintance with their religious code to command the respect of their own community...'. Aligarh consequently got a quite unusual amount of British patronage, including a personal donation of ₹10,000 from the Viceroy, Lord Northbrooke. As Francis Robinson has pointed out, it was through British support, above all, that 'a man whose religious views were so unorthodox that the majority of his co-religionists branded him an infidel was raised up as the advocate of his community'. (*Separatism among Indian Muslims*, p. 131)

The social basis for Sayyid Ahmed was provided by U.P. Muslim landlords (numerous in the Aligarh-Bulandshahr region and comprising 76 out of the 272 *taluqdar* families of Avadh) and traditional service families—a privileged but slowly declining group, which held 63.9% of subordinate judicial and executive posts in the province in 1857, 45.1% in 1886–87, and 34.7% in 1913 (the percentage of Muslims to the total population in N.W. Provinces and Avadh was only 13.4 in 1886–87). Thus, contrary to Hunter's generalization on the basis of the rather special Bengal case (where urban upper or middle-class Muslims were relatively few in number), a generalization which was taken over by many British officials and Muslim leaders, separatism developed initially not for reasons of 'backwardness', but because a traditional elite felt increasingly threatened by Hindu trader, moneylender and professional groups buying up land, capturing municipalities and obtaining jobs at its expense. A similar case—in reverse—is to be seen in the Punjab, where Kenneth Jones links the growing appeal of Arya Samajist revivalism in part to a Muslim challenge to earlier Khatri, Arora and Badia predominance in business and the professions.

The initial British support for Aligarh was due not so much to the need for a counterpoise against Congress-type nationalism (which was not yet much of a threat), but to official fears concerning certain other trends within Indian Islam—the so-called 'fanaticism' and anti-foreign mentality preached by some religious leaders, which often seemed to find a ready response among what Peter Hardy has described as the 'pre-industrial lower middle class of petty landholders, country-town mullahs, teachers, booksellers, small shopkeepers, minor officials and skilled artisans...men literate in the vernacular...quick to be seized by religious passion.' (*Muslims of British India*, p. 58) Broadly similar groups among Hindus were being attracted to revivalism and Extremist nationalism by the late nineteenth century. In this case, memories of 1857 which exaggerated somewhat the specific role of the Muslims merged with the panic caused by the 'Wahhabi' frontier wars and conspiracies of the 1860s. By the next decade, however, the political, anti-British aspects of the Wahhabi (more correctly, *Tariqah-i-Muhammediyah*) movement had been suppressed; what survived was a sustained campaign of Islamization active particularly in rural Bengal, directed against syncretist cults, *shirk* and *bid'ah* (polytheism and sinful innovation). Such puritanical movements were thus curiously double-edged—heroically anti-British at times, they could also contribute to internal conflicts. An almost exact parallel here would be the Kuka sect among the Sikhs. Having faced British guns in 1872, they have been hailed occasionally as freedom-fighters, and yet their activities principally concerned bitter attacks on Islam on the cow-slaughter issue, culminating in the murder of some Muslim butchers at Amritsar and Ludhiana in 1871.

A more muted kind of anti-British temper survived in the religious seminary started at Deoband in 1867. Rigidly orthodox, unlike the Wahhabis, and hostile to Sayyid Ahmed for his theological innovations and political loyalism alike, Deoband attracted relatively poor students who could not afford Western education, remained influential through the *madrasah* teachers it produced and in the twentieth century provided fairly consistent support to Congress nationalism. What alarmed the British in our period much more, however, was the occasional evidence of pan-Islamic sentiments aroused by the distant figure of the Ottoman Sultan-Khalifa, particularly during the Balkan war of 1876–78 and the Graeco-Turkish war of 1896–97. The founder of modern pan-Islamism, Jamal al-Din al-Afghani, was himself in India between 1879 and 1882, writing and giving lectures in Hyderabad and Calcutta. Though Jamal al-Din made a violent attack on Sayyid Ahmed in a *Refutation of the Materialists* (1882), modern research has established that his real quarrel was against the latter's subserviency towards the British. Al-Afghani's own theological ideas were at least as heterodox, and he passionately pleaded for Hindu-Muslim unity in lectures to Calcutta students, one at the Albert Hall in College Street, now the Coffee House. The immediate impact seems to have been small, but a new trend was emerging, once again profoundly ambiguous. By the late 1890s, there is some evidence that even Calcutta Muslim jute workers were being taught to look upon the Sultan as a distant but mighty protector. Pan-Islamism contributed to the Calcutta riots of 1897; twenty years later it was to become for some time a powerful anti-imperialist force through the Khilafat movement.

As would be evident from the above survey, very many of the conflicts in late nineteenth century Indian society were intra-communal disputes among various trends within Hinduism or Islam, rather than confrontations between the two big religious communities. But 'communalism' proper was also acquiring, for the first time in the 1880s and '90s, something like an all-India dimension. The two principal issues were the Urdu-Devanagri controversy and cow-protection. The demand for the use of the Devanagri script, first made by some Benares Hindus in 1868 and granted by Lt.-Governor Macdonnell in 1900, was clearly connected with the tension between old and new elites in the U.P. It is interesting that Sayyid Ahmed started talking in terms of Muslims as a separate entity for the first time in 1869, and explicitly in the context of the script controversy—his Scientific Society had actually had more Hindu members than Muslim. Ultimately more significant, however, was the cow-protection issue, for it served as a link between elite and popular communalism, as McLane has shown in a recently-published study. Hindu defenders of the cow hoped and agitated for legislation on the subject, and in many U.P. municipalities passed by-laws restricting slaughter-houses and *kabab*-shops on allegedly 'hygienic' grounds. Muslim politicians feared that the Hindu majorities which would result from the introduction of elections would further curb what many felt was an essential part of their religion. Dayanand had published a pamphlet on the subject, *Gaukarunanidhi* in 1881, and local *gaurakshini sabhas* began springing up in many parts of northern India from the late 1880s, encouraged by the patronage of some lawyers and *zamindars,* as well as by the activities of some wandering *sadhus*. The cow was not only an age-old religious symbol, but also the most vital economic asset for the peasant, apart from his land—while educated Hindus were attracted by the argument that cow-protection would improve the health and prosperity of all Indians. *Gaurakshini sabhas* were becoming more militant after 1892–93, perhaps reflecting to some extent orthodox resentment at the passing of the Age of Consent Act the previous year. There were reports of forcible interference with the sale or slaughter of cows and even of setting up of *sabha* courts which punished sale to butchers by fine or social boycott. As Islamic revivalist trends were simultaneously insisting on the necessity of the Bakr-Id sacrifice, the ground was prepared for the large scale riots of June-July

1893. These started at Mau in Azamgarh, where a big Muslim population was attacked by crowds coming in from Ghazipur and Ballia districts. Riots were most organized in Ballia, where a Rajput *zamindar* was extremely active; most widespread (22 in all) in Saran, Gaya and Patna, the locale of many large cattle fairs; and most violent in Bombay city, where 80 were killed, and the disturbances were sparked off by the issue of whether Hindu processions could play music before mosques. The two other places affected were Junagadh and far-off Rangoon. This was rioting on a quite unprecedented, almost country-wide, scale—a poor augury, indeed, for the modern national movement which was only just getting into its stride.

The connection often assumed between revivalism and extremer varieties of nationalism appears a bit dubious in so far as the former led up to riots which Secretary of State Kimberley welcomed as cutting 'at the roots of the Congress agitation for the formation of a united Indian people'. (Kimberley to Lansdowne, 25 August 1893) Even otherwise, it must be remembered that the biggest single contribution made to nationalism in the 1905 period—the formulation of a systematic critique of the economic aspects of British rule through the drain of wealth theory—was the work of men like Dadabhai Naoroji, Ranade, G.V. Joshi and R.C. Dutt, all broadly associated with modernistic reformers. Nor were social reform enthusiasts always necessarily milk and water moderates in politics. In 1876, the Brahmo leader Sivanath Sastri inspired a group of young men (including Bepinchandra Pal) to take a remarkable pledge abjuring government service and declaring that 'self-government is the only form of political government ordained by God.' G.G. Agarkar, who started the Deccan Education Society and the journals *Kesari* and *Mahratta* along with Tilak but later quarrelled with him, had the reputation of being a radical in both social and political matters. Patwardhan, who succeeded Agarkar as editor of the reformist *Sudharak* after the latter's untimely death in 1895, was suspended as a teacher and threatened with sedition charges during the plague disturbances in Poona in 1897. Conversely, not all advocates of orthodoxy or revivalism were political firebrands. An orthodox rally of 10,000 at Benares in 1892 ended with three cheers for the Sanatan Dharma and Queen Victoria. Annie Besant became politically active only after her conversion to social reform, and the more orthodox Gurukul section of the Aryas kept away from nationalist politics, unlike Lajpat's College faction. As late as 1913, the Gurukul was parading its loyalism through an ostentatious welcome to Lt. Governor Meston.

What was happening from roughly the 1870s was a gradual, incomplete, often inconsistent, but still extremely important shift within the whole universe of discourse and action of the intelligentsia towards various forms of nationalism, a shift which affected many (though by no means all) reformers and revivalists alike. The attempt to explain this phenomenon in terms of growing educated unemployment is not entirely satisfactory. It is true that Indian newspapers (as well as many official reports) repeatedly complained of diminishing prospects for graduates (itself a product of colonialism, one must add: the very slow growth of industry and the humanistic bias given to English education right from its beginnings under Macaulay made over-crowding of the liberal professions and government services inevitable). Yet it has to be remembered that competition for jobs by itself could lead as easily to sectional consciousness along regional or communal lines. We have already seen examples of this happening, in the Hindu-Muslim elite conflict in U.P. and the growing unpopularity of Bengalis in much of northern India. The leaders and most of the participants in the early Congress were not unemployed youths, but successful and fairly prosperous professional men. Much more important factors were racism, of which the Ilbert Bill furore was only one major manifestation, and the growing awareness of the link between British policies and the stark poverty of the country (made more obvious by the repeated famines of the 1870s and '90s). If explanations are still to be sought at the micro-level, one could point to the fact that the successful lawyer leaders of the early Congress often had to overcome considerable white obstructions in their early careers. Pherozeshah Mehta, for instance, decided to concentrate on *mofussil* practice after complaining about unfair British competition in Bombay in 1873. W.C. Bonnerji was passed over for appointment to standing counsel in 1881, and Indian *vakils* in Madras and Calcutta won the right to appear without barristers in High Court original suits only after refusing to serve as junior counsels to whites. Patriotism of a necessarily more muted kind was bred also at times by discrimination within the Civil Service—in men like Brojendranath De, for example, who was repeatedly passed over in promotions after he had intervened on behalf of Indians ill-treated by white mine-owners at Ranigunj, and had then added to his sins by defending the Ilbert Bill against the wishes of his superior John Beames. Another, much more obscure Bengal official, a district *munsiff* named Gyanchandra Banerji, has left an unpublished diary marked throughout by remarkably intense anti-British feelings, sparked off by the twin issues of racial discrimination and mass poverty.

Patriotism in Literature

The initial, and natural form of expression of the patriotism of the intelligentsia was through literature in the regional languages. Modern literature in the various Indian languages (and particularly prose, which was largely undeveloped prior to the nineteenth century) everywhere emerged in close association with reform movements (one might recall, for instance, the role of Rammohun and particularly Vidyasagar in the development of Bengali prose). It was then taken over by the new patriotic mood. Bengal in the 1860s and '70s produced a large number of patriotic poems and songs bemoaning the plight of the country and at times even directly referring to the decline of handicrafts. Many of these were written for the Hindu Mela organized for some years from 1867 by Nabagopal Mitra with the backing of the Tagore family. The newly-established theatre was even more directly anti-British, from Dinabandhu Mitra's exposure of indigo-planters in *Nil-Darpan* (1860) down to certain plays in the 1870s which led directly to Lytton's Dramatic Performances Act in 1876. The greatest single influence was Bankimchandra, with his historical novels climaxed by *Anandmath* (1882) with its *Bande Mataram* hymn. Through essays as well as novels, Bankimchandra sought to evoke a new interest in the history of the country, striking a note typical of nationalism the world over. It is interesting, however, that the 1880s and '90s which saw Hindu revivalism at its height in Bengal seem to have been marked by a certain decline of political interest. The theatre was now dominated by Girishchandra Ghosh's sentimental domestic dramas or plays on Puranic themes with little direct political content. In 1903 Bepinchandra Pal stated that since the Ilbert Bill days, 'Politics have been neglected in the interest of abstract religion. And in consequence religious songs have supplanted the old national songs.' (*New India,* 19 March 1903)

A broadly similar pattern of connection between nationalism and the development of regional literature can be seen in other parts of the country, along a varied time-scale which again corresponded roughly to the emergence of patriotic activity in particular areas. M.G. Ranade's *Note on the Growth of Marathi Literature* (1898) catalogued the rapid increase in the number of Marathi publications (only 3 between 1818–27, 102 in 1847–57, 1530 in 1865–74, 3824 in 1885–96), and emphasized the move to publish new editions of the medieval Marathi *bhakti* poets from the 1840s onwards. This was followed by publications of old Marathi chronicles (*bakhars*), and Ranade's own historical works and articles in a sense began the cult of Shivaji which Tilak took up from 1895. Ranade, however, tried to portray the seventeenth century revival as a kind of protestant movement inspired by *bhakti* saints who sought to transcend caste differences. He felt that the orthodoxy of the later Peshwas was partly responsible for the Maratha decline. A quite different view of Shivaji, emphasizing the role of his *guru* Ramdas as an apostle of Hindu militancy, was put forward from the 1890s by Tilak, Kelkar and Rajwade; it is obvious that contemporary differences were being projected back into the past on both sides. There was also a third view, projecting Shivaji as a Shudra king, as Jotiba Phule tried to do in a ballad composed in 1869. More directly political themes were developed, again from contrasting points of view, by 'Lokahitavadi' Gopal Hari Deshmukh in his *Satapatra* series (1848–50) which called for social reforms, advocated indigenous enterprise, but broadly welcomed British rule, and a generation later by Vishnukrishna Chiplunkar's journal *Nibandhamala* (1874–81) with its strong revivalist and anti-British note.

As the examples of Bengali and Marathi make clear, however, the development of patriotic literature in the languages of the various Indian peoples contained certain ambiguities. It tended to foster, more or less at the same time, national, regional and communal consciousness. Thus Bankimchandra was concerned essentially with the history of Bengal, repeatedly asserted that Bengal had lost her independence with Bakhtiyar Khilji and not with Plassey, emphasized the harmful effects of Mughal centralization on regional life, and liberally distributed abuse of Muslims in his later historical novels (particularly *Anandamath, Debi Chaudhurani,* and *Sitaram).* Tod's romantic mythmaking about Rajput chivalry and valour directed against Muslim invaders was taken up on a large scale in Bengali poetry, drama, novels and even books for children. Attempts were made also to import the cult of Shivaji, though the principal historical link of Bengal with the Maratha power had been through the extremely destructive *bargi* raids of the 1740s. Thus developed what Bipan Chandra has appropriately called 'vicarious nationalism', which has been justified at times by the argument that it would have been dangerous (for Bankim as a government official, for instance) to write openly against British rule. But the use of Muslims as convenient whipping-boys for the British could not but have extremely harmful consequences. Bankimchandra was idolized by *swadeshi* Hindu youth particularly from 1905, but even Muslim journals like the *Mussalman,* broadly sympathetic to nationalism, repeatedly attacked him for the abuse of *Yavanas* contained in many of his works. Muslim intellectuals were soon developing their own variety of vicarious nationalism, glorifying precisely the periods and figures (like Aurangzeb) abused by the Hindus and evoking nostalgic feelings for the lost glories of Islam on a world scale. This was the note struck by late-nineteenth century Urdu poets like Altaf Husain Hali and Shibli Nomani. In Bengal, this trend was expressed by the Muslim poet Kaikobad.

Things were even more complicated in two major regions—Tamilnadu, and what is today described as the 'Hindi' belt. The evocation of Tamil history and classical Tamil literature, encouraged by British scholars like

Robert Caldwell and J.H. Nelson, was acquiring by the early twentieth century a strongly anti-Brahmanical note which could easily become anti-north Indian Aryan also—a development occasionally encouraged, as we have seen, by British officials like Governor Grant-Duff in 1886. Literary Hindi, again, was very much of an artificial creation closely associated with Hindu-revivalist movements. 'Bharatendu' Harishchandra (1850–85), often regarded as the 'father' of modern Hindi due to his plays, poems and journalism, combined pleas for use of *swadeshi* articles with demands for replacement of Urdu by Hindi in courts, and a ban on cow-slaughter. He remained also fundamentally a loyalist in politics. In the eighteenth and much of the nineteenth century, Urdu had been the language of polite culture over a big part of north India, for Hindus quite as much as Muslims. As late as the decade 1881–90, 4380 Urdu books had been published in U.P. as compared to 2793 in Hindi, while the corresponding circulation figures for newspapers were 16,256 for Urdu and 8002 for Hindi. Even Premchand wrote mainly in Urdu down to 1915, till he found publishers difficult to obtain. The campaign for Hindi in the Devanagri script launched by Arya Samajists and orthodox Hindus did have a certain populist appeal, for Persianized Urdu had been the language of an elite. But the highly Sanskritized Hindi which was increasingly propagated, and later sought by some enthusiasts to be given the stature of the 'national' language, was really quite far removed from the various popular vernaculars of the region (Punjabi, Haryanvi, Pahari, Rajasthani, Avadhi, Bhojpuri, Maithili, Magadhi, etc.). What was much more ominous was the way in which differences of script and language came to be progressively identified with differences in religion, embedding communalism at a very deep level in the popular consciousness. Thus, in north India as well as in the south, problems were emerging that have remained to trouble independent India right up to the present day.

Nationalist Economic Theory

Much less ambiguous in its import was the second major form of expression of nationalism—the economic critique of foreign rule for which the phrase drain of wealth may serve as a convenient shorthand. Conceptually, this is what really demarcates the post-1870 generation of Indian intellectuals from their predecessors. Rammohun, it is interesting to remember, in his evidence before the House of Commons Select Committee of 1831 did refer to what a later generation would call the drain, and even attempted an estimate of its amount—only to suggest European colonization as a solution, for then the profits made by whites in India would not leave the country! Starting with Naoroji, however, a whole tradition of nationalist economics began developing from the 1870s and found expression through a vast literature of books, newspaper articles, speeches and memorials which serve as the basis for Bipan Chandra's authoritative work on the subject. The nationalist critique directly related the abysmal and growing poverty of India to certain deliberate British policies, more particularly to drain of wealth through an artificial export-surplus, destruction of handicrafts followed by hindrances to modern Indian industry, and excessive land revenue burdens—the three recurrent themes of R.C. Dutt's *Economic History of India* (1901–03). The remedies repeatedly suggested were a reversal of these policies and all-out Indian efforts at industrial development. The early nationalists, in fact, formulated with a fair amount of clarity a perspective of independent development along capitalist lines. As early as 1873, Bholanath Chandra (an early Bengali critic of deindustrialization, who also suggested 'non-consumption' of English goods as a solution) appealed to his countrymen to make industrial enterprise 'the ocean to the rivers of all their thoughts', and twenty years later Ranade was expressing the hope that industrialization 'will soon become the creed of the whole Nation, and ensure the permanent triumph of the modern spirit in this Ancient Land'. Tilak's *Mahratta* echoed the same theme: 'We must become capitalists and enterprisers... a nation of traders, machine-makers, and shopkeepers.' (13 February 1881)

Judged in the light of more recent and sophisticated research summarized in the previous chapter, the nationalist critique did have certain limitations. There was little understanding of India's vital role in the total imperial economy of Britain, and the woes of the country were all too often attributed to certain individual 'un-British' policies which men like Naoroji for long thought could be reversed through gentle persuasion and pressure. The concentration on government policies also led to neglecting the role of private British capital. Above all, there was the definite slurring-over of tensions within Indian society. Thus, if as Naoroji and R.C. Dutt rightly argued, the peasants were having to forcibly sell their produce and this was being funnelled away through foreign export agencies to maintain the export-surplus necessary for the drain, the reason lay not just in revenue extortion, but also in exploitation by Indian *zamindars* and moneylenders. Many Indians, too, were subordinate beneficiaries and agents of colonial exploitation, and the nationalists generally ignored this. Nationalist opinion also usually refused to concern itself with the plight of Indians working in Indian-owned factories, in sharp contrast to that of those employed by foreigners, for whom (as for the Assam coolies) humanitarian sentiments were often expressed. The Factory Acts, which put certain fairly minimal and ill-enforced restrictions on the employment of women and children, and which the government passed mainly at the instance of a Lancashire worried by Bombay competition, were opposed by most nationalist newspapers. Only an overriding concern for the future of India's cotton textile industry can explain (though not excuse) the callous brutality of statements like that of the *Amrita Bazar Patrika* of 2 September 1875: 'A larger death-rate amongst our operatives is far more preferable to the collapse of this rising industry.'

Yet despite such limitations, Moderate economic thought remains extremely impressive. It was to provide the core of the Indian critique of foreign rule throughout the later phases of nationalism, whether Extremist, revolutionary-terrorist, Gandhian, or even socialist. The drain of wealth theory did provide a rough approximation to the underlying realities of colonial exploitation. Thus it was much less of a false consciousness than the varieties of ideologies and movements we have been considering so far, which had sought a solution for the country's sorrows through social reform, revivalism, communal alignments, or regional loyalties. In a more immediate sense, drain of wealth logic served as the theoretical underpinning for the demands and activities of the early Moderate-led Congress.

Foundations of the Congress

The nucleus of the Congress leadership consisted of men from Bombay and Calcutta who had first come together in London in the late-1860s and early-'70s while studying for the ICS or for law—Pherozeshah Mehta, Badruddin Tyabji, W.C. Bonnerji, Manmohan and Lalmohan Ghosh, Surendranath Banerji, Anandamohan Bose, and Romeshchandra Dutt, who all fell under the influence of Dadabhai Naoroji who was then settled in England as businessman-cum-publicist. Those among this group who did not join the civil service (or, as in the case of Surendranath was thrown out of it), along with some others like a Sadharan Brahmo group headed by Dwarkanath Ganguli in Calcutta, Ranade and G.V. Joshi in Poona, K.T. Telang in Bombay, and a little later G. Subramaniya Iyer, Viraraghavachari and Ananda Charlu in Madras, took the initiative in starting a number of local associations. These were 'middle-class'—professional rather than *zamindar*-led in composition. The most important of these organizations were the Poona Sarvajanik Sabha (1870), the Indian Association (1876), which organized the first all-India agitations in 1877–78 on the civil service and the press act issues, the Madras Mahajana Sabha (1884), and the Bombay Presidency Association (1885). From the early 1880s onwards, there had been numerous suggestions and attempts at a coming-together of such groups on an all-India scale, and the Indian Association even organized two 'National Conferences' at Calcutta, in 1883 and 1885. But eventually only the attempt launched at the initiative of Allan Octavian Hume succeeded on a permanent basis, and 72 largely self-appointed delegates met for the first session of the Indian National Congress at Bombay in December 1885.

Some unnecessary controversy has been caused by the statement of W.C. Bonnerji in 1898 that Hume was acting under the direct advice of Dufferin. Originally put forward no doubt as a means of gaining respectability, this version of the foundation of the Congress later came to be studied together with Hume's pleas to officials for concessions to educated Indians to stave off mass violence which he repeatedly prophesied was just around the corner. The result was a theory with considerable appeal for later radical critics of the Congress (like R.P. Dutt, for instance)—the Congress, it was argued, had been deliberately created by a British Viceroy acting through a British ex-civilian to act as a 'safety-valve' against popular discontent. This 'conspiracy theory', however, has been discredited by the opening of Dufferin's private papers, which reveal that no one in ruling circles took Hume's Cassandra-like predictions of imminent chaos very seriously. Hume did meet Dufferin at Simla in May 1885, but the Viceroy's main immediate reaction was to advise the Governer of Bombay to keep away from the proposed 'political convention of delegates'. (Dufferin to Reay, 17 May 1885) In any case, the whole story greatly exaggerates the personal role of Hume. Something like a national organization had been in the air for quite some time. Hume only took advantage of an already-created atmosphere; though he was perhaps helped by the fact that he was more acceptable to Indians as free of regional loyalties. Indians probably also had an exaggerated idea of Hume's potential influence in official circles—an impression which he did nothing to dispel.

The Moderate Congress: Objectives and Methods

It is customary to discuss the first twenty years in the history of the Congress—its Moderate phase—as a single bloc, and certainly a broad uniformity in objectives and methods of activity seems fairly obvious over the entire period. The Congress met at the end of each year for three days in what became a great social occasion as well as a political assembly, heard and applauded a long Presidential address and numerous speeches (almost always in English), and dispersed after passing a roughly similar set of resolutions dealing with three broad types of grievances—political, administrative and economic. The principal political demand was reform of Supreme and Local Legislative Councils to give them greater powers (of budget discussion and interpellation, for instance) and to make them representative by including some members elected by local bodies, chambers of commerce, universities, etc. Thus the immediate perspective fell far short of self-government or democracy, and as late as 1905, Gokhale's presidential address asserted that the educated were the 'natural leaders of the people', and explained that political rights were being demanded 'not for the whole population, but for such portion of it as has been qualified by education to discharge properly the responsibilities of such association'. There was however also an expectation that freedom would gradually broaden from precedent to precedent on the British pattern, till India entered the promised but distant land of what Naoroji in 1906 described with considerable ambiguity as 'Self-Government or Swaraj like that of United Kingdom or the colonies'. Among administrative reforms, pride of place went to the demand for Indianization of services through simultaneous ICS examinations in England and India—a demand raised not really just to satisfy the tiny elite who could hope to get into the ICS, as has been sometimes argued, but connected with much broader themes. Indianization was advocated as a blow against racism; it would also reduce the drain of wealth in so far as much of the fat salaries and pensions enjoyed by white officials were being remitted to England, as well as help to make administration more responsive to Indian needs. Other administrative demands included separation of the judiciary, extension of trial by jury, repeal of the Arms Act, higher jobs in the army for Indians, and the raising of an Indian volunteer force—demands which evidently combined pleas for racial equality with a concern for civil rights. The economic issues raised were all bound up with the general poverty of India-drain of wealth theme. Resolutions were repeatedly passed calling for an enquiry into India's growing poverty and famines, demanding cuts in Home Charges and military expenditure, more funds for technical education to promote Indian industries, and an end to unfair tariffs and excise duties. The demand for extension of the Permanent Settlement was also related to the drain of wealth argument, for over-assessment was held to be responsible for forced sale by peasants leading to the export surplus. That the early Congress was not concerned solely with the interests of the English-educated professional groups, *zamindars,* or industrialists is indicated by the numerous resolutions on the salt tax, treatment of Indian coolies abroad, and the sufferings caused by forest administration. Resolutions condemning forest laws were passed every year between 1891 and 1895. In addition, the Indian Association launched a campaign exposing the horrors of indentured labour in Assam tea gardens in the late 1880s, and its assistant secretary Dwarkanath Ganguli even went to the Assam plantation areas at considerable personal risk to bring back information about the slave labour conditions prevailing there. The Congress, however, refused to take this up on the ground that it was a local issue.

What made the Moderate Congress increasingly a target of criticism was not so much its objectives as its methods and style of functioning. The keynote here had been struck by Naoroji's phrase, 'un-British rule'—and the early Congress concentrated on building-up through petitions, speeches and articles a foolproof logical case aimed at convincing, not so much the 'sun-dried' bureaucrats of British India, but the presumably liberal-minded public opinion of the land of Cobden, Bright, Mill and Gladstone. Even these politics of what Extremists were to describe as 'mendicancy', moreover, were tried out in a rather intermittent manner. Politics remained for the bulk of the Moderates very much a part-time affair—the Congress was not a political party, but an annual three-day show, plus one or two secretaries, and the local associations which were quite numerous on paper were no more than tiny coteries, usually of lawyers, which met occasionally to 'elect' among themselves the Congress delegates for the year or to pass resolutions on some immediate grievances, and otherwise enjoyed long spells of complacent hibernation.

All this is well-known; the more interesting question is why this should have been so. The answer perhaps lies in the nature and social composition of the early Congress leaders and participants. The Moderate leaders tended to be Anglicized in their personal life and highly successful men in their professions. The first bred ambivalent attitudes towards Englishmen, with criticism of specific policies balanced by general admiration and even a belief in the 'providential' nature of British rule. The second meant little time left over for political activity; as Wacha complained to Naoroji on 18 November 1887, 'Pherozeshah is nowadays too busy with his professional work.... They are already rich enough...Mr Telang too remains busy. I wonder how if all remain busy in the pursuit of gold can the progress of the country be advanced?' Success also bred complacency, a belief that things would improve gradually, since after all some concessions like the 1892 Council Act had been obtained. Above all, many top Congressmen had developed a highly elitist life-style (Mehta travelled in a special railway saloon, Gandhi recalls J. Ghoshal asking him to button his shirt for him during the Calcutta Congress in 1901, and even the less Anglicized Ranade visited Simla in 1886 with 25 servants), and this often led to feelings of mingled contempt and fear of the 'lower orders', and a dependence on the British for law and order which must have been strengthened by the revivalist frenzies and communal riots of the 1890s. Thus Wacha in his *Shells from the Sands of Bombay* recalled the blowing from British guns of 1857 rebels without the slightest sympathy; Mehta in 1874 was mobbed during a Parsi-Muslim clash by what he described as 'this beggarly rabble and scum of the Mahomedan population'; Surendranath during a temperance campaign in 1887 found the lower classes utterly alien; and food rioters at Nagpur in 1896 chose a Congress leader's house as a principal target—no doubt because he was also a landlord and moneylender. Recent research, as we have seen, is bringing out the connections between the early Congress professional intelligentsia and propertied groups—a few industrialists in Bombay, commercial magnates like the Tandons of Allahabad, landholders or tenure holders practically everywhere. Such groups were not likely to support radical programmes or unrestrained mass agitation.

Phases of Moderate Politics

So far we have been talking of uniformities, but certain interesting variations over time and between regions are also being 'revealed by current research. Though the broad pattern of Congress resolutions remained on the whole the same, Council reform hardly figured much between 1892 and 1904—some concessions had after all been obtained here, and Congress leaders were being elected to the new local and imperial legislatures. Repeated famines and the cotton excise issue, however, focussed increasing attention on economic matters. Gokhale's speech on the budget in 1901 expounded nationalist economic theory on the floor of the Imperial Legislative Council for the first time, and, as Bipan Chandra has pointed out, the drain of wealth doctrine served as a radicalizing force, for at this crucial level things were evidently getting worse rather than better. Naoroji was an old man who became more extreme with age, even developing some contacts with British socialists like H.M. Hyndman. British efforts to woo peasants and develop the image of a paternalist *sarkar* (as against alleged Congress elitism) through measures like the Punjab Land Alienation Act (1901) for restricting transfers outside 'agricultural tribes', also compelled some Congress rethinking on the thorny issue of land relations. Though the Hindu urban trader-dominated Punjab Congress was bitterly opposed to the Act, the Lahore session (1900) made a significant concession by dropping the resolution on that subject. Again, while early movers of resolutions advocating Permanent Settlement had more or less equated it with a settlement with *zamindars,* R.C. Dutt in the late 1890s developed a broader formula. The 1899 session over which he presided passed a resolution clearly demanding both permanent fixation of revenue in *raiyatwari* areas and a ceiling on *zamindari* rent. Incidentally, McLane's detailed study also reveals British pro-peasant 'righteous rhetoric' to be largely a myth. Surendranath's opposition in 1898 to certain pro-*zamindar* modifications of the 1885 Bengal

Tenancy Act, for instance, was immediately followed by the transfer of a Council seat from municipalities to *zamindars*.

Turning to the activities and organization of the Congress, three broad phases can be distinguished within the Moderate era. Till 1892, the Congress was largely dominated by Hume as general secretary and sole full-time activist. Erratic, paternalistic and domineering, his presence did impart a certain dynamism which was to be conspicuously absent in the succeeding years. Congress attendance figures rose rapidly for the first five sessions, from 72 in 1885 to nearly 2000 in 1889. The detailed studies of Washbrook and Bayly have revealed the sessions of 1887 (Madras) and 1888 (Allahabad) to have been unusually broadbased as compared to the Congress of the 1890s, and to have aroused widespread interest. Funds for the Madras session, for instance, were raised through mass collections—₹5500 in amounts between one anna and ₹1–8 annas from 8000 persons, and another ₹8000 from donations ranging from ₹2 to ₹30. Faced with the opposition from the old U.P. elite led by Sayyid Ahmed (which initially included Hindu aristocrats like the Maharaja of Benares as well as Muslims) to Congress demands for elected Councils and service recruitment through examinations, Hume made a determined effort to woo Muslim support in 1887–88, utilizing the personal contacts of Badruddin Tyabji and evolving a formula (at the 1887 session) by which a resolution would be rejected if it was opposed by the bulk of any community. Even more notable was the unique attempt, again at Hume's initiative, to rally peasant support in 1887 through two popular pamphlets translated into no less than twelve regional languages. Hume himself wrote an imaginary dialogue exposing arbitrary administration in villages, while Viraraghavachari's *Tamil Catechism* attacked existing legislative councils as sham, and is said to have been sold in 30,000 copies. Nothing quite like this was to be attempted again till the 1905 days.

Such efforts, however, were short-lived and not particularly successful. The Aligarh Muslim elite still felt that they had a lot to lose from elected Councils which Hindus would be sure to dominate and from competitive recruitment where the latter's lead in English education would give them an advantage. The 1893 riots strengthened Muslim alienation, and the percentage of Muslim delegates in Congress, which had averaged 13.5 of the total between 1885 and 1892, fell to only 7.1 between 1893–1905. Even the latter figure is artificially swollen by the high local Muslim attendance at the Lucknow session (1899)—313, out of a total of 761 Muslims who attended all sessions in the 1893–1905 period. However, the Congress leaders were not particularly worried, as no rival Muslim political organization had as yet emerged. Theodore Beck's Muhammedan Anglo-Oriental Defence Association (1893) proved to be quite shortlived. No special attempt seems to have been made after 1887–88 to woo Muslim opinion. The peasant strategy of Hume was abandoned even more quickly as soon as it was found to have aroused intense official suspicion and hostility. The U.P. Lt. Governor Auckland Colvin tried to obstruct the holding of the Allahabad session and Dufferin in November 1888 in a famous speech denounced the Congress as a 'microscopic minority'—no doubt precisely because there were a few signs that it might soon become somewhat less microscopic. A badly frightened Congress leadership privately rebuffed Hume, and the bid for mass contact was abandoned.

A frustrated Hume left for England in 1892, with the parting shot of a circular prophesying imminent peasant revolution (unless Congress became more energetic and the British more responsive) which officials condemned as 'incendiary' and other Congress leaders repudiated. The Congress fell into the doldrums in the 1890s. Decisions were taken by a caucus consisting usually of Surendranath, W.C. Bonnerji, Ananda Charlu, and Pherozeshah Mehta with Ranade as adviser behind the scenes, but no effective leadership emerged, till Mehta decided to take more active interest in the Congress from 1899 and established his predominance. Hume was still elected general secretatry despite his absence, for the want of any agreed substitute. These were the years when failures in India led to a shift in emphasis almost entirely to campaigning in England through the British Committee of the Congress headed by Wedderburn, Hume and Naoroji with its journal *India*. The bulk of the fairly paltry Congress funds were sent over to this London committee (about ₹32,000 annually), and though Dinshaw Wacha was made joint-secretary from 1895, the money alloted to him was minimal. Yet in England, too, the hopes aroused by the 1892 Act and the snap Commons resolution supporting simultaneous examinations in 1893 were quickly dissipated, particularly after the Tories returned to power and Naoroji was unseated in the 1895 elections. Meanwhile interest in the Congress in India was waning. This was indicated for instance by the rising proportion of local delegates at its sessions, which had varied from 43.5% to 59.5% between 1885–93, but went up to between 64.7% to as high as 88.6% during 1894–1903. A decline in the activities of local or regional bodies like the Indian Association, the Poona Sarvajanik Sabha or the Madras Mahajana Sabha was also marked in the late-1890s. It needed the provocative policies of a Curzon (to be studied in the next chapter) to breathe some new life into the Moderates—that, and the rise of a new leader in Gokhale, with his assets of an attractive personality (unlike the rather abrasive Pherozeshah Mehta), youth (he was ten years younger than Tilak), and undoubted self-sacrifice and devotion to full-time public work.

Roots of Extremism

Yet if Curzon's assessment in November 1900 that the Congress was 'tottering to its fall' (Curzon to Secretary of State, Hamilton, 18 November 1900) was soon to be proved ludicrously off the mark, this was principally due to the fact that the Moderate Congress was increasingly 'reflecting only a small segment of nationalist sentiment'. (McLane) British unpopularity was increasing under the impact of famines and plagues the countervailing excise and Curzon's package of aggressive measures. The potential base for political activity was expanding fast, with the circulation of vernacular newspapers going up from 299,000 in 1885 to 817,000 in 1905. It was significant that some of the most popular journals were those which were critical of the Congress for a variety of reasons, like the Calcutta *Bangabasi* or the *Kesari* and *Kal* of Poona. The soil was becoming ripe for the rise of Extremism.

Historians of the 'Cambridge school' have been trying in recent years to present the emergence of Extremist dissent as basically a set of factional quarrels between 'ins' and 'outs' for the control of the Congress. Certainly there was no lack of factionalism in Congress circles during the 1890s. In Bengal, Surendranath and his newspaper, the *Bengalee,* had a running quarrel with the *Amrita Bazar Patrika* group of Motilal Ghosh ever since the former's Indian Association had overshadowed the shortlived India League in 1875–76. Factionalism was particularly acute in the Punjab, with three groups within the Lahore Brahmo Samaj, a major split within the Aryas, and a conflict between Lala Harkishan Lal and Lala Lajpat Rai. Washbrook has tried to analyse Madras politics in terms of a triangular conflict between the 'Mylapore clique' (V. Bhashyam Iyengar and S. Subramania Iyer in the 1880s, followed by V. Krishnaswami Iyer—the 'in' group, according to him), its less successful 'Egmore' rivals, also Madras city based (C. Sankaran Nair, Kasturi Ranga Iyengar), and *mofussil* 'outs' like T. Prakasam and Krishna Rao in coastal Andhra or Chidambaram Pillai in Tuticorin who allied with some 'Egmore' politicians to constitute Madras Extremism after 1905. In Poona, too, it has been argued, Tilak's quarrel in the late-1880s with Agarkar and Gokhale was over the control of the Deccan Education Society and had little to do initially with differences on political or even social reform issues.

Faction-analysis does have a certain utility, particularly in the context of earlier tendencies to present conflicts within nationalism in terms of debates between more-or-less disembodied ideals. Yet Cambridge scholars surely press it much too far. It is difficult to understand why dissidents should have been so eager to capture the Congress—not yet a real political party with power and patronage opportunities, it must be remembered, but no more than an annual platform with very inadequate funds—unless it was because they had certain alternative strategies and ideals to put forward. Above all, such scholarship ignores entirely the fairly systematic critique of Moderate politics which was emerging in the 1890s, most notably in the three principal bases of later Extremism—Bengal, Punjab and Maharashtra.

The starting-point of the new approach was a two-fold critique of the Moderate Congress—for its 'mendicant' technique of appealing to British public opinion, felt to be both futile and dishonourable, and for its being no more than a movement of an English-educated elite alienated from the common people. Instead of prayers and petitions, self-reliance and constructive work became the new slogans—starting *swadeshi* enterprises, organizing what came to be called national education, and emphasizing the need for concrete work in villages. Self-help, use of the vernaculars, utilization of traditional, popular customs and institutions like the village fair or *mela,* and, increasingly, an evocation of Hindu revivalist moods—came to be regarded as the best ways of bridging the gulf between the educated and the masses. The overall reaction against Moderate 'agitation' took in the end, three main forms, which become distinct only after 1905 but can be seen in germ from the 1890s—a somewhat non-political trend towards *self-development* through constructive work, ignoring rather than directly attacking foreign rule; political Extremism proper, attempting mass mobilization for *Swaraj* through certain new techniques which came to be called *passive resistance;* and *revolutionary terrorism,* which sought a short-cut to freedom via individual violence and conspiracies.

The first really systematic critique of Moderate politics was made in 1893–94 in a series of articles entitled *New Lamps for Old* by Aurobindo Ghosh, then living in Baroda, having returned from England after a highly Anglicized upbringing against which he had begun to react sharply. Aurobindo rejected the English model of slow constitutional progress admired by the Moderates as much inferior to the French experience of 'the great and terrible republic'. He attacked Congress mendicancy ('a little too much talk about the blessings of British rule'), and striking a remarkable class-conscious note which was no doubt derived from his recent European experience, urged as the most vital of all problems the establishment of a link between 'the burgess, or the middle class' which the Congress represented and 'the proletariate... the real key of the situation... the right and fruitful policy for the burgess, the only policy that has any chance of eventual success, is to base his cause upon an adroit management of the proletariate.' But the 'proletariate' to Aurobindo was surely no more than the common people of town and country in general, and the 'key' to its heart, which he was already seeking through revivalist Hinduism in the 1894 essays on Bankimchandra, in the end eluded the Extremists. By the turn of the century, Aurobindo was trying to organize secret societies, and sending Jatindranath Banerji and Barindrakumar Ghosh to Bengal as emissaries. He was also, however, to elaborate a programme of mass passive resistance when the anti-Partition upsurge revealed for a time the possibilities of a broader movement. We shall see such an oscillation fairly often in other Extremist figures, too.

In Bengal, disillusionment with the Congress was voiced by Aswinikumar Dutt, who described the Amraoti session of 1897 as a 'three days' tamasha'. Dutt was a Barisal school teacher who through a lifetime of patient social work in his district built up a unique kind of mass following and made his region the strongest base of the *Swadeshi* movement in the 1905 days. It was voiced memorably also by Rabindranath Tagore, already Bengal's leading literary figure (which he was to remain for fifty years), who was contributing to patriotism not only through magnificent poems and short stories evoking the beauty of the Bengal countryside and describing the life of its people, but also more directly through attacks on Congress mendicancy, repeated calls for *atmasakti* (self-reliance) through *swadeshi* enterprise and national education, and extremely perceptive suggestions for mass contact through *melas, jatras* and the use of the mother-tongue in both education and political work. By the early years of the twentieth century, Vivekananda's message was also being given a more direct political colour by his disciple, the Irish Sister, Nivedita (Margaret Noble), with her experience of Irish and other European revolutionary movements. The Bengali *bhadralok* was also turning to *swadeshi* industrial enterprise—the scientist Profullachandra Roy started his Bengal Chemicals in 1893, for instance—and Satis Mukherji through his Dawn Society and Rabindranath through his Santiniketan *asrama* were experimenting with new forms of education under indigeneous control. All this obviously contributed much more to Bengal Extremism than the petty factionalism of Surendranath and Motilal Ghosh.

In the Punjab, both Harkishan Lal (who started the Punjab National Bank) and Arya Samajists of the College faction were active in *swadeshi* enterprise from the 1890s. Congress delegates from the Punjab also pressed from 1893 onwards for a formal constitution, evidently to reduce the powers of the informal Bombay-Bengal axis which dominated the organization. They managed to set up a permanent Indian Congress Committee at the 1899 session, only to see it successfully sabotaged two years later by the

Pherozeshah caucus. In two articles published in the *Kayastha Samachar* of 1901, Lajpat Rai advocated technical education and industrial self-help in place of the fatuous annual festival of the English-educated elite which was all that the Congress amounted to. He also argued that the Congress should openly and boldly base itself on the Hindus alone, as unity with Muslims was a chimera. Once again we see the chalking-out of Extremist themes and limitations.

But the man who really blazed the trail for Extremism was Bal Gangadhar Tilak of Maharashtra. Tilak was a pioneer in many ways—in the use of religious orthodoxy as a method of mass contact (through his alignment against reformers on the Age of Consent issue, followed by the organization of the Ganapati festival from 1894), in the development of a patriotic-cum-historical cult as a central symbol of nationalism (the Shivaji festival, which he organized from 1896 onwards), as well as in experimenting with a kind of no-revenue campaign in 1896–97. The countervailing cotton excise of 1896 produced intense reactions in western India on which Tilak tried to base something like a boycott movement—the first trial use of a method which was to become the central nationalist technique from 1905 onwards. Tilak, who had pointedly declared that 'we will not achieve any success in our labours if we croak once a year like a frog', seemed to be groping his way towards the techniques of mass passive resistance or civil disobedience when in a speech in 1902 he declared: 'Though down-trodden and neglected, you must be conscious of your power of making the administration impossible if you but choose to make it so. It is you who manage the railroad and the telegraph, it is you who make settlements and collect revenues...'.

Before 1905 revealed the possibilities of mass action, however (and also afterwards, as we shall see, whenever mass participation prospects dwindled), the obvious reaction to Moderate methods was a call for individual violence. Constitutional agitation and terrorism were opposite poles united on a common base of elite action; a shift from the one to the other was really much easier and socially less dangerous than a breakthrough towards genuine mass action. Hence the bitter feelings aroused by tactless British handling of the Poona plague situation in 1897 culminated, not in any effective mass action, but in the first outbreak of revolutionary terrorism—the murder of Rand and Ayerst by the Chapekar brothers. Damodar Chapekar's autobiography reveals a complex inter-mixture of patriotic fervour (he had dreamt of guerrilla warfare in his boyhood, while passing by train through the Ghats), Brahmanical revivalism, and hatred of social reformers at least partly because they were successful men while he himself came from the struggling lower middle class. The British accused Tilak of sedition, on the strength mainly of a *Kesari* article which had justified Shivaji's assassination of the Bijapur general Afzal Khan. He was jailed for two years. The entire Congress public protested, for though many disliked Tilak, they all realized that what was at stake was the question of civil rights and a free press. The political tempo in Maharashtra declined rapidly, however—only to rise again, along with that of a considerable part of India, after Curzon's folly of partitioning Bengal in 1905.

Chapter 4
POLITICAL AND SOCIAL MOVEMENTS
1905-1917

THE VICEROYALTY OF CURZON

Lord Curzon's administration has remained famous—and notorious—for its intense activity and veritable cult of efficiency. 'Efficiency of administration is, in my view, a synonym for the contentment of the governed', the Viceroy declared in a budget speech in 1904. The net result was the beginning of quite a new phase in the history of Indian nationalism with the struggle against the Partition of Bengal.

Bepinchandra Pal's *New India* offered the following contemporary analysis of Curzon's policies. 'Lord Ripon's ideal was to secure, by slow degrees, autonomy for the *Indian people*. Lord Curzon's is to secure it for the *Indian Government*'. (20 August 1903) Two years later, the same journal referred to Curzon's efforts 'to win the goodwill of people, and to prevent any powerful combination between them and the educated middle classes'. (15 July 1905) Discounting the usual mythmaking about Ripon, we have here a fairly accurate description of a paternalist despotism, quite in the Tory tradition but more aggressive than was usual, together with a less typical effort to make the Secretary of State and even the Cabinet dance to the Viceroy's tune.

Foreign Policy

Curzon's bid to direct policies from India was at its most blatant in foreign relations, where his extreme Russophobia often embarrassed British Governments already taking the first ambiguous steps towards what in 1907 was to become the Triple Entente between England, France and Russia. The Viceroy repeatedly expressed a desire to establish a definite British sphere of interest over the Persian Gulf and Seistan. London after much hesitation agreed only to a Monroe Doctrine type of British declaration concerning the Gulf, warning off other powers (May 1903), and reluctantly permitted a flag-waving mission in the region by Curzon himself. Extension of British influence over Kuwait and Bahrain was to prove vitally important, however, in the oil politics of the twentieth century. Curzon suggested a move on Kandahar when the new Afghan Amir Habibullah insisted on the old arms subsidies, without any renegotiation of the Durand border agreement as desired by the Viceroy. 'For Heaven's sake do not let Curzon get us into a row there', implored a thoroughly alarmed Joseph Chamberlain, 'Remember that it ruined Dizzy's [Disraeli's] government.' Louis Dane's mission to Kabul in 1904 eventually returned with the old agreements confirmed. Curzon was more successful in Tibet, where he used the Tibetan adventurer Dorjieff's meeting with the Tsar to play up for all he was worth the Russian bogey. Ignoring repeated Cabinet warnings, the Younghusband expedition (1903–04) marched right up to Lhasa, and though the only evidence it could find of the Russian presence consisted of a couple of rifles, insisted on a heavy indemnity and occupation of the Chumbi Valley for 75 years. A trade agreement and clauses excluding other foreign influences were also extorted at the point of the gun. The Cabinet, however, got the indemnity and period of occupation reduced.

Administrative Reforms

The drive for efficiency through cutting-down administrative red-tape was pursued with enormous fan fare, yet even the highly adulatory near-contemporary biography by Lovat Fraser admitted that expenditure on office stationary almost doubled under Curzon. The Viceroy's scathing comments on subordinates in official minutes or private letters make delightful reading for historians today (like the celebrated outburst against 'departmentalism'— 'Round and round, like the diurnal revolution of the earth, went the file, stately, solemn, sure and slow.'); its contemporary impact often must have been unnecessary irritation. It is not at all surprising that no school of devoted officials developed around Curzon in India (unlike Milner in Africa), and that his resignation in August 1905 came over an extremely petty dispute with Kitchener over the status and choice of the Military Supply Member in the Viceroy's executive. Curzon's habit of picking unnecssary quarrels is shown also by his insistence upon Indian princes getting permission before going abroad. The Gaekwar of Baroda, who had already irritated the Viceroy by employing R.C. Dutt, went off without seeking permission, and ultimately it was Calcutta which had to retreat.

Curzon's administration was lucky in coming near the end of a cycle of famines, the last of which was in 1899–1900 (though plague continued unabated, with annual mortality figures passing the one million mark in 1904), and he also had a run of surplus budgets. Depreciation of the silver rupee had stopped after free minting had been closed and the gold exchange standard adopted in the late 1890s. With Home Charges no longer a growing burden as they had been with a falling rupee, some tax concessions became possible. Remissions of land revenue were made after the famine of 1899–1900 (even though Curzon repeatedly rejected Congress pleas for Permanent Settlement and argued that weather rather than excessive taxes lay at the root of famine). The salt tax was reduced, and the income-tax exemption limit raised from ₹500 to ₹1000 a year in 1903–04. The government could also push ahead with railway construction, setting up a Railway Board and opening 6100 miles of new lines (the greatest expansion under any Viceroy), as well as devote somewhat greater attention to irrigation through the Irrigation Commission of 1901–03. Curzon's interest in economic matters was revealed also by the setting-up of a Department of Commerce and Industry in 1905, and the establishment of the Pusa Institute for research on agriculture. In much of this, as usual, the benefits went to whites, or at best to select groups of Indians. New railways, for instance, meant more engineering contracts for British firms in England or in India; Englishmen constituted an important proportion of income-tax payers in India; while even the departure from free trade policies through the import duty on bounty-fed European beet-sugar in 1899 helped Mauritius planters and white owners of sugar factories like Begg Sutherland and Company of Kanpur. Curzonian 'paternalism' was somewhat better represented by the Punjab Land Alienation Act (1901) restricting transfer of peasant property to urban moneylenders, and legislation in 1904 promoting cooperative credit societies among agriculturists. The former caused some embarrassment to nationalists, as Punjab Congressmen often had Hindu urban trader connections while a big section of the peasants were Muslim or Sikh. Both measures ultimately benefited rich peasants, who turned moneylenders themselves and often dominated the cooperative societies as well.

Curzon did show a genuine interest in India's ancient monuments, and passed a valuable Act for their preservation. Less laudable were his grandiose plans for the somewhat bizarre Victoria Memorial in Calcutta, while the Durbar for Edward VII in 1902 was a sheer waste of more than two million rupees. In his early years, he also won some popularity among Indians by punishing white soldiers for a collective rape incident at Rangoon (1899), disciplining the 9th Lancers for beating an Indian cook to death at Sialkot (1902), and trying (unsuccessfully) to get the Calcutta High Court to revise a lower court sentence of only six months jail for an Assam tea manager who had murdered a coolie (Bain case, 1904). Such things made Anglo-Indians furious for a time, but Curzon had no intention of risking another Ilbert Bill agitation, and so never attempted the only real remedy—ending all-white juries in multi-racial cases. On basic matters he was as racist as anyone, and even at his most benevolent tended to speak 'of Indians in tones one normally reserves for pet animals'. (S. Gopal, *British Policy in India* p. 227) In a letter to Secretary of State Hamilton on 23 April 1900, Curzon expressed his concern about the increasing number of higher posts 'that were meant and ought to have been exclusively and specifically reserved for Europeans... being filched away by the superior wits of the natives...' And even in public pronouncements, he could be at times quite fantastically and unnecessarily insulting: 'I hope I am making no false or arrogant claim when I say that the highest ideal of truth is to a large extent a Western conception.' (Calcutta University Convocation Address, 1905)

What made Curzon's administration ultimately so significant was in fact his consistent hostility towards educated Indian aspirations as represented by the Congress, along with a not unrelated determination to strengthen, streamline and enforce the authority of the Raj. He had decided from the beginning, long before nationalist hostility towards him had manifested itself, to treat the Congress as an 'unclean thing... never taking notice of it', as 'in so far as it is innocent, it is superfluous, and in so far as it is hostile to Government or seditious, it is a natural danger'. (Curzon to Ampthill, 15 June 1903) It is not surprising that police reforms found an important place in his plans, as well as a tightening of security through an Official Secrets Act (1904). The recommendations of a Police Commission (1902–03) with Andrew Fraser as Chairman brought about significant improvements in the number, training and salaries of the police force at an additional expenditure of ₹15 million annually. A separate Department of Criminal Intelligence was also set up to tackle political crimes, in place of the quaintly named *Thuggee* and Dacoity Department.

Curzon and Nationalists

The real confrontation between Curzon and the nationalist intelligentsia came through three successive measures: changes in the Calcutta Corporation in 1899, the Universities Act of 1904, and the Partition of Bengal in 1905. The first reduced the number of elected Indian members, and was a move directly connected with the interests of the Calcutta European business community, which had often complained about delays in the grant of licenses or other favours. It is interesting that Alexander Mackenzie, then the Lt. Governor of Bengal who apart from Curzon was the man principally responsible for the changes, happened to be the brother of a Burn Company partner who was also the representative in the Legislative Council of the Bengal Chamber of Commerce. Universities reform was formulated at a secret and purely white conference at Simla in September 1901, and worked out by a Universities Commission whose sole Indian member, Gurudas Banerji, strongly disagreed with its recommendations. Trumpeted by Curzon as a move 'to raise the standard of education all round', the Act cut down the number of elected Senate members, transferred the power of ultimate decision in matters of college affiliation and school recognition to government officials, and tried to fix minimum college fees. Educated Indian opposition on grounds of the Act's undemocratic and restrictive nature was hardly unnatural. Claims that educational improvement was the principal aim consorted oddly with the fact that total expenditure on education was only ₹20.46 million in 1903–04 and ₹24.49 million in 1905–06—only slightly more, it will be noted, than the increase in police expenses during the same period and a paltry 2.5 per cent or so of the total budget. The new emphasis on universities becoming postgraduate teaching rather than primarily examining bodies did produce some good results in the end, particularly at Calcutta where it was implemented by a Vice-Chancellor of great vision, Asutosh Mukherji. But much more important in the immediate context were the new official controls on affiliation and grants-in-aid. These were to be liberally used from 1905 onwards to curb student militancy, and so the Universities Act really deserves a place alongside the Police Commission in the strengthening of British defences against the rising nationalist tide.

Partition of Bengal

Curzon's most unpopular measure—the Partition of Bengal—has also aroused the most controversy among historians, with apologists tending to emphasize administrative convenience as its prime motive against contemporary and later nationalist charges of deliberate 'divide and rule'. Down to 1903, administrative considerations were certainly predominant in official circles. The size of the Bengal Presidency had worried many at various times (hence the stray proposals to reduce it going back to the 1860s, the separation of Assam and Sylhet in 1874, and the Assam Chief Commissioner William Ward's proposal in 1896–97 to attach Chittagong Division, Dacca and Mymensingh to his province), and there was an increasing interest in the development of Assam into a more viable province. Ward's proposal was revived by Bengal's new Lt. Governor Andrew Fraser in a note of 28 March 1903, accepted by Curzon in a minute on territorial redistribution in India (1 June 1903), and, suitably edited for public consumption, and announced for the first time in Home Secretary Risley's letter of 3 December 1903. Relief of Bengal and improvement of Assam were the two grounds offered by Risley in support of the transfer plan. It needs to be pointed out, however, that 'administrative convenience' was not something abstract or impartial but often closely related to the convenience of British officials and British businessmen. Thus an expansion of Assam was needed, argued

Risley, to 'give to its officers a wider and more interesting field of work', and provide 'a maritime outlet in order to develop its industries in tea, oil and coal' (all dominated by whites, it may be added).

Between December 1903 and the formal announcement of 19 July 1905, a transfer plan was transformed into a full-scale Partition by Fraser, Risley and Curzon, with the new province of 'East Bengal and Assam' eventually including Chittagong, Dacca and Rajshahi divisions. Hill Tippera and Malda apart from Assam. Secret official minutes, comments and private papers make the public denial of political motives difficult to maintain, particularly during this second phase. The contemporary and later nationalist charge of deliberate encouragement of Hind-Muslim tensions finds some support in Curzon's much-quoted speech at Dacca in February 1904 offering east Bengal Muslims the prospect of 'unity which they have not enjoyed since the days of the old Mussulman viceroys and kings'. But the really important political motive at this time was a division among the predominantly Hindu politicians of West and East Bengal. Home Secretary H.H. Risley summed it all up with clarity and frankness in two notes dated 7 February and 6 December 1904 while analysing the arguments of the critics of the Partition: 'Bengal united is a power; Bengal divided will pull in several different ways. That is perfectly true and is one of the merits of the scheme.... It is not altogether easy to reply in a despatch which is sure to be published without disclosing the fact that in this scheme as in the matter of the amalgamation of Berar to the Central Provinces one of our main objects is to split up and thereby weaken a solid body of opponents to our rule.' Marathi-speaking Berar, newly acquired on perpetual lease from the Nizam in 1902, had not been attached to Bombay since, as Curzon said, 'We hear quite enough of Sivaji as it is.' Alternative plans to relieve Bengal administration by setting up an executive council or by detaching linguistically-distinct Bihar and Orissa (the ultimate 1911 solution) were repeatedly dismissed by Curzon on political grounds—the latter proposal, he argued in a telegram to the Secretary of State who had been toying with the idea, 'would tend to consolidate the Bengali element by detaching it from outside factors, and would produce the very effect that we desire to avoid. The best guarantee of the political advantage of our proposal is its dislike by the Congress Party.'

Bureaucrats like Risley anticipated present-day Cambridge historians in their fondness for interpreting opposition to Partition entirely in terms of elitist interest-groups. Vikrampur babus were worried about their clerical jobs, *zamindars* with estates in both Bengals disliked having to appoint two sets of agents and pleaders, the Bhagyakul Roy family with raw jute and rice trading interests near Calcutta were jealous of a possible rise of Chittagong, and Calcutta lawyers were afraid that a new province would ultimately mean a new High Court cutting into their practice. In addition, the east Bengal political elite felt its chance of sitting in legislative councils slipping away (this was in the earlier phase, when parts of Bengal were being sought to be transferred to the Chief Commissioner's province of Assam which had no elected legislatures), and Calcutta politicians would find their influence gravely curtailed. None of the factors listed by Risley in his note of 7 February 1904 were invented by him—all of them in fact repeatedly appear in early pamphlets on the subject like *An Open Letter to Lord Curzon* (Dacca, April 1904), *The Case Against the Break-up of Bengal* and *All About Partition* (Calcutta, September 1905). But the related bureaucratic expectation that protests would die down quickly, and in any case would never leave the beaten track of meetings and petitions, was soon totally belied by events in Bengal and some other provinces. With startling rapidity, after July 1905, the movement broke away from traditional moorings, developed a variety of new and militant techniques, attracted larger numbers than before, and broadened into a struggle for *Swaraj*.

What the British had clearly underestimated was first of all the sense of unity among the Bengalis—rooted to some extent in a history marked by long periods of regional independence and greatly fostered, at least among the literate, by the cultural developments of the nineteenth century. Calcutta had become a real metropolis for the educated Bengali *bhadralok*. It attracted students from all districts, sent out teachers, lawyers, doctors and clerks all over the province and often beyond it, and contributed to both regional writing and regional pride through the evolution of a standard literary language, a growing number of newspapers and periodicals and a modern literature which with Rabindranath Tagore was on the threshhold of world recognition. Such things—along with less worthy factors like the evident (though gradually diminishing) educated Bengali lead in professions, government services, and politics over much of India due to the advantage of earlier English education—fostered a new self-confidence which came to be further stimulated by the growing Hindu revivalist mood best typified by Vivekananda. International developments also played a part—British reverses in the Boer War, the unexpected Japanese victory over Russia in 1904–05 which sent a thrill of pride through Asia and was ecstatically hailed by the Bengal press (even children were given nicknames like Togo or Nogi, after Japanese leaders), news of the Chinese boycott of American goods in protest against immigration laws and of the popular revolution against autocracy in Russia.

In this atmosphere of strong regional unity and growing self-confidence and pride, Curzon's provocative actions culminating in a virtually behind-the-scenes Partition decision (very little had been said about it publicly by officials between February 1904 and July 1905) was regarded above all as a national insult. Inevitably it became associated, not only with political disappointments over the paltry achievements of twenty years of Moderate agitation which perhaps directly affected only a limited circle, but with much more widely-felt grievances about racial discrimination and white arrogance. The diary of Gyanchandra Banerji vividly reflects all this: a *munsiff* getting ₹200 as against the white district judge's ₹2000, a distant whistle brings to him memories of racial discrimination suffered aboard steamers and trains, and he finds solace in 'signs of national reawakening', the achievements of the scientist Jagadischandra Basu, and 'the rise of Japan as a world power'.

Banerji began his journal (in October 1904) with a reference to the growing poverty of India. Though the Bengali *bhadralok* was seldom directly affected by famine or plague, the ravages of both in the 1890s could not but have stirred his conscience—and made faith in the 'providential' British connection increasingly difficult to maintain, particularly in face of that other, intrinsically subversive, aspect of Moderate theory: the 'drain of wealth' explanation of Indian misery. More direct economic grievances perhaps also played a part. The liberal professions were getting overcrowded (a *Swadeshi* pamphlet in 1905 complained that there were 80 pleaders in the single east Bengal subdivision of Madaripur) making the *bhadralok* often more dependent on petty *zamindari* or intermediate tenures which sub-division through inheritance made progressively less remunerative. And prices had suddenly started rising fast, the all-India unweighted index numbers constructed by K.L. Dutta (1890–94 = 100) being 106 for 1904, 116 for 1905, 129 for 1906, and 143 for 1908. The curve in fact was steepest between 1905 and 1908—precisely the years of maximum political unrest.

The *Swadeshi* strongholds in the East Bengal countryside—Bakarganj, Madaripur, Vikrampur, Kishoregunj—were areas of Hindu *bhadralok* concentration, multiplicity of intermediate tenures and considerable spread of English education (with consequent overcrowding of professions and spread of nationalist ideology). Rising prices probably stimulated nationalism among such groups and areas, while sections of industrial labour were also prodded by inflation into strikes which represented an important—though often forgotten—aspect of the 1905 days. But economic discontent could also turn against the immediate oppressor—the (usually Hindu) rentier, moneylender or trader in East Bengal, and thus contribute to communal riots. The *Swadeshi* intelligentsia in Bengal added to these problems by getting increasingly involved in Hindu revivalist postures, and completely failing to develop, as we shall see, anything like a radical agrarian programme. Higher prices and problems in getting jobs made them cling more strongly to rent-incomes, however small. Gyanchandra Banerji had only a meagre ancestral holding in Vikrampur, yet his diary indignantly denounces the Tenancy Act of 1885 for having embittered agrarian relations. An extremely interesting vernacular pamphlet on Bengal's land relations written in 1904 even developed a curious theory about the ancient Aryan' origins of intermediate tenure-holders, self-defined as usual as a 'middle class'. They were being squeezed out, it complained, by big *zamindars* (allegedly usurpers created by the Muslims and the British) on the one side, and by 'insolent raiyats' encouraged by tenancy legislation, on the other. (Amritalal Pal, *Banger Bhumi-Rajasya o Prachin Arya Gramya Samiti*, Calcutta, 1904) Another pamphlet, the *Open Letter to Curzon* (1904), quoted Edmund Burke to equate public opinion with the views of men 'above menial dependence', and confidently asserted that the 'educated classes' were the 'natural leaders' of the masses. The *bhadralok's* distance from the peasantry thus had fairly clear class roots, rather than mere aversion to manual labour.

While the Extremist intelligentsia—whether in Bengal or in other provinces—failed to link up nationalist slogans with the immediate economic grievances of the peasantry (attempting usually a short-cut to mass contact through religious appeals which often proved disastrous in so far as the Muslims were concerned) there is some evidence also of a certain slackening of pressures from below. Famine and plague must have caused considerable exhaustion in a large part of the country, while among the survivors the fall in population may have reduced somewhat the pressure on land and therefore agrarian tensions. British remedial legislation after the rural disturbances of the 1870s and 1880s—consolidating occupancy rights in Bengal, restricting passage of land to outsider *mahajans* in Bombay and Punjab—also tended to pacify for some time the upper stratum of the peasantry which had been the most active element in conflicts with moneylenders or landlords. The price-rise was closely associated with a boom in the export of agricultural raw materials, and in fact seems to have been primarily caused by it. Another factor behind the inflation was a currency expansion, itself connected with the inflow of gold and silver due to the export surplus. While the major beneficiaries of this boom must have been British export agencies and Indian merchant intermediaries, perhaps some sections of the peasantry (the richer cultivators of jute in east Bengal for instance) also made marginal gains. The first decade of the twentieth century seems to have been marked by some growth in per capita national income according to Sivasubramonian's estimate, calculated on the basis of 1938–39 prices, from ₹49.4 in 1900–01 to ₹60.4 in 1916–17. (*National Income of India 1900–01 to 1946–47*, Delhi University mimeograph, 1965) All this helped to keep apart the currents of national and social discontent during the Extremist phase of Indian nationalism.

THE SWADESHI MOVEMENT IN BENGAL: 1905–1908

Down to July 1905, the partition plan had been opposed through an intensive use of the conventional 'Moderate' methods of press campaigns, numerous meetings and petitions (particularly in Dacca and Mymensingh districts), and big conferences at the Calcutta Town Hall in March 1904 and January 1905 attended by many district delegates. The evident and total failure of such techniques led to a search for new forms—boycott of British goods (first suggested by Krishnakumar Mitra's weekly *Sanjivani* on 13 July 1905, and accepted by the established leaders like Surendranath Banerji after considerable hesitation at the Town Hall meeting of 7 August) and Rabindranath's and Ramendras under Trivedi's imaginative appeals for *rakhi-bandhan* and *arandhan*. Wristlets of coloured thread were exchanged on Partition Day (16 October) as symbol of brotherhood, and the hearth kept unlit as a sign of mourning. The British crackdown on student picketers through measures like the Carlyle Circular (published on 22 October) threatening withdrawal of grants, scholarships and affiliation from nationalist dominated institutions led to a movement for boycott of official educational institutions and organization of national schools which received a great fillip from the spectacular donation of rupees one lakh by Subodh Mullik on 9 November. Tensions mounted with further measures of repression (the posting of Gurkhas in Barisal, the *lathi*-charge smashing up the provincial conference there in April 1906, numerous 'Swadeshi' cases against picketers), and soon internal differences cropped up within the movement in Bengal. With some, boycott became the starting-point for the formulation of a whole range of new methods, and the abrogation of the Partition came to be regarded as no more than the 'pettiest and narrowest of all political objects' (Aurobindo Ghosh in April 1907)—a mere stepping-stone in a struggle for '*Swaraj*' or complete independence. With others, like Surendranath, boycott was a last desperate effort to get Partition revoked by pulling at the purse-strings of Manchester. The established Moderate leaders managed to call off the educational boycott by 16 November 1905, and were soon taking advantage of the appointment of Morley with his great liberal reputation as Secretary of State to get back to the safer shores of 'mendicancy'.

Such internal differences evidently had a factional aspect, with individuals or groups more-or-less kept out of nationalist leadership so far (like Motilal Ghosh with his *Amrita Bazar Patrika,* or Bepinchandra Pal, or Aurobindo Ghosh) trying to muscle in on hitherto closed preserves and seeking to break up the 'rings of lawyers' which, Pal complained, had monopolized politics till then in the district towns. Yet to present the whole story in terms of a conflict between 'ins' and 'outs' would be to grossly oversimplify things, and rob the *Swadeshi* era in Bengal of its real interest and significance.

Trends

At a theoretical level, three major trends can be distinguished in the political life of Bengal between 1905 and 1908 apart from the well-established Moderate tradition. There was first what may be termed 'constructive *Swadeshi*'—the rejection of futile and self-demeaning 'mendicant' politics in favour of self-help through *Swadeshi* industries, national schools, and attempts at village improvement and organization. This found expression through the business ventures of Prafullachandra Roy or Nilratan Sircar, Satischandra Mukherji's journal *Dawn* and his Dawn Society which played a seminal role in the national education movement, and above all in Rabindranath, who in his *Swadeshi Samaj* address (1904) had already sketched out a blue-print for constructive work in villages, through a revival of the traditional Hindu *'samaj'* or community. Aswinikumar Dutt's Swadesh Bandhav Samiti in Barisal (Bakargunj) claimed to have settled 523 village disputes through 89 arbitration committees in its first annual report (September 1906), and about a thousand village *samitis* were reported to be functioning in Bengal in a pamphlet dated April 1907. In all this there were clear anticipations of much of the later Gandhian programme of *Swadeshi*, national schools and constructive village-work.

Such a perspective of slow and unostentatious development of what Rabindranath called *atmasakti* (self-strengthening) had little appeal to the excited educated youth of Bengal, who felt drawn much more to the creed of a more political Extremism. Journals like Bepin Pal's *New India*, Aurobindo Ghosh's *Bande Mataram,* Brahmobandhab Upadhyay's *Sandhya* and the *Yugantar* (brought out by a group associated with Barindrakumar Ghosh) from 1906 onwards were calling for a struggle for *Swaraj*. In practice, as later events showed, many of the Extremist leaders would agree to settle for less—Tilak in January 1907, for instance, expressed his willingness to take 'half a loaf rather than no bread', though with the intention 'of getting the whole loaf in good time'. The more fundamental difference was really therefore over methods, and here the classic statement came from Aurobindo in a series of articles in *Bande Mataram* in April 1907, later reprinted as *Doctrine of Passive Resistance*. Ridiculing the ideal of 'peaceful ashrams and swadeshism and self-help' as inadequate, he visualized a programme of 'organized and relentless boycott' of British goods, officialized education, justice, and executive administration (backed up by the positive development of *swadeshi* industries, national schools, and arbitration courts), and also looked forward to civil disobedience of unjust laws, a 'social boycott' of loyalists, and recourse to armed struggle if British repression went beyond the limits of endurance. The *Sandhya* of 21 November 1906 had chalked out a similar perspective: 'If...the chowkidar, the constable, the deputy and the munsiff and the clerk, not to speak of the sepoy, all resign their respective functions, feringhee rule in the country may come to an end in a moment.' Once again we have practically the entire future political programme of Gandhism, minus the dogma of non-violence, and—significantly enough—no tax or no-rent calls, which Aurobindo explicitly ruled out in his April 1907 articles as going against a *zamindar* community in Bengal which was assumed to be basically patriotic.

In practice, Bengal Extremism wasted a lot of energies in purely verbal or literary violence and in-fighting over the Congress organization, though it did contribute (along with others), as we shall see, to building up an impressive chain of district organizations or *samitis* and in providing some novel political leadership to labour unrest. Already by 1907, however, the mass-movement perspective was being challenged from within its own ranks by calls for elite-action terrorism: 'And what is the number of English officials in each district? With a firm resolve you can bring English rule to an end in a single day.... If we sit idle, and hesitate to rise till the whole population are [sic] goaded to desperation, then we shall continue idle till the end of time.... Without blood, O Patriots! will the country awake?' (*Yugantar,* 3 March, 26 August 1907).

Cutting across the debate over political methods or goals was another controversy over cultural ideals, between modernistic and Hindu-revivalist trends. The *Swadeshi* mood in general was closely associated with attempts to combine politics with religious revivalism, which was repeatedly used as a morale-booster for activists and a principal instrument of mass contact. Thus Surendranath claimed to have been the first to use the method of *Swadeshi* vows in temples, national education plans often had a strong revivalist content, boycott was sought to be enforced through traditional caste sanctions, Extremist leaders insisted in May 1906 on a Shivaji *uttsava* complete with image-worship; and radical politics and aggressive Hinduism often got inextricably combined in the pages of *Bande Mataram, Sandhya* or *Yugantar.* Yet there were dissidents in every group. Brahmo-edited journals like *Sanjivani* or *Prabasi* were critical of obscurantism, and bluntly declared that 'the patriotism which glorifies our past as ideal and beyond improvement and which rejects the needs for further progress is a disease' (Sibnath Sastri in *Prabasi,* Jaistha 1313/1906). Krishnakumar Mitra's Anti-Circular Society boycotted the Shivaji *utsava* out of consideration for its 'numerous Mahomedan workers and sympathisers', and even some revolutionary terrorists like Hemchandra Kanungo later bitterly denounced the prevalent religiosity. Perhaps most interesting of all is the evolution of Rabindranath—considerably swayed by revivalism for some years, but then breaking away sharply in mid-1907 under the impact of communal riots and vividly expressing the tensions and ambiguities of the age through two of his finest novels, *Gora* (1907–09) and *Ghare-Baire* (1914).

The anticipations of Gandhian constructive work and mass *satyagraha* proved extremely shortlived, and by the end of 1908 Bengal politics was once again confined to the opposite, but not unrelated, poles of Moderate 'mendicancy' and individual 'terrorism'. The central historical problem of the period is why this became so—since an explanation in terms of the external factor of British repression alone is hardly sufficient. Despite much talk in nationalist circles about police 'atrocities' and *Swadeshi* 'martyrs', the total number of prosecutions directed against the open movement down to 1909 was only 10 in Bengal and 105 in the new province, the accused getting sentences from two weeks to a year. The only two cases of firing in this period had as their targets Jamalpur rail workers on strike (August 1906) and Muslim rioters in Sherpur (September 1907), not *Swadeshi* demonstrators. What is needed therefore is a closer look at the strength and internal limitations of the principal components of the 1905–08 movement: boycott and *Swadeshi,* national education, labour unions, *samitis* and mass contact methods.

Boycott and Swadeshi

The history of boycott and *Swadeshi* in Bengal vividly illustrate the limits of an intelligentsia movement with broadly bourgeois aspirations but without as yet real bourgeois support. Boycott did achieve some initial success—thus the Calcutta Collector of Customs in September 1906 noted a 22% fall in the quantity of imported cotton piecegoods, 44% in cotton twist and yarn, 11% in salt, 55% in cigarettes and 68% in boots and shoes in the previous month as compared to August 1905. The decline in Manchester cloth sales had a lot to do with a quarrel over trade terms between Calcutta Marwari dealers and British manufacturers, resulting in a spectacular drop in 'Lucky Day' contracts for the following year in October 1905 from 32,000 packages to only 2500. Once this dispute was settled, however, the Marwaris went back to their compradore business, while in the districts merchants of the Shaha community often became the principal targets of social boycott due to their refusal to subordinate profits to patriotism. Bombay mill-owners on their part seized the opportunity to hike up prices, despite numerous appeals from Bengal. Bombay could not yet manufacture the finer types of yarn and cloth being imported from Manchester, and therefore was not too enthusiastic about boycott. It is significant also that the sharpest decline was in commodities like shoes and cigarettes, where, as the Collector of Customs pointed out, the demand was mainly from 'Indian gentlemen of the middle class, such as clerks, pleaders etc.... (*Government of India, Home Public* B. October 1906, n. 13).

The *Swadeshi* mood did bring about a significant revival in handloom, silk-weaving, and some other traditional artisan crafts—a point emphasized by two official industrial surveys in 1908. There was also a related, near-Gandhian, intellectual trend glorifying handicrafts as the Indian or Oriental way to avoid the evils of largescale industry. Satischandra Mukherji in 1900, for instance, quoted Engels to prove the horrors of industrial revolution, and wanted big factories only where absolutely indispensable—preferring wherever possible smallscale 'individual family organization' explicitly run on a caste basis. Such theoretical departures (often associated with revivalism) from Moderate economics did not prevent, however, a number of attempts to promote modern industries. An association had been set up in March 1904 by Jogendrachandra Ghosh to raise funds for sending students abroad (usually to Japan) to get technical training. The Banga Lakshmi Cotton Mills was launched with much fanfare in August 1906 with equipment bought from an existing Serampore plant, and there were some fairly successful ventures in porcelain (the Calcutta Pottery Works of 1906), chrome tanning, soap, matches and cigarettes. The patrons and entrepreneurs included a few big *zamindars* (like Manindra Nandi of Kasim-bazar) but otherwise came mainly from the professional intelligentsia. Lack of capital thus became the crucial limiting factor, as the established Indian business community, in the words of a leading Calcutta merchant as quoted in an official report, felt 'that it is much easier to make money by an agency in imported goods than by investment in industrial enterprise'. One *Swadeshi* pamphleteer, Kalisankar Sukul in 1906, did argue that efforts should be concentrated first on distribution channels rather than starting one or two mills slowly building up through trade, a new type of business class since the old was essentially unpatriotic—but his views found few takers. *Swadeshi* thus could never seriously threaten the British stranglehold over the crucial sectors of Bengal's economy.

National Education

As in other fields, a considerable variety may be noticed within the national education efforts in *Swadeshi* Bengal, ranging from pleas for more technical training, through advocacy of the vernacular medium (urged most powerfully by Rabindranath), to Tagore's Santiniketan and Satis Mukherji's somewhat eclectic Dawn Society plans to combine the traditional and the modern in a scheme for 'higher culture' for selected youth. National education with its negligible job prospects failed to attract, however, the bulk of the student community. What survived after a couple of years was the Bengal National College (planned initially as a parallel university under the National Council of Education set up in March 1906, but quite falling to get any colleges affiliated to it), a Bengal Technical Institute set up by a breakaway group with closer Moderate links, and perhaps potentially the most significant—about a dozen national schools in West Bengal and Bihar and a considerably larger number in East Bengal districts. It was the latter development which for a brief while alarmed the authorities—the attempt 'to extend these schools to the villages and get hold of primary education' (*Home Political A*, March 1909, p. 10–11) involving schools in Mymensingh, Faridpur and Bakarganj which occasionally had large numbers of Muslim and low-caste Namasudra pupils. The Calcutta-based National Council, however, largely ignored such district or village schools (it was spending only ₹12,000 on them out of a total budget of ₹125,000 in 1908), and they shared in the general decline of mass-oriented movements. What survived in the end in East Bengal were certain schools which became virtually recruiting centres for revolutionaries, of which Sonarang National School near Dacca was the most famous.

Labour Unrest

An official survey entitled *Administration of Bengal under Andrew Fraser 1903–08* described 'industrial unrest' as 'a marked feature of the quinquennium', and noted the role of 'professional agitators' as quite a novel phenomenon. Strikes in white-controlled enterprises (as most industrial units were in Bengal), sparked off by rising prices and also quite often by racial insults, now obtained from nationalist quarters considerable newspaper sympathy, occasional financial help, and even aid in setting up trade unions. Four men in particular deserve to be remembered as pioneer labour-leaders: the barristers Aswinicoomar Banerji, Prabhatkusum Roychaudhuri, Athanasius Apurbakumar Ghosh; and Premtosh Bose the proprietor of a small press in north Calcutta. In September 1905, the entire *Swadeshi* public hailed a walk-out of 247 Bengali clerks of Burn Company in Howrah in protest against a new work-regulation felt to be derogatory. The next month saw a tram strike in Calcutta, settled through the efforts of Banerji and Ghosh, and reports of 16 October convey a *bandh-like* flavour, with most offices closed down, carters off the roads, and strikes in some jute mills and railway workshops. The first real labour union followed soon after: the Printers Union, set up on 21 October in the midst of a bitter strike in government presses. In July, 1906, a strike of clerks on the East Indian Railway led to the formation of a Railwaymen's Union and efforts to draw in the coolies through meetings at Asansol, Ranigunj and Jamalpur addressed by *Swadeshi* political leaders like Bepin Pal, Shyamsundar Chakrabarti and Liakat Husain apart from A.C. Banerji, A.K. Ghosh and Premtosh Bose. There was one massive proletarian intervention, at the Jamalpur workshop on 27 August which led to firing. The strike, however, failed, and the union collapsed with it. Jute strikes were also frequent between 1905 and 1908, affecting at various times 18 out of 37 mills. The private papers of A.C. Banerji show him organizing an Indian Millhands' Union at Budge Budge in August 1906. They also reveal what was to be a recurrent problem for the Indian labour movement—contacts with workers were inevitably often through the 'babus' (clerks) and *sardars,* yet a memorial signed by 28 labourers of the Budge Budge Jute Mills reveal such people as petty exploiters charging bribes and *puja* fees.

The labour movement at its height appeared formidable enough for the Anglo-Indian journal *Pioneer* on 27 August 1906 to thunder that the politician might 'agitate about and against the partition to his hearts' content, but when he... threatens the welfare of the whole province by sowing discontent among the ignorant labourers... it is time that a government of law and order asserted itself.' Some Extremist journals occasionally speculated about the great potentialities of the 'Russian method' of the political general strike: 'The workers of Russia today are teaching the world the methods of effective protest in times of repression—will not Indian workers learn from them?' (*Naba sakti,* 14 September 1907, after Pal had been jailed). As in so much else, however, all this remained no more than interesting anticipation. There were no really political strikes (unlike in Bombay during Tilak's trial in 1908), plantation and mine labour remained unaffected, *Swadeshi* contacts were developed in the main only with clerks or at best Bengali jute workers (hence the importance of mills like Fort Gloster or Budge Budge, where the upcountry element was less prominent than elsewhere)—and nationalist interest in labour slumped suddenly and totally after the summer of 1908, and would not be renewed before 1919–22.

Samitis

The sudden emergence of the *samitis* or 'national volunteer' movement was one of the major achievements of the *Swadeshi* age. Hindsight has too often led to an equation of such organizations with incipient terrorist societies. Actually, down to the summer of 1908, most *samitis* were quite open bodies engaged in a variety of activities: physical and moral training of members, social work during famines, epidemics or religious festivals, preaching the *Swadeshi* message through multifarious forms, organizing crafts, schools, arbitration courts and village societies, and implementing the techniques of passive resistance. Apart from Calcutta, with 19 *samitis* reported by the police in 1907, the main strength of the movement was in East Bengal. This included a central bloc consisting of Bakargunj, Faridpur, Dacca and Mymensingh districts (where originated the five principal *samitis* which were to be banned in January 1909—Swadesh Bandhav, Brati, Dacca Anushilan, Suhrid, Sadhana), strong organizations in Rangpur, Tippera, Sylhet and the part of the old province lying to the east of the Hooghly river, and some societies in all districts except Sibsagar, Goalpara and Garo hills. A police report of June 1907 gave an estimate of 8485 volunteers for East Bengal; Bakargunj and Dacca topped the list with more than 2600 each. As in other things, there was a lot of variety within the *samiti* movement. Thus the Calcutta-based Anti-Circular Society stood out due to its secularism (it was the only *samiti* with important Muslim associates, like Liakat Husain, Abul Hossain, Dedar Bux, and Abdul Gafur). The Barisal Swadesh Bandhav did acquire something like a genuine mass base—175 village branches were reported in 1909, and through sustained humanitarian work (as during a near-famine in 1906) its leader Aswinikumar Dutt acquired remarkable popularity among the peasants of his district, Muslims as well as Hindus. The Dacca Anushilan founded by Pulin Das in sharp contrast concentrated from the beginning on secret training of cadres through physical culture and a paraphernalia of initiation vows steeped in Hinduism—things conspicuously all but absent in the much looser but mass-oriented structure of Swadesh Bandhav. Still, down to 1908 efforts at mass contact formed the principal staple of the activities of the bulk of the *samitis,* and this again took on a variety of, at times, extremely imaginative forms: not only a multitude of journals, pamphlets and speeches (all increasingly in the vernacular) but a flood of patriotic songs, plays and use of folk media like *jatras* (particularly those of Mukunda Das in Bakargunj), the organization of festivals, and the cultivation of a traditionalist religious idiom. Increasingly Hinduism was sought to be used as the principal bridge to the masses, appealing both to the imagination as well as to fear (e.g., the use of caste sanctions in the social boycott of loyalists).

Yet during 1908–09, in face of the very first round of repression, the open *samiti* either disappeared (as with the Swadesh Bandhav), or became a terroristic secret society, the Dacca model driving out the Barisal. Even Aswinikumar Dutta's organization had not really developed a peasant membership (as distinct from some ill-comprehending attendenee at meetings and respect for a benevolent babu)—the village societies invariably consisted 'of the bhadralok of the village', and it is significant that at Sarupkhati (in Bakargunj district), for instance, 'nearly half the volunteers (were)... persons with a tenure-holding interest in the land'. (*Home Political Deposit.* October 1907, n. 19) An ominously large number of *Swadeshi* cases involved disputes between *zamindari* officials and Muslim vendors, landlord closing of village markets became a principle boycott method, and social boycott often took the form of pressurizing of tenants or sharecroppers by *zamindars* or tenure-holders. Rabindranath's *Ghare-Baire* would later vividly portray the oppressive *zamindar* turned *Swadeshi* hero in Harish Kundu, and that this was not sheer invention is indicated by a November 1907 case in Tangail (Mymensingh district) where a Muslim sharecropper charged his Hindu landlord of having burnt his Manchester cloth in order to terrorize him into relinquishing his lease.

Hindu-Muslim Relations

The situation thus was almost tailor-made for British divide-and-rule methods. In October 1907, *Swadeshi* sympathizers in north Calcutta found themselves being beaten up by police backed up by some elements drawn from the urban poor, described repeatedly in the non-official enquiry report on the disturbances as 'ruffians and low class people, such as dhangars, mehters, sweepers etc'. But the really serious development was the rapid growth of Muslim separatism. Despite eloquent pleas for communal unity, some memorable scenes of fraternization (like the 10,000-strong joint student procession in Calcutta on 23 September 1905), and the presence of an extremely active and sincere group of *Swadeshi* Muslim agitators (men like Ghaznavi, Rasul, Din Mahomed, Dedar Bux, Moniruzzaman, Ismail Hussain Siraji, Abul Husain, Abdul Gafur, and Liakat Husain—some of whom figured in the very first list of proposed prosecutions for sedition in May 1907), the British propaganda that the new province would mean more jobs for Muslims did achieve considerable success in swaying upper and middle class Muslims against the *Swadeshi* movement. The elite-politics of the Salimulla group and the Muslim League (founded at Dacca in October 1906) will be considered later; much more relevant in the present context is the rash of communal riots in East Bengal: Iswargunj in Mymensingh district in May 1906, Comilla (March 1907), Jamalpur, Dewangunj and Bakshigunj, all again in Mymensingh, in April-May 1907. 'Ordinary Muhammadans of the lower class in the bazaar' (*Home Public A, May 1907, n. 163*) were prominent in the riot in Comilla town, while a strong agrarian note pervaded the Mymensingh disturbances. The targets were Hindu *zamindars* and *mahajans,* some of whom had recently started levying an *Iswar britti* for maintaining Hindu images. Debt-bonds were torn at many places, and at times the riots took on the colour of a general 'plunder of the rich by the poor' with even Hindu cultivators joining in at places (*Home Political A, July 1907, n. 16*). *Maulvis* are said to have spread rumours that the British were handing over charge to Nawab Salimulla of Dacca, who was painted in the rather unlikely colours of a messiah in the communal leaflet *Nawab Sahaber Subichar.* Such religious leaders often had connections with emerging rich peasant-elements made relatively prosperous by jute, and Muslim propaganda literature like the *Red Pamphlet* (1907) or the later *Krishakbandhu* (1910) visualized a kind of *kulak* or capitalist farmer development side by side with identifying the *zamindar-mahajan* exploiter with the Hindu.

In a series of remarkably perceptive articles written in 1907–08, as well as in his presidential address to the Pabna provincial conference (February 1908), Rabindranath pointed out that simply blaming the British for the riots was quite an inadequate response. 'Satan cannot enter till he finds a flaw', and the crucial problem was that 'a great ocean separates us educated few from millions in our country'. Till that gulf was bridged, no short-cuts like verbal extremism or terrorist action were likely to succeed. Tagore's alternative, however—patient unostentatious constructive work in villages in which he hoped *zamindars* would take the lead in a paternalistic fashion (as he was trying to do himself in his own estates)—had little appeal to militant youth increasingly provoked by British repression, nor did he really have any concrete social or economic programme of mass mobilization. His, therefore, was increasingly a voice crying in the wilderness: as recognized implicitly in *Ghare-Baire,* whose noble but quite ineffective and isolated hero Nikhilesh stands in significant contrast to the optimistic ending of his earlier novel *Gora.*

To the vast majority of nationalists, the Muslim rioters were no more than hired agents of the British, the equivalent, as the *Bande Mataram* put it, of the Russian counter-revolutionary Black Hundreds. Volunteer organization in fact was greatly stimulated by the 1907 riots, and Extremist propaganda took on aggressive Hindu colours and simultaneously veered towards terrorism—an almost inevitable development, as 'revolution' with the vast masses inert or hostile could mean in practice only action by an elite.

The Shift to Terrorism

The first revolutionary groups had been started round about 1902 in Midnapur (by Jnanendranath Basu) and Calcutta (the Anushilan Samiti, founded by Promotha Mitter and Aurobindo's emissaries from Baroda, Jatindranath Banerji and Barindrakumar Ghosh), but their activities had been confined initially to physical and moral training of members and were not particularly significant till 1907 or 1908. An inner circle within the Calcutta Anushilan under Barindrakumar Ghosh and Bhupendranath Dutta (with the behind-the-scenes advice of Aurobindo) started the *Yugantar* weekly in April 1906 and attempted one or two abortive 'actions' in the summer of the same year (like a plan to kill the very unpopular East Bengal Lt. Governor Fuller which misfired). Hemchandra Kanungo, probably the most remarkable figure among this first revolutionary generation, then went abroad to get military (and some political) training, which he ultimately obtained from a Russian emigre in Paris. After Kanungo's return in January 1908, a combined religious school and bomb factory was set up at a garden house in the Maniktala suburb of Calcutta. Gross carelessness on the part of the leadership (and particularly of Barindrakumar Ghose) however, led to the arrest of the whole group including Aurobindo within hours of the Kennedy murders (30 April 1908), by Kshudiram Basu and Prafulla Chaki— the target, a particularly sadistic white magistrate named Kingsford, escaping unscathed. Terrorism of a more efficient variety was meanwhile developing in East Bengal, spearheaded by the much more tightly organized Dacca Anushilan of Pulin Das, with the Barrah dacoity (2 June 1908) as its first major venture.

Apart from a wealth of patriotic songs and other considerable cultural achievements (among which may be mentioned a new interest in regional and local history and folk traditions, the scientific work of J.C. Bose and P.C. Ray, and the Calcutta school of painting founded by Abanindranath Tagore), revolutionary terrorism was to constitute in the end the most substantial legacy of *Swadeshi* Bengal, casting a spell on the minds of radical educated youth for at least a generation or more. The 'revolutionary' movement took the forms of assassinations of oppressive officials or traitors, *Swadeshi* dacoities to raise funds, or at best military conspiracies with expectations of help from foreign enemies of Britain. It never, despite occasional subjective aspirations, rose to the level of urban mass uprisings or guerrilla bases in the countryside. The term 'terrorism' hence remains not inappropriate.

Elite 'revolution' did make substantial contributions to the national struggle. The British were often badly frightened, rare examples were set of death-defying heroism in the cause of complete independence (a goal which the Congress as a whole would formally accept only in 1930) and world-wide contacts were sought in quests for shelter and arms, leading, as we shall see, to important ideological consequences. Hemchandra Kanungo, to cite the earliest example, came back from Paris as an atheist with some interest in Marxism. Terrorist heroism evoked tremendous admiration from very wide circles of educated Indians, and sometimes from others, too—a street-beggar's lament for Kshudiram, for instance, could still be heard in Bengal decades after his execution. Yet British administration was never in serious danger of collapsing, and the admiration felt was usually no more than a vicarious satisfaction at the self-sacrifice of others. The intense religiosity of most of the early secret societies (a note which however was to partly disappear over time) helped to keep Muslims aloof or hostile. The emphasis on religion had other negative aspects, too, as Hemchandra later pointed out. The much-quoted *Gita* doctrine of *Nishkama karma* stimulated a rather quixotic heroism, a cult of martyrdom for its own sake in place of effective programmes: 'The Mother asks us for no schemes, no plans, no methods. She herself will provide the schemes, the plans, the methods...'. (Aurobindo in April 1908). And religion could also become a royal road for an honourable retreat, as when Aurobindo departed for Pondicherry, or Jatindranath Bandopadhyay ended his days as a Ramakrishna Mission *swamiji*.

Above all, elite action postponed efforts to draw the masses into active political struggle, which in turn would have involved conscious efforts to link up national with socio-economic issues through more radical programmes. The social limitations of Bengal revolutionary terrorism remain obvious; in a 1918 official list of 186 killed or convicted revolutionaries, no less than 165 came from the three upper castes, Brahman, Kayastha, and Vaidya.

EXTREMISM IN OTHER PROVINCES: 1905–1908

So far we have been concentrating on Bengal alone; it is time now to broaden our focus, and consider to what extent similar trends were emerging in other provinces, and how Extremists faced Moderates at an all-India level.

While Curzon's actions, and particularly the Bengal Partition, aroused widespread resentment throughout educated India, the extent and nature of specific responses were naturally determined by regional or local factors. In Bihar, Orissa and Assam, for instance, the educated Bengali was becoming increasingly unpopular due to his dominant position in the services and professions. 'Counter-elite' movements developed with the spread of education, ultimately demanding separate provinces for Orissa and Bihar. Such trends tended to keep away from a radicalism primarily associated with Bengal and reaching these provinces mainly via the educated Bengali immigrants, though sympathy was often expressed for 'non-political' *Swadeshi* enterprise (by Madhusudan Das's Utkal Union Conference, for instance).

Extremism failed to make very much of an impact also on the United Provinces, where Congress political activity had died down after an initial spurt in the late 1880s. Leaders like Madanmohan Malaviya or Motilal Nehru, Bayly argues in his study of Allahabad, still felt that considerable local gains could be made through a policy of cooperation with a provincial government which under Mac Donnell had begun to lean a little towards the Hindus. The Nagri resolution (1900) giving Hindi equal status with Urdu in courts, government grants to the Nagri Pracharini Sabha, and a fairly helpful official stance towards proposals for a Hindu University at Benares, all these kept Malaviya contented. The British also seemed quite sympathetic towards non-political *Swadeshi* and particularly to demands for protection of U.P. sugar, and Malaviya and Chintamani were invited to the officially sponsored Industrial Conference at Nainital in 1907. Tilak's U.P. tour in January 1907 did cause a stir among the students, but most influential political leaders kept away. Malaviya had already annexed to his brand of politics the emotional forces of Hindi and Hindu revivalism which otherwise might have been used by radicals, and no serious attempt seems to have been made by any intelligentsia group to approach the peasantry till about 1917. Extremism in fact became a formidable force only in Benares, with its big Marathi and particularly Bengali communities, and here a revolutionary group speedily emerged, maintaining contacts with Calcutta through Mokhodacharan Samadhyay (the editor of *Sandhya* after Brahmobandhab's death in December 1907), and producing an outstanding leader in Sachindranath Sanyal. U.P. student recruits to Extremism like Sunder Lal were also quickly drawn into terrorism, since prospects for mass politics were evidently poor, and the province (and specifically Benares) because of its goegraphical position came to occupy an important place in revolutionary plans as the meeting-place of Bengal and Punjab groups.

Another region where Extremism failed was in the Gujarati-speaking districts of Bombay Presidency. In 1907, Pherozeshah Mehta engineered the transfer of the Congress session from Nagpur to the safe Moderate stronghold of Surat. Some of the complexities of the situation are indicated, however, by the interesting case of the brothers Kunvarji and Kalyanji

Mehta, rich Gujarat peasants who attended the Surat session, came back enthused by the Lal-Bal-Pal trio, and started organizational work through the Patidar Yuvak Mandal which culminated in the 1920s in their becoming the 'real makers' of the great Gandhian success-story of Bardoli.

Punjab

In the Punjab, with its well-established traditional business communities (mostly belonging to the Khatri, Aggarwal or Arora castes), constructive *Swadeshi* in the fields of banking, insurance and education had roots going back to the 1890s, and there had also been some moves to organize a boycott of foreign cloth after the countervailing excise of 1895. Arya Samajists connected with the 'College' faction had been prominent in such self-help efforts, along with a rival Brahmo-leaning group headed by Lala Harkishan Lal which ran the *Tribune* newspaper. Among the Aryas (and even to some extent the Punjabi Brahmos), constructive *Swadeshi* often got inextricably combined with militant Hindu consciousness. As his very revealing autobiography makes clear, it was the Hindi-Urdu controversy of the 1880s which made Lajpat Rai become 'wedded to the idea of Hindu nationality'. The boyhood influence of a heavily Islamicized father was obliterated by government school textbooks full of stories of Muslim tyranny, and Lajpat began making pro-Hindi speeches even before learning the Devanagri alphabet (to him, as to many north-Indian Hindu intellectuals of his age, Urdu was really the much more natural form of literary expression). Connections of this Punjab group with the Congress—often felt to be both too mendicant and too Westernized or secular—were in contrast much more sporadic, as we have already seen.

Punjab's swing towards a rather shortlived Extremism between 1904 and 1907 was determined partly, but as usual by no means solely, by factional considerations. The Arya group of Lajpat and Hans Raj had quarrelled bitterly with Lala Harkishan Lal over the management of the Punjab National Bank and Bharat Insurance, and they started the *Panjabee* (with its motto of 'self-help at any cost') in October 1904 as a radical challenge to the *Tribune*. Down to late 1906, however, the Punjab variety of Extremism was much milder than that of Bengal, concentrating in practice on constructive work rather than boycott, and often seeking joint platforms with moderate Congressman as well as with a Muslim group headed by Muhammed Shafi and Fazal-i-Husain.

What made the Punjab situation very different for a few months in 1907 were a series of provocations from the British. The Punjab intelligentsia was infuriated by the prosecution of the *Panjabee* for writing about racist outrages at a time when violent abuse of Indians in the pages of the *Civil and Military Gazette* passed unnoticed by officials. The trial of the *Panjabee* editor led to demonstrations and stray attacks on whites in Lahore in February 1907 and again in May. Proposals to tighten up the Land Alienation Act irritated urban Hindu commercial and professional groups. What really frightened the British, however, were signs of discontent and militancy among the peasantry in certain areas, Sikh and Muslim as well as Hindu, and particularly ominous since Punjab supplied one-third of the man power for the British Indian army. In the Chenab canal colony centred around Lyallpur which British irrigation measures had made fertile, land had been granted in large blocs to peasant immigrants, ex-soldiers, and sometimes to urban investors (whose estates at times exceeded 2500 acres). The whole area was controlled in a rigidly bureaucratic and dictatorial manner by white Colonization Officers (who imposed heavy fines for violations of their orders), and the system was sought to be tightened up further by the Chenab Colonies Bill introduced in October 1906. A protest movement began to be organized from 1903 by Siraj-ud-din Ahmad with his journal *Zamindar* (the term in the Punjab context meant peasant proprietor and not landlord), and by early 1907 the Chenab colonists (who included Muslims, Sikhs and Hindus, and were marked at this time by remarkable communal amity) were eagerly looking for a broader political leadership. Meanwhile the British added to their own troubles by sharply enhancing in November 1906 the canal water rate in the Bari Doab region (Amritsar, Gurdaspur and Lahore districts, inhabited mainly by a Sikh peasantry) by 25% or sometimes even 50%, and there was a land revenue hike in the Rawalpindi district too. The ravages of the plague and the general price rise contributed to widespread discontent, and labour was also becoming restive. There were several strikes among revenue clerks, and the sympathy aroused by the North-Western State Railway strike in early 1907 (the N.W.S.R. line went across the Chenab colony) evoked particular alarm in the mind of the Punjab Lt.Governor Denzil Ibbetson.

Though Lajpat was to be deported in May 1907 on charges of instigating the peasants, his personal role as described in his autobiography seems to have been rather limited. He went to Lyallpur to address meetings of Chenab colonists twice, in February 1907 and again in March during a big cattle fair, but only with considerable hesitation ('I kept putting (it) off', he tells us), and tried to play there a clearly restraining role. Much more important really were the activities of Ajit Singh (uncle, incidentally, of Bhagat Singh), who organized the Extremist Anjuman-i-Mohibban-i-Watan in Lahore with its journal *Bharat-Mata*—a combination of 'Muhammadan and Hindu names' which alarmed Ibbetson. Like many Bengal *samitis,* Ajit Singh's group would later turn to terrorism, but in 1907 it was extremely active in urging nonpayment of revenue and water rates among Chenab colonists and Bari Doab peasants. Ibbetson in his minute of 30 April 1907 urging drastic action described moves towards 'a combination to withhold the payment of Government revenue, water rates and other rates' as 'an inconceivably dangerous suggestion'. There were reports of sepoys attending seditious meetings at Ferozepur, and a government move to debar five leading Rawalpindi lawyers from the courts for having sponsored an Ajit Singh meeting led to massive protests in the latter city (including strikes by Muslim and Sikh arsenal and railway engineering workers and attacks on sahib bungalows).

Punjab Extremism died down quickly, however, after the government struck in May 1907 with a ban on political meetings and the deportation of Lajpat Rai and Ajit Singh, repressive measures which were soon intelligently balanced by some concessions: a Viceregal veto of the Chenab Colonies Bill, reductions in water rates, and the release of the deportees in September 1907. Arya Samajist leaders hastened to protest their loyalty and as the radical movement collapsed and swung back sharply towards communal politics. Hindu *Sabhas* had largely replaced defunct Congress bodies in most districts by 1908–09. Ajit Singh and a few close associates (like Sufi Amba Prasad from Moradabad in U.P., and the radical Urdu poet Lal Chand 'Falak') in sharp contrast developed into full-scale revolutionary terrorists, along with a few Aryas like Bhai Paramanand and the brilliant Delhi student Har Dayal.

Madras

In Madras Presidency, Extremist ideas acquired considerable influence in two widely-separated areas: the Andhra delta region, and Tirunelveli district in the extreme south. Washbrook relates this entirely to factional conflicts. The dominant 'Mylapore' clique headed at this time by V. Krishnaswami Iyer was being challenged by a combination (led by G. Subramaniya Iyer, who had been prominent in the 1880s, but had then been pushed into the background) of some 'Egmore' politicians and *mofussil* 'out' groups (T. Prakasam of Rajamundry, M. Krishna Rao of Masulipatam, V.O. Chidambaram Pillai of Tuticorin in Tirunelveli district). 'Egmore' was now controlling the influential newspaper *Hindu* of Madras, and Prakasam and Krishna Rao had started the radical *Kistnapatrika* from Masulipatam in 1904. The factional conflict was no doubt real enough, but an account which dismisses in a couple of lines what is described as the work of 'student and workers mobs' in some Andhra towns in 1907 and Tuticorin and Tirunelveli in March 1908 can hardly be considered adequate.

Meetings were being held in sympathy with Bengal in Andhra delta towns like Rajamundhry, Kakinada, and Masulipatam from onwards, and what had come to be called the *Vandemataram* movement received a major fillip from Bepin Pal's tour in April at the invitation of M. Krishna Rao. Repressive measures against Rajamundhry students for wearing *Vandemataram* badges and attending Pal's meetings led to a student strike followed by a movement to start national schools in Andhra. There was also a crowd attack on the Kakinada European Club on 31 May 1907, after a sahib had boxed the ears of a boy for shouting *Bande Mataram*. The *Swadeshi* atmosphere also contributed heavily to a new interest in Telugu language, literature and history (an influential *Andhrula Charitramu* or *History of the Andhras* was published in 1910), and after the decline of Extremism leaders like Prakasam, Konda Venkatappayya and Pattabhi Sitaramayya—all future Gandhian stalwarts—began organizing the Andhra Mahasabha to demand a separate linguistic state for the Telegu-speaking people.

Much more alarming immediately from the government point of view were developments in Tirunelveli district centered around Tuticorin port. An official report in December 1906 singled out Tirunelveli as the only district in Madras from where significant anti-British feelings were being reported. G. Subramaniya Iyer toured the district several times in 1906 and 1907, the Tuticorin *vakil* V.O. Chidambaram Pillai developed into a major Extremist leader, and in October 1906 a Swadeshi Steam Navigation Company was started in Tuticorin to run steamers up to Colombo. The bitter hostility towards this *Swadeshi* venture (backed by rupees six lakhs capital, and indicating therefore considerable participation by local business groups) shown by the British India Steam Navigation Company sharpened anti-foreign feelings in Tuticorin. A sharp lurch towards radicalism became apparent from January 1908 with the arrival of Subramania Siva, a plebian agitator from Madura who began addressing almost daily meetings on Tuticorin beach together with Chidambaran Pillai, preaching the message of *Swaraj*, extended boycott, and (if police reports are to be believed) occasionally urging more violent methods. By late February they were striking a new note of direct appeal to workers: 'If the coolies stood out for extra wages European mills in India would cease to exist' (Siva on 26 February)—and there was even a statement (by the same orator on 23 February) 'that the Russian revolution had benefited the people and that revolutions always brought good to the world'. Allegedly as a direct result of such speeches, the workers went on strike at the foreign-owned Coral Cotton Mills, and a 50% rise in wages was obtained in the first week of March. British efforts in mid-March to stop meetings and prosecute Siva and Pillai led to closing of shops, protest strikes by municipal and private sweepers and carriage-drivers in

Tuticorin, attacks on municipal offices, law courts, and police stations at Tirunelveli, and firing in both towns on 11–13 March 1908. The Calcutta *Bande Mataram* on 13 March hailed the Tuticorin events as forging a 'bond...between the educated class and the masses, which is the first great step towards *swaraj*...every victory for Indian labour is a victory for the nation...'. As in Bengal, however, this 'first great step' remained beyond the reach of Extremism, and after the removal of Siva and Pillai Tirunelveli radicals either became inactive or formed a small terrorist group which was responsible for the murder of district magistrate Ashe in June 1911. The small group of Tamilian revolutionaries incidentally included a major poet, Subramaniya Bharati, a Tirunelveli Brahman critical of caste who contributed heavily to emerging Tamil nationalism. A political exile in Pondicherry from 1910, he followed a path sharply different from his fellow emigre V.V.S. Iyer who became a disciple of the Hindu revivalist Savarkar. Bharati before his untimely death in 1921 had started writing poems hailing the Russian Revolution of 1917.

Maharashtra

Despite a considerable biographical literature on Tilak, generally recognized as the most outstanding Extremist leader, no really detailed account seems to be available as yet (at least in English) on the movement in Maharashtra between 1905 and 1908. The *Swadeshi* mood naturally led to a rapid development of radical journalism, with the *Kesari* reaching a circulation of 20,000 by 1907, and the creed of *Swaraj* and extended boycott or passive resistance was energetically preached by Tilak and his close associates (like Khaparde and Munje) both in Maharashtra and in other provinces. Speeches like Tilak's *Tenets of the New Party* (Calcutta, January 1907) remain Extremist classics, together with Pal's Madras lectures and Aurobindo's *Bande Mataram* articles. There was a revival of the religio-political festivals already pioneered by Tilak in the 1890s (Ganapati, Shivaji, Ramdas), bonfires of foreign cloth were organized (as at Poona on 8 October 1905), and a Swadeshi Vastu Pracharini Sabha was set up in Bombay city to carry the new message to what was still a Moderate citadel so far as the established political leadership was concerned. Bombay industrialists (overwhelmingly Parsi or Gujarati—there was only one Maharashtrian mill-owner in 1908), as we have already seen, were at best only lukewarm supporters *of Swadeshi,* and in September 1906, a later police History Sheet of Tilak tells us, the Extremist leaders' bid through Dinshaw Wacha to persuade mill-owners to sell *dhoties* at more moderate prices was met by the blunt reply 'that they could not be supplied except at market rates'. *Swadeshi* enthusiasm for indigenous cloth, however, contributed, first to the super profits made by Bombay and Ahmedabad during 1905–06 (a contemporary estimate calculated the profits made by Bombay mill-owners to have been ₹3.25 crores in 1906, as compared to a wage-bill of ₹1.68 crores), and second, in staving off a major slump in 1906–07 when Japanese competition began sharply curtailing the Chinese yarn market. The major breakthrough represented by the floating of the Tata Iron and Steel project in August 1907 (the projected share capital of ₹2.5 crores was subscribed in three weeks, mainly from Bombay) probably also had some connections with the new mood of self-confidence and patriotism generated by political developments.

Two major new initiatives are associated with Tilakite activity in Maharashtra and Bombay city in late 1907 and early 1908—mass picketing of liquor shops, and efforts to develop contacts with the predominantly Marathi working-class of Bombay. The first—which anticipated a major Gandhian technique—had the twin advantages of reducing government excise revenue, and appealing at times to trends towards a 'Sanskritizing' imitation of Brahmanical norms by lower castes. The second was easier in Bombay than in Calcutta, as a big part of the factory-workers at the latter place were non-Bengalis—while in Bombay 49.16 per cent of mill-workers in 1911 came from Tilak's home-district of Ratnagiri. Some philanthrophic work had been started already among Bombay workers in the 1880s, though the initiative had come at first not from the predominantly Brahman nationalist intelligentsia but from men like N.M. Lokhande associated with Phule's anti-Brahman Satyashodhak Samaj movement. More important probably was an emerging tradition of militancy—for if Bombay workers had at times plunged into fratricidal communal strife (as in 1893), they had also mounted spontaneous but powerful strikes—in 1892–93 and 1901 against wage-cuts, and again in September-October 1905 against a fantastic 15 to 16 hour working-day which mill-owners were trying to enforce through introduction of electric lights.

Nationalist opinion had generally refused to concern itself with labour conditions in Indian-owned—as sharply distinct from foreign—enterprises, and in 1881 the first Factory Act (pushed through by a Lancashire jealous of low wage-costs in Bombay) had been opposed by Ranade's *Quarterly Journal* and Tilak's *Mahratta* with equal vehemence. Tilak's activities in 1907–08 do not represent as much of a break here as sometimes imagined, as the speeches he made at labour meetings in December 1907 and June 1908 in the Chinchpoogly industrial area of Bombay were remarkably free of class-war tones. The emphasis throughout was on boycott of foreign goods and liquor. *Swadeshi* was advocated as through it 'the work in Mills would increase and the employees would be benefited', and the plight of workers was related to deindustrialization forcing people to leave villages. Tilak is reported also to have 'advised the millhands, specially the Jobbers and Head Jobbers, to form committees of millhands'. The jobbers in fact had enormous influence, since they were the main agents in hiring workers, and tended to belong to the same caste and region as the men they engaged. Themselves petty exploiters, the Marathi jobbers often had their own grievances about the predominantly Parsi or white managers and senior foremen. Police reports also pointed out that 'every mill has its Brahman clerks, who possess more or less influence amongst the jobbers', and that such clerical groups were very much under the sway of Extremism. Jobbers in fact were to play a crucial role in later Bombay labour organization too—till the Communist-led Girni Kamgar attempted a sharp break in 1928.

Yet if the Extremist leadership had obvious limitations, the massive outburst of proletarian anger in Bombay when Tilak was put on trial in July 1908 (for certain *Kesari* articles on Bengal terrorism) and given six years' transportation remains a major landmark in our history. Nationalist speeches and leaflets and clerical-jobber manipulation apart, the workers must have come to realize from their own experiences that officials and policemen were their natural enemies, as purely economic strikes sparked off by truly intolerable living and working conditions were crushed time and again through police intervention. The police commissioner had personally led a force to smash the Phoenix mill strike, for example, in October 1905. Sporadic strikes, stone-throwing, and clashes with the police began with the opening of Tilak's trial on 13 July, and soon the army was also called out. When Tilak was convicted on 22 July, cloth shop employees of the Mulji Jetha Market called for a six-day *hartal* (one for each year of Tilak's imprisonment)—a vow which the Bombay working-class kept to the letter by staging a massive walk-out till 28 July which at its height affected 76 out of 85 textile mills, as well as the railway workshop of Parel (which had witnessed big economic strikes already in May 1907 and January 1908). The police and the army fired repeatedly, and official reports speak of 16 killed and 43 wounded.

Tilak's imprisonment was followed by one major *mofussil* riot, at the pilgrimage centre of Pandharpur (Sholapur district) on 29 July. Both participants and organizers are described in the official report as lower caste people—a fact which, like the Bombay strike, consorts oddly with the oft-repeated theory of Extremism in Maharashtra being no more than a Chitpavan conspiracy. But as in other provinces, mass contact and participation proved very short-lived. What survived of Maharashtra Extremism after the removal of Tilak largely took to the path of individual terror, with the Nasik-based Abhinava Bharat group as the most important. This had emerged in 1907 from out of the Mitra Mela founded in 1899 by the Savarkar brothers, and pistols sent secretly from London by V.D. Savarkar were used to kill the Nasik district magistrate in December 1909. There was also a similar Nava Bharat group in Gwalior, where the experience of working under Sindhia's autocracy led to a complete break with illusions still often cherished in this period by other Indian revolutionaries and nationalists. The Nava Bharat Society proclaimed its goal to be a republic, 'since all Native princes are mere puppets'. Terrorism in Maharashtra, however, never became anywhere near as formidable as in Bengal, and we hear little more about it after the Nasik and Gwalior conspiracy cases of 1909–10.

The Congress Split

From 1905 to 1907, the struggle between various trends within the national movement was fought out also at the annual sessions of the Congress, culminating in the Surat split of December 1907. To describe this as the 'most conspicuous form' of Extremism, and to define the latter as 'an all-India coalition of dissidents, who... tried to reverse at the top the defeats they had suffered in the localities' (Anil Seal, p. 347), is, however, not particularly convincing. The Congress, we must remember, was as yet not a proper political organization worth 'capturing' but no more than an annual forum whose deliberations have been given perhaps somewhat exaggerated significance—and the Extremists down to 1907–08 had certainly not been 'defeated' in their regional bases of Bengal, Punjab, parts of Madras and Maharashtra. A few efforts were made in this period to give to the Congress a more substantial form, most notably through a resolution at the Calcutta Congress (1906) recommending the formation of 'District Associations... for sustained and continuous political work'. Numerous district conferences were organized in 1907 and early 1908 in a number of provinces, mainly though by no means entirely at Extremist initiative. Some of the Moderate leaders also tried to adjust themselves to the new atmosphere. Industrial conferences began to be held from December 1905 onwards, along with the Congress sessions, to promote a kind of non-militant *Swadeshi*. Gokhale in June 1905 launched his Servants of India Society, combining strictly Moderate goals with an insistence on self-sacrifice, moral purity, and full-time national work on a salary of no more than ₹65 per month. The Society had managed to recruit no more than 20 members, however, by 1909. For the rest the Congress remained what it had been previously; persuading it to adopt Extremist resolutions would mean good publicity and added prestige, but not much more.

At Benares in December 1905, the Extremist challenge was still rather weak. Gokhale's Presidential address and a separate resolution condemned Partition and repressive measures in Bengal but the only reference to boycott described it in noticeably half-hearted language: 'perhaps the only constitutional and effective means left to them (Bengalis) of drawing the attention of the public...' (Resolution XIII, moved by Surendranath and Malaviya). Tilak, Lajpat and Motilal Ghosh opposed in the Subjects Committee a resolution which 'most humbly and respectfully' welcomed the coming visit of the Prince of Wales, but eventually by a compromise arrangement they and their followers kept away from the open session which passed this resolution 'unanimously'.

By December 1906, Extremism had advanced considerably, and forged a certain degree of intra-provincial contacts (through visits like that of Tilak to Calcutta in June 1906, for instance). Moves to elect Tilak or Lajpat as president for the coming Calcutta session could be scotched by the dominant Bombay caucus (Pherozeshah Mehta, Wacha and Gokhale) only by inviting the universally respected father-figure, Dadabhai Naoroji. Calcutta in a way marked the height of Extremist influence over the Congress with its resolutions on Boycott, *Swadeshi,* National Education, and Self-Government, though an element of equivocation was frequently present. Naoroji redefined the goal of the Congress in deliberately ambiguous terms: 'Self-Government or Swaraj like that of the United Kingdom or the Colonies'—there would remain considerable difference between the political systems of Britain and the colonies or Dominions till at least the Statute of Westminster of 1926. Bepin Pal's effort to extend the resolution on boycott to cover other provinces and boycott of honorary offices as well as of foreign goods was promptly repudiated by Malaviya and Gokhale, and differing interpretations were given of all four major resolutions throughout 1907.

Mehta managed to shift the venue of the next session from Nagpur to Surat, and as by convention the local Reception Committee chose the President, ensured in this way the election of the very moderate Rashbehari Ghosh. Both sides came prepared for a confrontation, there were uproarious scenes on the opening day as rumours spread that the four Calcutta resolutions would be dropped, and on 27 December Tilak's abortive move for an adjournment (ruled out by Reception Committee Chairman Malvi) was followed by the famous throwing of the Marathi *chappal* and the dissolution of the session into total chaos. Precise responsibility for the actual clash has remained controversial (there is no doubt that many Extremists had come with *lathis*), but on a broader view the major provocation seems to have come from the Moderates. Certainly not only Lajpat (regarded at this time as the mildest among the Extremist figures) but also Tilak and most of his Bengal friends repeatedly tried for a reunion of the Congress in the months following Surat. But the Bombay Moderate group remained inflexible, and the Allahabad Convention (April 1908) made the split definitive by drawing up a constitution which fixed the Congress methods as 'strictly constitutional' and limited to bringing about 'steady reform of the existing system of administration' and—most important of all—restricted delegate election to 'recognised bodies of over three years' standing'. Every effort was thus made to deliberately exclude Extremists from future sessions.

The most important factor responsible for the sudden rigidity of the Moderate leadership was an expectation of reforms, as the Liberals were in power in England and the famous Liberal political thinker John Morley was Secretary of State. It is to the evolution of British policies, therefore, that we must turn now.

REPRESSION, CONCILIATION, AND DIVIDE AND RULE: 1909–1914

Morley and Minto

Discussions of British Indian Government policy have often become debates over who originated a particular measure, the Viceroy or the Secretary of State. This has been markedly evident with Morley and Minto, due to the early publication of extracts from their correspondence by the ex-Secretary of State and the Viceroy's wife. A massive literature exists on this subject, but the question is really a rather trivial one, for the differences between the Liberal scholar Morley and the Viceroy (appointed by an outgoing Tory administration, and a man who preferred horses to politics) were, as we shall see, seldom over fundamentals. The really important theme is the way in which both contributed, together with many other officials, to the formulation of a set of policies for tackling political unrest which was to remain more or less standard for the remaining years of British rule in India. Three major components may be distinguished here—outright repression, concessions to 'rally the moderates', and (closely connected with the second) divide and rule, best typified by the device of separate electorates.

After 1906, repressive measures were adopted at first with considerable hesitation and uncertainty, since their target would have to be educated Indians for whom (unlike tribal or peasant rebels, workers on strike, or indentured labourers) civil liberties and the rule of law had been on the whole both a reality and an important ideological instrument for keeping them contented. They were first tried out by the Lt. Governor of the new province of East Bengal and Assam, Bampfyld Fuller, who unleashed Gurkhas on Barisal, banned the *Bande Mataram* slogan, and tried to get schools disaffiliated for participation in politics. Minto, and much more so, Morley, were rather embarrassed and readily accepted Fuller's resignation in August 1906 over a clash on the disaffiliation issue. More systematic repression began in 1907–08, after the Punjab events and, above all, the Bengal bombs. The major instruments forged included banning of 'seditious' meetings in specific areas (May and November 1907) newspaper acts enabling seizure of presses (June 1908, February 1910) the Criminal Law Amendment Act of December 1908 which permitted a ban on the principal *samitis* in Bengal, and deportations (Lajpat and Ajit Singh in May 1907, 9 Bengal leaders in December 1908). Morley frequently made the appropriate Liberal noises, expressed the feeling that he was becoming 'an accomplice in Cossack rule' (letter to Minto, 7 May 1908), but did or could do little except getting deportation terms somewhat reduced. After 1910, the tough line was continued under Hardinge's Home Member Reginald Craddock, to reach its culmination in the wartime Defence of India Act of 1915.

After a series of fairly fruitful meetings with Gokhale, Morley did initially prod Minto into balancing a maintenance of the unpopular Partition (which the Secretary of State declared to be a 'settled fact' in March 1906, much to the disappointment of his Indian admirers) with some reforms. 'Cast-iron bureaucracy won't go on for ever', some more Indians should be allowed into Legislative and, perhaps, even Executive Councils, more time should be given for budget debates and amendments permitted—though 'of course officials would remain a majority', and there was no question of introducing English political institutions into India—'Assuredly not in your day or mine'. (Letters to Minto, 1 June and 15 June 1906). Minto and other officials in India were quite determined, however, that reform proposals should be seen as coming from Calcutta, and firmly scotched Morley's proposal for a Parliamentary commission of enquiry. They took their own time over preparing a reform scheme, and the final Government of India Despatch on Reform was sent only on 1 October 1908. Morley and Minto also differed on the kind of 'moderates' who could be rallied. While Morley would have liked adjustments with Congress Moderates of the Gokhale brand, the Viceroy seems to have usually meant by the term loyalists outside the Congress. He suggested at first something like a Council of Princes (thus anticipating a favourite British ploy of the 1920s and '30s), and then eagerly accepted upper-class Muslims as the necessary counter-weight. Minto and his Political Secretary Harcourt Butler in fact inaugurated a significant departure in British policy towards the princely states, when the Viceroy in his Udaipur speech of 1909 emphasized the principle of 'non-interference in the internal affairs of Native States.... It is easy to overestimate the value of administrative efficiency.' Minto made an explicit reference also to joint action against sedition as a further proof of the princes 'devotion and loyalty to the Crown'. Thus the post-Mutiny policy of alliance with feudal chiefs was being extended in face of the nationalist danger, and Curzonian interference for the sake of efficiency being given up.

The Indian Councils Act of 1909 did allow somewhat greater powers of budget discussion, putting questions and sponsoring resolutions to members of legislative councils, and for the first time formally introduced the principle of elections. Details of seat allocation and electoral qualifications were left to be made by regulations in India, to be settled in accordance 'with the specific recommendations of the Local Governments'—leaving ample scope for bureaucratic whittling-down of reforms by themselves hardly very generous. There was to be special provision in addition 'for representation of professional classes, the landholders, the Mahomedans, European commerce and Indian commerce'. An official majority was retained in the Imperial Legislative Council, (which would have only 27 elected members out of 60. The 'non-official majorities' in Provincial Councils were an illusion, since they included some nominated members. In Bengal, the only province given formally an elected majority, four among the latter were to be returned by British commercial interests. The Government of India was given general power of disallowing politically dangerous candidates. Above all, no less than 8 out of 27 elected seats in the Imperial Council were reserved for the Muslim separate electorate (they captured 3 of the general seats, too, in the 1910 elections). Electoral rules were also made markedly invidious: the income qualification for Muslim voters being considerably lower, for instance, than for Hindus. It must be added that though officials and Muslim leaders always talked in terms of entire communities, in practice only particular elite groups among Muslims were being preferred throughout by government policy. Thus when separate electorates were extended to U.P. local bodies in 1916, government servants, pensioners and landlords heavily outnumbered less reliable groups, like professional men, traders, or *ulama* in the 'Muslim franchise'.

Simla Deputation and Muslim League

Thus a remarkable success had attended the efforts of the predominantly U.P. and Aligarh-based Muslim elite group which had organized the Simla Deputation to Minto on 1 October 1906, pleading for separate electorates and representation in excess of numerical strength in view of 'the value of the contribution' Muslims were making 'to the defence of the Empire'. The same group quickly took over the Muslim League, initially floated by Salimulla at Dacca in December 1906. Admirers of the Muslim League have indignantly sought to refute the nationalist (as well as Hindus communalist) charge that this entire movement had been stage-managed by the British, and was no more than a 'command performance' (Mohammed Ali's oft-quoted term for the Simla Deputation at the Kakinada Congress of 1923). The Sayyid Ahmed group had been pleading for special Muslim representation by nomination from the 1880s, and as elections became unavoidable, a demand for separate electorates was bound to emerge. Very significant also were signs of internal differences among politically-conscious Muslims. Sayyid Ahmed's political heir, Mohsin-ul-Mulk, informed Principal Archbold on 4 August 1906 that a more active political line was necessary, as 'young educated Mohammadens seem to have sympathy for the Congress'— referring probably to Aligarh 'young gentlemen' like Hasrat Mohani or Mohammed Ali or the *Zamindar* editor Zafar Ali Khan of Lahore. The Aligarh students union had in fact passed a resolution advocating Hindu-Muslim political cooperation in May 1906. Mohsin-ul-Mulk insisted on removing from Archbold's initial draft a sentence pledging 'aloofness from political agitation', since the radicals he wanted to counter were already saying 'that the policy of Sir Syed and that of mine has done no good to Muhammedans'.

Yet British responsibility for the encouragement of communal separatism remains an undeniable fact. Fuller had been 'playing off the two sections of the population against each other' in the new province, admitted Minto to Morley on 15 August 1906, and his successor had continued the policy of favouring Muslims in new appointments. He also pressed Minto to sanction a ₹14 lakh loan to Nawab Salimulla of Dacca as 'a political matter of great importance'. There is ample evidence that through Principal Archbold, Mohsin-ul-Mulk and other Muslim leaders kept in close touch with the Viceroy's private secretary Dunlop Smith, as well as with officials like the Lucknow Commissioner Harcourt Butler (in whose private papers historians have recently discovered a first draft of the Simla Memorial). While organizing the Muslim League, the Aga Khan assured Dunlop Smith on 29 October 1906 that he had instructed Mohsin-ul-Mulk 'not to move in any matter before first finding out if the step to be taken has the full approval of Government privately'.... More important than direct inspiration, however, was an objective similarity of interests, which would repeatedly manifest itself in succeeding decades between officialdom and both Muslim and Hindu upper-class communalists. It may be mentioned in parenthesis that at a meeting of the Bharat Dharma Mahamandal in December 1906, the Maharaja of Darbhanga had declared that 'with the Hindus Loyalty or

Rajbhakti is an element of religion'. Nothing else can explain how an infant and really quite weak organization like the Muslim League (with a membership of only 400 in December 1907, an annual subscription of no less than ₹25, and a minimum eligibility qualification of ₹500 annual income), pursuing 'mendicant' techniques identical with those of the early Congress, could still be so successful within three years of its foundation. A deputation under Ameer Ali in early 1909 was able to quickly scotch a move by Morley to replace separate electorates by a mixed electoral college, since the contacts it had established with Tories were alarming for a Liberal administration engaged in a bitter fight over internal reforms. 'I cannot see that they (Muslims) are in the least entitled to the number of seats that will now be allotted to them', Minto confessed to Morley in private on 11 November 1909—but neither felt it at all incumbent to do anything about it. The basic weakness of the Muslim League was to be revealed soon enough, when, ignoring its loud protests, the new province of Eastern Bengal and Assam which had undoubtedly helped the Muslim elite was suddenly wound up in December 1911.

The Indian Councils Act of 1909 proved to be the most short-lived of all of Britains 'constitutional' experiments in India, being totally revised within nine years by the Montagu-Chelmsford Report of 1918. It quickly revealed itself to be a failure, both in rallying moderates and in keeping politically-active Hindus and Muslim apart. The moderates at their Madras Congress (1908) had welcomed the proposed reforms as 'large and liberal'. By 1909, however, a closer look had made men like Malaviya extremely critical of the excessive concessions to Muslims. As Bayly has shown in detail in his micro-study of Allahabad, developments like the uneasiness caused by violations of civil liberties in the suppression of radicals and further extension of separate electorates into local bodies were making an important section of the old Moderate leadership think in terms of somewhat greater militancy by about 1915–16. For the moment, however, Congress politics remained 'very dull' (as Jawaharlal Nehru recalls in his *Autobiography*) in the immediate pre-war years. Attendance at Congress sessions fell off sharply, and Moderates without Extremists to prod them on seemed capable of only making eloquent speeches. Gokhale did that with some effect on the floor of the reformed Imperial Council, pleading for universal primary education, attacking repressive policies, and drawing public attention to the plight of indentured labourers and the condition of Indians in South Africa.

The Muslim political elite got a rude shock in December 1911, when George V announced the revocation of the Partition at the Delhi Durbar. The king had personally suggested this as a suitable 'boon': he had seen something of the Bengal agitation at first hand, having visited India as Prince of Wales in 1905–06. After some initial hesitation, Viceroy Hardinge and Secretary of State Crewe found the idea quite attractive as it involved little extra expenditure unlike other possible 'boons'. The suggestion was strongly endorsed by Home Member Jenkins, who was deeply worried by the continuing revolutionary terrorism in Bengal, and felt that 'until we get rid of the partition ulcer, we shall have no peace...'. The Government of India despatch of 25 August 1911 linked the reunion of Bengal under a Governor-in-Council with a transfer of the capital to Delhi, both as a sop to Muslim sentiments and, much more important, on the rather farsighted argument that Viceregal authority should be insulated from provincial pressures as ultimately 'a larger measure of self-government' was inevitable in the provinces.

Muslim opinion was not mollified by the bid to recall Delhi-based Mughal glory, and was in fact further alienated by Britain's refusal to help Turkey in her Italian and Balkan wars (1911–12); Hardinge's rejection of proposals for a Muslim University at Aligarh in August 1912; and the August 1913 riot in Kanpur over demolition of a platform adjoining a mosque. The so-called 'Young Party' captured the Muslim League in 1912, and began steering it towards greater militancy, some kind of accommodation with nationalist Hindus, and increasing pan-Islamism. Its leaders included Wazir Hassan, T.A.K. Sherwani and the more radical Ali brothers (Muhammad and Shaukat) and Hasrat Mohani in U.P., the Extremist veteran Zafar Ali Khan in Punjab, and Fazlul Huq in Bengal (a rising young lawyer who for fifty years would combine sophisticated politicking with a genuine rustic mass appeal). Unlike 'Old Party' veterans like Salimulla, Nawab Ali Chaudhuri and Shansul Huda in Bengal or Mohsin-ul-Mulk in U.P., these were seldom titled *zamindars,* (though in U.P. they did get the support of the Raja of Mahmudabad for a time). Francis Robinson has shown that in U.P. the Young Party tended 'to belong to the class which occasionally had a small pittance in rents from land but generally...had to find employment in service or the professions'—(p. 177) very similar in social composition, it may be noted, to radical Hindu nationalists. Journals like Muhammad Ali's *Comrade* (Calcutta), Abul Kalam Azad's *Al-Hilal* (Calcutta) or Zafar Ali Khan's *Zamindar* (Lahore) were soon attracting police attention by their pan-Islamist and anti-British tone. The Ali brothers backed by Abdul Bari's Lucknow-based Firangi Mahal school of *ulama* organized the Anjumen-i-Khuddam-i Kaaba in 1913 to raise funds to protect the Muslim holy places, and in 1912–13 Ansari and Zafar Ali Khan led a medical mission to help Turkey in the Balkan wars. Wazir Hassan as the new secretary of the Muslim League pushed through in March 1913, a resolution stating colonial self-government through constitutional means to be the League's aim, bringing it in tune with the Congress. The stage was being set for the Khilafat movement and a period of general Hindu-Muslim political cooperation.

Revolutionary Terrorism

Meanwhile revolutionary terrorism had shown no signs of abatement in Bengal, being quite unmoved by the royal 'boon' of December 1911 abrogating the Partition. The tightly-organized Dacca Anushilan, which now had branches throughout the province and even beyond it, concentrated on 'Swadeshi dacoities' to raise funds and assassinations of officials and traitors. The Yugantar 'party' led by Jatindranath Mukherji represented a much looser confederation of groups, which on the whole tried more to conserve their resources and build international contacts so as to organize a real military conspiracy at an appropriate time. Rashbehari Bose and Sachindranath Sanyal knit together a far-flung secret organization spanning centres in Punjab, Delhi and U.P., and staged a spectacular bomb attack on Hardinge while he was making his official entry into the new capital on 23 December 1912.

Increasingly, however, the need for shelter, the possibility of bringing out revolutionary literature immune from Press Acts, and the quest for arms took Indian revolutionaries abroad. In London, Shyamji Krishnavarma had started in 1905 a centre for Indian students (India House), a journal (*Indian Sociologist*), an Indian Home Rule Society, and a little later a scholarship scheme to bring radical youth from India. Krishnavarma's own militancy remained a bit theoretical, and was confined largely to a theory of passive resistance (of which the *Indian Sociologist* was in fact an early proponent), but from 1907 his India House was taken over by a revolutionary group led by V.D. Savarkar from Nasik. Madanlal Dhingra of this circle assassinated the India Office bureaucrat Curzon-Wyllie in July 1909, and went to the scaffold with a memorable declaration of patriotic fervour: 'Neither rich nor able, a poor son like myself can offer nothing but his blood on the altar of Mother's deliverance... may I be reborn of the same Mother and may I redie in the same sacred cause, till my mission is done and she stands free for the good of humanity and to the glory of God'. London became too hot for Indian revolutionaries now, particularly after Savarkar had been extradited in 1910 to be given life transportation in the Nasik conspiracy case. New centres emerged on the Continent—Paris and Geneva, from where Madame Cama, a Parsi revolutionary who developed close contacts with French socialists like Jean Longuet, brought out the *Bande Mataram*; and, increasingly important as Anglo-German relations worsened, Berlin, which Virendranath Chattopadhay chose as his base from 1909 onwards.

Indians in Britain and Europe could be no more than fairly isolated emigre groups; in British Columbia and the Pacific coast states of U.S.A., however, the revolutionary movement for the first time acquired something like a mass base. A colony of about 15,000 Indians, mostly Sikhs, had come into existence here by 1914, consisting of fairly prosperous traders and workers, yet suffering acutely from various forms of racial discrimination about which the British Indian government did nothing. The famous Ghadr movement began in 1913 in San Francisco, founded by Sohan Singh Bhakna and including among its early leaders the brilliant though somewhat mercurial intellectual Har Dayal from St. Stephens College, Delhi. It took its name from the weekly *Ghadr*, brought out from 1 November 1913 in Urdu, Gurmukhi and later several other Indian languages, which began its first issue with the following dramatic passage: 'What is our name? The *Ghadr* (Revolution). In what does our work consist? In bringing about a rising.... Where will this rising break out? In India. When will it break out? In a few years...'. The Ghadr movement represented one of the two main contributions made by Indian colonies abroad to the cause of India's freedom struggle in this period. The other, the experience of *satyagraha* in South Africa, will be discussed a little later in connection with the emergence of Mahatma Gandhi.

Apart from the real threat they came to represent to British rule for a few years during the First World War, the wanderings of Indian revolutionaries abroad helped to end the intense Hindu religiosity, relative parochialism, and rather limited social outlook of early militant nationalism. The aggressively Hindu *Bhawani Mandir*-pamphlet of Aurobindo Ghosh (1905) spoke of 'a need to *Aryanize* the world', wanted to unite all classes through 'the link of a single and living religious spirit', and had even explicitly desired 'to promote sympathy between the zamindars and the peasants and to heal all discords'. The pamphlet *Oh Martyrs* (1907) brought out by the London group evoked, however, the memory of the joint Hindu Muslim upsurge of 1857: "How the Firinghee rule was shattered to pieces and the swadeshi thrones were set up by the common consent of Hindus and Mahomedans...'. A vision of international anti-imperialist struggle was emerging: 'Dhingra's pistol shot has been heard by the Irish cottier in his forlorn hut, by the Egyptian fellah in the field, by the Zulu labourer in the dark mine...'. (*Bande Mataram* London 1909). Contacts with Irish radicals were particularly close—the New York *Gaelic American* of G.F. Freeman, for instance, was being constantly seized by Indian customs along with journals like *Indian Sociologist, Bande Mataram,* Chattopadhyay's *Talvar* (Berlin), Taraknath Das *Free Hindustan* (Vancouver), and the *Ghadr*. And links were being developed with the international socialist movement too. Hyndman of the British Marxist Social Democratic Federation addressed meetings at Krishnavarma's *India House,* Madame Cama unfurled the flag of free India at the Stuttgart Congress of the Second International in August 1907, and Har Dayal served as secretary of the San Franscisco branch of the anarcho-syndicalist Industrial Workers of the World—he also wrote perhaps the earliest Indian article on Karl Marx in the *Modern Review* (Calcutta) of March 1912. It is not accidental that the first Indian Communsits would emerge from this milieu after the October Revolution in Russia— men like the Yugantar leader Naren Bhattacharji (M.N. Roy), Virendranath Chattopadhyay, Abani Mukherji and some Ghadr veterans.

WAR AND INDIAN POLITICS

The First World War (1914–18) brought about really crucial changes in the political life and socio-economic conditions of India. Leaving the more profound consequences for later discussion (in relation to the emergence of mass all-India nationalism in the immediate post-war years to which they contributed heavily), we may concentrate first on the varying reactions to the war among already-active Indian political groups.

Revolutionary Activities

For revolutionaries striving for immediate complete independence, the war seemed a heaven-sent opportunity, draining India of troops (the number of white soldiers went down at one point to only 15,000) and bringing the possibility of financial and military help from German and Turkish enemies of Britain. It was the one point of time when a successful *coup d'etat* appeared not impossible. Britain's war with Turkey (the seat of the Khalifa, claiming religio-political leadership of all Muslims) brought about close cooperation between Hindu nationalists and militant Muslim pan-Islamists, and important Muslim revolutionary leaders emerged-men like Barkatulla in Ghadr and the Deoband *mullahs* Mahmud Hasan and Obeidulla Sindhi.

In Bengal, the revolutionaries achieved a major success in August 1914, when a large consignment of 50 Mauser pistols and 46,000 rounds of ammunition was appropriated by them from the Rodda firm in Calcutta through a sympathetic employee. The curve of political dacoities and murder reached its highest point now—12 and 7 in 1914–15, and no less than 23 and 9 in 1915–16. Most Bengal groups united under Jatin Mukherji (nicknamed 'Bagha Jatin'), and planned the disruption of rail communications, seizure of Fort William in Calcutta (contacts had been made with the 16th Rajput Rifles stationed there), and landing of German arms (for arranging this Naren Bhattacherji was sent to Java). The grandiose plans were ruined, however, by poor coordination, and Bagha Jatin died a hero's death near Balasore on the Orissa coast, where he had been tracked down by the police through the help of local villagers (September 1915)—a tragic reminder of the essential social isolation of the Bengal revolutionaries.

The Bengal plans were part of a far-flung conspiracy organized by Rashbehari Bose and Sachin Sanyal in cooperation with returned Ghadrites in Punjab. The latter had started coming back in their thousands after the outbreak of the war to fight for the country's freedom. Passions were inflamed further by the Komagata Maru incident (29 September 1914)—a ship-load of would-be Sikh and Punjabi Muslims immigrants, turned back from Vancouver by Canadian immigration authorities, clashed with the police on their return at Budge Budge near Calcutta, and 22 were killed. Many of the Punjabis who returned after 1914 were quickly rounded up by the British (by 1916, 2500 had been interned and 400 jailed, out of a total of about 8000), and the plan for a coordinated revolt on 21 February 1915 based on mutinies by Ferozepur, Lahore and Rawalpindi garrisons was foiled at the last moment by treachery. Rashbehari Bose had to flee to Japan, and Sachin Sanyal was transported for life for having tried to subvert garrisons at Benares and Danapore. Though the plan for an all-India revolt misfired badly, its organizers—and particularly the Ghadrites—were still pioneers in taking revolutionary ideas to the army and to the peasants. There were some scattered mutinies, most notably at Singapore on 15 February 1915, of the Punjabi Muslim 5th Light Infantry and the 36th Sikh battalion under Jamadar Chisti Khan, Jamader Abdul Ghani and Subedar Daud Khan—37 were executed after its suppression, and 41 transported for life. The Punjab political dacoities of January-February 1915 also had a somewhat new social content. In at least 3 out of the 5 main cases, the targets were village moneylenders and the raiders burnt debt bonds before decamping with the cash. The lowly Ghadr peasant and sepoy heroes have been much less remembered than the *bhadralok* Bengal terrorists who remain household names at least in their own province—yet surely they deserve a better fate. They included men like Kartar Singh Sarabha, 19-year-old organizer of mutiny among Punjab garrisons, who died with the words: 'If I had to live more lives than one, I would sacrifice each of them for my country's sake'. Memorable too are the parting words of Abdulla, solitary Muslim in a group of rebel sepoys executed at Ambala, who spurned offers to betray his *kafir* comrades: 'It is with these men alone that the gates of heaven shall open to me.'

Efforts to send help to revolutionaries from abroad were centred during the war years in Berlin, where the Indian Independence Committee was set up in 1915 under Virendranath Chattopadhyay, Bhupen Dutta, Har Dayal and some others in collaboration with the German foreign office under the so-called 'Zimmerman Plan'. An Indo-German-Turkish mission tried to stir up anti-British feelings among tribes near the Indo-Iranian border, and in December 1915 Mahendra Pratap, Barkatulla and Obeidullah Sindhi set up a 'Provisional Government of Free India' at Kabul, with some backing from crown prince Amanullah but not from Amir Habibulla. The U.S.A. was a third centre, where the remaining Ghadr leaders like Ramchandra and New York agents of the Berlin Committee headed by Chandra Chakrabarti received considerable German funds but squabbled among themselves. The 'Hindu Conspiracy Case' (1918) after U.S. entry into the war ended such activities. Funds were channelled also through German embassies in the Far East, and from Japan Rashbehari Bose and Abani Mukherji made several efforts to send arms after 1915. The gun-running attempts all failed with depressing regularity, however, and in any case came too late, for in India the flash-point of possible armed revolt had come and gone in early 1915.

The British met the war-time threat by a formidable battery of repressive measures—the most intensive since 1857—and above all by the Defence of India Act passed in March 1915 primerily to smash the Ghadr moment. Large numbers of suspects were held without trial for years in Bengal and Punjab, and special courts handed down extremely severe sentences. One estimate of the Ghadr trials lists 46 executions and 64 life sentences, excluding numerous court-martials of army men. Apart from Bengal terrorists and Punjab Ghadrites, radical pan-Islamists also aroused considerable British alarm, and the Ali brothers Azad, and Hasrat Mohani were interned for years during the war and in some cases even afterwards.

Unity at Lucknow

Indian politicians who were not revolutionaries supported the war effort—in 1918 Tilak and Gandhi would even go to the extent of trying to raise money and men for the British through village tours—but with the hope that the rulers would grant major political reforms in return for such loyalty. 'Purchase war debentures, but look to them as the title deeds of Home Rule', was Tilak's plea in 1918. An objective basis thus emergied during the war years for a kind of joint platform of Moderates, Extremists, and the 'Young Party'-controlled Muslim League around a programme for putting constitutional but still quite intense pressure on the beleagured British Government in return for war support. The ever pragmatic Tilak seemed eager to make up with his old Congress enemies after returning from his Mandalay exile in 1914, and while Pherozeshah Mehta proved obdurate till his death in 1915, other Moderates like Bhupendranath Bose of Calcutta expressed their willingness to 'accept any means to lift the Congress out of the present bog' (letter to Gokhale, 26 November 1914). A major new element which helped the reunification process was the sudden rise to political prominence of the Theosophist leader Annie Besant from 1914. Besant, as subsequent events were to reveal, was far from being a consistent anti-imperialist, but she had come to feel that a substantial measure of self-government was necessary for Indo-British friendship, and that the only way of achieving this goal was through effective and nation-wide agitation and organization modelled on the British Radical and Irish Home Rule movements.

In December 1915, the Tilak group was allowed to re-enter the Congress, and both the Congress and Muslim League, meeting simultaneously at Bombay, set up committees to draft a platform of minimum constitutional demands through mutual consultation. Nineteen non-official members of the Imperial Council jointly petitioned the Viceroy in October 1916, calling for representative government and dominion status for India. At Lucknow in December 1916, a common demand was raised again for elected majorities in Councils, while Hindu-Muslim political differences were sought to be resolved through the famous Lucknow Pact by which Congress accepted separate electorates and a bargain was struck over distribution of seats. The Muslim leaders accepted under-representation in Muslim-majority areas (only 40% of seats in Bengal, for instance), in return for over-representation in provinces like Bombay or United Provinces (where 30% was to be assigned to them). The Pact clearly reflected on the Muslim side the interests of the U.P.-based 'Young Party' led by Wazir Hassan and Mahmudabad, and aroused some resentment in Bengal despite the support given to it by the Fazlul Huq group.

Home Rule Agitation

The Congress, however, remained a purely deliberative body not geared to any sustained agitation, and Tilak's proposal at Lucknow to set up a compact Working Committee as a first step towards converting it into a real party was ruled out of order by the president. Agitational work had therefore to be organized through the two Home Rule Leagues of Tilak and Annie Besant. Besant had announced plans for such a League in September 1915, and worked to that end through her Madras newspapers *New India* and *common weal,* followed by the Bombay *Young India* started in early 1916. Tilak forestalled her, partly in order to maintain his old Maharashtra base, by starting his Home Rule League in April 1916. This remained confined to Maharashtra and Karnataka, but claimed a membership of 14,000 in April 1917 and 32,000 by early 1918. Besant's League, which had more of an all-India character but relied heavily at first on its founder's old Theosophical contacts, was set up in September 1916. While Tilak and Kelkar tried to run a fairly centralized organization from Poona, the Adyar (Madras) headquarters of Besant's League maintained only loose supervision over its 200-odd local branches (132 of them in Madras Presidency). At its height in mid-1917 the Besant Home Rule League had 27,000 members.

The activities of the Home Rule Leagues consisted in organizing discussion groups and reading-rooms in cities, mass sale of pamphlets, and lecture tours—no different in form from older Moderate politics, but significantly new so far as intensity and extent were concerned. Tilak's League in its first year sold 47,000 copies of 6 Marathi and 2 English pamphlets, and Besant's organization had already brought out 300,000 copies of 26 English tracts by September 1916. There was some talk too, of passive resistance when Besant and her two principal Theosophist colleagues, Arundale and Wadia, were interned in June 1917. While the bulk of the propaganda was centred around the some-what abstract and intellectual concept of Home Rule, a few speeches of Tilak which have survived do reveal interesting efforts—repeatedly pointing towards later Gandhian themes—to relate this ideal to more specific and concrete popular grievances. 'Zulum has been exercised upon us in connection with the Forest Department, liquor has spread more in connection with the Abkari department' (Tilak's speech at Belgaum, 1 May 1916)—and references were made also to revenue pressures and the salt tax. Nor was Tilak's movement a purely Chitpavan Brahman affair: membership lists of his Home Rule League show considerable participation of non-Brahman traders in Poona, and Gujars and Marathas outnumbered Brahmans in districts like Khandesh. Home Rule Leaguers like B.P. Wadia also started some trade union activity, though of quite a moderate kind, among the Madras city working class.

The real importance of the Home Rule agitation, and particularly of Besant's League, lay, however, in the extension to new areas, groups, and something like a new generation—a point emphasized by H.F. Owen in the only substantial account of the movement available so far. Apart from Maharashtra, the other two old Extremist bases were relatively quiet. Punjab and Bengal had been the main targets of British repression during the war years, making any kind of open militant agitation difficult—though in Bengal the Bhawanipur Provincial Conference (April 1917) marked the entry into active politics of a major new leader: Chittaranjan Das. The Besant League found its main support from Tamil Brahmans of Madras city and *mofussil* towns, urban professional groups in the United Provinces (Kayasthas, Kashmiri Brahmans, some Muslims), the Hindu Amil minority in Sind, and younger Gujarati industrialists, traders and lawyers in Bombay city and Gujarat.

Theosophy with its combination of a modicum of social reform, theories of ancient Hindu wisdom and glory, and mystic claims that all the achievements of the modern West had been anticipated by the *rishis,* had won recruits mainly from such groups, perhaps because other reform or revivalist movements like Brahmoism or the Arya Samaj had not reached them very much. There was also something like a political vacuum, for with the exception of the cities of Bombay and Madras these were areas without strongly established political traditions, whether Extremist or Moderate. Besant herself soon broke sharply with radical politics, along with many of her closest associates in Madras (Wadia, Arundale, and C.P. Ramaswamy Iyer—the latter was to become in the end an extremely authoritarian and conservative Diwan in Travancore state). But among the young men activized by the Home Rule movement were numerous future leaders of Indian politics from the 1920s onwards: Satyamurti in Madras, Jitendralal Banerji in Calcutta. Jawaharlal Nehru and Khaliquzzaman in Allahabad and Lucknow, and in Bombay and Gujarat men like the wealthy dye importer Jamnadas Dwarkadas, the industrialist Umar Sobhani, the rich man's son Shankerlal Banker, and Indulal Yajnik. Besant's League had 2600 members in Bombay city, and held meetings of up to 10–12,000 at Shantaram's *Chawl* in a area inhabited by government employees and industrial workers. Gujarat and many parts of U.P. were also being activized for the first time—portents of the future, when these areas would constitute the backbone of Gandhian nationalism.

Besant performed a somersault in late-1917, when Montagu's promise of 'responsible government' converted her almost overnight into a near-loyalist. Tilak, too became increasingly involved in a libel suit against Valentine Chirol, and left for England to fight his case in September 1918. Meanwhile Gandhi was winning his first political spurs in India, at Champaran, Kheda, and Ahmedabad during 1917–18. Before turning to the interrelated processes of constitutional reform, the beginnings of Gandhism, and the broader impact of the War on Indian life, however, it is necessary to consider briefly certain developments during 1905–1917 below the level of all-India politics which also contributed greatly in the end to the transformation of the Indian scene after 1919: tribal and peasant unrest, lower-class communalism, caste associations, and the development of regional sentiments.

MOVEMENTS FROM BELOW: 1905–1917

Tribal Revolts

As in the nineteenth century, tribal outbreaks remained an endemic feature of many parts of India. In the Nallamalai hills of Cuddapah and Nellore (present-day south Andhra), for instance, the very primitive food-gathering Chenchu tribe found its traditional rights to forest producte being increasingly restricted by the government from 1898 onwards, though the latter was somewhat inhibited by the fear that pure repression might lead to the 'total destruction by fire of the Nallamalai forests'. (Thurston and Rangachari, *Castes and Tribes of Southern India Volume II,* pp 32–35). The tightening up of restrictions for conservancy and revenue purposes by a Forest Committee in 1913 directly contributed to a powerful 'forest *satyagraha*' in Cuddapah during the Non-Cooperation movement. The old 'Rampa' country of the Godavari hills also remained restive, with a *fituri* or revolt in 1916 serving as a prelude to the major rebellion under Aluri Sitarama Raju in 1922–24 which will be described in the next chapter. In 1910, British troops suppressed a rising in the Jagdalpur region against the Raja of Bastar; though partly provoked by a succession dispute, the main cause was again the recent imposition of forest regulations banning shifting cultivation and free use of forest produce. The rebels disrupted communications, attacked police stations and forest outposts, burnt schools (which were being built by forced labour and compulsory levies on tribals), and even tried to beseige Jagdalpur town. In the Orissa feudatory state of Daspalla in October 1914, a Khond rebellion which began over a disputed succession quickly took on a different colour, as rumours spread that a war had started and soon 'there would be no sahebs left in the country' and the Khonds would 'live under their own rule'. The British feared a general Khond rising which could 'set ablaze the whole of the vast inaccessible mountain tracts streching along the Eastern Ghats so far as Kalahandi and Bastar', and so went about burning Khond villages. (*Home police B,* March 1915, p. 153). News of the war produced interestingly similar results among the Oraons of Chote Nagpur, the neighbours of the Mundas. Here a movement started by Jatra Bhagat in 1914 calling for monotheism, abstention from meat, liquor and tribal dances, and a return to shifting cultivation briefly took on a more radical millen-arian colour in the following year as rumours spread of the imminent coming of a saviour variously identified with Birsa or a 'German' or 'Kaiser Baba'. Quick repressive action stamped out this militant strand, but a more pacific 'Tana Bhagat' movement survived among the Oraons and developed important links with Gandhian nationalism from the 1920s. British efforts to recruit tribal labour for menial work on the Western Front led to a Santal rising in Mayurbhanj and a rebellion in Manipur among the Thadoe Kukis in 1917. Guerrilla war went on here for two years, fuelled also by other grievances like *pothang* (tribals being made to carry the baggages of officials without payment), and Government efforts to *stop jhum* (shifting cultivation). Meanwhile in southern Rajasthan more than a thousand miles away, the Bhils of Banswara, Sunth and Dungarpur states (adjoining Mewar) had been stirred to action by a reform movement under Govind Guru. This began as a temperance and purification movement, but in late 1913 developed into a bid to set up a Bhil raj. 4000 Bhils assembled on Mangad hill, and the British were able to disperse them only after considerable resistance in which 12 tribals were killed and 900 taken prisoner. (*Home police B,* December 1913, n. 108–11).

Peasant Movements

Mewar was also the scene of a number of important peasant movements. By a curious coincidence these began in 1905, at a time when in far-off Bengal patriotic intellectuals like R.C. Dutt, D.L. Roy, Abanindranath Tagore and Rabindranath were writing novels, plays, stories and poems extolling the chivalry and heroism of the medieval Ranas of Chitor. The latter's modern descendents combined abject servility towards the British with the grossest forms of feudal exploitation of the peasantry. At Bijolia, a big Mewar *jagir* held by a Parmar Rajput, there were 86 different types of cesses on *kisans,* and in 1905 and again in 1913 the latter collectively refused to cultivate lands and tried to emigrate to neighbouring areas. The 1913 protest was led by a *sadhu,* Sitaram Das, while in 1915 a new element was introduced by the externment in this region of an ex-revolutionary connected with Sachin Sanyal's group named Bhoop Singh, alias Vijay Singh Pathik. Pathik in exile developed into a peasant leader, and persuaded a state official, Manik Lal Verma, to jointly lead a no-tax movement against the Udaipur Maharana in 1916. Peasant refusal to contribute to war-loans was another element in the Bijolia movement, which later developed Gandhian contacts and continued into the 1920s. Both Pathik and Verma later became important Congress leaders in Rajasthan.

Peasant movements contributed directly and very substantially to the birth of Gandhian nationalism in two areas: Champaran in north-west Bihar and Kheda in Gujarat. While Gandhi's intervention was indispensable in raising the local issues here to the level of all-India politics, there is ample evidence in both cases of discontent and protest long before the coming of the Mahatma, and of the existence of what Jacques Pouchepadass in his study of Champaran has called 'upward pressure from the rural masses themselves'. There had been sporadic resistance in Champaran since the 1860s to the *tinkathia* system by which European planters holding *thikadari* leases from the big *zamindars* of Ramnagar, Bettiah, and Madhuban made peasants cultivate indigo on part of their land at unremunerative prices. As indigo declined from about 1900 in face of competition from synthetic dyes, the planters tried to pass the burden on the peasants by charging *sharahbeshi* (rent-enhancement) or *tawan* (lump-sum compensation) in return for releasing them from the obligation to grow indigo. Widespread resistance developed in the Motihari-Bettiahi region between 1905-08, affecting an area of 400 square miles and involving some violence (the murder of Bloomfield, a factory manager), 57 criminal cases, and 277 sentences. The better-off section of the peasantry continued the struggle over the next decade through petitions, cases, and contacts with some Bihar Congress leaders and journalists, and it was as a part of this on-going confrontation that Raj Kumar Shukla, a prosperous peasant-cum-petty moneylender, contacted Gandhi at the Lucknow Congress of 1916. At Kheda, too, collective refusals to pay revenue had become increasingly common well before the entry of Gandhi. An emerging rich peasant stratum, which had benefited in the late nineteenth century from expanding markets for tobacco and dairy produce and had started calling themselves Patidars instead of Kanbis, had been struck by plague and famine between 1898 and 1906, and government revenue enhancements added to their burdens. At Bardoli in Surat district, the other main centre of Gandhian activity in Gujarat, a certain amount of organization had started developing from 1908, initially on caste lines: the Patidar Yuvak Mandel, founded by Kunvarji Mehta.

Communalism

As already noted in a previous chapter, lower-class discontent often took on the much less clear-cut, 'sectional' form of different types of communal, caste or regional consciousness. At Kamariarchar in the Jamalpur sub-division of Mymensingh, for instance, a *praja* conference in 1914 formulated a charter of *raiyat* demands : rent-reduction, an end to cesses, relief for indebtedness, the right to plant trees and dig tanks without paying *nazar* to *zamindars,* as well as honourable treatment of Muslim tenants at the Hindu *zamindar's* court. The conference was organized by an affluent Muslim *raiyat,* Chaudhuri Khos Mohammed Sarkar; it remained significantly silent about possible grievances of share-croppers, and was attended by a number of Bengal poltical leaders, all of them Muslim—Fazlul Huq, Akram Khan, Abul Kasem and others. Here was the beginning of a *Praja* movement which was to play an important part in the Bengal politics of the 1920s and '30s, reflecting agrarian discontent (more precisely perhaps, rich peasant or *jotedar* demands), but also contributing in the end to Muslim separatism. This happened mainly as a result of the mistakes and limitations of the predominantly Hindu Bengal Congress. Very little study has been made so far of the roots of such relatively 'popular', as distinct from elite, communalism, whether Muslim or Hindu. One would have liked to known much more, for example, about the possible social dimensions of the massive Bihar riots of October where crowds of up to 50,000 Hindus attacked Muslims in 124 villages in Shahabad, 28 in Gaya and 2 in Patna. Though the immediate and ostensible issue was cow-protection, there were widespread rumours that British rule was collapsing, rioting crowds shouted '*Angrej ka raz uth gaya*' and '*German ki jay*' and the area affected in Shahabad coincided very closely with what had been Kunwar Singh's base in 1857–58. It has also been suggested that upper-caste landholders were utilizing communalism to regain a local leadership threatened by emerging class tensions. Cow-protection propaganda by Sanatan Dharma Sabha and Arya Samajist agitators certainly played an important role in provoking such riots—and it is another interesting index to the volatise nature of early peasant mobilization that a prominent Sanatan Dharma activist in the Allahabad region of U.P., Malaviya's protege Inder Narayan Dwivedi, combined religious lectures and the propagation of Hindi with Home Rule politics and the starting of Kisan Sabhas in 1917. In the Calcutta riots of September studied in some detail by J.H. Broomfield, Marwari businessmen of Burra Bazar were attacked by their poorer Muslim neighbours. The latter had been aroused in part by the pan-Islamic propaganda of some non-Bengali Muslim agitators (Habib Shah, Fazlur Rehman, Kalami) and up-country *ulama*. Both Hindu revivalism and pan-Islamism could thus oscillate between expression of lower-class discontent, communal frenzy, and anti-imperialist politics.

Caste Movements

An important feature of the early decades of the twentieth century was the proliferation of caste conferences, associations, and movements. Such bodies were organized mainly by fairly small groups of educated men belonging to intermediate or (less often) lower castes. Latecomers in the race for professional or service jobs, they found caste a useful rallying-points to attack the lead established by Brahman or other upper-caste elements which usually had also been the first beneficiaries of English education. While Cambridge historians not unexpectedly emphasize this factional aspect, sociologists tend to relate case movements to the upward mobility through 'Sanskritization' of particular *jatis* as a whole and have sometimes hailed caste associations as a valuable link between 'tradition' and 'modernity'. A third kind of approach is that developed by Gail Omvedt in a very interesting recent study of the non-Brahman movement in Maharashtra: this seeks to explain caste-conflicts as a distorted but important expression of socio-economic and class tensions, and finds the Sanskritization concept too narrow, since it cannot explain emergence of some radical and popular anti-caste movements like the Satyashodhak Samaj in Maharashtra or the Self-Respect agitation in Tamilnadu.

While caste associations were by no means uncommon in provinces like Bengal (tending to become more prominent after 1908 as the national movement declined), they acquired much greater social and political importance in south India and Maharashtra. These were regions marked by a more clear-cut Brahman predominance and greater caste rigidity (in Kerala for instance the lower castes were supposed to pollute not only by touch but by sight). Among the untouchable Nadars of south Tamilnadu, a prosperous group of traders had emerged by the late nineteenth century in the towns of Ramnad district which raised community funds for educational and social welfare activities, claimed Kshatriya status, imitated upper-caste customs and manners, and organized a Nadar Mahajan Sangam in 1910. The Sanskritization model seems fairly appropriate here, provided we remember that such upward mobility hardly affected the lowly toddy-tappers of Tirunelveli who still went on being called by the old caste-name of Shanar at a time when their successful brethren in Ramnad had appropriated the more prestigious title of Nadar. Politically far more significant was the 'Justice' movement launched in Madras around 1915–16, by C.N. Mudaliar, T.M. Nair and P. Tyagaraja Chetti on behalf of intermediate castes (Tamil Vellalas, Mudaliars and Chettiars, above all, but also Telugu Reddis, Kammas and Balija Naidus and Malayali Nairs) which included numerous prosperous landlords and merchants and therefore felt jealous of Brahman predominance in education, the services, and politics. Only 3.2% of the population, Brahmans in the Madras Presidency held 55% of deputy collector and 72.6% of district munsiff posts in 1912. Brahmans at times were also big landowners, particularly in Thanjavur, and upper-caste taboos on agricultural work and professional activities in towns made them usually absentees. The predominantly Brahman Home Rule League agitation of Annie Besant aroused fears which British officials, journalists, and businessmen in Madras were quick to exploit. T. Earle Welby, editor of the *Madras Mail* and spokesman of British business interests in Madras city, violently attacked Montagu's promise of responsible government ('And England's voice, no more the lion's they knew/Becomes the whisper of this Wandering Jew'—*Madras Mail,* 19 September 1917) and cultivated the emerging Justice Party. The latter paraded its loyalism in the hope of getting more service jobs and special representation in the new legislatures, and the Non-Brahman Manifesto of 20 December 1916 expressed opposition to any moves 'to undermine the influence and authority of the British Rulers, who alone...are able to hold the scales even between creed and class...'. The alliance was facilitated by the fact that the Justice leaders were an extremely elitist group heavily dependent on landlord finance. But non-Brahman grievances were real enough, as shown by the organization in September 1917 of a pro-nationalist Madras Presidency Association which too demanded separate representation—and in the late-1920s a radical and populist anti-Brahman and anti-caste movement would develop in Tamil Nadu under E.V. Ramaswami Naicker.

In the princely state of Mysore, a mainly urban Brahman community (3.8% of the total population) held 65% of gazetted posts in 1918, while Vokkaligas and Lingayat constituted the dominant rural groups. A Lingnyat Education and Association and a Vokkaliga Sangha emerged in 1905–06, and in 1917 C.R. Reddi, a Madras non-Brahman politican teaching in the Mysore Maharaja's College, founded the state's first political organization—the Praja Mithra Mandali—on an anti-Brahman platform. These bodies remained urban professional lobbies, however, trying to influence court politics through personal contacts alone.

In Travancore state, the tiny elite of Nambudiri Brahmans (less than 1% of the population) living off big tax-free *jenmi* estates largely kept away from the race for education and jobs. Non-Malayali Brahmans (Marathi Desastha or Tamil in origin), however, enjoyed a privileged position in the state administration, holding in 1891 about the same number of posts as the local dominant caste of Nairs, though they were only 28,000 as against the latter's strength of half a million. An unusual feature of Travancore life was the high degree of literacy, brought about by intense missionary activity among Ezhava and other lower castes in this old centre of Christianity, as well as by the efforts to promote education among upper castes under Dewan Madhava Rao (1860–72). Urban literacy in Travancore in 1901 stood at 36%—a figure higher than Calcutta. The Nairs felt excluded by the non-Malayali Brahmans and threatened at the same time by Syrian Christians (a community which included numerous landlords and prosperous traders in north Travancore, and were pioneers in modern journalism) and the beginning of an upthrust among the Ezhavas. They had numerous internal problems, too: the traditional unwieldy *taravad* (matrilineal joint family) of the Nairs was increasingly felt to be unsuited to modern economic conditions, and many *taravads* held relatively small blocs of land and were hard-hit by rising prices (creating a situation similar to that faced by the gentry-based intelligentsia in many other provinces). Western education also made many Nair social customs appear embarrassing and retrograde, particularly the rule of Nair women having to appear bare-breasted before Nambudiri visitors and to enter into temporary liasons (*sambandham*) with them.

The cumulative result was the early and almost simultaneous emergence of trends towards social reform, anti-Brahman sentiments, patriotism, and even elements of radicalism. Thus Kerala's first modern novel, Chander Menon's *Indulekha* (1889), attacked Nambudiri social domination and *taravad* constraints on romantic love, while C.V. Raman Pillai's historical novel *Martanda Varma* (1891) attempted an evocation of lost Nair military glory through its hero Ananda Padmanabhan. Raman Pillai was the principal organizer of the Malayali Memorial of 1891 attacking Brahman predominance in state jobs—primarily a Nair move, though there were also some Christian and Ezhava signatories. While Raman Pillai's group was fairly easily accommodated within the official elite by the late 1890s, a more energetic Nair leadership emerged after 1900 under K. Ramakrishna Pillai and Mannath Padmanabha Pillai. The latter founded the Nair Service Society in 1914 which still exists, combining caste aspirations with a measure of internal social reform. The former edited the *Swadeshabhimani* from 1906 till 1910, when its attacks on the court and demands for political rights led to Ramakrishna Pillai's explusion from Travancore. Ramakrishna Pillai had some connections with T.M. Nair's Justice movement, but two years before his untimely death in 1916 he had also published the first biography of Karl Marx in Malayalam.

Nor were such multifarous activities a Nair monopoly. The awakening of the Ezhavas—traditionally lowly tappers and tenders of the coconut palm, but developing a relatively prosperous segment as the market for coconut products expanded—was centred around the religious leader Sri Narayan Guru (c 1855–1928) and his Aruvipuram temple. The Sri Narayana Dharma Paripalana Yogam was founded in 1902-03 by Sri Narayan Guru, Dr Palpu the first Ezhava graduate, and the great Malayali poet N. Kumaran Asan. The successful industrial exhibition organized by it at Quilon (January 1905) was followed by a spate of Nair-Ezhava riots. The S.N.D.P. Yogam under T.K. Madhavan would establish important links with Gandhian nationalism in the 1920s, while the next generation of Ezhavas would swing decisively over to the Communists. A quick transition from social reform, initially sought often through caste associations, to thoroughgoing radicalism was to be in fact a recurrent feature of Kerala life: E.M.S. Namboodiripad, too, began in the 1920s as a Nambudiri Welfare Association activist.

But the most interesting of the caste movements was that of the Satyashodhak Samaj in Maharashtra, which Gail Omvedt's research has revealed to have had two distinct strands. The first trend, very similar to the Justice movement in Madras, relied largely on the patronage of the Kolhapur ruler Shahu (who had his own quarrels with Brahman courtiers), and concentrated on getting more jobs and political favours for an elite. But there was also a much more populist and radical trend, claiming to speak in the name of the 'bahujan samaj' against the *shetjis* and *bhatjis* (the Brahman priests, but also the merchants and the rich in general). Under leaders like Mukundrao Patil, who from 1910 brought out the most important Satyashodhak paper, *Din Mitra,* from his home village of Taravdi, the Samaj acquired a unique rural base in the Maharashtra Deccan and the Vidarbha-Nagpur region. Its populist character is well indicated by the fact that practically the entire Satyashodhak literature is in Marathi and not in English. The 1917 annual conference of the Samaj received reports from 49 branches spread over 14 districts, and no less than 30 of these local units were in villages of less than 2000 inhabitants. The predominant note at this level was a rejection of caste oppression and hierarchy, and not a Sanskritizing demand for a higher status within the existing structure. No doubt the social base was primarily rich-peasant, but in this period there were certain common interests of the entire peasantry against largely upper-caste *mahajans* and landlords. The Satyashodhak message was spread over the countryside through a refashioning of the traditional folk drama or *tamasha* (a method which the Communists would use again in the 1940s through the Indian People's Theatre Association), and in Satara, where such *tamasha* groups were most active, a peasant rising would break out in 1919 under local Satyashodhak leaders.

Regional Sentiments and Languages

A final significant feature of our period was the development of regional sentiments along linguistic lines. While associated at times with the demand for more jobs for relatively under-privileged groups of educated youth, such feelings often struck much deeper roots, bound up as it was with the emergence of powerful literary and cultural trends in the different regional languages. A movement for a separate province began developing in the Andhra districts of Madras from about 1911, fuelled by complaints about Telegu under-representation in the services voiced through journals like the *Deshabhimani* of Guntur, and inspired also by works like *Andhrula Charitramu.* Annual Andhra Conferences (later called the Andhra Mahasabha) were held from 1913 onwards, whose resolutions demanded also the use of the mother-tongue as medium of instruction. The main support came from the Krishna-Godavari delta region, where prosperous urban elements had fairly close connections with a broad middle peasant stratum, creating a wider base for political agitation than anywhere else in Madras Presidency. Nationalist leaders like Konda Venkatappayya and Pattabhi Sitaramayya were active in the Andhra movement, and in 1918 Congress conceded the demand for a separate 'Andhra Circle', within its own organization.

While a clear-cut demand for a linguistic state had as yet emerged only in Andhra, the development of regional languages everywhere fostered a variety of sometimes contradictory political trends. Malayalam, as we have seen, had become a powerful vehicle for social reform and patriotism. 'Thy slavery is thy destiny, O Mother! Thy sons, blinded by caste, clash among themselves/And get killed; what for is freedom then?' wrote the Ezhava poet Kumaran Asan in 1908, and in the 1920s Vallathol's poetry would become a major force in the propagation of Gandhian ideas in Kerala. Anti-Brahman movements in Tamilnadu were closely associated with the formation of Tamil Sangams in Madura, Madras, and other towns which stimulated interest in ancient Tamil classics and began emphasizing the pre-Sanskrit and non-Aryan 'Dravidian' heritage of the south. The *Ramayana* was turned on its head to glorify Ravana against Rama, and it is interesting that in Maharashtra, too, Satyashodhak propaganda sometimes included songs mourning the murder of Shambuk the untouchable boy by Rama, and revived an old Maratha peasant cult of Bali-Raj slain by Sugriv and Rama. From Phule onwards, who in 1869 had written a ballad hailing Shivaji as 'Shudra king', non-Brahmans also developed an image of Shivaji quite distinct to that propagated by Tilak or Ranade—not the orthodox anti-Muslim hero inspired by Ramdas to protect cows and Brahmans, nor the liberal unifier of high and low castes through *bhakti,* but a rebel against caste tyranny whose work was ruined by the later Brahmanical Peshwa usurpation.

Bengal in 1905 had given the first clear proof of the strength of regional sentiments, and C.R. Das in his 1917 Bhowanipur address tried to strike that same chord: 'The Bengalee might be a Hindu or Musalman or Christian, but he confined to be a Bengalee all the same'. More than ever before, Tagore dminated the cultural world of the educated Bengali (particularly after winning the Nobel Prize in 1913), though there was one important innovation which he took up but did not directly initiate—the use of the colloquial form in literature, pioneered by the *Sabuj Patra* literary group in 1915. Politically, however, Rabindranath was out on a limb after 1908: having broken with a nationalism he considered to be over-narrow and revivalist, he was preaching a universal humanism which his critics (like C.R. Das, for instance) considered somewhat unrealistic.

The educated Bengali with his lead in jobs and professions was very unpopular among his neighbours, and in Bihar an agitation by Kayastha professionals under Sachchidananda Sinha for a separate province, complete with university and high court, accompanied and followed the formation of the new province of Bihar and Orissa in 1911. Over much of northern India, Urdu remained the prime literary language, with a rich tradition best represented in this period by Muhammed Iqbal. Hindu-revivalist pressures were gradually leading, however, to its decline in the face of Hindi—a gain for populism, to some extent (limited by the fact that literary Hindi was often a highly Sanskritized and artificial construct), but a major blow to communal unity. Even Prem Chand began his literary career in Urdu, switching over to Hindi after 1915 as he found publication difficult. His early writings already struck a distinative political note: *Soz-i-Vatan* (1908), a collection of short stories, referred in its preface to the partition of Bengal as having 'awakened ideas of revolt in the hearts of the people', and the novel *Jalvai-i-Isar* (1912) modelled its hero on Vivekananda.

Indian society and politics were thus full of complexities and contradictions. From 1919 onwards, all-India nationalism under Gandhi would begin to plumb with varying success some of these lower depths.

Chapter 5
MASS NATIONALISM—EMERGENCE AND PROBLEMS: 1917–1927

WAR, REFORMS AND SOCIETY

The Montford Reforms

The war and the immediate post-war years witnessed truly dramatic changes in Indian life, the three universally accepted crucial landmarks being constitutional reforms (Secretary of State Montagu's declaration of 20 August 1917, followed by the Montagu-Chelmsford Report of 1918 and the Government of India Act of 1919), the emergence of Gandhi as leader of a qualitatively new all-India mass nationalism, and important shifts in India's colonial economy. Considerable differences exist, however, as regards the precise nature and significance of these new features and their mutual interaction.

Liberal-imperialist scholars have at times been ecstatic about the 'Montford' reforms as positive proof of basic British good intentions. Montagu's 20 August Commons declaration that British policy in India would henceforth have as its overall objective 'the gradual development of self-governing institutions, with a view to the progressive realization of responsible government in India as an integral part of the British Empire', certainly seems a clear break with the old line of British Indian development towards at best 'representative' government (elected legislators, even elected majorities, but with no control at all over the executive). The problems of realizing 'responsible government' 'progressively' was tackled in 1919 by provincial autonomy and the peculiar device of 'dyarchy', transferring certain functions of provincial governments (education, health, agriculture, local bodies) to ministers responsible to legislative assemblies while keeping others subjects 'reserved'. As with the Morley-Minto reforms, there has been some controversy about the respective contributions of London or Delhi, the Secretary of State or the Viceroy, in making the reforms. Montagu on the whole has enjoyed a much better press, thanks in large part to his own *Indian Diary* (1930) where he portrayed himself as a crusading reformer; Chelmsford has recently found his advocate, however, in P.G. Robb.

A closer look at the reform process reveals it to have been considerably less novel or far-reaching. Devolution for financial motives, shifting local expenditure on locally raised and managed revenues, goes back, as we have already seen, to Mayo and Ripon, and in 1907 a Decentralization Commission had been appointed to go into the whole question. Hardinge's despatch of 25 August 1911 had implicitly argued that the next dose of political concessions should take the form of some kind of provincial autonomy and self-government since this would keep the central authority safely with the British. Though Secretary of State Crewe had then rejected the whole idea of any kind of Indian self-government as something 'as remote as any Atlantis or Erehwon', war pressures and weaknesses soon caused considerable rethinking. Chelmsford's administration made a number of concessions to Indian public opinion—'lubricants', as Montagu was to later describe them. War finance demanded a hike in cotton import duties, and these were raised from 3½% to 7½% in March 1917 without increasing the countervailing excise on Indian textiles. Indian opinion had always been critical of the export of coolies through the indentured labour system, and now that the army, too, wanted a ban on emigration to help military recruitment, Chelmsford readily accepted the demand in 1917. The Viceroy also urged a hesitant Secretary of State (Austin Chamberlain) to come forward with a general statement of objectives. His telegram of 18 May 1917 made interesting references, not only to the Home Rule agitation (at its height during these months, and making the Bombay Governor Willingdon an ardent advocate of some such declaration), but to the possible impact on India of the overthrow of Tsarist autocracy in Russia in March 1917. Chamberlain's replacement by Montagu in July 1917 only hastened an already well-advanced process. Robb has acclaimed Chelmsford's foresight and liberalism in advocating a statement of goals; more cynical historians might feel that such a declaration was preferable from the British point of view precisely because it dangled a vague and general promise without involving any definite immediate action.

At the level of specific reforms, the Government of India's Despatch of 24 November 1916 had visualized elected majorities in the provinces but not any kind of executive responsibility. It was being increasingly felt, however, that such an extension of the Morley-Minto line of development would only create a powerful permanent opposition in councils, without adding to the number of Indian collaborators. Here an important role was played by an influential group around the London journal *Round Table* (Lionel Curtis, Philip Kerr, William Duke, and others), which felt that it would be disastrous to give elected non-officials more power without some amount of executive responsibility, and came forward with the idea of dyarchy in provinces.

The Government of India Act of 1919 set up a bicameral system at the centre (Council of State and Legislative Assembly, with elected majorities but no control over ministers and a Viceregal veto plus 'certificate' procedure of pushing through rejected bills) and considerably enlarged electorates to 5½ million in provinces and 1½ million for the Imperial Legislature. The basic innovation—dyarchy—transferred only departments with less political weight and little funds to ministers responsible to provincial legislatures, skillfully drawing Indian politicians into a patronage rat-race which would probably also discredit them, as real improvements in education, health, agriculture, and local bodies required far more money than the British would be willing to assign to these branches. Officials remained in control of more vital departments like law and order or finance, and provincial governors too had veto and certificate powers. Revenue resources were divided between the centre and the provinces, with land revenue for instance going to the latter while income tax remained with the Government of India. Despite some theoretical criticism made of separate electorates in the Montagu-Chelmsford Report, communal representation and reservations were in practice not only retained but considerably extended, the British conceding with suspicious ease Justice Party demands for reservations for non-Brahmans in Madras.

Recent Cambridge historiography has contributed considerably to the development of this less starry-eyed view of the 1919 Reforms, relating them rather to the twin imperial requirements of financial devolution and need for a wider circle of Indian collaborators. Much more controversial, however, is the direct cause-effect relationship which it sometimes seeks to establish between the Reforms and the emergence of mass politics. The Act of 1919 broadened electorates, it is argued, and therefore politicians were forced to cultivate a more democratic style. As elsewhere, the Cambridge interpretation is not incorrect, but seriously incomplete; it may well explain certain types of politics and politicians, but hardly the basic fact of the tremendous post-war mass awakening. The Justice Party in Madras or non-Brahman and (a little later) 'depressed classes' movements in Maharashtra were no doubt greatly stimulated by the reality or possibility of special reservations. Even among nationalists, Malaviya's protege Indra Narain Dwivedy started a United Provinces Kisan Sabha with Allahabad Home Rule League funds in February 1918 with a fairly obvious electoral purpose, and Jawaharlal's wanderings among the *kisans* were welcomed by his father as late as June 1920 as improving the former's election chances. Yet U.P. itself gives us a convincing counter-example, in the emergence of an initially quite autonomous grass-roots Kisan Sabha in Pratapgarh and Rae-Bareli under Baba Ramchandra in 1920. The most substantial section of Indian politicians did after all boycott elections under Gandhian leadership for some years, and the massive anti-imperialist upsurge of 1919–22 is surely much too big a thing to be explained by a paltry extension of voting rights to at most between one and three per cent of the adult population.

Impact of the War

Far more significant were the economic and social consequences of the First World War, bringing to the surface and sharpening the numerous contradictions between Indian and British interests already discussed in a previous chapter—drain of wealth, the decline of handicrafts, revenue pressures and obstacles to indigenous capitalist growth. In more specific terms, the War affected Indian life through massive recruitments, heavy taxes and war loans, and a very sharp rise in prices, and may be directly related to the two-fold extension of the national movement—towards considerable sections of the peasantry and towards business groups—which manifested itself immediately afterwards under Gandhi. In both cases—as well as with industrial labour which, also made a spectacular entry onto the national stage in the immediate post-war years—what is repeatedly evident is a combination of multiplying grievances with new moods of strength or hope: the classic historical formula for a potentially revolutionary situation. It must be added that the war affected different sections of the Indian people in varied and sometimes even opposite ways, and so simultaneously sharpened tensions within Indian society, too.

The 'drain of wealth' took on during the War years the character of a massive plunder of Indian human and material resources. The Indian army was expanded to 1.2 million, and thousands of Indians were sent off to die in a totally alien cause in campaigns which were often grossly mismanaged (like some of the offensives on the Western front, or in Mesopotamia where there was a first-class scandal in 1916 compelling Austin Chamberlain's resignation). Theoretically, voluntary recruitment often became near-compulsory, most notably in the Punjab under Lieutenant-Governor Michael O'Dwyer, where the Congress enquiry after the 1919 disturbances found numerous instances of coercion through *lambardars* (village chiefs). No less than 355,000 were recruited from the Punjab, and O'Dwyer in August 1918 boasted that the proportion of soldiers to the adult male population had been forced up from 1:150 to 1 : 44 in a single year in Gujranwala—a district which was to be noticeably militant during the Rowlatt Act disturbances. As for the pumping out of grain and raw materials for army needs, the following private comment of Bombay Governor Lloyd to Montagu on 10 January 1919 is illuminating: 'Large quantities of valuable fodder are being exported from here to Mesopotomia by the Army... Luckily the Horniman Press [a reference to the nationalist *Bombay Chronicle* edited by B.G. Horniman] have not tumbled to the fact that fodder is being exported while the Deccan starves'. (Quoted in A.D.D. Gordon, *Businessmen and Politics: Rising Nationalism and a Modernising Economy in Bombay, 1918–1933*, Delhi, 1978, pp. 33–4)

The 300% increase in defence expenditure inevitably meant not only war loans (again at times semi-compulsory) but a sharp rise in taxes and in fact significant changes in the entire financial structure. Though land revenue remained a major burden (provoking Gandhi's second campaign in India, the Kheda *satyagraha* of 1918), in general the land tax was by now governed by regulations permitting enhancements in temporarily settled areas only at 30-year intervals, and the British also could not afford to further alienate the class which was supplying the bulk of recruits. The axe had to fall heavily for the first time on trade and industry. Between 1913–14 and 1920–21, the share of customs in the total revenue of the Government of India went up from 8.9% to 14.8%, and in 1917, as we have seen, Lancashire protests had to be disregarded while imposing an import duty on cotton textiles of 7½%. Even more significant was the new importance of income tax, yielding only 2% of gross revenues in 1911–12, but 11.75% in 1919–20. Individual returns were demanded for the first time from 1917–18, and this helped to draw into the net large numbers of Indian merchants following traditional business practices. In the same year a supertax was imposed on both companies and undivided Hindu business families, followed in 1919 by a temporary excess profits duty.

War expenditure and transport bottlenecks and disruption (e.g., the sharp fall in shipping-space available for non-military needs, causing a decline in imports) led to a big increase in prices. An official Statistical Abstract on prices gave the following all-India index numbers: (1873=100)

1913	1914	1915	1916	1917	1918	1919	1920	1921	1922	1923
143	147	152	184	196	225	276	281	236	232	215

(Judith Brown, *Gandhi's Rise to Power 1915–1922*, p. 125)

Even more significant than the absolute increase was its differential character. Prices of industrial goods were inflated by war demand, those of imported manufactures also went up sharply as supply declined due to lack of cargo space and diversion of European industries to military needs. Export prices of Indian gricultural goods did not go up (specially raw jute) in the same proportion due to the dislocation in world economic relations. Thus a peasant in Champaran in 1917, for instance, would find himself paying considerably more for cloth, salt or kerosene, while the prices of the agricultural exports of his district like indigo or rice were not increasing to anything like the same extent. The shift in the terms of trade against agriculture thus adversely affected better-off peasant groups producing for the market. Poorer peasants or landless labourers who had to buy the bulk of their food were hit hard by yet another differential which seems to have been a long-term tendency—prices of coarse foodgrains which constituted the staple of the poor tended to go up faster than that of higher-quality crops like rice or wheat, though the latter of course remained more expensive. This was clearly a trend connected with commercialization which encouraged a shift in acreage to higher priced crops. To take an example again from another early Gandhian base, in Ahmedabad district, taking 1873=100, the price of wheat was 166 and 259 in 1914 and 1918, that of *bajra* 220 and 410. Price statistics in United Provinces reveal a similar picture : thus wheat went up by 250% between 1861–65 and 1917–21, but barley by 300% and *arhar* by 400%.

While the war meant misery and a fall in living standards for the majority of the Indian people (the consumption of cotton piecegoods, for instance, went down from 5102 million yards in 1913–14 to 2899 million yards in 1919–20), it also contributed to fabulous profits by business groups taking advantage of the War demand (of cloth for uniforms, for example), the decline in foreign competition, the price-differential between agricultural raw materials (raw jute or raw cotton) and industrial goods, and the stagnation or decline in real wages. The super-profits were partly dissipated by excessive dividends, but still enabled substantial industrial expansion during a short but intense post-war boom (1919–20 to 1921–22). The benefits in eastern India went mainly to British jute mill magnates: raw jute prices collapsed during the war years due to the cutting-off of European demand, war needs boosted the prices of jute manufactures (e.g., sandbags or canvas) and the ratio of net profits (excluding interests) to paid-up capital in jute mills was as high as 75 in 1916. A rising group of Calcutta based-Marwari businessmen, however, also accumulated considerable wealth during these years through speculation in the jute trade, and soon after the war, G.D. Birla and Swarupchand Hukumchand would start the first Indian-owned jute mills around Calcutta. But the really decisive change was in the cotton-textile industry of Bombay and Ahmedabad, where the slackening of Lancashire competition enabled a real breakthrough by Indian capitalism. The war brought about an element of fiscal protection due to government financial needs (the 7½% import duty of 1917, while the excise on Indian textiles remained unchanged at 3½%), a sharp decline in import of piecegoods and yarn, a rise in Indian textile mills production, a decline in handlooms (hit both by the higher cost of imported yarn and by Indian factory competition) and—a portent of future problems—the beginning of an invasion of Indian markets by Japanese cotton goods. Amiya Bagchi gives us the following figures illustrating these tendencies (*Private Investment in India,* pp. 226–7, 238).

(All figures in million yards.)

	Import of Cotton Piecegoods from U.K.	*Import of Cotton Piecegoods from Japan*	*Indian Handloom Production of Cotton Piecegoods*	*Indian Mills Production of Cotton Piecegoods*
1913–14	3104	9	1018.8	1171.1
1914–15	2378	16	1136.0	1175.9
1915–16	2049	39	943.2	1496.1
1916–17	1786	100	645.6	1606.1
1917–18	1430	95	741.2	1615.6
1918–19	867	238	890.0	1481.8
1919–20	976	76	506.0	1630.0
1920–21	1292	170	931.2	1563.1
1921–22	955	90	938.0	1716.0
1922–23	1453	108	1084.0	1720.8

Thus Indian mill production had surpassed Lancashire imports—a decisive change which proved irreversible.

The war years also led to certain shifts in British Indian Government policy towards Indian industrial development out of a combination of financial demands (which led to hikes in import duties) and the realization that a certain minimum of economic self-sufficiency was a strategic necessity. An Indian Industrial Commission was set up in 1916 under Thomas Holland, and the Montford Report was accompanied by the 'Fiscal Autonomy Convention'—a Joint Parliamentary Committee recommendation that London should not override Indian fiscal decisions so long as the Government of India and the new Legislature were in agreement. Such things did represent some modification of earlier British policies. In 1910, Morley had halted the efforts being made by Alfred Chatterton (an unusually enterprising Madras civilian who had tried to promote at state initiative aluminium and chrome tanning industries) through a note bluntly asserting the principles of *laissez-faire*. It would be unhistorical, however, to overemphasize the significance of this shift. As his later career as head of the department of industries in Mysore State revealed, Chatterton wanted at best to develop certain light industries. (e.g., sandalwood oil and soap in Mysore) which would not have affected in any basic way the total structure of dependence. Mysore's remarkable Dewan Visvesvaraya (1911–18), in sharp contrast did attempt something like a total change, through his very ambitious projects of the Krishnaraja Sagar Dam and the Bhadravati Iron Works—and in 1918 the British played a notable part in forcing his resignation. As for the much lauded Fiscal Autonomy Convention, the proviso requiring agreement between Viceroy and Legislature robbed it of much of its value, for the Viceroy after all was a British official.

The new strength of Indian capitalism was accompanied by the development of country-wide connections (particularly among Marwaris) and a sense of accumulating grievances over issues like war taxation and post-war uncertainties in the rupee-sterling exchange ratio. The rising Bombay nationalist lawyer Bhulabhai Desai organized a petition in September 1918 against compulsory income-tax returns which small traders following traditional business methods were finding particularly irksome. The exchange ratio fluctuated wildly—going up to 2s 4d in December 1919 and then down to 1s in early 1921 before the Hilton-Young Commission of 1926 pegged it to 1s 6d. The British made repeated efforts to maintain a high ratio, since this would minimize the Government's sterling expenditure on Home Charges, benefit Englishmen interested in repatriating pensions or profits, and stimulate import of Lancashire goods by lowering prices. Indian business groups in contrast persistently demanded a lower, 1s 4d ratio throughout the 1920s and 30s to make imports more expensive and boost exports of Indian cotton manufactures and agricultural raw materials by reducing their prices. In the short-run context of 1919–21, the fluctuation in the exchange-ratio were resented also by Indian importers of Lancashire goods since it made keeping of contracts with British exporting firms difficult—a point on which the Nagpur Congress of December 1920 was to pass a special resolution.

Greater business interest and involvement in nationalism were thus in the logic of things. As we shall see, this was to be an important feature of Gandhian movements from the beginning, Thus the Sabarmati *asrama* (1915) received substantial financial support from the Ahmedabad mill-owner Ambalal Sarabhai, 74% of the 680 signatories in Bombay city to Gandhi's March 1919 *satyagraha* pledge were merchants, Bombay contributed no less than ₹37½ lakhs out of the ₹1 crore raised for the Tilak Swaraj Fund in 1921, and collective pledges by Indian merchants not to indent British goods became a principal form of the boycott (in sharp contrast to Swadeshi Bengal). Yet business support was to remain always equivocal and very far from uniform. For the moment we need only note that small and middling traders tended (both in 1919–22 and again during Civil Disobedience) to be more pro-nationalist than big industrialists. Thus A.D. Gordon's recent micro-study of the Bombay business world between 1918 and 1933 reveals a complex pattern of mill-owners and cotton exporters utilizing Government contacts to regulate and reduce raw cotton prices in the immediate post-war years. The 'marketeers' or traditional merchants who brought raw cotton into Bombay city expressed their resentment partly through support to nationalism at a time when the business magnate Purshottamdas Thakurdas with considerable cotton-exporting interests was organizing an Anti-Non-Cooperation Association (1920–21).

The loyalism of most big industrialists can be related also to their need for state support against labour unrest. A significant increase had taken place in the number of the working class. Employment in organized industries and plantations went up from 2,105,824 in 1911 to 2,681,125 in 1921. Wages remained low in a period of high prices and super-profits for employers, and a relative labour-shortage in the immediate post-war years (due to rapid industrial expansion at a time when the influence epidemic of 1919 was discouraging emigration to towns) created for a brief while a somewhat stronger bargaining position. The result was what Chelmsford was to describe in December 1920 as 'a sort of epidemic strike fever'. While the really big strike wave began in late 1919 and will be discussed in a later section, its precursors included the Ahmedabad strike of March 1918 led by Gandhi, and the great Bombay textile strike of January 1919. Ravinder Kumar's detailed study of the latter emphasizes its basically spontaneous nature, though jobbers did play some part in organizing it as in 1908. Workers of C.N. Wadia's Century Mills went on strike from 31 December for a 25% increase in wages and a month's salary as bonus. An 80–100% rise in foodgrain prices had been counterbalanced by only a 15% increase in wages in Bombay city between 1914–18, even though the Wadia enterprises had made a fantastic profit of ₹22.5 lakhs in 1918—on a capital investment of ₹20 lakhs! The Century Mills workers began persuading other labourers of the Parel industrial area to join them from 9 January. Soon the entire textile working class of more than 100,000 were on the streets, closing down all 83 mills, and the strike spread to clerks of mercantile houses, dock labourers of the Royal Indian Marine, and Parel railway engineering workers. Leadership was sought to be provided by a few radical lawyers and Home Rule League politicians (H.B. Mandavale, Kanji Dwarkadas, Umar Sobhani) who addressed labour meetings, as well as by S.K. Bole's Kamgar Hitvardhak Sabha which had been trying to mobilize workers through their jobbers on non-Brahman lines since 1909. But it is interesting that labour rallies repeatedly rejected the counsels of moderation offered by such would-be leaders, and the mediation efforts of Police Commissioner

C.A. Vincent could succeed in ending the strike (on 21 January) only after he had persuaded the mill-owners' Association to grant a 20% increase in wages and a special bonus.

The war and immediate post-war years mark the real beginning of the Indian trade union movement. The first organization with regular membership lists and subscriptions, the Madas Labour Union of April 1918, was started by two young men connected with Annie Besant's *New India* (G. Ramanajulu Naidu and G. Chelvapathi Chetti) and presided over by Besant's colleague B.P. Wadia. An important part was also played by T.V. Kalyanasundar Mudaliar (popularly known as Thiru Vi Ka), leading Madras city Congress and non-Brahman nationalist leader and Tamil literary figure. Home Rule Leaguers like Baptista and the *Bombay Chronicle* of B.G. Horniman also made some contributions to the beginning of trade unions in Bombay. Unions came in a flood in 1920, some 125 of them being recorded by November of that year when the first All-India Trade Union Congress met at Bombay. In general, however, as in Bombay in January 1919, the pressures for militancy came from below rather than from these early unions which usually played a restraining role. The early middle-class union leaders were at best inspired by nationalism, but often were quite loyalist in their politics, like N.M. Joshi in Bombay or K.C. Roychaudhuri in Calcutta. The restraining role was most unequivocal, as we shall see, in the Gandhian Textile Labour Association (Majoor Mahajan) of Ahmedabad, but Wadia, too, opposed a strike in Binny's in July 1918 on the ground that soldiers needed uniforms.

Strikes were only one form of expression of acute popular distress and discontent caused by factors like rising prices, a poor harvest and scarcity conditions over much of the country in 1918–1919, the influenza epidemic of 1918–19, and artisan unemployment (handloom cotton production, as the table on p. 149 indicates, touched an all-time low in 1919–20). A more elemental form was that of food riots: the looting of small-town markets and city grain shops, and the seizure of debt-bonds. 115 grain shops were looted in the Bombay mill area in the food riots of early 1918, while the account books of Marwaris were seized by railwaymen. There were food riots in the Krishna-Godavari delta region in May 1918, followed by three days of intensive riots in Madras city in September in which textile and railway workers played an important part. In Bengal 38 *hat* looting cases with 859 convictions were reported from Noakhali, Chittagong, Rangpur, Dinajpur, Khulna, 24 Parganas and Jessore districts in 1919–20. Such outbursts could take on varying significance depending on local political conditions: contributing to anti-Marwari rioting by Muslims in central

Calcutta in September 1918, but also playing a significant part in the very widespread Anti-Rowlatt Act upsurge in many Indian cities in April 1919.

It would be quite inaccurate, however, to relate the post-war mass awakening to specific economic factors, alone. We cannot afford to forget that what was happening in India was in the broadest sense a part of a worldwide upsurge, anti-capitalist in the developed countries and anti-imperialist in the colonies and semi-colonies. In ways almost impossible to document but none the less important, Indian soldiers coming home from distant lands must have carried back with them something of the new world-wide revolutionary mood. Military service certainly made Kazi Nazrul Islam of Bengal into a poet with definite socialist leanings, while in an agrarian riot at Karhaiya in March 1921 (on the border between Rae-Bareli and Pratapgarh districts in U.P.) police reports spoke of the local leader Brijpal Singh as an ex-sepoy who 'obviously had great control over the crowd which was not lacking in a certain degree of military discipline'.

Most far-reaching of all ultimately was the impact of the Bolshevik Revolution of November 1917. British fears on this score were certainly grossly exaggerated. In a panic reminiscent of that caused by the French Revolution, official reports from 1919–20 onwards discovered Bolshevik ideas and Soviet agents everywhere, with even people like Gandhi or C.R. Das at times not above suspicion. ('Honest, but a Bolshevik and for that reason very dangerous', was the Bombay Governor Willingdon's description of Gandhi on 5 May 1918). To give only two examples, a C.I.D. report on the U.P. *kisan* agitation in February 1921 discovered notions that 'distinctly smack of Bolshevism', while Wilkinson's account of a peasant movement in far-off Mewar in the same year alleged that the Maharana was 'said to have been threatened to be meted the fate of Czar'. Wildly inaccurate so far as specific connections are concerned, this imperialist panic still had an objective basis in the rumours about 1917 that were spreading among wide sections of the Indian people. Revolutionary nationalists quickly saw in Bolshevik Russia a potentially replacing defeated Germany, and early visitors to Moscow, as we shall see, included Mahendra Pratap, M.N. Roy, Abani Mukherji, Virendranath Chattopadhyay and Bhupen Dutt. For the nationalist-minded educated Indian public, the very fact that the British rulers so obviously hated and feared revolutionary Russia was a factor contributing to a sympathetic interest and response. The soaring idealism and internationalism of early Soviet foreign policy under Lenin and Trotsky had a major impact: the call for an immediate peace without annexations and indemnities, the proclamation of the right of nations to self-determination (quickly implemented in the case of Finland), and the publication of secret treaties which had promised Russia enormous territorial gains (including Constantinople) and privileges, and which were all 'torn to pieces and repudiated' within days of the Bolshevik seizure of power. And while definite news about Russian internal developments was extremely difficult to obtain, vague rumours were spreading about a total change, a world being turned upside down with the dispossessed coming into their own.

It is in this total context that we have to place the rise of Mahatma Gandhi, a relative outsider in Indian politics when he returned from South Africa in 1915, who attained a position of supreme leadership by the end of 1920.

MAHATMA GANDHI

The Appeal of Gandhi

The South African experience (1893–1914) contributed in a number of different ways to the foundations of Gandhi's ideology and methods, as well as to his later achievements in India. Down to 1906, Gandhi as a rising lawyer-politician had followed the usual 'Moderate' techniques of prayers and petitions in the struggle against racial discrimination affecting Indians in Natal (disenfranchisement and restrictions on landholding and trade), and his movement had essentially been one of merchants and lawyers alone. A totally new departure began with the three campaigns of passive resistance (soon redefined as *satyagraha* in 1907) of 1907–08, 1908–11, and 1913–14. The issues involved were the 1906 Transvaal ordinance on compulsory registration and passes for Indians, the 1913 immigration restrictions, the derecognition of non-Christian Indian marriages while deciding the cases of new entrants, and the £3 tax on ex-indentured labourers. The peculiar conditions of South Africa allowed the amalgamation into a successful movement of people of disparate religions, communities and classes: Hindus, Muslims, Parsis and Christians, Gujaratis and south Indians, upper-class merchants and lawyers as well as Newcastle mine-workers whom Gandhi led in a memorable strike and cross-country march in October 1913. It needs to be emphasized that this experience made Gandhi into potentially much more of an all-India figure from the beginning of his work in India than any other politician, all of whom (like Tilak, Lajpat or Pal, for example) had essentially regional bases. Gandhi's life-long recognition of the necessity and possibility of Hindu-Muslim unity certainly goes back to his South African movements in which Muslim merchants had been extremely active. South Africa also made him something of an international celebrity, while the connections which many South African Indians still had with their original homes in parts of the country helped to spread the name of Gandhi throughout India. Thirteen out of the first 25 inmates of the Sabarmati *Asrame* (1915) came from Tamilnadu—something which would have been inconceivable then for any other Indian leader.

The basic Gandhian style was worked out in South Africa after 1906. This involved careful training of disciplined cadres (in the Phoenix Settlement and the Tolstoy Farm), non-violent *satyagraha* involving peaceful violation of specific laws (compulsory registration, entry permits, trade licenses, etc.), mass courting of arrests, and occasional *hartals* and spectacular marches. It included a combination of apparently quixotic methods together with meticulous attention to organizational and particularly financial details; a readiness for negotiations and compromise, at times leading to abrupt unilateral withdrawals which were by no means popular (like the January 1908 withdrawal of the first *satyagraha* on the strength of a verbal promise from Smuts which was soon broken—Gandhi was beaten up by a militant Pathan after this unexpected retreat); and the cultivation of what non-disciples usually considered to be the Gandhian 'fads' (vegetarianism, nature-therapy, experiments in sexual self-restraint, etc). The net impact had a clear two-fold character: drawing-in the masses, while at the same time keeping mass activity strictly pegged down to certain forms predetermined by the leader, and above all to the methods of nonviolence.

Non-violence or *ahimsa* and *satyagraha* to Gandhi personally constituted a deeply-felt and worked-out philosophy owing something to Emerson, Thoreau and Tolstoy but also revealing considerable originality. The search for truth was the goal of human life, and as no one could ever be sure of having attained the ultimate truth, use of violence to enforce one's own necessarily partial understanding of it was sinful. As a politician and not just a saint, Gandhi in practice sometimes settled for less than complete non-violence (as when he campaigned for military recruitment in 1918 in the hope of winning post-war political concessions), and his repeated insistence that even violence was preferable to cowardly surrender to injustice sometimes created delicate problems of interpretation. But historically much more significant than this personal philosophy (fully accepted only by a relatively small group of disciples) was the way in which the resultant perspective of controlled mass participation objectively fitted in with the interests and sentiments of socially-decisive sections of the Indian people. Indian politicians before Gandhi, as we have seen, had tended to oscillate between Moderate 'mendicancy' and individual terrorism basically because of their social inhibitions about uncontrolled mass movements. The Gandhian model would prove acceptable also to business groups, as well as to relatively better-off or locally dominant sections of the peasantry, all of whom stood to lose something if political struggle turned into uninhibited and violent social revolution. In more general terms, as we shall see, the doctrine of *ahimsa* lay at the heart of the essentially unifying, 'umbrella-type' role assumed by Gandhi and the Gandhian Congress, mediating internal social conflicts, contributing greatly to joint national struggle against foreign rule, but also leading to periodic retreats and some major reverses.

A third, crucial, aspect of the Gandhian appeal lay in his social ideals, put forward most unambiguously in *Hind Swaraj* (1909). The basic point made in this pamphlet is that the real enemy was not British political domination, but the whole of modern industrial civilization. Taking over and extending the Romantic critique of industrialism developed by mid-nineteenth century English writers like Carlyle and Ruskin, (whose *Unto His Last* remained a favourite text of his), Gandhi argued that mere political *Swaraj* would mean 'English rule without the Englishmen', while 'It would be folly to assume that an Indian Rockefeller would be better than the American Rockefeller. Railways, lawyers and doctors have impoverished the country'—railways have spread plague and produced famines by encouraging the export of foodgrains, lawyers have stimulated disputes in their greed for briefs and helped to maintain British rule by manning the law courts, western medicine is expensive and ruins natural health measures. The central passage reads: 'India's salvation consists in unlearning what she has learnt during the past 50 years or so. The railways, telegraphs, hospitals, lawyers, doctors and such like have all to go, and the so-called upper class have to learn to live consciously and religiously and deliberately the simple life of a peasant.'

The Gandhian social utopia as outlined in *Hind Swaraj* is undoubtedly unrealistic and indeed obscurantist if considered as a final remedy for the ills of India or of the world, and it never had much appeal for sophisticated urban groups which by the 1930s and 40s would turn increasingly to either capitalist or socialist solutions based on industrialization. But it did represent a response to the deeply alienating effects of 'modernization' particularly under colonial conditions. For the artisan ruined by factory industries, the peasant to whom law courts were a disastrous trap and going to a city hospital usually an expensive death-sentence, as well as to the rural or small-town intelligentsia for whom education had brought few material benefits, the anti-industrial theme had a real attraction, at least for some time. After his return to India, Gandhi concretized his message through programmes of *khadi,* village reconstruction, and (somewhat later) Harijan welfare. Once again, none of these really solved problems in the sense of changing social or economic relations, but, when tried out with sincerity and patience by devoted Gandhian constructive workers, they could improve to some limited extent the lot of the rural people. The message of self-reliance and self-help of the *Swadeshi* period thus acquired wider dimensions. It must be added that the peasant appeal of Gandhi was greatly helped also by his political style: travelling third-class, speaking in simple Hindustani, wearing a loin-cloth only from 1921 onwards, using the imagery of Tulsidas's Ramayana so deep-rooted in the popular religion of the north Indian Hindu rural masses. (Such use had its problems so far as Muslims were concerned, but more of that later on.)

The Role of Rumour

Yet the tremendous breadth of Gandhian movements cannot be explained purely by what Gandhi as a personality thought, stood for, or actually did. What we have to understand also is the role of rumour in a predominantly illiterate society going through a period of acute strain and tensions. From out of their misery and hope, varied sections of the Indian people seem to have fashioned their own images of Gandhi, particularly in the earlier days when he was still to most people a distant, vaguely-glimpsed or heard-of tale of a holy man with miracle-working powers. Thus peasants could imagine that Gandhi would end *zamindari* exploitation, agricultural labourers of U.P. believed that he would 'provide holdings for them' (Viceroy Reading to the Secretary of State, 13 October 1921—*Reading Collection*), and Assam tea coolies left the plantations en masse in May 1921 saying that they were obeying Gandhi's orders. A C.I.D. report on the *kisan* movement in Allahabad district in January 1921 makes the same point in vivid detail: 'The currency which Mr Gandhi's name has acquired even in the remotest villages is astonishing. No one seems to know quite who or what he is, but it is an accepted fact that what he says is so, and what he orders must be done. He is a Mahatma or sadhu, a Pundit, a Brahman who lives at Allahabad, even at Deota... the real power of his name is perhaps to be traced back to the idea that it was he who got *bedakhli* (illegal eviction) stopped in Pratapgarh... as a general rule, Gandhi is not thought of as being antagonistic to Government, but only to the zamindars.... We are for Gandhiji and the Sarkar.' (*Home Political Deposit,* February 1921, No. 13) That a Gandhi-type leadership with strong religious overtones was something like a historical necessity in this period is indicated, as we shall see, by the emergence of a number of somewhat similar regional or local leaders in the early 1920s: Swami Viswananda and Swami Darshanananda among Bengal and Bihar miners, Swami Vidyananda in north Bihar, Baba Ramchandra in Pratapgarh, Swami Kumarananda in Rajasthan, Ananda Swami in Maharashtra, Alluri Sitarama Raju among the 'Rampa' tribals of Andhra. The dual nature of this process of image-building needs to be emphasized. As the Allahabad C.I.D. report indicates, peasants were giving the vague rumours about Gandhi a radical, anti-*zamindar* twist. But at the same time they were attributing their own achievements to him—for, if *bedakhli* had been restricted in Pratapgarh, it was due to peasant struggle under local leaders like Baba Ramchandra; Gandhi or the Congress leadership, as we shall see, had little or nothing to do with it directly. If, as would happen repeatedly from 1922 onwards, the Mahatma categorically ordered a retreat, the bulk of the masses would obey. The peasants still needed to be represented by a saviour from above—a crucial limitation which is perhaps at times underestimated by some recent scholars who, reacting against elite historiography, tend to somewhat romanticize the spontaneous revolutionary potential of the rural misses.

The millenarian vision faded in course of time, and was in fact curbed by the very growth of Gandhian Congress organization and discipline. Thus a recurrent pattern in Gandhian movements would be a kind of inverse relationship between organizational power and the strength of elemental, often violent and radical, popular outbursts.

Champaran, Kheda, Ahmedabad

Gandhi returned from South Africa in 1915 having won a partial victory there. Smuts' Indian Relief Act of June 1914 abolished the £ 3 tax and recognized Indian marriages, though discrimination certainly did not end and the broader question of white racist exploitation of Africans and Indian alike had hardly been touched upon as yet. During the next three years, Gandhi acquired the reputation of a man who would take up local wrongs (of Champaran indigo cultivators, Ahmedabad textile workers, and Kheda peasants) and usually manage to do something concrete about them—a political style in sharp contrast to the established Congress (and Home Rule League) pattern of starting with somewhat abstract all-India issues or programmes and proceeding from top downwards. Judith Brown has argued that the main importance of these early movements lay in the recruitment of 'sub-contractors' who would serve as his life-long lieutenants—like Rajendra Prasad, Anugraha Narayan Sinha and J.B. Kripalani in Champaran, or Vallabhbhai Patel, Mahadev Desai, Indulal Yajnik and Shankarlal Banker in the two Gujarat movements. But her own and other available accounts reveal other important dimensions, too: the existence in every case of pressures from below, a note of millenarian appeal at times, and the first indications also of a restraining role.

Champaran, as we have seen, had a long history of anti-planter discontent and agitation. Jacques Pouchepadass's detailed analysis makes clear that the crucial mediating role in peasant mobilization was played not so much by Gandhian converts from the small-town intelligentsia (*vakils* like Rajendra Prasad, A.N. Sinha, or Braj Kishore Prasad, or the Muzaffarpur College teacher J.B. Kripalani—the 'subcontractors' of Judith Brown) but by a somewhat lower stratum of rich and middle peasants (Rajkumar Shukla who had gone to Lucknow to invite Gandhi, Sant Raut, Khendar Rai), local *mahajans* and traders who resented planter competition in moneylending and trade, and a few village *mukhtars* (attorneys) and school-teachers (Pir Muhammad, Harbans Sahai). Gandhi's own role was at first sight confined to instituting an open enquiry in July 1917 (after a local ban on his entry had been rescinded by higher authorities in face of a *satyagraha* threat), and giving all-India publicity to the grievances of the Champaran indigo cultivators—an enquiry and a publicity which led to the abolition of *tinkathia*. Yet the psychological impact far surpassed the concrete activities: Gandhi 'is daily transfiguring the imaginations of masses of ignorant men with visions of an early millenium', reported the Bettiah S.D.O. on 29 April 1917. A *raiyat* compared Gandhi to Ramchandra, and declared before the enquiry committee that 'tenants would not fear the Rakhshasa—planters now that Gandhi was there'. Rumours were current that Gandhi had been sent by the Viceroy or the King to overrule all local officials and planters; and even that the British would leave Champaran in a few months. There were some signs of militancy going beyond Gandhian limits—a few attacks on indigo factories and cases of incendiarism, for instance. By late 1917, peasants were at times refusing to pay even the reduced *sharahbeshi* which had been accepted by the Gandhian settlement. Gandhi left behind him a group of fifteen volunteers who tried to start constructive village work, and told Rajendra Prasad that the only real solution 'was the education of raiyats and a constant process of mediation between them and the planters'—but such efforts do not seem to have been particularly successful at Champaran, where only three village-level workers were still active by May 1918.

The Gandhian intervention proved much more of a permanent success at Kheda district of Gujarat, a land of relatively prosperous Kanbi-Patidar peasant proprietors producing foodgrains, cotton and tobacco for nearby Ahmedabad (and not of big *zamindars,* planters, and extremely impoverished petty tenants, as Champaran was). Many Patidars had gone to South Africa as traders, and primary education was fairly widespread among them. As David Hardiman has pointed out in a recent micro-study of Kheda, a late-nineteenth century 'golden age' here was succeeded by repeated famine and plague after 1899, making revenue payments (which were seldom reduced) very difficult. The 'lesser Patidars', living in villages occupying a lower position in the marriage network within the caste, were the worst affected, for the superior Patidars could accumulate extra wealth through dowries and often got employment also in the civil service of nearby Baroda state—and it was the former group which was to provide the most permanent support to Gandhian nationalism. In 1917–18, a poor harvest coincided with high prices of kerosene, ironware, cloth, and salt, while the low-caste Baraiyas whom the Kheda Patidars employed as farm labour had successfully forced up wages. 'We have to pay six annas for labour which we used to get for three', a Patidar complained in April 1918. The initiative for no-revenue (to press the case for remissions in the context of the poor harvest) really came not from Gandhi or Ahmedabad politicians, but from local village leaders like Mohanlal Pandya of Kapadvanj *taluka* in Kheda in November 1917; it was taken up by Gandhi after a lot of hesitation only on 22 March 1918. The delay proved unwise, as by that time the poorer peasants had already been coerced to pay up revenue, and a good *rabi* crop had weakened the case for remissions. Kheda, the first real Gandhian peasant *satyagraha* in India, consequently proved a rather patchy affair, affecting only 70 villages out of 559, and having to be called off in June after no more than a token concession. But sustained village work would build up over the years a solid Gandhian base in Gujarat, particularly in the Anand and Borsad *talukas* of the rich tobacco and dairy-farming Charotar tract of Kheda, and Bardoli *taluka* of Surat (where Gandhians linked up with the constructive work already started by Kunvarji Mehta's Patidar Yuvak Mandal). The deep Patidar faith in Gandhian non-violence followed not just from traditional Vaishnava-*bhakti* influences, but from the fact that 'as property-owners they did not want violent revolution'. The Kheda *satyagraha* has been followed in fact by a spate of dacoities in Patidar houses by Baraiyas who apparently felt that British law and order was collapsing. That the Gujarat peasants had a mind of their own, and were not simply responding to strings pulled by Gandhi's 'sub-contractors' as Judith Brown likes to assume, is proved by the extremely poor response that Gandhi and his followers obtained in Kheda for their war recruitment campaign in the summer of 1918—'villagers who had met them previously with, garlands, now refused them food', (quotations from Hardiman, *Peasant Agitations in Kheda District, Gujarat, 1917–1934*, Sussex thesis, 1975, pp. 113, 158, 151).

Unlike the Champaran and Kheda movements against white planters and revenue authorities, Gandhi's intervention in Ahmedabad in February-March 1918 was in a situation of purely internal conflict between Gujarat mill-owners and their workers. The textile magnate Ambalal Sarabhai had been an early contributor to the Sabarmati *Asrama* finances, while his sister Anasuya Behn had become a Gandhian disciple, visiting Kheda during the *satyagraha* and starting nightschools among mill-workers. The mill-owners' attempt to end the 'plague bonus' of 1917 in a period of rising prices led to a confrontation despite Gandhi's mediation attempts, with the workers demanding a 50% wage-hike in lieu of the plague bonus (later reduced under Gandhi's advice to 35%) and the owners offering only 20%. The Ahmedabad strike of March 1918 under Gandhi's leadership was notable for the Mahatma's first use of the weapon of the hunger-strike (from 15 March). Conventionally this is described as a successful attempt to rally the flagging spirit of the workers, an alternative to militant picketing which Gandhi strictly forbade. The District Magistrate's report quoted by Judith Brown gives an interestingly different version: the workers, we are told, had 'assailed him (Gandhi) bitterly for being a friend of the mill-owners, riding in their motorcars and eating sumptuously with them, while the weavers were starving', and Gandhi allegedly began his fast 'stung by these taunts'. Whatever its motives, the hunger-strike successfully won for the workers a 35% wage-increase. The Gandhian hold on the Ahmedabad workers was consolidated through the Textile Labour Association of 1920, grounded on the philosophy of peaceful arbitration of disputes, interdependence of capital and labour, and the concept of owners being 'trustees' for the workers. Gandhi's excellent personal contacts with Ahmedabad mill-owners and workers alike made such methods a success here. It is significant, however, that this Gandhian model, which rejected not only politicization along 'class-war' line but also militant economic struggles, never spread beyond Ahmedabad. Gandhi himself, unlike many other nationalist leaders, kept strictly aloof from the AITUC right from the beginning, long before the Communists became important within it. The message of class peace and mutual adjustment had much greater success among the peasantry than with the proletariat, for in the countryside exploitation at times took on a 'paternalistic' colour and issues like land revenue or the salt tax provided unifying grievances.

Down to early 1919, Gandhi's interventions in matters of all-India politics had been relatively minimal, being mainly confined to protests against the internment of Annie Besant and repeated pleas for the release of the Ali brothers (through which he had already started developing important contacts with Muslim religious leaders like Abdul Bari of Lucknow). He showed little interest in the Reform proposals, which were engrossing the attention of most other politicians. The provocative enactment of the Rowlatt Act in February 1919 made him turn to an all-India *satyagraha* campaign for the first time.

ROWLATT SATYAGRAHA

The so-called 'Rowlatt' Act (embodying some of the recommendations of the Sedition Committee of 1918 under Justice Powlatt) was rushed through the Imperial Legislative Council between 6 February and 18 March 1919, against the unanimous opposition of all non-official Indian members. Representing an attempt to make war-time restrictions on civil rights permanent through a system of special courts and detention without trial for a maximum of two years (even for actions like mere possession of tracts declared to be seditious), the Act was probably a bid to conciliate the considerable segment of official and non-official white opinion which had resented Montagu's liberal promises and the grant of dyarchy. It was accompanied by Viceregal assurances that the civil service and British commercial interests would not suffer from the coming Reforms. From the Indian point of view, the Rowlatt Act directly affected only active politicians, but any move to give further powers to the police was bound to evoke much more widespread alarm, considering the latter's notoriety everywhere as petty oppressors.

While all sections of Indian political opinion deeply resented the Rowlatt Act, it was left to Gandhi to suggest a practicable form of all-India mass protest, going beyond petitioning but not intended to be unrestrained or violent. The plan initially was a rather modest one of volunteers courting arrest by public sale of prohibited works; it was extended by Gandhi on 23 March to include the novel and far more radical idea of an all-India *hartal* on 30 March (later postponed to 6 April). The brakes were there from the beginning, however: the *hartal* was deliberately fixed for a Sunday, and Gandhi explicitly declared that 'employees who are required to work even on Sunday may only suspend work after obtaining previous leave from their employers'. He also rejected the Arya Samajist leader Swami Shraddhanand's suggestion for a no-revenue call ('Bhai Saheb! You will acknowledge that I am an expert in Satyagraha business!'), and urged the old Moderate leader Dinshaw Wacha to accept his programme with the argument that 'the growing generation will not be satisfied with petitions, etc,... Satyagraha is the only way, it seems to me, to stop terrorism" (letter to Wacha, 25 February 1919).

In organizing his *satyagraha,* Gandhi tried to utilize three types of political networks—the Home Rule Leagues, certain Pan-Islamist groups, and a Satyagraha Sabha which he himself started at Bombay on 24 February. Younger, radical members of the two Home Rule Leagues were in need of a leader, as Besant had suddenly turned into a moderate (she was shouted down for supporting the Montford reforms at the Delhi Congress of 1918), while Tilak had left for England in September 1918. Besant Home Rule

League enthusiasts in Bombay city like Jamnadas Dwarkadas, Shankerlal Banker, Umar Sobhani and B.G. Horniman supplied most of the men and finances for the Satyagraha Sabha. Some of Tilak's younger followers also joined Gandhi, though the former's principal lieutenants like N.C. Kelkar or G.S. Khaparde remained aloof. Gandhi had already developed excellent relations with some Muslim leaders, and particularly with Abdul Bari of the Firangi Mahal *ulama* group at Lucknow—the religious preceptor of the Ali brothers who were still interned. With the defeat of Ottoman Turkey and the spread of rumours regarding very harsh peace terms being prepared by the victorious Allies, concern about the future of the Sultan-Khalifa was spreading among Indian Muslims. The Delhi session of the Muslim League (December 1918) was marked by an important change in leadership, for the more moderate section of the 'Young Party' (Wazir Hasan, Mahmudabad) who wanted to accept the Montford reforms were ousted by an alliance of somewhat more radical politicians like Ansari and a large group of *ulama* brought by Abdul Bari. Ansari had hailed Gandhi at this session as 'the intrepid leader of India...who has...endeared himself as much to the Musalmans as to the Hindus', and Bari came out in favour of *satyagraha* against the Rowlatt Act after a meeting with Gandhi in mid-March 1919. The specific organization started for the movement, the Satyagraha Sabha, concentrated on publishing propaganda literature and collecting signatures to a *satyagraha* pledge, while Gandhi himself embarked on a whirl-wind tour visiting Bombay, Delhi, Allahabad, Lucknow, and a number of south Indian cities between March and early April. The Congress as such was not in the picture at all. It had no machinery as yet for real agitational politics in most parts of the country; where something of that sort did exist, as with the old Extremist networks in Bengal and Maharastra, resistance to Gandhi would in fact be the strongest.

What emerges from all this is that the organizational preparation was extremely limited and patchy, and quite remarkably disproportionate to the storm which arose in April 1919—the biggest and most violent anti-British upsurge which India had seen since 1857. Signatories to the *satyagraha* pledge numbered only 982 in mid-March: 397 in Bombay City, 400 in Gujarat, 101 in Sind, and only 84 outside Bombay Presidency. In the province that was to be most affected, Punjab, the Home Rule League network had been weakest (due to wartime restraints), nor did Gandhi have time to visit it before the explosion.

The Hunter Commission and the Congress Punjab Inquiry Committee Reports (1920), and the recent valuable collection of research papers edited by Ravinder Kumar (*Essays on Gandhian Politics*), together give us a picture of an elemental upheaval, sparked off by a combination of post-war economic grievances, rumours about Gandhi that were potent precisely in their vagueness and inaccuracy, and brutal provocation and repression particularly in the Punjab. The movement seems to have been almost entirely urban, with lower middle class groups and artisans on the whole more important than industrial workers. While there were *hartals* in most Indian towns on 30 March and 6 April, the places most affected by the ensuring disturbances were Amritsar, Lahore, Gujranwala and a number of smaller towns in the Punjab, Ahmedabad, Viramgam, and Nadiad in Gujarat, and Delhi, Bombay and (to a lesser extent) Calcutta.

Lieutenant-Governor O'Dwyer's Punjab administration had become thoroughly unpopular already before 1919 due to ruthless recruitment and war exactions, severe repression following the Ghadr outbreaks of 1915, and tactless speeches abusing educated groups (a point perhaps over-emphasized in the Congress Inquiry Report with its assumption that the latter were 'the natural leaders of the people', p. 24). Ravinder Kumar's micro-study of Lahore pinpoints some more specific factors: a foodgrains price-rise of 100% between 1917 and 1919 while artisan wages went up by only 20–25%; O'Dwyer's active connivance in 1913 in the collapse of the Peoples Bank of Punjab's top *Swadeshi* entrepreneur Harkishan Lal, causing a major set back to the economic ambitions of the predominantly Hindu trading community of Lahore; the spread of anti-British political ideas by Arya Samajist barristers with business connections like Mukund Lal Puri and Gokul Chand Narang (as well as by the old Extremist Ram Bhuj Dutt and the Sanatan Dharma Sabha patron Ram Saran Das); and a Muslim awakening, inspired by the journalist Zafar Ali Khan and above all by the poetry of Iqbal in his first, nationalist, phase (when he was writing the famous patriotic hymn *Hindustan Hamara,* and proclaiming: 'Your temples and mosques, where the Priests chant and the mullahs cry—disgust me....I seek God in the soil of my country.')

What seems to have frightened O'Dwyer ard other British officials most was the remarkable Hindu-Muslim-Sikh unity of early 1919 in a province noted both before and afterwards for its communal divisions. The *hartals* of 30 March and 6 April at Amritsar were peaceful but massive affairs, and the 9 April Ram Navami procession here was later described by the Hunter Commission 'as very largely participated in by Muhammedans...a striking demonstration in furtherance of Hindu-Muslim unity—people of the different creeds drinking out of the same cups publicly'. The local leaders of Amritsar, Kitchlew and Satyapal, were deported the same evening, and orders were issued restraining Gandhi from entering Delhi and the Punjab. Firing on a peaceful demonstration near Hall Bridge in Amritsar on 10 April was followed by attacks on the symbols of British authority—banks, post offices, the railway station and the town hall. Martial law was clamped down on the town on 11 April, with General Dyer in command. On 13 April, a peaceful unarmed crowd, consisting in large part of villagers who had come for a fair and had not been told of the ban on meetings, was attacked without the slightest warning by Dyer in an enclosed ground, Jallianwalla bagh. Official estimates later spoke of 379 killed, unofficial accounts gave much higher figures. Dyer's only regrets before the Hunter Commission were that his ammunition ran out, and that the narrow lanes had prevented his bringing in an armoured car—for it was no longer a question of merely dispersing the crowd, but one of 'producing a moral effect'. During the following weeks, Dyer with the full backing of the Lieutenant-Governor went on with his job of 'producing a moral effect' through indiscriminate arrests, torture, special tribunals, public flogging, recruiting lawyers to work on menial jobs as special constables, insisting on 'natives' salaaming all sahibs, and making Indians crawl down Kucha Kauchianwalla lane where a white woman had been insulted.

At Lahore, peaceful *hartals* and demonstrations marked once again by remarkable communal unity on 6 and 9 April were followed by violent clashes with the police on the tenth as rumours about Gandhi's externment and the Amritsar events reached the city. Muslim artisans and workers were particularly militant, while established leaders like Rambhuj Dutt made desperate efforts to control the crowds. On 11 April, there were strikes at the Mughalpara railway workshop (employing 12,000) and many factories, and the situation became so serious that the British withdrew from the city into the cantonment area. An enormous rally at the Badshahi Mosque endorsed the formation of a People's Committee, which virtually controlled the city from 11 to 14 April. This Committee, however, consisted of middle-class politicians who did not know what to do with the power so suddenly thrust into their hands by the people. Accustomed to pressure-politics, and certainly not prepared for revolution, they did little apart from organizing some kitchens to provide food during the *hartal,* and their effort on 13 April to call off the *hartal* itself at a Town Hall meeting was blocked only by mass resentment. There were a few, very short lived, signs of an alternative, more militant leadership: a 40-member 'Danda Fauj' under Chaman Din paraded the streets with *lathis* and toy guns, and put up inflammatory posters: 'O Hindu, Muhammadan and Sikh brethren, enlist at once in the Danda army and fight with bravery against the English monkeys.... Leave off dealings with the Englishmen, close offices and workshops. Fight on. This is the command of Mahatma Gandhi.' The British returned in force on 14 April, deported the People's Committee leaders, and smashed the popular movement by martial law.

Five districts in the Punjab were seriously affected by the Rowlatt disturbances: Gujranwala, Gujarat, and Lyallpur, apart from Amritsar and Lahore. The British were seriously worried by the threat of a general strike on the North-Western railway line linking Gujarat, Gujranwala, Lahore and Amritsar with Delhi, and though this did not take place, the Hunter Commission found 'railway staff' to have been 'specially infected', along with 'the lower orders of the town populations'. The Hunter Commission agreed with the Congress Committee Report that 'the vast masses of peasantry' were unaffected. The pattern everywhere was of sporadic attacks on government buildings, communications (there were 54 cases of disruption of telegraph lines between 10 and 22 April) and occasionally on individual whites— followed by far more violent, brutal and ruthless repression. The latter included aerial bombing of Gujranwala and surrounding villages on 14 April, 258 sentences of flogging by martial law tribunals and 'fancy punishments' like rubbing noses on the ground and making the entire population stand the whole day under the scorching Punjab sun (at Kasur on 1 May— where a boy of eleven was charged with waging war against the King). The total disproportion between popular and government violence is indicated by the fact, brought out by the Congress Report, that in the whole of the Punjab only 4 whites were killed, while Indian casulties were at least 1200 dead and 3600 wounded.

At Delhi, the transfer of capital in 1912 had been followed by something like a political awakening. A Home Rule League branch had been active since February 1917 under Ansari, the city had become a centre of Pan-Islamic activity, Shraddhanand enjoyed a unique influence over the Hindu lower middle class, and five radical vernacular newspapers had been started between November 1918 and February 1919 whose editors (like Indra of *Vijaya,* Asif Hussain Haswi of *Congress* and *Inquilab,* and Qazi Abbas Hussain of *Qaum*) were to play a more prominent and radical part in April 1919 than established leaders like Ansari or Hakim Ajmal Khan. D.W. Ferrell's study also notes importance of economic factors. The influenza epidemic had killed 7000 in the city, salt was selling at four times the 1914 price, while kerosene had become unobtainable, the (predominantly) Hindu traders were irritated by war taxation, and the big artisan community (largely Muslim) had been hard hit by the decline in handicrafts. The number employed by the lace and embroidery trade, for instance, went down from 18,000 to 4000 between 1911 and 1921. The Rowlatt movement went through three phases in Delhi city. The *hartal* of 30 March, marked by two cases of police firing near the railway station and on Chandni Chowk, was followed by a relative lull, during which took place the memorable rally (4 April) at the Jama Masjid where Muslims and Hindus alike kissed the feet of Swami Shraddhanand. News of the externment of Gandhi set off a continuous *hartal* from 10 to 18 April, accompanied by a strike of bank clerks and an attempted rail strike on 13 April. As at Lahore, lower-class militancy soon frightened the established leaders and even the more radical journalists—'the informal alliance between the middle classes and the lower classes began to dissolve as unobtrusively as it had formed'.(Ferrell). After another round of firing on Chandni Chowk on 17 April, the city quickly returned to normal.

The news of the action taken against Gandhi provoked a massive and really violent upsurge in Ahmedabad on 11 April, when 51 government buildings were burnt down by rioters consisting mainly of textile workers. Official estimates speak of 28 being killed and 123 injured in the action subsequently taken under martial law. On 12 April, crowds of mill-hands went on the rampage also in the nearby town of Viramgam. While there was a spontaneous two-day *hartal* in Bombay city on 10–11 April, things remained more or less peaceful—and here Gujarati merchants and professional groups were far more prominent than industrial workers, the main centre of demonstrations being south-central Bombay (Wards C and D), not proletarian Parel. Gandhi's presence definitely acted here as a restraining factor—and at Nadiad in Kheda district, mass violence was averted by the 'teaching of one of Mr Gandhi's followers who came from Ahmedabad on 11 April and exhorted the people to remain quiet'. (Hunter Report) The Bombay Government's reactions were also much more restrained than in the Punjab, which was a frontier province supplying the major part of soldiers for the Indian army.

Calcutta witnessed *hartals* on 6 and 11 April, a joint Hindu-Muslim rally at Nakhoda mosque on the 11th and clashes with the police and army in the cosmopolitan Harrison Road—Chit-pur-Burra Bazar area on the 12th, with the British using machine guns to kill nine people. A significant feature of the Calcutta demonstrations was the prominence of up-country Hindus, Marwaris and Muslims and the relative unimportance of the Bengali student element—in very sharp contrast to the *Swadeshi* days. The Madras city protest remained non-violent, but included a number of big labour meetings on the Beach, addressed by T.V. Kalyanasundara Mudaliar (Thiru Vi Ka), Congressman and one of the chief organizers of the pioneer Madras Labour Union of 1918, and Subramaniya Siva, the Extremist veteran of the Tuticorin strike of 1908. The response elsewhere in the country was not very remarkable—in the Central Provinces, for instance, the only places affected by *hartals,* complete or partial, were Chhindwana, Akola and Amravati.

The unprecedented scale of British repression seems to have frightened most Indian politicians for some time. At Calcutta, for instance, it proved impossible to organize a public protest meeting, and it was left to Rabindranath Tagore to voice the agony and anger of a nation through a famous letter renouncing his Knighthood (30 May 1919). The official Congress reaction to the Punjab horrors remained confined in 1919 to the well-worn device of a non-official enquiry committee. As for Gandhi himself, the widespread violence—particularly on his home-ground of Ahmedabad—led him to confess to a 'Himalayan blunder' (18 April) and quickly call off the *satyagraha*. Henceforward Gandhi would be extremely wary about starting movements without adequate organizational and ideological preparations and controls.

Together with the short-lived hopes aroused by the royal amnesty for prisoners not accused of violence which accompanied the formal assent to the Reforms in December 1919, this caution probably explains the rather surprising alignments at the Amritsar Congress in the same month. The Congress had already taken up a stand critical of the Montford Reforms at Delhi the previous year, leading to a breakaway by the old Moderate remnants who formed the National Liberal Association under Sapru, Jayakar and Chintamani. At Amritsar, however, Gandhi gave his full support to a resolution thanking Montagu and promising cooperation in working the new Councils. A compromise clause describing the Act as disappointing was added at the insistance of C.R. Das, Tilak, Rambhuj Dutt Chaudhuri and Hasrat Mohani, despite Gandhi's opposition. The alignments were to be totally reversed by September 1920, with Gandhi pressing hard for Council boycott and Non-Cooperation and Das' and Tilak's followers holding back—but by then Gandhi through his use of the Khilafat issue had acquired a commanding position over both Congress and overall national politics.

1919–1920: LEADERS AND MASSES

Gandhi, Khilafat and the Congress

The recent writings of Richard Gordon, Judith Brown, and Francis Robinson have described in great detail the process of Gandhi's 'rise to power' or 'capture' of national leadership in the course of 1919–20, with the accent always on the whole thing being no more than a very skilful top-level political game.

With rumours about a harsh peace treaty to be imposed on the defeated Ottoman Empire fast becoming a certainty, the Khilafat movement was rapidly gaining momentum in 1919–20. Its three central demands, presented by Mohammad AH to diplomats in Paris in March 1920, were that the

Turkish Sultan—Khalifa must retain control over the Muslim sacred places, must be left with sufficient territory to enable him to defend the Islamic faith, and that the *Jazirat-ul-Arab* (Arabia, Syria, Iraq, Palestine) must remain under Muslim sovereignty. As was to be expected, the movement developed a moderate and a radical strand. The first had its focus in the Central Khilafat Committee, organized by prosperous Bombay merchants like Chotani; the second consisted of lower middle class journalists and *ulama* with considerable influence over small towns and villages, particularly in the United Provinces, Bengal, Sind and Malabar. The Bombay leaders (who initially controlled the purse-strings, till the broadening movement enabled mass collection of funds) would have liked to confine the agitation to sober meetings, memorials, and deputations to London and Paris. The radicals, led by the Ali brothers after their release from internment in early 1920, pressed for country-wide *hartals* (as on 17 October 1919 and 19 March 1920) and it was from this group that the call for Non-Cooperation first came, at the Delhi all-India Khilafat Conference on 22–23 November 1919.

Gandhi, Judith Brown tells us, made himself vital to both groups by initially playing a mediating role. He was also the indispensable link with Hindu politicians—and Khilafat leaders were extremely eager for Hindu-Muslim unity, without which any Non-Cooperation movement involving boycott of services or Councils was evidently impossible. Their eagerness was reflected by the December 1919 Muslim League resolution calling for the giving-up of the Bakr-Id slaughter of cows. It is noteworthy that Hindu leaders then or later on never offered the obvious *quid pro quo* of abandoning music before mosques, even though the latter was hardly an indispensable part of Hinduism while Bakr-Id was a central religious function. Till May 1920, Gandhi on the whole sided with the Bombay group, opposing for instance Hasrat Mohani's call for boycott of British goods at the Khilafat Conference of November 1919 (the bulk of Bombay Muslim merchants were importers and retailers of such goods). The turning point came with the publication of the very harsh terms of the Treaty of Sevres with Turkey on 14 May 1920, followed on 28 May by the Hunter Commission Majority Report on the Punjab disturbances—bitterly described by Gandhi as 'page after page of thinly disguised official whitewash'. The Government of India had already protected its officers by an Indemnity Act—and now O'Dwyer was acquitted of blame, the House of Lords rejected the censure passed on Dyer, and the *Morning Post* raised a purse of £ 26,000 for the butcher of Jallianwallabagh.

The Allahabad meeting of the Central Khilafat Committee (1–3 June 1920), which was attended by a number of nationalist Hindu leaders, saw the victory of the radicals, now backed by Gandhi. A programme of four-stage Non-Cooperation was announced (boycott of titles, civil services, police and army, and finally non-payment of taxes), and Gandhi began pressing the Congress to adopt a similar plan of campaign around the three issues of the 'Punjab wrong', the 'Khilafat wrong' and 'Swaraj'—the last being left, quite deliberately, undefined. Full support initially came only from Gujarat and Bihar. Motilal Nehru (unlike his son) was at first hesitant about the crucial issue of boycott of council elections (scheduled for November 1920), and C.R. Das and the Tilakites bitterly opposed it. The dramatic conversion of the established leaders to Gandhi's programme between September and December 1920 has been explained by Gordon and Brown largely in terms of political calculation of election prospects. Thus Lajpat Rai, we are told, supported election boycott on 25 June, as the Punjab election rules announced in mid-June offered little chance for the urban Hindu-based Congress of that province. The opposition to Council boycott was, conversely, strongest in Bengal and Maharashtra, old Extremist strongholds where electoral chances were relatively bright. Motilal allegedly realized that the U.P. Congress was organizationally unprepared for elections, and his support proved decisive at the Calcutta Special Congress (4–9 September 1920), which approved a programme of surrender of titles, the 'triple boycott' (of schools, courts and Councils), boycott of foreign goods, and encouragement of national schools, arbitration courts, and *khadi* by a 144 to 132 vote at the Subjects Committee and a much wider margin (1855 to 873) at the open session. No mention was made here, however, of resignations from services, police, or the army, or of no-tax. The Nagpur Congress (December 1920) saw the dramatic switch-over of C.R. Das, who spent ₹36,000 on financing a big opposition delegation from Bengal, but eventually moved the central resolution accepting 'the entire or any part of the non-violent non-cooperation scheme, with the renunciation of voluntary association with the Government at one end, and the refusal to pay taxes at the other, (to be) put in force at a time to be determined by either the Indian National Congress or the AICC.' Council elections were over in any case, and Gandhi's promise of 'Swaraj within one year' (first made in a *Young India* article on 22 September) possibly implied a tacit understanding that the whole issue could be reopened if *Swaraj* did not come through Non-Cooperation within the stipulated period. For the time being, at least, the whole Congress lay at Gandhi's feet. Its creed was modified to read 'the attainment of Swaraj by all legitimate and peaceful means'—*Swaraj* being again left deliberately vague. Crucial changes were made at Gandhi's insistence in Congress organization, in an effort to make it into a real mass political party for the fiist time: a regular four-anna membership; a hierarchy of village-taluka-district or town committees;

reorganization of PCCs on a linguistic basis, with the number of delegates to be fixed in proportion to population; and a small 15-member Working Committee as the real executive head.

Pressures from Below

Electoral calculations may have played some part in the 'conversions' of individual leaders to Non-Cooperation, though even here we must not underestimate the element of real emotion and anger aroused by the Khilafat and Punjab issues: 'My blood is boiling over since I read the summaries [of the Hunter Report] you have sent. We must hold a Special Congress now and raise a veritable hell for the rascals.' (Motilal Nehru to Jawaharlal, 27 June 1920) Judith Brown herself has given ample evidence of a kind of populist groundswell virtually forcing more radical courses on both Khilafat and Congress leaders: the 180 peasant delegates whose support ensured victory for the Non-Cooperation resolution at the Bihar Provincial Conference at Bhagalpur in August 1920, the enormous gap between voting figures at the Subjects Committee and the open session at Calcutta, the 14,582 delegates at Nagpur (the highest ever in Congress history). At Calcutta and Nagpur, crucial support for Gandhi came from the country-wide network of Marwari businessmen and traders, from Muslim Khilafatists, and from relatively submerged regions like Andhra whose demands for linguistic reorganization had been taken up by Gandhi from April 1920 onwards and given a place in the revised Congress constitution at Nagpur. The apparently distant and unreal Khilafat issue was fast acquiring new dimensions through the diverse interpretations given to it at local levels. Lower-class Muslims in U.P. are said to have related Khilafat to the Urdu word *khilaf* (against), and used it as a symbol of general revolt against authority, while in Malabar the ever-restive Moplahs would soon convert it into a banner of anti-landlord revolt.

An additional factor arousing Muslim sentiments and hopes was the anti-British stance of the new Amir Amanullah of Afghanistan, who fought a brief war with British India in May-June 1919 and developed some contacts with Bolshevik Russia. In June 1920, no less than 20,000 Muslim *Muhajirin* trekked from Sind and North-West Frontier Province into Afghanistan in a massive *hijrat* away from the government which had dishonoured the Khalifa. In August 1920, the *Zamindar* editor Zafar Ali Khan was sentenced to five years' transportation for a speech proclaiming that 'it was time for the advent of the Mahdi'—the Islamic saviour. Soaring millenarian hopes were aroused also by the very vagueness and lack of realism of Gandhi's promise of *Swaraj* within a year. Above all, 1919 and 1920 were also years of widespread labour unrest, organization, and peasant awakening—aspects entirely ignored by Cambridge scholars.

A near-contemporary account gives the following list of the high-lights of the strike-wave of late 1919-early 1920: 'November 4 to December 2, 1919, woollen mills, Cawnpore, 17,000 men out; December 7, 1919 to 9 January 1920, railway workers, Jamalpur, 16,000 men out; January 9–18, 1920, jute mills, Calcutta, 35,000 men out; January 2 to February 3, general strike, Bombay, 200,000 men out; January 20–31, mill-workers, Rangoon, 20,000 men out; January 31, British India Navigation Company, Bombay, 10,000 men out; January 26 to February 16, mill-workers, Sholapur, 16,000 men out; February 24 to March 29, Tata Iron and Steel workers, 40,000 men out; March 9, mill-workers, Bombay, 60,000 men out; March 20–26, mill workers, Madras, 17,000 men out; May 1920, mill workers, Ahmedabad, 25,000 men out'. (R.K. Das, *Factory Labour in India,* Berlin, 1923, pp. 36–7). There were 110 strikes in Bengal during the second half of 1920 alone. Trade unions tended to follow rather than precede strikes, and were often little more than shortlived strike committees. Their numbers still heralded a new age in labour organization—a Bengal Government confidential report listed 40 relatively stable 'Labour Unions and Associations' in 1920, 55 in 1921, and 75 in 1922, while of the 53 unions active in Bombay in 1926, only 7 dated from before 1920 while no less than 29 had been formed between 1920 and 1923.

Union leadership, necessarily in the main middle-class, came from a variety of political trends—moderate near-loyalists like N.M. Joshi of Bombay; followers of Besant like Wadia in Madras and Baptista in Bombay; B.G. Horniman's *Bombay Chronicle* group, together with some of the younger followers of Tilak; Thiru Vi Ka, the Madras Congress leader; Khilafatist agitators and nationalists with old Extremist connections in Bengal (Prabhatkusum Roychaudhuri, Byomkesh Chakrabarti, S.N. Haldar, I.B. Sen), together with younger radicals who were to become very important in the 1920s like Jitendralal Banerji, Hemantakumar Sarkar, and Mrinalkanti Basu. There were also some political *sanyasis,* like Swami Darshananand in Ranigunj and Swami Viswanand the leader of the Jharia mine workers. The predominantly nationalist middle-class leadership often acted as a brake on labour militancy, particularly in Indian-owned enterprises: thus the Jamshedpur Labour Association founded by S.N. Haldar and Byomkesh Chakrabarti in the course of the February 1920 strike could provide only a very compromising and inept guidance to the Tata workers. Baptista perhaps spoke for most of these early labour leaders when, at the inaugural session of the AITUC in Bombay on 31 October 1920 (where he became Vice-President with Dewan Chaman Lal as secretary on a rather high salary of ₹500 per month), he deplored the *via dolorosa* of workers but held out to them 'the higher idea of partnership... They (workers and employers) are partners and co-workers, and not buyers and sellers of labour.' Already, however, a few individuals and groups on the fringes of the labour movement were beginning to lean towards Marxism—the radical young student S.A. Dange in Bombay, who talks of his rapid transition from being a *chela* (disciple) of Tilak to that of Lenin in the course of 1920–21, or the elderly lawyer Singaravelu Chettiar in Madras. It is interesting that though Lajput Rai presided over the first AITUC session and quite a galaxy of leading Indian politicians attended it (Motilal Nehru, Vithalbhai Patel, Annie Besant, even Jinnah), Gandhi kept sternly aloof, not even sending a message, and his Ahmedabad Majoor Mahajan never sought affiliation to the AITUC even when it was controlled by entirely moderate groups. The very effective and non-violent, but socially far-reaching, weapon of the political general strike would never be allowed to enter the armoury of Non-Cooperation.

In the political backwater of Rajasthan, the anti-feudal peasant unrest, endemic, as we have seen, from the early years of the century, touched a new peak in the 1920s. Wilkinson's Rajputana Agency Report of 1921 described Mewar as 'becoming a hotbed of lawlessness. Seditionist emissaries are teaching the people that all men are equal. The land belongs to the peasants and not to the state or landlords. It is significant that the people are being urged to use the vernacular equivalent of the word "comrade"... the movement is mainly anti-Maharana but it might soon become anti-British and spread to the adjoining British area!' We might legitimately suspect some alarmist exaggeration, here, but certainly Vijai Singh Pathik and Manik Lal Verma had built up a powerful *kisan* movement around the old centre of Bijolia, and some concessions in the shape of reduced cesses and *begar* were wrested from the *jagirdar* in 1922. Meanwhile Motilal Tejawat, an Udaipur spice merchant who adopted tribal dress and claimed to be Gandhi's emissary, started organizing the Bhil tribals of Mewar, while a no-revenue campaign began under Jai Narayan Vyas in Marwar. Pathik developed close contacts with the U.P. Congress leader Ganesh Sankar Vidyarthi, who gave some publicity to the Bijolia movement in the Kanpur *Pratap*. A move at the 1921 Congress to censure the Mewar government was blocked, however, by Madan Mohan Malaviya, who claimed that the Udaipur Maharana was his friend and that he would be able to persuade him to give concessions to the peasants.

Stephen Henningham in a recent article has analysed the powerful peasant movement which developed in 1919–20 on the estates of the enormous Darbhanga Raj, spread over the districts of Darbhanga, Muzaffarpur, Bhagalpur, Purnea and Monghyr in north Bihar. High prices adversely affected all those who had to buy part or all of their food (small tenants, share-croppers, agricultural labourers), while population pressure led to conflicts over land, grazing areas and timber, with the Darbhanga estate renting out old pastures and asserting new claims over trees. The *amlas* or agents employed by the estate were often petty *zamindars* made more oppressive by financial pressures. Peasant meetings voicing grievances began to be held from the summer of 1919, starting with a rally at Narar village on 26–30 June in the Madhubani sub-division of north Darbhanga district. The inspiration came from Bishu Bharan Prasad, son of a prosperous occupancy tenant with 30 *bighas* in Saran, who had taken the name of Swami Vidyanand, had been inspired by Gandhi's Champaran movement, and who often claimed to be a disciple of Gandhi. The demands raised concerned mainly extortion by *amlas* and threats to customary rights of better-off tenants (e.g., the Bhumihar brahman occupancy *raiyats* of Madhubani), though we do hear of sharecroppers in S.E. Darbhanga being inspired by Vidyanand to demand a change to cash rents (which they naturally preferred in a period of rising grain prices), and the original Narar petition had also complained of extortion of *ghee* and oil from lower-caste Yadavs and Telis. The movement remained peaceful and restrained, except for some forcible cutting-down of trees and a clash at Kothia Dumai (20 June 1920) when *lathials* of the nearby Bhawara indigo factory (leased out from Darbhanga) broke up a meeting of Vidyanand. The efficiently organized Darbhanga Raj bureaucracy defused the situation by giving some concessions to the better-off tenants in January 1920 (e.g., reduction of fees for transfer of land, and waiving of some timber rights). Vidyanand himself got diverted to electoral politics in late 1920 (five *kisan* candidates won in north Darbhanga and north Bhagalpur against *zamindar* nominees); and the movement had died down by the end of the year. The Darbhanga Raj was helped considerably by the attitude of the Bihar Congress leadership, which repeatedly turned down Vidyanand's appeals for support. In April 1920, the Bihar Provincial Conference at Rajendra Prasad's insistence shelved the plea for an enquiry into Darbhanga tenant grievances, and after the Bhawara incident, Congress leaders Hasan Imam, Mazhar-ul-Haq and Rajendra Prasad were easily persuaded not to attend meetings of Vidyanand. According to a secret Bihar Government report,—'alarm was widespread amongst the Indian zamindars of the Tirhut Division... they were prepared to make common cause with the indigo planters against what they regarded as a most dangerous attack on zamindars as a class. A deputation of zamindars came to Patna to interview Mr Hasan Imam...'. (Letter dated 7 August 1920, in *Government of India Home Political Deposit*, September 1920, No. 50).

The best-known of the early *kisan* movements, studied in detail recently by Majid Siddiqi and Kapil Kumar, was the one that developed in 1920–21 in the Pratapgarh, Rae Bareli, Sultanpur and Fyzabad districts of the Avadh region of the United Provinces. The British had done their best to win over the Avadh *talukdars* (who had proved so formidable in 1857) through what Harcourt Butler (Lieutenant-Governor of U.P. in the 1920s) called the 'policy of sympathy'. This in effect meant giving *talukdars* a free hand with regard to thier tenants (occupancy rights remained almost non-existent in Avadh, in sharp contrast to Agra province), so that rent could outstrip the steadily increasing revenue demand (land revenue per head of population in Avadh in 1921–22 was almost four times that in Permanently-Settled Bengal). The Oudh Rent Act of 1886 gave in practice little or no protection, as the 7- year fixity of rent and ceiling of 6¼% on enhancement given to the new category of 'statutory tenants' were evaded by landlords through *nazrana* (premium charged for renewal of tenancy after seven years—often this became much more than the rent), extorted under threat of *bedakhli* (eviction). The peasants also suffered from a variety of cesses and the extortion of unpaid labour (*begar*—as when the landlord used their plough-teams gratis in what was called *hari*) while the congruence of caste with class domination made the *jajmani* system an effective instrument of exploitation—the lower castes being obliged to supply *ghee,* cloth or hides free or at below-market rates to higher caste landlords or better-off *kisans*. Rising prices made such customary levies much more oppressive, while enforced recruitment and *Larai Chanda* (war contributions) collected by *talukdars* added to peasant greivances during the war years. A U.P. Kisan Sabha had been started in February 1918, as we have seen, by Malaviya's protege Indra Narain Dwivedi, with some 450 branches set up at the initiative of Allahabad Home Rule League and Congress leaders mainly in Agra province. This rather superficial movement from the top split in late 1920 on the Council boycott issue, with Dwivedi trying to rally *kisan* votes for liberal candidates and his colleague Gaurishankar Misra joining Non-Cooperation and establishing links with the grassroots peasant movement which had emerged by then in the Rae Bareli-Pratapgarh region. The latter was founded by Jhinguri Singh, a disgruntled under-proprietor of Pratapgarh, and Baba Ram Chandra, a *sanyasi* who had come to that district after a, spell as an indentured labourer in Fiji. Baba Ram Chandra's movement characteristically combined appeals for *kisan* solidarity with considerable use of the *Ramayana* and caste slogans. Thus Roor village in Pratapgarh was selected as a base for the first Kisan Sabha, apparently because of an alleged mention of it in Tulsidas, and the recently discovered private papers of Baba Ram Chandra contain references to a 'Kurmi-Kshatriya Sabha' later founded by him. The demands and methods were fairly moderate—abolition (or, more usually, reduction) of cesses and *begar,* refusal to cultivate *bedakhli* land, social boycott of oppressive landlords (*nai-dhobi bundh*) organized through *panchayats*. But the strength of the *kisan* movement was vividly revealed in September 1920, when a peaceful but massive peasant demonstration at Pratapgarh obtained the release of Baba Ram Chandra, who had been arrested on a trumped-up theft charge a few days before. Meanwhile contacts had been established with Gauri Shankar Misra and Jawaharlal Nehru following a trip to Allahabad in June 1920 by Ram Chandra accompanied by several hundred peasants, and Jawaharlal began his 'wanderings among the kisans' which he was to describe so vividly later on in his *Autobiography*. By October 1920, with the foundation of the Oudh Kisan Sabha headed by Nehru, Misra and Ram Chandra (with 330 branches in Pratapgarh, Rae Bareli, Sultanpur and Fyzabad set up by the end of the month), the Gandhian Congress was well on the way towards establishing its hegemony over the peasant movement in U.P. The results, as we shall see, were to be by no means uniformly fortunate from the peasant point of view.

1921–1922: NON-COOPERATION AND KHILAFAT

An adequate understanding of the Non-Cooperation upsurge of 1921–22 requires an analysis at three levels: the phases of the all-India movement as sought to be determined by the Gandhian Congress leadership, the role of distinct social groups and classes, and—most interesting and important of all, perhaps—the regional and local variations.

The All-India Movement

Four phases may be distinguished in what may be termed the 'official, movement, specifically responding to successive calls from the Working Committee or AICC. From January to March 1921, the central emphasis was on students leaving government controlled schools and colleges and lawyers giving up practice. Even the *charkha* programme initially had a strong intelligentsia orientation, with students and educated urban people in general being urged to take up spinuing on a voluntary basis, as a symbol of identification with the rural masses and as a quick road to *Swadeshi*. After a spectacular beginning, with massive student strikes at Calcutta and Lahore and top lawyers like C.R. Das and Motilal Nehru giving up their practice, this exclusively intelligentsia movement soon began showing signs of decline. In April, the Vijayawada session of the AICC found the country 'not yet sufficiently disciplined, organized and ripe' for civil disobedience, and decided to concentrate on raising ₹1 crore for the Tilak Swaraj Fund, enrolling one crore Congress members, and installing 20 lakh *charkhas,* by 30 June. In face of mounting pressures from below, the Bombay AICC meeting of 28–30 July adopted a somewhat more militant stance, concentrating on boycott of foreign cloth (including public bonfires) and boycott of the coming visit of the Prince of Wales in November, though full-scale civil disobedience through non-payment of taxes was again postponed. Gandhi here gave a call for flooding the prisons with volunteers—'Our triumph consists in thousands being led to prisons like lambs to the slaughter-house' and organization of volunteer bands was now given top priority. Viceroy Reading quickly grasped the significance of the new mass orientation involved in the strategy of large-scale enrolment of volunteers, militant picketing, and courting of arrest by tens of thousands: '…the change from Gandhi's appeal to intellectuals to his appeal to ignorant masses…has altered [the] situation, but it has the advantage of bringing intellectuals and persons of property more closely to us.' (Telegram to Secretary of State, 15 October 1921, *Reading Collection*) The Prince of Wales was greeted with an extremely successful countrywide *hartal* on 17 November, and there were violent clashes in Bombay, which made Gandhi declare that 'Swaraj…has stunk in my nostrils' and postpone once again plans for civil disobedience in the selected single *taluka* of Bardoli.

Despite the brakes, however, developments in the fourth phase, between November 1921 and February 1922, very nearly brought the government to its knees. Khilafat leaders like Hasrat Mohani, angered by the jailing of the Ali brothers in November (for speeches at the Karachi Khilafat Conference in July calling on Muslims to resign from the army) were demanding complete independence (as at the Ahmedabad Congress in December) and giving-up of the non-violence dogma. The new government policy of large-scale arrests and ban on meetings and volunteer groups threatened to alienate the Liberals, while much of the country seemed, as we shall see, on the brink of immensely variegated, disorganized, but formidable revolt. In December 1921, Reading in secret telegrams to Montagu suggested not only release of prisoners, but a Round Table Conference and an early revision of the just-implemented Reform scheme (telegrams of 15, 17 and 18 December)—an interesting anticipation of the 1930s which was scotched by Gandhi's refusal of any compromise at this point, combined with reluctance of the British Cabinet to go anywhere near so far. Gandhi finally decided on a no-revenue compaign at Bardoli, on the issue of infringed liberties of speech, press and association, to begin from the second week of February 1922. As is well-known, this, together with virtually the entire movement, was abruptly called off on 11 February at Gandhi's insistance, following the news of the burning-alive of 22 policemen by angry peasants at Chauri Chaura, in Gorakhpur district of U.P., on 5 February 1922.

Social Composition

Available data concerning the impact of Non-Cooperation give some indication of the varying response of different social groups. The initial appeal for self-sacrifice by the upper and middle classes was hardly very successful. Only 24 titles were surrendered out of 5186, and the number of lawyers giving up practice stood at 180 in March 1921. Polling was low in many places in the November 1920 elections, falling to only 8% in Bombay city and 5% in Lahore, but candidates offered themselves in all but 6 out of 637 seats, and Council functioning could not be disrupted. The educational boycott was more effective, particularly in Bengal, where about 20 headmasters or teachers were resigning per month till April 1921, and where there was an exodus of 11,157 out of 103,107 students attending government or aided institutions. All-India figures collected in Intelligence official Bamford's confidential *History of the Non-Cooperation and Khilafat Movements* (1925) reveal the impact to have been considerable in colleges but non-existent at the primary level:

NUMBER OF STUDENTS

	Arts Colleges	Secondary Schools	Primary Schools
1919–20	52,482	1,281,810	6,133,521
1921–22	45,933	1,239,524	6,310,451

(Bamford, p. 103)

A considerable number of national schools and colleges were also founded (like the Jamia Millia Islamia in Aligarh, later shifted to Delhi, the Kasi Vidyapith at Banares and the Gujarat Vidyapith) with 442 institutions started in Bihar and Orissa, 190 in Bengal, 189 in Bombay, and 137 in U.P. Many of these proved short-lived, as the pull of conventional degrees and jobs naturally reasserted itself when *Swaraj* failed to come in a year—but quite a few survived, to serve as valuable seminaries of nationalism.

The economic boycott was far more intense and successful than in 1905–08, with the value of imports of foreign cloth falling from ₹102 crores in 1920–21 to ₹57 crores in 1921–22. Import of British cotton piecegoods was 1292 million yards and 955 million yards respectively in the same years. While picketing remained important, a new feature was the taking of collective pledges by merchants not to indent foreign cloth for specific periods, and we hear also of interesting forms of business pressure, as when a Delhi trader's threat not to honour *hundis* of Rohtak, led the latter town into joining a *hartal* in February 1920. For importers of Lancashire cloth, nationalism in 1921 neatly coincided with short-term business interests, as with the fall in the rupee-sterling exchange ratio from 2s to 1s 4d by late 1921, Indian merchants were being asked to pay much more for British goods than previously contracted for. Possible industrialist hostility to the *charkha* was sought to be reduced by numerous articles by Gandhi in his *Young India,* which argued that what his movement wanted to do 'at the present moment is to supplement the production of yarn and cloth through mills.' (*Young India,* 19 January 1921) The same article declared that Gandhi had 'no design upon machinery as such, at least for the present'.

Business support was decisive in bringing about a qualitative change in the Congress funds situation. The AICC had only ₹43,000 in its coffers in 1920, but was able to collect more than ₹30 lakhs between 1921 and 1923— while no less than ₹37½ lakhs out of the Tilak Swaraj Fund of ₹ 1 crore came from the city of Bombay alone. British alarm at business backing of Non-Cooperation probably contributed to the decision in October 1921 to set up a Fiscal Commission with Indian representatives to go into the question of tariff protection for Indian industries. A significant section of big business, however, still remained hostile, and an Anti-Non-Cooperation Association was started in 1920 by Purshottamdas Thakurdas, Jamnadas Dwarkadas, Cowasji Jehangir, Pheroze Sethna, and Setalvad. While the textile industry was certainly helped by the nationalist *Swadeshi* upsurge (in October 1921 the average of cotton mill share prices, taking 1913 as 100, stood at 275, as against a general share price average of 248) fear of labour unrest (at its peak in 1920–21) was probably crucial in keeping industrialist—as distinct from merchant—attitudes ambivalent. *Capital,* the organ of British business in Calcutta, made the point neatly on 13 July 1922. Nationalist politics, it declared, had 'promoted the influence of millowners and enhanced the sale of their goods. The only fly in the ointment is the liability of labour to run amock.' (Sabyasachi Bhattacharji, 'Cotton Mills and Spinning Wheels, Swadeshi and the Indian Capitalist Class 1920–22', *Economic and Political Weekly,* 20 November 1976)

Labour did seem to be 'running amock' throughout 1921, with 396 strikes involving 600,351 workers and a loss of 6,994,426 workdays. By the middle of 1920, the post-war boom had been succeeded by a recession particularly in the Calcutta jute industry, with the mill-owners trying to cut back production with a four-day week. The workers fought back, and there were 137 strikes in Bengal jute mills in 1921, involving 186,479 labourers. Swami

Viswanand and Swami Darsananand tried to organize the coal miners of the Raniganj-Jharia belt, initially with some help from Indian mine-owners fighting European hegemony. The Jharia session of the AITUC in December 1921 was marked by considerable participation of actual workers—something which would become conspicuously absent for some years from 1922 onwards. Regional Congress leaders were active in some strikes, most notably, as we shall see, in Bengal and Madras. But Gandhi's own stand was unequivocal: strikes 'do not fall within the plan of non-violent non-cooperation.' (*Strikes, Young India* 16 February 1921) 'In India we want no political strikes.... We must gain control over all the unruly and disturbing elements.... We seek not to destory capital or capitalists, but to regulate the relations between capital and labour. We want to harness capital to our side. It would be folly to encourage sympathetic strikes.' ('The Lesson of Assam', *Young India,* 15 June 1921).

For the peasant—always given theoretical primacy by the Mahatma—the Gandhian programme of village reconstruction through self-help envisaged an economic revival through the spinning wheel and hand-woven cloth (*charkha* and *khadi*), *panchayats* or arbitration courts, national schools, and campaigns for Hindu-Muslim unity and against the evils of liquor and un-touchability. *Panchayats* proved very popular in Bihar and Orissa, while in Bengal 866 arbitration courts in all were set up between February 1921 and April 1922—at their height in August 1921, 'they considerably outnumbered the Government courts.' (*History of Non-Cooperation in Bengal— Bengal Government, Political Confidential, 395/1924).* The anti-liquor campaign became quite formidable, perhaps partly because lower castes found in it an opportunity for 'Sanskritizing' social upliftment. Excise revenues went down in 1921–22 by ₹33 lakhs in the Punjab, and the decline caused a ₹65 lakh deficit in the Madras budget. No definite statistics seem available about the impact of the *charka* drive, but handloom cloth production did go up fairly sharply between 1920 and 1923. (See above, p. 172) The Khilafat alliance made Hindu-Muslim unity a powerful, though temporary, fact. Progress regarding untouchability was much less marked, though Gandhi deserves all credit for bringing the issue to the forefront of national politics for the very first time. Even in his own Gujarat, a decision not to recognize as national schools institutions debarring the *Antyajas* caused a near-crisis in late 1920 (*Young India,* 24 Nov. 1920), while at a Bardoli village a year later, untouchables waiting for Gandhi were kept at a distance by upper-caste villagers till the latter were rebuked by Kalyanji Mehta. (Krishnadas, *Seven Months With Mahatma Gandhi,* Part II, p. 37).

Thus the emphasis was always on unifying issues and on trying to cut across or reconcile class divisions. Hence no-revenue was planned—and that after enormous hesitation—for a *raiyatwari taluka* like Bardoli, and not in any *zamindari* region where it would inevitably involve no-rent. After the U.P. agrarian riots of early 1921 (see below, p. 192) Gandhi in a speech at Fyzabad 'deprecated all attempts to create discord between landlords and tenants and advised the tenants to suffer rather than fight, for they had to join all forces for fighting against the most powerful zamindar, namely the Government.' (*Leader,* 13 Feb. 1921, quoted in *Collected Works,* XIX, p. 352) A month later, the *Instructions to U.P. Peasants* warned against disturbances if *kisan* leaders were arrested, and categorically ordered: 'We may not withhold taxes from the Government or rent from the landlord.... It should be borne in mind that we want to turn zamindars into friends.' (*Young India,* 9 March 1921, quoted in *ibid,* pp. 419–20)

Regional Variations

The varied dimensions and contradictions of Non-Cooperation can best be appreciated, however, through regional and local studies—and for that recent research is rapidly accumulating data, though many gaps still remain.

Non-Cooperation began in the Punjab with a fairly successful Lahore student walk-out inspired by Lajpat Rai in January 1921, but the movement in the cities here seems to have remained relatively weak unlike in April 1919—perhaps precisely because memories of ruthless British reprisals at that time were still very fresh. The Sikh-dominated central Punjab countryside was stirred to its depths, however, by the powerful Akali upsurge, initially quite an independent religious reform movement which for a time got closely identified with Non-Cooperation. The Akalis were fighting to wrest control over the Sikh shrines (Gurudwaras) from corrupt *mohants,* who had established a mutually profitable alliance with British officials. Arur Singh, the government-appointed manager of the Amritsar Golden Temple, had even gone to the extent of inviting General Dyer to become a honorary Sikh 'even as Nikalseyan Sahib' (Nicholson, the butcher of Delhi in 1857) 'became a Sikh'. Tensions mounted after the Nankana tragedy of 20 February 1921, where about a hundred Akalis were massacred by the *mohant,* and the Sikhs suspected, with some reason, a certain amount of complicity and instigation on the part of the Lahore Divisional Commissioner. In November 1921, the British refusal to hand over the keys of the Golden Temple treasury led to a direct confrontation, with mass courting of arrest by Akalis. The coincidence in time with the peak of the Non-Cooperation movement led to a British retreat, the keys being handed over and the prisoners released by mid-January 1922. The bulk of the 15,506 Akali volunteers listed in a government report of January 1922 came from the Jat Sikh peasantry, particularly of the Jullundur, Hoshiarpur, Amritsar, Shaikhupura and Lyallpur districts. While the official Akali movement led by the Shromani Gurdwara Prabandhak Committee firmly adhered to non-violent methods, a dissident, 'Babbar Akali' group emerged in March 1921 in Jullundur and Hoshiarpur under Kishan Singh and Mota Singh, calling for no-revenue movements and eventually adopting terroristic methods against loyalists and (occasionally) moneylenders. The Akali struggle continued till the Sikh Gurdwaras and Shrines Act of November 1925 established SGPC control over the Gurdwaras. What was gradually lost after 1922, however, was the link with the broader national movement and the remarkable communal unity of 1921 in a province otherwise noted for its religious divisions—what an alarmed Viceroy described as the 'closest possible connection between Khilafat and Congress Committees and various Sikh organisations.' (Telegram to Secretary of State, 9 November 1921, *Reading Collection*)

The deeply-feudal princely states of Rajasthan reveal an interesting deviant pattern of powerful peasant movements preceding and contributing very directly to a much later urban nationalism, which was just emerging in 1920 in the British enclave of Ajmer with the Rajasthan Seva Sangh. The Bijolia movement in Mewar, as we have seen, won a partial victory in 1922, while agitation against cesses and *begar* on the *khalisa* lands of the Udaipur Maharana began with a peasant rally in May 1921 at the traditional annual Matri Kundiya fair. The Bijolia leader Maniklal Verma would found the nationalist Mewar Praja Mandal much later, in April 1938. The Bhil tribal movement under Motilal Tejawat acquired a more militant millenarian flavour in 1921–22, and in December 1921 Meos from Alwar attacked a police station in the neighbouring Gurgaon district and had to be suppressed through a joint operation by British Indian police and Alwar State troops.

In Bombay Presidency, the Muslim traders and peasants of Sind were aroused to great enthusiasm by the Khilafat call. The Hindu minority produced two important leaders in Jairamdas Daulatram, close associate of Gandhi, and Swami Govindanand, jailed for five years on a sedition charge in May 1921, who later became a radical critic of Congress orthodoxy.

The specifically Gandhian movement was naturally strongest of all in Gujarat, where Krishnadas' account of a 'tour of inspection', with the Mahatma, of Bardoli *taluka* in December 1921 gives a vivid impression of a peasant awakening, at once massive and tightly-controlled and disciplined. (*Seven Months With Mahatma Gandhi, Vol. II*, pp. 27–40) The discipline of non-violence fitted in perfectly with the interests of the Patidar peasant-proprietors, for a more uninhibited movement could have raised problems of control over lower-caste or tribal agricultural labourers and village servants (e.g., the Baraiyas in Kheda or the *Kaliparaj* or 'black people' of Bardoli as distinct from the caste Hindu 'fair-skinned' *Ujaliyat*). Though Anand and Barsad in Kheda remained important bases, Gandhi eventually preferred Bardoli as the first civil disobedience centre, probably because the *Kaliparaj* were more backward and docile than the perennially restive Baraiyas. Baraiya social banditry in fact touched a new peak in Kheda in 1921, with 70 dacoities—many of them committed by a gang led by Babar Deva who had become a kind of folk hero among the lower castes. (Hardiman, *Peasant Agitations,* pp 201, 206)

Things were more complicated in Bombay city. While enthusiastic support came from Gujarati businessmen, professional and clerical groups, Maharashtrians still revering the memory of Tilak (more than 200,000 attended his funeral on 1 August 1920) tended to be somewhat suspicious of Gandhi, and there were serious problems of control so far as industrial labour and lower-class Muslims were concerned. The *hartal* on 17 November 1921 quickly developed into large-scale riots, with Maharashtrian mill-workers and Muslims inflamed by the jailing of the Ali brothers attacking whites, Christians, Anglicized Parsis, and sometimes anyone wearing European clothes. About twenty were killed, though Gandhi could find some comfort in the fact that his decision to go on a fast helped to end the riots by 23 November. Of greater long-term significance than this brief outburst was the emergence during 1921 of a radical student group under S.A. Dange, R.S. Nimbkar, V.D. Sathaye and R.V. Nadkarni (later joined by S.V. Deshpande and K.N. Joglekar), very active in Non-Cooperation but increasingly critical of Gandhi and developing an interest in Marxism through literature supplied by a millionaire with socialist leanings named R.B. Lotwalla. In his *Gandhi versus Lenin,* written in April 1921, Dange attempted a point-by-point comparison of the philosophy of Gandhi (which he traced back to Tolstoy) with that of Lenin, and visualized a *swaraj* which would nationalize big factories, impose a ceiling on wealth and redistribute *zamindari* land among peasants. While accepting non-violence as an effective tactic, the pamphlet emphasized the need to use the weapons of no-tax and the political general strike—'If we win, we will win only by the help of the proletariat, i.e. the labourers and peasantry.'

Non-Cooperation remained relatively weak in Maharashtra, where the established Tilakite political leadership was unenthusiastic about Gandhi, and where non-Brahmans till the 1930s felt with some reason that the Congress was a Chitpavan-led affair. As elsewhere, however, the weakness of Gandhian controls led to some sporadic local outbursts. At Malegaon, a Muslim pocket in Nasik district, a Khilafat crowd burnt three policemen to death on 25 April 1921, following the arrest of some of their leaders.

Peasants of Mulshi Peta, near Poona, adopted *satyagraha* methods to defend their lands, which Tata with government support was trying to acquire for a hydro-electric project. The Poona Congress took up their cause in April 1921, and the struggle continued intermittently for years.

The truly all-India nature of the Non-Cooperation-Khilafat upsurge is best indicated by its penetration of the south. Of the four linguistic regions of south India, only Karnatak remained largely unaffected—its political awakening would come in the 1930s. As elsewhere, the initial appeal to upper and middle class professional groups had only limited success in Madras Presidency, with only 6 out of 682 title-holders surrendering their honours, 36 Tamil and 103 Andhra lawyers giving up their practice, and only 92 national schools were established with some 5000 pupils. The highlight of the Madras city movement was rather a labour upsurge culminating in a four-month-long strike at the white-owned Buckingham and Carnatic textile mills from July to October 1921 which received the full support of local Non-Cooperation leaders like Thiru Vi Ka. The government (which after the 1921 elections included anti-Brahman Justice Party ministers) tried to break the strike by egging on untouchable Adi-Dravidas against caste-Hindu strikers, while the nationalist leadership made a somewhat unrealistic bid to link the labour movement with Gandhian strategy by distributing *charkhas* in place of strike funds. The experience of trying to combine nationalism with a labour movement set an elderly Madras lawyer and volunteer organizer, Singaravelu Chettiar, on the road to becoming the first Communist in south India. In an open letter to Gandhi dated 5 May 1921, Singaravelu condemned the brakes he was imposing on *kisan* movements, urged the use of non-violent Non-Cooperation against 'capitalistic autocracy' and suggested a rather eclectic 'Communism' which would include the *charkha,* through which 'each and every house-hold in the land could become independent of an employer.... Just so, I wish each and every one of us should own a piece of land...'

Orthodox Brahman sentiments, Sanskritizing ambitions of non-Brahman castes like Nadars, Saurashtras and Komatis, and the resentment of liquor dealers against Government efforts to enhance revenue through increasing license rates—all combined to make picketing of liquor-shops one of the most successful forms of Non-Cooperation in coastal Andhra and interior Tamilnadu. The Madras Government was seriously worried, for by the early 1920s more than 20% of its revenue came from excise, a much higher proportion than in other provinces. Such movements were throwing up a new, specifically Gandhian leadership based in interior Tamilnadu and headed by Rajagopalachari, a Salem lawyer who gave up his practice in 1921. Madras city nationalists like Satyamurthi or Kasturi Ranga Iyengar, in contrast, had adopted Non-Cooperation only half-willingly, like the Tilakites of Maharashtra or C.R. Das in Bengal.

Non-Cooperation attained its greatest strength, however, in the Andhra delta region, with outstanding leaders like Konda Venkatappayya, A. Kaleswara Rao, T. Prakasam and Pattabhi Sitaramayya, considerable merchant support (from the Mothey family of Ellore, for instance, or the Rajahmundri Chamber of Commerce which virtually functioned as the local Non-Cooperation committee), and a broad middle peasant stratum unlike the Tamilnadu 'dry' areas. The broad sweep, as well as the internal tensions, of the Andhra political awakening of 1921 were vividly reflected in Unnava Lakshminarayana's Telegu novel *Maalapalli* (1922). Its hero advocates Gandhian methods for solving the tensions between caste-Hindu landlords and untouchables, but has an impatient brother who turns into a kind of social bandit and composes a ballad evoking the lost equality of men and referring to the international solidarity of toilers.

Among the highlights of the Andhra upsurge was the resistance of the small town of Chirala-Parala in Guntur district to the government move to make it a municipality (which implied a sharp hike in local taxes from ₹4000 to ₹30,000). Led by Duggirala Gopalakrishnayya, its 15,000 inhabitants refused to pay taxes and collectively migrated for eleven months to a new settlement named Ramanagar. A powerful movement for nonpayment of land-revenue developed in the delta region between December 1921 and February 1922. This was spearheaded by mass resignations of village officers who had their own grievances about recent government moves to restrict their considerable privileges, but was fuelled also by peasant distress due to a poor monsoon and the general feeling, stated by a Guntur villager to a British official, that 'Gandhi Swaraj was said to be coming and they were not to pay taxes'. (M. Venkatarangaiya, *Freedom Struggle in Andhra Pradesh*, Vol. III, p. 276) Attaining its maximum intensity in the Pedanandipad subdivision of Bapatla *taluka* near Guntur town and in Raghudevapuram *firka* near Rajahmundri, the movement brought down revenue collection from ₹14.73 lakhs to only ₹4 lakhs for the month of January 1922—before Andhra Congress leaders called it off on 10 February at Gandhi's insistence.

Andhra in 1921–22 was also the scene for a pioneer link-up of tribal and poor peasant grievances against forest restrictions with nationalism, the 'forest *satyagrahas*' in Rayachoti *taluka* of Cuddapah and Palnad *taluka* of Guntur. The Cambridge historian C.J. Baker has tried to reduce this to an interested agitation of prosperous cattle breeders of the coastal area against higher grazing fees imposed on cattle other than locally owned, but there is ample evidence of a much more elemental and lower-class movement.

'Enormous crowds' of villagers had greeted Gandhi in Cuddapah in September 1921 in the brief 'that he would get their taxes reduced and the Forest Regulations abolished'. While Congress leaders like Venkatappayya tried to confine the agitation to social boycott of forest officials, peasants began sending cattle into forests without paying grazing fees, some forest villages in Palnad proclaimed *swaraj* and attacked police parties, and forest administration in both Palnad and Rayachoti virtually collapsed in face of 'large bands of men imbued with the idea that Gandhi Raj was either in being or about to be established and that the forest was theirs to work their will upon'. (*Madras Forest Administration Report,* 1921–22, p. 30). Such apocalyptic rumours repeatedly acted as catalysts in 1921–22: a jail break by ordinary convicts at Trichinopoly in May 1921, for instance, was 'based on the belief that Gandhi's Swaraj was about to replace British rule'. (Viceroy to Secretary of State, 20. June 1921, *Reading Collection*)

By far the most violent of the millenarian outbursts of 1921 developed among the ever-restive Moplahs of Malabar. While previous Moplah outbreaks had a 'ritualistic' character, with actual participants no more than a handful, rumours of imminent collapse of British authority now converted endemic protest into massive popular rebellion. Given the already described social context of Hindu *jenmis* exploiting Muslim leaseholders and cultivators and a long tradition of Muslim religious militancy (see above, Chapter 3), the outburst inevitably had a 'communal' aspect—which, however, seems to have been much exaggerated. A tenant-rights agitation, developing in Malabar from 1916, was taken up by the Khilafat movement after the Manjeri conference of April 1920. Peasants were encouraged to air their grievances at Khilafat meetings, and the local leader Ali Musaliar is said to have promised that in the coming Muslim state 'there will be no expensive litigation.... No one shall have more than what he actually wants... We do not want the present system of police...'. The arrest of established Congress and Khilafat leaders like K. Madhavan Nair, U. Gopala Menon, Yakub Hasan and P. Moideen Koya in February 1921 left the field clear for such radical leaders preaching an egalitarian millenium. On 20 August 1921, a police raid on Tirurangadi mosque in search of arms sparked off a major rebellion, with widespread attacks on police stations, public offices, communications, and houses of oppressive landlords. The British totally lost control over Ernad and Walluvanad *talukas* of south Malabar for several months, and 'Khilafat Republics' were set up at a number of places under 'Presidents' Kunhammad Haji, Kalathingal Mammad, Ali Musaliar, Sithi Koya Thangal, and Imbichi Koya Thangal. 'The situation now is clearly actual war', reported a British G.O.C. on 26 September, asking for artillery reinforcements—with the Moplah resistance 'framed upon guerilla warfare...getting stronger...

the armed fighting gangs probably total 10,000...'. (Viceroy to Secretary of State, 28 September 1921, *Reading Collection*)

Hindu opinion generally condemned the Moplahs as being no more than communal fanatics, and it is true that about 600 Hindus were killed and some 2500 forcibly converted (according to an Arya Samajist source). These figures, however, are really rather low, considering the facts that the 'fanatics' controlled for months an area inhabited by four lakh Hindus including many oppressive landlords and moneylenders, and numerous collaborators with the British. The first case of forcible conversion occurred only on 10 September, and K.N. Panikkar in a recent article gives interesting details of a 23 mile march by a Moplah band across a Hindu area merely to burn the records of a particularly oppressive Hindu landlord without injuring anyone on the way or even the family of the *jenmi*. Even more startling is the fact that the very first batch of Moplah prisoners included a Nambudri and four Nairs. (Secretary of State to Viceroy, 3 November 1921, enclosing a letter from a Coimbatore District Judge) The central fact remains that of a massive and armed anti-imperialist revolt, the bloody suppression of which left 2337 rebels killed, 1652 wounded, and no less than 45,404 prisoners. As in 1857 or 1919, the mask of British liberalism fell off completely in face of a really formidable threat. At Podanur on 20 November, the bodies of 66 asphyxiated Moplah prisoners were found in a railway wagon into which they had been shut in. Every English school boy knows of Sirajud-daulah's Black Hole—a grossly exaggerated story, if not entirely a myth; surprisingly few even in independent India have heard of the absolutely indisputable 'black hole' of Podanur.

In the usually isolated province of Assam, Non-Cooperation attained a strength which no later phase of the national movement would ever equal. The most important development was in the tea-gardens of Surma valley, where at Chargola in May 1921 coolies demanded a big wage increase with 'shouts of Gandhi Maharaj Ki Jai', followed by a massive exodus of some 8000 (52% of the labour force here) again amidst declarations that such was Gandhi's order. Rumours had apparently spread that Gandhi-Raj was coming to give them land in the villages from where they had been so forcibly or deceitfully torn away. It is significant that the bulk of plantation labour in Chargola valley came from the eastern U.P. districts of Basti and Gorakhpur where Non-Cooperation had become very powerful. In October and again in December sporadic strikes and disturbances were being reported from tea gardens in Darrang and Sibsagar districts, and officials repeatedly complained that Non-Cooperators were active among tea garden labour. Most Assam Congress leaders, however, were not at all enthusiastic about strikes in plantations, since some of them (like N.C. Bardaloi) were planters themselves. A Congress activist's memoirs recall how his heart 'was almost frozen' when some workers came to him one night with a strike proposal. (P. Barthakur, *Swadhinata Ranar Samsparshat,* quoted in Amalendu Guha, *Planter Raj to Swaraj,* pp. 137–9) There were signs also of a no-revenue movement among peasants, and even after Gandhi's Bardoli retreat, a route march of the Assam Rifles was ordered in Sibsagar 'for the special benefit of tea garden coolies' (Viceroy to Secretary of State, 20 February 1922). The 1921 days left a deep impression on Assamese literature, through the poetry of 'Assam-Kesari' Ambikagiri Roychaudhuri, as well as numerous folksongs where 'Gandhi-Raja' was substituted for Krishna in Vaishnava lyrics.

The Non-Cooperation-Khilafat alliance made 1921–22 was possibly the point of greatest strength and unity in the entire history of the national movement in Bengal. It is true that most Bengal political leaders accepted Gandhi very late, only with C.R. Das's conversion at Nagpur, after which even the terrorists agreed to give Gandhian methods a trial for a year. Sophisticated Calcutta intellectuals never showed much enthusiasm for some Gandhian ways. Rabindranath started a celebrated controversy with his 'Call of truth' (*Modern Review,* October 1921), which hailed the Mahatma's achievement in arousing the destitute millions, but sharply criticized elements of narrowness, obscurantism and unthinking conformity in the cult of the *charkha.* The literary outcrop of Non-Cooperation in Bengal was quite meagre if compared to that of the 1905 days, and nationalists in the 1920s and '30s had to make do very often with the old *Swadeshi* songs. But all this pales into relative insignificance when set beside the unique communal unity (particularly important for Bengal, where Hindus and Muslims were more or less evenly matched in numbers), the effective political leadership provided by C.R. Das and his three young lieutenants (Birendranath Sasmal in Midnapur, J.M. Sengupta in Chittagong, and Subhas Bose in Calcutta), and—above all—the elemental awakening of urban and rural masses.

After the initial student upsurge of early 1921, Non-Cooperation in Bengal reached its second major climax following the Gurkha assault on coolies fleeing from the Assam tea-gardens on 20–21 May at the East Bengal port of Chandpur. 'In an incredibly short time the whole of Eastern Bengal was in a ferment', recalled an official report in 1924—with widespread *hartals* followed by strikes paralysing railway and steamer services under the leadership of J.M. Sengupta. The steamer strike continued till early July, that on the Assam-Bengal railway till September; both were thoroughly disliked by Calcutta Marwari business circles as well as by Gandhi. A relative lull then set in from July to October, well-utilized, however, by nationalists who concentrated on building up volunteer groups, organizing arbitration courts, and holding innumerable meetings (no less than 4265 between early June and mid-November). The third, and greatest, wave began with the coming of the Prince of Wales in November and continued till February 1922 and even beyond. The 17 November *hartal* was a massive success in Calcutta, with control of streets passing into the hands of volunteers, and quite a few resignations by policemen. A police official reported disaffection among his men in no less than seven districts in December 1921. Repression was countered by mass courting of arrest (more than 3000 had gone to jail in Calcutta by the end of the year). Volunteers going to jail now included for the first time both upper-class women (following the lead of Basanti Debi, the wife of C.R. Das) and large numbers of (mainly Muslim) mill-workers. Khilafat agitators like Muhammad Osman had been active among Muslim workers in Calcutta's industrial suburbs from early 1921 simultaneously organizing volunteer groups and trade unions. The 349 volunteers arrested in Calcutta in the first week of January 1922 included 123 millhands, a considerable number of 'boat manjhis and low-class Muhammadans', and only 39 students—a social composition utterly different from the *Swadeshi* days. As in Bombay and Madras, the experience of 1921—and of subsequent disillusionment—contributed to the formation in Calcutta of pioneer Communist groups, led in this case by Muzaffar Ahmad, who was contacted by an *emissary* of M.N. Roy, Nalini Gupta, in late 1921.

In the countryside, Non-Cooperators had attempted a jute boycott in February 1921, urging peasants to give up jute cultivation for paddy and cotton in a move calculated to hit British owned jute mills, reduce foodgrain prices, and encourage *khadi*. Peasant response was meagre, as jute was after all more profitable. Much more effective was a campaign against the white-owned Midnapur Zamindari Company on the Rajshahi-Nadia Pabna-Murshidabad border, where peasants already fighting against indigo cultivation were provided able guidance by the Calcutta student Someshwarprasad Chaudhuri. Chaudhuri recalled in a later autobiography that Das had encouraged him in private, at the same time warning him that the Congress officially would not support no-rent moves.

The best-organized of the village movements was the anti-Union Board agitation in the Contai and Tamluk sub-divisions of Midnapur led by Birendranath Sasmal. The newly-introduced Union Board meant a heavy increase in local taxes, and Sasmal was able to organize a very effective no-tax movement among the predominantly Mahishya substantial tenantry of Midnapur in November-December 1921 which forced the government to withdraw the new regulation from the district. In the winter of 1921–22, peasants resisted Settlement operations in Puban, Bogra, and particularly in the Rampurhat sub-division of Birbhum, where the movement was led by Jitendralal Banerji.

These were essentially movements of relatively better-off peasants, led by local lawyer-politicians; there were mounting signs, however, of a more elemental groundswell. On 24 March 1921, no less than 669 convicts broke out from Rajshahi jail, declaring that Gandhi Raj had arrived. An official report speaks of 'a great wave of lawlessness' in the first quarter of 1922— 'the movement had got beyond the control of the leaders...the spirit of violence and contempt of all authority...was not of the leaders, but of the masses.' Even in well-organized Midnapur, district leaders' pleas for payment of *chaukidari* taxes after the Union Board was withdrawn (in December 1921) often went unheaded, there was considerable withholding of rent, and Santals in the Jhargam sub-division were looting *hats* and *zamindar* owned forests. In Jalpaiguri in February 1922, police were attacked by Santhals wearing Gandhi caps, which they claimed made them immune from bullets. In the neighbouring north Bengal district of Rangpur, nonpayment of *chaukidari* tax 'soon developed into a refusal to pay rent', and Muslim peasants of Nilphamari set up a 'Swaraj thana' under a 'Gandhi daroga'. Chittagong witnessed a veritable invasion of reserved forests—a widespread looting which 'was not the work of volunteers, but of ordinary villagers out to help themselves'. In the Chaudagram sub-division of Tippera, the village police stopped work from November 1921. 'No taxes were being paid, and no agricultural rents collected either by Government or by private landlords...the agitation was entirely Muhammadan, but not religious. The people were simply out to assert themselves...'. (*Government of Bengal, Political Confidential*, 395 of 1924: *History of the Non-Cooperation and Khilafat Movements in Bengal*) It needs to be noted that Rangpur, Chittagong and Tippera were all outlying districts, seldom visited by top leaders, and that official reports repeatedly note efforts by local volunteers or politicians to restrain the masses, without success. A theory of 'subcontractors' or instigation by elite-politicians seems utterly irrelevant here.

If Bengal manifested a repeated tendency to burst Gandhian bounds, Bihar won the Mahatma's praise as 'a Province in which the most solid work is being done in connection with Non-Cooperation. Its leaders understand the true spirit of non-violence...(*Young India*, 2 March 1921). 41 high and 600 primary and middle national schools with a total of 21,500 pupils had been established by June 1922, and 48 depots had been set up in 11 districts to distribute cotton and *charkha*. 300,000 *charkhas*, 89,000 handlooms, and a *khadi* production of 95,000 yards per month were reported from Bihar in August 1922, though Congress leaders admitted that *khadi* was 'not very popular' because of its high price and it was being worn by only 1% of the population. Liquor boycott made substantial progress, and some contacts were established with Chotanagpur tribals, particularly with the Tana Bhagat sect. Against this general impression of a powerful but strictly restrained movement, however, must be set sporadic incidents like 35 cases of *hat*-looting in Muzaffarpur, Bhagalpur, Monghyr and Purnea in January 1921 (with men who claimed to be Gandhi's disciples trying to enforce just prices at some places), the attack on Giridih just after the arrest of a Khilafat volunteer, leading to firing on 25 April 1921, an epidemic of illicit distillation in some tribal areas, and widespread tension in Champaran and Muzaffarpur districts over appropriation of traditional village pastures by *zamindars* and indigo planters. Bhumihar villagers of Sonparsa in Bhagalpur attacked Gurkhas employed by a European landlord in January 1921, a dispute regarding grazing rights led to the burning of the Chauterwa indigo factory near Motihari in Champaran in November 1921, while Sitamarhi sub-division in Muzaffarpur earned a reputation as a storm-centre, with punitive police sent there in January 1922 to check a possible no-tax movement. There was no revival, however, of the *anti-zamindar* peasant agitation which had plagued the Darbhanga estate in 1920, and from which the Bihar Congress leadership had firmly dissociated itself. In the summer of 1921, white coal mine owners of the Chotanagpur region expressed fears that Non-Cooperation propaganda in labour recruitment areas combined with the activities of Swami Viswanand (who got some support from Marwari mineowners like Ramjas Agarwala in Jharia) might lead to an exodus from the mines in the Assam pattern. At Giridih 'the miners had themselves organised a trade union', even before the entry of Congressmen. (*Home Political, 43/1921*)

The United Provinces during Non-Cooperation became one of the strongest bases of the Congress, with 328,966 members in July 1921 (a figure exceeded only by Bihar which claimed 350,000), and U.P. won from this time a leading position in national politics which it has retained till today. 1920–21 marks the beginning of the continuous political careers of a host of a leading nationalists—Jawaharlal Nehru, Purushottamdas Tandon, Ganesh Shankar Vidyarthi, Govind Ballabh Pant, Lal Bahadur Shastri. 90,0000 volunteers had been enrolled by the Congress in U.P. by the beginning of 1922, and there was a massive growth also in Khilafat volunteer associations. 137 national educational institutions had been set up in the province by July 1921, of which the Kashi Vidyapith was the most prominent. The deep Gandhian impact on the U.P. intelligentsia was vividly reflected in the novels of Premchand, who resigned his post in a Gorakhpur government school in February 1921 to work for the nationalist journal *Aj* and for the Kasi Vidyapith. His *Premasharam* (1921) depicts a landlord with Gandhian leanings, while *Rangbhumi* (1925) has as its hero a blind beggar, Surdas, who fights a prolonged, non-violent struggle to prevent the pastures of his village being taken over for an Anglo-Indian cigarette factory. The latter novel also had two characters who turn revolutionaries, Vinay Singh and Sofia.

Organized Non-Cooperation in U.P. was mainly an affair of cities and small towns; as elsewhere, however, more elemental movements in the countryside were perhaps equally significant. The U.P. Congress leadership was marginally more responsive to peasant outbursts than that of Bihar, perhaps because the Avadh *talukdar* was notoriously loyalist, though a restraining role was repeatedly evident at crucial points. The peasant upsurge in south and south-east Avadh associated with Baba Ramchandra culminated in widespread agrarian riots in Rae Bareli, Pratapgarh, Fyzabad and Sultanpur between January and March 1921. The targets included not only the houses and crops of *talukdars,* but bazars and merchant property. Fursatganj bazar in Rae Bareli, for instance, was attacked by a crowd of 10,000 on 6 January which complained of 'dearness of grain and cloth' and demanded that 'all the shopkeepers should at once be ordered to sell cloth at 4 annas per yard and flour at 8 seers per rupee'—an instance of attempted popular fixation of prices, reminiscent of the 'Maximum' sought to be imposed by plebian violence before and during the French Revolution. There were several violent clashes with the police, and instances of peoples' courts dispensing rough peasant justice. A Shah Naim Ata proclaimed himself 'King of Salon', and in Fyzabad a pretender 'Ramchandra' appeared, preaching non-payment of rent and land to the landless, all in the name of Gandhi.

Gandhi's own condemnation of this plebian outburst has been mentioned already, but it is interesting that in 1921 Jawaharlal's stand was no different— he recalls in his *Autobiography* that at a meeting in Fyzabad he persuaded those who had indulged in violence to put up their hands, knowing full well that the police were present and the men would be jailed. Khilafatist and Congress leaders persuaded Baba Ramchandra to keep away from the affected area, and when the latter was arrested on 10 February, Motilal Nehru and Gauri Shankar Misra hastened to issue a leaflet which insisted: 'We must not be unhappy over this and must not even try to get him released.' Ramchandra in an autobiographical fragment written in the 1930s charged the Congress with betrayal, but in 1921 he seems to have willingly followed the lead of his nationalist mentors.

By the summer of 1921, the *kisan* movement seems to have been largely swallowed up by Non-Cooperation, with specific peasant demands relegated to the background, while an alarmed U.P. Government persuaded *talukdars* to agree to a few concessions by the Oudh Rent Act of 1921 (like life-tenancies in place of seven year-leases). Things threatened to get out of hand again in late-1921 and early 1922 in N.W. Avadh (Hardoi, Bahraich, Bara Banki and Sitapur districts), where the 'Eka' movement started by some local Congressmen was taken over by the much more radical Madari Pasi. The basic demand here was the conversion of produce rents (*batai*) into cash (which would have favoured the peasants as prices were rising), and an elaborate ritual of *mantras* and vows seems to have been devised. The police managed to crush the movement and arrest Madari Pasi only in June 1922.

The British in U.P. were alarmed also by signs of disaffection even lower down the social scale. Hill-tribes were on the rampage in the summer of 1921, burning down thousands of acres of reserved forests in the Kumaon Division (Viceroy to Secretary of State, 10 July 1921, *Reading Collection*). In October 1921, Reading expressed his concern that in the Avadh, countryside, 'the majority of those attending meetings, nominally held for cultivators, are men who have lost their land and who believe that it would be restored to them by Gandhi and low-class laboureres who believe that Gandhi will provide holdings for them.' (*Ibid*. 13 October 1921).

Chauri-Chaura

The Chauri Chaura incident which proved the last straw for Gandhi took place in a Gorakhpur village, unaffected by the Kisan Sabha or Eka agitation, but with a well-organized volunteer body which had started picketing the local bazar in a campaign directed both against liquor sales and high food prices. Gandhi himself admitted that there had been ample provocation—the police had beaten up the volunteer leader (an army pensioner named Bhagwan Ahir), and then opened fire on the crowd which had come to protest before the police station. British alarm at the incident was vividly reflected by the fact that the sessions court initially sentenced not less then 172 of the 225 Chauri Chaura accused to death (eventually 19 were hanged, and the rest transported). It must remain a matter of shame that there were virtually no nationalist protests against the barbarous attempt to take 172 lives in return for the 22 policemen killed—the only recorded protests being those made by M.N. Roy's emigre Communist journal, *Vanguard,* and by the Executive Committee of the Communist International—and that even today at Chauri Chaura there remains a police memorial, but nothing in honour of the peasant martyrs.

Jawaharlal Nehru later recalled that Gandhi's abrupt and unilateral decision to suspend the entire movement after Chauri Chaura was deeply resented by 'almost all the prominent Congress leaders' and 'naturally even more' by the 'younger people' (*An Autobiography,* p. 82). Gandhi's own defence, as stated in *Young India* on 16 February 1922, used two arguments. A passionate reiteration of faith in non-violence ('I would suffer every humiliation, every torture, absolute ostracism and death itself to prevent the movement from becoming violent') was accompanied by the following revealing plea—'Suppose the nonviolent disobedience of Bardoli was permitted by God to succeed, the India Government had abdicated in favour of the victors of Bardoli, who would control the unruly element...?' As R.P. Dutt pointed out in what has become the standard Left criticism, the Working Committee's Bardoli Resolution of 12 February confirming the withdrawal emphasized in two of its seven clauses that 'withholding of rent payment to the zamindars is contrary to the Congress resolutions', (No. 6) and assured the *zamindars* 'that the Congress movement is in no way intended to attack their legal rights...' (No. 7) (*India Today,* p. 290). Yet rent was not directly involved at all in the Chauri Chaura incident, and no-rent by itself was no more inevitably violent than picketing of cloth or liquor or non-payment of revenue.

In fairness to Gandhi, it may be argued that he had given repeated and ample warning that he was prepared to lead only a specific type of controlled mass movement, and was not interested at all in class struggle or social revolution. The fact that the entire movement collapsed when Gandhi called it off also reveals its own basic weakness—there was ample combustible material in the India of 1919–22, perhaps even at times an objectively revolutionary situation, but nothing at all in the way of an alternative revolutionary leadership. The masses had been inspired by the vague vision of Gandhi Raj, had interpreted it in their own diverse, sometimes near-revolutionary ways, but they still looked up to the Mahatma alone for guidance. Congress leaders in jail like Motilal Nehru, Lajpat Rai or C.R. Das who disliked the Bardoli retreat were certainly not in any way more radical or less socially inhibited than Gandhi. The disagreement was probably no more than tactical, over a question of timing. Motilal and C.R. Das felt, with some justice, that acceptance of the British peace feelers during the Prince of Wales visit in December 1921 would have brought some concrete gains in the shape of constitutional concessions, whereas Gandhi, who had rejected all compromise then, had now called off civil disobedience without any returns.

The British, who had not dared to touch Gandhi so long even while arresting practically every prominent Congressmen, plucked up courage on 10 March 1922 to arrest him and award a six-year jail sentence, in what was little more than an act of sheer vindictive revenge for the fright he had given them. Gandhi made the occasion memorable by a magnificent court speech: 'I am here, therefore, to invite and submit cheerfully to the highest penalty that can be inflicted upon me for what in law is deliberate crime, and what appears to me to be the highest duty of a citizen.' The crucial fact, however, was that there was not a ripple of protest anywhere in India as Gandhi went to jail.

1922-1927: DECLINE AND FRAGMENTATION

The years from 1922 to 1927 are at first sight dominated entirely by a sense of anti-climax, all the more acute because Gandhi's promise in 1920 of *Swaraj* within a year had aroused such soaring expectations. By March 1923, Congress membership (for the 16 out of 20 provinces which had sent reports to the AICC) had fallen to 106,046, less than one-third of what U.P. alone had claimed two years before. The No-Changer-Swarajist rift threatened to break up the national movement, there were strong tendencies towards a return to near-mendicant politicking, and the Hindu-Muslim unity of 1919-22 was quickly succeeded by communal riots on an unprecedented scale. And yet below the surface other forces must have been gathering strength, for the announcement of the all-white Simon Commission in November 1927 would be followed by a national resurgence culminating in Civil Disobedience. Our account of the intervening years must take note of both aspects, of decline but also of the beginnings of a renewal.

No-Changers and Swarajists

Within the Civil Disobedience Enquiry Committee set up by the AICC in June 1922 to recommend the future course of action, Ansari, Rajagopalachari, and Kasturiranga Iyengar advocated concentration on Gandhian constructive rural work, while Motilal Nehru, Vithalbhai Patel and Hakim Ajmal Khan argued that the changed situation demanded Congress participation in Council elections. Orthodox Gandhians like Vallabhbhai Patel and Rajendra Prasad rallied round the first view, while the latter received the powerful support of C.R. Das, President of the Gaya Congress (December 1922), who put forward a justification of Council entry in radical terms. The Congress should enter the Councils, Das argued, to wreck them from within by total obstruction of their proceedings, creating a deadlock which would force the British to concede further reforms. At the Dehra Dun U.P. Provincial Conference two months before Gaya, Das had also enunciated his famous formula that *Swaraj* must be for the 'masses' and not for the 'classes' alone. The Gaya session rejected Council entry by 1740 votes against 890, but Das and Motilal Nehru went ahead in March 1923 to set up a Swaraj Party to contest the coming elections in November. At the Delhi Special Congress (September 1923) and the regular Kakinada session (December 1923) a compromise was struck by which Congressmen were allowed to stand for elections even while faith in the constructive programme was reiterated and an All India Khadi Board was set up to organize its most important element. Gandhi's release from jail in February 1924 for a time seemed to tilt the balance again on the side of the 'No-Changers'. At the AICC session at Ahmedabad in June 1924, Gandhi pressed for a minimum spinning qualification for Congress membership, removal of those who had entered Councils from the ranks of Congress office-bearers, as well as for total condemnation of a recent terrorist incident in Bengal. The first two resolutions were defeated, and the condemnation of Gopinath Saha, bitterly opposed by Das and most Bengal delegates, was carried by only 78 votes against 70. Gandhi declared himself to be 'Defeated and Humbled' (*Young India,* 3 July 1924), and came to an agreement with Das and Motilal Nehru in November 1924 permitting Swarajists to work within Councils 'as an integral part of the Congress organization', while in return a spinning qualification would be introduced for Congress membership (but which could be fulfilled either personally or by asking a substitute to spin the required 2000 yards). Next year Gandhi decided to place the entire organizational machinery of the Congress at the disposal of the Swarajists, and set up a separate All India Spinners Association to implement his own ideas. His announcement that 1926 would be a 'year of silence' for him, even led to rumours that Gandhi was retiring from politics.

Nagpur, Borsad and Vaikom

The internecine quarrel inevitably reduced the Congress's ability to conduct big agitations. The Nagpur Flag *satyagraha,* started in mid-1923 against a local order banning the use of the Congress flag in some areas of the city, proved a rather tame affair and ended in a compromise, though Gujarat under Vallabhbhai Patel again revealed its organizational strength by sending large numbers of volunteers. The continuing Akali agitation seemed for a brief while to focus the energies of restless radicals like Jawaharlal. The Guru-ke-Bagh *satyagraha* (August 1922-April 1923) originated from a very trivial dispute over the cutting of a tree on land disputed between the ousted *Mohant* of the shrine and the new SGPC management, but it aroused country-wide sympathy due to the atrocious police beating-up of thousands of absolutely peaceful Akali volunteers. Next year the abdication under British pressure of Maharaja Ripudaman Singh of Nabha, a major patron of the Akali movement, led to a *satyagraha* at Jaito which Jawaharlal briefly joined. The astute new Governor of Punjab, Malcolm Hailey, was able however to defuse the whole Akali issue through the Sikh Gurdwaras and Shrines Act of 1925 accepting SGPC control over Sikh religious centres. A somewhat similar, though much more localized, issue briefly emerged in Bengal in 1924, with the Tarakeswar *satyagraha* against a corrupt *Mohant*, started by Swami Viswananda and taken up by C.R. Das.

The two really significant *satyagrahas* of these years, however, were those at Borsad (in Kheda district) in 1923–24 and Vaikom in Travancore state in 1924–25. Vallabhbhai Patels Borsad movement has been described by Hardiman as the first really successful Gandhian *satyagraha* in rural Gujarat. Directed against a poll-tax of ₹2-7-0 imposed in September 1923 on every adult in Borsad to pay for police required to suppress a wave of dacoities (these were largely commited by low-caste Baraiyas, and the Patidars felt that they were being unjustly penalized for supporting the Congress), the movement took the form of total non-payment of the new levy by all the 104 affected villages in December, and the tax had to be cancelled on 7 January 1924. The victory revived Gandhian Congress prestige, which had been somewhat lowered by the abrupt retreat of February 1922. A pioneer attempt to extend Gandhian *satyagraha* to a princely state—the no-revenue movement against a recent tax-hike in Petlad *taluka* of Baroda (adjoining Kheda) in 1924—failed, however, to get off the ground, as Baroda state officials showed much greater flexibility than the British by quickly making some concessions. The Vaikom *satyagraha* was the first 'temple-entry' movement—more precisely, it was an attempt along strict Gandhian lines to assert the right of low caste Ezhavas and untouchables to use roads near a Travancore temple. It was led by the Ezhava Congress leader T.K. Madhavan, together with Nair Congressmen like K. Kelappan and K.P. Kesava Menon. Multi-caste support for the *satyagraha* was indicated also by the participation of the Nair caste association leader Mannath Padmanabha Pillai, but the important Christian community was unnecessarily alienated by a statement by Gandhi asking them to keep away from a Hindu affair. Gandhi visited Vaikom in March 1925, but the *satyagraha* petered out after 20 months when the government constructed diversionary roads for use by untouchables.

Constructive Work

Occasional *satyagrahas* on local issues apart, the Gandhian 'No-Changers' during these years concentrated on constructive work in villages. This included impressive relief work (often far outdistancing government efforts) in emergencies like floods (as in Bengal in 1922, and Gujarat in 1927), national schools, the promotion of *khadi* and other cottage crafts, anti-liquor propaganda, and social work among low castes and untouchables. Considered as a solution to the social and economic problems of rural India, the programme was clearly a failure. National schools, as the experience of numerous efforts since 1905 clearly revealed, flourished only in the brief periods of high political excitement and could not overcome the lure of degrees and jobs in more normal times. Gandhi admitted privately to Motilal in 1927 that *khadi* was proving an uphill task (Motilal to Jawaharlal Nehru, 11 August 1927)—it was still so much more expensive, after all, than either imported cloth or Indian mill-cloth. 'Acchutoddhar'—renamed 'Harijan' welfare and enormously extended after 1932 for political reasons—did not tackle at all the basic economic issue of landless and often semi-servile agricultural labour which constituted the bulk of the 'untouchables'. Even as pure social reform, it was considerably hindered in the 1920s by Gandhi's refusal to condemn the caste system in principle. During his Travancore visit of 1925, the Mahatma had expressed his disagreement about the radical anti-caste ideas of the Ezhava religious leader Sri Narayan Guru, and militant non-Brahmans in Tamil Nadu like E.V.R. Naicker were extremely disappointed by his speeches in Madras in 1927 defending Varnashrama ideals.

Yet recent detailed research (e.g., Hitesh Sanyal on Bengal, Gyan Pandey on U.P., and David Hardiman on Kheda) is increasingly bringing out the considerable *political* importance of Gandhian constructive work in building up rural support for Congress and, above all, in establishing Congress hegemony over low castes and untouchables. National schools, Khaddar Bhandars, and social service associations (like Lajpat Rai's Lok Sevak Mandal, active in Punjab and U.P.) trained up and provided financial support to considerable numbers of full-time Congress cadres. If national education served mainly urban lower middle class and rich peasant groups (not a single untouchable emerged as a Congress worker from such schools in U.P. in the 1920s), *khadi* did provide marginal relief for the rural poor, even apart from the clear political advantage of 'forcing elite politicians to dress as peasants' (Hardiman). Even in a province like Bengal with its generally 'non-Gandhian' reputation, much useful work was done by institutions like Satis Dasgupta's Khadi Pratisthan of Sodepur and Suresh Banerji's Khadi Asrama of Comilla, while Hitesh Sanyal has emphasized the sustained activities from 1922 onwards of men like Prafulla Sen in the very backward and poverty-stricken Arambagh region of Hooghly district. Arambagh was certainly not an area of rich peasant development, though in this it may not have been typical of most Gandhian rural bases. As could nave been expected, constructive work attained its greatest success in Gujarat, particularly in Kheda and Bardoli with their chain of *asramas* and numerous truly dedicated *gram sevaks*. Constructive work here helped to extend Gandhian influence considerably beyond its initial, 'lesser Patidar' base. Work among the Bardoli *'Kaliparaj'* and Kheda Baraiyas combined genuine, if marginal, upliftment with a process of 'taming' unruly elements. Ravisankar Maharaj's wandering as a *sadhu* and social reformer in Baraiya villages, for instance, contributed to reducing the number of dacoities in Borsad *taluka* from 20 in 1921 to one each in 1927–29. The centres of constructive work everywhere provided the initial bases for Civil Disobedience activities in 1930, and the deep roots struck by nationalism among the peasants of Kheda was vividly revealed when 14 Borsad villages pressed on their own initiative for a no-revenue movement during the Dandi March. Harvests that year had been excellent, there had been no recent revenue enhancement, and the late-1930 collapse in agricultural prices still lay well in the future. Narrow material interest cannot always or totally explain the workings of Indian nationalism.

Swarajist Politics

Swarajist electoral and Council activity during these years was outwardly much more spectacular, though ultimately perhaps of less permanent significance. The Swarajists won a majority in the 1923 elections in the Central Provinces, where the old Maharashtrian followers of Tilak like N.C. Kelkar who had never been particularly enamoured of Non-Cooperation had swung strongly behind Motilal and Das. The party did well in Bengal, too, where its candidate B.C. Roy routed the old stalwart Surendranath Banerji who had become a minister in 1921; it was able to capture 47 out of the 85 elected general Hindu and Muslim seats, including no less than 21 Muslim constituencies. The Bengal victory was made possible by the extremely skilful and effective leadership of 'Deshbandhu' Chittaranjan Das, who was able till his untimely death in June 1925 to preserve a broad coalition of Calcutta politicians, district leaders with mass experience like Birendranath Sasmal, revolutionary cadres (28 ex-detenues had been taken into the BPCC by 1924) and—most important of all—Muslim leaders. The Muslim leaders were won over by Das' Bengal Pact (December 1923) which promised to the Muslims 55% of the administrative posts in the province after *Swaraj*, the stopping of music before mosques, and non-interference with Bakr-Id cow-slaughter. The programme of discrediting the Councils from within started off with a bang with refusal of salaries to dyarchy ministers in C.P. and Bengal, compelling them to resign and forcing the Governors to repeatedly use their 'certificate' powers to push through legislation—thus 'exposing' dyarchy to be no real constitutional advance. In the Central Assembly, a resolution was passed at Swarajist initiative in February 1924 demanding a Round Table Conference to discuss reforms leading up to responsible government, and men like Motilal Nehru and Vithalbhai Patel revealed considerable talents as Parliamentarians. Another consequence was the development of considerable links between Indian business groups and Swarajist politicians, for the latter proved extremely helpful in prodding the government into granting protection to Tata's steel industry in 1924, under the new policy of 'discriminating protection' enunciated by the Fiscal Commission of 1921. Meanwhile the Congress had captured local bodies and municipalities all over the country—most notably Calcutta under Das and Subhas Bose, Allahabad under Jawaharlal and Ahmedabad under Vallabhbhai Patel—and these proved useful arenas for some limited welfare activities, and probably more important, a valuable source of patronage and funds. Certainly Bengal politicians from 1924 onwards would always display a not entirely seemly concern about the intricacies of Calcutta Corporation politicking.

Very soon, however, the politics of Council entry was leading to a host of problems and internal divisions. Once dyarchy had been shown to be a sham, the question arose as regards what to do next, since the Viceroy or the Governors could still push through any legislation they liked by means of the certificate procedure. The Bengal Swarajists could do nothing, for instance, when in October 1924 Subhas Bose was detained without trial, along with 80 others suspected of terrorist links, under an Ordinance similar to the wartime Defence of India regulations which the certificate procedure made into an Act in April 1925. While elected Ministers in dyarchy had little real power, they did and control considerable patronage—and proximity to possible loaves and fishes of office soon encouraged a trend towards 'Responsive Cooperation' with acceptance of executive posts. Even C.R. Das seems to have toyed with the idea just before his death, offering cooperation in return for release of prisoners and talks on constitutional reforms in his Faridpur Conference speech of May 1925. S.B. Tambe took the plunge in C.P., accepting a ministerial post in October 1925; he was bitterly denounced by Motilal Nehru, but got the support of Maharashtrian and Bombay Swarajists like N.C. Kelkar, B.S. Moonje and M.R. Jayakar. Patronage possibilities, in the emerging party bureaucracy as well as in local bodies and government offices, sharply enhanced factional rivalries. In Bengal, the death of C.R. Das was followed by a bitter succession war, in which J.M. Sengupta ousted Birendranath Sasmal in 1927 but was challenged by Subhas Bose on his release from detention soon afterwards. On the eve of the 1926 elections, Motilal's old rival Madanmohan Malaviya formed an Independent Congress Party in alliance with Lajpat Rai and the

Responsive Cooperators, with a programme which combined political moderation with uninhibited Hindu communalism.

Communalism

The quite unprecedented growth of both Hindu and Muslim communalism was in fact by far the most serious and permanent negative development of these years. There was a violent anti-Hindu outburst at Kohat in the N.W. Frontier Province in September 1924, with 155 killed. Three waves of riots in Calcutta between April and July 1926 killed 138; there were disturbances the same year in Dacca, Patna, Rawalpindi and Delhi; and no less than 91 communal outbreaks in U.P., the worst-affected province, between 1923 and 1927. The recurrent ostensible issues were the Muslim demand for stopping music before mosques, and Hindu pressures for a ban on cow-slaughter. Communal bodies proliferated, and political alignments were made increasingly on a communal basis.

Even at the height of Hindu-Muslim fraternization in 1919–22, Congress and Khilafat volunteer organizations had usually remained separate bodies, united because of the alliance between their leaders, but potentially divisive if the leaders quarrelled. Khilafat had brought orthodox *mullahs* into politics on a large scale, and the December 1921 programme of the Jamiyat-al-Ulama-i-Hind visualized free India as a kind of federation of religious communities. Congress propaganda, particularly at lower levels, had also been far from consistently secular—Ram-Rajya, after all, was not a concept with much meaning or attraction for Muslims. The alliance between Congress and Khilafat leaders, weakened by Gandhi's unilateral withdrawal of February 1922, lingered on till early 1925, when Mohammad Ali, who as late as December 1923 had presided over the Kakinada Congress, broke with Gandhi in the wake of repeated riots. The Khilafatists in any case had been deprived of their principal slogan when Kamal Attaturk abolished the Ottoman Caliphate in 1924.

So far as divisions among politicians and educated people are concerned, the crucial factor behind the growth of communalism in the 1920s lay in the very logic of participation in the post-1919 political structure. The Montford reforms had broadened the franchise, but preserved and even extended separate electorates; there was, therefore, a built-in temptation for politicians working within the system to use sectional slogans and gather a following by distributing favours to their own religious, regional or caste groups. A second, related, factor was the considerable spread of education in the 1920s, without corresponding growth in employment opportunities. 'The resentments and bitternesses of school, office and shop...(were) sharpened by the disappointment of rising expectations' (P. Hardy, *Muslims of British India,* p. 204)—as had started happening from the 1880s, but on a much larger scale now, the scramble for scarce resources fed communal rancour. Lower down the social scale, economic and social tensions, as before, could often take a distorted communal form, particularly now that an appropriate ideology was very much present. In a city like Kanpur, for instance, the background to the massive riot of March 1931 had been set partly by the decline during the 1920s in predominantly Muslim handloom weaving at a time when Hindu merchants and industrialists were forging ahead. A Bengal Government report of November 1926 related communal tensions in the Mymensingh countryside to 'the economic rivalry of Hindu landlords and Muhammadan talukdars or jotedars in this district, which is reflected in the keen interest taken by the Muhammadan electors in the fate of the Bengal Tenancy Act Amendment Bill'. (*Government of Bengal Political Confidential 516 [1–14] of 1926*) The entire Swarajist leadership in Bengal, including even the 'Leftist' Subhas Bose, took up a pro-*zamindar* stand in the discussions on the tenancy amendment which went on intermittently between 1923 and 1928, and thus contributed directly and heavily to Muslim alienation.

The link between elite and popular communalism was provided by the rapid growth of communal associations and ideologies. The Muslim contribution here is well-known—the spread of *tabligh* (propaganda) and *tanzim* (organization) from 1923 onwards, the Kohat outburst of 1924, the revival of the Muslim League as Khilafat bodies petered away, the murder of Swami Shraddhanand in 1926. At its Lahore session in 1924 presided over by Jinnah (the first since 1918 to meet separately from the Congress), the Muslim League raised the demand for federation with full provincial autonomy to preserve Muslim-majority areas from the danger of 'Hindu domination', apart from separate electorates—a slogan that would remain basic to Muslim communalism till the 1940 demand for Pakistan. It needs to be emphasized, however, that much of this was a reaction against the very rapid spread of Hindu communalism in these years. *Tabligh* and *tanzim* were in large part a response to Arya Samajist *shuddhi* and *sangathan,* started after the Moplah forcible conversions and extended in 1923 by Shraddhanand to western U.P. in a determined bid to win back for Hinduism Malkana Rajput, Gujar and Bania converts to Islam. The Hindu Mahasabha, started at the Hardwar Kumbh Mela in 1915 by Madan Mohan Malaviya along with some Punjabi leaders, had become practically defunct in the Non-Cooperation years. A major revival began from 1922–23, and the Banares session of August 1923, which incorporated the *shuddhi* programme and called for Hindu self-defence squads, represented an alliance of Arya

Samajist reformers with Sanatan Dharma Sabha conservatives in a common Hindu-communal front presided over, as usual, by Malaviya. While the emphasis on the link between Hindu and Hindi in much Mahasabha propaganda led to its specific appeal remaining largely confined to north India (86.8% of delegates to the 1923 session came from U.P., Delhi, Punjab and Bihar—as contrasted to only 6.6% from Bengal, Bombay and Madras combined); a development of ultimately very great significance was the foundation, at Nagpur in 1925, of the Rashtriya Swayam Sevak Sangh by K.B. Hedgewar, an associate of Tilak's old follower Moonje.

Despite their theoretical secularism, No-Changers and Swarajists alike failed to adequately counter Hindu communalism, or even often to clearly disassociate themselves from its organizations and ideology. Gandhi went on a 21-day fast after the Kohat riot in September 1924, staying at Muhammad Ali's Delhi house and bringing about a very temporary reduction of tension through a Unity Conference of leaders. He also denounced, in words which still have great contemporary relevance, the barbaric folly of killing human beings for the sake of the life of a cow. (*Young India,* 29 May 1924) Yet in U.P. No-Changers like Purushottamdas Tandon kept close relations with Malaviya, and Gandhi himself never broke with him. At places like Banares, the Swaraj party and the Hindu Sabha were virtually the same organization. From 1925 onwards, Malaviya made very effective use of Hindu communalism in his bitter rivalry with Motilal Nehru, organizing with the help of Lajpat Rai an Independent Congress Party which was little more than a Mahasabha front. Election preparations often involved direct encouragement of Hindu communalist intransigence, as at Allahabad in 1925–26 where repeated Muslim offers of compromise on the music-before-mosques issue (including in May 1926 a plea that music should be stopped only for five or ten minutes during the evening prayer) were rejected. In Bengal, Das' Hindu-Muslim Pact was abrogated in 1926, and Sasmal who had tried to defend it was defeated next year in a Midnapur election by fellow-Congressmen using the slogan of Hinduism in danger. Even Motilal before the 1926 elections descended at times to communalist appeals, trying desperately and unsuccessfully to woo some Hindu Sabha groups to counter the propaganda that he was pro-Muslim and a beef-eater.

In the 1926 elections, the Swarajists went down everywhere except in Madras before the combination of Hindu Mahasabha and advocates of Responsive Cooperation. The sharpening communal alignment was indicated by the fact that in Bengal Swarajists still won 35 out of 47 Hindu seats, but only one Muslim seat out of 39. Much more important was the fact that the searing memories of the mid-'20s contributed greatly to the general Muslim aloofness in the next round of struggle against foreign rule in

1930–34. The real winner was British imperialism. It is not always remembered that the Hindu communalist leadership's record in bolstering up British rule is not much less notable than that of the Muslim League—from Madan Mohan Malaviya, the apostle of 'Hind-Hindi-Hindu' who bitterly opposed Non-Cooperation in 1921, to Shyamaprasad Mukherji the later founder of the Jana Sangh, who was a minister in Bengal in August 1942 at a time when the British were drowning the Quit India movement in blood.

EMERGENCE OF NEW FORCES: 1922–1927

A deeply despondent Motilal Nehru was writing to his son on 30 March 1927: 'In short conditions in India have never been worse. The reaction of the NCO movement which set in 1922–23 has since been slowly but surely undermining all public activity... The only education the masses are getting is in communal hatred'—and Congressmen were vying with each other for Government favours. Yet the end of 1927 would mark the beginning of a new upswing in the national movement, and it is time now to consider the factors behind this dramatic reversal.

Political and Economic Tensions

The basic objective contradictions between British political and economic domination and most sections of the Indian people made it impossible for the pulls towards compromise and collaboration to go too far. Politicians of all hues were getting increasingly frustrated by the clear signs in the mid-1920s that British policy in India was stiffening now that the post-war anti-imperialist upsurge had died down. Lloyd George in August 1922 in his notorious 'steel-frame' speech declared that 'one institution... we will not deprive of its functions and privileges, and that is the British Civil Service in India'. The implications were spelt out by a 1924 Royal Commission and the 1926 Indian Sandhurst Committee, which visualized a 50% Indianization of the ICS after 15 years and of the police and army in 25 years (i.e., in the case of the army, only in 1952!). The 1920s were the years when the white Dominions were winning virtually complete independence, a process which culminated in the Statute of Westminster of 1931. Government spokesmen, like Home Member Malcolm Hailey in February 1924, hastened to make clear that 'the objective of the Government of India Act (of 1919) is not full Dominion Status but Responsible Government'. For Birkenhead, Tory Secretary of State in 1925, nothing apparently had changed since the days of Lytton or Curzon. 'The door to acceleration (of

Reforms, as demanded by Swarajists) is not open to menace', he thundered in the House of Lords on 7 July 1925—and it was absurd to speak of India as an entity: 'There never has been such a nation.... If we withdraw from India tomorrow, the immediate consequences would be a struggle *a le outrance* between the Muslim and the Hindu population.'

Even more significant perhaps was the fact that after a brief spell of concessions (the Fiscal Commission of 1921 and steel protection in 1924), the economic contradictions were definitely sharpening from the mid-1920s. The policy of discriminating protection meant in practice long delays while Tariff Boards deliberated on the pleas of Indian industries, and then the government sometimes held back the implementation of higher import duty recommendations—as with the Textile Tariff Board of 1927. In eastern India, the Birla group was trying to make headway against entrenched British jute interests, while the Scindia Steam Navigation venture of Walchand Hirachand and Lalji Narainji in Bombay faced tremendous and unscrupulous opposition from British shipping interests headed by Lord Inchcape. The most serious bourgeois grievance of all concerned the 1s 6d rupee-sterling exchange ratio fixed by the Hilton-Young Commission of 1926. Purshottamdas Thakurdas, the near loyalist of 1921, spearheaded the unanimous Indian opposition: the over-valued rupee would cheapen and so encourage foreign imports at the cost of Indian textiles, raise prices of raw material exports and thus possibly reduce the market for Indian agriculturists (and Thakurdas's own business interests, it may be added, were largely in raw cotton exports), and lead to deflationary measures which reduced investment possibilities. The 1s 6d ratio also clearly meant a bonus for British officials and businessmen repatriating pensions or profits from India. Such things were resented all the more because Indian capitalism itself was gathering strength during these years, and beginning to organize itself on a nationwide scale. On 7 December 1923, Birla was writing to Thakurdas: 'I have been watching very closely the activities of the Associated Chambers [the all-India organization of British capitalists, founded in 1920] for the past few years, and I feel that their strong organization will be very detrimental to Indian interests if steps are not taken immediately to organize a similar institution of the Indians.' (*Thakurdas Papers, F.N. 42 [III]*) Birla and Thakurdas founded the Federation of Indian Chambers of Commerce and Industry in 1927, and though the Tatas were too dependent on government favours to join, and Bombay millowners also largely kept away, the FICCI within a few years had become the accredited spokesman of the class interests of a decisive section of the Indian bourgeoisie.

For the masses, the 1920s witnessed no improvement in living conditions, and possibly some deterioration. While the Indian population curve took a sharp upward turn after the 1921 census, agricultural productivity stagnated everywhere except in the Punjab and marginally in Madras. Average productivity per acre for all crops at 1938–39 prices, estimated at ₹26.5 in the period 1920–21 to 1924–25, went down to ₹25.7 in 1925–26–1929–30 (Amiya Bagchi, p. 95). The 1920s were also the decade when land revenue revisions became due in large parts of Bombay and Madras under the thirty year *raiyatwari* settlement. The working class faced a major employer offensive through wage-cuts and rationalization in cotton textiles, jute, and railway workshops. Indian textiles were again confronting renewed Lancashire and Japanese competition (imports of piecegoods, went up from 1090 million yards in 1921–22 to 1973 million yards in 1927–28—Bagchi, p. 205), and jute exports were stagnating even before the great depression of the 1930s. Indian and British capitalists alike tried to shift the burden on to the workers, and a government committee in 1926 planned a massive retrenchment of 75,000 from railway workshops.

Tribal and Peasant Movements

The elemental lower-class upsurge unwittingly called forth in many areas by the Non-Cooperation movement did not subside immediately with the Bardoli retreat. Bara Banki with its Eka movement, for instance, was still worrying U.P. officials in March 1922, and order was not fully restored in the Tippera and Chittagong districts of Bengal till July. But the most striking evidence of continued popular militancy came from the ever-restive semi-tribal 'Rampa' region north of the Godavari, scene of a veritable guerilla war between August 1922 and May 1924 led by Alluri Sitarama Raju—a truly remarkable man who has become a folk hero in Andhra but is almost unknown elsewhere. The grievances, as recorded vividly in an official report of August 1924, were basically the old ones of exploitation by moneylenders, and forest laws restricting shifting cultivation and age-old grazing rights. An unpopular *tashildar,* Bastian of Gudem, provided the immediate occasion by trying to construct forest roads with unpaid tribal labour. But this time the leadership came not from any local chief, but from an outsider who had wandered among the tribals since 1915 claiming astrological and healing powers, and who had been inspired by Non-Cooperation to start village *panchayats* and a campaign against drink. The movement combined in a fascinating way elements of what Hobsbawm would call 'primitive rebellion' with modern nationalism. Raju allegedly claimed that he was bullet-proof, and a rebel proclamation announced the imminent coming of Kalki-*avatar.* Yet in meetings with local officials during the rebellion, Sitarama Raju 'spoke highly of Mr Gandhi', but considered 'that violence is necessary', and expressed his regret 'that he was not able to shoot Europeans as they were always accompanied and surrounded by Indians whom he did not want to kill'—and at the Damarapalli ambush of 24 September 1922 the rebels in fact allowed an advance party of Indians to pass and then shot down two British officers. Raju also won the grudging admiration of the British as a formidable guerilla tactician, who had armed his followers by successful raids on police stations, and whose rebel band of about a hundred seems to have been like fish in water, enjoying the sympathy 'of the majority of the local hill population over an area of about 2500 square miles'. It cost the Madras Government ₹15 lakhs to suppress the rebellion with the help of the Malabar Special Police and the Assam Rifles. Raju was captured on 6 May 1924, was promptly reported shot in an 'attempt to run away'—an unpleasantly familiar formula—and resistance finally stamped out in September 1924.

Rajasthan throughout the 1920s remained a centre of antifeudal peasant movements. The Mewar police burnt down two whole villages in May 1922 in a bid to suppress the Bhil movement inspired by Motilal Tejawat, and Bijolia was once again in the forefront from 1927, with peasants under Vijaysingh Pathik, Maniklal Verma and Haribhau Upadhyay adopting *satyagraha* methods to fight fresh cesses and *begar*. At Neemuchana in Alwar state in May 1925, there was a veritable massacre of peasants protesting against a 50% increase in land revenue, with the State police killing 156 and wounding 600. The Congress, however, refused to get itself officially involved in any movement in the princely states (a policy changed only at Haripura, in 1938), though urban middle-class Praja Parishads with nationalistic ideas had started emerging (the first of them in Baroda, in 1917, followed by one in the Kathiawar region in 1921, the proximity to Gujarat being important in both cases). A States Subjects' (later renamed Peoples') Conference met annually from 1923 onwards but was as yet a very tame affair, Peasant radicalism definitely preceded urban nationalism in princely states like Mewar.

Disillusioned by the repeated Congress failure to unequivocally take up their demands, some peasant activists by the mid-20s had started groping towards new ideologies. In 1922 Swami Vidyanand raised the demand for abolition of *zamindari,* and Baba Ramchandra in November 1925 referred to Lenin as 'the dear leader of the kisans... the peasants are still slaves except in Russia.' (*Pratap,* 23 November 1925, quoted in Majid Siddiqi's *Agrarian Unrest in North India,* p. 195) The strong links of Congressmen—whether Swarajists or No-Changers—with *zamindari* or intermediate tenure-holding made it generally unresponsive to peasant demands for rent-reduction and share-cropper efforts at a fairer division of the harvest in Bengal,

Bihar and U.P. This-was clearest and ultimately most disastrous in Bengal, a province where share-cropping (*barga*) was rapidly spreading in the 1920s. The Swarajists here bitterly opposed any proposal to give tenancy status to *bargadars,* and showed no sympathy at all for a number of Namasudra and Muslim *bargadar* movements in the mid-1920s in districts like Mymensingh, Dacca, Pabna, Khulna and Nadia. The U.P. Congress did take up a slightly more pro-peasant stance, and in 1924 started a U.P. Kisan Sangh to pressurize the government into modifying some pro-*zamindar* clauses in a tenancy amendment bill then being discussed for Agra province. It was made clear, however, that 'the policy of the Sangha has been not to antagonise the zamindars by saying even one word against them, but to attack the Government in whose hands the zamindars are blindly playing.' (AICC, *F.N. 23/1924*).

The one peasant grievance about which Congress was generally unequivocal was revenue enhancement in *raiyatwari* areas. Enhancement was resisted with some success in Tanjore in 1923–24, with its prosperous *mirasdars*. In coastal Andhra, N.G. Ranga started work among the upper stratum of the peasantry in 1923, founding the first Ryot's Association in Guntur in that year. The British bid in 1927 to enhance revenue by $18¾\%$ in the Krishna-Godavari delta led to a powerful *kisan* movement in coastal Andhra which was taken up by local Congress leaders like Venneti Satyanarayana in east Godavari and Dandu Narayanaraju in west Godavari, as well as by more well-known nationalist figures like T. Prakasam and Konda Venkatappayya. Bardoli under Vallabhhai Patel would provide the principal inspiration for all such movements from 1928 onwards.

Caste Movements

As in earlier periods, the varied contradictions of Indian society often found expression through caste associations and movements, which could be divisive and basically conservative, but at times also potentially quite radical. The anti-Brahman Justice Party in Madras was outspokenly loyalist, and made dyarchy a success in that province from the British point of view—the only other example of harmonious cooperation between officials and elected ministers coming from the Punjab, where Fazl-i-Husain's Unionist Party was able to build a powerful 'agriculturist' (i.e., landlord and rich peasant) lobby including Jats as well as Muslims against predominantly urban nationalism. Bhaskarrao Jadav's non-Brahman Party tried to play a similar loyalist role in Maharashtra, and was bitterly hostile to a Congress which it charged with being a mask for Brahman ambitions—an accusation which some aspects of Tilakite ideology helped to strengthen.

Yet if the Justice Party and non-Brahman leaders like Jadav revealed themselves in practice to be interested mainly in job-reservations for a counter-elite and Sanskritizing imitation of upper-castes, other, much more radical and more genuinely plebian movements were also emerging in the 1920s.

A Bihar Government report of May 1925 described the Goalas or Yadavs of Patna, Monghyr, Darbhanga and Muzaffarpur districts as 'agitating for the improvement of the social status of their caste, and pari passu with taking the sacred thread they have been proposing to refuse menial and other services hitherto rendered to their landlords.' It may be added that Swami Sahajanand Saraswati, the most prominent Bihar and indeed all-India *kisan* leader of the next decade, began in the 1920s as organizer of a Bhumihar Brahman Sabha with an *asrama* at Bihta in Patna district.

The radical potentialities of some elements within the Satyashodhak movement of Maharashtra have been noted before. Satyashodhak rural agitators led an anti-landlord and anti-*mahajan* upsurge in Satara district in 1919–21, affecting 30 villages and involving some violent clashes; and from the mid-1920s Keshavrao Jedhe and Dinkarrao Javalkar began providing the leadership, from Poona, of a new type of non-Brahman movement which was quite as anti-British as the Brahman-dominated Tilakite Congress. In course of the next decade, the Maharashtra Congress would be able to establish links with and ultimately absorb this trend, making Satara the strongest fort of nationalism in Bombay by 1942.

But while the Maratha landholding peasantry could be assimilated, the untouchable Mahars developed an autonomous movement from the 1920s under Dr Ambedkar, their first graduate. Their demands included separate representation, the right to use tanks and enter temples, and abolition of the 'Mahar watan' (traditional services to village chiefs). By 1927, the year of the first Mahar political conference, some of Ambedkar's followers had started burning the *Manusmriti* as symbol of a sharper break with Hinduism.

Congress leadership in Tamil Nadu proved less flexible than that of Maharashtra, and here 'Periyar' E.V. Ramaswami Naicker, who had been active in Non-Cooperation, broke with the Congress in the mid-20s to develop a populist and radical alternative to Justice elitism. His journal *Kudi Arasu* (1924), written in racy Tamil, and the 'Self-Respect Movement' which he founded next year, progressed from advocating weddings without Brahman priests to forcible temple-entry, the burning of the *Manusmriti*, and outright atheism at times.

In Kerala, too, the mild Vaikom *satyagraha* had failed to satisfy the Ezhava leader Sri Narayana Guru, who wanted *satyagrahis* to 'scale over the barricades' and not only walk along the prohibited roads but enter all temples. T.K. Madhavan's Sanskritizing and Gandhian leadership of the SNDP Yogam (of which he had become secretary in 1927) came under attack from radical Ezhavas like K. Aiyappan and C. Kesavan, who increasingly considered temple entry to be a minor issue and became outspoken atheists.

It is interesting that in all these regions, militant lower caste movements contributed to the emergence of Leftist trends. Sahajananda joined the Congress Socialists and then the Communists, while Nana Patil, who had participated in the Satyashodhak movement in Satara in 1919–21, headed the 1942 parallel government there and later became Maharashtra's best-known Communist peasant leader. Early Tamil Communists like Singaravelu and P. Jeevanandan cooperated with 'Periar' for a time in the early 1930s, and Aiyappan and Kesavan set many Ezhavas in Kerala on the road leading to the Communist Party even though they never joined it themselves.

Labour

In the history of the labour movement, the years from 1922 to 1927 are marked at first sight by a definite decline. The number of strikes as calculated by the Royal Commission of Labour (1931) went down from a peak figure of 376 in 1921 to about 130 annually between 1924 and 1927. Though AITUC membership went up, with 183 affiliated unions listed in January 1925, the leadership remained very moderate, being either Liberal or Congress in political temper, and sessions lacked the elan and rank-and-file participation of the Jharia conference of 1921. Yet if strikes were less numerous, they also tended to be more prolonged and bitter in face of the major employer offensive of these years. The number of working-days lost, 70 lakhs in 1921, exceeded that figure every year from 1924 onwards, and 1927 was definitely the beginning of a new labour upsurge, with a 202 lakh loss in working-days and the emergence in some centres of a much more radical and increasingly Communist leadership. In 1926, trade unions got some legal protection for the first time through an Act which was otherwise quite heavily loaded against labour interests—fund collection by unregistered unions was made virtually illegal, a ceiling of 50% was imposed on 'outsider' presence in union executives, and the use of union funds for civic and political purposes was banned (in sharp contrast to British practice, where trade unions comprised the major financial support for the Labour Party).

In the last days of Non-Cooperation, Darsanananda and Viswananda had led a powerful East Indian Railway strike which lasted from February to April 1922; it is significant that no Congress leader seems to have thought of utilizing the potentialities of this movement in pressurizing the government. The Jamshedpur Labour Association, founded during the 1920 strike by Bengal Congress leaders like S.N. Haldar, was a restraining rather than inspiring force. A recent detailed study has shown that the Tata strike in September 1922 came about almost entirely due to spontaneous working-class pressure, while the union tried to utilize it to gain recognition for itself, more or less ignoring other labour demands. Thanks to its excellent Congress links, the J.L.A was able to pressurize Tata to set up a conciliation board headed by C.R. Das and C.F. Andrews during the 1924 Assembly debate on steel protection, for which Swarajist support was necessary. Recognition of the union came at last in August 1925, after C.F. Andrews had become its president and during Gandhi's visit to Jamshedpur, where he was given a great reception by the management and returned the compliment by a speech emphasizing the need for harmony between capital and labour. The management volunteered to deduct union dues automatically from wages, and it is not surprising that by 1928 workers were describing the J.L.A. under Andrews as a Company union. In Ahmedabad, 56 out of 64 textile mills were closed down by a massive strike in April 1923 against a 20% wage-cut at a time when, perhaps significantly, Gandhi was in jail—for in 1925 he would urge Ahmedabad workers not to embarrass their employers during a period of trade depression: 'Faithful servants serve their masters even without pay.'

Yet there were repeated signs that the labour movement was straining against the brakes being sought to be imposed on it. Madras city remained as before an important centre, with four more strikes in the Buckingham Carnatic mills in 1922–23, and it was on Madras beach that the first May Day was celebrated in 1923, at a rally organized by Singaravelu. The massive strike on the North-Western Railway from April to June 1925, sparked off by the dismissal of a Union leader, was made memorable by a procession in Lahore carrying flags stained red with the workers' own blood. The biggest strikes of all, however, were in the textile mills of Bombay, in January-March 1924 and again September-December 1925. The 1924 strike of 150,000 workers was against the refusal of bonus (paid during the last four years). After the government had set up an enquiry committee (which eventually decided against labour, linking bonus to profits instead of treating it as a kind of deferred wages), Baptista and N.M. Joshi advised workers to call off the strike, but the latter held out for two months in face of police repression and firing, getting little or no help from the national movement, till starvation defeated them. In the following year, a wage-cut of 11.5% on the ground of an alleged crisis in the textile industry led to a second massive strike in September. Bombay mill-owners argued that the cut could not be restored, unless the government gave their industry a concession by lifting the 3½% excise duty, which had been a standard nationalist and bourgeois complaint ever since it had been imposed in 1894 to help Lancashire. As the strike showed no signs of breaking up, on 1 December 1925 the government suspended the cotton excise duty, after which the mill-owners restored the wage-cut. The Bombay proletariat had thus won for the country a central nationalist demand of 30 years standing—as late as September 1925, a Swarajist resolution for suspending the duty had been carried in the Assembly but promptly vetoed by the Viceroy—though this achievement of theirs has seldom been remembered. Even before the great strike of 1928, labour militancy and organization in Bombay textiles had been able to push wages significantly higher there than in the British-dominated jute mills of Calcutta—average monthly wages, which were ₹24.75 and ₹16.40 in 1919 in Bombay and Calcutta, stood at ₹34.56 and ₹19.60 in 1927 (Bagchi, p. 126). While the recognized Bombay Textile Labour Union (registered in 1926, the first union to do so under the new Act) was led by the Liberal humanitarian N.M. Joshi, something like an autonomous grassroots movement had started in the Bombay mills from 1923, with the Girni Kamgar Mahamandal under two militants who were or had been mill-hands themselves, A.A. Alve and G.R. Kasle—a trend which the Communists would take over and convert in 1928 into the famous Girni Kamgar (Lal Bavta) Union.

Emergence of the Communists

Despite repeated allegations of British officials and some later scholars that the whole movement was no more than a foreign conspiracy organized from Moscow, Indian Communism really sprang, as we have already seen, from roots within the national movement itself, as disillusioned revolutionaries, Non-Cooperators, Khilafatists, and labour and peasant activists sought new roads to political and social emancipation. Its founder was the famous Yugantar revolutionary, Naren Bhattacharji (alias Manabendra Nath Roy), who came into contact with the Bolshevik Mikhail Borodin in Mexico in 1919, helped to found a Communist Party there, and went to Russia in the summer of 1920 to attend the second Congress of the Communist International. Here he embarked on a celebrated and significant controversy with Lenin concerning the strategy of Communists in the colonial world. Lenin urged the necessity of broad support to the predominantly bourgeois-led national movements in the colonies and semi-colonies; Roy with the enthusiasm and sectarianism of a new convert argued that the Indian masses were already disillusioned with bourgeois-nationalist leaders like Gandhi and were 'moving towards revolution independently of the bourgeois-nationalist movement'. The attitude towards the 'national bourgeoisie' and the nationalist mainstream in general would remain the basic issue in Communist controversies in India and elsewhere down to and even beyond independence.

In October 1920, M.N. Roy, Abani Mukherji (another ex-terrorist convert who later quarrelled bitterly with Roy) and some *muhajirs* (Khilafat enthusiasts who had joined the *hijrat* in 1920 and crossed over through Afghanistan into Soviet territory) like Mohammad Ali and Mohammad Shafiq founded a Communist Party of India in Tashkent, together with a political-cum-military school. When hopes of penetrating India through Afghanistan faded away in early 1921, some of the new Indian recruits joined the Communist University of the Toilers of the East at Moscow. Roy himself shifted his headquarters to Berlin in 1922, starting from there the fortnightly *Vanguard of Indian Independence* and publishing (in collaboration with Abani Mukherji) *India in Transition,* a pioneering attempt at a Marxist analysis of Indian economy and society. Other emigre Indian revolutionary groups were meanwhile turning towards Marxism—most notably the old Berlin group headed by Virendranath Chattopadhyay, Bhupendranath Dutt and Barkatullah, whose efforts in 1921 to win Soviet backing were blocked by Roy out of essentially factional motives, but who started an India Independence Party in Berlin in the following year. By the mid-1920s, an important section of the Ghadr movement in exile had also turned Communist, under Rattan Singh, Santokh Singh and Teja Singh Swatantra.

By the end of 1922, through emissaries like Nalini Gupta (another ex-terrorist) and Shaukat Usmani (who had been a *muhajir*), Roy had been able to establish some tenuous and often-intercepted secret links with embryonic Communist groups which had emerged from out of the Non-Cooperation and Khilafat experience in Bombay (S.A. Dange), Calcutta (Muzaffar Ahmad), Madras (Singaravelu) and Lahore (Ghulam Hussain). Abani Mukherji made similar though less successful efforts on behalf of the rival Chattopadhyay group. Left-nationalist journals like *Atmasakti* and *Dhumketu* in Calcutta and *Navayuga* in Guntur had started publishing eulogistic articles on Lenin and Russia and sometimes paraphrasing extracts from the *Vanguard,* while from August 1922 Dange was bringing out the weekly *Socialist* from Bombay, the first definitely Communist journal to be published in India. In a letter to Dange on 2 November 1922, Roy outlined a plan for 'a dual organisation, one legal and another illegal'—a secret Communist nucleus working within a broad-front workers' and peasants' party. The *Socialist* of 16 September had in fact made a similar suggestion already, proposing a 'Socialist Labour Party of the Indian National Congress', and Singaravelu in May 1923 announced the formation of a Labour Kisan Party. Singaravelu created a minor sensation at the Gaya

Congress (December 1922) by speaking openly in the name of the 'great order of the world communists', bluntly stating that the Bardoli retreat had been a 'disaster', and emphasizing the need to combine Non-Cooperation with 'national strikes'. Till the 'Left' turn at the VIth Comintern Congress of 1928, it may be noted, Indian Communist groups on the whole tried to work within the nationalist mainstream even while sharply criticizing the Congress leadership for its many compromises with imperialism. Roy regularly prepared Communist programmatic statements for circulation among delegates at the annual sessions of the Congress, while the analysis of Gandhi made in the early issues of *Vanguard* (May-June 1922), though sharply critical, was very far removed from post-1928 descriptions of him as a mere bourgeois 'mascot'. It acknowledged Gandhi's 'deep love for his suffering countrymen, a love nonetheless noble for having made great tactical mistakes', and warmly hailed in him 'a strength that dreadnoughts cannot conquer nor machine-guns subdue.' (G. Adhikari, *Documents of History of CPI,* I, 458, 438)

The veritable British panic in face of the emergence of a few tiny Communist groups in India—the Home Political files of the 1920s are at times obsessed with the 'Bolshevik menace'—far exceeded the real immediate significance of such activities, and can be explained only by the world-wide ruling class fear inspired by 1917, so reminiscent of the panic after the French Revolution. *Muhajirs* trying to reenter India were tried in a series of five Peshawar Conspiracy Cases between 1922 and 1927, and in May 1924 Muzaffar Ahmad, S.A. Dange, Shaukat Usmani and Nalini Gupta were jailed in the 'Kanpur Bolshevik Conspiracy Case'. The setback caused by such repressive measures, however, proved only temporary. An open 'Indian Communist Conference' was held in Kanpur in December 1925, organized by Satyabhakta—who proved very much of a bird of passage—and with Hasrat Mohani as chairman of the Reception Committee and Singaravelu as president. Though floated by rather diverse groups, which emphasized their independence from the Comintern in order to preserve legality, the skeleton organization set up by this Conference was soon taken over by more determined Communists like S.V. Ghate of Bombay, and the united C.P.I, in 1959 acknowledged the 1925 meeting to have marked the formal foundation of the Party. Of much greater practical significance, however, was the embodiment, in a number of organizations set up between 1925 and 1927, of the 1922–23 idea of a broad-front workers' and peasants' party to serve as a legal cover. The Labour-Swaraj Party, soon renamed Peasants and Workers Party, was set up in Bengal in 1925–26 by Muzaffar Ahmad, his friend the well-known radical poet Nazrul Islam, Qutubuddin Ahmad, and the radical Swarajist Hemantakumar Sarkar who had been

C.R. Das' secretary. It was joined in 1927 by a group of ex-Anushilan cadres headed by Gopen Chakrabarti and Dharani Goswami, and published two Bengali journals, the *Langal,* followed by *Ganabani.* In Punjab, a similar group was formed in 1926 around the journal *Kirti,* edited by the Ghadr veteran Santokh Singh; this drew in some survivors of the radical Babbar Akali movement, and became the Kirti Kisan Party under Sohan Singh Josh. A Workers and Peasants Party was founded in Bombay, too, in January 1927 by S.S. Mirajkar, K.N. Joglekar and S.V. Ghate, with a Marathi journal, *Kranti.* Most important of all was the fact that Communists were at last achieving real links with the working-class. Communists were quite prominent in the Kharagpur railway workshop strikes of February and September 1927, giving expression to the discontent of the workers against the highly moderate Union leadership of V.V. Giri and Andrews. When Andrews opposed the very sensible Communist suggestion that efforts should be made to extend the strike beyond Kharagpur to workshops like Lilluah, Dange attacked him for wanting to be 'the Hume of the trade union movement—to divert and mislead it. That shall not be—workers shall become the masters of their own destiny.' Communist influence grew rapidly among the Bombay textile workers, too, from 1926 onwards, but there was little penetration as yet into the countryside anywhere. The visit of Shapurji Saklatvala, the Indian who had become a British Communist member of Parliament, in 1927 aroused general interest in Communism, with Congress-controlled municipalities giving him civic receptions and even Gandhi entering into a fairly friendly debate with him. The Mahatma praised 'Comrade Saklatvala's transparent sincerity', criticized—with some point—the Communist neglect of the peasantry, but ended with the hope that 'though we may for the moment seem to be going in opposite directions, I expect we shall meet some day'. In fairness to the early Communists, it may be pointed out that sheer paucity of cadres made dispersal into villages very difficult in the 1920s, even apart from the theoretical primacy given to work among the city proletariat before the experience of the Chinese Revolution. Communist programmatic documents right from the beginning also raised demands for abolition of *zamindari* and redistribution of land—themes which the Congress would begin taking up with great hesitation only from the mid-1930s.

Revolutionary Terrorism

The post-1922 mood of disillusionment with established Congress leaders led to a renewed attraction for the methods of revolutionary terrorism among sections of educated youth in Bengal, U.P. and Punjab. From 1922 onwards,

Bengali journals like *Atmashakti, Sarathi* and *Bijoli,* often edited by ex-detenues, published numerous memoirs and articles extolling the self-sacrifice of the old revolutionaries. Sachin Sanyal's *Bandi-Jivan,* which was circulated also in Hindi and Gurmukhi versions, was a major influence on the younger generation, while Bengal's most popular novelist, Sarat Chandra Chatterji, published in 1926 his *Pather Dabi* glorifying the path of urban middle class violent 'revolution'. The government ban on Chatterji's novel only enhanced its popularity. A brief revival of terrorism in Bengal in 1923–24, climaxed by the murder of an Englishman named Day by Gopinath Saha in January 1924 (the real target had been Calcutta's notorious Police Commissioner, Tegart), was quickly followed by large-scale arrests under the Bengal Ordinance of October 1924 which effectively stopped revolutionary action—as distinct from spread of ideas—in the province till the detenues were gradually released in 1927–28. Meanwhile Sachin Sanyal and Jogesh Chandra Chatterji, Bengalis living in U.P., had organized the Hindustan Republican Association and started raising funds through dacoities. After the Kakori train holdup of August 1925, most members of this Association were arrested, but the remnants drew in new recruits (including Ajoy Ghosh, future general secretary of the C.P.I), established links with an emerging Punjab group under the brilliant young student Bhagat Singh, and constituted the famous Hindustan Socialist Republican Army in September 1928.

Actual terrorist actions during the mid-'20s obviously cannot stand comparison with what had happened during the war and what was to happen in the movement's last and most intense phase between 1930 and 1934. What was significant, however, was a process of development and rethinking within some of the revolutionary groups. In Bengal, veteran *dadas,* living on their past, still engaged bitterly in the old quarrels of Yugantar *vs* Anushilan. They got increasingly involved in Congress factional politics through the Karmi Sangha, and had started losing credibility in the eyes of enthusiastic young recruits like the 'Revolt Group' in Chittagong under Surjya Sen, who were eager for immediate and dramatic action. Apart from some individual converts to Communism, and a few efforts at combining the old and the new in what came to be called 'Terro-Communism', the sheer weight of the established terrorist tradition still prevented serious rethinking on matters like Hindu religiosity, individual terror and the cult of heroic self-sacrifice by the few. Two veterans of 1905–08, however, Hemchandra Kanungo and Bhupendranath Dutta, wrote important memoirs in the 1920s sharply criticizing many aspects of the old tradition. A 1925 pamphlet written probably by Sachin Sanyal on behalf of the Hindustan Republican Association went much further. Though still justifying individual terror by the argument that 'chaos is necessary to the birth of a new star', this declared the final aim to the 'the abolition of all systems which make the exploitation of man by man possible', and mentioned also the need to start 'labour and peasant organizations'. With Bhagat Singh, such rethinking would lead soon to complete atheism and an espousal of clear-cut socialist aims.

Subhas and Jawaharlal

Even apart from definite Communist and terrorist trends, the general restiveness of the rising generation in the middle and late-'20s was giving birth to a variety of student and youth organizations, critical of both Swarajist and No-Changer leaders, demanding more consistent anti-imperialism in the shape of the slogan of Purna Swaraj, and with a vague but still important awareness of international currents and of the need to combine nationalism with social justice. Subhas Bose after his release in 1927 to some extent expressed such gropings, though his growing popularity among Bengali urban youth owed quite as much to a considerable pandering to regional sentiments. For the other rising star of Indian youth, Jawaharlal Nehru, a 1926–27 visit to Europe proved of decisive importance. Experience of communal riots had already convinced him that 'religion in India will kill that country and its peoples if it is not subdued'. S. Gopal has emphasized that 'the turning-point in Jawaharlal's mental development' came with his active participation in the Brussels Congress against Colonial Oppression and Imperialism in February 1927, giving him a vision of anti-imperialist solidarity of socialist and Third-World nationalist forces which he often did not live up to but never totally abandoned. Jawaharlal was appointed an honorary president of the League against Imperialism and for National Independence which was started at Brussels, and in November 1927 he and his father were invited to the Soviet Union. The articles he wrote for the *Hindu* covering this visit (published in 1928 as *Soviet Russia*) vividly reveal the deep impact made on Jawaharlal by the 'country of the hammer and sickle, where workers and peasants sit on the thrones of the mighty'—and the title-page of his book quoted Wordsworth on the French Revolution: 'Bliss was it in that dawn to be alive. But to be young was very heaven.'

With the announcement of the all-white Simon Commission in November 1927, the forces for renewal began to coalesce leading towards a new great wave of anti-imperialist struggle.

Chapter 6
NATIONALIST ADVANCE AND ECONOMIC DEPRESSION: 1927–1937

AN OVERVIEW
Cross-Currents in Politics

The nine-and-a-half years between the appointment of the Simon Commission in November 1927 and the formation of popular ministries in the provinces in July 1937 were full of complex and often contradictory political developments. The national movement, deliberately and insultingly ignored through the setting-up of an all-white Commission to consider the next instalment of constitutional changes, fought its way through the First Civil Disobedience campaign to a position of near-equality with the Gandhi-Irwin Pact of March 1931. This was followed by a major British counter-offensive under Willingdon and Ramsay Macdonald's National Government, which had apparently smashed the Congress by 1933–34. The victory was soon proved illusory, however, by the sweeping Congress electoral triumph of March 1937 which for the first time gave the national movement some real, though very partial, control over the state machinery at the provincial level.

The general advance of Indian nationalism, despite the obvious ups and downs, was remarkable enough, but it remained a process full of contradictions. These have been illuminated by a recent study of the United Provinces by Gyan Pandey. (*The Ascendancy of the Congress in UP, 1926–34*) The pattern already vaguely discernable in 1919–22 becomes clearer in the 1930s: the advance and consolidation of the Congress organization meant also the assimilation and curbing of more elemental and potentially radical lower-class outbursts. The Congress, as we noted at the beginning of this volume, while fighting the Raj was also becoming the Raj, foreshadowing the great but incomplete transformation of 1947. This was not just a question of party organization throttling lower-level spontaneity; what was involved was the gradual establishment of a kind of hegemony (never absolute or unqualified, however, as we shall see) of bourgeois and dominant-peasant groups over the national movement. The Congress repeatedly aroused expectations and aspirations which it could not satisfy, and so the development of a Left challenge through trade unions, Kisan Sabhas, radical student organizations, Congress Socialists and Communists, and Right-Left confrontations within the Congress organization itself increasingly became an important part of the country's life from the mid-1930s onwards. The disillusionment of radical middle-class youth with Gandhian constraints—which found initial expression through a last outburst of terrorism in Bengal and Punjab between 1928 and 1934—was also contributing significantly to the growth of the Left by the end of this period, as revolutionaries abandoned the path of individual violence for mass struggle and Marxism.

As in earlier periods, political awakening often also took sectional forms, and an increasingly cornered British government tried to utilize these more than ever before. Thus developed a 'crisis of Indian unity' which R.J. Moore rightly relates (in a book of that title) to the basic British strategy of 'devolution' of power by stages. The post-1857 utilization of princes against nationalism found its logical conclusion in the 'Federation' moves of the 1930s, where the offer of responsible government at the Centre (subject to numerous 'reservations' and 'safeguards') was firmly tied up with the creation of a powerful nominated princely contingent in the Central Assembly. All-out attempts were made, as before, to encourage Muslim fears of Hindu domination, while the very legitimate and natural resentments of the 'untouchables' which were finding expression through Ambedkar's movement were played off against nationalist demands for a quick advance towards independence. Yet another facet of colonialist strategy was the encouragement of tribal separatism in regions like Chotanagpur, and the 1935 Act gave provincial Governors 'discretionary powers' of administering 'backward' tribal areas without consulting the popular ministers.

The national movement sought to counter such divide-and-rule methods with varying degrees of success. States' peoples movements against princely autocracy gathered increasing momentum, though the Congress leadership (and particularly Gandhi) for long hesitated in giving open support to agitations which in the context of the near-total lack of political rights and rampant feudal oppression characteristic of many states had considerable socially radical potentialities. Though Ambedkar's movement could not be assimilated, Gandhi from 1932 onwards devoted the bulk of his time to work among the Harijans, and the Congress in the 1930s did succeed in rallying to its cause non-Brahman intermediate caste movements in regions like Maharashtra, Mysore, and (to a lesser extent) Tamil Nadu. Tribal support was sought to be mobilized through welfare activities, and forest *satyagrahas* became an important component of Civil Disobedience. As for the Muslims, hindsight has sometimes traced the decisive break back to the Nehru Report discussions of 1928–29, and certainly the community kept largely aloof from Civil Disobedience except in the North-West Frontier Province. But perhaps the situation really remained open for quite some time longer, for Jinnah's League could win only 109 out of the 482 Muslim seats in the 1937 elections, and in any case, as we shall see, Jinnah himself became an uncompromising communalist only after repeated rebuffs from aggressive Hindu leaders like Moonje, Jayakar and Malaviya. In the crucial Muslim-majority provinces of Bengal and Punjab, the League lost in 1937 not to the Congress, but to predominantly Muslim regional parties (Krishak-Praja and Unionist) which claimed to espouse the cause of peasants against landlords or urban traders and moneylenders. Congress failure to develop radical agrarian programmes was particularly marked in both provinces, and in the long run proved disastrous for the unity of the country.

The 'Cambridge school' in recent years has sought to revive interest in the constitution-making processes of the 1930s—which progress of research on broader political and social movements had made into a rather unfashionable subject—by suggesting a direct causal link between British policies and the ups and downs of the national movement. 'Gandhi's all-India role was in part made possible by the British', argues Judith Brown in her latest book (*Gandhi and Civil Disobedience,* 1977, p. 12) echoing Willingdon's assessment that the Mahatma's 'influence has varied greatly with the treatment that he has received from the Government'. (Viceroy to Secretary of State, 25 June 1932, *Templewood [Hoare] Collection*) The Congress revived after the Simon Commission made constitutional changes an immediate national issue, Irwin gave Gandhi a new stature by talking with him as an equal, British use of Ambedkar made Gandhi concentrate on Harijans, and Willingdon's refusal to hold any negotiations whatsoever with the Congress led to the nationalist collapse of 1932–33. Yet, as in the case of the alleged link of the Montford Reforms with the upsurge of 1919–22, a closer look raises doubts about this entire thesis, for British polices often changed in response to nationalist pressures rather than vice-versa. If the all-white Simon Commission, set up during a period of ebb-tide for nationalism, planned a retreat from Montagu liberalism in several respects, the nationalist revival from 1928 onwards soon compelled Irwin to make his 'offer' of 31 October 1929 and Ramsay Macdonald to hold out the promise of some kind of responsible government at the Centre in January 1931. The millions who participated in Civil Disobedience could have had little understanding of, or interest in, the constitutional niceties being debated at the Round Table Conferences. Yet it was their pressure and heroic self-sacrifice, above all, which forced Irwin to negotiate with Gandhi and turned the apparent Congress defeat of 1932–33 into the sweeping electoral victory of 1937. History was not made by elite-politicians alone, whether British or Indian.

Depression and India

The mass upsurges of the 1930s were closely related to decisive economic changes. The world-wide Depression which set in from late-1929 affected India in two main ways: through a very sharp fall in prices, particularly of agricultural commodities, and by bringing about a major crisis in the entire export-oriented colonial economy. The all-India general price-index (1873=100), 203 in 1929, fell to 171 in 1930, 127 in 1931, 126 in 1932, 121 in 1933, and 119 in 1934; it rose slightly thereafter, but was still only 136 in 1937. Agricultural prices had started declining from 1926, in fact, but the collapse from 1930 in India was truly catastrophic. The all-India average of raw cotton prices (1873 = 100), 133 in 1929, fell to 70 in 1931. In Bengal, the price of winter rice (1929 = 100), went down to 45.9 in 1932, while that of jute had slumped to 43.5 by 1934. In the United Provinces, wholesale prices (1901–05 = 100) fell from 218 in 1929 to 162 in 1930, 112 in 1931, and 103 in 1934 (C.J. Baker, *Politics of South India 1920–37*, p. 174; B.B. Chaudhuri. 'The Process of Depeasantisation in Bengal and Bihar 1885–1947', *Indian Historical Review*, July 1975, p. 117; G. Pandey, p. 160). Depression sharply enhanced the burdens of revenue, rent and interest payments, and the people worst affected were the relatively better off or 'middle' peasants with a surplus to sell (unlike the post-1918 inflation which had hurt the poorest sections hardest). What we know about the pattern of mobilization in the 1930s fits in well with this economic situation. The Congress (and, a little later and in some regions, Left-inclined Kisan Sabhas) rallied peasant proprietors and tenant smallholders (rather than share-croppers or agricultural labourers) around issues like reduction of revenue, irrigation charge, and rent and debt burdens, return of alienated land, or—the most radical slogan of this period—abolition of *zamindari*. The movement spread much more widely over the countryside than in Non-Cooperation and set up relatively stable organizations, but lacked, in the main, the sporadic and elemental millenarian flavour of 1919–22. Congress support for even such specific *kisan* demands was often inhibited by its landlord links, and, as Hardiman has shown, a tendency towards growing conservatism by rich peasants was manifesting itself by the mid-1930s in areas like Gujarat, making Vallabhbhai Patel, the hero of Bardoli, ultimately the greatest stalwart of the Congress Right.

The Depression brought about a qualitative shift in the overall pattern of British colonial exploitation of India, which, though somewhat weakened by the First World War, had remained fundamentally unchanged till 1929. Down to the late-1920s, India still took in about 11% of British exports (including no less than 28% of Lancashire textiles). Her export-surplus with non-U.K. countries of agricultural raw materials remained crucial for Britain's balance of payments, while India was still a vital field for British capital investment in extractive and export-oriented industries (mining, tea and jute). The Depression brought down the value of Indian exports from ₹311 crores in 1929–30 to ₹132 crores in 1932–33 (imports fell off in the same period from ₹241 crores to ₹133 crores), and the Home Charges could be met only by massive exports of gold through distress sales by Indians (Claude Markovits, *Indian Business and Nationalist Politics,* pp. 19–20). Lancashire trade faced a major crisis which proved Irreversible: imports of cotton piece-goods from U.K. fell from 1248 million yards in 1929–30 to 376 million yards in 1931–32, and—after a slight recovery—to 145 million yards by 1939–40. (Amiya Bagchi, p. 238).

British—and particularly Lancashire—efforts to retrieve the situation underlay much of the political counter-offensive under the National Government from 1932 onwards. That the Lancashire trade could not be saved, and New Delhi due to financial difficulties went in for more protective duties (on cotton, paper and sugar) of considerable benefit for Indian industrial growth, have been construed sometimes as proof that India won real economic independence long before 1947. 'If London did not surrender control to elected Indian legislatures [by the financial provisions of the 1935 Act], it did hand power over to the Government of India.' (B.R. Tomlinson, *Indian National Congress and the Raj 1929–1942,* p. 30) Things in actual fact were considerably more complicated. Protective tariffs, as we shall see, were repeatedly linked to Imperial Preferences for Britain, and Lancashire in any case represented diminishing interest within the overall structure of British capitalist colonialism. By 1935–36, non-traditional items like electrical goods, telecommunication and wireless apparatus, and sugar machinery had almost caught up in value with textiles in British exports to India. Along with the setting up of subsidiary manufacturing units behind tariff walls in India by foreign companies (Lever Brothers and Metal Box in 1933, Dunlop and Imperial Chemicals by 1936–37), as well as the device of foreign-controlled 'India Limited' groups, these represented a new kind of imperialist interest in certain types of dependent Indian industrialization. Such moves towards indirect economic control through collaboration with Indian business groups in fact paralleled the constitutional developments of the same period. If commercial domination was ending, financial controls were defended bitterly and with considerable success. The rupee remained tied to sterling at the artificially high 1s 6d rate, the Reserve Bank was kept insulated from legislative influence, and the 1935 Act armed the Viceroy with a whole battery of financial 'reservations' and 'safeguards'. As Basudev Chatterji has shown in a recent thesis, India's invisible remittances to the

U.K. (Home Charges, dividends on private capital investments, insurance and bank remittances, freight charges, royalties—what nationalists somewhat crudely called the 'drain of wealth', in other words) represented 16.31% of British's total invisible earnings in 1922, 14.77% in 1931, and 15.75% still in 1936. (*Lancashire Cotton Trade and British Policy in India*, p. 27)

From the point of view of the Indian bourgeoisie, though Depression did create a number of problems, the slackening of at least the older forms of colonial economic ties meant opportunities for a major advance. Indian mill production of piecegoods went up from 2356.5 million yards in 1929–30 to 2982.7 in 1932–33 and 3905.3 in 1938–39, far surpassing Lancashire imports, though Japan still represented a major threat, particularly to Bombay. Sugar, cement and paper industries developed rapidly in the 1930s, while Tata Steel was strong enough to do without protection after 1934. Indian capitalist advance was no longer confined to the Bombay-Ahmedabad region, for the 1930s saw significant progress in Calcutta, U.P., south India (the number of cotton mills in Madras province, for instance, being 26 in 1932 and 47 in 1937) as well as certain princely states (Baroda, Mysore, Bhopal, etc.). Apart from market protection, provided by the Lancashire crisis and government tariffs, Indian industry also benefited from the fact that agricultural prices declined much more sharply than industrial, while commercial and rural depression probably led to a transfer of capital from trade, usury and land-purchase to industry.

The political consequences of this growing strength of Indian capitalist groups were by no means unambiguous, for there were, as the following sections will indicate, considerable regional variations in attitudes and repeated conflicts between short-term and long-term interests. For the moment, we may confine ourselves to the general statement that the overall weight of bourgeois groups in national politics expanded massively in course of the 1930s, and at times proved quite decisive in Civil Disobedience, constitutional discussions, and ministry-making alike. Certainly the private papers of British officials (like Irwin, Hoare, or the Bombay Governor Sykes) reveal an almost obsessive concern with Indian business attitudes, while the recently-opened papers of a number of leading businessmen (Purshottam-das Thakurdas, H.P. Mody, Walchand Hirachand and Pheroze Sethna among Indians, Edward Benthall among the British) have become a most important source which confirms the same conclusion.

Capitalist growth, particularly under conditions of weakening but still formidable colonial domination and world-wide Depression, inevitably meant growing burdens on the working class. Atrocious working conditions were made worse by repeated 'rationalization' drives (in 1928–29 and again after 1934), wage-cuts, and lay-offs. The pattern of consequent labour unrest involved a peak-point in 1928-29 (with 203 strikes and lock-outs involving 506,851 workers and the loss of 31,647,404 working days in 1928), a decline in face of repression (the Meerut trial of 1929-33) and splits, and a revival again from the mid-1930s (379 strikes and lock-outs involving 647,801 in 1937—R.P. Dutt, *India Today,* p. 337). As already noted for the 1919-22 period, the high-points of labour militancy and general nationalist upsurge somehow never coincide—a disjunction of possibly quite considerable significance for the modern history of our country.

While the weakening of ties with Britain and the capitalist world economy did lead to some indigenous industrial growth, this was more than counterbalanced for the country as a whole by the deep agrarian depression. Sivasubramanian's calculations indicate a decline in the per capita national income during the 1930s, and problems were sharpened by a significant demographic change from the 1920s. Population had risen by little more than 20 million between 1901 and 1921, from 284 to 306 millions; the corresponding figures for 1931 and 1941 were 338 and 389 million—a jump of about 80 million in an equivalent period. Economic stagnation and mass poverty remained the dominant features of late-colonial India: at constant (1938-39) prices, per capita national income has been estimated as ₹60.4 in 1916-17, and only ₹60.7 in 1946-47.

1928-29: SIMON BOYCOTT AND LABOUR UPSURGE

Simon Commission and Nehru Report

The announcement of the all-white Simon Commission (8 November 1927) had a two-fold and somewhat contradictory impact on Indian politics. Stung by the deliberate insult (compounded by Birkenhead's taunt that Indians were quite incapable of agreeing on any workable political framework), liberal politicians like Sapru and Muslim leaders headed by Jinnah joined hands with the Congress to formulate a Dominion Status Constitution—till communal differences broke up the united front of such relatively moderate groups in late 1928. At the same time, the Simon boycott movement stimulated the rapid growth of radical forces, demanding not only complete independence but a variety of socio-economic changes in a socialistic direction.

Prospects for Indian unity seemed bright towards the end of 1927, as practically all established political groups (except the Justice Party in Madras and the Punjab Unionists) decided to boycott the Simon Commission and began preparing for an All-Parties Conference to draw up a constitution. Already at a conference in Delhi in March 1927, Jinnah had persuaded a number of Muslim leaders to come out with a compromise formula. Separate electorates—the central plank in Muslim programmes ever since 1906—would be given up in return for joint electorates with reserved seats for minorities, a promise of one-third Muslim representation in the Central Assembly, representation in proportion to population in Punjab and Bengal, and three new Muslim-majority provinces (Sind, Baluchistan, North-West Frontier Province). The offer was repeated at the December 1927 session of the Muslim League (which also called for a boycott of the Simon Commission), though a breakaway League session at Lahore under Mohammed Shafi refused to give up separate electorates and decided to cooperate with the Commission.

Though the AICC in May 1927 and the Madras Congress session in December 1927 had accepted the Jinnah offer, Hindu-communalist pressure from Punjab and Maharashtra soon forced a disastrous retreat. The All-Parties Conference which met at Delhi in February 1928, at Bombay in May, and finalized the so-called Nehru Report (drafted mainly by Motilal Nehru and and Tej Bahadur Sapru) at Lucknow in August, got involved in tortuous negotiations and squabbles on the issue of communal representation. The Jabalpur session of the Hindu Mahasabha under N.C. Kelkar (April 1928) adopted aggressive resolutions calling for conversion of non-Hindus, and Hindu communalists in general bitterly opposed the creation of new Muslim-majority provinces and reservation of seats for majorities in Punjab and Bengal (which would ensure Muslim control over legislatures in both). They also demanded a strictly unitary structure, setting a pattern that would be repeated at the Round Table Conferences of 1930–31. The Nehru Report made a number of concessions to the Mahasabha. While there would be joint electorates everywhere, reserved seats were conceded only at the Centre and in provinces with Muslim minorities (and not in Punjab and Bengal). Sind would be detached from Bombay and made into a separate province only after India acquired dominion status and subject to a weightage for the Hindu minority there, and the political structure would be broadly unitary with the Centre keeping residual powers. Jinnah, who had broken with the Shafi-Fazl-i-Husain group of Punjab Muslims on the joint electorates issue and who could legitimately accuse Congress leaders of going back on their 1927 promises, made a desperate attempt at unity in the last December 1928 session of the All-Parties Conference in Calcutta. He pleaded for an immediate separation of Sind, residual powers to provinces, one-third of Central Assembly seats for Muslims, and reserved seats in Punjab and Bengal till adult suffrage was established, and ended with a passionate plea for unity; 'We are all sons of this land. We have to live together...Believe me, there is no progress for India until the Musalmans and Hindus are united...' (Uma Kaura, *Muslims and Indian Nationalism*, Delhi, 1977, p. 45). The Mahasabha leader M.R. Jayakar brushed aside all such pleas for compromise, with the result that Jinnah rejoined the Shafi group and in March 1929 put forward his famous 'Fourteen Points'. These repeated the demands for new provinces, one-third seats at the Centre, and federation with complete provincial autonomy, and revived the slogan of separate electorates—till such time as the other points were accepted by the Hindus.

Jinnah later described the acceptance by the All-Parties Conference of Jayakar's standpoint as the 'parting of the ways'. There is probably considerable exaggeration here: agreement among politicians on the basis of the 1927 offer would not have touched the deeper socio-economic and ideological roots of the communal conflict, and surrender of separate electorates in return for firm Muslim majorities in five provinces would not have necessarily eliminated or even weakened the sense of a separate Muslim political identity. But the 1928 breakdown did contribute considerably to the aloofness and positive hostility of most Muslim leaders towards Civil Disobedience two years later. Not for the first or last time, Hindu communalism had significantly weakened the national anti-imperialist cause at a critical moment.

Apart from the abortive bid to solve the problem of communal representation, the Nehru Report remains memorable as the first major Indian effort to draft a constitutional framework for the country, complete with lists of central and provincial subjects and fundamental rights. As was natural for a predominantly moderate body like the All-Parties Conference, the Report, even while demanding responsible government both in the Centre and in the provinces, advocated Dominion Status and not complete independence, much to the chagrin of the growing number of younger radicals in the Congress among whom Motilal's son was fast becoming the most prominent. It did raise the demand, however, for universal suffrage for adults of both sexes, something never conceded in any constitution made by the British for India down to 1947—a significant comment, this, on the oft-repeated argument that the Indian nationalists were elitist politicians, while the white rulers were seeking to protect the interests of the masses.

A constitution-making exercise inevitably raised the question of the future status of the princely states—an issue which the Congress had so long largely evaded. From Minto onwards, the British had been trying to consolidate their alliance with the princes as bulwarks against nationalism. The Montford Reforms had set up a consultative Chamber of Princes (February

1921), which became the forum for middle-sized states like Bikaner and Patiala. Bigger states (Hyderabad, Mysore, Travancore or Baroda) kept away, preferring independent negotiations with New Delhi as more dignified. At the height of the Non-Cooperation upsurge in early 1922, an alarmed Chamber of Princes had pleaded for a reduction of central claims to Paramountcy in the context of a possible transition to democracy at the all-India level, in order to avoid, as Bikaner frankly informed Reading, the fate of 'loyalists in Ireland'. In the mid-1920s, the British felt less need for conciliating princes as the Congress challenge had weakened, and Reading administered a major snub to the Nizam in 1926, rejecting his demand for an independent tribunal to decide the question of return of Berar to Hyderabad. Paramountcy, Reading argued, was not based on specific treaties alone, but existed independently of them, and the British had a right of interference in internal matters also since they were ultimately responsible for the security of the whole country. With the revival of nationalism in 1927–28, British need to conciliate princes and princely demands for restrictions of Paramountcy became prominent once again. Though the Nehru Report made no recommendation for immediate internal changes in states, it did visualize a complete transfer of Paramountcy to the fundamentally unitary and democratic centre of the future, and the first session of the All India States Peoples' Conference (Bombay, December 1927), organized by politicians with Congress sympathies, demanded extension of responsible government to princely India. Irwin modified Reading's policy to the extent of setting up a Committee to go into the Paramountcy question under Harcourt Butler (famous for his pro-*talukdar* policy in U.P.) in the same month. The Butler Report (March 1929) reasserted that 'Paramountcy must remain paramount', but explicitly stated that it was not automatically transferable from the Crown to any future self-governing centre enjoying Dominion Status. Paramountcy would be exercised by the Viceroy directly, not by the Governor-General in Council—a clear attempt to remove relations with the Princes away from the orbit of a possible Congress-dominated central government—and an ominous portent for the unity of the country.

The basic conservatism of the makers of the Nehru Report was revealed also by their acceptance in August 1928 of an amendment by Malaviya guaranteeing 'all titles to private and personal property'. This was attacked at the Calcutta session of the All-Parties Conference, interestingly enough, by 'Babu Ramchandra (member of the U.P. Kisan Sabha)', as well as by two delegates from Bengal, Naresh Sengupta and J.L. Banerji, who declared that 'one of the first duties of the new state of Bengal...will be to unsettle the Permanent Settlement.' But Malaviya easily won his point. (*Indian Annual Register,* 1928) The Indian response to Simon, however, was by no means confined to constitutional discussions. 'Go Back Simon' demonstrations, black flags and *hartals* rocked city after city as the Commission toured the country, and 1928 was marked by the beginnings of a renewed movement for boycott of British goods, The highlights of the anti-Simon campaign included the countrywide *hartal* of 3 February, massive demonstrations in Calcutta on 19 February when Simon reached that city, simultaneous meetings in all 32 wards of Calcutta calling for boycott of British goods on 1 March, a major clash with the police at Lahore on 30 October (seriously injuring Lajpat Rai, who died on 17 November), and very effective protest demonstrations in Lucknow on 28–30 November—in which Khaliquzzaman floated kites and balloons with 'Go Back Simon' slogans over a *talukdars'* reception to the Commission at Kaiserbagh, and Jawaharlal and Govindballav Pant were beaten up by the police.

Youth Movements

Middle-class students and youth dominated such urban demonstrations, and 1928 and 1929 were years full of student and youth conferences and associations, raising demands for complete independence and radical social and economic changes. Educated unemployment may have had something to do with this wave of youth unrest. The transfer of education to elected ministers under dyarchy had led to a significant increase in the number of students (from 5.04% of the total population in 1922 to 6.91% in 1927, according to the Simon Report), while employment opportunities were little better than before. In 1929 both FICCI and the Birla-dominated Indian Chamber of Commerce expressed concern about this phenomenon. The Congress tried to rally young men through the Hindustani Seva Dal, started in the mid-1920s by N.G. Hardikar in Karnataka, and throughout 1928 and 1929 Jawaharlal Nehru and Subhas Bose were kept busy addressing youth conferences in many parts of the country. At Calcutta in December 1928, for instance, Jawaharlal presided over a Socialist Youth Congress which called for independence as 'a necessary preliminary to communistic society', while Subhas addressed another Youth Congress in a somewhat vague manner indiscriminately hailing youth movements of 'Germany, Italy, Russia and China'. Relations between the two rising stars of the Congress Left, however, were already bedevilled by a strong note of personal competition and jealousy.

A year before at Madras, Jawaharlal had become President of a Republican Congress, which had demanded complete independence, called for close links with the League Against Imperialism, and passed resolutions hailing Alluri Sitarama Raju as well as Sacco and Vanzetti (the Italian labour martyrs of U.S.A.). At the Madras Congress itself (December 1927) which Gandhi did not attend, Nehru had been able to push through a snap resolution advocating complete independence, though delegates rejected supplementary clauses defining it to mean immediate and complete British withdrawal, and the Congress creed of undefined *Swaraj* remained unchanged. Gandhi sharply warned Jawaharlal in private that he was going too fast, and, in a pattern which would be repeated often in the future, the latter drew back from any open or total breach: 'Am I not your child in politics, though perhaps a truant and errant child?' (Nehru to Gandhi, 23 January 1928—Gopal, p. 112). When the Nehru Report opted for Dominion Status, Jawaharlal and Subhas organized the Independence for India League as a pressure-group within the Congress to carry on the campaign for acceptance of the goals of complete independence and what the U.P. branch of the League in April 1929 described as a 'socialist democratic state in which every person has the fullest opportunities for development...[with] state control of the means of production and distribution'. In yet another pattern destined to recur, however, Congress Left theoretical radicalism failed to find anything like adequate expression in concrete action or organization. In July 1929, Jawaharlal confessed to Gandhi that the Independence for India League had proved a 'hopeless failure...I have not the politician's flair for forming groups and parties'. (*Selected Works,* IV, 156)

The H.S.R.A.

Dissatisfied with such largely verbal radicalism, sections of educated urban youth turned once again towards the methods of revolutionary terrorism. In Bengal, the elderly Anushilan and Yugantar *'dadas'* advised patient preparations, discouraged any immediate action, and engrossed themselves in the meantime in Congress factional squabbles. Yugantar backed Subhas and Anushilan Sengupta in the bitter struggle which developed from 1928 soon after Bose had been released. Younger 'Revolt groups' emerged, disregarding the advice of their elders; one of them was smashed in December 1929 in the Mechuabazar bomb case, but the most formidable group, led by Surjya Sen of Chittagong, went on with effective preparations for a really dramatic action. The weight of an established revolutionary terrorist tradition in Bengal on the whole prevented much rethinking on broader social goals or methods. *Youths of Bengal,* a leaflet brought out by the Mechuabazar group, still insisted on the cult of heroic self-sacrifice by a handful: '...it would be a matter of pride if you will have to stand alone at the outset against the despotism of the blood-thirsty English'—and there was no trace of any socio-economic programme.

A remarkable openness to new ideas, in sharp contrast, was the striking feature of at least some of the leaders of the Hindustan Socialist Republican Army, founded in September 1928 at a meeting in the romantic setting of the ruins of Ferozeshah Kotla in Delhi by Bhagat Singh and his Punjab group, Sachin Sanyal's brother Jatindranath and Ajoy Ghosh from U.P. and Phanindranath Ghosh from Bihar. Bhagat Singh in particular was marked by an increasingly deep commitment to Marxian socialism and—equally remarkable, perhaps, given the strong Hindu religiosity of the earlier terrorists—militant atheism. H.S.R.A. actions included the murder of Saunders in Lahore in December 1928 as revenge for the assault on Lajpat Rai, bombs thrown in the Legislative Assembly by Bhagat Singh and Batukeswar Dutta on 8 April 1929, an attempt to blow up Irwin's train near Delhi in December 1929, and a whole series of terrorist actions in Punjab and U.P. towns in 1930 (26 incidents being recorded that year in Punjab alone). While the activities themselves might appear conventionally terrorist, the H.S.R.A. and the open youth organization under its influence, the Naujawan Bharat Sabha, really had a much broader perspective. As Bhagat Singh clarified in his trial, revolution to him was 'not the cult of the bomb and pistol', but a total change of society culminating in the overthrow of both foreign and Indian capitalism and the establishment of the dictatorship of the proletariat. 'Revolution is the inalienable right of mankind. Freedom is the imperceptible birthright of all. The labourer is the real sustainer of society....To the altar of this revolution we have brought our youth as incense, for no sacrifice is too great for so magnificent a cause. We are content. We await the advent of revolution. Inquilab Zindabad.' The Assembly bombs were meant to be purely demonstrative, and the occasion, significantly enough, was the anti-labour Trades Disputes Bill. Awaiting execution for the murder of Saunders, the young man of 23 began a systematic study of Marxism, and wrote a profoundly moving piece entitled *Why I am an Atheist,* defending total rejection of all religion on grounds of human dignity and rationalist logic. One of Bhagat Singh's close associates, Ajoy Ghosh, would one day become General Secretary of the Communist Party of India.

The H.S.R.A. heroes and martyrs attained remarkable popularity. When Jatin Das died in jail in September 1929 on the 64th day of a hunger strike for improvement in the status of political prisoners, a two-mile long procession followed his bier in Calcutta. Jawaharlal in his *Autobiography* later recalled the 'sudden and amazing popularity' of Bhagat Singh in Punjab and north India, and a confidential Intelligence Bureau account, *Terrorism in India (1917–1936)* went so far as to declare that 'for a time, he bade fair to oust Mr. Gandhi as the foremost political figure of the day'.

Labour Upsurge and the Communists

Bhagat Singh's transition to Marxism must be placed in the context of what was in some ways the most striking feature of 1928–29—a massive labour upsurge (particularly in railways, cotton textiles, and jute), accompanied by considerable Communist penetration into trade unions.

In Bengal, the Kharagpur strikes of 1927 were followed by a long and bitter struggle at the Lillooah rail workshop (January-July 1928), headed by Gopen Chakrabarti, Dharani Goswami (both Communists), Kiran Mitra and Sibnath Banerji. Its highlights included police firing at Bamungachi (28 March), and several spectacular workers' marches through the industrial suburbs of Calcutta. Activists of the Communist-dominated Workers' and Peasants' Party played a leading role also during 1928 in a Calcutta Corporation scavengers' strike and strikes at jute mills in Chengail and Bauria, along with independent labour leaders like Prabhabati Dasgupta and Congressmen with growing Communist sympathies like Bankim Mukherji and Radharaman Mitra. Nationalist support for labour came easier in Bengal than elsewhere, for most big employers were British or at least non-Bengali. The involvement of top Bengal Congress leaders still remained rather intermittent and marginal, and a request for funds for Bauria strikers, for instance, had to be relayed to Subhas Bose via Jawaharlal Nehru (Nehru to Subhas, 24 January 1929—*Selected Works,* Vol. IV).

In December 1928, the Calcutta working-class gave a striking demonstration of its growing political involvement and maturity when, led by the Workers' and Peasants' Party, thousands of workers marched into the Congress session, occupied the *pandal* for two hours, and passed resolutions demanding *Purna Swaraj*. Congress organizers did not like this at all, and it is said that Subhas Bose, 'GOC' of the volunteers, even wanted to call in the police, though in the end a confrontation was avoided.

Bose showed greater interest in the Jamshedpur labour movement, where workers dissatisfied with the very moderate leadership of C.F. Andrews' Jamshedpur Labour Association went on partial strikes several times during 1928. The situation was sought to be utilized by a rather opportunistic local lawyer with a grudge against the Tatas, Manik Homy, as well as by Bose; the consequent factional rivalry led to the defeat of the movement. The limits of nationalist involvement in labour struggle in Indian-owned enterprises are revealed in a very interesting letter of G.D. Birla to Purshottamdas Thakurdas (16 July 1929), reporting a conversation of the former with Subhas. 'Mr. Bose mishandled has been', Birla remarked, but 'I feel in a position to assure that Mr. Bose could be relied upon to help the Tata Iron and Steel Works whenever necessary provided properly handled. When we deal with them we ought. To study their psychology.' (*Thakurdas Papers,* F.N. 42)

In July 1928, there was a brief but very bitter strike on the South Indian Railway which was smashed by intense government repression. Its leaders, Singaravelu and Mukundlal Sircar, were given jail sentences, and a worker-militant, Perumal, was actually transported for life to the Andamans. But the most famous strike of all was that of the Bombay textile workers from April to October 1928. Throughout the late 1920s, textile magnates had been trying to shift on to the workers the burdens imposed on the industry by the government's refusal to give tariff protection against Lancashire and Japan, and the 1928 strike was directed against a rationalization drive involving wage-cuts. The famous Communist-led Girni Kamgar Union, which developed during the strike as a radical alternative to the moderate Textile Labour Union of N.M. Joshi, had its basis in a kind of grass-roots 'workers' control' movement whose leaders, A.A. Alve and G.R. Kasle, had come into touch with Bombay Communists like Joglekar, Mirajkar and Dange from 1926–27. The heart of the GKU in its moment of greatest strength lay in fact in the elected *girni samitiya* or mill-committees, 42 of which were functioning in April 1929. The 1928 strike conducted by it was massive, total, and peaceful. 'It is really amazing how the men are holding out....I have been considerably disturbed by the fact that the mill owners opened a section of their mills on several occasions, and although adequate police protection was given, not a single man returned to work', admitted the Bombay Governor in a secret letter to the Secretary of State on 16 August. The strike ended only when the mill-owners agreed to restore the 1927 wages, pending the report of an official enquiry committee. The Girni Kamgar at its height had about 60,000 members, as against 9800 of its rival under N.M. Joshi; even the well established Gandhian Ahmedabad Textile Labour Association had only 27,000. By late-1928, Communist influence was spreading fast in Bombay, particularly among G.I.P. railway workers and oil depot employers.

The situation inevitably called forth a massive capitalist and government counter offensive. Pathans were deliberately employed as strike-breakers in Bombay, leading to a major communal riot in February 1929. The non-Brahman minister, Bhaskarrao Jadav, tried to encourage anti-Brahman sentiments among the predominantly lower caste textile workers (the Communist leaders were mainly Brahman), and was able to win over Kasle; it was rumoured that part of the money for this propaganda came from Homi Mody, boss of the Bombay Mill-owners Association. The correspondence of Bengal Governor Jackson and Bombay Governors Wilson and Sykes during 1928–29 reveals a mood of real alarm, and a note of unequivocal support for Indian capitalists against Indian workers which was conspicuously absent on issues likes tariff protection or rupee-sterling ratio. Wilson for instance informed Irwin on 22 August 1928 that he was 'seeing practically every one of them [mill owners] personally, and pointing out the danger of their giving way...' The government pressed for a Public Safety Bill, which would give it power to summarily deport Philip Spratt and Ben Bradley, British Communists helping to organize Bengal and Bombay workers. The Trades Disputes Act of April 1929 imposed a system of tribunals, and tried to ban strikes 'undertaken for objects other than furtherance of a trade dispute or if designed to coerce Government and/or inflict hardship on the community'. The Congress officially opposed both bills, though it was noted by the *Indian Quarterly Register* that 'an unusually large number of Congress members were absent' during the debate on the Public Safety Bill. The principal government move, however, was the round-up on 20 March of 31 labour leaders (most of them, but by no means all, Communists). They included Dange, Mirajkar, Ghate, Joglekar, Adhikari, Nimbkar, Alve and Kasle from Bombay; Muzaffar Ahmed, Kishorilal Ghosh, Dharani Goswami, Gopen Chakrabarti, Radharaman Mitra, Gopal Basak, and Sibnath Banerji from Calcutta; Sohan Singh Josh from Punjab; P.C. Joshi and Viswanath Mukherji from U.P.; as well as three Englishmen, Bradley, Spratt, and Hutchinson. The conspiracy trial was to be staged at Meerut, since the British 'could not...take the chance of submitting the case to a jury', as the Home Member, H.G. Haig, admitted in a confidential note on 20 February 1929. The trial in the end proved somewhat counter-productive, for the Communists in fact made good use of it to propagate their ideals through defence speeches. But as it lasted for nearly four years, and heavy jail sentences were imposed in January 1933 (much reduced, however, on appeal and after considerable international agitation), the most experienced and active labour leaders were kept locked up for much of the early 1930s. The entire national movement condemned the Meerut prosecution, which incidentally involved no less than eight members of the AICC.

Labour militancy was not immediately cowed down by Meerut. When the Fawcett Committee report proved unfavourable, and the Wadias started large-scale dismissals, the Girni Kamgar, now led by Deshpande and B.T. Ranadive, organized a second general strike (April-August 1929). The mill committees were more militant than ever, and an official enquiry condemned the 'chaos' brought about 'by young, inexperienced and illiterate operatives asserting their authority in various ways'. But the strike was perhaps unwisely prolonged, and its defeat greatly weakened the G.K.U. The first general strike in jute mills took place in July-August 1929, under the Bengal Jute Workers' Union which was largely controlled by Communists; it successfully beat back the employers' bid to extend working-hours from 54 to 60 per week. Communist influence over the AITUC seemed greater than ever at the December 1929 Nagpur session, for the Liberal group under N.M. Joshi walked out to form the All India Trade Union Federation, while Nehru remained and presided over the rump session. The AICC set up a Labour Research Department under Bakar Ali Mirza in 1929, and there were signs that some Congress leaders like Bose in Calcutta and Bhulabhai Desai in Bombay were trying to take advantage of the removal of established Communist trade unionists to extend their own influence over labour. The Congress took a lot of interest, for instance, in the Golmuri tin-plate strike near Jamshedpur—a foreign-owned concern which had benefited incidentally from Swarajist pleas for protection. Bose organized a sympathy strike at Budge Budge, and even Rajendra Prasad visited Golmuri. British officials were considerably alarmed by the possible Congress-labour link-up, but found solace in the thought that Congress efforts 'will meet with very active opposition on the part of those leaders of a Communist complexion who heretofore seem to have exercized by far the most considerable influence over Labour'. (Note by Intelligence Chief Petrie, 9 October 1929)

In February-March 1930, there was a big, though eventually unsuccessful, Communist-led strike on the G.I.P. railway. On the very eve of Civil Disobedience in Calcutta (April 1930), a young Communist militant, Abdul Momin, led an extremely successful carters' strike against a ban on transport of goods during afternoons. Momin worked out the very effective strategy of using carts as virtual barricades paralyzing city transport. There were violent clashes with the police, in which nationalist youth eagerly joined the carters, and Police Commissioner Tegart hastily pressed the government to come to an amicable settlement. But there were ample signs by 1930 that the labour movement as a whole was declining fast. The Communists were weakened, not just by repression (which was important enough, since they were still no more than a handful) but by a major change in their strategy. Down to the end of 1928, they had followed a unity-cum-struggle policy with regard to the Congress, criticizing its limitations but striving still to build an anti-imperialist united front. The Congress should be opposed only on well-defined, specific issues, the Executive Committee of the Bengal Workers' and Peasants' Party had argued in its report for 1927–28, for otherwise 'we shall enable our opponents to claim that we are anti-Congress or even anti-national and that we stand merely for the sectional claims of labour'. But in December 1928 the Sixth Comintern Congress executed a sharp 'Left' turn, and Indian Communists began to keep aloof from the nationalist mainstream in a highly sectarian manner, and followed Stalin's curious policy of 'concentrating fire on the middle of the road forces' by attacking above all relatively Left Congress elements like Nehru (who was expelled from the League Against Imperialism in 1930). Congress interest in labour had always been intermittent and limited, and the Gandhian leadership, firmly back in saddle with the onset of Civil Disobedience, had no intention at all of using what it considered to be the highly divisive and dangerous weapon of general strikes. Above all, the economic situation was becoming unfavourable for labour movements. With the onset of Depression, unemployment increased while prices went down, thus weakening labour's bargaining power while reducing somewhat the discontent of the employed.

Peasant Movements and Bardoli

Though the Workers' and Peasants' Parties always advocated in theory very radical anti-feudal peasant programmes, they could make little inroads into the countryside as their handful of cadres tended to be engrossed wholly in trade union activities. The Bengal unit did acquire some influence, however, among predominantly Muslim peasants of Kishoregunj in East Bengal. Bhagat Singh's H.S.R.A. talked about the 'dictatorship of the proletariat', but remained vague on peasant issues. Yet discontent was deepening in many parts of the country, as agricultural prices stagnated or slowly declined while revenue reassessments became due in *raiyatwari* areas.

Congress attitudes to peasant demands varied sharply. Bengal represented one extreme, where all sections of the Swarajists (the radical Subhas Bose as much as Sengupta) woefully failed to defend peasant and sharecropper interests during the debate on the Bengal Tenancy Amendment Bill (August-September 1928). Jitendralal Banerji did support some additional rights for *raiyats* against *zamindars,* but even he opposed an amendment to give *bargadars* (sharecroppers) tenancy rights and thus reduce *jotedar* domination. Hindu *jotedars* and Muslim *bargadars* had already clashed in Pabna in August 1926, in a 'communal riot' which a Calcutta Hindu paper had declared to be a 'class war'. Muslim Council members in 1928 took up a (at times somewhat demagogic) pro-peasant stance, though many Muslim *zamindars* also opposed the *bargadar* clause. The tenancy bill issue provided the occasion for the formation of the Praja Party (under Akram Khan, Abdur Rahim and Fazlul Huq in July 1929), which included at first a few socially-radical Hindus (Jitendralal Banerji, Naresh Sengupta, Atul Gupta) but was otherwise overwhelmingly Muslim in leadership and Muslim *jotedar* in social support.

A somewhat similar pattern was emerging in the Punjab, where Fazl-i-Husain's efforts to protect agriculturists from urban Hindu moneylenders were generally opposed by the Congress-Hindu Mahasabha combine. The Unionists, though predominantly Muslim (who constituted 33 out of 36 elected Council members of the Party in 1926, for instance), were able to retain for quite some time Haryana Jat support through Fazl-i-Husain's alliance with Chhotu Ram and the advocacy of an agriculturist vs urban programme. The 'pro-peasant' stance of the Praja Party and the Unionists had considerable limitations, being oriented in practice in both cases mainly towards relatively prosperous farmers rather than the mass of cultivators, share-croppers, or agricultural labourers. The Congress in both provinces was still losing valuable potential support, through a combination of Hindu communalism and failure to develop even a moderately reformist agrarian programme. In east Punjab with its predominantly Sikh peasantry, the Akalis during the late 1920s were engaged in a struggle with Maharaja Bhupinder Singh of Patiala, who was suspected of having been mainly responsible for the forced abdication of the Nabha ruler Ripudaman Singh in 1923. The continued detention in Patiala of the Akali activist Sewa Singh Thikriwala provided the major issue. While the factional, even princely element in this struggle is evident, it also acquired wider dimensions as a peasant-based movement for civil and political rights and agrarian reforms in the east Punjab princely states. The Punjab Riyasti Praja Mandal, founded in July 1928 at Mansa, in course of the Akali leader Kharak Singh's tour of Patiala, raised demands like cancellation of the 19% hike in land revenue imposed by Patiala in 1926 and abolition of the Maharaja's reserved *shikar* lands (as the wild animals there gave trouble to the peasants). After Thikriwala's release in August 1929, some of the Akalis began to respond to the overtures coming from Bhupinder Singh, while the more radical peasant activists in the Riyasti Praja Mandal moved towards Marxism. The latter included Jagir Singh Joga and Master Hari Singh, later Punjab Communist peasant leaders.

Zamindari pulls on the Congress were strong in permanently-settled Bihar, too, but here there was no coincidence of communal with agrarian class distinctions, and caste ties (as among the Bhumihar Brahmans) could at times unite medium and petty *zamindars* with the upper stratum of the peasantry. What was to become the biggest *kisan* movement in pre-1947 British India had its roots in the activities of Swami Sahajananda Saraswati in the 1920s. Born in a petty *zamindar* family of Ghazipur (east U.P.), Sahajananda become a *sanyasi* in 1907, was active in Congress politics during Non-cooperation, started an *asrama* at Bihta (Patna district) in 1927 initially to promote the social advancement of Bhumihars, and then began organizational work among *kisans*. The Bihar Provincial Kisan Sabha was founded by him in November 1929 on an initially quite moderate basis (the Congress Council leader, Srikrishna Sinha, was its first Secretary), but

Sahajananda and the movement he inspired were to develop far beyond such modest beginnings.

Congress support for peasant movements could be much less inhibited in *raiyatwari* areas, where government revenue enhancements provided a unifying and socially safe issue. In coastal Andhra, the Madras Government's proposal in 1927 to raise revenue rates by 18¾% led to a powerful agitation during 1928–29 in an area marked by the existence of a broad rich and middle peasant stratum. Leaders like T. Prakasam and Dandu Narayanaraju in west Godavari, Konda Venkatapayya and Vennati Satyanarayana in east Godavari, and Unnava Lakshminarayana (the well-known author of the novel *Malapalli*) in Guntur had built up a formidable *kisan* base for the Congress by the eve of Civil Disobedience, and there were already considerable pressures for a full-scale no-revenue campaign. In scattered pockets in many other provinces, too, rural bases had been slowly built up through unostentatious but sustained constructive village work by Gandhian No-Changers; one may mention as examples, Arambagh in the Hooghly district of Bengal under Prafulla Sen, and Baba Raghava Das in Gorakhpur of eastern U.P.—both of whom in course of time acquired the reputation of being the 'Gandhis' of their particular regions.

The first real breakthrough for specifically Gandhian methods of rural organization and agitation came with the spectacular success story of Bardoli (Surat district of Gujarat) in 1928. Gandhian constructive work centres had carried on extremely successful humanitarian and organizational work since 1922 in this *taluka* of 137 villages with a population of 87,000. The dominant peasant landholding caste of Kanbi-Patidars had been organized from 1908 onwards under local leaders like Kunvarji and Kalyanji Mehta through the Patidar Yuvak Mandal, the journal *Patel Bandhu,* and a Patidar *asrama* running a student hostel at Surat. The Patidars tilled their land with traditional debt-serfs, who were Dubla tribals known as *Kaliparaj* ('black people'), and who constituted 50% of the population of Bardoli. The *Kaliparaj* were extremely backward and were praised by Gandhi's secretary Mahadeb Desai in his *Story of Bardoli* (1929) as most 'innocuous and guileless' and 'law-abiding'. As Jan Breman has shown in his study of broadly similar relations between Anavil Brahmans and Dublas of south Gujarat, debt-servitude was 'a form of unfree labour that was complicated and mitigated by a lelationship of patronage'. (*Patronage and Exploitation,* California, 1974, p. 67). The *Kaliparaj* bonded labourer was assured of a minimum of food and clothing by the Patidar, and the realities of exploitation were somewhat veiled by an element of traditional mutuality. Gandhian constructive workers had been active, too, among the *Kaliparaj* (whom they renamed *Raniparaj*—forest dwellers', in place of 'dark people') from the early 1920s.

When the Bombay Government announced a revenue-hike of 22% in Bardoli in 1927, even though cotton prices had been declining, the Mehta brothers persuaded Vallabhbhai Patel to organize a no-revenue campaign which proved as determined as it was peaceful. Peasants refused to be cowed down by largescale attachments of cattle and land, while the *Kaliparaj* on the whole rejected the bait of land on easy terms being offered by government officials. Patel and the other local leaders made extremely skilful use of caste associations, social boycott, religious appeals and *bhajans* or devotional songs. Tribal audiences were told that their gods, Siliya and Simaliya, had become old and had now deputed Gandhi to look after them—and did not the Mahatma wear a loin-cloth like them, and drink goat's milk rather than the more expensive buffalo-milk? (Ghanshyam Shah, 'Traditional Society and Political Mobilization', *Contributions to Indian Sociology*, 1974) Speeches and articles in the daily *Satyagraha Patrika* (brought out from Surat in editions of 10,000) harped on the theme of the peasants and rural labourers being the only 'real producers of wealth...the two main pillars of the state'. This was combined with a repeated emphasis on rural class unity and traditional mutuality—'The sahukar (moneylender) is merged in the tenant like milk in water. It is not possible to separate them.' (A speech of Patel), quoted in Mahadev Desai, p. 169)

Bardoli soon became a national issue. Ahmedabad workers raised ₹1300 through one-anna collections, while the Indian Merchants Chamber representative in the Bombay Council, Lalji Naranji, resigned his seat in protest when Bombay business efforts at mediation failed in July. The Bardoli movement in leadership and ideology was obviously far removed from the Girni Kamgar strike going on at the same time in Bombay under Communist leadership, and yet the secret correspondence of Governor Wilson with Secretary of State Birkenhead reveals the interesting fact that the British did fear a link-up between the two. Plans for sending armed police and even troops to Bardoli in late July were suddenly reversed in the first week of August, and a settlement was reached on the basis of a judicial enquiry and return of confiscated lands. 'My police officers inform me that they were practically certain that the Communists would use the Bardoli situation, if Government took action there, to call a general strike, both on the BB and CI and GIP (railways), and they think that they would have got the men out.' (Wilson to Birkenhead, 7 August 1928, *Birkenhead Collection*) The Max-well-Broomfield Enquiry Committee admitted the Bardoli assessment (and, by implication, assessments elsewhere in the province) to have been defective, and enhancement was cut down in Bardoli from ₹187,492 to ₹48,648. With Patel planning anti-revision campaigns throughout Gujarat and Maharashtra and organizing a Bombay Presidency Land League, the Bombay Government on 16 July 1929 abandoned revenue revisions till the completion of the current round of constitutional reforms. In Kheda, the 1890s revenue rates remained, and in fact were not basically raised till the 1940s. Gandhian nationalism certainly brought some concrete benefits for the peasant proprietors of Gujarat.

Business Attitudes

If 1928 and 1929 were years marked by the growing militancy of urban educated youth, workers and peasants, Indian business groups were also becoming increasingly restive about certain British policies. To the standing general grievance of the 1s 6d exchange ratio was added in June 1927 the goverment's rejection of the Cotton Tariff Board's proposals for raising import duties from 11% to 15% in face of Japanese and Lancashire competition. In January 1928, the Bombay Indian Merchants' Chamber endorsed the Simon boycott call; its leaders, Purshottamdas Thakurdas and Lalji Naranji, had actively opposed Non-Cooperation eight years earlier. Walchand Hirachand and Lalji Naranji's Scindia Steam Navigation was engaged in an uphill fight with British shipping interests headed by Lord Inchcape. The government refused to implement the Indian Mercantile Marine Committee's recommendations for reservation of coastal shipping to indigenous companies, and Haji's bill on the subject (March 1928) came up against bitter white and official opposition. G.D. Birla's letters to Thakurdas and the private papers of Edward Benthall (head of Bird Company) vividly reveal a growing conflict between Calcutta Marwari business groups and entrenched British jute interests. 'We are organising Indian trade in Calcutta in every direction, and all the newly-formed Associations are getting themselves affiliated to the Indian Chamber of Commerce.... The Europeans are getting very jealous of all these... The Imperial Bank in some cases is not behaving properly.' (Birla to Thakurdas, 2 May 1928) British financial control through the Imperial and Exchange banks was another major Indian capitalist grievance, and Thakurdas in his minute of dissent to the Indian Banking Enquiry Committee Report (1929–30) sharply attacked the monopoly exercised by the Exchange banks.

Yet Indian business attitudes remained ambivalent and diverse. Labour militancy made Bombay mill-owners in particular dependent on government support. Chairman Homi Mody's annual report to the Bombay Millowners' Association in March 1929 did mention issues like exchange ratio and lack of tariff protection, but the central focus was very definitely on the 'unprecedented general strike'. He 'naturally' supported the Trades Disputes Bill, and wanted total ban on picketing—'peaceful picketing does not really exist' (a point with very interesting implications for nationalist politics). The Bombay textile industry was increasingly threatened by cheap Japanese goods more than by Lancashire (whose finer cottons competed rather with Ahmedabad), thus providing some economic justification, too, for a pro-British alignment. The most successful and enterprising Indian industrial capitalist group, the Tatas, were also on the whole the most loyalist, since an industry like steel depended heavily on government contracts and patronage and had in any case won tariff protection in 1924. In 1929, in the context of the veritable 'Red scare' produced by the Girni Kamgar, Dorabji Tata, Cowasji Jehangir and Ibrahim Rahimtulla tried to start a specifically capitalist organization, distinct from the Congress, and openly aligned with European employers 'to stand up against the Red leaders of disruption' (N.N. Majumdar of Tata's to Thakurdas, 22 May 1929). H.P. Mody, Ness Wadia, Lalji Naranji, and M.R. Jayakar (Liberal lawyer with numerous capitalist connections) also seriously considered financing a Bombay Marathi paper to 'bring about a better atmosphere of understanding between capital and labour'. (Lalji Naranji to Jayakar, 18 October 1929, *Jayakar Papers*). The Bombay Governor had the same idea six months before. 'Encourage well-disposed capitalists to establish a good Indian 'Daily Mirror'. (Sykes to Irwin, 22 May 1929, *Sykes Collection*).

Birla pursued a different strategy, more 'nationalist' and certainly much more subtle and far-seeing. In August 1928, his Indian Chamber of Commerce cold-shouldered a proposal by the Calcutta Marwari Association (a body confessedly 'very greatly interested in the piecegoods and yarn trade') to do something about the decline in Lancashire imports which was adversely affecting the more purely compradore section of the Marwari business community. Far from supporting the Tata idea of a separate capitalist party, Birla in 1929 was trying to strengthen the Swarajists in Council by mediating between Malaviya (whom he had backed in the 1926 elections) and Motilal. Both Birla and Thakurdas strongly opposed the Tata move: 'I have not the least doubt in my mind that a purely capitalistic organization is the last body to put up an effective fight against Communism. What we capitalists can do...is to...cooperate with those who through constitutional means want to change the government for a national one.' (Birla to Thakurdas, 30 July 1929) Yet the differences among the capitalists must not be exaggerated or oversimplified. After a private talk with Birla in May 1929, Benthall expressed the hope that 'having made his position in the market...we may find him (Birla) adopting less aggressive tactics in the future'. (*Benthall Diary,* entry for 15 May 1929) The precise tone of the Thakurdas letter to N.M. Majumdar (7 June 1929) rejecting the Tata proposal would also repay closer attention. Thakurdas emphasized the need to retain links with the nationalists instead of trying 'to join hands with the European commercial community without making it clear to them that we are Indians first and merchants and industrialists afterwards'. But his next sentence reads: 'I am convinced that it is better to join hands a little later and on surer grounds than today.'

From Dominion Status to *Purna Swaraj*

Throughout 1928 and 1929, Gandhi acted as a brake on mounting pressure for another round of all-India mass struggle, aimed this time explicitly at complete independence. He had strongly disapproved of Jawaharlal's snap Independence resolution passed in his absence at the Madras Congress (1927), and at Calcutta next year was able to push through a compromise formula which accepted the Nehru Report's dominion status objective provided the British granted it by the end of 1929, failing which the Congress would be free to go in for Civil Disobedience and *Purna Swaraj*. Bose's amendment calling for immediate reiteration of the complete independence objective was backed by Jawaharlal, Satyamurti of Tamil Nadu, a large number of Bengal delegates, and the Bombay Communists, Nimbkar and Joglekar, but was defeated by 1350 votes against 973. Gandhi tried to confine Congress activities during 1929 to constructive work in villages, prohibition, and boycott of British goods, plus redress, along Bardoli lines, of 'specific grievances'. He encouraged public bonfires of foreign cloth (for which he was arrested in Calcutta in March, and awarded a token fine), and toured the country collecting funds for *khadi*, but repeatedly rejected pressures for any all-out struggle.

While Gandhi's restraint during 1928–29 obviously coincided with bourgeois hesitations and ambiguities, its roots probably lay more in the fact that the regions and social groups most prominent in these years (urban educated youth of Bengal, Punjab, and Bombay, and industrial workers of Bombay and Calcutta) were precisely those over whom he had least influence or control. He bluntly declared in July 1929: 'I know well enough how to lead to civil disobedience a people who are prepared to embark upon it on my own terms. I see no such sign on the horizon.' The state of Congress organization was another reason for (legitimate) hesitation: membership was down to only 56,000 in May 1929, and through an energetic drive spearheaded by Jawaharlal did raise it to half-a-million six months later, quotas for members and funds were still not met by most provinces. Gandhi's supreme ability of extending his hegemony over potentially divisive and rebellious forces was vividly revealed in the same month, when he insisted on making Jawaharlal president of the coming Congress session in the teeth of opposition from most P.C.C.s (10 had wanted Gandhi, 5 Vallabhbhai, and only 3 Nehru) and considerable reluctance of Jawaharlal himself Jawaharlal, said Gandhi, is 'undoubtedly an extremist, thinking far ahead of his surroundings. But he is humble and practical enough not to force the pace to the breaking point.... Steam becomes a mighty power only when it allows itself to be imprisoned.... Even so have the youth of the country of their own free will to allow their inexhaustible energy to be imprisoned, controlled and set free in strictly measured and required quantities.' (*Young India,* September 1929)

The choice of Jawaharlal was still an indication that things were moving towards a confrontation, particularly since the Calcutta Congress deadline of a year was nearing its end. Matters were complicated briefly by the 'Irwin offer' of 31 October 1929, in which the Viceroy declared Dominion Status to be the 'natural issue' of India's constitutional progress and promised a Round Table Conference after the Simon Report had been published. The Viceroy had been privately urging the need for such a gambit from December 1928 in the context of the strength of the Simon boycott. The new Labour Government (June 1929) endorsed his move, but most Tories and Liberals did not like it at all, as they made clear in a Commons debate after the offer which considerably reduced the credibility of the whole move. On 2 November, Gandhi, Motilal and Malaviya joined the Liberals in accepting the offer, subject to four conditions: the Round Table Conference should discuss the details of Dominion Status, not the basic principle which the British should accept immediately; the Congress must have majority representation in the Conference; and there should be an amnesty and a policy of general conciliation. Bose refused to sign this 'Delhi Statement', Nehru signed but soon developed strong doubts and wanted to resign. Negotiations broke down in any case at Gandhi's meeting with Irwin on 23 December, for the Viceroy flatly rejected the Congress conditions.

Jawaharlal graced the Lahore Congress (December 1929) with the first of his stirring Presidential addresses, boldly sketching out a new internationalist and socially-radical perspective for the freedom movement—a perspective so far confined to small Leftist sects. 'I must frankly confess that I am a socialist and a republican, and am no believer in kings and princes, or in the order which produces the modern kings of industry ...' He attacked Gandhi's pet 'trusteeship' solution for *zamindar*-peasant and capital-labour conflicts: 'Many Englishmen honestly consider themselves the trustees for India, and yet to what a condition they have reduced our country!' Yet the proceedings details show Gandhi firmly in command.

Bose's alternative proposal for immediate 'non-payment of taxes', 'general strikes wherever and whenever possible', and a 'parallel Government' was rejected. Gandhi insisted on a resolution condemning the bomb attack on Irwin's train (passed by the fairly narrow majority of 942 to 794), and pushed through the main resolution (which included a friendly reference to Irwin, justified the initial stand of the Working Committee on the Irwin offer, and refused to close the door totally for future negotiations) with the argument that the delegates would have to accept or reject it 'in *toto*'. Above all, though Nehru as well as Subhas had visualized a Civil Disobedience which would culminate in general strikes, the details of the action programme were left to be worked out entirely by the AICC and in effect by Gandhi. Yet, with all such qualifications, it must be emphasized that the anti-imperialist movement in the world's biggest colony did enter a radically new phase when at midnight on New Year's Eve, the Congress at long last adopted the creed of *Purna Swaraj,* and the national tri-colour was unfurled amidst cries, no longer just of *Bande Mataram,* but *Inquilab Zindabad.*

1930–1931: CIVIL DISOBEDIENCE

Towards Salt *Satyagraha*

The Lahore Congress was followed by a two-month lull while the country and the government waited for Gandhi to decide on the precise methods of non-violent struggle for *Purna Swaraj.* An independence pledge was taken at innumerable meetings throughout the country on 26 January, denouncing the British for having 'ruined India economically, politically, culturally and spiritually', asserting that it was 'a crime against man and God' to submit any longer to such a rule, and calling for preparations for 'civil disobedience, including non-payment of taxes'. Congress legislators were ordered to resign on 6 January—a directive generally but not universally obeyed, the dissenters including N.C. Kelkar, Satyamurti and Muslim Congress leaders like Ansari (who since the breakdown of the Nehru Report negotiations had been unhappy about another round of national struggle without some kind of communal pact). For the rest, a powerful Communist-led G.I.P. railway strike based on Bombay and Nagpur was allowed to go down in defeat in February 1930. Gandhi's 11 point ultimatum to Irwin on 31 January seemed to many a sad climb-down from the *Purna Swaraj* resolution, since no demand was made for any change in the political structure, not even Dominion Status. The choice of salt as the central issue also appeared somewhat eccentric at first, and Nehru later recalled his initial sense of bewilderment (*An Autobiography* p. 210). 'At present the prospect of a salt campaign does not keep me awake at night', Irwin complacently informed Secretary of State Wedgewood-Benn on 20 February 1930.

Events soon proved the sceptics wrong and Gandhi at least partly right. If the 11 points were a kind of retreat, they also concretized the national demand and related it to specific grievances. The letter to Irwin combined issues of general interest (50% cuts in army expenses and civil service salaries, total prohibition, release of political prisoners, reform of the C.I.D., and changes in the Arms Act allowing popular control of issue of firearms licenses) with three specific bourgeois demands (lowering of the rupee-sterling exchange ratio to 1s 4d, textile protection, and reservation of coastal shipping for Indians) and two basically peasant themes—50% reduction in land revenue, and abolition of the salt tax and government salt monopoly. It is interesting and significant that a Mercantile Marine Conference in January 1930 had failed to settle the dispute between British shipping interests and Walchand Hirachand and Lalji Naranji's Scindia Steam Navigation, while the March 1930 Annual Report of the Bombay Millowners' Association declared that protection against British and Japanese competition had 'become a matter of life and death to the industry'. The government tried with some success to detach Bombay textile magnates in March 1930 by raising duties on piecegoods to 15% on British and 20% on non-British imports, but the implicit note of Imperial Preference was bitterly resented by most Indian business leaders outside Bombay. Birla joined the walk-out against the Bill in the Legislative Assembly, stating that Bombay 'has lost her nerve' and warning mill-owners that if Japan was ousted through Imperial Preference, 'they will be knocking their heads against a wall of stone if they wanted any protection in the future'. (G.D. Birla, *The Path of Prosperity,* p. 193) Thakurdas carried a unanimous resolution denouncing the 1s 6d ratio at the FICCI annual session of 14 February 1930, and G.D. Birla as president of the same meeting launched a bitter attack on the stranglehold of British capital over the Indian economy and attacked government fiscal policies as 'discriminating free trade' rather than discriminating protection. On 5 March, Birla's close adjutant D.P. Khaitan declared at a special meeting of the Calcutta Indian Chamber of Commerce: '... at long last there is dawning upon our minds the realization of the stubborn fact that unless India attains Self-Government it is difficult for her to improve her economic position.'

As for peasant issues, Gandhi clearly had little or no intention of endorsing Jawaharlal's radical suggestions for *anti-zamindiri* no-rent campaigns expressed at a *kisan* rally in Rae Bareli on 5 February—'In my opinion the zamindar community is quite superfluous.' Jawaharlal's resolution at the

United Provinces P.C.C. meeting of 26 February calling for abolition of landed intermediaries was promptly shelved. But Gandhi's speeches and articles in January and February 1930 did repeatedly emphasize peasant woes, and salt linked up in a flash the ideal of *Swaraj* with a most concrete and universal grievance of the rural poor (and one that unlike no-rent had no socially divisive implications). It afforded, like *khadi*, the chance of paltry but psychologically important extra income for peasants through self-help, and— like *khadi,* once again—offered to urban adherents the possibility of a symbolic identification with mass suffering. 'You planned a fine strategy round the issue of salt', Irwin would admit to Gandhi in February 1931.

Gandhi's Dandi March (12 March-6 April), from Sabarmati to the sea through the heartland of Gujarat with 71 *asrama* members drawn from all parts of India attracted enormous publicity and attention from the entire country and even on a world scale. Wholesale illegal manufacture and auctioning of salt should begin, Gandhi declared on 11 March, after he had himself violated the law at Dandi; it could be accompanied by boycott of foreign cloth and liquor, and indeed 'everyone (would have) a free hand', subject to the pledges of non-violence and truth, after his own arrest, though local leaders should be obeyed. The existence, right from the beginning, of pressures from below was vividly revealed as village officials began to resign their posts all along Gandhi's route; and on 19 March Patidars of Ras (in Borsad *taluk* of Kheda district) demanded permission for starting immediate non-payment of revenue—a plea which Gandhi accepted with considerable reluctance. In mid-May, after Gandhi's arrest, the Working Committee sanctioned non-payment of revenue 'in provinces where the ryotwari system prevails', a no-*chaukidari* tax compaign (not no-rent, significantly enough) in *zamindari* provinces, and violation of forest laws in the Central Provinces.

Chittagong, Peshawar, Sholapur

Till towards the end of April, British reactions remained fairly moderate, though Patel was arrested on 6 March and Jawaharlal on 14 April and there were violent police-crowd clashes in Karachi, Calcutta and Madras. Things changed dramatically with three major outbursts, all outside or going beyond the confines of Gandhian Civil Disobedience, at Chittagong, Peshawar and Sholapur. The Chittagong group of revolutionaries headed by Surjya Sen brought off the most spectacular coup in the entire history of terrorism on 18 April, seizing the local armoury, issuing an Independence Proclamation in the name of the 'Indian Republican Army' and fighting a heroic pitched battle on Jalalabad hill on 22 April where 12 revolutionaries were killed. Though obviously very far removed in methods from Gandhi, the revolutionaries still celebrated the seizure of the armoury with a cry of 'Gandhiji's Raj has come!' Chittagong proved the curtain-raiser for an extremely intense wave of terrorism in Bengal, with no less than 56 incidents reported for 1930 (as against 47 for the entire decade 1919–29), including a spectacular raid on government headquarters in Writers Building in Calcutta on 8 December. The H.S.R.A. had also become very active in the Punjab, from where 26 incidents were reported in 1930.

Even more alarming perhaps from the British point of view was the popular upsurge in Peshawar, capital of the traditionally sensitive border area of North-West Frontier Province. Abdul Ghaffar Khan, son of a prosperous village chief of Utmanzai near Peshawar, had started educational and social reform work among his Pathan countrymen from 1912, deriving inspiration successively from the Deoband Muslim nationalist group, the Khilafat movement, and the modernistic reforms of Amir Amanullah (the Afghan king whose progressive and pro-Soviet policies led to his overthrow in 1928). 'Badshah Khan', as he was coming to be known by the mid-1920s, started the first Pushto political monthly *Pakhtun* in May 1928, and organized in the next year a volunteer brigade, Khudai Khidmatgar, which wore red shirts because these got less soiled on village tours. By 1929, Ghaffar Khan had become a fervent disciple of Gandhi. The creed of non-violence helped to mitigate the traditional blood-feuds among Pathans, and as elsewhere served as a check on internal social tensions (for the Khudai Khidmatgar included small and middling landlords, tenant farmers, as well as poor peasants and agricultural labourers). After the Lahore Congress, which Ghaffar Khan attended with a large contingent of Pathans, membership of the Khudai Khidmatgar shot up from 500 to 50,000 in six months, and a government communique on 5 May 1930 also alleged a certain amount of Communistic activity in the villages around Peshawar by a local branch of the Naujawan Bharat Sabha. The arrest of Badshah Khan and a number of other leaders on 23 April led to a massive upsurge in Peshawar, with crowds confronting armoured cars and defying intensive firing for three hours at Kissakahani Bazar. Thirty were killed here according to the official communique, while non-official estimates ranged from 200 to 250. A platoon of Garhwal Rifles, Hindu soldiers facing a Muslim crowd, refused to open fire. 'We will not shoot our unarmed brethren, because India's army is to fight India's enemies without. You may blow us from the guns, if you like', they would declare before their court-martial later on. The British were able to restore order in Peshawar only ten days later, on 4 May, and a reign of terror and martial law was unleashed in the N.W.F.P. Irwin reported to

Wedgewood-Benn that the N.W.F.P. Chief Commissioner was in 'a state of mental prostration', and the sudden and massive anti-British upsurge in a province that was 92% Muslim threatened to upset all government stereotypes and calculations. Though Ghaffar Khan's own movement was confined to the settled districts of Peshawar, Kohat, Bannu, Dera Ismail Khan and Hazara, there were also a series of tribal incursions in the latter part of 1930 against which aerial bombardment was freely used. The tribal raiders this time significantly refrained from looting villages, and with moving simplicity raised demands for the release of Badshah Khan, 'Malang Baba' (the 'naked fakir', Gandhi) and 'Inquilab' (they had heard the slogan *Inquilab Zindabad,* and had assumed 'Inquilab' to be another great leader in prison).

At the industrial city of Sholapur in Maharashtra, the news of Gandhi's arrest led to a textile strike from 7 May. Crowds, composed mainly of millhands, burnt liquor shops and attacked police outposts, law courts, the municipal building, and the railway station; order could be restored through martial law only after 16 May. Though all liquor shops were broken into, there were virtually no cases of drunkenness, and—to the evident chagrin of the authorities—Bakr-Id on 10 May passed off without any communal incident despite the burning-alive of three Muslim policemen two days before. Something like a parallel government seems to have been set up for a few days: 'Congress volunteers were directing traffic and I am informed that a hierarchy of the officials from the district magistrate downwards was appointed'—reported the Sholapur District Magistrate on 13 May (*Home Political 512/1930*). It is interesting that the working class, predominant in the Sholapur upsurge, was quite active in some other centres, too, in the early days of Civil Disobedience—dock-labourers in Karachi, Choolai Mill workers on strike in Madras, and Calcutta up-country transport workers and Budge Budge mill-hands in the clashes with the police after the arrest of Nehru in mid-April and Gandhi on 4 May. Such things happened despite the total ignoring of specific workingclass grievances in the 11-points and in Congress strategy in general, and the general aloofness of Communists from Civil Disobedience due to their new ultra-Left line.

Phases of Civil Disobedience

In sharp contrast to what had happened after Chauri Chaura, Gandhi made no move to call off the movement despite the violent incidents at Chittagong, Peshawar and Sholapur. In an article in *Young India* on 27 February 1930, he had in fact given an assurance that he knew 'now the way—not the retracing as at time of Bardoli', but pushing ahead with the non-violent mainstream despite sporadic incidents which were realistically recognized now as more or less inevitable: 'Civil disobedience once begun this time cannot be stopped and must not be stopped...' in this as well as in several other respects, 1930 marked a definite advance in radicalism over 1921–22. The stated objective now was complete independence, not the remedying of two specific 'wrongs' plus a very vague *Swaraj,* and the methods from the beginning involved deliberate violation of the law, not mere non-cooperation with foreign rule. The number of jail-goers consequently was at least three times the 1921–22 figure—Jawaharlal later estimated it to have been 92,124 (*AICC, GI/1931*), with the largest contingents coming from Bengal (15,000), Bihar (14,251), U.P. (12,651) Punjab (12,000), N.W.F.P. (5000), Bombay city (4700), Delhi (4500), Gujarat (3549), Tamil Nadu (2991), Andhra (2878), and C.P. Hindusthani (2255). Participation, it needs to be emphasized, now involved much greater risk then in 1921, for a frightened government from May onwards adopted a policy of senseless brutality even towards absolutely peaceful *satyagrahis.* At Dharasana on the Bombay coast in May 1930, a horrified foreign journalist, Webb Miller, watched 'unresisting men being methodically bashed into a bloody pulp', and Thakurdas bitterly complained about 'the beating of women and little children of ten and twelve years of age by the police'. Apart from life and limb, the meagre property of the poor was very much at stake, for non-payment of land revenue or *chaukidari* tax was met by wholesale confiscation of household goods, implements and even land. Another significant feature was the participation of women and teenagers: of the 29,054 prisoners on 15 November 1930, no less than 2050 were below 17, while 359 were women. Civil Disobedience marked in fact a major step forward in the emancipation of Indian women—a point admitted by a U.P. police official in a note full of male chauvinist overtones: 'The Indian woman is struggling for domestic and national liberty at the same time and like a woman she is utterly unreasonable and illogical in her demands and in her methods, but like a woman she has enormous influence over the stronger sex...many loyal officials including police officers have...suffered more from taunts and abuse from their female relatives than from any other source.' (Note of U.P. Police Inspector-General Dodd, 3 September 1930, *Home Political 249/1930*).

Yet it would be a considerable over-simplification to present Civil Disobedience as an unqualified advance in every respect over Non-Cooperation. The stirring Hindu-Muslim unity of 1919–22 was obviously a thing of the past in 1930, for between the two movements stood not only the breakdown of the Nehru Report negotiations, but a decade of intensive communal organization and fratricidal strife. Outside the N.W.F.P. and a few isolated pockets like Delhi where the official Fortnightly Report in September 1930 admitted the 'appreciable success' of the Congress in winning over 'a large contingent of the lower-class Muhammadans' (*Home Political 18/X /1930*), Muslim participation remained low throughout the Civil Disobedience years. In U.P., for instance, where the Congress-Khilafat alliance had been so formidable in 1921–22, only 9 out of 679 Civil Disobedience prisoners in Allahabad between 1930 and 1933 were Muslims. (Gyan Pandey, p. 112) Unlike Non-Cooperation, once again, Civil Disobedience did not coincide with any major labour upsurge. 'The most satisfactory feature of the situation in Bombay city is that at present the mill population appears to be quite unaffected...the operatives have not forgotten the effects of the strikes of last year',—an otherwise alarmist official report noted in June 1930 (*Home Political 257/V/1930*). Yet another contrast lay in the evident decline in the older, more purely intelligentsia forms of protest like lawyers giving up their practice and students leaving official institutions to start national schools and colleges. Gandhi at the Lahore Congress rejected a call for boycott of schools and courts as unpractical—'I do not see today the atmosphere about us necessary for such boycott.' A Bihar Congress report of July 1930 admitted that there had been 'practically no response from lawyers and students' (*AICC F.N. G/80/1930*), and cyclostyled bulletins issued by the Bombay Congress repeatedly denounced 'our lifeless students'.

The lag in respect of labour and the urban intelligentsia was counterbalanced, however, by the massive response obtained from business groups and large sections of the peasantry. A social history of Civil Disobedience will have to be written largely in terms of the participation—varying between regions as well as over time—of these two basic social classes. Organizationally, too, the Congress now was much stronger in most parts of the country than in 1921–22, when it had just taken the first step on the road towards becoming a mass party. This had, as we have already mentioned in passing, a somewhat contradictory impact. Organizational discipline and strength made movements on selected, specific issues much more effective, but also sometimes acted as a brake on elemental popular enthusiasm and radicalism. Once again, variations over space and time were extremely important here. In regions like the Central Provinces, Maharashtra, Karnatak or tribal areas of central India, where Non-Cooperation had made little inroads and Gandhian ideas still had the flavour and vagueness of novelty, an elemental and near-millenarian fervour could still be seen which was no longer much in evidence in well established Gandhian strongholds like Gujarat, U.P., Bihar, or coastal Andhra. Yet the basic Gandhian strategy of courting arrest meant that established leaders and cadres were fairly quickly removed from the scene, and this often provided an opportunity for sporadic but militant movements from below, a kind of less inhibited 'second wave' which gathered strength in the countryside particularly in the context of the deepening slump in agricultural prices from the autumn of 1930 onwards.

September-October 1930 may be taken in fact as a rough dividing-line between two broad phases of Civil Disobedience. The first phase saw the high point of bourgeois participation in towns and controlled peasant mobilization on issues selected by the Gandhian leadership (salt, no-revenue, picketing of liquor shops, and non-payment of *chaukidari* tax) in the villages. 'Sykes (the Bombay Governor) tells me that in Bombay the mercantile community has already given to Gandhi a measure of support which it refused him until the later stages of the Non-Cooperation movement of 1921-22', Irwin reported to Wedgewood-Benn on 24 April 1930. Among business leaders, G.D. Birla donated from one to five lakh rupees to the movement according to British Intelligence estimates, and his letters preserved in the Thakurdas Papers reveal him as actively trying to persuade Calcutta Marwari foreign piecegoods importers to establish trade contacts instead with Ahmedabad and Bombay cotton mills. While Jamnalal Bajaj was unique among capitalists in being a fullscale Congress activist (he served as AICC Treasurer for many years, and went to jail in 1930), Walchand Hirachand urged fellow-businessmen in a letter to FICCI on 28 April 1930 to give up the policy of 'sitting on the fence'—if the Government of India did not wish to see eye to eye with Indian commercial opinion, we will be obliged to throw in our lot with those that are fighting with Government for Swaraj'. *Walchand Hirachand Papers, F.N. 8 (i)*). The FICCI in May 1930 decided to boycott the Round Table Conference as long as Gandhi stayed away from it and till the Viceroy made a definite promise regarding Dominion Status. The loyalists of 1921, Lalji Naranji and Thakurdas, were signatories to this FICCI protest, and though Thakurdas maintained close connections with officials throughout, even he demanded from Irwin on 12 May 1930 full Indian control over 'finance, currency, fiscal policy and Railways'. (*Thakurdas Papers, F.N. 99/1930*). Congress relations with Bombay mill-owners, it is true, remained bedevilled by the problems of excessive cloth prices, the passing off of mill-cloth as *khadi,* use of foreign yarn, and piecegoods import business of some mill-agents, and 24 Bombay mills were blacklisted as non-Swadeshi in August 1930. Though the Ahmedabad mill-owners, Ambalal Sarabhai and Kasturbhai Lalbhai, cooperated with Motilal Nehru in trying to remove such difficulties, merchants and petty traders as in 1921) were on the whole much more enthusiastic supporers of the national movement than industrialists. Collective ledges by merchants not to indent foreign goods became very common in Bombay, Amritsar, Delhi and Calcutta (where Marwari importers took such a pledge on 30 April), and represented a more effective form of boycott than the spectacular picketing by (often largely women) volunteers. The fall in prices due to the world depression no doubt sometimes made cancellation of further import orders profitable as well as patriotic, but two successive official reports from Bombay bear testimony to more long-term and ideological considerations. 'Bombay businessmen have for a long time been dissatisfied with the economic and financial policy pursued by the Government of India.... They feel that it is worthwhile making appreciable sacrifices now, if this is going to secure for them the economic and financial autonomy which they strongly desire.' (H.G. Haig, 13 June 1930, *Home Political F.N. 457/V/1930*)... 'a highly impressive feature is that many of the ordinary, sober and sensible businessmen seem quite prepared to continue the movement, even though ruin is staring them in the face'. (Petrie, 20 August 1930, *Home Political F.N. 504/1930*)

The net impact was a remarkable fall in British cloth imports, from £26 million in 1929 to £13.7 million in 1930, and, quantity-wise, from 1248 million yards in 1929–30 to only 523 million yards in 1930–31. It is true that trade was contracting on a world scale due to the depression, but Homi Mody's presidential speech to the Bombay Millowners' Association in March 1931 still makes significant reading: 'The Swadeshi movement... undoubtedly helped the (Indian) industry during a period of grave difficulty', and now 'the future may be regarded as full of hope'. Other British imports also suffered, and from May to August 1930 the British Trade Commissioner's office was flooded with panic-stricken reports and complaints from Imperial Tobacco, Dunlop and other 'white' firms.

In the countryside, the early 'official' type of Gandhian Civil Disobedience had its natural starting-points and strongest bases in pockets which had already witnessed some amount of Gandhian rural constructive work through local *asramas*—Bardoli and Kheda in Gujarat, Bankura and Arambagh in Bengal, Bihpur in Bhagalpur district of Bihar, to give only a few better-known examples. Salt provided the initial vital catalyst, but illegal manufacture became difficult with the onset of the monsoon, and in any case could become the basis for a sustained campaign only in coastal like parts of Bombay Presidency, Balasore in Orissa, or Midnapur in Bengal. Picketing of liquor shops and of excise license auctions became an important form both in small towns and villages, while peasants in many areas (north and central Bihar districts, and Midnapur, for instance) firmly refused to pay the *chaukidari* tax despite enormous physical coercion and sale of property. Rural administration was sought to be paralyzed by largescale resignations of village officials: thus 224 out of 655 *mukhis* had resigned in Kheda by 21 June. Anand, Borsad and Nadiad *talukas* of Kheda district and Bardoli of Surat became centres of a very successful no-revenue campaign, with Patidars taking refuge in neighbouring Baroda state in a *hijrat* which at its height in October involved over 15,000 peasants in Kheda. Only ₹20,000 out of Bardoli's revenue quota of ₹397,000 could be collected till the signing of the Gandhi-Irwin Pact. In the Central Provinces, Maharashtra and Karnatak, the Congress leadership tried to utilize in a controlled manner the potentially explosive issue of poor peasant and tribal grievances regarding forest laws, setting up training camps for 'forest *satyagrahis*' (as at Sangamner in Ahmednagar district), carefully selecting *satyagraha* centres (106 in Berar for instance between July and September), and seeking to restrict the movement to boycott of Forest Department auctions, peaceful mass violation of grazing and timber restrictions and public sale by auction of illegally-acquired forest produce. The Karnatak Satyagraha Mandal even tried to specify the kind of trees that were to be cut down.

The strength of Civil Disobedience in its first phase was vividly reflected in the firm stand taken by the national leadership at the abortive Yeravda jail negotiations, attempted by Sapru and Jayakar as mediators in July-August 1930. Gandhi did vacillate a little in his initial note to the Nehrus via Sapru (23 July), admitting a possible discussion of transitional 'safeguards', but he made clear at the same time that 'Jawaharlal's must be the final voice....I should have no hesitation in supporting any stronger position upto the letter of the Lahore resolution.' The 15 August joint letter from Yeravda of Gandhi and the Nehrus unequivocally reiterated demands for right of secession, a 'complete national government' with control over defence and finance, and an independent tribunal to settle British financial claims. Not surprisingly the talks broke down at this point. The strength of the movement was also revealed by the fairly successful boycott of the September 1930 Legislative Assembly elections. Only 8% voted in the urban Hindu constituencies of Bombay, while the all-India average of participation fell from 48.07% in 1926 to 26.1%.

Just six months later, in his talks with Irwin at Delhi in February-March 1930, Gandhi would adopt a remarkably different and far more moderate stance. The explanation must lie in large part in the changing course of Civil Disobedience itself.

From September 1930 onwards, official reports repeatedly emphasize a decline in enthusiasm and support from urban merchants, with dealers breaking Congress-imposed seals on foreign cloth at Benares, Amritsar traders selling foreign cloth on the sly at Fazilka, and, even in Bombay, merchants 'with large stocks of last year's goods on their hands' beginning, 'to show signs of rebelling against the Congress mandate'. (*Home Political 18/X/1930*) If merchants were having second thoughts mill-owners had never been too enthusiastic, for the gains from *Swadeshi* demand were counter-balanced by what Homi Mody in March 1931 described as 'frequent *hartals* which dislocated trade and industry' and created a feeling of considerable uncertainty. Though Birla-supported Gandhi's stand at Yeravda (letter to Thakurdas, 6 September), Lala Shri Ram a few days later wanted the FICCI to reconsider its May decision to boycott the Round Table Conference, and Thakurdas warned Motilal through Lalji Naranji that 'the capacity of the commercial community for endurance' was reaching its limits (*Thakurdas Papers, F. N. 104/1930*). Thakurdas reiterated the same point more sharply in a letter dated 8 October to Birla's close associate, Deviprasad Khaitan: 'My impression gathered on the journey is that at Delhi, Amritsar and Cawnpore etc. the piecegoods importer and dealer is getting tired of picketing and of the loss involved on the dealer of imported cloth.... But for Bombay the rest of India is well under control and will on the whole die out before long... I fear that the Congress will have a set back and with it the country will suffer heavily.' (Ibid., *F. N. 99/1930*)

The alarm-signals from business groups calling for compromise, as well as the ultimate nationalist response to them, were probably connected also with developments in the countryside. Here the more purely Gandhian forms based on relatively proper-tied peasant groups were losing some of their early potency in the face of ruthless British policies of distraint. At the same time, there were signs of a 'second wave', taking less manageable and socially dangerous forms, like no-rent or tribal rebellion. The *Fortnightly Report* from Bombay in November 1930 described Kheda Patidars camping in abject misery across the Baroda border—'there is no sign of insolence, much less of violence, in their attitudes. They seem disheartened.' Yet at about the same time, in Chanakpur (Nasik district) on 20 October, Koli tribals, 'filled with stories that the British Raj had been replaced by Gandhi Raj....armed with spears, swords and other weapons...started to shout Congress slogans....refused to disperse (and) hurled down stones 'in the face of police firing.' (*Home Political 18/XI–18/XII/1930*). Among the Kolis of the western Ghats and the Gonds of the Central Provinces, forest *satyagraha* had long passed beyond Gandhian controls, with repeated violent attacks on police pickets and largescale and indiscriminate cutting-down of trees. Elsewhere, too, in scattered incidents throughout the country peasants were resisting the arrests of their leaders and the seizure of their property, mobilizing neighbouring villages through the blowing of conch-shells, and surrounding and attacking police parties. Pressures for no-rent were mounting as prices fell, and the U.P. Congress had to reluctantly sanction it in October 1930.

Regional Studies

We have been talking about Civil Disobedience so far as an all-India movement. As with Non-Cooperation, however, a brief study of regional variations is now evidently necessary, to illustrate the contradictory developments and internal tensions which led up to the Gandhi-Irwin Pact.

Metropolitan Bombay remained throughout 1930 the principal citadel of Civil Disobedience. Home Member H.G. Haig reported in acute alarm on 13 June: 'Gandhi caps fill the streets, volunteers in uniform are posted for picketing with the same regularity and orderliness as police constables', and massive processions (one of them, on 23 May, organized by no less than 28 Indian commercial bodies) were 'brushing aside...the ordinary functions of police control of traffic'. Muslims, it is true, remained largely aloof, and the combined effects of the 1929 strike defeat, economic depression reducing prices and threatening unemployment, and the ultra-Left politics of the Communists kept most workers away. But the Bombay Governor admitted that the movement in Bombay city could not be tackled 'on the theory that we are dealing with a limited political clique', for Civil Disobedience had the 'support of practically whole of the very large Gujarati population of Bombay, great majority of whom are engaged in business trade or as clerks...' (Sykes to Irwin, 5 and 20 June, *Irwin Papers*). The orthodox Gandhian leadership was represented in the city by Jamnalal Bajaj and Patel's protege S. K. Patil but a radical strand was emerging among the Congress youth, headed by K. F. Nariman and Yusuf Meher Ali who were to become prominent Socialist leaders a few years later. By the last quarter of 1930, Congress volunteers were making serious efforts to rally working-class support in mill and dock areas, and cyclostyled bulletins of the Bombay Satyagraha Committee were violently attacking business leaders like Thakurdas.

The classic land of Gandhian controlled mass movement was, as before Gujarat—or, more precisely, Anand, Borsad, and Nadiad *talukas* in Kheda, Jambusar in Broach and Bardoli in Surat, all of which reported significant arrears in revenue collections due to political reasons in 1930–31. Yet even in Kheda, some Patidars had reached 'the stage of transition from non-violence to violence' (Hardiman) by early 1931 in the face of wholesale confiscation of land. Peasants had resisted the arrest of their leaders in some cases, summoning aid from neighbouring villages by beating drums (as at Od, in Kheda, on 30 August), and there had been at least one instance of a village official in Borsad being murdered by lower caste Dharalas for refusing to resign (*Home Political 14/20/1931*).

Despite an initial mob-police clash on 16 April in Karachi over the trial of *salt-satyagrahis*, and the presence of one or two radical leaders like Swami Govindanand, Civil Disobedience remained weak in Sind, as the Muslims (who numbered almost 90% in the villages) largely kept aloof. There was even a communal riot at Sukkur in August 1930. The contrast with Non-Cooperation worked in the opposite direction in the Mahahrastra districts, for here the Congress had at last outgrown its traditional reputation of being a predominantly Chitpavan Brahman affair. A new generation of Congressmen headed by N. V. Gadgil (who had some Socialist leanings) had succeeded in building bridges with non-Brahman Satyashodhak Samaj radicals like Keshavrao Jedhe of Poona by extending support to a temple entry movement in 1929, even while the old Tilakites like Kelkar and Munje were moving away from the nationalist mainstream to become Hindu Mahasabha leaders. The Congress, however, failed to win over the emerging political movement of the untouchable Mahars, whose leader, Dr. B.R. Ambedkar, attended the Round Table Conference in 1930 and raised there the demand for separate electorates.

A similar pattern could be seen in the Central Provinces, from where the Governor reported on 23 July that Civil Disobedience was 'sweeping up from Bombay into Berar and Mahratta country. The popular attitude towards it is semi-religious, and to a considerable extent ignores considerations of personal loss'. (*Sykes Papers*). In Maharashtra, C.P., as well as Karnatak (which had been another area more or less untouched by Non-Cooperation), forest *satyagraha* speedily became the most widespread and militant form of Civil Disobedience. AICC files report peaceful but truly massive violations of forest laws by 100,000 villagers at Sangamner in Ahmednagar, (22 July), by 70,000 at Bagalan in Nasik (5 August), and at 32 places in Satara district on 28 August (*G/148/1930*), while large areas in the Central Provinces (including the districts of Chanda, Amraoti, Betul, Raipur, Bhandara and Seoni) and Sirsi and Siddapur *talukas* of north Kanara also became storm-centres. Everywhere the forest movement tended to get out of hand, with leaders emerging from among the tribals themselves like Ganjan Korku of the Gonds in Betul. Violent attacks on forest guards and police parties became extremely common in all these regions, and a later official catalogue of 'Congress violence' lists 10 instances in the Central Provinces between July and October and 20 in Bombay Presidency between May and October 1930 (*Home Political 14/14 and 14/19/1931*). By early 1931, preparations for a no-revenue movement had started in some Karnatak districts, while a *Fortnightly Report* dated December 1930 referred to attempts being made in parts of Maharashtra 'to influence the Khots not to pay their revenue by inducing their tenants to withhold their rent'. There were some signs also of a spill-over of popular agitation into neighbouring princely states. Volunteers from Mysore participated in the Kanara movement, while a powerful no-tax campaign developed in the central Indian state of Chhatarpur in Bundelkhand between October and December, headed, interestingly enough, by a 'notorious dacoit, Mangal Singh' who demanded reduction in land revenue and was 'said to have visions of carving out a state for himself. On 30 December, a crowd of 20,000, including about a thousand armed with rifles, could be dispersed only by the timely arrival of a military contingent from British India; otherwise they would have 'advanced on Chhatarpur and forced the Maharaja to accede to all their demands'. (*Home Political 18/X1–18/Xiii/1930*).

In Tamil Nadu, the onset of Civil Disobedience enabled the Gandhian No-Changer leader C. Rajagopalachari (who had established his headquarters at Tiruchengodu *asrama* in Salem district in 1925) to oust his Madras city-based Swarajist rivals, Satyamurti and Srinivasa Iyengar, from leadership of the provincial Congress in March 1930. Rajaji emulated his master by organizing a march from Trichinopoly to Vedaranniyam on the Tanjore coast to break the salt law in April 1930. This was followed by widespread picketing of foreign cloth shops, and, as in 1921, the anti-liquor campaign gathered considerable force in interior Tamil Nadu towns like Coimbatore, Madura, and Virudhanagar (where Kamaraj began his political career, breaking away from the loyalist Justice Party politics of the Nadar caste association). Rajaji did his best to keep Civil Disobedience a strictly non-violent and controlled affair, and deliberately avoided areas inhabited by the low-caste poor-peasant and labourer Kallars during his march to the sea. But, as elsewhere, Civil Disobedience in Tamil Nadu 'thrived upon the violent eruptions of the masses and the violent repression of the police.' (Arnold in *Congress and the Raj*, p. 265) These began with largescale clashes on Madras beach (27 April), to which police action against salt *satyagrahis* and official efforts to break the Choolai mills strike both contributed. Unemployed weavers attacked liquor shops and police pickets at Gudiyattam in north Arcot in July, and peasants suffering from falling prices rioted in August at Bodinayakanur in Madura. A link between Depression and discontent seems clear also in Madura town, where the movement acquired considerable strength due to support from merchants and weavers of the Saurashtra community. Baker's attempt (in his *Politics of South India*, p. 179) to explain such involvement entirely in terms of a struggle to capture the municipality seems singularly incomplete.

In Malabar, salt marches were organized by Kelappan, a Nair Congress leader who had established contacts with the lower-caste Ezhavas through the Vaikom temple *satyagraha* of the mid-1920s. The political fame of

P. Krishna Pillai, future founder of the Kerala Communist movement, began with his heroic defence of the national flag in the face of police *lathis* on Calicut beach on 11 November 1930.

Organizationally the Congress in Madras Presidency had its strongest base in coastal Andhra, where the No-Changer-Swarajist rift had been much less acute than in Tamil Nadu, and where, as we have seen, an agitation against revenue enhancement had been going on since 1927. District salt marches were organized in east and west Godavari, Krishna and Guntur, merchants contributed readily to Congress funds, and dominant-caste Kamma and Raju cultivators defied repressive measures which included withholding of irrigation water to 1420 acres in west Godavari (Stoddart in *Congress and the Raj*, p. 121). Yet despite (or possibly because of) the effective organization, the elemental fervour of 1921–22 was largely absent in costal Andhra. Official fears of a no-revenue movement proved groundless except in a single Nellore village. Andhra would develop a very powerful *kisan* movement on class issues, but significantly, this would happen in 1931 and again from 1934 onwards, when Civil Disobedience had been suspended or had collapsed. In the tribal belt, an isolated attack on a police party took place at Kalyanasingapur in the Vizagapatam Agency on 22 January 1931, but the Congress made no attempt to revive forest *satyagraha* in what had been its initial base in 1921. Civil Disobedience convictions in Andhra in 1930 totalled only 2878; together with 2991 in Tamil Nadu, this came to less than 6% of the all-India figure more than 90,000.

In Orissa, which had a strongly Gandhian leadership from the 1920s under Gopabandhu Chaudhuri, salt *satyagrapha* proved a very effective movement in the coastal areas of Balasore, Cuttack and Puri districts. In Balasore in particular, 'a considerable section of the local population' was reported in April 1930 to be 'distinctly sympathetic, partly no doubt through dislike of the statutory prohibition of the old Orissa industry of salt-making'. (*Home Political 252/1/1930*)

In Assam, like Andhra, Civil Disobedience failed to regain the heights attained in 1921–22, due mainly to a whole series of divisive issues: the growing conflicts between Assamese and Bengalis, Hindus and Muslims, and the tensions developing from the inflow of Muslim peasant immigrants from densely-populated east Bengal. Of the established Congress leaders, Tarunram Phookan was hostile to Civil Disobedience, and N.C. Bardaloi unenthusiastic. There was a fairly successful student strike in May against the Cunningham Circular banning participation in politics, and 3117 out of 15,186 Government school pupils left their institutions. Sylhet became the principal base of the movement, and no less than 892 out of the 2373 arrests during 1930–31 came from this single district. There was a certain amount of poaching in reserved forests, necessitating a route march of the Assam Rifles through north Kamrup in January 1931 and Mrs Chandraprabha Saikiani was reported in December to be inciting the aboriginal Kachari villages in that region to break forest laws. But the Assam Congress leadership refused to take up forest *satyagraha* officially. There was no link at all this time with plantation labour, and, again on the Andhra pattern, Raiyat Sabhas became important only from about 1931.

The Bengal Congress was peculiarly faction-ridden, with Subhas Bose and J.M. Sengupta setting up rival organizations to conduct Civil Disobedience and wasting a lot of their energy in Calcutta Corporation electioneering even at the height of the 1930 movement. Factional squabbles, the undoubted alienation of most Calcutta *bhadralok* leaders from the rural masses, and the relative failure of the Congress in the 1937 elections, have all been taken as proof of the proposition that throughout the 1930s the Congress was 'in decline' in Bengal (Gallaghar in *Locality, Province and Nation*). Yet Bengal provided the largest contingent of 1930–31 arrests (15,000) as well as the highest incidence of violence (136 excluding terrorist actions according to one official estimate. (*Home Political 14/20/1931*), and the relative weakness of Congress organization (as compared to Gujarat, Andhra, U.P. or Bihar) perhaps led to a more multifarious and violent, though also more fragmented, kind of movement. In Midnapur, Arambagh and a number of other rural pockets, powerful movements developed around the issues of salt and *chaukidari* tax, and the Gandhian constructive workers who often provided the initial impetus here were quite as much critical of the urban *bhadralok* bias of the Calcutta leaders as any latter-day historian. In areas without previously established Gandhian centres (the Ghatal sub-division of Midnapur, for instance, in contrast to nearby Arambagh which remained strictly non-violent), as well as elsewhere after the removal of the frontranking leadership, peasant mobilization often took the form of militant confrontations with the police, while middle-terrorism had also entered its last and most energetic phase following the Chittagong Armoury Raid of April 1930. Still the contrast with 1921 remains clear, in the lack of an effective central leadership which C.R. Das had then provided, the relative passivity of industrial labour, the absence of elemental tribal and poor peasant upsurges of the type then seen in outlying areas like Jhargram, Rangpur, Chittagong and Tippera, and above all in the general aloofness of the Muslims. Early trends towards some amount of Muslim participation were cut short by communal riots, in Dacca town in May and Kishoreganj villages in July 1930. Recent research indicates that in both places communalism was a distorted expression of social tensions which a more radical nationalist leadership could have possible harnessed to the anti-imperialist cause. Houses, shops and godowns of Hindu moneylenders and merchants were the principal targets, and rioters seemed interested in snatching away debt-bonds rather than in issues like cow-slaughter or music before mosques. The Kishoreganj disturbances began with an attack on a Muslim *talukdar's* house, and here a movement started on class lines by a branch of the Workers' and Peasants' Party was taken over by communal *mullahs* after the Communists had been removed by arrest. The pattern first made evident in the *Swadeshi* days was being repeated once again: the basic nationalist weakness in Bengal remained the failure to develop any clear *anti-zamindar* or anti-moneylender programme, and this at a time when rural tensions were mounting due to the sharp fall in prices. The rural Gandhians had no urban *bhadralok* bias, but they too fought shy in 1930–31 of any no-rent calls, while the questions of *jotedar*-sharecropper relations also remained outside the sphere of Congress theory or practice.

A somewhat similar pattern can be seen in the Punjab, where the Congress reputation of being a predominantly urban Hindu trader party made mobilization of Muslim and Sikh peasants difficult now that there were no unifying religious issues like Khilafat or purification of Gurdwara management. The Unionist bloc was firmly loyal, while Akali attitudes varied, Tara Singh backing the Congress while Kharak Singh kept aloof. The British were still acutely nervous about the Punjab, due to its link with the army, proximity to a Frontier Province where the Khudai Khidmatgar remained a serious problem and the existence of a radical fringe operating on the border line of terrorism and Marxism: the Naujawan Bharat Sabha and the Kirti Kisan group. Merchant support made boycott initially extremely effective, monthly sale of British cloth at the principal trade centre of Amritsar dropping from ₹25 lakhs to only ₹2 lakhs in July, but by September, as in other provinces, *Fortnightly Report* were speaking of 'the growing restiveness of the cloth merchants, many of whom were faced with imminent bankruptcy'. (*Home Political 18/X/1930*) In sharp and significant contrast, radicalism among urban youth was stimulated further by the death sentence passed on Bhagat Singh on 7 October, while the Punjab Governor on 18 October was expressing 'acute anxiety' about falling agricultural prices—'The mischief-makers are already busy with the zamindars and cultivators and urging the non-payment of land taxes'. (*Irwin Collection*) Though the Akali-led Punjab Zamindar Sabha founded in October pleasantly surprised the British by remaining quite moderate, the Riyasti Praja Mandal combined support to Civil Disobedience with propaganda among the Sikh peasantry in the Phulkian states against the Patiala Maharaja. Even more interesting perhaps were a number of more-or-less spontaneous outbursts : peasants in Hissar district refusing rent and forcibly seizing crops of landlords in April;

defiance of forest grazing regulations in Kangra in September; and, in December, widespread social banditry in Rohtak, with Jats 'assisted by others from lower castes' attacking moneylenders and grain-dealers, robbing their property and burning their account-books. '...there is little doubt that the sympathies of the Jat villagers are to a large extent with these Dick Turpins... If it was not a case of Hindus on both sides we should hear much more of it in the press'. (Governor Montmorency to Irwin, 7 December 1930)

The strength as well as the limitations of Civil Disobedience in Bihar were clearly revealed in a report from the P.C.C dated 21 July 1930. There had been 'practically no response from lawyers and students'. The movement is practically entirely in the villages and in the hands of village people'; and Deep Narain Singh, newly appointed provincial 'dictator', was being recommended for Working Committee membership as 'a big zamindar and an old nationalist'. (*AICC, G/80/1930*) While most big *zamindars* remained loyalist, the Congress had established a powerful and well-organized base among small landlords (who were particularly numerous in Bihar) and better-off tenants through Gandhian constructive work, and the strength of the organization was indicated by the P.C.C. claim in the same report that 'we have organized our own mail (*Dak*) system'. Organizational strength may have initially dampened elemental outbursts, for Governor Stephenson reported in July that things were much better than during Non-Cooperation, and that 'the semi-religious hysteria manifest in Bombay and C.P. was absent (Simla Governors' Conference Report, included in *Sykes Papers*). Officials soon began singing a different tune, however, as emphasis shifted from an ineffective salt campaign (for which physical conditions were obviously unsuitable) to a very powerful no-*chaukidari* tax agitation. Nearly 11,000 were in jail by November, whole districts were refusing payment of *chaukidari* tax, foreign cloth and liquor sales dramatically declined, and administration had virtually collapsed in pockets like the Barhee region of Monghyr (G. McDonald in *Congress and the Raj*). The provincial leadership with its strong small-landlord links firmly refused, however, to take up no-rent despite growing *kisan* distress as prices fell. It is significant that the autonomous Kisan Sabha movement which had started developing in Bihar under Swami Sahajanand in 1929 seems to have totally disappeared in the next year, swamped by the atmosphere of multi-class national unity; it would revive only after the defeat of Civil Disobedience, in 1933–34, following the pattern already noted in Andhra or Assam. Gandhian restraints on non-violence were breaking down even in Bihar, however, towards the end of 1930 and early 1931, with a series of attacks on police parties. In December, an anti-*chaukidari* tax demonstration in a Saran village defied

27 rounds of buckshot, and on Independence Day in the following month at Begusarai (Monghyr) a crowd chased the sub-divisional officer into a ditch and could be dispersed only after 146 rounds of firing. The tribal belt of Chotanagpur was also astir, with Bonga Majhi and Somra Majhi leading a movement in Hazaribagh which combined socio-religious reform along 'Sanskritizing' lines with Congress sympathies (followers were asked to give up meat and drink, and use *khadi* only), while Santals elsewhere were reported to be taking up illegal distillation on a largescale under the banner of Gandhi. But such instances of lower-class militancy were accompanied by declining enthusiasm among small landlords and better-off tenants in the face of ruthless British attachment of property, and the Bihar Congress leadership welcomed the March 1931 truce with a sense of relief (McDonald, in *Congress and the Raj*).

The pattern of two phases in Civil Disobedience was perhaps clearest in the United Provinces, and Jawaharlal Nehru summed it up neatly in a comment drawn from experiences during a brief spell out of jail in mid-October 1930—'The cities and the middle classes were a bit tired of the hartals and processions', but 'a fresh infusion of blood' could still come 'from the peasantry', where 'the reserve stocks...were enormous'. (*An Autobiography*, p. 232) Intelligentsia participation from the beginning was less than in 1921, with fewer resignations from schools or courts, and urban trader enthusiasm proved shortlived. In the countryside, however, pressures for no-rent and what a *Fortnightly Report* of early September described as 'the growing tendency towards violence and the defiance of authority' mounted as prices declined sharply from the autumn of 1930 onwards. After a tour of 21 districts, the U.P. Inspector General of Police reported on 3 September that Kanpur was the one major urban centre giving cause for anxiety, but that the situation in villages, particularly in the Bulandshahr-Meerut region dominated by the Jats, was becoming ominous. Another contrast with Non-Cooperation lay in the virtual absence of large-scale Muslim participation. This further weakened the movement in the towns (Muslims in U.P. were 37% of the urban population, though they numbered only 14.5% in the province as a whole), while the Congress seems to have deliberately avoided Muslim-dominated pockets in the countryside when selecting centres for active Civil Disobedience. There was a serious riot in Benares in February 1931, provoked by picketing of a Muslim cloth shop, and in March a Congress call for a *hartal* in honour of Bhagat Singh led to major communal disturbances in Kanpur in which 290 were killed—the police keeping strangely quiet and thus indirectly encouraging mobilization on both sides, a pattern witnessed in Dacca also, in the previous year.

The contrast with Non-Cooperation was double-edged, however, for Civil Disobedience in many areas in U.P. did become much more of a villagers' campaign, and Congress organization now was definitely more widespread, elaborate and disciplined (Gyan Pandey, *Ascendancy of the Congress in U.P.,* pp. 40–154,). The British with the experience of the Avadh *kisan* upsurge of 1920–21 were very nervous about no-rent from the beginning, and the provincial leadership in U.P., unlike that of Bihar, did give a call for a no-tax movement in October, advising *zamindars* to stop paying revenue and peasants to withold rents. Jawahar Lal's radicalism may have been partly responsible for the plunge, U.P. *zamindars* had also been demonstratively loyalist (a Lucknow conference of landlords had denounced the Independence Resolution in February 1930), while peasants with memories of a partly-successful struggle ten years earlier were difficult to restrain as prices fell catastrophically and in an unprecedented manner. But the ambivalent relationship between Congress organization and peasant militancy remain clear in U.P., too, as Gyan Pandey has shown through a study of local variations. Congress discipline was most marked in Agra under Sri Krishna Paliwal, an area with few big *zamindars* and a mass of small landlords and rich peasants, the latter mostly enjoying occupancy rights. Here the Bardoli pattern was successfully followed in villages like Barauda and Bhilaoti: non-payment of taxes, mass desertion of villages in face of police action, avoidance of anti-landlord agitation as well as of violence. In Rae Bareli, big *talukdars* were much more in evidence, only 1.5% of land was held by occupancy tenants, and the 1920–21 *kisan* agitation was a living memory; radical pressures from below were correspondingly much more acute, and a local leader, Kalka Prasad, was preaching no-rent and promising lower rents under *swaraj* already from June. Men like Kalka Prasad would be disciplined, however, in course of 1931 as the Congress organization tightened its hold over the district after the Gandhi-Irwin Pact. The most violent outbursts, including murder of some oppressive landlords, took place after March 1931, and not during the movement, and usually in areas relatively untouched by Congress agitation and organization—in the *doab tehsils* of Allahabad, for instance, which had been avoided by the Congress because here Muslim landlords faced Hindu tenants, and there was a danger of communal riots. At Bara Banki, *khadi* or *charkha* was little in evidence, but local, formally 'Congress' workers were preaching in mid-1931 that land was a gift of God and could not belong solely to the *zamindars*. (G. Pandey, Ch., 6–7)' Congress organization did make a success of no-tax in U.P. once the slogan was endorsed in October 1930, but all-India politics compelled the retreat of March 1931 and the urging of restraint on the peasantry throughout the months of the truce. As we shall see, this was probably the psychological moment from the *kisan* point of view, which was irrevocably lost. A Meerut Settlement Officer recalled in 1934: 'When at last Congressmen definitely launched their "no-rent" campaign in the autumn of 1931, they found...that they had "missed the bus".' (Ibid., p. 193)

Despite many local variations, available regional data thus seem to indicate a broadly similar pattern from the autumn of 1930 onwards of simultaneous decline and radicalization: a weakening in forms of struggle associated with bourgeois groups or peasant upper strata (e.g., urban boycott and no-revenue), accompanied by sporadic but fairly widespread tendencies towards less manageable forms (no-rent, tribal outbursts, popular violence). In such a situation, moves towards some kind of compromise settlement were only natural, both for the Gandhian leadership with its faith in controlled mass participation, as well as for business leaders with their counting-house mentality and fear of peasant radicalism (so many of them had interests in land, too, after all—even G.D. Birla was described by the *Indian Year Book* of 1939–40 as 'millowner, merchant and zamindar'). Developments in London at the first session of the Round Table Conference (November 1930–January 1931) meanwhile seemed to create an opportunity for compromise.

The Round Table Conference

While thousands of Indians were going to jail or facing *lathis,* bullets, and loss of property, a largely unrepresentative handful had gone to London for constitutional talks with the multiparty British delegation. The Congress had kept away, as had most Indian business leaders apart from Homi Mody; but Muslim politicians were there in strength (Muhammad Ali, Muhammad Shafi, Aga Khan, Fazlul Huq, Jinnah—while Fazl-i-Husain was an important behind-the-scenes influence as a member of the Viceroy's Executive), along with Hindu Mahasabha leaders (Moonje and Jayakar), Liberals (Sapru, Chintamani. Srinivasa Sastri), and a big princely contingent. The mass upsurge in India had made implementation of the Simon Commission Report of May 1930 (which promised responsible government in place of dyarchy in provinces, subject to some emergency powers reserved with Governors, but suggested no change at all in the central government) all but impossible. Irwin admitted privately to Wedgewood-Benn on 19 June that the Report 'will provoke an explosion here' by its 'stern refusal anywhere to mention Dominion Status'. Some sort of promise of a change at the centre was evidently necessary, and here the idea of federation including princely India came as a real godsend for the British. A federal assembly with a major section nominated by princes should prove a safe enough body, and so, as Prime Minister Ramsay MacDonald declared at the end of the Conference on 19 January 1931. 'His Majesty's Government will be prepared to recognize the principle of the responsibility of the Executive to the Legislature.' The idea formally came from the princes, specifically from the Dewans of Hyderabad (Akbar Hydari) and Mysore (Mirza Ismail), but Hydari had been persuaded initially by the British Resident, Lt. Col. Terence H. Keyes, and the suggestion was eagerly taken up by British officials like Malcolm Hailey and British politicians like Reading, Hoare, Zetland and the very moderate Labourite Secretary of State Wedgewood-Benn. Indian princes were interested in a weak centre which their entrance would also help to keep undemocratic, particularly at a time when mass pressure was threatening to bring about Dominion Status, at the very least with a central government dominated by the Congress—and here there was also an objective similarity of interests between princes and Muslim politicians alarmed by the prospect of Hindu majority rule. The British, in addition, carefully hedged in the promise of central responsibility with a series of 'reservations and safeguards' in the crucial spheres of defence, external affairs, and financial and economic control, as MacDonald made clear in his 19 January speech. Working out the details of the scheme would take almost five years, for it soon became clear that federation was chameleon-like, and had been accepted in January 1931 out of a variety of motives. The princes thought it would reduce paramountcy claims, Muslims liked the idea of a weak centre, Liberals like Sapru were attracted by the promise of a responsible centre, while most British politicians felt that through it they could grant 'a semblance of responsible government, and yet retain...the realities and verities of British control'. (R.J. Moore, *Crisis of Indian Unity*, p. 155)

A second development playing into British hands was the failure of the Minorities Committee of the Conference to come to any agreement, and here the responsibility lies very largely with the Hindu Mahasabha leaders, Moonje and Jayakar, along with Sikh representatives. Jinnah, Shafi, and the Aga Khan very nearly achieved an agreement with the Sapru group of Liberals on the basis of the 1927 compromise position of joint electorates with reserved seats for Muslims, but the breaking-point, as in 1928-29, came over the Mahasabha opposition to Muslim reservations in Punjab and Bengal, while an additional complication was introduced by the Sikh claim to 30% of the Punjab seats (they were 11% of the population, and had already about 19% representation). The Mahasabha argument that Muslims should not require reservations in Punjab and Bengal as they were the majority there was cogently answered by Muhammed Ali with the plea that the small numerical superiority of the Muslims in these two provinces could be outweighed by the social power of Hindu Banias in Punjab and Hindu *zamindars* in Bengal since universal suffrage was not being introduced. But

Jayakar and Moonje refused to yield an inch, and so yet another chance of at least elite-level unity was lost.

Gandhi–Irwin Pact

The Liberal delegates, not unnaturally from their own point of view, tried to present the Round Table Conference as a significant gain for India, and on returning from London pleaded with the Congress leaders (who had been released on 26 January) for a compromise. But Sapru and Jayakar had been pressing for a settlement throughout 1930, their appeals had been firmly rejected at Yeravda, and Gandhi's initial reaction this time too seems to have been quite negative. 'I do not believe that MacDonald's statement grants us anything', he declared on 31 January, and he went on expressing deep pessimism about the prospect of any agreement in both public statements and private correspondence right up to 11 February. Yet a sudden retreat began from 14 February (the date of Gandhi's letter seeking an interview with the Viceroy), and in the talks with Irwin at Delhi. Gandhi quickly accepted Irwin's insistence on three 'lynch-pins...Federation; Indian responsibility; reservations and safeguards'. (Irwin's version of 17 February interview). Clause 2 of the Delhi Pact of 5 March firmly pegged down the scope of future discussions to the scheme outlined at the first R.T.C. session, and defined 'reservations and safeguards' to cover 'such matters as, for instance, defence; external affairs; the position of minorities; the financial credit of India, and the discharge of obligations.' While Civil Disobedience prisoners were to be released, relatively little attempt seems to have been made for saving the life of Bhagat Singh, and token concessions regarding salt and non-political *Swadeshi* propaganda were more than counterbalanced by Gandhi giving up, after some strenuous negotiations, his demands for enquiry into police atrocities and return of confiscated lands already sold to third parties (a concession which aroused very adverse reactions particularly in Gujarat). The contrast with Yeravda and with repeated Congress statements throughout 1930 about a 'fight to the finish', could hardly have been sharper; no wonder that radicals like Jawaharlal felt deeply let down: 'This is the way the world ends/Not with a bang but a whimper.' (*An Autobiography*, p. 259)

The historical puzzle concerning the change in Gandhi's attitudes cannot be solved in terms of pressure from Liberal leaders alone (personally respected but with virtually no support in the country). Nor can it be seriously argued that Gandhi was simply won over by Irwin's charm, or had become suddenly attracted by the very vague R.T.C. promise of responsible government in the centre, limited as it was by a federation where princes would have a very big say and whose details all remained to be worked out, a string of reservations and safeguards, and an unsolved communal tangle. There is some evidence that the crucial role was played by business pressures. A surcharge of 5% had been imposed on cotton piecegoods imports in early February, despite some Cabinet opposition and loud protests from depression-affected Lancashire, and this time the government did not levy any additional charge on non-British imports, avoiding Imperial Preference for the time being obviously on political grounds. The Bombay Governor reported to the Viceroy on 7 February that 'a number of Gandhi's followers, particularly among mercantile community, are contemplating a breach with him unless he adopts reasonable attitude', and Irwin informed Wedgewood-Benn on 11 February that 'Purshottamdas will probably go to see Gandhi at Allahabad in order to try to put commercial pressure on him'. Thakurdas was in Delhi during the negotiations, and helped in resolving the final hitch over Gujarat land confiscations on 4 March. And on 11 February, Birla's close adjutant D.P. Khaitan had declared in his presidential address to the Calcutta Indian Chamber of Commerce: 'it may not be amiss to suggest to Mahatma Gandhi and the Congress that the time has come when they should explore the possibilities of an honourable settlement.... We all want peace.' The coincidence of dates is once again striking and significant.

MARCH–DECEMBER 1931: UNEASY TRUCE

Ambiguities

The logic of events between March 1931 and the wholesale British counter-offensive which compelled the Congress to embark on the second Civil Disobedience movement in January 1932 was determined in large part by the profoundly ambiguous consequences of the Gandhi–Irwin Pact.

The frustration and anger of radical nationalists was sharpened by the execution of Bhagat Singh, Sukhdev and Rajguru on 23 March, just before the opening of the Karachi Congress, and the Naujawan Bharat Sabha organized a demonstration against Gandhi at the Karachi railway station. Yet the Karachi session is significant mainly as revealing the weaknesses of the Left critics of Gandhi. Jawaharlal had utilized his spell in jail from October to January to work out a fairly radical agrarian programme and to formulate what became a basic element in Left-nationalist strategy of the mid-1930s by suggesting a Constituent Assembly as the central political slogan (Notes in Naini prison, December 1930, *Selected Works,* Vol. IV, pp. 437–51). He spent some sleepless nights after the Delhi Pact, but then surrendered easily to Gandhi and agreed to move the key resolution endorsing the agreement at Karachi. The death of Motilal (6 February) perhaps had made him more psychologically dependent on Gandhi, and he was acutely aware of his own limitations, as compared to the Mahatma, so far as empathy with the peasantry was concerned. It is significant that in the *Autobiography* published five years later, discussion of the Delhi Pact was followed immediately by an appreciation of Gandhi as representative of 'the peasant masses of India'. A sense of helplessness and passivity is noticeable also in the speeches at Karachi of other critics of the Delhi Pact. Yusuf Meherali, soon to become a prominent Socialist leader, denounced unequivocally 'the politics of compromise' and 'change of heart', and bitterly attacked 'the Birlas, Purshottamdas Thakurdas', Walchand Hirachands, Husainbhai Laljis, who are now out and busy in making efforts to obtain the fruits of the suffering and sacrifices of others'. But his concluding note was strangely tame: Gandhi would again have to give the call for struggle, as the Round Table Conference was bound to fail, and then the radicals would get their chance—'We patiently await the call to fight. *Inquilab Zindabad.*'

The Karachi session passed a resolution on fundamental rights and economic policy which has often been interpreted as a major concession to placate the Left. It is true that some officials suspected in it the hand of M.N. Roy, and some months later Ambalal Sarabhai circulated a note among FICCI members sharply attacking parts of the resolution as threatening to bring about 'a Government on Russian model' (*Walchand Hirachand Papers, F.N. 8 (ii)*. But there was in reality precious little of 'socialism' in the 20 points of the Karachi Resolution, which combined general democratic demands (civil liberties, legal equality, adult suffrage, free primary education, and a state policy of religious neutrality) with much of Gandhi's 11-points of 1930, plus fairly modest promises to labour (living wages, an end to forced labour, trade union rights, etc.), a vaguely worded clause about control by the state of key industries and mineral resources, and a very moderate programme indeed of agrarian change. Only 'substantial reductions' were promised in land revenue and rent, there was no reference to the burning issue of rural indebtedness, and obviously no intention at all of eliminating landlordism or redistributing land.

So the Karachi Congress submitted to Gandhi as usual, and, as in February 1922, this was an indication of certain basic weaknesses of the entire movement, and not just of the leader. Civil Disobedience had been marked by much scattered potentially radical manifestations, but no real alternative leadership had emerged. In its absence rural militancy remained either entirely spontaneous, sporadic, and uncoordinated, or under the leadership of village Gandhians with a limited outlook. Labour organization and militancy had declined sharply since 1928–29, and the Communists, already weakened by the Meerut arrests, were going through a Left-sectarian phase in which they concentrated their fire on Left-nationalists, expelling Nehru from the League Against Imperialism in April 1930, and quarrelling with Bose to the point of bringing about a second split in the AITUC at its Calcutta session in July 1931. They kept aloof from Civil Disobedience, and spent most of their energies quarrelling among themselves.

Yet the Pact disappointed many others outside the rather narrow circle of conscious radicals with more or less definite socialist leanings. The Patidars of Kheda, Hardiman points out, 'considered the pact a betrayal' since revenue had not been reduced and even the forfeited land remained largely unrestored, in sharp contrast to the Bardoli victory of 1928. 'The pact, rather than police lathis, broke the morale of the Patidars' (Hardiman, *Peasant Agitations in Kheda District,* p. 289). Brian Stoddart and Gyan Pandey have come to similar conclusions about coastal Andhra and U.P. For both regions, 1931 was probably the psychological moment for full-scale no-revenue and no-rent movements in face of the first blast of the Depression, but for a crucial period of nine months the Congress held back the peasantry, trying to honour the truce. 'It was the conclusion of the Gandhi-Irwin Pact, rather than the Government's repressive policies, which altered the Congress hold on the coastal districts of Andhra'. (Stoddart in *Congress and the Raj,* pp. 121–2)

At the same time, it would be an over-simplification of a rather complex reality to describe the impact of the Gandhi-Irwin Pact in entirely negative terms. Whatever the concessions made by Gandhi, and however paltry the concrete nationalist gains, the Viceroy had been forced to treat the national leader on an entirely novel basis of courtesy and equality—a fact of profound psychological significance, and as such deeply resented from the beginning by most British officials in India. The average Congress worker released from jail seems to have gone back to his village or town almost as a victor, a mood vastly different from the near-total disenchantment and frustration of 1922. While Congress organization had virtually collapsed after the Bardoli retreat, 1931 was marked by a considerable extension of party machinery in many areas. By May 1931, for instance, the single district of Rae Bareli in U.P. had 32 Congress offices, 8040 Congress members, 13,081 volunteers, and 1019 villages flying Congress flags. (Gyan Pandey, p. 41) What is more significant, a combination of economic pressures, heightened morale of the average Congress activist, official Congress reluctance to take up radical programmes, and perhaps a certain disenchantment with the leadership, all produced a variety of pressures from below, making the truce increasingly fragile, and stimulating secret official moves for an all-out counter-offensive.

Pressures from Below

In Bengal, where the disillusionment of educated youth about Gandhian non-violence could only have been enhanced by the Delhi Pact, terrorism surpassed all previous records in 1931, with 92 incidents including 9 murders (two of them of District Magistrates, Peddie of Midnapur in April and Stevens of Tippera in December). Stevens was assassinated by two schoolgirls, Santi and Suniti Chaudhuri, marking a new level of participation of women in the revolutionary movement. Nor was terrorism any longer confined to towns alone, at least in Chittagong, where no less than 52 villages were declared disturbed areas in May. A really frightened British government went in for draconian methods of repression, imposing a night curfew on *all* Hindu *bhadralok* youth between 16 and 25 in Chittagong town, and shooting down detenues in jail at Hijli on 16 September. Rabindranath addressed the protest meeting in Calcutta after this incident despite his general aloofness from nationalist politics during these years and well-known hostility to terrorism. A sweeping Ordinance was issued on 29 October permitting indiscriminate arrest of alleged terrorist sympathizers. Meanwhile at the other end of the country in the N.W.F.P., the rapid growth of the Khudai Khidmatgar, made formally a part of the Congress in August 1931, led to further official complaints that the Congress was violating the March truce.

The most serious threat, alike to the British and to the policy of compromise now being sought to be followed by the Congress leadership, came from deepening rural discontent as prices touched a record low (in U.P. the index of wholesale prices taking 1901–05 as 100 fell from 218 in 1929 to 162 in 1930 and 112 in 1931 (Pandey, p. 160) and revenue, rent, and debt burdens became correspondingly unbearable. In Kheda and Bardoli, purchasers of confiscated land and newly-appointed village officials were socially boycotted, and revenue collections fell off again from May. Since the Gujarat rural base was so very vital, Gandhi spent much of his time in these two districts between March and his departure to attend the second session of the R.T.C. on 29 August. He threatened to cancel his trip to England if remedial action was not taken in Gujarat, and eventually, through talks with Willingdon and Home Member Emerson in Simla on 25–27 August, obtained an official enquiry into Bardoli Congress grievances as a special case.

The U.P. rural situation proved less tractable and much more explosive. The Congress here tried to act as an arbitrator between *zamindars* and tenants, asking *kisans* to send applications for rent-reductions to the local Congress offices; the bureaucracy not unnaturally disliked this intensely, considering it as an attempt 'to establish institutions parallel to those of Government'. Gandhi issued a Manifesto to U.P. *kisans* on 24 May, suggesting a compromise by which non-occupancy tenants should pay a minimum of 8 annas in the rupee of the current rent, and occupancy tenants 12 annas. The edge of this appeal was clearly directed against agrarian radicalism: 'let me warn you against listening to the advice if it has reached you that you have no need to pay the zamindars or taluqdars any rent at all.' But officials soon complained that peasants were taking Gandhi's minimum rates as the maximum, and often stopping all payments, while local leaders and activists were emerging, all using the Congress name, but preaching a far more radical message—like Kalka Prasad in Rae Bareli, for instance, or Anjani Kumar in the same district who picketed the house of the Raja of Sheogarh as a protest against eviction of defaulting tenants. Sheogarh, interestingly enough, had started a Khadi Vidyalaya, employing as a teacher there the wife of Sitala Sahai, the local Congress leader closest to Jawaharlal. (*Home Political 33/24/1931*) Despite official charges of Congress instigation, there is ample evidence that the leadership—including even Jawaharlal—acted on the whole as a restraining force. Kalka Prasad was driven out of the district Congress, and things quietened down considerably in Rae Bareli after Jawaharlal's tour there in June. Agra with its very powerful Congress machinery and Gram Seva Sangh financed by Seth Achal Singh, a nationalist landlord, remained very quiet apart from one isolated riot, while the main centres of agrarian radicalism, apart from Rae Bareli, were in Bara Banki, with little Congress organization, and Manjhanpur *tehsil* in Allahabad, which the nationalists had avoided in 1930 due to the presence there of Muslim *zamindars*. In December 1931, with R.T.C. negotiations clearly breaking down, the U.P. Congress did at last authorize no-rent in some districts, but by then Governor Malcolm Hailey's policy of judicious combination of repression and conciliation (₹108 lakhs revenue and ₹412 lakhs rent was remitted in the end), had taken much of the edge out of peasant militancy. Yet the U.P. peasants had achieved something, winning remissions which, however inadequate, were still much in excess of those granted in other provinces or in earlier years of distress, and forcing on the Congress leadership a partial but growing recognition of the importance of questions of agrarian relations for the future of the national movement. By 1936, the U.P. leadership would come to advocate, at least in theory, the abolition of the *zamindari* system, well in advance of the Congress in other provinces.

The months of the truce were marked by movements in many other regions, too, though these have received less publicity than the U.P. events.

Anti-autocratic and anti-feudal agitations were emerging in some of the princely states—in Kashmir, for instance, in July 1931, where the inevitable confrontation between an overwhelmingly Muslim subject population and a Hindu ruling dynasty did acquire at times a certain communal tinge, but where the foundations were also being laid in these years of the powerful National Conference movement. The agitation started by a group of Muslim graduates including Sheikh Abdulla culminated in a mass attack on Srinagar jail on 13 July, when 21 were killed in police firing. While the immediate result was a communal outburst, repressive measures in September 1931 led to attacks on police rather than Hindus, and the situation soon required British military intervention to help the Maharaja. In Jammu there were anti-moneylender riots in Mirpur, Kotli and Rajouri *talukas,* and eventually the state set up a Grievances Enquiry Commisson with some non-official members on 12 November. At Pudukottah, a small state near Trichinopoly in July there was for some days what the *Indian Annual Register* described as 'mob rule': crowds protesting against new taxes overpowered the police and military, burnt court records, released prisoners from jail, and forced the ruler to cancel the additional levy for the time being. In Bihar, the Congress leadership stuck to a strongly pro-*zamindar* line, but a strong Kisan Sabha movement was emerging in Gaya district under Jadunandan Sharma, later one of Sahajanand's closest associates. The Utkal P.C.C. decided to set up 'Krushak Sanghas' throughout Orissa in September 1931, and officials complained that Congress village work was worsening *zamindar*-tenant relations in districts like Puri. In coastal Andhra, pressures were mounting for a no-revenue campaign by late-1931, under local leaders like Duggirala Balaramakrishnayya of Krishna district, whose Telegu ballad *Gandhi Gita* popularized both agrarian and nationalist agitations. Andhra peasants living in *zamindari* areas were also being organized for the first time, particularly on the vast Venkatagiri estate covering 2117 square miles in Nellore. A forest *satyagraha* began here in 1931, against grazing fees through which the *zamindar* was curtailing traditional peasant rights to fodder and timber; leadership was provided by N.V. Rama Naidu and N.G. Ranga. There was a spate of anti-*mahajan* riots in the districts of Krishna and Guntur in September 1931, involving crowds of up to 4000. In Kerala, with its particularly atrocious forms of caste discrimination, the Guruvayoor temple *satyagraha* which was started under the Congress leader Kelappan in November 1931 had a major radicalizing impact. Volunteer *jathas* covered on foot large parts of both Malabar and the princely states of Travancore and Cochin, and despite the onset of Civil Disobedience, *satyagraha* continued in Guruvayoor till called off at Gandhi's orders in September 1932. Among the activists at Guruvayoor was a school-teacher named A.K. Gopalan, soon to become Kerala's most popular Communist peasant leader.

Official Attitudes

Mounting popular pressures during the truce months strengthened the tendency in British official circles to plan a wholesale counter-offensive through a pre-emptive strike. D.A. Low has shown in an important article that the shift in British attitudes, usually attributed to Irwin's successor Willingdon, really had its roots in some official thinking already during the first Civil Disobedience movement and in the strong bureaucratic reaction to the Viceroy's treatment of Gandhi as an equal in February-March 1931. The basic idea, as Low puts it, was of 'civil martial law': empowering civil officials with sweeping, near-military powers, instead of directly calling in the army as at Amritsar in 1919. (D.A. Low in *Congress and the Raj*, Ch. 5) Home Member Emerson emphasized in May 1931 that maintenance for the time being of the Delhi Pact must be 'accompanied by the determination to strike at once and strike hard, if and when the Settlement breaks down', and a draft Emergency Powers Ordinance was prepared months before the actual crack-down of January 1932.

The hardening of official attitudes in India was helped by a simultaneous shift to the Right in British politics, with the Tory-dominated National Government headed by the renegade Labour leader Ramsay MacDonald assuming office in September 1931, and with a Lancashire and British business counter-offensive developing as the world economic crisis deepened. The new Tory Secretary of State, Samuel Hoare, threatened to override the fiscal autonomy convention in September 1931, when the Government of India, in serious financial difficulties as revenues from customs, income tax and railways were all declining due to the economic crisis, decided to raise the cotton duty from 20 to 25% without imposing politically explosive countervailing excises or Imperial Preference. In a pattern which would be often repeated during the 1930s, the Home authorities eventually agreed to the new tariff despite Lancashire protests, but insisted on keeping the rupee tied to sterling at 1s 6d when Britain went off the gold standard on 21 September 1931. A floating rupee would have devalued considerably, adversely affecting payment of Home Charges and remittance of profits; metropolitan financial considerations were thus given top priority, even at the cost of some sacrifice for the sectional interests of Lancashire. At the second session of the Round Table Conference (September-December 1931), officials and British business representatives insisted that the Viceroy should retain enormous reserved powers in finance. Birla calculated that under the proposed Federal structure, the supposedly 'responsible' Indian finance minister would effectively control only ₹15 crores out of a total revenue of ₹130 crores (Birla to Sapru, 31 October 1931, G.D. Birla, *In the Shadow of the Mahatma*, p. 46). British business delegates like Benthall also pressed hard for commercial safeguards, guaranteeing foreign capital in India against 'discrimination' by nationalist governments. At the political level, too, there were signs of a return towards 'Simonism'—Indians must be 'more and more forced back upon Provincial Autonomy as the first step to be taken' Hoare informed Willingdon on 2 October 1931. (R.J. Moore, p. 232)

The overall situation made Gandhi's participation at the Round Table Conference singularly futile. The session was soon deadlocked on the minorities issue, with separate electorates being demanded now not only by Muslims but by depressed castes, Indian Christians, Anglo-Indians, and Europeans, and all these groups came together in a 'minorities' pact' for joint action on 13 November. Benthall in particular cultivated the Muslim delegates, obtaining their support in return for a promise 'that we should not forget their economic plight in Bengal and...do what we can to find places for them in European firms...' (Benthall note, quoted in Uma Kaura, p. 77). Gandhi desperately fought against the concerted move to make all constitutional progress conditional on a solution of the communal problem. That solution, he argued, would be 'the crown of the Swaraj constitution and not its foundation', and on 5 October Gandhi even offered to accept all Muslim claims provided they supported the Congress demand for *Swaraj*. But the Muslim delegates bluntly rejected the offer, and Gandhi's generosity was certainly not shared by the Mahasabha delegates, who along with the Sikhs bitterly opposed anything that could give a majority to Muslims in the Punjab. On the Federation question, too, the princes were now speaking in different voices and seemed much less enthusiastic then in 1930, for the threat of an immediate change in the centre had diminished now that Congress had called off its movement. A British move to postpone discussion of changes at the centre altogether was scotched only because of opposition from the otherwise pliable Sapru, Jinnah and Ambedkar, and MacDonald ended the session on 1 December with a reiteration of his 19 January stand, announcement of two new Muslim-majority provinces (N.W.F.P. and Sind), the setting up of an Indian Consultative Committee and three expert committees (on franchise, finance, and States), and holding out the prospect, both humiliating and dangerous from the nationalist point of view, of a unilateral British communal award if the Indians failed to agree.

The whole thing had been a pointless exercise, inevitably so because Gandhi had given up during the Delhi negotiations the demand for majority representation for his party which had led to the rejection of the Irwin offer in December 1929. The Congress instead had accepted parity at the R.T.C. with a variety of sectional interests, some of them quite minor or unrepresentative. An obviously out-manouevred Gandhi returned to India on 28 December, to find Nehru and Ghaffar Khan in jail and large-scale repressive measures already under way in Bengal, U.P. and N.W.F.P. Willingdon rudely turned down Gandhi's request for an interview, leaving the Working Committee with no option but to resume Civil Disobedience. On 4 January 1932 the long-prepared plans for preemptive strike went into operation, with a battery of Ordinances (Emergency Powers, Unlawful Association, Unlawful Instigation, and Molestation and Boycotting) banning Congress organizations at all levels, arresting leaders, activists and sympathizers, and providing for confiscation of property. There was to be 'no drawn battle this time', declared Hoare: no less than 272 associations were banned on the very first day in Bengal alone.

1932-1934: SECOND CIVIL DISOBEDIENCE MOVEMENT

Repression and Resistance

Out-manouevred and facing repressive measures on an entirely unprecedented scale, the national movement under the Congress still fought on valiantly for about a year and a half before admitting defeat. Estimates of arrests during the fifteen months between January 1932 and March 1933 go up to as high as 120,000, though it must be added that this is not a valid indication of relative strength as compared to the figure of 90,000 for 1930-31. Many more were arrested this time because repression had become so much more intense and systematic. There was also a significant and quite rapid decline over time. An official break-up of 74,671 convictions up to April 1933 lists 14,803 for January 1932, 17,818 in February, 6909 in March, and 5254 in April. The monthly figure never exceeded 4000 thereafter and Willingdon was reporting conditions as 'well under control' by 4 April 1932 and Civil Disobedience to be 'almost in a moribund condition' on 6 November of the same year. (*Templewood Collection*) Provincial breakups for convictions give high percentages relative to total population for Bombay Presidency (14,101; 0.064%), Bihar and Orissa (14,903; 0.040%), U.P. (14,659; 0.030%), Bengal (12,791; 0.026%) and C.P. (4014; 0.026%)—as contrasted to only 0.008% in Punjab and 0.007% in Madras. Though Muslim participation remained generally low, the percentage of convictions in N.W.F.P. was the highest for the entire country (6053; 0.25%). Women numbered 3630, and the extent to which the Congress had become a real mass movement is indicated by the fact that illiterates comprised 759 out of 904 in Madras and 1550 out of 2004 in U.P. in an early 1932 estimate; 1397 out of this U.P. figure were described as tenants or labourers. (*Home Pol.,* F.N. 3/11/1933-q. in Judith Brown, *Gandhi and Civil Disobedience,* pp. 284–6)

Civil Disobedience in 1932–33 comprised a wide range of activities, in part because so very many things had now become illegal, and civil liberties almost totally suppressed. Willingdon while finalizing plans for the 4 January attack confessed that he felt he was 'becoming a sort of Mussolini in India', (letter to Hoare, 20 December 1931) The forms of defiance included picketing of cloth and liquor shops, closing of markets and boycott of white or loyalist business concerns, symbolic hoisting of Congress flags, holding in public of illegal Congress sessions (as near the Chandni Chowk Clock Tower in Delhi in April 1932, and on the Calcutta Maidan next year), salt *satyagrahas,* non-payment of *chaukidari* taxes, no-rent as well as no-revenue, forest law violations, and a certain amount of illegal Congress functioning (including even a secret ratio transmitter near Bombay in August 1932) and use of bombs—the latter two methods later strongly condemned by Gandhi.

Willingdon's letter of 4 April 1932 described Bombay city and Bengal as the 'two black spots'. Bombay city to its Governor remained 'the keep of Gandhism', where the 'Congress have got a deeper hold...than anywhere else in India'. (Sykes to Hoare, 6 March 1932, *Sykes Collection, MSS Eur., F. 150*). Massive participation by the Gujarati business community, and particularly, it seems, of the smaller traders, badly disrupted the central Mulji Jethe raw cotton market till October 1932, when the government decided to help white firms threatened with ruin by very effective blacklisting and pushed through a law establishing official regulation of the cotton trade. But mill-workers remained aloof, as in 1930, and Muslims at times hostile—there was in fact a major series of communal riots in Bombay city between May and July 1932. In the countryside, whether in Bombay or elsewhere, response on the whole seems to have been less than in 1930, for the Congress had spiked its own guns during the 1931 truce and missed the psychological moment for an all-out no-revenue and no-rent movement. Kheda and Bardoli were handicapped this time by the British success in pressurizing Baroda to close its borders and only 15 villages were withholding revenue in Kheda by February 1932. A village like Ras, in Kheda, however, was still refusing revenue in 1933, though its Patidars had lost by then 2000 acres of land, and some of them had been stripped naked, publicly whipped, and given electric shocks by the police. A powerful no-tax movement developed in parts of Karnataka, particularly in Ankola and Siddapur *talukas* of north Kanara where more than 200 villages withheld revenue, and the AICC reports refer to scattered outbursts of forest *satyagraha* in many parts of central and south India. In Ankola on 1 May 1932, for instance, 4000 villagers poured into the *taluka* headquarters carrying freshly cut firewood for auction, and in Betul in C.P. in the same month, forest *satyagraha* was offered under tribal leaders like Mannu Gond and Chaitu Koiku. The Kerala PCC also reported forest *satyagraha* in Kasergod *taluka* of Malabar in August and October 1932. (*AICC, F.N. 1/1932*)

Civil Disobedience was weaker in Tamilnadu and Andhra as compared to 1930, though there were some active centres of urban picketing (e.g., Madras City, Madura and Virudhanagar in Tamilnadu), and the British were seriously alarmed for a while in 1933 by signs of a revival of no-revenue movements in coastal Andhra. In Bihar, there were several mass attacks on police stations in Monghyr and Muzaffarpur districts in February 1932 by crowds of up to 7000, and excise revenues continued to decline till 1933. In U.P., though a secret AICC bulletin of March 1932 reported no-rent movements in a number of districts (*R.E. Hawkins Papers* in Cambridge South Asian Centre), Civil Disobedience was now becoming much more of an urban affair, Agra district for instance was now quiet except for an isolated no-rent movement in Barauda village, while 80% of land revenue due from Rae Bareli had been collected by July 1932, two months before time (G. Pandey, pp. 177, 187).

In Bengal, the March 1932 AICC bulletin reported revival of salt *satyagraha* in coastal areas, non-payment of *chaukidari* taxes and Union Board boycott in many districts and no-rent in Arambagh sub-division of Hooghly and parts of Tippera, Sylhet and Jalpaiguri. The continued failure of the Congress leadership to espouse agrarian radicalism even in Depression conditions, however, encouraged Muslim peasant movements to develop increasingly on separatist lines. The Praja movement gathered strength during these years, and in December 1932 Maulana Bhasani, who throughout his career would combine genuine agrarian populism with communalist appeals, organized a big Praja Sammelan at Sirajgunj which demanded abolition of *zamindari* and scaling-down of debts. Bengal remained a nightmare for the British, however, because of terrorism. Though the new governor Anderson was a specialist in repression ever since the Irish Civil War days, the number of terrorist cases was the highest ever in 1932 (104), before declining to 33 in 1933 and 17 in 1934. Two more white district magistrates were killed in Midnapur, Governor Jackson was attacked at the University Convocation by a girl student, and Surjya Sen could be arrested only in February 1933. More than 3000 were detained at concentration camps in Buxa, Hijli and Deoli, while the Chittagong prisoners were sent to the Andamans.

The second Civil Disobedience movement coincided with significant upsurges in two princely states. In Kashmir, the concessions offered by the Grievances Enquiry Commission in April 1932 (steps to promote Muslim education, return of government-occupied Muslim religious buildings, partial suspension of a grazing tax, and payments for state-requisitioned labour) failed to stop a growing movement. The Muslim Conference was started in October 1932, and though it would be renamed the National Conference only six years later, its leader Sheikh Abdulla had already started to develop close contacts with a group of anti-autocratic Jammu Hindus under P.N. Bazaz. In the Rajasthan state of Alwar in early 1933, there was a formidable rising against Maharaja Jaisingh Sawai's revenue enhancements, *begar,* grazing dues, and reservation of forests for hunting. The Meos, a self-contained semi-tribal peasant community with a largely formal affinity to Islam, began guerrila war on a large scale. On 12 February 1933, Willingdon reported the Alwar conditions to be 'getting as bad as they can be', and the *Indian Annual Register* spoke of 80–90,000 Meos participating in what it predictably but mistakenly dubbed 'communal trouble'. While the Punjab Muslim leader Mohammed Yasin Khan did try to give the anti-Maharaja movement a communal (as well as pro-British) colour, an alternative, consciously radical trend was also developing, associated with Syed Mutalabi Faridabadi, and, interestingly, enough, K.M. Ashraf, soon to become one of India's first Marxist historians. Eventually the British decided to pack off the unpopular Maharaja to Europe, and take over Alwar administration for some years (Chaudhuri Abdul Haye's article in H. Kruger (ed.), *K.M. Ashraf,* Delhi, 1969).

By the second half of 1932, Civil Disobedience was evidently going down in defeat. It is true that the decline in peasant participation evident for instance in Gujarat, Andhra or U.P. was clearly a submission to overwhelmingly superior force rather than any loss of faith in the Congress, and the halo of sacrifice and martyrdom won by the latter during 1930–34 helped decisively in the winning of elections from 1934 onwards. Yet Hardiman has a point when he reminds us that 'voting was not the same as agitating....The days of the classic Gandhian satyagrahas had passed'. Propertied peasants would go on voting Congress, but were no longer so ready to sacrifice their land, now that Gandhi had failed to get it restored for them in 1931; and in some areas, most notably Gujarat, they would also become more prosperous after Depression was succeeded by a war boom (when tobacco prices went up 500% in Kheda) and, correspondingly, less militant. Rural capitalism developed only in a few scattered pockets before 1947, and peasant radicalism retained its potentialities in the greater part of the country, and particularly so in the *zamindari* areas. This was a radicalism, however, which from the mid-1930s would increasingly seek forms of expression outside the Congress proper, through Left-leaning Kisan Sabhas as well as sometimes through communal organizations.

Business Realignments

If peasant response was becoming increasingly contradictory, urban bourgeois attitudes towards Civil Disobedience also showed considerable ambivalence. Gujarat merchant support throughout 1932 made the Bombay movement formidable, the Indian Merchants Chamber of that city was captured by a nationalist group in early 1932 against the opposition of Thakurdas, and, when Civil Disobedience was resumed, the FICCI decided to keep away from constitutional discussions for the time being. But G.D. Birla, who had pleasantly surprised Benthall by appearing quite accommodating in private discussions during the 1931 Round Table session, hastened to assure Hoare on 14 March 1932 that the door to cooperation was by no means entirely closed, and that the resolution boycotting the R.T.C. had been unwillingly taken by the FICCI leaders under great pressure from member-bodies (*In the Shadow of the Mahatma*, pp. 54–5). As the mass movement declined, political 'realism' plus certain sectional economic calculations pushed some business groups towards collaboration. At the Ottawa Imperial Economic Conference in the summer of 1932, India conceded lower import duty rates for a number of British commodities in return for preferential treatment in the U.K. for some raw material exports, most of which, like tea or hides and skins, faced little competition in any case. Though strongly denounced by nationalists as well as, in public, by Birla, the Agreement was ratified fairly easily in the Legislative Assembly. Bombay textile magnates in 1932–33 were much more worried by Japanese competition in coarser piecegoods than by an evidently weakened Lancashire, and this provided the basis for the notorious Lees–Mody Pact of October 1933, by which Bombay agreed to further preferences for British textiles imports in return for a Lancashire promise to buy more Indian raw cotton. Japan had been cutting down its Indian raw cotton purchases as retaliation for high import duties in India, and so a new outlet for Indian cotton was needed if anti-Japanese tariff walls were to be retained. Nationalists were furious at this 'betrayal' through acceptance of lower tariffs for Lancashire, and so were Ahmedabad textile magnates who produced fine cloth in competition with Lancashire and had no desire to see the long-staple cotton it needed flowing away to the U.K. But Bombay mill-owners and Tatas (who signed a similar agreement with British steel interests in face of Belgian competition soon afterwards) together represented a formidable combination, and politically, too, Thakurdas was pleading for 'some understanding' by June 1932, and Birla repeatedly tried his hand as mediator between the government and Gandhi during 1932–34.

Yet strong objective compulsions, both economic and political, existed to prevent anything like total sell-out or unqualified collaboration by Indian business groups. British insistence on retaining the 1s 6d ratio remained a permanent grievance, for it encouraged imports and required for its maintenance deflationary fiscal and monetary policies. Governments elsewhere in the capitalist world were fighting Depression by greatly extending public expenditure, but in India so-called 'sound finance' remained a dogma, and investments in railways and irrigation were drastically cut down (Bagchi pp. 18, 46–7). The massive gold exports which began from 1931 (due to the decline in the gold value of the rupee after sterling had gone off the gold standard) helped the government to meet Home Charges and debt payments at a time when commodity exports were declining catastrophically. They were deeply resented, however, by Indian business and public opinion, which attributed them to distress sales by Depression-affected peasants, and Congress volunteers tried to picket gold export shops in Bombay—though radical nationalists also suspected at times that men like Thakurdas and Birla were secretly making 'lakhs...from this immoral traffic'. (Illegal Bombay Congress Bulletin, 17 October 1932, *Thakurdas Papers F.N. 101*). Lalji Naranji, who had opposed Non-Cooperation publicly in 1921, warned the Liberal leader Jayakar on 27 January, 1932 that 'I in my commercial way of thinking believe more in Gandhiji's policy', for 'Government indifference to us' has driven 'we capitalists to work with socialistic organizations like Congress ...'. On a purely temporary and limited basis, Naranji hastened to add. If the British stopped export of gold, gave protection to Indian textiles, modified currency, excise, and fiscal policies, and relaxed their near-monopoly on banking, insurance and shipping, he felt that Congress would soon withdraw Civil Disobedience, of which 'they are not fond...particularly Mahatmaji is sure to withdraw if we are given what we want'. (*M.R. Jayakar Papers, F.N. 456*)

Above all, collaboration was made difficult by the fact that the years 1932–34 were marked by a full-scale counter-offensive by British business interests, with Lancashire in particular closely aligning itself with the ultra-Tory opposition led by Churchill to any constitutional concession going beyond the Simon framework. Demands were raised for indefinite postponement of any changes in the centre, or alternatively for stringent commercial and financial safeguards which would virtually abrogate the Fiscal Autonomy Convention of 1919. Lancashire pressure led to suppression of the December 1932 Tariff Board recommendations for higher cotton import duties without preferences to Britain, and efforts were made during 1934 to get the Lees-Mody concessions formalized. The Indo-British Supplementary Agreement of January 1935 brought cotton duties, previously excluded from the Ottawa arrangement, within its scope, and visualized a reduction in the 25% import duty as soon as finances allowed. (Basudev Chatterji, Ch. 6) Birla dramatically warned Thakurdas on 14 November 1934: 'I think Lancashire has now tasted the human blood and they are no longer satisfied with Mody-Lees Pact'. (*Thakurdas Papers, F.N. 126*)

The ultimate result of the opposite pressures towards collaboration and conflict was an important re-alignment of business attitudes in support of a change in Congress policy, away from mass agitation and towards Assembly and eventually ministerial participation. This re-alignment enabled Indian capitalists to overcome the fairly sharp split between near-loyalists and nationalists within their own ranks which had become quite marked during the early 1930s. It also fitted in with developments within the Congress leadership as it came to terms gradually with the evident decline of Civil Disobedience in face of overwhelming repression.

Harijan Campaign

By the second half of 1932, Gandhi in jail had probably started thinking in terms of an honourable retreat from a confrontation which had failed—something made very difficult this time because of the obstinate British determination to hold no political discussions with him. His instinctive first reaction, as after 1922, was to shift to constructive village work, and Macdonald's Communal Award of August 1932 with its creation of separate electorates for untouchables helped to focus his attention primarily on 'Harijan' welfare. Gandhi began a 'fast unto death' on the untouchable separate electorate issue on 20 September, and was able to secure an agreement between caste Hindu and untouchable leaders (Poona Pact) by which the Award was modified. The Hindu joint electorate was retained with reserved seats for untouchables who were given greater representation than by MacDonald. This was essentially the system which continued after 1947 also. Harijan upliftment now became Gandhi's principal concern; starting an All India Anti-Untouchability League (September 1932) and the weekly *Harijan* (January 1933) even before his release, going out on a 12,500 mile 'Harijan tour' between November 1933 and August 1934, and even attributing the terrible Bihar earthquake of 15 January 1934 to divine punishment for the sins of caste Hindus—an obscurantist flourish which deeply shocked Rabindranath. Civil Disobedience was gradually allowed to slip into the background. It was suspended temporarily in May 1933, Gandhi personally decided to abstain from it after his final release from jail on 23 August 1933, and the movement was formally withdrawn in April 1934.

Like so many of Gandhi's programmes, the Harijan campaign was richly ambiguous in motives and significance. Radical nationalists like Jawaharlal felt it to be a harmful diversion from the main task of anti-imperialist struggle—a feeling encouraged by the British readiness to let Gandhi conduct Harijan work even from jail. At the same time, orthodox Hindus within the Congress increasingly disliked the new emphasis: Malaviya, for instance, who had been very close to Gandhi in the mid-1920s, now began to drift away. Hindu communalist resentment was sharpened by Gandhi's refusal to concern himself overmuch with other provisions of the MacDonald Award which had given Muslims 49% of seats in the Punjab and 48.6% in Bengal (i.e., together with European members, majorities in both provinces). Orthodox Hindu opinion in Bengal bitterly attacked the acceptance of a permanent caste Hindu minority status by the Poona Pact, but the Congress Working Committee in June 1934 adopted a compromise 'neither rejection-nor-acceptance' formula which led Malaviya to start a breakaway Congress Nationalist Party. Gandhi's Harijan meetings had been disrupted in April and July 1934 in Buxar, Jasidih and Ajmer by Sanatanists, and there was even a bomb attack on his car in Poona on 25 June. The British Government, too, despite its claims to be a modernizing influence, had no intention at all of alienating orthodox opinion, and official members helped to defeat the Temple Entry Bill in the Legislative Assembly in August 1934.

From a more long-term point of view, Harijan welfare work by Gandhians must have indirectly helped to spread the message of nationalism down to the lowest and most oppressed sections of rural society, and Harijans in most parts of the country did come to develop a traditional loyalty towards the Congress which would greatly help the party after independence, too. Like other Gandhian mass movements, extension was combined with control, for Gandhi deliberately confined the Harijan campaign to limited social reform (opening of wells, roads, and particularly temples, plus humanitarian work), delinking it from any economic demands (though very many Harijans were agricultural labourers) and also refusing to attack caste as a whole. He advised caution on inter-dining and inter-marriage, and went on defending the original *Varnasrama* system—with the result that Ambedkar refused a message to the *Harijan* weekly on the ground that 'nothing can emancipate the outcaste except the destruction of the caste system'. (Tendulkar, Vol. III, pp. 236–8) As with peasant movements, Gandhian Harijan work seems to have been in part a bid to establish hegemony over potentially more radical pressures from below. In Tamil Nadu, E.V. Ramaswami Naicker's Self-Respect Movement advanced rapidly in the early 1930s, developing a populist style of anti-Brahmanism quite distinct from the loyalist and elitist Justice Party. Naicker after a trip to Soviet Union in 1932 built a 'Stalin Hall' in Coimbatore and opened his journal, *Kudi Arasu,* to the atheist and socialist writings of the elderly Communist Singaravelu Chettiar. Though Naicker's 'socialism' proved a passing flirtation, some Self-Respect cadres like P. Jeevanandan did later become Communist leaders. Gandhi encountered an anti-religious mood in Kerala, too, for here the Ezhava caste organization, SNDP-Yogam, had been captured after the death of the Gandhian T.K. Madhavan in 1930 by leaders like C. Kesavan and K. Aiyappan, radicals who thought temple-entry to be relatively trivial, and who became militant atheists, inspiring many to take the Communist road though never becoming Marxists themselves. In general, however, the Indian Left failed to devote sufficient attention to the complex inter-relations of caste and class, and Gandhi surely had a point when he rebuked Narendra Dev on 2 August 1934 for forgetting to mention untouchability in the draft programme of the Congress Socialist Party. (Tendulkar, Vol. III, p. 344)

Return to Council Politics

While Birla contributed financially to the Harijan campaign, and even agreed to preside over the Anti-Untouchability League, business groups in general were much more interested (now that Civil Disobedience had failed), in having the Congress back in the legislatures as an effective pressure-group which could lobby for them. The prospect of full responsible government in provinces added to the attraction, which was strongly felt also by the bulk of the Congress leaders. Plans for a return to electoral politics through a revived Swarajya Party were floated by Satyamurti in October 1933, and quickly taken up by Bhulabhai Desai, Ansari and B.C. Roy in April 1934. Things were somewhat complicated by the breakaway of the Hindu-communalist Malaviya-Aney group on the Communal Award question, but the trend back towards conventional politics was clear. It is significant that Gandhi in a letter to Birla in April 1934 acknowledged 'that there will always be a party within the Congress wedded to the idea of Council-entry. The reins of the Congress should be in the hands of that group'. (*In the Shadow of the Mahatma,* p. 138). Council-entry supporters in Tamil Nadu in 1934 included Rajagopalachari, the staunch No-Changer of the 1920s, as much as the Swarajist veteran Satyamurti. The mid-1930s would be marked by a gradual coming-together of orthodox Gandhian constructive-workers and advocates of Council-entry (and soon of ministry-formation, too) in a common front against a growing challenge from the Left, and there is ample evidence that business advice and pressures played an important part in this process of formation of a definite Congress Right. 'I should like you to keep yourself in touch with Bhulabhai (Desai)', Birla advised Thakurdas on 12 April 1934. 'If the Swaraj Party is to be successful, they will have to collect some fund for fighting the new election and I would suggest that fund should not be supplied from Bombay without being satisfied that the right type of men are being sent.' And again, on 3 August 1934, 'Vallabhbhai, Rajaji and Rajendra Babu are all fighting Communism and Socialism. It is therefore necessary that some of us who represent the healthy Capitalism should help Gandhiji as far as possible and work with a common object.' [*Thakurdas Papers, FN 126. 42(vi)*].

The Left Alternative

The emergence of the Left alternative which obviously alarmed such men lay in the logic of Civil Disobedience itself, for it had inevitably aroused expectations which it could not satisfy. World events also played a notable part: while world capitalism was afflicted by the absurdity of a crisis of over-production, and was breeding in Nazism the negation of all human and democratic values, the Soviet Union seemed to go ahead through Five Year Plans with constructing what two life-long critics of Marxism would soon hail as a 'new civilization'. Its image had not yet been tarnished by Stalinist purges or a Nazi-Soviet Pact.

In May 1933, when Gandhi suspended Civil Disobedience for the first time, Subhas Bose and Vithalbhai Patel issued a statement from Europe repudiating his leadership. More significant, as representing an ideological alternative, was Jawaharlal's intellectual radicalization in prison. His letters to his daughter, later published as *Glimpses of World History* (1934), and the *Autobiography* written in jail in 1934–35, mark the height of Nehru's interest in and partial commitment to Marxian socialist ideas. Out of jail for a brief period between July 1933 and February 1934, Nehru made clear his theoretical differences with Gandhi in letters and articles published as *Whither India?* 'repeatedly emphasized the need to combine nationalist objectives with radical social and economic programmes, and also bitterly attacked Hindu communalism. (The Hindu Mahasabha at its October 1933 Ajmer session had combined calls for Hindu 'self-defence' with denunciation of 'any movement advocating extinction of capitalists and landlords as a class'). As always, however, Nehru drew back from any total breach with Gandhi and saw no reason why he 'should walk out of the Congress leaving the field clear to the social reactionaries'. He did not approve of the moves being made then to start a socialist party. Gandhi was not particularly alarmed, 'His communist views need not...frighten anyone' (*Bombay Chronicle* interview, 18 September 1933) but many British officials considered Nehru to be 'the high-priest of Communism', and packed him off to jail again at a time when practically every other leader was being released.

The idea of a distinct Socialist ginger-group, working within the Congress but trying to push it Left-wards, had been floated in Nasik jail meetings in 1933 where the participants included Jayaprakash Narayan, Achhut Patwardhan, Yusuf Meherali, Ashok Mehta and Minoo Masani. The U.P. Congress leader Sampurnanand drew up 'A Tentative Socialist Programme for India' in April 1934, and the Congress Socialist Party was formally started next month at a conference in Patna chaired by Narendra Dev. Ambiguities were there from the beginning, for the C.S.P. wanted to remain within the Congress, but was sharply opposed to its leadership and ready to cooperate with non-Congress Leftist groups. The ideology of its founders ranged from vague and mixed-up radical nationalism to fairly firm advocacy of Marxian 'scientific socialism', which Narendra Dev at the Patna meeting distinguished sharply from mere 'social reformism'. Right-leaning Congress leaders disliked the new trend intensely, Sitaramayya going so far as to describe its founders as 'scum' in a letter to Patel on 21 September 1934, and the Working Committee in June 1934 condemned 'loose talk about confiscation of private property and necessity of class war' as contrary to nonviolence. Nehru was sympathetic, but never formally joined the C.S.P., and it is interesting that Gandhi in his already-cited letter to Narendra Dev (2 August 1934) felt that Jawaharlal 'who has given us the mantra of socialism...would have hastened slowly' if he had been out of jail. The letter went on to make the prediction that Nehru would be 'the natural wearer of the Congress crown of thorns when I and other elderly men and women retire'—a point which Gandhi repeated soon afterwards for the benefit of Vallabhbhai Patel, too. (Tendulkar, Vol. III, p. 386)

The C.S.P.'s quick advance in provinces like U.P. (where 7 out of 11 members of the Provincial Congress Executive were described as Socialists by a government source already in September 1934) was somewhat illusory. Much of the support was purely opportunistic, coming from groups with factional quarrels with the established Congress leadership at various levels, and most of the C.S.P. founding-fathers were to have extremely chequered and by no means consistently Leftist political careers in the future. Yet C.S.P. propaganda did help considerably in stimulating thinking in Congress ranks and leadership on questions like radical agrarian reform, problems of industrial labour, the future of princely states, and non-Gandhian methods of mass mobilization and struggle—Narendra Dev's 'general strike of workers and peasants' which Gandhi found 'intoxicating' and 'too dangerous' in August 1934.

C.S.P. activists were able to develop close connections with the emerging Kisan Sabha movement, particularly in Bihar and Andhra. Several *kisan* marches were organized in 1933–34 through coastal Andhra districts, the Ellore Zamindari Ryots Conference in 1933 demanded abolition of *zamindari,* and the C.S.P. leader N.G. Ranga started an Indian Peasant Institute at Nidubrolu to train *kisan* cadres. In Bihar, a section of the Congress leadership had initially encouraged Sahajananda in 1933 to revive the Kisan Sabha, which had been allowed to go defunct during Civil Disobedience, as a counter to the moves of the loyalist *zamindar*-dominated United Party to woo peasants for electoral purposes through concessions on minor issues like right to plant trees, dig wells, and transfer holdings after paying *salami.* The United Party kept silent on the much more important questions of rent-remissions, landlord efforts to increase *zerait* (private holdings), and *bakasht,* land on which hereditary tenants were being replaced by short-term leases during the Depression years. Sahajananda was able to quickly mobilize large sections of the peasants of central and north Bihar around such issues, and the membership of his Kisan Sabha shot up to 80,000 by 1935. He was initially opposed to any calls for abolition of *zamindari* or clearcut class struggle, but sustained C.S.P. pressure-cum-persuasion led to the acceptance of this radical programme by Sahajananda and the entire Bihar Provincial Kisan Sabha at its third, Hajipur session in November 1935. It needs to be added that the C.S.P. throughout the mid and late-1930s acted objectively as a kind of bridge across which radical nationalists passed on their road to the full-fledged Marxism of the Communist Party. N.G. Ranga later complained bitterly that the C.P.I. captured one-third of the 2000 peasant youths he had trained at Nidubrolu, and no less than 90% of the original Andhra C.S.P. membership. (*Revolutionary Peasants,* pp. 75–6) The C.S.P. also was made use of as a legal 'front' or cover by growing numbers of convinced Communists, as the C.P.I. remained illegal from 1934 to 1942.

1933 and 1934, finally, were years of a significant labour revival, closely associated, like the late-1920s, with Communist activity. The number of strikes, which had touched the lowest ever figure since 1920 in 1932, began rising again from next year:

Year	Number of Strikes	Number of Workers Involved	Work Days Lost
1932	118	128,099	1,922,437
1933	146	164,938	2,168,961
1934	159	220,808	4,775,599

C. Revri, *Indian Trade Union Movement,* (1972), pp. 183–5

British jute and Indian cotton mill-owners alike tried to pass the burden of Depression on to the workers through retrenchment, rationalization and wage cuts. Average daily earnings in Bombay textiles, for instance, had fallen by 16.94% in December 1933 as compared to July 1926, and despite the counter-balancing effect produced by falling prices, even real wages had started declining in 1934. (Revri, p. 176; Bagchi, p. 122) The trade union movement had been gravely weakened by the Meerut arrests and the repeated splits in 1929 and 1931, creating the moderate National Trade Union Federation and the Communist Red Trade Union Congress as rivals to the AITUC. Though the jailed leaders were soon replaced by younger Communist militants headed by men like B.T. Ranadive and S.V. Deshpande in Bombay and Abdul Halim, Somnath Lahiri and Ranen Sen in Calcutta, the 'ultra-Leftism' of the early 1930s led to a multiplicity of mutually hostile groups and general isolation from the nationalist mainstream. Things were further complicated by the efforts of the Comintern dissidents, M.N. Roy and Soumendranath Tagore, to start groups of their own and the Royists soon achieved considerable success in trade union activities through leaders like V.B. Karnik, Maniben Kara and Rajani Mukherji. A 'Labour Party' was started in Calcutta by Niharendu Dutta Majumdar, a barrister who developed into an effective trade union leader.

From 1934 onwards, however, there were clear signs both of renewed labour militancy and of tendencies towards reunion of Communist and trade union factions. Communists and Royists tried to organize a general strike in textiles in 1934, and there were big strikes in Sholapur (February-May), Nagpur (May-July), and, above all, a Bombay general strike from April. The alarm caused in government circles by this renewed labour and Communist militancy is indicated by the flood of official papers dealing with the subject in 1934, and the C.P.I. was formally banned on 23 July under the old 1908 Act against seditious associations. Unlike in 1929, however, repression failed to seriously weaken the Communist movement, for the mid-1930s would be marked rather by consolidation and advance through a new 'United Front' strategy, with Communists progressively developing contacts with Left-nationalist elements by work within the C.S.P. and the Congress. The formal shift in party line was clearly associated with the United Front perspective worked out in Dimitrov's report to the Seventh Comintern Congress in 1935 in the context of the menace of Fascism. But it needs to be emphasized that there were probably some internal pressures, too, for the aftermath of Civil Disobedience brought into the Communist movement a new generation of disillusioned Gandhian nationalists and revolutionary terrorists with much wider contacts with and prestige among the nationalist mainstream than the Bombay and Calcutta sects of the 1920s could have possibly enjoyed. In Kerala, for instance, leaders like P. Krishna Pillai, E.M.S. Namboodripad and A.K. Gopalan were by the mid-1930s simultaneously rebuilding a Congress organization shattered by repression, forming the local unit of the C.S.P., and laying the foundations of the Communist Party in Kerala, and absorbing in that process the small and rather sectarian Trivandrum Communist League group which had been the first avowedly Marxist circle in the region. In Bengal, too, the real spread of Communism into the districts came with the large scale conversion of terrorists to Marxism in detention camps and in the Andamans during the mid-1930s through intense ideological debates and heroic self-searching. From terrorism came Bengal Communist leaders of the stature of Bhowani Sen and Harekrishna Konar, and the Party eventually was able to recruit a big majority of the most prestigious revolutionary group of all—the heroes of the Chittagong Armoury Raid.

The stage had thus been set for a major confrontation between Right and Left within the national movement, and increasingly from 1935 a touchstone was provided by the opportunities and snares offered by the new constitutional structure being imposed by the British.

1935-1937: THE CONSTITUTION AND THE CONGRESS

The 1935 Act

In August 1935, the long and tortuous process started eight years earlier with the appointment of the Simon Commission at last ended with the Government of India Act. From 1932 onwards, real Indian participation in the making of this 'Constitution' had become negligible. A largely formal and unimportant third and last session of the Round Table Conference held in November-December 1932 with only 46 delegates present (as against 112 in 1931), was followed by the British Government issuing a White Paper (March 1933) and setting up a Joint Select Committee of Parliament with a provision merely for 'consulting' Indians. The final Act emerged after intense debates within the British Parliament alone. Not unnaturally, many of the admittedly limited concessions offered in 1930-31 under pressure of Civil Disobedience were reduced through this process, and the resultant Act was criticized by virtually all sections of Indian public opinion (by Liberals and by Jinnah, as well as the Congress) as representing little real advance over 1919. Right Wing Tory pressure, for instance, spearheaded by Churchill with Lancashire support, replaced direct by indirect elections at the Federal level, and extended and tightened up the machinery of official 'discretionary powers', 'reservations' and 'safeguards'.

The only significant steps forward were in the provinces, where dyarchy was replaced by responsible government, theoretically in all departments, and the electorate was increased from 6½ to about 30 million. But Governors retained 'discretionary powers' regarding summoning of legislatures, giving assent to bills, and administering certain special regions (mostly tribal)— and on these matters Ministers were not entitled to give advice. They were also empowered 'to exercise individual judgement'—Ministers could give advice 'but their views could be rejected, on matters like minority rights, privileges of civil servants, and prevention of discrimination against British business interests. The Governor in addition could take over and indefinitely run the administration of a province under the notorious Section 93 clause of the 1935 Act. The proposed Federal structure, to come into effect only after 50% of the princes had formally acceded to it, introduced a kind of dyarchy in the administration of what remained a fairly strong centre. The subjects 'transferred' to elected Ministers were limited by 'safeguards' of the type created in the provinces, while foreign affairs and defence remained entirely under Viceregal control. The new Central Reserve Bank was carefully kept outside Assembly control, as well as Railways, while debt services and ICS salaries were also reserved subjects, and legislation on currency and exchange required prior Viceregal permission. Ultimate financial control, it is true, was transferred by the Act from London to New Delhi, a point much emphasized by some recent historians like Tomlinson; one may be permitted a little scepticism, however, over the real significance of a shift from a Secretary of State to a Viceroy also appointed by the British Government. In the bicameral Central Legislature, members nominated by princes would occupy 30 to 40% of the seats (104 out of 276 in the Council of State and 125 out of 375 in the Federal Assembly), while Muslims and other special electorates were also given considerable weightage both in the centre and in the provinces through the inclusion in the Act of the Macdonald Award (as revised by the Poona Pact). A further, very dangerous, provision of the Act was the transfer of relations between the

Crown and Indian states to the 'Crown Representative'—in practice, the Viceroy himself but functioning not through responsible ministers but via the purely official Political Department, local Residents and Political Agents. The Federal part of the 1935 Act in any case proved to be a total non-starter, as the princes had become quite unenthusiastic once with the decline of Civil Disobedience the prospect of a real Congress takeover of the central government had receded, and once the realization had spread that the British were quite unwilling to reduce paramountcy claims in return for accession to Federation. Muslim political leaders, too, felt that the proposed Federal structure was still too unitary, and hence subject to the danger of Hindu majority domination, while all sections of the Congress denounced Federation as a sham. The British on their part were clearly not too unhappy with a deadlock which allowed the 1919 system of total official control at the centre to continue unchanged indefinitely. Finally, it needs to be emphasized that six years after the much-trumpted Irwin offer of November 1929, the 1935 Act remained entirely silent about Dominion Status. Linlithgow, Chairman of the Joint Parliamentary Committee and Viceroy from 1936, offered perhaps the best (though naturally private) estimate of the Act. He stated that the Act had been framed 'because we thought that way the best way... of maintaining British influence in India. It is no part of our policy, I take it, to gratuitously to hurry the handing over the controls to Indian hands at any pace faster than that which we regard as best calculated, on a long view, to hold India to the Empire' (Linlithgow to Zetland, 21 December 1939, quoted in R.J. Moore's article in *Congress and the Raj,* p. 379)

The years 1935 and, particularly 1936, saw the emergence of a pattern in Indian politics which would be repeated often, both before and after Independence. Outwardly, all the signs were of a significant lurch to the Left: growing Socialist and Communist activity (despite the 1934 ban on the CPI), numerous labour and peasant struggles, the formation of several Left-led all-India mass organizations, and Congress Presidential addresses by Nehru at Lucknow and Faizpur (April and December 1936) which formally seemed to embody virtually all the radical aspirations and programmes of the Left. Yet in the end the Right within the Congress was able to skillfully and effectively ride and indeed utilize the storm, and by the summer of 1937 Congress ministries were being formed to work a significant part of the Constitution which everyone had been denouncing for years.

Labour and *Kisan* Movements

On the labour front, a slightly more favourable situation for trade union struggles was created by the partial lifting of the Depression from about 1934.

Employment figures were rising (thus 14,247 new workers were taken in by jute mills in 1935, while in the following year the 54-hour week was reintroduced, ending the short-time imposed in 1931) but discontent was more acute than ever, since both white and Indian capitalists tried to retain the wage-cuts they had enforced during the preceding years. Notable strikes included those affecting the Kesoram Cotton Mills in Calcutta and Ahmedabad textiles in 1935, the Bengal-Nagpur Railway in December 1936–February 1937, and a series of labour disputes in Calcutta jute and Kanpur textile mills during 1936 culminating in the next year in massive general strikes in both centres. Meanwhile the legacy of the 1929 and 1931 splits was being successfully overcome. In April 1935, the Red Trade Union Congress of the Communists rejoined the AITUC, controlled at this time by followers of M.N. Roy plus some Socialists, and a Joint Labour Board was set up a few months later to explore possibilities of united action with the moderate National Trade Union Federation, too. The Communists by 1936 under their new General Secretary, P.C. Joshi, had become warm advocates of a United Front strategy, and the implication of this new line, formulated by Dimitrov at the Seventh Comintern Congress in the summer of 1935, were spelt out for India in an article by R.P. Dutt and Ben Bradley in the British Communist Journal *Labour Monthly* in March 1936. This called for work within the Congress with the aim of converting it into an 'anti-imperialist people's front'. Trade Unions and peasant organizations should be given collective affiliation to the Congress, elections should be fought on a radical programme, but office entry firmly repudiated, and the principal positive slogan should be a Constituent Assembly elected by universal suffrage. Nehru in fact had suggested such a demand already in 1930, and Dutt and Bradley had met him at Lausanne shortly before writing this article. The Lucknow Presidential Address repeated a month later the two concrete demands of collective affiliation and Constituent Assembly.

The new spirit of unity among Left-nationalists, Socialists and Communists found expression also through the formation of the All India Kisan Sabha during the Lucknow and Faizpur Congress sessions. The initiative at first had come from Andhra, where N.G. Ranga, leader since 1933–34 of the Provincial Ryot's Association and a separate Zamin Ryot's Association for *zamindari* tenants, had been trying from 1935 both to extend the Kisan movement to the other three linguistic regions of Madras Presidency, as well as to draw in sections of agricultural labourers. A South Indian Federation of Peasants and Agricultural Labour, started in April 1935 with Ranga as General Secretary and E.M.S. Namboodripad as a Joint Secretary, suggested in its conference of October 1935 the immediate formation of an All India Kisan body. The Socialists took up the idea at their Meerut

Conference in January 1936, and though Bihar (the other main base of the early Kisan movement) seems to have been unenthusiastic at first about what was feared would be a rather formal unity, Sahajanand Saraswati eventually agreed to preside over the first session of the All India Kisan Sabha in Lucknow in April 1936. Another notable pioneer was Indulal Yajnik, the disillusioned Gandhian veteran from Gujarat who became Editor of the *Kisan Bulletin*. As was probably inevitable, the Kisan Sabha focussed mainly on the grievances of peasants with some (and at times considerable) land vis-a-vis zamindars, traders, money-lenders, and the Government. The Kisan Manifesto of August 1936 demanded abolition of zamindari, a graduated tax on agricultural incomes in excess of ₹500 in place of the present land revenue, and cancellation of debts. It included also a minimum charter of demands: 50% cut in revenue and rent, full occupancy rights to all tenants, abolition of *begar,* scaling-down of debts and interest-rates, and restoration of customary forest rights. The problems of class-differences within the peasantry, and of tensions between landholding peasants and landless labourers, would remain to plague the Kisan Sabha (and the entire Left) throughout both in theory and practice. But the Kisan Manifesto did suggest transfer of uncultivated government and zamindari lands to peasants with less than five acres and to the landless, who would hopefully get organized into cooperatives; there was no demand, however, for any general ceiling on landholding. Sahajanand in an early issue of the Kisan Bulletin wanted an enquiry into agricultural wages, and visualized improvement in agrarian labour conditions 'by negotiating with the peasants, and by assisting their organized strike against zamindars and planters'—an interesting, but not unnatural, distinction.

The early activities of the Kisan Sabhas included the holding of spectacular peasant marches, the celebration of an All India Kisan Day (1 September 1936; when a hundred village meetings were reported from the single district of Guntur in Andhra), and numerous local struggles. The Bihar Kisan Sabha, for instance, began a big movement at Barhaiya Tal, in Monghyr District, from November 1936 against zamindar attempts to evict occupancy tenants and convert their lands into *bakasht.* The All-India Conferences gave a great fillip to the formation of new provincial bodies. Bengal delegates returning from Lucknow, for instance, took the initiative in contacting already active scattered local activists to constitute the Bengal Provincial Kisan Sabha at a conference in Bankura district in March 1937.

The most formidable and oppressive strongholds of feudalism lay in the princely States, and, as we have seen, these had already witnessed numerous spontaneous local peasant outbreaks—the most recent incidents being in Sikar *thikana (jagir)* of Jaipur, against revenue—enhancement in the midst of Depression, and at Lohanu in Punjab where an agitation against a tax on camels had led to firing in 1935. The All-India States Peoples Conference, however, had so far been a very moderate and elitist body, confined to drawing up petitions and issuing pamphlets, while the Congress still stuck to a strict policy of non-interference. As late as 1934, Gandhi had reiterated the 'helplessness' of the Congress, and had expressed the hope that princes could be persuaded to behave as good 'trustees' for their subjects. Bhulabhai Desai, the strongly Right-wing leader of the Congress Assembly Party, even gave an assurance while visiting Mysore in 1935 that princes would have the sole right of determining relations with any future Federation. 1936 marked the clear beginning of a change. Nehru's address to the fifth session of the States Peoples' Conference urged the need for mass contacts in place of mere petitions, and the session for the first time drew up a programme of agrarian demands: a one-third cut in land revenue, scaling-down of debts, and an enquiry into peasant grievances in the context of the 'tragedies of Kashmir, Alwar, Sikar (Jaipur) and Loharu.' Next year, the formation of Congress ministries would set off a veritable upsurge in large parts of princely India.

Leftism in Literature

The foundation, again in 1936, of the All India Students Federation and the Progressive Writers' Association indicated the growing Left influence on educated youth and intelligentsia. Unlike Non-Cooperation, Civil Disobedience did not leave a strong impression on the literary world, which was marked by growing disillusionment with Gandhian rigidities and a search for more radical ways. Premchand's last and greatest novel, *Godan* (1936), is a stark and unrelieved picture of peasant misery, totally lacking the Gandhian idealism and optimism of *Rangbhumi* (1925); at the same time, the essay, *Mahajani Sabhyata,* written just before his death, combined a bitter critique of the capitalist profit motive with appreciation of the Soviet experiment. In Andhra, a vogue for realistic novels about toilers was started after the translation in 1932 of Gorky's *Mother,* and the rising poet Sri Sri, the first to use spoken Telegu in verse, was inspired by Bhagat Singh's martyrdom to compose the famous *Mare Prapancham* ('Another world, another world, another world is calling') which ended with an evocation of the red flag. The Bombay labour movement influenced Modkholkar and Mama Warerkar's Marathi stories about textile strikes. In Bengal, where the urban intelligentsia had never been particularly attracted by Gandhi, Rabindranath remained aloof from Civil Disobedience and positively hostile to terrorism (as shown by his novel *Char-Adhya,* 1934), but his *Letters from Russia* (1930) were warmly though not uncritically appreciative. The Calcutta high-brow literary monthly *Parichay* (founded in 1931), to give another example, combined indifference towards contemporary Gandhian nationalist and even peasant movements with considerable interest in international developments, the world-wide struggle against fascism, and Marxist theory and practice.

The initiative for starting an All India forum for Left leaning writers was taken by a group of Urdu-speaking intellectuals headed by Sajjad Zahir, who drew up a manifesto in 1935 while still studying in London which urged the necessity 'to bring the arts into the closest touch with the people' through focussing on 'the problems of hunger and poverty, social backwardness and political subjugation'. Premchand presided over the first session of the Progressive Writers Association in Lucknow in April 1936, and Rabindranath in 1938 sent a warm and unusually self-critical message regretting his own relative isolation from the masses. As an all-India movement, the P.W.A. attained its greatest strength in the world of Urdu, no doubt in part because of its inter-regional (though also largely urban and at times somewhat elitist) span, and its leading figures included Hasrat Mohani (the radical politician who was also a distinguished composer of *ghazals*), Josh Malihabadi, Firaq Gorakhpuri and Krishan Chander. Though the united-front approach of the Association's Leftist organizers sometimes involved elements of opportunism and quest for big names, there were also some interesting efforts at genuine mass contact like the very successful conference of peasant poets at Faridabad (near Delhi) in the summer of 1938, or Kaifi Azmi's 'revolutionary mushairas' among Bombay workers. Such things foreshadowed the major Communist efforts at revitalization of folk culture through the Indian Peoples' Theatre Association in the 1940s.

Lucknow and Faizpur

Nehru became Congress President (as in 1929, at Gandhi's insistence) soon after his return from Europe, and his addresses at Lucknow and Faizpur (April-December 1936) at first sight seemed to indicate the climax of the Left influence over the national movement during these years. While disclaiming any intention of forcing his socialist ideas on the Congress, Nehru at Lucknow explicitly stated that he was using the term socialism— 'the only key to the solution of the world's problems and of India's problems'—'not in a vague humanitarian way but in the scientific, economic sense'. He hailed the Soviet Union, despite its faults, as a 'new civilization', and declared that 'we who labour for a free India... inevitably... take our stand with the progressive forces of the world which are ranged against

Fascism and Imperialism'. The two sessions were persuaded by Nehru to pass resolutions condemning Italian and Japanese aggression and expressing solidarity with Abyssinia, China and Republican Spain, all symbolizing the new international perspective which was one of Jawaharlal's most notable contributions to our freedom movement. Internally, he advocated fighting elections on a radical programme, refusal to take office, and a central slogan of a Constituent Assembly based on universal suffrage, which, he warned at Lucknow, could come about only in 'a semi-revolutionary situation'. The Congress, Nehru hoped, could be converted into a real anti-imperialist 'joint popular front', and he suggested as a first step 'corporate membership' of trade unions and Kisan Sabhas. Nehru also explicitly criticized as 'authoritarian' the trend in Congress organization which Gandhi had insisted upon at the previous, Bombay, session (October 1934): reduction in the number of delegates, a *khadi* qualification for office-bearers, and tighter control by the President and the Working Committee nominated by him. Nehru's Working Committee after Lucknow included three Socialists (Jayaprakash, Narendra Dev, Achyut Patwardhan), and the socio-economic clauses of the Congress Election Manifesto (August 1936) and the provisional Agrarian Programme adopted at Faizpur, while mainly reiterating the Karachi resolution, did go some way towards incorporating the minimum demands of the Kisan Manifesto of the A.I.K.S.: reductions in revenue and rent, agricultural income tax, fixity of tenure, scaling down of debts, end of forced labour, recognition of forest rights and of peasant unions. Nehru emerged as the most energetic and successful compaigner for the Congress in the 1937 elections, thus beginning a career as his party's most effective vote-catcher which would last for almost three decades.

Right Consolidation and Business Pressures

Yet closer scrutiny reveals the Left advance during 1935–37 to be somewhat illusory and verbal, at least in so far as crucial decision-making was concerned. It is true that Liberal or communalist Right-wing groups outside the Congress, lacking the prestige of a heroic though unsuccessful national struggle, seemed to be getting increasingly discredited. Despite the confusion caused by the Communal Award issue, Malaviya and Aney's Congress Nationalist Party did badly in the 1934 elections losing all eight Legislative Assembly seats to the Congress in U.P., for instance—whereas a similar breakaway group (under, Malaviya and Lajpat) had captured six seats to the Swarajists two in 1926. Jinnah's desperate efforts before the 1937 elections to revive the Muslim League through a single All-India Muslim Parliamentary Board was also not too successful. He failed to rope in the two major agriculturist-based regional parties in Punjab and Bengal, the Unionists and the Krishak Praja, and the Muslim League could capture only 109 out of 482 Muslim reserved seats in the Provincial Assembly elections of 1937.

But the really important development was the consolidation of a Right-wing within the Congress, based on a rapprochement between advocates of conventional Assembly-politics and Gandhian constructive workers, and backed, as we have seen, by considerable business pressures and patronage from about 1934 onwards. Through skilful manouevres, combining pressure with (largely verbal) concessions, the Right was able to preserve its hegemony over the national movement throughout this period. The partial opening to the Left in the form of radical Presidential addresses, programmatic declarations, and election speeches was in fact indispensable in the context of the Civil Disobedience mass awakening and the five-fold expansion of the electorate.

The Thakurdas Papers give illuminating details about the ways in which Indian businessmen tackled the phenomenon of Congress Leftism, as symbolized in these years above all by Nehru. H.P. Mody's move in August 1935 to start anew, openly capitalist-backed, moderate party unless Congress ceased its 'flirtations with extreme socialist elements' cut little ice with more far-seeing and tactful fellow-businessmen like Thakurdas or Birla who found judicious cultivation of Congress leaders like Bhula-bhai Desai or Vallabhbhai Patel a much better strategy. Nehru's Lucknow address did initially frighten 21 leading Bombay businessmen (including both anti-Congress elements like H.P. Mody and nationalists like Walchand Hirachand and A.O. Shroff) into issuing an angry manifesto in May 1936 denouncing socialism as a threat to all property, religion and personal liberty. Birla, however, sharply rebuked Walchand and Thakurdas for gross tactlessness—'it looks very crude for a man with property to say that he is opposed to expropriation...'. That should be left to 'those who have given up property', and 'if we can only strengthen their hands, we can help everyone'. (Birla to Walchand Hirachand, 26 May 1936, *Thakurdas Papers, F.N. 177*) Birla in fact had been remarkably happy about Lucknow: 'Mahatmaji kept his promise...he saw that *no new commitments were made.* Jawaharlalji's speech in a way was thrown into the wastepaper basket...Jawaharlalji seems to be like a typical English democrat...out for giving expression to his ideology, but he realises that action is impossible and so does not press for it...things are moving in the right direction' (Birla to Thakurdas, 20 April 1936). The differences among the capitalists were only tactical, for Thakurdas in his reply of 23 April stated that 'I never had any doubt about the bonafides of J., only I feel that a good deal of nursing will have to be done to keep J. on the right rails all through.'

The Congress leadership had always contained elements like Bhulabhai Desai or B.C. Roy, men unenthusiastic about even Gandhian forms of mass struggle and much more at home in the world of municipal or Assembly politicking. What was new in the mid-1930s was the big increase in their strength through a remarkable shift in the attitudes of men like Vallabhbhai Patel, Rajendra Prasad, or Rajagopalachari, the No-changers of the 1920s with considerable stature as rural constructive workers and mass leaders. A partial explanation in some cases might well be the opportunism of middle age replacing youthful ardour. More important was the fact that the twin Gandhian strategies of constructive work and peaceful controlled mass *satyagraha* seemed to be failing. Civil disobedience, it had been revealed after 1932, had little or no chance if faced with a really determined and ruthless government, while the All-India Village Industries Association floated by Gandhi in 1934–35 proved a virtual non-starter: a Bihar official in December 1935 described it as a 'very damp squib'. Gandhi himself was probably prepared to concentrate on slow rural work and upliftment on a long-term basis. He formally retired from the Congress at the end of 1934, and his Secretary Mahadev Desai reported to Birla on 20 August 1936: 'Bapu is getting more and more absorbed in his village work.... The fact is that he is turning his mind off from the Congress and all other outside activities and reverting it entirely on the village and its problems.' (*In the Shadow of the Mahatma,* p. 204). But relatively few even among his close associates had that amount of patience or idealism, while all-including Gandhi—felt acutely threatened by the new Left challenge, posing for the first time a country-wide alternative mass strategy which was considered unacceptable primarily for class reasons.

The months after Lucknow clearly revealed the foresight of Birla, Jawaharlal and the three Socialist Working Committee members (out of 14) became increasingly prisoners of the Right, without effective power, yet hindered by their office from frank criticism of the way the Congress was going. Nehru's socialist speeches were made the pretext for a resignation threat on 29 June 1936 by 7 Working Committee members headed by Rajendra Prasad, Rajagopalachari, Patel and Kripalani, who drafted their protest letter from Gandhi's headquarters at Wardha. Gandhi then patched up the quarrel, but it is clear that it was Nehru who as usual had made the concessions—Gandhi in fact rebuked him sharply for 'intolerance', and pointedly reminded him that 'you are not in power yet. To put you in office was an attempt to find you in power quicker than you would otherwise have been' (letters dated 8 and 15 July, Nehru *Bunch of Old Letters,* pp. 198, 204). At Lucknow itself, the scheme for corporate membership of labour and peasant associations had been diluted beyond recognition, despite

Socialist opposition, by the mere setting-up of a Mass Contact Committee in which Jayaprakash would be more than counterbalanced by Rajendra Prasad and Jairamdas Daulatram; not surprisingly, the Committee had not yet finalized its report at Faizpur. The agrarian programme was repeatedly stalled by delaying tactics adopted by the PCCs. The Faizpur draft blurred all the sharp edges of the Kisan Manifesto of the A.I.K.S. (e.g., 'substantial reductions' in rent, revenue and debt burdens, instead of 50% cuts and a 6% ceiling on interest), and demands for abolition of zamindari and redistribution of uncultivated government or landlord land were dropped altogether. When Patel came down heavily on N.G. Ranga for trying to get Andhra Congress election candidates sign a pledge supporting minimum demands of the *kisan* as a precondition for Kisan Sabha support, Nehru failed totally to support Ranga, brushing aside the whole thing as a 'misunderstanding', and advising him to 'drop the controversy'—and Ranga, too, released the Congress candidates from the Kisan pledge (*Indian Annual Register,* July-December 1936, p. 286). On the crucial political issue of office-entry, the Right ultimately got its way by repeatedly postponing the issue, at Lucknow and again at Faizpur. Once elections had been won, pressure for Ministry-making would soon prove irresistible, despite all the bold radical rhetoric of the Congress President and the entire Left. Again Birla had been an accurate prophet: 'The election which will take place will be controlled by 'Vallabhbhai Group', and if Lord Linlithgow handles the situation properly, there is every likelihood of the Congressmen coming into office.' (Birla to Thakurdas, 20 April 1936)

CHAPTER 7
POLITICAL MOVEMENTS AND WAR
1937–1945

1937–1939: THE CONGRESS-MINISTRIES

Elections and Ministry-Making

The Congress did extremely well in the 1937 elections, winning 711 out of 1585 provincial assembly seats, with absolute majorities in five provinces out of eleven (Madras, Bihar, Orissa, C.P. and U.P.) and a near-majority in Bombay (86 out of 175). Official backing failed to save from utter rout loyalist landlord-based groups like the Nawab of Chhatari's National Agriculturist Party in U.P. and the Justice Party in Madras. Even the poor showing in the Muslim constituencies (the Congress contested only 58 out of 482 reserved seats, and won 26) was somewhat counterbalanced by the evident failure of the Muslim League to make good its claim to be the sole representative of the Muslims. The League failed to win a single seat in the N.W.F.P. and could capture only 2 out of 84 reserved constituencies in the Punjab and 3 out of 33 in Sind. The Congress also won most scheduled caste seats, except in Bombay where Ambedkar's Independent Labour Party captured 13 out of 15 seats reserved for Harijans.

For millions of Indians, particularly in the Hindu-majority general constituencies, the 'vote for Gandhiji and the yellow box' signified appreciation of patriotic self-sacrifice, plus some hopes of socio-economic change. The Congress Election Manifesto and the Faizpur Agrarian Programme had, after all, marked a considerable advance over previous statements of party policy even while falling much short of Left aspirations. At the same time, elections on a wider (but by no means universal) franchise demanded both more money and considerable cultivation of links with local dominant groups, businessmen in towns and landlords and dominant peasant groups in the country-side. Birla contributed ₹5 lakhs for the Congress Central Parliamentary Board headed by Patel, while R.K. Dalmia provided ₹27,000 out of ₹37,000 raised by the Bihar PCC. Since such amounts were evidently inadequate (election costs came to at least ₹2000 per seat), most candidates were expected to provide their own finance—which meant in practice a clear preference for propertied men. In Bihar, for instance, numerous Kisan Sabha militants were deprived of nomination under local landlord pressure, and the Congress leader A.N. Sinha admitted that most of his party's candidates came from the zamindari class. (Tomlinson, *Indian National Congress and the Raj,* pp. 82–5). As throughout this entire period, simultaneous but contradictory pressures on the Congress in a 'Right' as well as a 'Left' direction thus were inherent in the total situation.

Electoral success strengthened and soon made irresistible pressures for ministry-formation by the Congress. The AICC session of March 1937 accepted a resolution moved by Rajendra Prasad and Patel on 'conditional acceptance' of office, the condition being that the leader of the Congress assembly party of a province 'is satisfied and is able to state publicly that the Governor will not use his special powers.' Jayaprakash's Left amendment demanding total rejection of office was defeated by 135 votes against 78, and Birla hailed the decision as a great triumph for the right wing of the Congress' in a letter to Viceroy Linlithgow's private secretary. (*In the Shadow of the Mahatma,* p. 214) Though Linlithgow refused to give any public assurance that the Governor's powers would not be used, Gandhi had made up his mind by July 1937, and Mahadev Desai informed Birla on 16 July that it must be said 'to the credit of Jawahar that it did not prove difficult to persuade him'. The Working Committee had permitted office-acceptance a week earlier on the rather specious plea that though British assurances were not satisfactory, the situation 'warrants the belief that it will not be easy for the governors to use their special powers.' Congress ministries took office in U.P., Bihar, Orissa, C.P., Bombay, and Madras, and a few months later also in the N.W.F.P. In September 1938, a Congress ministry was established in Assam through somewhat sordid assembly manouevres and floor-crossings in which, interestingly enough, the Left President of the Congress, Subhas Bose, played a prominent role.

So over the major part of the country, the persecuted of yesterday had become ministers, the new assemblies met to the strains of the *Bande Mataram,* and the national flag for which so many had faced *lathis* and bullets flew proudly over public buildings. Congress ministries initially gave a major stimulus to all sections of the anti-imperialist movement. Congress membership shot up from half a million in 1936 to 3.1 million in 1937 and 4.5 million in 1938, Left-leaning student, labour and *kisan* movements and organizations forged ahead, and the installation of popular ministries soon stimulated a massive anti-autocratic and anti-feudal upsurge in a large number of princely states. The more negative and contradictory sides of the assumption of ministerial responsibility, however, were also not slow to manifest themselves. There were the inevitable paradoxes of a party committed to Purna Swaraj and bitterly critical of the 1935 Constitution working within its framework, with powers limited by official reservations and safeguards as well as by restricted financial resources, and having to implement decisions through a civil service and a police with which its relations had so long been extremely hostile. Though the Working Committee at Gandhi's insistence imposed a ceiling of ₹500 per month on ministerial salaries, the sudden access to power and patronage bred the usual evils of opportunistic place-hunting and factional squabbles. An AICC Inspector's report on the state of the party in Bihar confessed in 1938 that 'nothing in particular has been done except elections to local bodies being contested by the Congress in certain districts (quoted in Tomlinson, Ibid, p. 87). In the Central Provinces in July 1938, N.B. Khare was pushed out from premiership by Ravi Shankar Shukla backed by D.P. Mishra, and though this was given the colour of a regional conflict of Hindi-speaking Raipur and Jabalpur versus the Marathi districts of which Khare had been the leader, factional considerations were probably much more important (Mishra had backed Khare against Shukla only the year before). But the most serious problem was the balancing of diverse interests of communities and classes. Despite its national and multi-class ideals, the Congress as a ruling party found it almost impossible to go on pleasing Hindus and Muslims, landlords and peasants, or businessmen and workers at the same time. A steady shift to the Right, occasionally veiled by 'Left' rhetoric, increasingly characterized the functioning of the Congress ministries as well as of the party High Command between 1937 and 1939.

Congress and Bureaucracy

The Right shift helps to explain the otherwise surprising absence of major conflict with officialdom, till the outbreak of war in September 1939 created a totally new situation. The one crisis was in February 1938, when the ministries of Govindballav Pant in U.P. and Srikrishna Sinha in Bihar briefly resigned because the Governors had refused to allow immediate release of all political prisoners. Prisoners' release had become a major national issue following a hunger-strike in Andaman jail in July 1937, the Congress had been bitterly attacking the non-Congress Fazlul Huq ministry of Bengal for doing nothing about the large number of detenues in that province, and some kind of gesture was obviously needed to silence the Left on the eve of the Haripura Congress session. The resignations were withdrawn a few days after the session had ended, with the Governors retaining the principle of individual rather than immediate and total release.

The Congress ministries began by repealing the emergency powers inherited from 1932. By October 1937, however, Rajagopalachari was prosecuting for seditious speeches in Madras and repressive measures were increasingly used in all Congress provinces against communal riots and Left-led labour and peasant movements alike. In September 1938, the AICC gave a virtual blank cheque of support to 'measures that may be undertaken by the Congress Government for the defence of life and property', and condemned 'people, including Congressmen...found in the name of civil liberty to advocate murder, arson, looting and class war by violent means....' The imperialist historian Coupland found 'little to distinguish' Congress ministries in their last year from the other government or from pre-1937 bureaucracies in so far as maintenance of order was concerned. He was ready to give Congress a patronizing pat on the back. '...the Congress Governments can be said to have stood the test imposed on them in the field of law and order.' (R. Coupland, *The Constitutional Problem in India,* Part II, p. 135)

The Communal Problem

Coupland combined such praise with a bitter attack on the alleged 'totalitarianism' of the Congress High Command, which, he argued, had 'completely undermined the federal principle, and, together with a number of pro-Hindu measures of Congress ministries, led to a decisive alienation of the Muslims. (Ibid, p. 99) This in fact was the standard Muslim League critique, put forward for instance by Jinnah at the Patna session of the League (December 1938) when he denounced 'Congress Fascism'. Others besides League spokesmen have also attributed fundamental importance in the process of Muslim alienation to certain Congress attitudes and policies between 1937 and 1939: Azad, for instance (in his *India Wins Freedom,* 1959), as well as British writers on the Partition years like Penderel Moon and H.V. Hodson.

Since the great post-1937 League revival was centred in the United Provinces, Congress rejection of a coalition in that province has often been interpreted as peculiarly decisive. Congress-League relations in U.P. during the elections had been quite friendly, as both were fighting Chhatari's National Agriculturist Party. On an all-India plane, too, the League Election Manifesto had adopted a critical stance towards the 1935 Act quite similar to that of the Congress, and had visualized cooperation on the basis of the Lucknow Pact (1916) principles. After the elections, however, the Congress with its absolute majority in U.P. spurned the coalition offer by Khaliquzzaman (a League leader who as late as 1934 had also been a member of the Congress Parliamentary Board). Talks with Nehru and Azad broke down partly over choice of ministers, but more because the Congress insisted in July 1937 on a total absorption of the Muslim League assembly party. In mid-1937, such an insistence was not unnatural or perhaps even unjustified.

The League in U.P. as Khaliquzzaman frankly admits, was very much bound up 'with zamindari and the services, military and civil'. (*Pathway to Pakistan,* p. 173) Its all-India Election Manifesto had denounced 'any movement that aims at expropriation of private property', and Khaliquazzaman at the October 1937 Lucknow session of the League ruled out land reforms even while pleading for improvement of conditions of Muslim peasants. Nehru and Congress Leftists like Narendra Dev or K.M. Ashraf consequently feared that a coalition on any terms falling short of a total surrender by the League would render impossible any radical socio-economic reforms, and they preferred to try to win over Muslims through a 'mass contact' drive for which Ashraf was given responsibility. The Congress in addition had a big majority in U.P. (134 out of 228), enjoyed the support of the Deoband ulama group which dominated the Jamiat-ul-Ulema-i-Hind, and was being backed in northern India also by the Ahrar Party formed a few years back by ex-Khilafatists in the Punjab. An Ahrar Conference in May 1937 denounced Jinnah as an 'out-of-date politician...making a fetish of constitutionalism', and the League as 'a coterie of a few knights, Khan Bahadurs, and Nawabs.'

From its Lucknow session onwards the League made a determined and ultimately successful effort to build up a more populist image. It accepted complete independence with effective minority safeguards as its creed, denounced the Congress for creating 'class bitterness and communal war', recruited 100,000 new members in the U.P. within a few months, and was able to obtain the (as yet largely formal) adherence of the premiers of Punjab and Bengal, the Unionist Sikander Hayat Khan and the Krishak Praja leader Fazlul Huq. 'All students of Indian politics know that it was from the U.P. that the League was reorganized' (Khaliquzzaman p. xiii). It may be argued, however, that what proved disastrous was not the rejection of a coalition, but the failure to develop and implement, in the U.P. as well as elsewhere, genuine socially radical measures. Muslim 'mass contact' remained largely on paper, and secularist and radical rhetoric in the end merely alarmed Muslim vested interests without winning over the Muslim masses.

Ministry-formation in Bengal was associated with somewhat similar—and perhaps less justifiable—developments. Under pressure from relatively radical elements like Abul Mansur Ahmad, Shamsuddin Ahmad and Nausher Ali, Fazlul Huq's Krishak Praja Party in April 1936 had adopted an election programme calling for abolition of *zamindari* without compensation, immediate rent reduction, and compulsory primary education. Preelection negotiations with Jinnah broke down partly on the *zamindari* abolition issue, and the K.P.P. proved a tough electoral opponent of the League, with Fazlul

Huq winning the prestigious Patuakhali seat against Khwaja Nazimuddin. The Congress leadership in Bengal, however, had seldom espoused agrarian reform even for purposes of rhetoric, perhaps partly because unlike in U.P. zamindars tended to be overwhelmingly Hindus while Avadh *talukdars* had a strong Muslim component. Coalition talks with the K.P.P. broke down, with the Congress insisting on immediate release of prisoners while Abul Mansur Ahmed argued that priority should be given in the ministry's programme to tenancy reforms as the prisoners' issue might very well lead to a Governor's veto and consequent resignation. Fazlul Huq was thus more-or-less pushed into an alliance with the League.

Throughout the twenty-seven months of Congress rule in provinces, the League kept up an intense propaganda barrage, climaxed by the Pirpur Report (late-1938), the Shareef Report on Bihar (March 1939), and Fazlul Huq's *Muslim Sufferings under Congress Rule,* December 1939). The charges included failure to prevent communal riots, local bans on Bakr-Id cow-slaughter, singing the Bande Mataram with its 'idolatrous' passages on public occasions, and encouragement of Hindi and Hindustani in the Devanagri script at the cost of Urdu. Much in all this was clearly exaggerated, and it is significant that the League rejected a Congress offer of an enquiry into the charges by Chief Justice Maurice Gwyer. League leaders before the 'Pakistan Resolution' of March 1940 were disgruntled politicians without a clear programme, for the old demands of separate electorates, provincial autonomy, full provincial status for N.W.F.P. and Sind, and Muslim political predominance in Punjab and Bengal had all been more-or-less accepted by the British and the Congress alike. Jinnah in his talks with Bose in May 1938 therefore insisted on recognition of the League as sole representative of Muslims—a totally unjustified claim at any time before the mid-1940s, for the League, though strong among Muslim minorities in U.P., Bombay and Madras, was still fairly weak in Bengal, negligible in the N.W.F.P. and Punjab, and had failed to form a government even in Sind (where a Congress-backed ministry under Allah Baksh had been installed in March 1938). Khaliquzzaman admits with frankness that Congress rejection of Jinnah's position was 'a piece of good luck for us', for 'If Congress had accepted the position at the time when the demand was made by the League, I wonder what positive demands we could then have made.' (Khaliquzzaman, p. 192)

Coming to specific charges, that of High Command 'totalitarianism makes curious reading, for an all-India party could hardly be blamed for trying to consolidate its organization, and Jinnah himself would be spending much of his energies during the decade 1937–47 trying to assert his control over provincial Muslim leaders. Communal riots were frequent in Congress provinces, but not significantly more so than elsewhere—60 in 8 Congress states between October 1937 and September 1939, as against 25 in 3 non-Congress provinces (Coupland, p. 131). The Congress Working Committee in October 1937 decided to drop the closing stanzas of *Bande Mataram,* recognizing 'the validity of the objection raised by Muslim friends to certain parts of the song'. If the League attacked the Wardha basic education scheme as too Hinduized, the Hindu Mahasabha denounced it for including Urdu in the curriculum, and the distinguished Muslim intellectual Zakir Hussain was prominent both in the Wardha scheme as well as in preparing Urdu textbooks for Bombay schools which the League condemned as anti-Islamic.

Yet Nehru admitted to Rajendra Prasad on 18 October 1939 that 'there is no doubt that we have been unable to check the growth of communalism and anti-Congress feeling among the Muslim masses'. (Uma Kaura, p. 123) In the one Muslim-majority province under Congress rule, the N.W.F.P., Khan Saheb's ministry began to lose support among Muslim peasants for failing to take adequate measures to reduce rural indebtedness in face of opposition from Hindu and Sikh traders and moneylenders. (A.K. Gupta, *NWFP Legislature and Freedom Struggle, 1932–47.* p. 93). In much of northern and central India, Congress-led rural populism was often associated with Hinduism and the use of Hindi, for Muslims tended to be more urbanized and literate and Urdu had been the language of upper-class culture. If top Congress leaders in the late-1930s now insisted more than ever before on the need for secularism, their attitudes were by no means universally shared, or sincerely implemented, lower down in the party hierarchy or even by all Congress ministers. Azad, for instance, complained in 1937 that C.P. Congressmen could not join the League, but were often to be found active in the Hindu Mahasabha, and it was only in December 1938 that the Working Committee declared Mahasabha membership to be a disqualification for remaining in the Congress. The Hindu Mahasabha was gaining strength during these years, and its new president, the Maharashtrian ex-revolutionary V.D. Savarkar, declared at the Nagpur session (December, 1938) that 'We Hindus are a Nation by ourselves...Hindu nationalists should not at all be apologetic to being called Hindu communalists'. Most ominous of all was the growth of para-military communalist bodies: Inayatullah Khan Mashriqi's Khaksars, founded among Punjab Muslims in 1931, and the Rashtriya Swayamsevak Sangh of K.B. Hedgewar. Patronized initially by the old Tilakite Mahasabha leader, B.S. Moonje, the RSS spread in the 1930s from its Nagpur base to U.P., Punjab, and other parts of the country. By 1940, when Golwalkar took over the leadership, it numbered 100,000 trained and highly disciplined cadres pledged to an ideology of uncompromising communalism.

Hindsight derived from the later experience of the Partition days perhaps exaggerates the significance of communal issues to contemporaries in the late-l930s. Certainly most Congressmen did not yet regard the League as a very serious challenge and were busy trying to utilize the existence of Congress ministries in diverse and often contradictory ways: as opportunities for personal gain, for the implementation of sincerely held Gandhian ideals, in the development of plans for national economic advance in collaboration with Indian business leaders and in efforts to improve the conditions of the down-trodden.

Gandhian Reforms

An education conference at Wardha in October 1937 endorsed Gandhi's proposals for 'basic education' through the vernacular medium, linked with manual productive work. Schools along these lines were set up in the Congress provinces with some government help. While embodying interesting ideals of simplicity, reduction of differences between mental and manual labour, and schools becoming self-sufficient through sale of their own manufactures, basic education never really became a viable alternative to conventional schools or colleges, and the link with cottage crafts was felt by many to be an unrealistic and archaic Gandhian fad. Gandhi also insisted on prohibition, though this had not been mentioned in the election manifesto. Despite heavy financial losses, Congress ministries were prodded by the High Command to take quick steps in the direction of total prohibition, particularly in Bombay and Madras. Madras also went in for some temple-entry legislation, but otherwise not much seems to have been done for the other major Gandhian concern of Harijan welfare. Ambedkar by the late-1930s had become almost as bitter a critic of the Congress as the League, and even joined Jinnah in celebrating the resignation of Congress ministries in October 1939 as a 'day of deliverance'.

For growing numbers of Congressmen, many of Gandhi's ideas seemed increasingly unpractical and irrelevant, more particularly his theoretical hostility to big industry. A very significant feature of the years of Congress rule in provinces was the foundation of what Claude Markovitz has called 'a durable alliance' between Indian business and the Congress party.

Capitalists and Congress

This was not a process free of contradictions or variations over regions and time. While Birla declared himself to be 'simply overwhelmed with joy' upon hearing the news of Congress acceptance of office, industrialists based on Congress-ruled provinces (rather than Calcutta) were initially rather nervous that popular ministries would be more open to trade union pressures. A Congress Labour Committee in October 1937 did formulate an ambitious programme of welfare legislation, and the U.P. ministry insisted on recognition of the Mazdur Sabha which led a series of formidable strikes in Kanpur textiles during 1937 and 1938. J.P. Srivastava, a U.P. magnate who later joined the Viceroy's Executive Council, later told Wavell that 'after the Congress...assumption of office in U.P. in 1937, the leading industrialists—all I think Hindu—got together and decided to finance Jinnah and the Muslim League and also the Mahasabha, as the extreme Communal parties to oppose Congress who they feared might threaten their financial profits—a truly illuminating admission (Wavell, *The Viceroy's Journal,* entry for 30 November 1944, p. 402). A second potential source of conflict lay in finance. The Bombay Government in February 1939 imposed an urban property tax and a sales tax on cloth to meet the deficit caused by the Gandhian 'fad' of prohibition. New Delhi also made some gestures to conciliate Indian capitalists, when it accepted an Assembly resolution terminating the Ottawa and the supplementry Indo-British trade agreement of 1935, and invited Birla, Thakurdas and Kasturbhai Lalbhai to act as its 'unofficial advisers' in the tortuous negotiations about a new trade pact with Britain which continued from August 1936 to March 1939. The crux of these negotiations was a bargain through which more Indian exports would go to England in return for lower import duties against Lancashire. The Government of India had a stake of its own in expansion of Indian exports, for this would facilitate the outflow of remittances, while Bombay on its part was now firmly in control of the home market for textiles and so was not entirely unwilling to make some concessions regarding import duties. (Basudev Chatterji, Ch. VII)

Despite such problems, signs of a firmer understanding between Indian capitalists and decisive sections of the Congress leadership became evident from about mid-1938 onwards. Businessmen benefited from the *swadeshi*-oriented stores purchase policy of Congress ministries, and close relations with capitalists were developing particularly in Bombay. The Thakurdas Papers, for instance, show Patel directly helping Walchand Hirachand to take over the Bombay Steam Navigation Company from Killick Nixon (Markovitz, p. 222). Maintenance of cotton import duties was a prestige point with nationalists, and the unofficial advisers quit under Congress pressure in September 1938—unlike 1933, no significant section of Indian capitalists could now afford to alienate a party ruling in eight out of eleven provinces. The March 1939 Indo-British trade agreement concluded by New Delhi on its own established a sliding scale of cotton import duties proportionate to British off-take of Indian raw cotton and textile imports into India. All business M.L.As joined the Congress in voting against the pact, which had to be passed through the Viceroy's certificate procedure.

More fundamental economic developments were leading to significant modification in both business and Congress attitudes and permitting a closer alliance. The establishment behind Indian tariff walls of subsidiaries of giant British (and now also sometimes American) firms was a major threat. Lever Brothers, for instance, had displaced Godrej by 1937 as the major manufacturer of soap, Imperial Tobacco had started its Vazir Sultan subsidiary, and chemicals, engineering, and rubber were particularly affected by what the *Harijan* in a series of articles during 1938 denounced as 'the menace of India Limited'. The FICCI took up the issue in April 1939, and the Bombay Congress leader N.V. Gadgil moved a resolution on the issue in the Central Assembly the same month.

Meanwhile another industrial depression had set in from 1937, with over-production in sugar (effectively tackled by the U.P. and Bihar ministries by pressurizing manufacturers into forming a syndicate), a crisis in cement, and stagnation in textiles. The limits of growth through import-substitution in consumer goods industries were being reached, given the fact that a big expansion in the rural home market required structural changes like thorough-going land reforms which the Congress as well as the Indian bourgeoisie considered socially unacceptable. Intermediate and capital goods development required heavy initial investment, technical know-how, and readiness to accept low initial profits. The logical alternatives therefore were either encouragement of investments of the 'India Limited' type (and foreign capital was not really interested in low-profit capital goods), or efforts to promote basic industries through state initiative, investment and planning. While British officials like Finance Member Grigg had become notorious for their rigidly laissez-faire attitudes so far as industrial development and public investments were concerned, M. Visvesvaraya, the ex-Dewan of Mysore, had called for state planning already in 1934. As later developments have repeatedly shown, the more far-sighted sections of the bourgeoisie in an under-developed country would be quite ready to accept a measure of state regulation, planning, public investments in basic industries to create a favourable infrastructure for their own growth, and even 'socialist' rhetoric—so long as socialism did not mean wholesale nationalization along revolutionary lines. Subhas Bose's initiative in starting a National Planning Committee in October 1938 under Nehru was thus quite eagerly accepted by Indian businessmen. Birla, Lala Shri Ram, and Visvesvaraya were invited to the Congress industries ministers' conference which set up the N.P.C., business representatives were important members of the 29 sub-committees constituted by the latter, and Nehru on his part conceded the need to accept 'to a large extent the present structure, at any rate as a jumping-off ground.' (letter to K.T. Shah, 13 May 1939, Markovitz, p. 236) The use of phrases like 'socialistic planned structure', or a long-term goal of state ownership or control over key industries, consequently did not worry overmuch Indian capitalists, who judged the Congress more by the quite unsocialistic performance of its ministries. Thus there were signs in 1938–39 of a novel and very significant realignment. Indian capitalists, while retaining close ties with elements in the Gandhian 'Right' like Patel and Rajaji, had also started cultivating sections of the Congress 'Left' Nehru's vision of a modern industrialized India, after all, fitted in much better with bourgeois aspirations than the Gandhian evocation of rural simplicity and handicrafts, and there were enough indication already that the former's socialist flourishes were eminently manageable.

Congress and Labour

Rapproachment with the bourgeoisie naturally involved shifts in attitudes towards labour. The formation of popular ministries initially stimulated labour organization and militancy. Trade union membership went up by 50% in 1938 as compared to 1937, and labour unity was strengthened by the coming together of the AITUC and the moderate N.F.T.U.—the two held a joint session in Nagpur in April 1938. The major industrial disputes of these years included the great general strike in Bengal jute mills (March-May 1937), a series of stoppages in Kanpur cotton mills, textile strikes in Amritsar, Ahmedabad and particularly in Madras province (where the number of workers involved during 1938 exceeded that in Bombay), the strike in Martin Burn's Kulti and Hirapur iron and steel works in 1938, and the bitter six month-long struggle in the Digboi oil works in Assam (April-October 1939). Despite some Congress efforts to rally the working class (as when Nehru and Bose appealed to workers to 'unite, organize, and join hands with the Congress' at a big labour rally in Calcutta in October 1937, or a Hindustan Majdur Sabha was set up in 1938 by leaders like Patel, Rajendra Prasad and J.B. Kripalani), the bulk of the trade union movement remained under either Liberal or Leftist (mostly Communist) leadership. The Ahmedabad textile strike of November 1937 revealed some Communist penetration into even that old Gandhian stronghold.

The Working Committee expressed solidarity with Bengal jute workers (April 1937), and denounced repressive measures taken by the Fazlul Huq ministry in Bengal and Sikandar Hayat Khan's Unionists in the Punjab. But an early, relatively pro-labour stance taken by Congress ministries soon came under formidable capitalist pressures. Birla complained of rampant 'indiscipline' in Congress provinces (letter to Mahadev Desai, 4 September 1937, *In the Shadow of the Mahatma,* p. 227), and there were threats of a flight of capital from Congress-ruled Bombay and U.P. to the princely states where labour laws hardly existed. Congress desire to placate the bourgeoisie and curb labour unrest in the strongest base of the Communists was reflected in the very drastic provisions of the Bombay Trades Dispute Act (November 1938), which Governor Lumley described as 'admirable'. Rushed through in two months without select committee discussions, the Act imposed compulsory arbitration, six months jail for illegal strikes (but no corresponding penalties for lockouts), and new trade union registration rules making things very difficult for unions not recognized by the management. With the exception of the Ahmedabad Gandhian labour leaders (Gulzarilal Nanda and Khandubhai Desai), the entire trade union movement opposed the Act, along with most non-Congress parties (including the Muslim League). 80,000 attended a protest rally in Bombay on 6 November addressed by Dange, Indulal Yajnik and Ambedkar, and next day there was a partially successful general strike throughout the province. During the Digboi strike of 1939 against the British-owned Assam Oil Company, formal expressions of Congress sympathy were more than counterbalanced by the failure of the N.C. Bardoloi ministry to implement a pro-labour award by an ICS official, and in October the Congress ministry allowed free use of the newly introduced wartime Defence of India rules to smash the strike. It is interesting that apart from some criticism of the registration clause, Nehru found the Bombay Act 'on the whole...a good one' (Marko-vits, p. 218), while the Leftist President of the Congress, Subhas Bose, made some private protests to Patel but refused to make it an issue for any public break. (Bose to Nehru, 29 March 1939, *A Bunch of Old Letters,* p. 341)

Congress and *Kisans*

The Congress with its not unjustified claims to be primarily a *kisan* party was bound to undertake a measure of agrarian reform. Debt burdens were sought to be reduced in most Congress provinces through fixation of interest rates, statutory tenants of Avadh were raised to the level of hereditary occupancy *raiyats,* enhancements restricted and rents somewhat reduced in U.P. and Bihar *bakhast* lands from which occupy *raiyats* had been evicted during the 'Depression partly restored in the latter province' and *khoti* sub-tenants of *raiyatwari* landholders given some rights in Bombay. Forest *satyagraha* found partial fulfilment in the abolition of grazing fees in Bombay and their reduction in Madras. Yet Coupland found the chief merit of Congress agrarian legislation to be that 'its treatment of the landlords was not intolerably severe.... Congress policy might almost be called conservative.' (pp. 140, 138) Of the two proposals he described as really radical, the Prakasam committee recommendations in Madras suggesting *raiyat* ownership and rent-reduction to the level of 1802 in *zamindari* areas were quickly shelved, while an Orissa act fixing *zamindari* rents at a level only 12½% above revenues in adjoining *raiyatwari* areas was vetoed by the Governor—and the Congress did not make of this an issue demanding resignation. Congress legislation fell well short of even the moderate proposals of the Faizpur session, and the resolutions of the U.P. and Bihar PCCs in 1936 and 1937 advocating abolition of *zamindari* were forgotten once the party was in power. Faced with a threat of 'civil disobedience' from *zamindars* in September 1937, the Bihar ministry considerably watered down its tenancy bill, and Azad and Rajendra Prasad negotiated a secret agreement with landlords in Patna three months later. At a subsequent landholder's conference, a delegate praised the Bihar government as 'very reasonable...some concessions were secured by zamindars in Bihar which no other government would have allowed' (W. Hauser, *The Bihar Provincial Kisan Sabha,* unpublished thesis, Chicago 1961, pp. 121, 129) The pattern in fact was not dissimilar from that in the non-Congress provinces. The Fazlul Haq ministry restricted rent-enhancements and interest rates, but passed on the question of *zamindari* abolition to the Floud Commission, whose recommendation of state take-over with compensation (1940) would be implemented only after independence. Unionist moves in the Punjab to tighten up the 1900 Land Alienation Act were denounced as 'black bills' by the Hindu Mahasabha leaders and even by the local Congress till the High Command intervened.

Behind the limited agrarian reforms of 1937–39 lay the pressure of a massive peasant movement. Kisan Sabha membership shot up to half a million in 1938, with Bihar alone claiming 250,000, followed by Punjab (73,000), U.P. (60,000), Andhra (53,000), and Bengal (34,000). Spectacular *kisan* marches had become very common, and Bihar *kisans* for instance marched right into the Assembly house and occupied its seats for some time in the first session under the Congress ministry—much to the horror of G.D. Birla, who complained that 'the rank and file seems to be confusing freedom with indiscipline'. (*In the Shadow of the Mahatma,* p. 228) There were numerous local struggles: as examples may be cited the movement against canal water rates in Burdwan district in Bengal (1937); the movement of Hajong tribals under Moni Singh in the Garo Hills of north Mymensingh (East Bengal), in 1937–38, which was able to get produce-rent (*tanka*) reduced from one-half to one-fourth of the harvest; the Barhaiya

Tal agitation in Monghyr (Bihar) demanding restoration of *bakasht* lands which went on from 1936 to 1939 under the leadership of Karyananda Sharma, the future Communist leader; the anti-*zamindari* movements in Kalipatnam and Munagala in the Krishna district of Andhra (1938–39), where too Communists were prominent; anti-water tax agitations in Lyallpur (Punjab) and Sukur (Sind) and campaigns against revenue enhancement in Amritsar and Lahore, all during 1938–39; and powerful peasant movements in the coastal districts of Orissa. In Bihar rent-collection seemed on the point of collapse between autumn 1938 and mid-1939, and armed police pickets were often required to protect landlord harvests. Villages here resounded to Sahjanand's militant slogan: *Laga lege kaise/Danda hamara zindabad* How will you collect rent/Long live our lathis). Within the broad front represented by the A.I.K.S. Socialists and Communists were becoming increasingly prominent—a trend symbolized by the adoption of the red flag as banner by the Kisan Sabha in October 1937. Sahajananda himself was moving rapidly to the Left, through disillusionment with the performance of Congress ministries and contacts with the C.S.P. While still using the garb of a *sanyasi,* he is said to have declared in 1937 that 'as religious robes had long exploited the country now he would exploit those robes on behalf of the peasants. (Hauser, p. 86) The very successful Comilla Conference of the A.I.K.S. (May 1938), held in the heart of Muslim East Bengal in the teeth of opposition from the League as well as from some Congressmen, denounced Gandhian 'class collaboration', proclaimed 'agrarian revolution' to be the ultimate aim, and heard a passionate defence by Sahajananda of the *danda* in self-defence against *zamindar* attacks.

Despite occasional calls for unity with landless labourers (as at the Gaya Conference of April 1939), the Kisan Sabha remained essentially the organization of peasants with some land as small holders or tenants. Bhumihars prominated in the leadership and even the ranks of the Bihar unit, not Harijan or tribal agricultural labourers, and the Bengal Provincial Kisan Sabha memorandum to the Floud Commission concentrated on abolition of *zamindari* and failed to raise any specific demands for *bargadars* (sharecroppers). In Andhra, the initial Kisan Sabha (as well as Communist) base was among the fairly prosperous Kamma peasants of the Krishna-Godavari delta, while in the Punjab kisan movements concentrated almost entirely on the issues of revenue enhancement and irrigation taxes.

Congress ministers and leaders adopted an increasingly hostile attitude towards Kisan Sabha militancy. District Committees in Champaran, Saran, and Monghyr banned Congressmen from attending Sahajananda's meetings in Jate-1937, police pickets and Section 144 were freely used in Congress-ruled Bihar, U.P., Orissa and Madras, much was made of Sahajananda's advocacy of the *danda* as going against the creed of the non-violence, and the September 1938 AICC denunciation of 'class war' was made specifically in the context of Kisan Sabha agitations. All this happened while first Nehru and then Bose formally headed the Congress party. Coupland remarks that agrarian tensions were less acute in U.P. than in neighbouring Bihar in part because of the 'valuable support' given to the ministry 'in the matter of rent payment...by Pandit Nehru'. (p. 127) On 23 April 1938, for instance, Nehru advised Allahabad *kisans* not to obstruct the smooth working of the Congress ministry. Congress President Subhas Bose did not make an issue of the September 1938 resolution (moved by Bhulabhai Desai and powerfully backed by Gandhi); he would break with Gandhi next year, but only over the question of his own re-election as President.

States Peoples Movement

The most significant advance made by the national movement between 1937 and 1939 was in the princely states: the bulwarks of autocracy and rampant feudal exploitation which British Federation plans had increasingly exposed as key supports for imperialism in its efforts to keep India divided and subjugated. As in so many other phases of the national movement, the real initiative came from below rather than from top leaders or organizations. The All-India States People's Conference had become more active under its secretary Balwantrai Mehta, but it remained essentially an occasional gathering of middle class politicians, concerned with questions of civil rights and responsible government, and seldom raising specific peasant or tribal issues. Nor did it demand as yet any wholesale integration of states, merely suggesting (at its Ludhiana session in 1939, where Nehru presided) that very small non-viable states could be merged into neighbouring provinces. The Congress Right-wing on its part tried hard to stick to the old policy of non-intervention, and Gandhi himself at first showed exceptional rigidity on this point, openly expressing his displeasure over an AICC resolution in October 1937 which had appealed 'to the people of Indian states and British India to give all support and encouragement' to the popular struggle in Mysore. A compromise resolution at the Haripura session (February 1938) for the first time declared the Purna Swaraj ideal to cover the states as much as British India, but insisted that 'for the present' the Congress could give only its 'moral support and sympathy' to states peoples movements, which should not be conducted in the name of the Congress. Gandhi indicated a few months later that he would be statisfied if the princes granted a measure of civil liberties and independent courts, and reduced their privy purses—not even responsible government was demanded, far less integration. (R. L. Handa, *History of Freedom Struggle in Princely States,* New Delhi 1968, pp. 116–17)

In early 1939, in the context of the rapid advance of popular movements virtually throughout princely India, Gandhi decided to try out his specific techniques of controlled mass struggle for the first time in a native state. He allowed his close adjutant, the business magnate Jamnalal Bajaj, to lead a *satyagraha* in Jaipur, and, together with Vallabhbhai Patel, began a personal intervention in the movement in Rajkot which had been started by the local Praja Parishad under U.N. Dhebar. Virawala, the very unpopular Dewan of Rajkot, had imposed numerous monopolies disliked by local traders and stopped summoning an advisory elected council set up earlier, while nearly half the revenues of the state were swallowed up by the privy purse of its ruler. The choice of Rajkot by Gandhi is very significant: a tiny state surrounded by the firm Gandhian base of Gujarat, almost half its population lived in the capital and so there was little danger of agrarian radicalism swamping strictly non-violent *satyagraha*. Kasturba Gandhi and Manibehn Patel courted arrest in February 1939, and Gandhi himself went to Rajkot and started a fast on 3 March—just on the eve of the Tripuri Congress, where his leadership was being seriously challenged by the re-election of Bose. The Rajkot intervention, however, proved to be one of Gandhi's failures, for the British Political Department instigated Virawala to withdraw the concessions he had offered at one stage, as well as to skilfully encourage Muslim and untouchable demands for more seats in the proposed Reform Committee. Gandhi bowed himself out of the Rajkot affair in May 1939, declaring that his own fast had been of a coercive nature and therefore not sufficiently non-violent.

Meanwhile far more impressive and significant movements had developed in many other parts of princely India, most notably in Mysore, the Orissa states, Hyderabad and Travancore (as well as in parts of Rajputana and the Punjab states of Patiala, Kalsia, Kapurthala and Sirmoor).

Gandhian controls remained fairly firm in Mysore, where K.T. Bhashyam's State Congress, initially based on Brahman urban professional groups, extended its support through merger in October 1937 with the Peoples Federation of Non-Brahman rural landholders led by K.C. Reddy and H.C. Dasappa. A first round of agitation from October 1937 for legalization of the Congress and responsible government culminated on 11 April 1938 in a blood-bath at Viduraswatha village in Kolar district where 30 were killed by firing on a crowd of 10,000. In the following month Patel concluded a truce with Dewan Mirza Ismail which legalized the Congress, but failure to implement promises of significant constitutional reform led to another round of civil disobedience from September 1939. Effective Congress leadership of controlled mass movements built up a strength for the party in the Karnataka region which was rather unusual in south India, as post-1947 politics have often shown.

In the much more backward interior states of Orissa, issues like forced labour, taxes on forest produce, extortion of 'gifts' on festive occasions or tenancy rights inevitably were as much if not more important than demands for political reform. The C.S.P. leader Nabakrushna Chaudhuri led a *satyagraha* in Dhenkanal in December 1938, powerful movements developed in Nilgiri, Nayagarh, Talcher and Ranpur, and there were numerous violent incidents, with tribals fighting back with bows and arrows the armed power of the princes. Thousands emigrated from Talcher to camp at Angul and Kosala in Congress-ruled Orissa, and on 5 January 1939 the British Political Agent in Ranpur, Major Barzelgette, was stoned to death after he had fired on a crowd in front of the royal palace. Gandhi did his best to get the Orissan movements called off in return for some token political reforms in Dhenkanal and Talcher, and the question became a bone of contention between the Orissa Gandhians (led by Gopabandhu Chaudhuri) and the Socialists and Communists who were leading the Kisan Sabha in the province.

In the biggest princely state of all, Hyderabad, a small Muslim elite held 90% of government jobs, and Urdu was maintained as the sole official language and medium of instruction in a state which was 50% Telegu, 25% Marathi, and 11% Kannada-speaking. There was a total absence of elementary civil and political rights, and extremely crude forms of feudal exploitation, like *vetti,* or forced labour and compulsory payments in kind, prevailed in the Telengana region. Popular awakening initially took the form of middle-class language-based cultural associations—the Andhra Mahasabha in Telengana and the Maharashtra Parishad in Marathwada—petitioning for mild political reforms. The Congress policy of non-intervention gave an opportunity to Hindu-communalist forces, the Arya Samaj and the Hindu Mahasabha, to campaign against the tyranny of the Nizam and the Ittahad-ul-Mussalmaan even while the Mahasabha was denouncing Congress interference under the 'plausible slogan of responsible government' in states under Hindu princes (Nagpur session, December 1938). The Arya leader Pandit Narendraji started a purely Hindu *satyagraha* in Hyderabad city and the Marathwada region (adjoining the Marathi speaking districts of C.P., a stronghold of Hindu communalists) in October 1938, with the demand for more jobs for Hindus. At about the same time, a State Congress had been founded on a secular basis by Swami Ramananda Tirtha and Govinddass Shroff from Marathwada, Ravi Narayan Reddi from Telengana and a few Muslims like Sirajul Hasan Tirmizi from Hyderabad city. The State Congress began a parallel and more effective *satyagraha* from 24 October 1938, demanding its own legalization and responsible government, while a powerful 'Vande Mataram' movement developed among Osmania students, who left the University when the Nizam banned the singing of that patriotic hymn. The Congress movement, however, was called off at Gandhi's insistence in December 1938, ostensibly on the ground that it could get mixed up with the Hindu communalist agitation—'we could not understand the propriety of this decision', confessed Ramananda Tirtha later on. (*Memoirs of Hyderabad Freedom Struggle,* Bombay, 1967, p. 107) Soon 'the cream of Andhra workers who had given the lead' (Ibid, p. 87) under Ravi Narayan Reddi went over to the Communists. A Nizam State Committee of the C.P.I. was established secretly in 1939, guided initially by the already-strong movement in coastal Andhra. Using the broad front of the Andhra Mahasabha, the Communists penetrated into the Telengana countryside with amazing rapidity, building up within a few years the base that would sustain from 1946 to 1951 the greatest peasant guerrilla war seen in India so far.

In Travancore and Cochin, as in the adjoining Malayalee district of Malabar, the national movement was built up very largely under Leftist leadership and guidance. A.K. Gopalan has described in his autobiography how in the mid-and late-1930s activists like Krishna Pillai, E.M.S. Namboodripad and himself founded the C.S.P., converted the Congress for the first time into a real mass organization, and simultaneously moved towards Communism. (*In the Cause of the People,* Madras, 1973) Namboodripad eventually became secretary of the Kerala PCC, which remained under Leftist control till the nearly 1940s. In August 1938, the Travancore State Congress started a powerful agitation against the autocracy of Dewan C.P. Ramaswami Iyer. Despite brutal repression (including 12 cases of firing in two months), students joined the *satyagraha* in large numbers, and *jathas* marched into Travancore from many parts of Kerala (including one led by A.K. Gopalan), thus greatly contributing to the developing sense of regional-linguistic unity. Particularly impressive was the role of the working class. Alleppey coir workers led by Krishna Pillai went on strike in October 1938, demanding not only wage-increase and union recognition but release of political prisoners and responsible government based on universal franchise. The Dewan was forced to call off repressive measures against the Congress *satyagraha* in order to isolate the militant Alleppey workers. As elsewhere, the role of Gandhi and the Congress High Command was confined to advising withdrawal of the *satyagraha* once a few token concessions had been obtained.

The Left in the Congress

Labour and *kisan* organization and the upsurge in the princely states comprised issues around which a broad Left alternative could emerge within the Congress as a challenge to the increasingly conservative stance of the ministries and the majority in the High Command. The Left in this period included the Socialists, the followers of M.N. Roy (who remained quite important still in trade unions), and the illegal C.P.I. which worked through the C.S.P. and in fact provided many of its most effective mass leaders (Krishna Pillai, Namboodripad and Gopalan in Kerala, Jeevanandan in Tamil Nadu, Sundarayya in Andhra, Sohan Singh Josh in the Punjab). They obtained an uncertain and largely verbal support from the two Congress Presidents of these years, Nehru and Bose—support which was still felt to be valuable. There were some internal tensions, particularly the growing alarm felt by Socialists like Jayaprakash Narayan, Minoo Masani or N.G. Ranga at the rapid penetration of the rather amorphous party they led by dedicated and disciplined Communist cadres—a justified fear, for in 1939–40 the C.P.I. walked away with the entire Kerala unit and much of the Tamilnadu and Andhra membership. A measure of broad unity could still be preserved, till 1939 and in some ways till 1942. All sections of the Left agreed that remaining within the Congress was justified, and indeed, despite some inevitable compromises, it did seem to be bringing in rich dividends. Apart from the clear predominance established in trade unions and Kisan Sabhas, it was significant that students in regions like Bengal now tended to be attracted to one or other variety of the Left (terrorism had at last died out, and Gandhism had little appeal). The Bengal unit of the Communist-led All India Students Federation spread from Calcutta into mufassil colleges and schools through the prisoners' release campaign of 1937–38, followed up by movements for elected students unions, an adult literacy drive which was combined with anti-imperialist propaganda, and solidarity demonstrations with Spain and China. A pattern of student radicalism was being set which would last for at least a generation. (G. Chattopadhyay, *Swadhinata-Sangrame Banglar Chatra-samaj,* Calcutta, 1980)

The entire Left tried, without noticeable success, to persuade the Congress leadership to adopt a more sympathetic stance towards trade unions and Kisan Sabhas and to give open support to the States People's Movements. While the Congress periodically reiterated its opposition to British Federation plans based on Viceregal reserved powers and a central legislature with states members nominated by princes, it rejected Left demands for mass action on the issue, being apparently content with the provincial ministries for the time being.

In private letters Nehru repeatedly expressed strong misgivings about the conservative functioning of Congress ministries, even calling them 'counter-revolutionary' and 'merely carrying on the tradition (with minor variations) of the previous governments'. (Nehru to G.B. Pant, 25 November 1937, *A*

Bunch of Old Letters, p. 263). But actions are more significant than words (and particularly private doubts), and here, as we have repeatedly seen, both Nehru and Bose woefully failed to stem the drift to the Right.

On international issues, in sharp contrast, the Left clearly set the tone, thanks in large part to the consistent support and leadership it received here from Jawaharlal Nehru. Jawaharlal in fact increasingly sought in internationalist gestures a kind of surrogate for effective Left action at home—'I have felt out of place and a misfit. This was one reason...why I decided to go to Europe'. (Letter to Gandhi, 28 April 1938, *A Bunch of Old Letters,* p. 284) In the context of gathering war clouds, nationalist and Leftist opinion in general agreed that there was no question of any unconditional support this time to a British foreign policy characterized in the late-1930s by Chamberlain's appeasement of fascist aggression in Abyssinia, Spain, Austria, Czechoslovakia and China. *'Na ek pai na ek bhai'* (not a pie, not a man), was the slogan being raised already in the Punjab by Socialists and Communists in 1938—without very much impact, however, on army recruitment, for military salaries and pensions formed a principal basis for the relative prosperity of the Punjab peasantry. With Britain clearly abetting the aggressors and egging on Germany against the Soviet Union, there was no contradiction as yet between anti-British nationalism and anti-fascist internationalism. The entire Congress repeatedly denounced fascist aggression, Nehru went to Spain in 1938 to express his solidarity with the International Brigade defending Madrid, and the Congress responded to Chu Teh's appeal for help by sending a medical mission to China (one of whose members, Dr Kotnis, died a martyr to the cause of India-China friendship and anti-imperialist solidarity, working with the Communist Eighth Route Army guerrillas). Rabindranath too, repeatedly called for support to Republican Spain and denounced Japanese aggression in China. The shadows of fascism and impending world war gave a new tone to some of his poems in this period, which both in content as well as in the stark austerity of their style constituted a remarkable departure for a man in his late-seventies.

The Tripuri Crisis

Consensus on international issues which demanded little more in practice as yet than solidarity gestures, however, could be no substitute for radicalism on more immediately vital domestic problems, and here matters reached crisis point in early 1939 on the eve of the Tripuri session with Bose's decision to stand for re-election as President. Though the proposal initially came from eight C.S.P. leaders (all of them, incidentally, with Communist connections), and though Bose tried to link his candidature with a radical call for a 'National

Demand' for Swaraj in the form of a time-bound ultimatum to the British, it is difficult to avoid the impression that the issue was to a considerable extent personal. The Working Committee appointed by Bose after Haripura had not included a single Leftist apart from Jawaharlal (unlike Nehru's nominations in 1936), and he had done nothing to prevent the development of an increasingly hostile stance by the High Command and ministries towards labour and *kisan* militancy. The entire Left still rallied around Bose in his electoral confrontation with Sitaramayya, whom Gandhi explicitly declared to be his nominee after a third candidate, Maulana Azad, had withdrawn. Subhas was elected on 29 January 1939 by 1580 votes against 1377, with massive majorities in Bengal and Punjab and substantial leads in Kerala, Karnataka, Tamil Nadu, U.P. and Assam. The contest was very close in Maharashtra and Maha-koshal (C.P. Hindustani), and only Gujarat, Bihar, Orissa and Andhra voted more or less solidly for Sitaramayya.

Immensely superior tactics and Left lack of unity enabled Gandhi and the Congress Right to snatch victory from the jaws of an apparently decisive defeat. Gandhi immediately made the issue a matter of his own personal prestige by declaring Sitaramayya's defeat to be 'more mine than his'. (31 January) On 22 February 13 out of the 15 members of the old Working Committee resigned, on the ground that Subhas had publicly criticized them; they included, after the usual wobbling and on a somewhat different pretext, Nehru. The Tripuri session (8–12 March) found Bose temporarily almost incapacitated by illness, and Gandhi back from a fast in Rajkot which had won some concessions for the time being. The Right pressed home their offensive through the famous resolution moved by Govindballav Pant expressing confidence in the old Working Committee, reiterating faith in the Gandhian policies followed during the last 20 years, and asking Bose to nominate his new executive 'in accordance with the wishes of Gandhiji'. The resolution was carried by 218 to 133 votes in the Subjects Committee, and by an overwhelming majority through show of hands in the open session. Nehru's support was not unexpected: apart from his ultimate loyalty to Gandhi, his personal equation with Bose had never been happy. But Socialists, Royists, and Communists (except for some Bengal members like Bankim Mukherji) also failed to oppose the Pant resolution out of a desire to avoid a complete split. Jayaprakash even moved, and Nehru and the Communist Bhardwaj supported, the extremely diluted National Demand resolution which dropped Bose's idea of a time-bound ultimatum and merely called for preparations for a struggle to achieve a Constituent Assembly through strengthening the Congress.

The choice had been a difficult one for the Left, for Bose's previous record had not been one which could inspire a confidence unqualified enough to risk a total break. It may be argued that the more fundamental mistake from the Left point of view lay in the failure both before and after Tripuri to resist more effectively the increasingly anti-labour and anti-*kisan* policies of the Congress ministries. This was the result of a conception of a united front which in practice at times came to be identified with a desire to retain unity with top Congress leaders at all costs. C.P.I. General Secretary P.C. Joshi, for instance, argued in the party organ *National Front* in April 1939 that 'the greatest class struggle today is our national struggle' of which Congress was the 'main organ'—and so Congress-*kisan* unity had to be preserved.

Bose, who had already declared on 3 February that he considered his electoral victory meaningless if he failed to 'win the confidence of India's greatest man', tried for two months after Tripuri to set up an agreed Working Committee. The basic weakness of his position, particularly in the context of disunity within the Left, was made clear when he failed to take up Gandhi's challenge—'you are free to choose your own committee'—at the Calcutta session of the AICC on 29 April. He preferred to resign, and was replaced by the staunch Gandhian Right-winger Rajendra Prasad. On 3 May, Bose announced the formation of his Forward Bloc, initially with the idea of working within the Congress and also of uniting the various Left groups—for which purpose the Forward Bloc started a Left Consolidation Committee in June 1939. This received Communist support but both the Royists and Socialist leaders like Jayaprakash gave first priority to Congress unity and were critical of the formation of the Forward Bloc, which became in the end just another splinter group within the already fragmented Left. Subhas was now more popular in Bengal than ever, as the regional hero who had been given a raw deal, and he had his pockets of personal influence elsewhere, particularly in Bihar, Punjab, Bombay and Tamil Nadu. The High Command, however, was quite determined to finish him as a force within the Congress, and when Bose called for an all-India protest day on 9 July against a recent AICC resolution (moved by Patel) banning civil disobedience by Congressmen without previous permission from PCCs, disciplinary action was quickly taken against him. On 11 August the AICC removed Bose from the post of President of the Bengal PCC and debarred him from holding any Congress office for three years. An *ad hoc* committee was later set up to run the Bengal Congress, including Azad and Gandhians like P.C. Ghosh but also two members (B.C. Roy and Kiransankar Roy) of the 'big five' of Calcutta magnates who had once been Bose's main financial backers.

While Bose was firmly ousted, a total break with the Left would hardly have been wise from the High Command point of view. By late-1939, continuation of Congress ministries was proving to be somewhat counter-productive in terms of internal tensions and loss of party image. The ministries increasingly faced the problem of alienation of workers, *kisans* and all Left elements within the party, while not really pleasing landlords or business groups (who resented things like the Bombay urban property tax, which were inevitable, given the tight financial constraints under which provincial autonomy operated). Patel hinted in July 1939 that the ministries might have to resign unless the provinces received a greater share of the income tax. With the coming of war in September, there was the further danger that Congress ministers might have to use the new emergency powers against anti-war demonstrations by their own partymen. The resignation of Congress ministries on 29–30 October 1939 was thus logical and inevitable, even though the occasion was provided by Linlithgow's tactless obstinancy.

1939–1942 : WAR AND INDIAN POLITICS— THE FIRST PHASE

Bureaucratic Counter-Offensive

On 3 September 1939, the Viceroy unilaterally associated India with Britain's declaration of war on Germany, without bothering to consult the provincial ministries or any Indian leader. Congress hostility to fascist aggression had been incomparably more forthright and consistent than Britain's own record so far. Yet Linlithgow rejected numerous offers of full cooperation in the war effort provided some minimum conditions were met: a promise of a post-war constituent assembly to determine the political structure of a free India, and the immediate formation of something like a genuine responsible government in the centre. Such conditions, the Congress argued with considerable justice, were essential if Indian opinion was to be really mobilized for a war which in 1939 (and down to the Japanese attack of December 1941) was still a very distant one, for otherwise the Allied propaganda that the conflict was one between democracy and the principle of self-determination of nations against tyranny and aggression was bound to seem extremely hollow. Linlithgow's statement of 17 October 1939 merely repeated old offers of Dominion Status in an indefinite and presumably distant future, promised post-war 'consultations with representatives of the several communities' to modify the 1935 Act (and not any democratically-elected constituent assembly), and the settings-up for the present of a purely consultative group of Indian politicians and princely representatives with no real executive power whatsoever. Privately the Viceroy repeatedly declared his intention to 'lie back for the present' and avoid 'running after the Congress' (Linlithgow to Secretary of State, Zetland, 3 and 13 February 1940).

Linlithgow's attitude was not an aberration, but part of a general British policy to take advantage of the war to regain for the white-dominated central government and bureaucracy the ground lost to the Congress from 1937 or earlier. Even before war had been declared, an amendment to the 1935 Act had been rushed through the British Parliament giving New Delhi emergency powers in respect of provincial subjects. A Defence of India Ordinance restricting civil liberties came into force the day war was declared, and by May 1940 the Government had prepared a top-secret draft Revolutionary Movements Ordinance aimed at a crippling pre-emptive strike at the Congress at the first opportunity. As in 1931, an important section of British officialdom was eager to provoke the Congress into a confrontation at a time when the government had sweeping powers, could call upon (from early 1942 onwards) growing numbers of British and other Allied troops stationed in India, and could hope for an unusual amount of world-wide liberal and even Left-wing sympathy (after the Nazi invasion of the Soviet Union in June 1941) in suppressing a movement which could be portrayed as objectively helping Japan and Germany.

British Indian reactionary policies received powerful support and encouragement from Winston Churchill, who took over as head of a national coalition in May 1940 as the German *blitzkreig* smashed through the western front, swept the British into the sea at Dunkirk, and overran France in a matter of weeks. Churchill, the new Secretary of State Amery once whispered to Wavell at a Cabinet meeting, knew as much about the Indian problem as George III did of the American colonies. (Wavell, *Viceroy's Journal,* p. 21) 'I have not become the King's First Minister in order to preside over the liquidation of the British Empire', Churchill would declare in November 1942. Churchill's premiership more than counterbalanced the entry into the Cabinet of Labour leaders like Attlee and Cripps who had promised Nehru and Krishna Menon at a private meeting on June 1939 at Cripps' country house of Filkins that the next Labour Government would agree to a complete transfer of power to a constituent assembly based on universal franchise, subject to an Indo-British treaty protecting British obligations and interests in India for a transitional period. (P.S. Gupta, *Imperialism and British Labour,* pp. 257–9) In August 1940, while the 'battle of Britain raged over the skies of an isolated island, Amery and even Linlithgow were prepared for some concessions to win Indian support, but their proposals were whittled down drastically by Churchill. Linlithgow's 'August Offer' (8 August 1940) consequently was little more than a repetition of his 17 October 1939 statement: Dominion Status in the unspecified future, a post-war body to devise a constitution (but evidently subject still to ultimate British parliamentary sanction, and no mention was made of its being elected by universal franchise), immediate expansion of the Viceroy's Executive to include some more Indians, and a War Advisory Council. In July 1941, the Viceroy's Executive was enlarged to give Indians a majority for the first time (8 out of 12, but whites remained in charge of defence, finance and home) and a National Defence Council was set up with purely advisory functions. For the rest, no further initiative was taken, till the disasters in South-East Asia compelled the dramatic Cripps Mission of March-April 1942—and this too, as we shall see, would be effectively torpedoed by the Churchill–Linlithgow combine.

League and Pakistan

Encouragement of Muslim League claims formed an increasingly important part of war-time imperialist strategy. The 17 October 1939 statement referred to the need to consult representatives of the 'several communities' and the August offer made it clear that the British would not transfer responsibilities 'to any system of government whose authority is directly denied by large and powerful elements in India's national life.' This in effect conceded one of Jinnah's central demands since the outbreak of the war: not only was the League the sole spokesman for India's Muslims, there must also be a kind of League veto on future constitutional changes.

British instigation was not entirely absent in the final stages of the evolution of the Pakistan slogan which was adopted by the Lahore session of the Muslim League in March 1940. The genesis of this demand has sometimes been traced back to Iqbal's reference to the need for a 'North West Indian Muslim state' in his presidential address to the Muslim League in 1930, but the context of his speech makes it clear that the great Urdu poet and patriot was really visualizing not partition, but a reorganization of Muslim-majority areas in N.W. India into an autonomous unit within a single weak Indian federation. Choudhry Rehmat Ali's group of Punjabi Muslim students in Cambridge have a much better claim to be regarded as the original proponents of the idea. In two pamphlets, written in 1933 and 1935, Rehmat Ali demanded a separate national status for a new entity for which he coined the name *Pakstan* (from Punjab, Afghan province, Kashmir, Sind and Baluchistan). No one took this very seriously at the time, least of all the League and other Muslim delegates to the Round Table Conference who dismissed the idea as a student's pipe-dream. But the League after 1937, as we have seen, urgently needed some kind of a positive platform, while the Federal clauses of the 1935 Act showed less and less signs of ever coming near implementation and were in any case felt by Muslim leaders to envisage an unacceptably strong and Hindu-dominated central government. A number of alternative proposals were consequently put forward during 1938–39, and in March 1939 the League set up a subcommittee to examine the various schemes. While the Aligarh scheme of Zafrul Hasan and Husain Qadri suggested four independent states of Pakistan, Bengal, Hyderabad and Hindustan, most other plans stopped well short of complete partition, and wanted formation of distinct autonomous Muslim blocs within a loose Indian confederation. The Punjab Unionist premier Sikandar Hayat Khan, for instance, suggested a kind of three-tier structure with autonomous provinces grouped into seven regions having their own regional legislatures, together constituting a loose confederation with the centre having charge only over matters like defence, external affairs, customs and currency—an anticipation of the Cabinet Mission plan of 1946. Considerable British encouragement and prodding lay behind this sudden search for alternatives. Khaliquzzaman tells us that Secretary of State, Zetland had given a sympathetic hearing on 20 March 1939 to redefinition of Rehmat Ali's scheme, suggesting two Muslim Federations, one in the North West and the other in the East (covering Bengal and Assam). (*Pathway to Pakistan,* pp. 205–7) The recently-opened Linlithgow and Zetland papers make the British role even more evident. The Viceroy, for instance, told Jinnah on 6 February 1940, six weeks before the Lahore resolution, that British sympathy should not be expected 'for a party whose policy was one of sheer negation'—'If he and his friends wanted to secure that the Muslim case should not go by default in the UK, it was really essential that they should formulate their plan in the near future'. (quoted in Uma Kaura, p. 149)

The famous resolution of 23 March 1940, drafted by Sikandar Hayat Khan, moved (after considerable modifications) by Fazlul Huq, and seconded by Khaliquzzaman, demanded 'that geographically contiguous units are demarcated into regions which should be so constituted, with such territorial readjustments as may be necessary, that the areas in which the Muslims are numerically in a majority as in the north-western and eastern zones of India should be grouped to constitute 'Independent States', in which the constituent units shall be autonomous and sovereign.' The remarkably clumsy wording left ample—and probably deliberate—scope for vagueness, ambiguity and equivocation. Neither Pakistan nor Partition were explicitly mentioned, and in the early 1940s some Muslim politicians even argued at times that the Hindu press and politicians had started the Pakistan bogey by misinterpreting the resolution in order to block legitimate but more modest Muslim demands. 'Territorial readjustments' were not defined and 'Independent States' (within quotes) seemed to imply separation but could possibly mean no more than full autonomy within a loose federation. The use of the plural and the stress on the sovereignty of the units became very important after Partition, for they provided the theoretical basis for the Awami League agitation (started under Fazlul Huq) against a Punjabi-dominated unitary conception of Pakistan which eventually led to the break-away of Bangladesh.

In a much-quoted Punjab Assembly speech on 11 March 1941, Sikander Hayat Khan, leader of a Unionist bloc which included some Sikhs and Hindu Jats like Chhotu Ram, declared that he was opposed to a Pakistan which would mean 'Muslim Raj here and Hindu Raj elsewhere.... If Pakistan means unalloyed Muslim Raj in the Punjab then I will have nothing to do with it'. (V.P. Menon, *Transfer of Power in India,* p. 463) He reiterated his plea for a loose confederation, and claimed that his original resolution at Lahore had included references 'to the centre and coordination of the activities of the various units'. Few Muslim leaders in fact initially took Pakistan very seriously or literally, and even for Jinnah probably it began as a bargaining counter, useful to bloc possible British constitutional concessions to the Congress and gain additional favours for the Muslims. Yet Sikandar's speech admitted that though 'a vast majority of educated Muslims...do not believe in any of these schemes' (of Partition), its very vagueness and fluidity was increasingly making Pakistan 'a convenient slogan to sway the Muslim masses' (Ibid, p. 453). Unionist evocation of Punjab communal unity was associated with a general defence of the social and political *status quo* and open alignment with the British: Sikandar's successor, Khizar Hayat Khan, would be the one Indian politician to win the unqualified admiration of Wavell. In Punjab as well as in Bengal, a populist, demagogic communalism could consequently develop for a few years around the slogan of Pakistan, with an independent Muslim state being presented as a panacea to all problems. This still lay some years in the future, however. For the moment, Pakistan was useful for the British to maintain a constitutional deadlock in India, but while encouraging Jinnah within limits, they had no intention of surrendering to all his demands. League claims for Muslim non-official advisors in the provinces under Section 93, more seats in the expanded Executive Council, and parity with the Congress in it in case the latter decided to join in the future, were all rejected. Jinnah consequently in the end turned down the August offer, and next year compelled Sikander Hayat Khan and Fazlul Huq to decline membership of the new National Defence Council.

Trends within the Congress

Down to the winter of 1941–42, alignments within the Congress broadly followed the pattern set in the late-1930s. Gandhi and the Right-wing dominated High Command counselled restraint, tried repeatedly for some kind of agreement with the British, and later unwillingly sanctioned a movement characterized above all by its remarkably low-key and limited nature; the entire Left urged militant anti-War and anti-government actions. Though 'Congressmen seem to be expecting a big move', there was no immediate prospect of civil disobedience, Gandhi hastened to point out soon after the Congress ministries had resigned. Gandhi himself expressed occasional doubts as to whether his principles of *ahimsa* allowed direct support to war (he quixotically advised recourse to non-violent resistance even to Poland, France and Britain!), but the Working Committee repeatedly made it clear (as on 17 June 1940) that it was fully prepared to back the war effort if only the British gave some concessions on the two key demands of a post-war independence pledge and an immediate 'National Government' at the centre.

British obstinacy and Left pressures for action, however, eventually compelled some gestures towards a more militant policy. The Ramgarh Congress (March 1940) talked of civil disobedience 'as soon as the Congress organisation is considered fit enough for the purpose'—but left the timing and form of movement entirely to the personal discretion of Gandhi. After the August offer disappointment, Gandhi at last sanctioned civil disobedience, but of a peculiarly limited and deliberately ineffective kind. The sole issue was freedom of speech—more specifically, the right to make public anti-war pronouncements. Individual Congressmen (at first only those nominated by Gandhi himself, starting with Vinoba Bhave on 17 October and Jawaharlal on 31 October, later on a more general scale) would court arrest by making anti-war speeches. At its height in June 1941, about 20,000 had gone to jail, but the movement had petered out by the autumn of 1941, with most prisoners released. This was far and away the weakest and least effective of all the Gandhian national campaigns, and stands in the sharpest possible contrast to what would happen a year later, in August 1942. The aims clearly were not any serious embarrassment to the British, but merely to register the Congress presence and hostility to a war waged without consulting Indians, while at the same time giving Linlithgow no opportunity for a major crackdown. That the British would have been only too eager to use their wartime powers is indicated by the fantastic sentence of four years' rigorous imprisonment initially given to Nehru. In a conversation with Birla in January 1941, Gandhi made clear his desire 'to minimize any embarressment that may be caused by his movement' (there would be no *satyagraha,* for instance, during Christmas, on Sundays, or before 9 A.M.!) and expressed at the same time his concern about 'the mentality of our young men.... Communism appeals to youth, unfortunately.' (*Thakurdas Papers,* F.N. 177) As often before, the desire to sidetrack potentially more militant pressures seems to have been partly responsible for the twists and turns of Gandhian strategy.

With the exception of the M.N. Roy group which felt that the War was anti-fascist and therefore demanded unconditional support, the entire Left strained for militant anti-War struggles down to the end of 1941. Subhas Bose had no doubts at all that Britain's difficulties should be made into India's opportunity, and he presided over an Anti-Compromise Conference held alongside the Ramgarh session which bitterly denounced Gandhian moderation. Socialists were in an increasingly militant mood, with Jayaprakash Narayan for instance thinking in terms of armed struggle while in jail in 1941. Though Socialist-Communist relations had already worsened due to the C.P.I. capture of many of the best C.S.P. leaders and units, there was no major political difference till late-1941 so far as the attitude to war was concerned. The about-turn in Comintern policy after the Nazi-Soviet Pact of August 1939 was a serious embarrassment for Communists in Europe, but an asset for their comrades in India, allowing an easy synchronization of 'internationalist' support to Soviet policies with nationalist hostility to Britain's war—a situation which would be exactly reversed after Hitler's invasion of Russia on 22 June 1941.

Yet the Left as a whole was unable to sustain any significant movement in face of sharply intensified British repression. Subhas Bose led a successful *satyagraha* in Calcutta in July 1940 demanding the removal of the Holwell monument (a memorial to the British victims of the alleged Black Hole). Muslim students for once participated in large numbers in a movement linked with the honour of Siraj-ud-daulah the last independent Muslim ruler of Bengal, but Hindu-Muslim unity apart, the whole thing obviously had very limited significance. Bose excaped from home internment in January 1941, and used the Communist underground network in his flight through Afghanistan and Russia to Germany. He had embarked on the last and most dramatic phase of his patriotic career, but the decision to rely primarily on help from Britain's enemies was also in a sense a confession of the weakness of internal forces, and marked a kind of return to the methods of the revolutionary terrorists during the First World War. The Mysore State Congress (associated with the Socialist-dominated Karnataka PCC) staged a powerful three monthlong *satyagraha* from September 1939, winning significant peasant support: of the 2801 arrested 641 were agriculturists as against only 23 lawyers. (James Manor, *Political Change in an Indian State,* Delhi, 1977, p. 124) The other Left-controlled PCC, that of Kerala, organized a successful antirepression day on 15 September 1940 marked by police firing at Tellicherry, Mattanur and Morazha. In March 1941, a peasant-landlord clash in North Malabar led to four *kisan* teenagers being sentenced to death—the 'Kayyur martyrs' who acquired countrywide fame. In Purnea in north Bihar and the Thakurgaon sub-division of Dinajpur (north Bengal), Communist-led *kisan* movements acquired a new militancy, and spread down from middle peasants to tribal or semi-tribal sharecroppers (Santhals and Rajbansis) for the first time. But such scattered and localized militancy was obviously quite far removed from any country-wide challenge to British rule.

Economic Consequences

The relative weakness of the national movement between 1939 and 1941 probably also had certain economic roots. A war which was still a distant affair brought, on the balance, gains rather than losses for substantial sections of the population. The rise in agricultural prices was not as yet very sharp, and came as a relief for the bulk of the peasantry after a long decade of depression. As during the First World War, Indian industrial development received a major stimulus from war demand, cutting-off of imports, and forced reliance on indigeneous products, even though the British still did their best to discourage Indian efforts (by Walchand Hirachand and Diwan Mirza Ismail of Mysore, for instance) to start production of automobiles, ships and aircraft. Employment in factories went up by 31% between 1939 and 1942, whereas it had increased from 1,361,000 to 1,751,000 only between 1922 and 1939. (Wadia and Merchant, *Our Economic Problem*, 6th ed, Bombay, 1959, p. 335) Labour unrest which could have seriously threatened the war effort was kept in check in the big cities by substantial dearness allowances and supply of essential goods at subsidized rates. For Indian businessmen and traders in general, war meant an opportunity for fantastically quick profits, particularly so long as it remained distant and did not involve the threat of destruction of property through aerial bombardment or evacuation. Khaliquzzaman makes the interesting point that the Muslim League was pressed towards greater co-operation with the British by business magnates as well as by 'our Muslim taluqdars and zamindars... interested in smaller contracts for the supply of wood, charcoal and other small commodities. They could hardly be expected to forego the chance of a lifetime'. (*Pathway to Pakistan,* p. 243) It is surely not illegitimate to suspect the existence of similar pressures on the Congress, too.

The New Phase of the War

Two world developments in the latter half of 1941 transformed the Indian situation: Hitler's invasion of Russia, and the dramatic Japanese drive through South-East Asia from December 1941 which in four months swept the

British out of Malaya, Singapore and Burma and threatened to bring its empire in India to a sudden end.

The German invasion of Russia confronted Indian Communists with an agonizing choice. While British policies in India remained as repressive and reactionary as ever, Britain was now the ally of the world's only socialist state engaged in a life-and-death struggle for survival. After six months of hesitation and internal debate, the C.P.I. in January 1942 lined up with the rest of the international Communist movement in calling for full support to the anti-fascist 'people's war' even while reiterating the standard Congress demands for an independence pledge and immediate national government (which were now considered as valuable but no longer indispensable preconditions for support). Concern and sympathy for Russia was by no means confined to Communists. Rabindranath on his death-bed in August 1941 asked for news from Russia, and expressed his faith that the Soviets alone would be able to halt the 'monsters'. Nehru with his deep internationalist and anti-fascist commitment and admiration for embattled Russia and China sought desperately for a compromise enabling Indian support to war during the Cripps Mission negotiations, talked publicly in terms of the need to organize guerrilla resistance to Japanese invaders, and initially had very great reservations about the Quit India line. Such a global perspective, however, could hardly be expected from the vast majority of Indian patriots, whether Congress Right-wingers, Gandhians, Socialists, or followers of Bose, many of whom increasingly felt that Britain was going down in defeat and the time had come for a bold strike for freedom.

Cripps Mission

As the war daily came nearer India (Singapore fell on 15 February 1942, Rangoon on 8 March, the Andaman islands on 23 March), the British at long last felt obliged to make some gestures to win over Indian public opinion. Roosevelt raised the question of Indian political reform in his talks with Churchill in Washington in December 1941, on 2 January Indian Liberal leaders like Sapru and Jayakar appealed for immediate Dominion Status and expansion of the Viceroy's Executive into a National Government, and in February Chiang Kai-shek during his visit to India publicly expressed sympathy for 'India's aspirations for freedom'. All this provided an opening for relatively pro-Indian groups in Britain: Labour members of the War Cabinet like Cripps and Attlee, and the Quaker-dominated India Conciliation Group under Agatha Harrison set up during Gandhi's 1931 visit with which Nehru had developed friendly connections in 1938. Cripps had visited India privately in December 1939 and had decided after talks with the rising U.P.

League leader Liaquat Ali Khan that some modifications were needed in the Filkins formula of June 1938. 'There emerges a picture of a rather loose federation...with the right of provinces to withdraw if they wish'—the germ of the 'provincial option' idea which would form the basis of the Cripps plan two years later (R.J. Moore, *Churchill, Cripps and India 1939–45*, Oxford, 1979, p. 12).

In the first week of March, 1942, Cripps was able to persuade the War Cabinet to agree to a draft declaration promising post-war Dominion Status with right of secession, a 'constitution-making body' elected by provincial legislatures, with individual provinces being given the right not to join it, and with States being invited to appoint representatives. Paragraph (e) invited 'immediate and effective participation of the leaders of the principal sections of the Indian people in the counsels of their country' on urgent issues but insisted that the British during the war would have to retain 'the control and direction of the defence of India'. The declaration was not published immediately, but Cripps went out to India on 23 March to negotiate on its basis with Indian leaders. Linlithgow threatened to resign, but Churchill explained that: 'It would be impossible, owing to unfortunate rumours and publicity, and the general American outlook, to stand on a purely negative attitude and the Cripps Mission is indispensable to prove our honesty of purpose....If it is rejected by the Indian parties...our sincerity will be proved to the world...'. (Churchill to Linlithgow, 10 March 1942, N. Mansergh (ed), *Transfer of Power, Vol.I*, London 1970, pp. 394–5).

The Cripps Mission was plagued throughout, and ultimately torpedoed, by numerous ambiguities and misunderstandings. 'He is of course bound by the draft declaration which is our utmost limit', Churchill had assured Linlithgow, but Cripps seems to have gone considerably beyond that in his talks with Nehru and Azad, driven by his own desire for a settlement and a not unfavourable initial Congress response. The Congress was naturally very critical of the clauses regarding nomination of states representatives by rulers and the provincial option (which Amery on 2 March privately admitted to be 'the first public admission of the possibility of Pakistan', Ibid., pp. 282–3), and Gandhi deliberately kept very much in the background through-out-Cripps' stay in India. But the official Congress negotiators, Nehru and Congress President Azad, focussed the talks throughout on the provisions for immediate changes indicated in paragraph (e). They were apparently told by Cripps that the new Executive would approximate to cabinet government, not formally (as the 1935 Act could not be changed in wartime) but in practice through conventions—just as the Governor's special powers had not really hindered the Congress ministries from effectively ruling the provinces during 1937–39. In his cable to Churchill on 4

April, Cripps made a reference to the 'new arrangement whereby the Executive Council will approximate to a Cabinet...' (Ibid., p. 636).

The discussion consequently centred on control over defence, and here too an agreement seemed in sight on 9 April, thanks to the mediation efforts of Colonel Johnson, Roosevelt's personal representative who had come to New Delhi to discuss military problems. A compromise formula had been worked out by which an Indian would be in charge of the Defence Department while the British Commander-in-Chief would retain control over field operations and head a War Department whose functions were specified. But by this time Linlithgow and C-in-C Wavell were seriously worried that Cripps was conceding far too much real power to the Congress and, together with Churchill, they were able to block the settlement at the last moment. A War Cabinet telegram to Cripps on 9 April sharply pulled him up for not adequately consulting Linlithgow and Wavell and giving Johnson too much scope it further deplored 'allusions to a National Government', and emphasized the need 'to bring the whole matter back to Cabinet's plan which you went out to urge'. (Ibid., pp. 707–8) The Congress negotiators the same evening found Cripps singing a completely different tune and the talks broke down abruptly.

Nehru had desperately sought a settlement, largely because of his desire to mobilize genuine and effective Indian support in the anti-fascist war, while most Working Committee members and Gandhi himself had been apathetic or cynical. He was now placed in an extremely false position, and things were not helped by Cripps roundly and most unfairly blaming the Congress for the failure, no doubt partly to save his political career. The Congress side of the matter was summed up by Nehru's terse cable to Krishna Menon on 13 April: 'Cripps made clear early stages he envisaged national cabinet with Viceroy as constitutional head like King subject reservation defence. Discussion therefore centered on defence... Ultimately Cripps stated... no national cabinet with joint responsibility possible nor could assurances be given about use Viceroy's powers intervention veto. This entirely different picture from what Cripps originally suggested. Impossible call this national government or evoke enthusiasm people...' (R.J. Moore, pp. 129–30). It is difficult not to suspect an element of bluff and double-dealing here so far as the British were concerned, though opinions may well differ as to whether Cripps himself was a willing or unconscious agent in this game. For Churchill, certainly, 'it mattered not so much that something should be done as that some attempt should be seen to be made' (Tomlinson, *The Indian National Congress and the Raj*, p. 156), and he warmly congratulated Cripps' efforts on 11 April, as proving 'how great was the British desire to reach a settlement....

The effect throughout Britain and in the United States has been wholly beneficial.' (Mansergh, Vol. I, p. 739)

While responsibility for the failure of the Cripps Mission thus rests squarely on the British, it remains true that the bulk of the Congress leadership and ranks were probably unenthusiastic about it from the beginning. Things in fact were now rapidly moving towards the total confrontation of the Quit India movement.

1942-1945: QUIT INDIA, FAMINE, AND THE LAST PHASE OF WAR

Roots of Rebellion

The summer of 1942 found Gandhi in a strange and uniquely militant mood. Leave India to God or to anarchy, he repeatedly urged the British— 'this orderly disciplined anarchy should go, and if as a result there is complete lawlessness I would risk it.' (Linlithgow to Amery, reporting Gandhi's press interview of 16 May, Mansergh, Vol. II, p. 96) If the British withdraw, 'the Japanese would be bound to reconsider their plans' (*Harijan* article, 3 May), and in any case Indians should be left to tackle that problem in their own way. Though the need for non-violence was always reiterated, the famous 'Quit India' resolution passed by the Bombay session of the AICC on 8 August 1942 followed up its call for 'mass struggle on non-violent lines on the widest possible scale', 'inevitably' under Gandhi, with the significant rider that if the Congress leadership was removed by arrest, 'every Indian who desires freedom and strives for it must be his own guide...'. 'Let every Indian consider himself to be a free man.... Mere jailgoing would not do', Gandhi declared in his passionate 'Do or die' speech the same day. '...if a general strike becomes a dire necessity, I shall not flinch', was yet another most uncharacteristic remark, made by Gandhi in an interview on 6 August. Gandhi, it may be noted in parenthesis, was prepared for once to counterance political strikes, precisely at a moment when the Communists were bound to keep aloof from them—in very sharp contrast to his attitudes in previous periods of Left-led labour militancy in 1928-29 or the late-1930s and early '40s. The Wardha Working Committee resolution of 14 July had also introduced an unusual note of social radicalism: 'the princes, "jagirdars", "zamindars" and propertied and monied classes derive their wealth and property from the workers in the fields and factories and elsewhere, to whom eventually power and authority must belong.' (Mansergh, Vol. II, p. 388).

The new turn upset all older alignments within the Congress. At the crucial Working Committee session of 27 April–1 May after the collapse of the Cripps Mission, Gandhi's hard-line was backed by a combination of Right-wingers like Patel, Rajendra Prasad and Kripalani and Socialists (Achyut Patwardhan and Narendra Dev), while Nehru found himself in the strange company of the arch-moderates, Rajagopalachari and Bhulabhai Desai. Rajaji from early 1942 had been urging the need for some understanding with the Muslim League through recognition of the right of Muslim majority provinces to secede through plebiscites after independence had been obtained, and—in yet another strange realignment—the Communists took up a somewhat similar stand at the Bombay AICC pleading for a joint front with the League on the basis of the right of secession to any 'more or less homogeneous section' of the population. (Dr K.M. Ashraf and S.G. Sardesai's amendments to the 8 August resolution) Eventually Nehru swallowed his doubts, as so often before, and moved the Quit India resolution, which only the Communist members of the AICC opposed (Bhulabhai and Rajaji had resigned in July).

During and after the Quit India upsurge, the British in documents like Tottenham's *Congress Responsibility for the Disturbances* (February 1943) repeatedly attributed the Congress change of line to secret pro-Axis sympathies. Painting the whole outburst as a deliberate 'fifth-columnist' conspiracy was obviously the best way of winning world anti-fascist opinion or brutal repression of an undoubtedly massive popular rebellion. This smear-campaign deliberately ignored both the consistent anti-fascist international stance of the Congress throughout the 1930s (while the British were selling Spain, Austria and Czechoslovakia to the fascists), as well as numerous reiterations of sympathy for Russia and China and support for the Allied cause in the Allahabad, Wardha and Bombay resolutions of 1 May, 14 July and 8 August. 'I do not want to be the instrument of Russia's defeat nor of China's', Gandhi declared even in his 'Do or die' speech, and, in a private conversation in May (reported in a letter by a Communist to P.C. Joshi, and intercepted by the police), he had clearly stated his disagreement with those who felt that the Japanese could be 'liberators'. 'In fact, I believe that Subhas Bose will have to be resisted by us'. (1-B Note, 26 May, Mansergh, Vol. II, pp. 127–32) Yet there was a real difference (which in the case of the Communists became a chasm after August 1942) between a minority (including Nehru) who found the thought of a world with the Soviet Union destroyed and Hitler and Tojo victorious literally unendurable, and the bulk of the Indian patriots, provoked beyond endurance by British obstinacy and misrule, who considered it wiser to calculate India's national interest in the event of an Allied defeat. Gandhi's original draft for the Allahabad Working

Committee session of April had contained the sentences 'If India were freed her first step would probably be to negotiate with Japan.... India bears no enmity towards Japan'. These passages were omitted at Nehru's insistence. Jawaharlal possibly hit the nail on the head when he argued during the session that 'It is Gandhiji's feeling that Japan and Germany will win. This feeling unconsciously governs his decision.' (*Congress Responsibility for the Disturbances,* Appendix I) We must remember that an Allied defeat seemed very much on the cards in mid-1942, before the tide was turned at Stalingrad.

Yet calculations by Congress leaders can provide only a very partial explanation for the elemental and largely spontaneous popular outburst after the leaders had been removed by arrest in the early morning of 9 August. It needs to be emphasized that even the 'Quit India' resolution was remarkably vague about the details of the coming movement. Far from ruling out further negotiations, the whole thing may conceivably have been an exercise in brinkmanship and a bargaining counter which was followed by an explosion only because the British had decided on a policy of wholesale repression. Despite strenuous efforts, the British failed to establish their case that the Congress before 9 August had really planned violent rebellion. The confidential circular of the Andhra PCC dated 29 July 1942 which was quoted in the Tottenham report, for instance, merely urged Congressmen to 'be ready, organise at once, be alert, but by no means act...till Mahatmaji decides'. The six-stage programme outlined in the circular emphasized mainly traditional Gandhian items like salt, boycott of courts, schools and government services, picketing of foreign cloth and liquor, and no-tax in 'practically the last stage' (together with no-rent, but only 'if the zamindar will not join the movement'). It did talk of 'arranging labour strikes', and mentioned as 'not prohibited but not encourged' the stopping of trains 'by pulling chains only', travelling without tickets, and the cutting of telephone and telegraph wires. Even this somewhat extreme document fell very much short of the massive and violent attack on communications and all symbols of state authority which occurred in many parts of India after 9 August.

The element of British provocation is, therefore, absolutely clear. Right from the outbreak of the war, as we have seen, the bureaucracy had been planning a wholesale crackdown on the Congress on the pattern of 1932, rejecting all compromise efforts and obviously wanting a confrontation. But the British, too, got very much more than they had bargained for: instead of civil disobedience on the 1932 scale, which could be crushed with relative ease there developed from 9 August onwards what Linlithgow privately described on 31 August as 'by far the most serious rebellion since that of 1857, the gravity and extent of which we have so far concealed from the world for reasons of military security.' (telegram to Churchill, Mansergh Vol. II, p. 853) What we have to understand are the deeper factors underlying the new popular mood of August 1942, which Gandhi certainly sensed and reflected incomparably better than the Communists with their theoretically not unjustifiable people's war line.

The rout in South-East Asia following the victory of an Asian power not only shattered white prestige, it also revealed once again the gross racism of the rulers of India. The Europeans in Malaya, Singapore and Burma commandeered all forms of transport in their ignominious flight and left the Indian immigrants there to make their own way by trekking in atrocious conditions through forests and mountains. The resultant was a compound of anti-white fury and an expectation that British rule was ending—the typical popular mood which characterized August 1942. It is probably not accidental that east U.P. and west and north Bihar—the region where the 'August Rebellion' attained its maximum popular intensity—was also traditionally one of the principal catchment areas for Indian migrant labour going to South East Asia and other parts of the world. Azamgarh district, for instance, used to receive ₹30 lakhs annually from foreign money orders. (R.H. Niblett, *Congress Rebellion in Azamgarh,* Allahabad, 1957, p. 2) Evacuees wandering back home after the British had woefully failed to help them, and train loads of wounded soldiers returning from the Burmese front, combined to spread the mood of anger, hostility towards what to the vast majority of Indians was an alien and meaningless war bringing only suffering, and expectation of an apocalyptic end to foreign rule. The majority of British, American and Australian soldiers stationed in India certainly did not behave as idealist crusaders in a 'peoples war'. Cases of racial ill-treatment, particularly of rape multiplied, and the Congress repeatedly protested against molestation of women by foreign soldiers. Meanwhile prices were shooting up (a 60-point rise in foodgrains, for instance, in eastern U.P. between April and August 1942) and there were shortages particularly in rice (where Burmese imports had stopped) and salt. The British, who were running a most efficient war economy at home based on sternly egalitarian rationing, made little serious effort in their colony to check a rampant black-market, and profiteering in food would directly lead to the terrible famine of 1943 in Bengal. The synchronization of rising prices and shortages with the coming of a large number of Allied troops led to not unfounded fears that the food reserves of the country were being depleted to feed the army. Bureaucratic mismanagement of the war reached its climax in the Bengal order to seize all country boats and destroy them. The British in mid-1942 had little confidence in their own ability to defend Bengal and Assam in case of a full-scale Japanese invasion, and were preparing to withdraw to the Chota Nagpur plateau defence line. 'Scorched earth' was being effectively used in Russia, where the Soviets fighting a genuine patriotic peoples' war even blew up the Dnieper dam, their Five Year Plan's pride; the attempt to impose such methods on a subject country by bureaucratic fiat was a colossal blunder and provocation. Even house to house communication required boats in many parts of Bengal during the monsoon—'To deprive people in East Bengal of boats is like cutting off vital limbs.' (Gandhi in *Harijan*, 3 May 1942)

We have seen that there were sections of the Indian people who had benefited from the war in its first phase, particularly industrialists, traders, and businessmen in general profiting from war contracts. Such gains continued throughout the war—the bulk of the contractors and blackmarketeers were after all Indians—but for a brief period in 1942 other considerations seem also to have weighed considerably in the calculations of a significant section of the Indian business community. The Governor of the Central Provinces wrote to Linlithgow on 25 May 1942 that Indian business had been very pro-war two years earlier but 'the losses incurred in Malaya and Burma have stricken the Banias and Marwaris to the soul... a war which yields no profits, in the circumstances of the Excess Profits Tax, and which is accompanied by the sacrifices experienced at Singapore and Rangoon, is not at all to their tastes... It is fairly clear that the capitalist elements in the Congress Working Committee will go to almost any length to safeguard themselves and their property from the ill effects of a possible Japanese invasion.' (Mansergh, Vol. II, pp. 117–19) There has been no research so far on this subject, but it is not impossible that sections of Indian business for a brief while tended to give some covert support to a movement (even if violent) which might quickly push out the British, followed presumably by a separate peace, when faced with the alternative of evacuation and loss of property through scorched earth, bombing, or actual war. Certainly Jamshedpur and Ahmedabad were to be remarkably philosophical about the strikes that crippled both industrial centres during August-September 1942. Once the movement had been defeated, and the Japanese offensive clearly halted on the Assam border, calculations naturally changed, and Indian business happily went back to its more normal pursuits of speculation and profiteering through 'support' to the British war effort.

Detailed studies of the 'August Rebellion, are as yet relatively scanty, as compared to Non-Cooperation or Civil Disobedience. Yet we may attempt a similar arrangement of data, with an analysis of the all-India pattern and social composition followed by regional studies.

The All-India Pattern

The early-morning round-up of Congress leaders on 9 August unleashed an unprecedented and countrywide-wave of mass fury. As in earlier movements, the removal of established leaders left younger and more militant cadres to their own initiative, and gave greater scope to pressures from below. Amery's slander that the Congress had planned attacks on communications and sabotage boomeranged with a vengeance, for many (like K.G. Mashruwalla, for instance, who brought out two very militant issues of *Harijan* after Mahadev Desai had been arrested) believed that this really had been the Working Committee's plan. At a later stage, a number of 'instructions' were issued by various underground groups, all in the name of an AICC the vast majority of whose members were behind bars.

Three broad phases can be distinguished in the Quit India movement. The first, massive and violent but quickly suppressed, was predominantly urban, and included *hartals,* strikes, and clashes with the police and army in most cities. Bombay, as so often before, was the main storm-centre from 9 to 14 August, Calcutta witnessed *hartals* from 10 to 17 August, there were violent clashes with heavy casualties in Delhi, and in Patna control over the city was virtually lost for two days after a famous confrontation in front of the Secretariat on 11 August. The violence in Delhi was 'largely due to millhands on strike' (Linlithgow to Amery, 12 August), and the next day the Viceroy reported strikes in 'Lucknow, Cawnpore, Bombay, Nagpur and Ahmedabad'. (Mansergh, Vol. II, pp. 669, 682–3) The Tata Steel plant was totally closed down for 13 days from 20 August in a strike in which the sole labour slogan was that 'they will not resume work until a national government has been formed'. (Linlithgow to Amery, 21 August, Ibid., pp. 777) At Ahmedabad the textile strike lasted, for three and a half months and a nationalist chronicler later described the city as the 'Stalingrad of India'. (Govind Sahai, *'42 Rebellion,* Delhi, 1947, p. 128) The urban middle class was extremely prominent in this first phase, spearheaded by students.

From about the middle of August, however, the focus shifted to the countryside, with militant students fanning out from centres like Benaras, Patna and Cuttack, destroying communications on a massive scale, and leading a veritable peasant rebellion against white authority strongly reminiscent in some ways of 1857. Northern and western Bihar and eastern U.P., Midnapur in Bengal, and pockets in Maharashtra, Karnatak and Orissa were the major centres of this second phase, which saw the installation of a number of local 'National Governments', which were usually shortlived.

Weakened by brutal repression (no less than 57 army battalions were being used, the Indian Government informed the Secretary of State on

12 September, Mansergh, Vol. II, pp. 952–3), the movement from about the end of September entered its longest but also least formidable phase. This was characterized by terroristic activity by educated youth directed against communications and police and army installations, occasionally rising to the level of guerrilla war (such as the one along the north Bihar-Nepal border, led by Jayaprakash Narain). Part-time peasant squads engaged in farming by day and sabotage activities by right (the so-called 'Karnatak method'), and in some pockets secret parallel 'national governments' functioned, (most notably at Tamluk in Midnapur, Satara in Maharashtra and Talcher in Orissa). Extremely impressive and heroic by any standards, such activities, however, were no longer very much of a threat either to British rule or to the war plans of the Allies. Petty 'national governments' tucked away in a corner of the rather isolated district of Midnapur, for instance, did not seriously bother Calcutta or upset communications with the Arakan and Assam fronts—which is no doubt one reason why the 'Tamluk Jatiya Sarkar' could survive till September 1944.

Official statistics give some indication both of the extent of the upsurge, as well as of the intense repression which was unleashed to crush the movement. By the end of 1943, 91,836 people had been arrested, with the highest figures coming from Bombay Presidency (24,416), U.P. (16,796) and Bihar (16,202). 208 police outposts, 332 railway stations and 945 post offices had been destroyed or severely damaged, and there had been 664 bomb explosions. Bihar headed the list of police stations stormed by mass action (72 out 208), but recorded only 8 bomb incidents as compared to 447 in Bombay—a clear indication of greater popular participation in Bihar and more organized terrorist activity in Bombay. 1060 had been killed by police or army firing (almost certainly a gross underestimate), while 63 policemen had died fighting the upsurge and 216 had defected, no less than 205 of them in Bihar. (*Home Political,* 3/52/1943, quoted in Y.B. Mathur, *Quit India Movement,* Delhi, 1979, pp. 190–92). As for official atrocities, a Congress source listed 74 cases of rape in Tamluk sub-division, including 46 in a single village on 9 January 1943 (Satis Samanta, *et al., August Revolution and Two Years' National Government in Midnapur,* Calcutta, 1946, p. 40). R.H. Niblett, district magistrate of Azamgarh (east U.P.) who was removed for being too mild, has recorded in his fascinating diary numerous instances of a 'quite unnecessary... *terreur blanche'* (white terror), with the British unleashing an 'incendiary police' to 'set fire to villages for several miles'. Niblett speaks of 'bouts of official hysteria, with 'reprisals the rule of the day', and collective fines as a kind of 'official dacoity'. He recalls how he tried in vain to warn his men 'to remember you are neither out on *shikar,* nor on an errand of destruction'. (R.H. Niblett, pp. 26, 40,

44, 49). Free use was made of public flogging, as well as of refined methods of torture like inserting a ruler inside the rectum. Once again, the only real comparison is with 1857—with the difference that the British now commanded all the resources of modern military science, while the people were almost entirely unarmed. As early as 15 August, Linlithgow had ordered the use of 'machine-gunning from air' against crowds disrupting communications around Patna, and aeroplanes were used also in Bhagalpur and Monghyr in Bihar, Nadia and Tamluk in Bengal, and Talcher in Orissa.

Social Composition

A cross-section of the movement in social terms reveals, as we have seen, an early but rather short-lived and limited role of labour. Already by 14 August, Linlithgow was reporting that the 'mill element is dropping out', and Govind Sahai recalls that in Bombay city 'very little part was played by the labour in general and by textile labour in particular... (Mansergh, Vol. II, p. 691; Govind Sahai, p. 89). The Calcutta industrial belt was also largely quiet, and in both places Communist opposition to the movement probably played a considerable role in restraining the workers. Apart from Jamshedpur and Ahmedabad, labour participation remained considerable for several months in smaller centres like Ahmadnagar and Poona, where there had been little Communist activity and Gandhian influence had contributed to 'cordial relations between labour and capital'—'millowners did not resent the absence of their workers'. (Govind Sahai p. 110) Bangalore, where the Congress leader K.T. Bhashyam had been active for years in the trade-union field, saw brief strikes by about 30,000 workers. (James Manor, pp. 136–46). No detailed study has been made so far of the extent of business participation, but this is noted as having been considerable in Bombay by Sahai (p. 88). It is interesting that in December 1942 an illegal Socialist leaflet, *The Freedom Struggle Front,* warned that 'a virginly horror of outraging the class issues', should not 'stand in the way of seeking and taking' the financial help of 'the rich mill-owner or banker'. Stories are current also about considerable covert upper-class and even Indian high official support to secret nationalist activities in 1942. Such support enabled activists (most of whom, unlike the terrorists or the C.P.I., totally lacked underground experience) to set up a fairly effective illegal apparatus, including even a secret radio station under Usha Mehta for three months in Bombay.

Unlike in the Civil Disobedience days, middle class students were very much in the forefront in 1942, whether in urban clashes, as organizers of sabotage, or inspirers of peasant rebellion. What made the August movement so formidable, however, was the massive upsurge of the peasantry in certain areas, leading officials to make curious discoveries like an entire Bihar region (Saran) being 'notoriously a criminal district', or of students finding 'very willing allies in the widespread criminal population of the Bihar villages'. (Bihar Governor Stewart to Linlithgow, 22 August 1942, Mansergh, Vol. II, p. 790). The one available attempt at a statistical analysis of the 'crowd' in the east U.P. west Bihar region (by Max Harcourt, in *Congress and the Raj*), however, indicates that far from being a movement of habitual 'criminals' or rootless 'hooligans', 1942 (like earlier nationalist upsurges) was essentially an upsurge of peasant smallholders. Upper and middle castes predominated in the figures of those arrested (17% Brahman, 27.5% Rajput and Bhumihar—as against 7.4% untouchable and 4.2% tribal in a sample of 1214), while in another sample of 242 there were 36.5% *kisans*, 0.8% *zamindars* and 3.5% agricultural labourers. The samples, unfortunately, are small, the categories vague and ill-defined, and the whole paper rendered somewhat suspect by some startling errors (like describing Niblett's account as one of Ballia instead of Azamgarh); an enormous field of research obviously remains open here.

While 1942 clearly surpassed all previous Congress-led movements in its level of anti-British militancy, the very extent of anti-foreign sentiments, as in 1857, possibly reduced internal class tensions and social radicalism. The *Freedom Struggle Front* rather apologetically argued that 'the class war may have to come, but that is not yet, not till after the riddance of foreign exploitation', and secret instructions issued in the name of the AICC or 'Gandhi Baba' repeatedly confined no-rent only to cases where *zamindars* were loyalists. (*Congress Responsibility for the Disturbances*, Appendices V, VI, VII, VIII and XIII). 'The characteristic feature of this movement was that private property was not attacked' (Govind Sahai, p. 96) and even no-revenue was not as ubiquitous as in 1930–34. 'Strange to say, there was no particular difficulty about getting in the revenues', and 'only two or three instances of records being seized from patwaris and burnt', recalls Niblett about Azamgarh. 'There was only one attack on private property' in the district and that on the estate of an absentee white *zamindar*, while elsewhere 'even seed-stores were not plundered'. (Niblett, pp. 29–31, 17). Niblett's vivid account makes clear that the crowds beseiged *thanas* spurred by the belief that 'Swaraj had now been attained' (Ibid., p. 13); once that faith had been rudely shattered by British repression, the peasant upsurge tended to quickly melt away in the absence of concrete programmes geared to their more immediate needs. Attempts by underground leaders to revive the movement through improved technical methods alone (Jayaprakash's call for a proper revolutionary guerrilla army in his *To All Fighters For Freedom,* or the pamphlet *ABC of Dislocation,* seized by the police at Nasik, could not ultimately change the situation. It is interesting that, as we shall see, 'national governments' proved most long-lived in areas like Tamluk, Talcher or Satara where local circumstances seem to have forced somewhat more concrete and radical socio-economic policies on the militants.

Regional Variations

Regional studies of 1942 are all but non-existent, but a few general points about variations in the extent and nature of the movement may still be attempted. Punjab and even the Congress province of N.W.F.P. were unusually quiet, with only two cases of police firing and about 2500 arrests each. Politics in the Punjab was already set hard in the communal mould, Hindu, Muslim or Sikh, while wartime army employment and rising grain-prices kept quiet a peasantry which had developed a prosperous kulak-type upper stratum. Congress weakness in the N.W.F.P. reflected the continuing trend towards loss of Muslim support. Muslims almost everywhere kept aloof from 1942, though they remained neutral rather than actively hostile or pro-British—there were no major communal incidents during the movement. The movement was relatively weak also in Madras Presidency, except for scattered pockets like Guntur and West Godavari in coastal Andhra and Coimbatore and Ramnad in Tamilnadu. Rajaji's opposition may have been a significant factor in Tamilnadu, while Communist hostility helped to keep the agitation at a low key in Kerala. Despite appeals to states people by underground Congress and socialist leaders (like for instance in the *AICC's Twelve-Point Programme—Congress Responsibility for the Disturbances,* Appendix V), the movement in the princely states generally fell well below the intensity attained in 1938–39. Among the big states, only Mysore was seriously affected, the agitation here following the same three-stage pattern already noted at the all-Indian level: urban demonstrations and strikes in Bangalore, village movements (particularly in Hassan and Shimoga districts), and sabotage activities by secret student groups.

The four main storm-centres of Bihar-east U.P., Midnapur, Orissa, and Maharashtra-Karnataka present a totally different picture of really formidable mass rebellion. Both intensity and extent were greatest in Bihar—the province which in the 1930s had become the principal base of the Kisan Sabha, and where the bulk of the Kisan Sabha cadres had swung to the side of the socialists despite the new pro-war stance of the Communists and of Sahajanand. Patna for a time was cut off from all districts except Gaya save by air, and nearly 80% of police stations were captured or had to be temporarily evacuated in the ten districts of north and central Bihar. There was considerable tribal participation too, for a Congress source estimated the number of killed to be highest in Hazaribag district (533 out of 1761, followed by Saran—517 and Bhagalpur—447, Govind Sahai, p. 135). The tide of rebellion quickly swept from Bhojpuri-speaking west Bihar into the economically and culturally similar Benares division of U.P. All ten police stations were captured in Ballia, and brief national governments were set up both here (under the local Congress leader Chitu Pandey) and in neighbouring Ghazipur. Niblatt has left a fascinating description of the seige of Madhuban police sitation in Azamgarh on 15–17 August—crowds of 5000 marching on the '*thana* with *lathis* and spears, but also with 'plough-shares, hammers, saws and spades...in the distance their lathis and spears looked like a *sarpat* jungle on the move'. A veritable levy *en masse* of the rural population, in fact, though two *zamindars* secretly provided supplies to the beleaguered garrison (Niblett, pp. 13–18). It took several weeks and a really massive use of army and police to restore order and normal communications in the 16 seriously-affected districts of eastern U.P. and Bihar, and even then sporadic guerrilla activities went on till 1944, with a number of local parallel governments loosely connected with the Nepal frontier-based provisional government of Jaiprakash Narayan and Rammanohar Lohia.

The best available account of a rebel 'national government' comes from Tamluk sub-division of Midnapur, the chroniclers being local Congress leaders like Satis Samanta, the first *Sarbadhinayak* of the Tamluk Jatiya Sarkar. Tamluk and the neighbouring sub-division of Contai were old Gandhian bases, with a tradition of sustained constructive work. As compared to Bihar and east U.P., 1942 here was less elemental and violent, but perhaps better organized and sustained, and special circumstances (the need to resist the British 'denial' or scorched earth policy of destroying boats and bicycles and to provide relief after the terrible cyclone of 16 October 1942, followed in the next year by famine) forced a somewhat more radical economic policy. The Congress from mid-1942 had campaigned on the slogans of resistance to the denial policy and stopping grain exports from the region, and the first clash in Tamluk sub-division occurred on 8 September when villagers on their own blocked export of rice by a millowner at Danipur, and then sought the help of nationalist volunteers. On 29 September, a well-planned simultaneous attack was launched on communications and police stations in Tamluk, Mahishadal, Sutahata, and Nandigram (as well as Bhagabanpur in Contai), with massive crowds marching on the *thanas*. Sutahata *thana* was actually captured, but elsewhere there was a blood-bath, with 44 being killed on a single day— including Matangini Hazra, a 73-year-old poor peasant widow in Tamluk, who kept the national flag aloft even after being shot. Two weeks later a cyclone destroyed 50% of the crops and nearly 70,000 heads of cattle and killed about 4000 in Tamluk sub-division. In the absence (quite probably deliberate) of adequate official relief, Congress volunteers had to switch over to large-scale self-help measures, and this became a major function of the underground Tamralipta Jatiya Sarkar set up on 17 December 1942 with subordinate branches later on in Sutahata, Nandigram and Mahishadal. The Jatiya Sarkar, which lasted till September 1944, controlled an armed Vidyut Vahini, ran a hierarchy of arbitration courts which claim to have settled 1681 cases, provided grants to schools, organized relief amounting to ₹79,000, and—most interesting of all—tried to distribute the 'surplus paddy of the well-to-do...among the needy villagers.... The rich hoarders and profiteers were served with notices by the Jatiya Sarkar to stop exploitation and they were made to pay fair sums of money and paddy which were distributed among the distressed people'. (Satis Samanta, et. al., *August Revolution and Two Years' National Government in Midnapur,* Calcutta, 1946, pp. 32, 39).

In Balasore district of Orissa, bordering on Midnapur, the Congress organized plunder of salt depots, disruption of communications and village *swaraj panchayats* to hold on to food stocks. 35 were killed in a mass attack on Eram-Basudevpur police station on 28 September, and a national government functioned for some time in the Gurpal region. The official enquiry report on the Eram-Basudevpur firing alleged that the rumour had spread that 'Swaraj would be attained within a week...and that under a Swaraj Government no taxes would be paid and the paddy of the rich would be available to the poor.' Cuttack was another storm-centre, though here terrorist activity organized by a local *Rakta Vahini* soon became more important than mass action. Koraput with its large tribal population witnessed a massive upsurge, including no-rent movements against the Jeypore *zamindari,* invasion of reserved forests, and attacks on *thanas.* Leadership came from an illiterate villager, Lakshman Naik, who was hanged on 16 November for allegedly murdering a forest guard. (H. Mahtab, et. al., *History of Freedom Movement in Orissa,* Vol. IV, Cuttack, 1957–59, pp. 88–94, 68) In Talcher state, guerrilla activities continued till May 1943, with a *chasi-maulia* (peasant-labour) *raj* controlling nearly 400 square miles and staging an attack on Talcher town on 7 September 1942 which could be beaten back only with the help of aeroplanes. The immediate cause of the popular upsurge in Talcher, which had already witnessed a massive struggle against forced labour (*bethi*), forest laws and autocratic rule in September 1938, was a rumour that Pobitramohan Pradhan, President of the State Prajamandal, had been murdered. (Govind Sahai, pp. 420–2; *All India States Peoples Conference Papers,* File No. 164)

After the initial urban upsurge had been suppressed, the movement in Bombay Presidency took on two distinct forms: peasant guerrilla war in a few pockets, and more widespread terroristic activity and sabotage, carried on mainly by educated cadres, though obviously enjoying very great popular support. The main centres of peasant rebellion were east Khandesh and Satara in Maharashtra and Jambusar *taluk* in Broach district of Gujarat. That the Satara and Jambusar movements had some socially radical possibilities is indicated by the embarrassed comments made by the Congress historian Govind Sahai: in Satara 'criminal elements of the district took advantage' of the rebellion headed by Nana Patil, and both here and in Jambusar there were numerous 'dacoities' with a local 'bandit', Megzi, helping the Jambusar movement to set up a kind of liberated area for three months. (Sahai, pp. 118, 133) A recent detailed study by Gail Omvedt of the Satara *Prati sarkar* based on interviews of participants brings out a number of distinctive features. The Satara movement was closely related to the peasant-based non-Brahman *bahiajan samaj* tradition which had been very strong in this region. The parallel government developed rather late, from mid-1943, and maintained some kind of existence till as late as 1945–46. Its activities included the running of people's courts (*nyayadan mandals*) and constructive work along Gandhian lines apart from carrying on a guerrilla war. As elsewhere in 1942, nationalist militancy probably blunted to some extent the edge of social radicalism, for though in a few cases mortgaged land was returned to poor peasants and rape and exploitation of women by village big-wigs were severely punished activists recall that 'we did not touch property relations.' It is interesting also that the *prati sarkar* took effective measures against local dacoits possibly reflecting the needs of a propertied, though still oppressed peasantry as against lower-class social bandits who had been well established in the hilly parts of Satara. One may recall that in the French Revolution, too, peasant mobilization in 1789 had directed itself simultaneously against the rumoured 'aristocratic plot' and the 'brigands'. (G. Lefebvre, *The Great Fear of 1789*) Elsewhere in the Presidency, the Socialists organized an effective terroristic underground, controlled from Bombay city by leaders like Aruna Asaf Ali. 'Dislocation' activities in Karnatak included 1600 attacks on telegraphs lines, and raids on 26 railway stations and 32 post offices. But 'there was no no-tax campaign this time' (Govind Sahai, p. 96), and no-revenue did not figure even in Kheda and Bardoli, which saw a certain amount of terrorist activity by young men coming from superior Patidar families. 'The fervour of the lesser Patidars', Hardiman has argued, 'had been sapped by the return to prosperity': remittances from emigrants in East Africa, increase in tobacco cultivation, the war boom in agricultural prices, combined with the fact that there had been no revenue enhancement after 1928. (*Congress and the Raj*, p. 70) In general, one may hazard the tentative hypothesis that regions marked by some amount of agricultural progress and the emergence of a prosperous and broad rich peasant upper stratum tended to keep away from the 1942 rebellion: Punjab, western U.P., Gujarat, the Thanjavur delta in Tamilnadu. The main centres of peasant rebellion in contrast were in eastern India, where Blyn's figures show per capita agricultural production to have stagnated or even declined. The 'dominant peasants' about whom much is being heard in some recent historiography (cf. Low's introduction in *Congress and the Raj*) probably in the end benefited the most from Congress nationalism, but—as in the somewhat analogous case of business groups— the bulk of the participants generally came from lower down the social and economic scale.

Aftermath of Revolt

By the end of 1942, the British had definitely come out victorious in their immediate total confrontation with Indian nationalism, and the remaining two and a half years of the war passed without any serious political challenge from within the country. Yet the 'victory' was ambiguous and with severe limits, and had been possible only because war conditions had allowed really ruthless use of force. The British would never again risk such a confrontation, and that the decision in 1945 to try for a negotiated settlement was not just a gift of the new Labour government is indicated by the attitude of Wavell, the by no means ultra-liberal army commander who became Viceroy in October 1943. In a letter to Churchill dated 24 October 1944, Wavell pointed out that it would be impossible to hold India by force after the war, given the likely state of world opinion and British popular or even army attitudes (as well as the economic exhaustion of Britain, he might have added). 'We have had to negotiate with similar rebels before, e.g., De Valera and Zaghlul, and it would in fact be wise to start negotiations before the end of the war brought a release of prisoners and unrest due to demobilization and unemployment, creating 'a fertile field for agitation, unless we have previously diverted their (Congress) energies into some more profitable channel, i.e., into dealing with the administrative problems of India and into trying to solve the constitutional problem.' (Wavell, *The Viceroy's Journal,* Oxford, 1973, pp. 97–8) Churchill's pig-headedness delayed the process somewhat, but this was precisely what the British were able to persuade the Congress leadership to do after 1945.

From the point of view of the Congress leaders, imprisonment and defeat paradoxically brought certain benefits. Isolation in jail helped them to avoid taking a clear public stand on the pro-or anti-Japanese war issue—something which otherwise would have become very ticklish indeed for a few months in 1944 when Subhas Bose's Indian National Army appeared on the borders of Assam at a time when on a world scale the Allies were clearly winning the war. Much more important was the fact that, as D.D. Kosambi pointed out in a brilliant piece of contemporaneous history-writing in 1946, 'the glamour of jail and concentration camp served to wipe out the so-so record of the Congress ministries in office, thereby restoring the full popularity of the organisation among the masses.' ('The Bourgeoisie Comes of Age in India, reprinted in Kosambi, *Exasperating Essays,* Poona, n.d., p. 17) Rightist Congress leaders who throughout the late-1930s had urged more and more cooperation with the British and pursued increasingly conservative policies as ministers could now bask in the halo of patriotic self-sacrifice, as much as the Socialists who had done most of the actual fighting in 1942—while the Communist critics of both were branded in the eyes of a big section of nationalist public opinion as collaborators and traitors.

If the British ultimately came to realize the wisdom of a negotiated transfer of power from the Quit India experience, the 1942 rebellion and its aftermath thus also strengthened forces preferring a compromise on the nationalist side by giving a new prestige to the Congress Right. The Left alternative was in fact weakened in two ways through a struggle which, however, heroic and natural, was also perhaps untimely and doomed to failure, given the British control of massive military resources in 1942. Brutal repression must have exhausted many peasant bases, built up through years of Gandhian constructive work or radical Kisan Sabha activity. It is significant that Bihar, eastern U.P., and the Maharashtra, Karnataka and Orissa countryside played little or no part in the anti-imperialist upsurge of 1945–46, while most of the rural Gandhians of Midnapur and Hooghly found themselves largely pushed aside in the Bengal Congress politics of the post-war and post-independence years. In the second place, the Left was now divided as never before. The searing memory of 1942, with its charges and counter-charges of 'treachery' and 'fifth-columnist' activity, erected a wall between the Socialists and followers of Bose on the one side, and the Communists on the other, which has not been entirely overcome even after a generation.

The War and the Indian Economy: Famine and Super-Profits

The economic impact of the war on the whole aggravated this exhaustion of popular forces, even though it also led to acute discontent and occasional and sporadic near-revolutionary outbursts in 1945–47. Though India was spared actual military devastation (apart from the Kohima-Imphal border area in 1944 and occasional air-raids), mass suffering was none the less acute, for war meant rampant inflation (with notes in circulation shooting up from ₹2300 million in 1939 to ₹12,100 million in 1945), widespread corruption, shortages and blackmarket prices, and eventually a devastating famine in 1943. The food crisis was caused fundamentally by stoppage of rice imports from Burma and South-East Asia coinciding with the need to feed a vastly enlarged army, but it was greatly aggravated by gross mismanagement and deliberate profiteering. Rationing measures were extremely belated and confined to a few big cities, and even Wavell complained bitterly in private of London's indifference towards Indian food problems, and spoke of the 'very different attitude towards feeding a starving population when the starvation is in Europe' (referring to the ample supplies sent to Holland in early 1945, *Viceroy's Journal,* entry for 9 April 1945, p. 123). In the terrible summer and autumn of 1943, lakhs trekked to Calcutta to starve to death on its streets, begging no longer for rice, but just for the water in which it had been cooked. Between one and a half to three million perished in Bengal in a basically man-made famine. As starvation and malnutrition led to major epidemics of malaria, cholera, and small-pox, Bengal returned mortality figures considerably higher than normal for years after 1943. Direct British rule had begun with a famine in 1770; it was now drawing to a close with a comparable calamity. The worst-affected areas were the Tamluk-Contai-Diamond Harbour region of south-west Bengal, and the districts of Dacca, Faridpur, Tippera and Noakhali. Bengal's small-peasant economy suffered a shattering blow, with 600,000 tenants losing their holdings during 1943, and cattle wealth going down by 20% in a single year. Agricultural labourers, not unexpectedly, were the worst sufferers; in a survey of five Faridpur villages in 1944, 40.3% were found to have been 'wiped off' as against an aggregate morality of 15.2%). (A.K. Sen, 'Famine Mortality: A Study of the Bengal Famine of 1943, in Hobsbawm *et. al. Peasants in History*)

Yet war and famine also meant super profits for some, and as in 1914–18, a major step forward for the Indian bourgeoisie. Indo-British economic relations were significantly modified, with the U.S.A. displacing Britain by 1944–45 as the biggest source of India's imports, and with India's sterling debts being liquidated through British purchase of them to pay for war supplies from the country. By 1945, India had accumulated a sterling balance of more than £1000 million, and while these signified immediately no more than promissory notes issued in return for a vast wartime transfer of Indian material resources, they would also boost free India's foreign exchange reserves after Independence. One traditional item in the 'drain of wealth'—debt charges—thus finally disappeared. In the second place, war demand and enforced import-substitution led to advances in textiles, iron and steel, cement and paper, and some entry into engineering and chemicals, though the British still obstructed the development of indigenous shipping, automobile and aircraft production. Industrial growth remained fairly slow, however, gross production rising to only 120 in 1945 if 1937 is taken as base-year (though steel rose to 142.9, chemicals to 134.1 and cement to 196.5: Wadia and Merchant, p. 360).

The really fantastic increase was not in production but in profits, particularly speculative gains through profiteering in food, share-market operations and the black market in general. The Indian bourgeoisie was a specific kind of bourgeoisie, characterized by 'ravening greed' and a mania for speculation rather than initiative or efficiency in developing production (Kosambi, p. 14). Technological backwardness made it look for foreign collaboration, now that the changed economic and political position promised to give it additional leverage in conducting negotiations on somewhat less unequal terms. In the summer of 1945, Birla and Tata led an Indian business delegation to Britain and the U.S.A., and agreements were concluded during that year between Birla and Nuffield (setting up Hindustan Motors) and Tata and Imperial Chemicals. At the same time, bourgeois leaders were quite willing to accept or even urge Indian state investment in sectors like heavy industries, power, irrigation, etc., where initial profits were bound to be low, even while haggling over specific types of state intervention and complaining about neglect or too much controls. The 'Bombay Plan' of January 1944 drawn up by India's leading businessmen (including J.R.D. Tata, G.D. Birla, P. Thakurdas, Shri Ram, and Kasturbhai Lalbhai) visualized a doubling of the per capita national income in fifteen years through quick development of basic industries. While little more than a statement of objectives and vague on questions of distribution and degree of state control, the Bombay Plan was prepared to accept a 'temporary eclipse' in 'freedom of enterprise' in the interests of development, and made a number of surprisingly warm references even to the 'Russian experiment'. To quote Kosambi's contemporary analysis again, the bourgeoisie 'needs Nehru's leadership', just as in previous periods of mass struggle it had been intelligent enough 'to exploit for its own purposes whatever is profitable in the Mahatma's teachings and to reduce all dangerous enunciations to negative philosophical points'. (Ibid., p. 18)

As a class which had never had it so good amidst unprecedented mass misery, the bourgeoisie was naturally averse to any further round of popular struggle which could have unmanageably radical consequences, and its formidable influence was cast firmly on the side of a negotiated compromise settlement after 1945. The events of 1945–47, however, tragically proved that in the context of India the price of a negotiated 'transfer of power' was an encouragement of divisive forces culminating in Partition. A 'bloodless' winning of independence would be accompanied by an unimaginably bloody communal carnage.

The Advance of the League

The rapid advance of the Muslim League, which took full advantage of the suppression of the Congress, was in fact the most striking political development of the closing years of the war. By 1943, League ministries had been installed in Assam (August 1942), Sind (October 1942), Bengal (March 1943) and N.W.F.P. (May 1943), the League central leadership was asserting a tight control over provincial units and building up a volunteer corps (the National Guards), and Jinnah himself was well on the way toward establishing his claim to be sole spokesman of Muslims with the right to be treated on equal terms with the 'Hindu' Congress under Gandhi. The British role in facilitating this advance is fairly clear. The ministries of Saadullah in Assam and Aurangzeb Khan in the N.W.F.P. were made possible only because most Congress M.L.As were in jail. Allah Baksh, the pro-Congress Muslim premier of Sind, was dismissed by the Governor for renouncing his official honours, while in Bengal European M.L.As. propped up the Nazimuddin ministry. The two biggest Muslim-majority provinces, Punjab and Bengal, still gave Jinnah a lot of trouble, but the League central leadership in March 1943 was able to oust Fazlul Huq (who had become increasingly critical of Jinnah, and had formed on unexpected coalition in December 1941 with the Hindu Mahasabha leader Shyamaprasad Mukherji) with the help of the financial power of the Ispahanis, a Calcutta-based Muslim business family with all-India connections. The process of making Bengal Muslim politicians toe the all-India League line was not too dissimilar from that manifested earlier within the Congress, when Bose had been pushed out by a High Command which had close connections with Calcutta Marwaris like Birla. Jinnah's entry into the Punjab was helped by the death of Sikandar Hayat Khan in December 1942, though his weaker successor, Khizr Hayat Khan, was still resisting League pressures to break up the Muslim-Jat Unionist coalition in 1945.

Much more was involved in the League advance, however, than mere assembly intrigues and official patronage. The Pakistan slogan was catching on among rapidly increasing sections of Indian Muslims for a variety of reasons. To Muslim peasants of Bengal and Punjab, Pakistan was being presented as the end of Hindu *zamindar* and *bania* exploitation, and Abul Hashem, the dynamic secretary of the Bengal Muslim League from November 1943, did his best to cultivate a radical image for his party, promising abolition of rent-receiving interests in a manifesto issued in 1944. Of greater significance, perhaps, was the fact that Pakistan promised 'the hedging off of a part of India from competition by the established Hindu business groups or professional classes so that the small Muslim business class could thrive and the nascent Muslim intelligentsia could find employment.' (Amiya Bagchi, pp. 432–33) Such a prospect appealed particularly to Muslim professional groups and politicians in provinces like U.P. and Bombay where Muslims were a small minority; it was less attractive in Punjab and Bengal, where Pakistan could very well imply (and ultimately did result in) the disruption of well-established ties of regional unity and loss of valuable areas like Amritsar and Calcutta. It needs to be emphasized that the economic muscle behind Muslim separatism no longer came only from old-fashioned *talukdars* and *zamindars* as in the days of the Aligarh movement or of Nawab Salimulla of Dacca. The Ispahani and Adamjee business families financed the League press (the Calcutta evening newspaper *Star of India*, and the Delhi daily *Dawn* started in 1942), a Federation of Muslim Chambers of Commerce and Industry was started with Jinnah's blessings in April 1945 and Muslim banks and an airline company were planned soon after the war. The Indian bourgeoisie had never been immune from communal tensions (Hindu businessmen, for instance, were mostly extremely orthodox and had often had strong revivalist, cow-protectionist, and Mahasabha links), and there was no doubt that really big Muslim capitalists were relatively few in number. In west Punjab, big industries hardly existed before 1947, but a number of small entrepreneurs were coming up, connected with the flourishing agriculture of the region. Partition for such people did provide a major economic boon by insulating them from competition with established Indian large business houses.

Azad Hind

As the massive, though ultimately frustrated, anti-imperialist upsurge of the immediate post-war years was to reveal, exhaustion of popular energies and tendencies towards compromise and division did not make up the total picture of post-1942 India. The major inspiration for carrying on a relentless struggle against Britain came from Subhas Bose's adventures abroad. Bose had set up an Indian Legion in Berlin in 1941, but developed difficulties with the Germans when they tried to use it against Russia, and decided to go to South East Asia. He reached Japanese-controlled Singapore by submarine from

Germany in July 1943, issued from there his famous call, 'Delhi Chalo', and announced the formation of the Azad Hind Government and the Indian National Army on 21 October 1943. The link with the old revolutionary—terrorist tradition was emphasized by giving a post of honour in the government to Rashbehari Bose, who had been living in exile in Japan since 1915, while, despite all his quarrels with Gandhi, Subhas did not forget to ask for the blessings of the 'Father of the Nation' while starting his enterprise. Indian prisoners of war in Japanese camps provided a ready recruiting ground for the I.N.A., which was able to rally about 20,000 out of the 60,000 POWs, and financial aid and volunteers came from Indian trading communities settled in South East Asia. The I.N.A. was demonstratively non-communal, with Muslims quite prominent among its officers and ranks, and it also introduced the innovation of a women's detachment named after the Rani of Jhansi. Between March and June 1944, the I.N.A. was in action on Indian soil, besieging Imphal along with Japanese troops in a campaign which ended in total failure. The Japanese collapse in the next year made the I.N.A. men prisoners again, while Bose mysteriously disappeared, allegedly killed in an air-crash which some still believe to have been faked.

In assessing the significance of the last phase of Subhas Bose's career, it is important to distinguish between immediate achievement and ultimate (and mainly psychological) impact. The I.N.A. never amounted to very much in sheer military terms, and even if it had been far more effective, it obviously came too late, for everywhere the Axis powers were in retreat by 1944. The Forward Bloc underground in India, which might have backed up the Imphal-Kohima invasion, had been crushed even earlier (Secretary of State's memorandum on the Forward Bloc, 30 August 1945, Mansergh, Vol. VI, pp. 183–88) Yet we must not underestimate the impact on the patriotic imagination of an actual army fighting, however ineffectively, for the country's liberation, led by a Bengali—the least 'martial' of India's 'races' in traditional British stereotype. In November 1945, a British move to put the I.N.A. men on trial immediately sparked off massive demonstrations all over the country. Even more significant was the probable link between the I.N.A. experience and the wave of disaffection in the British Indian army during the winter of 1945–46, which culminated in the great Bombay naval strike of February 1946 and was quite possibly the single most decisive reason behind the British decision to make a quick withdrawal.

Communists and People's War

The other major factor behind the post-war anti-imperialist upsurge lay, paradoxically enough, in the organizational advance of the Communists—the most bitter opponents of Bose and his followers during 1942–45. The 'People's War' line had certainly isolated and discredited the C.P.I. very gravely, and they had added to their own troubles by adopting in August-September 1942 the curious 'Adhikari thesis' on 'Pakistan and National Unity'. This began with a not unreasonable emphasis on India as a multi-lingual and therefore multi-national country (consequently necessitating, as in the Soviet Union, the recognition of a right of secession which would permit genuinely democratic and voluntary federation), but then made a sudden jump to the peculiar concept of 'Muslim nationalities such as Sindhis, Baluchis, Punjabis (Muslims), Pathans', etc., and ended by asserting that the Muslim League leadership was now 'playing an oppositional role *vis-a-vis* imperialism in a way somewhat analogous to the leadership of the Indian National Congress itself (G. Adhikari, 'National Unity Now !' *Peoples Age,* 8 August 1942). The Communists consequently for a few years tried to discover 'Progressives' within the League (like Abul Hashem, for instance), pleaded repeatedly for an agreement between Gandhi and Jinnah, and came perilously near to accepting the Pakistan demand in what was perhaps an opportunistic bid to draw close to the other big national force now that relations with the Congress were so strained. In fairness, however, it should be added, as it very seldom is, that there were other individuals and groups in 1942 who appeared quite as 'unpatriotic' as the Communists. Rajagopalachari, the leading Gandhian and Congress Right-winger in the south, opposed Quit India and pleaded for negotiations on the Pakistan demand. Golwalkar's R.S.S. kept strictly aloof from the August rebellion, Savarkar on 4 September 1942 urged Hindu Mahasabha members of local bodies, legislatures and services to 'stick to their posts and continue to perform their regular duties', and Shyamaprasad Mukherji was actually a Bengal minister while Midnapur was being ruthlessly suppressed. Recently published documents clearly reveal that many officials deeply distrusted the sudden Communist offer of support, and particularly their requests for anti-Japanese guerrilla training: 'on the surface they are anti-Fascist and pro-War; below the surface they are anti-Imperial and their demand for arms may have as much relation to one as to the other of these lines of thought...' (Bihar Governor Stewart to Linlithgow, 6 May 1942, Mansergh, Vol. II, p. 46) M.N. Roy, in contrast, did receive government subsidies for his Indian Federation of Labour—a break-away from the now fully Communist-controlled AITUC—though not the seat in the Viceroy's Executive which he asked of Wavell. (*Viceroy's Journal,* 14 February 1944, p. 55)

Despite evident mistakes (even grotesque ones like calling Subhas a Quisling) and considerable unpopularity, the post-1942 years were by no means a totally negative experience in the history of the Indian Communist movement. Legalization (in July 1942) brought obvious organizational advantages, for Communists had been persecuted by the British right from the formation of their first groups in the early 1920s, and the Party had been illegal since 1934. Membership, only 4000 in 1942, shot up to 15,000 in May 1943, 53,000 in mid-1946, and over 100,000 at the time of the Second Party Congress in February 1948, while the AITUC doubled its strength, from two and a half to five lakhs between 1942 and 1944 (R.P. Dutt, *India Today,* p. 353). Isolation bred a sense of militancy, self-sacrifice, and idealism among cadres, and the Bengal unit in particular rehabilitated itself after 1942 through efficient and extremely dedicated famine relief work. The slogan of anti-fascist People's War, however incomprehensible to the masses (and particularly the peasants), did have a real appeal among intellectuals aware of world currents, and it was in these years that Marxism acquired a significant influence ovei the cultural life of middle-class Calcutta. The Party Secretary, P.C. Joshi, pioneered imaginative ways of utilizing folk media and cultural forms, and a striking achievement of 1944–45 was the Indian Peoples Theatre Association, with a central squad raising funds for starving Bengal through country wide tours. The IPTA and other cultural fronts were able to attract a veritable galaxy of talent: Balraj Sahani, Khwaja Ahmad Abbas, Kaifi Azmi, Salil Chaudhuri, Sambhu Mitra, Debabrata Biswas, Suchitra Mukherji, Sukanta Bhattacharji, to name only a few. In Bengal, Jyotirindra Maitra's *Nabajivaner Gan* and Bijon Bhattacharji's play *Nabanna* marked major cultural departures, while important literary figures like the novelist Manik Bandopadhyay or the poets Bishnu De, Samar Sen and Subhas Mukherji came close to or actually joined the Communist Party.

In the country-side, too, Kisan Sabha and share-cropper or agricultural labourer organizations advanced in areas where the bitter legacy of 1942 was not so evident: in Kerala, coastal Andhra and Telengana, north Bengal, as well as some pockets in Punjab, Maharashtra and Tamilnadu. By the end of the war, the C.P.I. with some justice could claim to be the third biggest party in the country, though obviously still incomparably weaker than the Congress or the League.

CHAPTER 8

FREEDOM AND PARTITION: 1945–1947

Two basic strands emerge from the maze of events during the last two years of British rule: tortuous negotiations between British, Congress and League statesmen, increasingly accompanied by communal violence, and culminating in a freedom which was also a tragic partition; and sporadic, localized, but often extremely militant and united mass actions—the I.N.A. release movement and the R.I.N. Mutiny in 1945–46, numerous strikes throughout the period, and, in 1946–47, the *Tebhaga* upsurge in Bengal, Punnapra-Vayalar in Travancore and the Telengana peasant armed revolt in Hyderabad. A mass of historical literature exists on the first theme, along with some collections of documents: the books of V.P. Menon, Campbell Johnson, H.V. Hodson, Penderel Moon, Wavell's Journal, Mansergh's volumes, Pyarelal's detailed study of Gandhi's last years, Sardar Patel's correspondence from 1945—to mention only the leading works. On popular movements, in very sharp contrast, there are some useful accounts by participants but hardly any systematic historical research so far. Yet, as always throughout the history of modern India, the decisions and actions of leaders, British or Indian, cannot really be understood without the counterpoint provided by pressures from below. Popular action, above all, made continuance of British rule untenable; fear of popular 'excesses' made Congress leaders cling to the path of negotiation and compromise, and eventually even accept Partition as a necessary price; and the limits of popular anti-imperialist movements made the truncated settlement of August 1947 possible.

1945–1946: 'THE EDGE OF A VOLCANO'

Prelude to Negotiations

The prelude to post-war negotiations was staged during the last months of the War, with occasional British efforts to obtain Congress and League participation in the existing structure of central government, as well as some abortive talks between Gandhi and Jinnah on the Pakistan issue. Tentatively in September 1943, even before assuming office, and more definitively after Gandhi had been released on 5 May 1944 on grounds of ill-health, Wavell urged the need to set up 'a provisional political government' at the centre based on a Congress-League coalition, to ensure fuller Indian cooperation in the war effort and, much more important, the diversion of Indian energies 'into some more profitable channel' than agitations (cf. his letter to Churchill, 24 October 1944, already cited on p. 345). As correspondence between Gandhi and Wavell quickly confirmed in July-August 1944, the Viceroy's offer fell very much short of the minimum Congress demands of a 'genuine national government' responsible to the Assembly, with only war operations temporarily under British control, and an immediate and unambiguous, promise of post-war independence. In any case, Wavell's proposals, like Cripps' in 1942, would almost certainly have been torpedoed at some stage by Churchill if they had shown signs of achieving anything. Churchill on 5 July 1944 sent 'a peevish telegram to ask why Gandhi had not died yet', displayed repeatedly what Amery in private called a 'Hitler-like attitude' on Indian matters and in March 1945 told Wavell that the problem should 'be kept on ice' for as long as possible. 'He seems to favour partition into Pakistan, Hindustan; Princestan, etc...' (*Viceroy's Journal*, pp. 78, 89, 120).

In July 1944, Gandhi braved bitter Hindu Mahasabha opposition and proposed talks with Jinnah on the basis of the 'Rajagopalachari formula' enunciated the previous April: a post-war commission to demarcate contiguous districts in N.W. and N.E. India where Muslims had an absolute majority; plebiscite of all inhabitants in such areas to decide whether they would prefer a separate Pakistan, mutual agreement in case of separation to run certain essential common services like defence or communications; and implementation of the whole scheme only after full transfer of power by the British (with the League endorsing the Congress demand for Independence and cooperating with it in forming an interim government in the transition period). Jinnah on 30 July, however, reiterated the demand for the separation of the whole of six provinces (Punjab, Sind, Baluchistan, N.W.F.P., Bengal and Assam), subject to minor adjustments, and attacked the formula as offering only 'a shadow and a husk, a maimed, mutilated and moth-eaten Pakistan'. He also argued that separation could not be deferred till after Independence, considered common services to be unnecessary, and felt that plebiscites with both Muslims and Hindus voting contradicted the basic principle of Muslims being a distinct nation with an inherent right of self-determination. The Gandhi-Jinnah talks of September 1944 consequently broke down, but this did not prevent growing cooperation between the League and Congress Central Assembly parties, and the spread of strong rumours (later repudiated by Jinnah) in January 1945 of an agreement between the two Assembly leaders, Bhulabhai Desai and Liaquat Ali Khan, by which the Congress and the League would form coalitions in the Centre and the province under the existing constitution as a war-time measure. The League position, it must be remembered, had become rather weak in early 1945. With the release of Congress M.L.A.s, the League ministry in N.W.F.P. was replaced by a Congress one under Dr Khan Saheb, Khizar Hayat Khan's Punjab Unionists had openly broken with Jinnah in mid-1944, and the Nazimuddin ministry in Bengal fell in March 1945, to be succeeded by Governor's rule; even the League ministries in Sind and Assam existed precariously on Congress sufferance. So far (till August 1946, in fact), there was little evidence also that the League would be able to organize real mass sanctions behind its Pakistan demand. Mass action had never been the League's *forte,* and the oft repeated slogan, *larke lenge Pakistan,* (we will fight and take Pakistan) still seemed largely verbal.

Simla Conference

With British elections just a month ahead, Churchill in June 1945 at last permitted Wavell to start negotiations with Indian leaders. On 14 June, Wavell ordered the release of all Congress Working Committee members, and proposed talks to set up a new Executive Council which would be entirely Indian except for the Viceroy himself and the Commander-in-Chief. 'Caste Hindus' and Muslims would have equal representation, the Executive would work within the existing constitution (i.e., it would not be responsible to the Central Assembly), but the door would be kept open for discussions on a new Constitution once the War had been finally won. At the Simla Conference (25 June–14 July 1945), the Congress naturally objected to what it felt was an attempt to reduce it to the status of a purely 'caste Hindu' party, and insisted on its right to include members of all communities among its nominees for the Executive. But the Conference really broke down due to Jinnah's intransigent demands that the League had an absolute right to choose all the Muslim members and that there should be a kind of communal veto in the Executive, with decisions opposed by Muslims needing a two-third majority. Given the existing political situation, the first demand was quite fantastic, for even apart from Congress claims (its Simla delegation, incidentally, was headed by Maulana Azad), the British had no intention of sacrificing the Unionists, who still controlled the Punjab government and had been in addition consistently loyalist and much less troublesome than the League. Yet by dissolving the conference in face of these two demands of the League, Wavell in effect gave Jinnah the veto he was asking for, as no attempt was made to call the League's bluff and go ahead with forming an Executive excluding it if necessary.

The massive Labour victory of July 1945 swept into power politicians associated with the Filkins talks with Nehru of 1938, as well as with the

Cripps offer of 1942. Wavell initially expressed some nervousness: the majority was 'too big', Labour might try to hand over 'India to their Congress friends as soon as possible', and it might become necessary for the Viceroy to shift from the 'accelerator' to the 'brake pedal...gently but firmly'. (*Viceroy's Journal,* pp. 159, 169–71) He realized soon enough that the subjective difference in attitudes was little more than marginal, with many Labour leaders—Foreign Secretary Bevin, for example—being 'in reality imperialists' who 'like everyone else hate(s) the idea of our leaving India but like everyone else...(have) no alternative to suggest'. (Entry for 24 December 1946, Ibid., p. 399) What was changing fast was the total objective situation, worldwide, as well as Indian. Nazi Germany had been destroyed, Japan surrendered after Hiroshima in August 1945, socially-radical regimes with Communist leadership or participation were emrging throughout Eastern Europe and seemed on the point of doing so even in France and Italy, the Chinese revolution was forging ahead, and a tremendous anti-imperialist wave was sweeping through South-East Asia, with Vietnam and Indonesia resisting efforts to restore French and Dutch colonial rule. With a war-weary army and people and a ravaged economy, Britain would have had to retreat; the Labour victory only quickened the process somewhat.

Despite Wavell's fears, the initial steps he was asked to take by the Attlee ministry were by no means very radical. The announcement of new elections in the coming winter which was made on 21 August 1945 was inevitable once the war had ended, for the last elections had been held in 1934 for the centre and in 1937 for the provinces. It was also essential, as the U.P. Governor Hallet pointed out to Wavell on 14 August, as the 'first step' towards providing 'constitutional activities for the agitators'. (Mansergh, Vol. VI, p. 68) After talks in England, Wavell on 19 September merely reiterated the promise of 'early realization of full self-government' (the term 'independence' being still avoided). Post-election talks were promised with M.L.A.s and Indian States for setting-up a 'constitution-making body' (a considerable step back, this, from the Filkins acceptance of a constituent assembly based on universal franchise), and renewed efforts would be made to set up an Executive Council which will have the support of the main Indian parties'. (*Viceroy's Journal,* pp. 170–71)

I.N.A. Trials

The decisive shift in British policy really came about under mass pressure in the autumn and winter of 1945–46—the months which Perderel Moon while editing Wavell's Journal (Chapter VIII) has perceptively described as

'The Edge of a Volcano'. Very foolishly, the British initially decided to hold public trials of several hundreds of the 20,000 I.N.A. prisoners (as well as dismissing from service and detaining without trial no less than 7000: Mansergh, Vol. VI, pp. 49–51). They compounded the folly by holding the first trial in the Red Fort, Delhi in November 1945, and putting on the dock together a Hindu, a Muslim and a Sikh (P.K. Sehgal, Shah Nawaz, Gurbaksh Singh Dhillon). Bhulabhai Desai, Tejbahadur Sapru and Nehru appeared for the defence (the latter putting on his barrister's gown after 25 years), and the Muslim League also joined the countrywide protest. On 20 November, an Intelligence Bureau note admitted that 'There has seldom been a matter which has attracted so much Indian public interest and, it is safe to say, sympathy...this particular brand of sympathy cuts across communal barriers.' A journalist (B. Shiva Rao) visiting the Red Fort prisoners on the same day reported that 'There is not the slightest feeling among them of Hindu and Muslim.... A majority of the men now awaiting trial in the Red Fort is Muslim. Some of these men are bitter that Mr Jinnah is keeping alive a controversy about Pakistan'. (Ibid., pp. 514, 564) The British became extremely nervous about the I.N.A. spirit spreading to the Indian army, and in January the Punjab Governor reported that a Lahore reception for released I.N.A. prisoners had been attended by Indian soldiers in uniform. (Ibid., p. 807)

A second issue was provided by the use of Indian army units in the bid to restore French and Dutch colonial rule in Vietnam and Indonesia. The impact this had on popular (at least urban) sentiments as well as on sections of the army bore vivid testimony to the tremendous advance in anti-imperialist consciousness brought about by the War. Wavell was very nervous about such use being made of the Indian army, but was overruled in October 1945 by Supreme Allied Commander Mountbatten. (Ibid., pp. 305–6, 360) Meanwhile the usual post-war problems of unemployment and high prices were being sharply aggravated by a major food crisis, with partial crop failures in Bombay and Bengal, a cyclone in Madras, and inadequate procurement in the surplus province of Punjab. Wavell on 29 January 1946 estimated a deficit of three million tons, while imports from the U.S.A. remained uncertain, and a drastic cut in rations reduced its calorie value to 1200 per head (wartime London in 1943 had got over 2800 calories, Ibid., pp. 868–9, 1006).

What the officials feared in the autumn of 1945 was another Congress revolt, a revival of 1942 made much more dangerous this time by the likely combination of attacks on communications with widespread agrarian revolt, labour trouble, army disaffection, and the presence of I.N.A. men with some military expertise (cf. for instance, C.P. Governor Twynham to Wavell, 10

November 1945, and C-in-C Auchinleck's appreciation of the internal situation, 1 December 1945, Ibid., pp. 468, 577–83). Wavell bitterly complained about violent speeches by Congress leaders (Nehru above all, but also at first Patel and regional leaders in Bihar, C.P., U.P. and elsewhere), glorifying the heroes and martyrs of 1942, demanding stern punishment for official atrocities, and calling for immediate release of I.N.A. prisoners. The British began to realize fairly quickly, however, that this sabre-rattling was essentially election propaganda combined with the need to accommodate the popular mood. 1942 after all was the electoral trump-card of the Congress, and as for the I.N.A., Asaf Ali in a private conversation in October was reported to have explained that his party 'would lose much ground in the country' unless it took up their cause, but if the Congress came to power it would certainly remove the I.N.A. men from the army and might even put 'some of them on trial'. (Ibid., p. 387) Another indication was the bitter campaign against the Communists, in which Nehru played a very active role, culminating in the resignation of the C.P.I. members from the Congress on 5 October and the formal expulsion of Communist AICC members in December. There were cases of assault on Communists, and a Congress mob inflamed by a speech by Nehru attacked the Party headquarters in Bombay. That more was involved here than legitimate anger about the C.P.I's war-time role is indicated by the fact that there was no such concerted campaign against the Hindu Mahasabha, some of whose leaders had actually been in ministries in August 1942, while Rajagopalachari, whose attitude on the Quit India and Pakistan issues in 1942 had been very similar to that of the Communists, remained a top Congress leader.

The forces which had restrained Congress militancy in the past were soon at work once again. The Governor of Sind on 3 November, Finance Member Rowlands on 17 November, and Secretary of State Pethick-Lawrence on 30 November independently referred to G.D. Birla as getting 'alarmed at the virulence of Congress speeches' (*Viceroy's Journal,* p. 185; Mansergh, Vol., VI, pp. 438, 572)—and Sardar Patel had by now largely 'taken the place of Bapu' in Birla's hot line with the Congress High Command. (*In the Shadow of Mahatma,* p. 328) 'There have recently been indications that the Congress leaders want to reduce the political tension by making it clear that there must be no mass movement until after the elections', Wavell informed Pethick-Lawrence on 5 December—'the strong capitalist element behind Congress...is becoming nervous about the security of its property'. And Birla the next day himself assured a London official: 'There is no political leader including Jawaharlal who wants to see any crisis or violence.... Popular impatience and the prevalent atmosphere are responsible for these strong speeches. Even leaders are often led. But I think unrestrained language will be heard less and less in the future'. (Mansergh, Vol. VI, pp. 602–3, 615)

The 'turning-point', which 'caused at least a temporary detente' (Wavell to George VI, 31 December, Ibid., p. 713), came with the popular explosion in Calcutta on the I.N.A. issue on 21–23 November 1945, which set a pattern of periodic upheavals in that city which went on for about a decade and are reminiscent in some ways of the famous *journees* or 'days' of Paris during the French Revolution. A student procession demanding release of I.N.A. prisoners and initially organized by the Forward Bloc sat down on Dharamtala street for the whole night on being prevented from entering Dalhouse Square. They were joined by Communist Student's Federation cadres—so long considered their bitterest enemies—as well as by students from Islamia College carrying the green flag of the League. Sarat Bose in sharp contrast, who had been adored as the brother of Subhas, refused to come to address them and later blamed the Communists for instigating violence. Spontaneously the students tied together the Congress, League, and Red Flags as symbol of all-in anti-imperialist unity. After the first round of police firing which killed two students (a Hindu and a Muslim), trouble spread all over the city on 22 and 23 November with strikes by Sikh taxi-drivers and Communist-led tramway-men as well as in many factories (Calcutta Corporation employees were already out on economic demands), burning of cars and lorries, crowds blocking trains, and barricades on streets. The police enquiry later noted as a new feature the fact that 'the crowds when fired on largely stood their ground or at most only receded a little, to return again to the attack'. (Governor Casey to Wavell, 2 January 1946, Ibid., p. 725) Order was restored only after 14 cases of firing, in which 33 were killed and about 200 civilians injured; 150 police and army vehicles had been destroyed, and 70 British and 37 Amercian soldiers suffered injuries. The reactions were very significant. Patel on 24 November at a Bombay election rally condemned the 'frittering away' of energies in 'trifling quarrels' with the police (*Indian Annual Register*), Gandhi began a fairly friendly dialogue with the Bengal Governor, and the Calcutta Working Committee session of 7–11 December strongly reaffiirmed its faith in non-violence in significant contrast to the September AICC session where many members had glorified every aspect of the by no means non-violent 1942 struggle. The British on their part realized the need for some concessions. On 1 December, it was announed that only I.N.A. members accused of murder or brutal treatment of fellow-prisoners would henceforward be brought to trial (instead of the sweeping charge of 'waging war against the King' used in the first case) and imprisonment sentences passed against the first batch were remitted in January. By February 1946, Indian soldiers were withdrawing from both Indo-China and Indonesia. On 28 November the British Cabinet sub-committee on India decided on a Parliamentary delegation; on 22 January 1946 the much more significant decision was taken to send a Cabinet Mission to negotiate with Indian leaders. Wavell meanwhile had started preparing a 'breakdown plan'. As presented to the Cabinet Mission in May 1946, this visualized as a 'middle course' between 'repression' and 'scuttle' a withdrawal of the British army and officials to the Muslim provinces of N.W. and N.E. India, handing over the rest of the country to the Congress. Though superseded by the Cabinet Mission proposals, the 'plan' is still interesting evidence of the British recognition that it would be impossible to suppress any future Congress-led rebellion, as well as of the desire in some high official circles to make of Pakistan an Indian northern Ireland.

The British had to face a second major crisis in February 1946 before they succeeded in finally bringing Indian leaders to the safer shore of negotiations. Between 11 and 13 February, Calcutta exploded again in protest against the seven years' rigorous imprisonment sentence passed on Abdul Rashid of the I.N.A. The League student wing gave a strike call, the Students Federation joined in, and as in November, there quickly developed a remarkable unity in the streets between students and workers, Muslims and Hindus. A Communist-led general strike paralyzed industrial Calcutta on 12 February, and a massive rally on the same day at Wellington Square was addressed by League leader Suhrawardy, Satis Dasgupta the Gandhian Congressman, and the Communist Somnath Lahiri. The police and army could restore order only after two days of street clashes in which 84 were killed and 300 injured according to official estimates (Gautam Chattopadhyay, 'The Almost Revolution', *Essays in Honour of S.C. Sarkar,* New Delhi, 1976). Meanwhile the all-India organizations of railway workers and postal employees, soon to be followed by government employees, were threatening strikes in the context of rising prices and the ration-cut imposed in January. The development of such effective country-wide labour organizations in strategic sectors gave a new muscle-power to the Indian trade union movement—strikes in the 1920s and '30s had been mainly confined to single industrial centres, primarily Bombay or Calcutta textiles. Though both the League and the Congress leadership accepted the ration cut (Azad on 3 March even welcomed it as 'far-sighted', and declared that strikes were 'out of place today', as the British were 'now acting as caretakers', Mansergh, Vol. VI, p. 1117), this did not prevent popular outbursts like a demonstration of 80,000 in Allahabad in mid-February which attacked ration-centres. (Ibid., p. 1006)

R.I.N. Mutiny

The greatest threat of all, however, was the naval mutiny in Bombay on 18–23 February 1946—one of the most truly heroic, if also largely forgotten, episodes in our freedom struggle. Wartime expansion of the Royal Indian Navy had brought in men from all parts of the country, weakening the old military tradition of recruitment from politically undeveloped 'martial races'. Racial discrimination continued unabated in this last bastion of Empire, while service abroad brought contact with world developments and the I.N.A. trials and the post-war popular upsurge in India had a growing impact. On 18 February, ratings in the Signals training establishment *Talwar* went on hunger-strike against bad food and racist insults. Next day the strike spread to Castle and Fort Barracks on shore and 22 ships in Bombay harbour, and the tricolour, crescent, and hammer-and-sickle were raised jointly on the mastheads of the rebel fleet. The ratings elected a Naval Central Strike Committee, headed by M.S. Khan, and formulated demands which combined issues of better food, equal pay for white and Indian sailors, etc., with the national political slogans of release of I.N.A. and other political prisoners and withdrawal of Indian troops from Indonesia. The men hesitated fatally, however, on the border-line of peaceful strike and determined mutiny, obeying orders to return to their respective ships or barracks on the afternoon of 20 February, only to find themselves surrounded by army guards. Next day fighting started at Castle Barracks when ratings tried to break out of their encirclement, with the ships providing artillery support, while Admiral Godfrey flew in bombers and threatened to destroy the navy. The same afternoon also saw remarkable scenes of fraternization, with crowds bringing food for ratings to the Gateway of India and shopkeepers inviting them to take whatever they needed. The pattern of events in fact unconsciously echoed the course of the mutiny on the Black Sea Fleet during the first Russian Revolution of 1905: that too, had begun over inedible food, and fraternizing crowds had been shot down in a scene immortalized later on in the 'Odessa steps' sequence of Eisenstein's film classic *Battleship Potemkin*. By 22 February, the strike had spread to naval bases all over the country as well as to some ships on sea, involving at its height 78 ships, 20 shore establishments, and 20,000 ratings. At Karachi, the *Hindustan* surrendered that morning only after a gun battle, while Hindu and Muslim students and workers demonstrated their support through violent clashes with the police and army.

At Bombay as well as elsewhere, two sharply different attitudes towards these dramatic developments became evident among Indian political groups by 22 February. The Bombay C.P.I. called for a general strike, which was supported by Congress Socialist leaders like Aruna Asaf Ali and Achyut Patwardhan. Sardar Patel in sharp contrast advised people 'to go about their normal business as usual', and S.K. Patil and Chundrigar, heads of the provincial Congress and League units, even offered volunteers to help restore order. Despite Congress and League opposition, 300,000 downed tools in Bombay on 22 February, closing down almost all mills, and violent street fighting with crowds 'erecting road blocks and covering them from nearby buildings' continued for two days particularly in the proletarian districts of Parel and Delisle Road. Two army battalions were needed to restore order in Bombay city, and the official casualty figures were 228 civilians killed and 1046 injured (plus 3 police deaths and 91 wounded). (*The R.I.N. Strike,* by a group of victimized ratings, Delhi, 1954, p. 93; Mansergh, Vol. VI, pp. 1082–3).

Patel, helped for once by Jinnah, managed to persuade the ratings to surrender on 23 February giving an assurance that the national parties would prevent any victimization—a promise soon quietly forgotten, for, as Patel wrote to Andhra Congress leader Viswanathan on 1 March 1946, 'discipline in the Army cannot be tampered with... We will want Army even in free India' (*Sardar's Letters,* Vol. IV, Ahmedabad 1977, p. 165). Nehru accepted Aruna Asaf Ali's invitation to come to Bombay, but quickly allowed himself to be 'impressed by the necessity for curbing the wild outburst of violence'—though he did later on hail the R.I.N, strike for breaking down the 'iron wall' between army and people. (Mansergh, Vol. VI, pp. 1084, 1117–18). Gandhi was as unequivocally hostile as Patel. On 22 February he condemned the ratings for setting 'a bad and unbecoming example for India', advised them to peacefully resign their jobs if they had any grievances, and made the very interesting statement that 'a combination between Hindus and Muslims and others for the purpose of violent action is unholy....' Aruna Asaf Ali made the pertinent comment in reply that 'It simply does not lie in the mouth of Congressmen who were themselves going to the legislatures to ask the ratings to give up their jobs.' She also made a tragically accurate prophecy that it would be far easier to 'unite the Hindus and Muslims at the barricade than on the constitutional front'. (*Sardar's Letters,* pp. 162–3) It is tempting to set beside Gandhi's statement of 22 February, Wavell's private comment of 30 May 1946: 'We must at all costs avoid becoming embroiled with both Hindu and Muslim at once'. (*Viceroy's Journal,* p. 485)

The R.I.N. ratings of February 1946, in sharp contrast to the men of the Azad Hind Fauj, have never been given the status of national heroes—though their action involved much greater risk in some ways than joining the I.N.A. as alternative to an arduous life in Japanese POW camps. The last message of the Naval Central Strike Committee deserves to be remembered far better than it is: 'Our strike has been a historic event in the life of our nation. For the first time the blood of men in the Services and in the streets flowed together in a common cause. We in the Services will never forget this. We know also that you, our brothers and sisters, will not forget. Long live our great people! Jai Hind!'. (*The RIN Strike,* p. 75)

1946 (MARCH–AUGUST): THE CABINET MISSION

Elections

Firmly rejecting mass confrontations, Congress leaders during the winter of 1945–46 concentrated all their energies on fighting the elections. As in 1937, Nehru was the star speaker, but Patel really controlled the machinery for selecting candidates. The former occasionally had misgivings 'that people who have played us false in the past' were being given nominations, but did little about it: 'I have no time and no inclination to enter into local squabbles' (Nehru to Patel, 31 October 1945, Durga Das (ed.), *Sardar Patel's Correspondence,* Vol. II, p. 66). The Congress did win massively in the general (i.e., non-Muslim) constituencies, capturing 57 out of 102 seats in the Central Assembly (against 36 in 1934) and 91.3% of non-Muslim votes. In the provinces, it won majorities everywhere except Bengal, Sind and Punjab. The Hindu Mahasabha was routed and the Communists, too, did badly, capturing only a handful of provincial seats (3 in Bengal, including Jyoti Basu from a labour constituency, 2 in Bombay, and 2 in Madras). But it was significant that the Communists had emerged as the principal contenders of the Congress in several provinces. Patel congratulated an Andhra Congress leader for 'defeating the Communists everywhere' after 'a very stiff contest' (Patel to A. Kaleswar Rao, 27 March 1946, Ibid., p. 243), and the Madras Governor reported that 'Congress right-wingers' were 'gloomily predicting' a Communist majority next time (Knight to Wavell, 5 April 1946, Mansergh, Vol. VII, p. 152).

The League's success in the Muslim seats was equally spectacular—all 30 reserved constituencies in the centre with 86.6% of Muslim votes, and 442 out 509 Muslim seats in the provinces. Unlike 1937, it had now clearly established itself as the dominant party among Muslims. But despite major advances in the Punjab (from 2 to 79 out of 175), a majority still eluded it in that key province, and Khizar Hayat Khan was able to strike a bargain with the Congress and the Akalis to remain in power for another year. The Congress won handsome majorities in two other provinces being claimed for Pakistan, N.W.F.P. and Assam, and the two League ministries that were set up—in Bengal and Sind—remained dependent on official and European support.

The most significant feature of the elections, however, was the prevalence of communal voting, in sharp contrast to the sporadic but very striking anti-British unity forged often in these months in the streets of Calcutta, Bombay, or even Karachi. Apart from the logic of separate electorates, it is possible that the extremely limited franchise (about 10% of the population in the provinces, less than 1% for the Central Assembly) may have had something to do with this disparity. The N.W.F.P. Governor, for instance, reported to Wavell in February 1946 that while Muslim officials and the 'bigger Khans' or landlords were all for the League, the Congress was still getting the support of the 'less well-to-do' Muslims due to its promises of economic reforms—promises, however, which were not implemented either after 1937 or in 1946–7. (Mansergh, Vol. VI, p. 1085) In this context, the tacit giving-up by the Congress of its central slogan of the late-1930s—a Constituent Assembly elected on universal franchise—acquires crucial significance in understanding the course of events. Of all Indian political groups, only the Communists in 1945–46 pressed this demand seriously—in P.C. Joshi's election pamphlet *For the Final Bid For Power* (1945), for instance, which posed as its key political slogan 'sovereign national constituent assemblies' elected by universal suffrage on the basis of linguistic regions and electing in their turn an all-India Constituent Assembly, with each region or 'nationality' retaining a right of secession. While sharply critical of Congress and League 'liberal illusions' about British good intentions, the pamphlet ended with a passionate call for 'Congress-League-Communist united front' in a 'last battle against the British rulers, against our common shame, for our common glory!' P.C. Joshi repeated the same demand for universal franchise in his meeting with the Cabinet Mission on 17 April 1946 (Mansergh, Vol, VII, pp. 291–3). Congress leaders, in sharp contrast, quietly accepted the election of the Constituent Assembly by the existing provincial legislatures based on limited voting rights. Much more was involved here than a question of abstract democratic principle. The League won its demand for Pakistan without its claims to represent the majority of Muslims being really tested, either in fully democratic elections or (as Congress claims had been) in sustained mass movements in the face of official repression (as distinct from occasional communal riots not unaccompanied often by official complicity). While the Congress after 1947 would win all-India elections for 30 years, the League was routed in East Pakistan in the very first vote held on the basis of universal franchise (in 1954), and failed to provide political stability even in W. Pakistan.

Cabinet Mission

From 24 March to June 1946, three members of the British Cabinet—Secretary of State Pethick-Lawrence, Cripps and Alexander—carried on together with Wavell long and often very tortuous negotiations with Indian leaders on the two issues of an interim government and principles and procedures for framing a new constitution giving India freedom. Attlee on 15 March raised Congress hopes considerably by a Commons statement promising speedy and full freedom and declaring that 'though mindful of the rights of minorities...we cannot allow a minority to place their veto on the advance of the majority'. (V.P. Menon, *Transfer of Power in India,* p. 237) Wavell was very suspicious of the Cabinet Mission being over-friendly with the Congress— Cripps for instance once horrified him by bringing a glass of water for Gandhi personally, and the *Viceroy's Journal* even accused the Mission of 'living in the pocket of Congress' (*Viceroy's Journal,* pp. 236, 324–5). Yet if the Cabinet Mission at times seemed to lean marginally towards the Congress, this was not basically due to Labour pro-nationalist sympathies or Cripps' old ties with Nehru, but to what Wavell himself on 29 March decribed as 'the necessity to avoid the mass movement or revolution which it is in the power of the Congress to start, and which we are not certain that we can control'. (Ibid., p. 232) It is difficult to avoid the conclusion that the Congress leadership once again spiked its own guns in its eagerness for quick and easy power and desire at all costs to preserve social order. There were widespread police strikes in April (in Malabar, the Andamans, Dacca, Bihar and Delhi), threats of an all-India railway stoppage throughout the summer, a postal strike in July, and on 29 July—less than three weeks before the Great Calcutta Killing of 16 August—a total, absolutely peaceful, and remarkably united *bandh* in Calcutta under Communist leadership in sympathy with postal employees. The Home Member on 5 April warned that he had doubts 'whether a Congress rebellion could be suppressed', particularly because 'a call to a general strike would be widely obeyed...labour is amenable mostly to Communist and Congress leadership'. (Mansergh, Vol. VII, p. 151) The strike-wave of 1946 in fact surpassed all previous records, with 1629 stoppages involving 1,941,948 workers and a loss of 12,717,762 man-days. The Congress High Command's attitude was well summed-up by a Working Committee resolution in August condemning the growing lack of discipline and disregard of obligations on the part of the workers. (Note on Labour by J.B. Kripalani, (*AICC G26/1946*). Yet the Congress leadership allowed itself to get engrossed in negotiations and ministry-making. Nehru much to Wavell's relief 'seemed to realize the unreasonableness of the (railway) men's demands and the danger of giving way to them', and Sarat Bose on becoming a minister in the Interim Government in September amused the Viceroy by calling for troops and British technicians at the first hint of a strike threat by Delhi electricity workers. (*Viceroy's Journal,* pp. 279, 352) And in the end the Cabinet Mission Plan and Interim Government manoeuvres became no more than stepping-stones on the road to a communal holocaust and Partition.

After initial negotiations had been stalled as usual on the rock of Jinnah's insistence on Pakistan, the Cabinet Mission on 16 May came out with a plan which for a brief moment promised to break the deadlock. This confronted Jinnah with a choice between a 'moth-eaten' Pakistan and a loose, three-tier confederal structure in which Muslims would have the chance of dominating the N.W. and N.E. province of a still-united country. A full-fledged Pakistan was impossible, the Mission pointed out, since it would include a very large number of non-Muslims (48.3% in Bengal and Assam, for instance); the very principle of communal self-determination being urged by the League would demand the separation of Hindu-majority West Bengal (including Calcutta, where Muslims numbered only 23.6%) and the Sikh and Hindu-dominated Ambala and Jullundur divisions of the Punjab. (Some Sikh leaders had already started demanding a separate state for themselves if the country was really partitioned). A Partition of Bengal and Punjab would go against deep-seated regional ties, raise any number of economic, administrative and military problems, and still fail to satisfy the League. The alternative suggested was a weak centre controlling only foreign affairs, defence and communications, with the existing provincial assemblies being grouped into three sections while electing the constituent assembly: Section A for the Hindu-majority provinces, Section B and C for the Muslim-majority provinces of the north-west and north-east (including Assam). The Sections would have the power to set up intermediate-level executives and legislatures of their own.

Maulana Azad later described the acceptance of this long-term plan by both the major parties (the League on 6 June, the Congress on 24 June), as a 'glorious event'. (*India Wins Freedom,* p. 151) Actually the agreement was bound to be short-lived, as it was based on mutually-opposed interpretations of the plan. The League wanted grouping to be compulsory, with Sections B and C developing into solid entities with a view to future secession into Pakistan. Jinnah in addition had thought that the Congress would reject the plan, in which case the British might ask the League alone to form the Interim Government at the centre—a hope fully shared by Wavell, who was deeply disappointed when the Congress accepted the long-term proposals. (*Viceroy's Journal* 25 June, p. 305) The Congress argued that compulsory grouping contradicted the otherwise oft-repeated insistence on provincial autonomy, and was not satisfied with the Mission's clarification (on May 25) that grouping would be compulsory at first, but provinces would have the right to opt out after the constitution had been finalized and new elections held in accordance with it. It was also critical of the absence of any provision for elected members from the princely states in the proposed Constituent Assembly. The new Congress President, Nehru, declared at a press conference on 10 July that the only commitment made by his party was to participate in Constituent Assembly elections. 'The big probability is that…there will be no grouping', as N.W.F.P. and Assam would have objections to joining Section B and C. The League responded on 29–30 July by withdrawing its earlier acceptance of the long-term plan and calling on the 'Muslim Nation' to go in for 'Direct Action' from 16 August to achieve Pakistan. (Mansergh, Vol. VIII, pp. 25–6, 139)

Meanwhile Wavell's parallel efforts to set up a short-term coalition Interim Government at the centre had also broken down. Jinnah wanted a ratio of five Congress Hindus, five League Muslims, one Sikh, one Scheduled Caste. The Congress rejected such 'parity' as a step back from even the Simla Conference, wanted the right to include Muslims and Harijans among its nominees, and demanded, as in 1942, that the new government should approximate to a genuine Cabinet, and not be a mere continuation of the old Viceroy's Executive. Wavell consequently had to set up a caretaker government of officials alone on 4 July. But within a few weeks the Viceroy began insisting on the need for somehow getting the Congress into the Interim Government, even if the League stayed out—a major departure from his stand at the Simla Conference, as well as from his preferences only a month earlier. The explanation once again lay in fear of possible mass action: July was the month of a threatened all-India strike in the railways and an actual postal walk-out. 'If Congress will take responsibility they will realize that firm control of unruly elements is necessary and they may put down the Communists and try to curb their own Left Wing. Also I should hope to keep them so busy with administration that they had much less time for politics.' (Wavell to Secretary of State, 31 July 1946, Mansergh, Vol. VIII, pp. 154). The Director of the Intelligence Bureau made the same point on 9 August '….the labour situation is becoming increasingly dangerous…Until a responsible Indian government is introduced at the centre, there is little that can be done…. I am satisfied that a responsible government, if one can be achieved, will deal more decisively with Labour than is at present possible'. (*Home Poll* (1) *12/7/1946*) Once again the Congress walked into the trap. By 5 August, Wavell had received information that Patel was 'convinced that the Congress must enter the Government to prevent chaos spreading in the country', and was even prepared to threaten resignation from the Working Committee if his views were not accepted (*Viceroy's Journal,* p. 329). The Viceroy did try to bully the Congress into accepting compulsory grouping by holding out the threat of not summoning the Constituent Assembly in an interview with Nehru and Gandhi on 27 August, but when the latter reacted strongly against Wavell's 'minatory' tone ('We are all plain men though we may not all be soldiers and even though some of us may know the law', Gandhi to Wavell, 28 August: Mansergh, Vol. VIII, p. 322) the Secretary of State in a 'panic-stricken telegram' insisted on avoiding any break (*Viceroy's Journal,* p. 343). On 2 September a Congress-dominated Interim Government was sworn in headed by Nehru—who had made it clear that his party was still opposed to compulsory grouping, though he did offer to refer the matter to the Federal Court envisaged by the Cabinet Mission plan.

1946-1947: COMMUNAL HOLOCAUST AND PEASANT REBELLION

Calcutta, Noakhali, Bihar, Punjab

From 16 August 1946, however, the whole Indian scene was rapidly transformed by communal riots on an unprecedented scale: starting with Calcutta on 16-19 August, touching Bombay from 1 September, spreading to Noakhali in east Bengal (10 October), Bihar (25 October), Garmukteswar in U.P. (November), and engulfing the Punjab from March 1947 onwards. While inflamed communal passions provided everywhere the common factor, the riots also showed significant variations so far as their form, extent or question of immediate responsibility was concerned. In Calcutta, where the League ministry had declared a holiday on Direct Action Day, large-scale Muslim attacks began after a Maidan rally where Chief Minister Suhrawardy had promised immunity from police and army interference. Suhrawardy 'spent a great deal of time in the Control Room in Lall Bazar, often attended by some of his supporters', and showed 'an exasperating pre-occupation with the sufferings undergone by members of his own community'. (Governor Burrows to Wavell, 22 August, Mansergh, Vol. VIII, pp. 297-300) Hindu and particularly Sikh toughs hit back strongly in what became 'a pogrom between two rival armies of the Calcutta underworld', leaving by 19 August at least 4000 killed and 10,000 injured, with 'the removal of the very large number of decomposed bodies' lying in the streets posing a major problem (Ibid., p. 302). Murder was the primary objective in the Calcutta riots, not—as often in earlier communal outbreaks—desecration of temples or mosques, rape, or attacks on the property of relatively privileged groups belonging to the opposite community. More Muslims seemed to have died than Hindus, a point made not only by Wavell (Ibid., p. 274) but also by Patel ('In Calcutta the Hindus had the best of it. But that is no comfort', letter to Cripps, 19 October, Ibid., p. 750). The British responsibility is equally clear: the army, in sharp contrast to November 1945 or February 1946, moved into action only after 24 hours, though the Governor was reminded of his First World War experiences in course of an early morning tour of the city on 17 August. There was a second round of riots in Calcutta between 26 March and 1 April 1947, followed by chronic disturbances and stabbing incidents till the very eve of independence; whole areas of the city remained out of bounds for members of one or other community for months.

In Bombay city, stray stabbing rather than largescale riots was the pattern from the beginning, though these were extensive enough to kill 162 Hindus and 158 Muslims in course of September 1946 (Mansergh, Vol. VIII, pp. 532, 648). A distorted social content was evident in Noakhali and Tippera, east Bengal districts with a tradition of agrarian unrest, where peasants were mostly Muslims while Hindus predominated among landlords, traders, and professional groups. In the October disturbances in northwest Noakhali and the adjoining south-west corner of Tippera, attacks on property and incidents of rape figured more prominently than murder in sharp contrast to the Calcutta riots. There were about 300 deaths, but loss of property amounted to crores of rupees, and in initial Hindu complaints attacks on *zamindars,* lawyers and other notables figured prominently. Burrows reported that the 'Trouble in South-East Bengal is not a general rising of Muslims against Hindus but activity (apparently organized) of a body of hooligans who have exploited existing communal feeling'; casualties were relatively 'low', but 'damage to property will probably prove heavy'. The League administration once again showed blatant bias: of the 1074 arrested only 50 were in jail by April 1947. (Mansergh, Vol. VIII, pp. 725, 745, 753; N.K. Bose, *My Days with Gandhi,* p. 33, 48, 302).

The Bihar riots in the wake of observance of 'Noakhali day' on 25 October revealed yet another pattern, more difficult to explain: a mass upsurge of Hindu peasants against Muslims, resulting in a massacre far more terrible rally than Noakhali, with at least 7000 deaths. A horrified and bewildered Nehru reported that 'a madness has seized the people' in what was an old Congress (as well as Kisan Sabha) stronghold; he suspected some landlord instigation, 'to divert the attention of their tenantry from agrarian problems', and noted that the Congress-run administration and many party members had also succumbed to Hindu communalism. 'The real picture that I now find is quite as bad, and even worse than anything that they (the League leaders) had suggested'. (Nehru to Patel, 5 November 1946, Durga Das, Vol. III, p. 165) Bihar was followed by Garhmukteswar in U.P. where Hindu pilgrims slaughtered a thousand Muslims. News of such massacres rapidly weakened the so long unassailable Congress position in the N.W.F.P. Nehru faced hostile tribal demonstrations during his tour of that province in late-October 1946, and riots in Hazara in January 1947 were followed by a Congress defeat in a crucial bye-election in Mardan.

Meanwhile Muslims, Hindus, and Sikhs alike were preparing for what proved to be the greatest holocaust of all—that in the Punjab. The Unionist bloc had been weakened by the death of the Haryana Hindu Jat leader Chhotu Ram in January 1945, and Baldev Singh's manoeuvre of propping up Khizar Hayat Khan's ministry through Congress and Sikh support even after elections had given the Unionists only 10 seats against the League's 79 only inflamed Muslim communalist and pro-Pakistan attitudes. A League campaign of civil disobedience from January 1947 brought down the Khizar ministry on 3 March. Next day a provocative Sikh demonstration in front of the Assembly Chamber in Lahore (with Tara Singh brandishing a sword and raising the slogan *Raj Karega Khalsa*: the Khalsa will rule) was followed by large-scale riots in Lahore, Amritsar, Multan, Attock and Rawalpindi, as well as in the rural areas of the last three districts. The main targets in these Muslim-majority regions were Sikh and Hindu traders and moneylenders. About 5000 had been killed by August 1947, but even this proved just a curtain-raiser to the war of extermination which began after Independence on both sides of the border, when refugee trains sometimes arrived carrying only dead bodies. Penderel Moon estimates that approximately 180,000 had been killed, of which 60,000 were from the west and 120,000 from the east. By March 1948, six million Muslims and four and a half million Hindus and Sikhs had become refugees, bringing about a virtually complete and forcible exchange of population, and leaving behind 4.7 million acres of land in east Punjab and 6.7 million acres in the west. On the whole 'Muslims lost the most lives, Hindus and Sikhs lost the most property'— thus in Bahawalpur in south-west Punjab where Moon was working in 1947, the 'Muslim population (mainly peasant) was less interested in blood than in the quiet enjoyment of Hindu property and Hindu girls'. Physical liquidation was more important in central and east Punjab where the opposite communities were more evenly matched, and the Sikhs in particular showed a grim determination in wiping out or driving-out Muslims so that land could be found for the two million Sikhs migrating from the West. (Penderel Moon, *Divide and Quit,* Ch. XIV)

The British, who as late as June 1946 had been making plans to bring five army divisions to India in the context of a possible Congress movement, (Mansergh, Vol. VIII, pp. 13–15) made no such move while presiding over this awesome human tragedy. Two examples, both taken from British sources, may suffice to indicate the extent of official passivity if not deliberate connivance. Wavell commented on 9 November 1946 in the context of Bihar Muslim requests to use aerial bombardment to stop the riots: 'Machine-gunning from the air is not a weapon one would willingly use, though the Muslims point out, rather embarrassingly, that we did not hesitate to use it in 1942'. (*Viceroy's Journal*, p. 374) In March 1947, the two main bazars of Amritsar were destroyed, while 'not a short was fired by the police'—and this, Penderel Moon pertinently recalls, was the city of the Jalianwala-bagh massacre. (Moon, pp. 78, 80–1)

The Interim Government of Nehru found itself presiding helplessly over this growing communal inferno. Despite the title, it was really little more than a continuation of the old Executive Council of the Viceroy, and Wavell overruled the ministers on the question of release of I.N.A. prisoners in his very last cabinet meeting on 19 March 1947. Collective, or for that matter any kind of functioning became all but impossible when Wavell persuaded Jinnah to join the government on 26 October on the basis of a League scheduled caste nominee (Jogen Mandal) balancing a Congress Muslim. The League was allowed to join without giving up its Direct Action programme, its rejection of the Cabinet Mission long-term plan, or its insistence on compulsory grouping with decisions being taken by majority vote by a section as a whole (which would in effect reduce opponents of Pakistan in Assam and N.W.F.P. to the position of a helpless minority. It refused also to attend the Constituent Assembly which had started meeting from 9 December, and which consequently had to confine itself for the moment to passing (in January 1947) a general 'Objectives Resolution' drafted by Nehru stating the ideal of an 'independent sovereign republic' with autonomous units, adequate minority safeguards, and having social, political and economic democracy as its fundamental aims. League obstructionism, in Congress eyes at least, included refusal to attend Nehru's 'tea-party Cabinets' (informal sessions to coordinate policies before meeting the Viceroy), and a rather demagogic budget moved in February 1947 by Finance Minister Liaquat Ali Khan imposing heavy taxes on big business (the major part of which was Hindu). Wavell considered this to be 'a clever move', since it 'drives a wedge between Congress and their rich merchant supporters like Birla, while Congress cannot object to its provisions' (*Viceroy's Journal,* 28 February 1947, p. 424)

Confronted by Calcutta, Noakhali, Bihar and Punjab, the secular ideals of many within the Congress ranks and leadership tended to evaporate. If Nehru consistently denounced Hindu communalism in Bihar and elsewhere, and Azad blamed Wavell for not calling out troops promptly in Calcutta to suppress 'the hooligans of Calcutta's underworld' unleashed by Suhrawardy (interview with Wavell, 19 August 1946, Mansergh, Vol. VIII p. 261), Patel sympathized with hostile Hindu reactions to Nehru's condemnation of Bihar. 'We would be committing a grave mistake if we expose the people of Bihar and their ministry to the violent and vulgar attacks of the League leaders.' (Patel to Rajendra Prasad, 11 November 1946, Durga Das, Vol. III, p. 171)

Communal riots, combined with the evident unworkability of the Congress-League coalition at the centre, compelled many by early 1947 to think in terms of accepting what had been unthinkable so far—a Partition, and these soon included Nehru as well as Patel. The most insistent demands for this surgical solution had now started coming from Hindu and Sikh communalist groups in Bengal and Punjab, alarmed by the prospect of compulsory grouping into Muslim-dominated sections which might very well later form themselves into Pakistan. The Hindu Mahasabha, for instance, set up a committee to investigate the feasibility of a separate Hindu province in West Bengal (V.P. Menon, p. 348). By 10 March 1947, Nehru was telling Wavell in private that though 'the Cabinet Mission Plan was the best solution if it could be carried through—the only real alternative was the partition of the Punjab and Bengal' (*Viceroy's Journal*, pp. 426–7). A month later, Congress President Kripalani informed Mountbatten: 'Rather than have a battle we shall let them have their Pakistan, provided you will allow the Punjab and Bengal to be partitioned in a fair manner.' (H.V. Hodson, *The Great Divide*, London 1969; p. 236)

The Mahatma's Finest Hour

To one man, however, the idea of a high-level bargain by which the Congress would attain quick power in the major part of the country at the cost of a Partition on religious lines still seemed unimaginably shocking and unacceptable. Gandhi had increasingly taken a back seat in the tortuous negotiations going on since 1945, apart from a few abortive moves through his personal emissary Sudhir Ghosh, and the suggestion—quixotic in the eyes of other Congress leaders—which he made to the Cabinet Mission and later to Mountbatten that Jinnah should be offered the Indian Prime Ministership with the British remaining for some time to protect, for a change, the interests of the majority community. Increasingly isolated from the Congress leadership, the old man of 77 with undiminished courage decided to stake his all in a bid to vindicate his life-long principles of change of heart and non-violence in the villages of Noakhali, followed by Bihar and then the riot-torn slums of Calcutta and Delhi. He lived with a handful of companions in hostile Muslim dominated villages, held out the threat of a fast unto death if Bihar Hindus did not mend their ways (6 November 1946), and from January 1947 set out barefoot through Noakhali village roads, once sweeping away with his own hands garbage strewn on his path by angry Muslims, and starting every morning with what had become his favourite hymn, Rabindranath's 'If there is none to heed your call, walk alone, walk alone'. Gandhi's unique personal qualities and true greatness was never more evident than in the last months of his life: total disdain for all conventional forms of political power which could have been his for the asking now that India was becoming free; and a passionate anti-communalism which made him declare to a League leader a month after Partition, while riots were ravaging the Punjab: 'I want to fight it out with my life. I would not allow the Muslims to crawl on the streets in India. They must walk with self-respect'. (Khaliquzzaman, *Pathway to Pakistan,* p. 404) A Calcutta resident who is otherwise very far from being an adherent of Gandhi still recalls how at prayer meetings he used to brush aside the very idea of Hindus and Muslims belonging to different nations with a gently-deprecating smile.

At times the presence of Gandhi really seemed to work miracles, as peace returned to Calcutta on the eve of 15 August after he had persuaded Suhrawardy to stay with him in riot-torn Beliaghata, and when a revival of communal strife in the city on 31 August was abruptly halted by a fast unto death from 1 to 4 September 1947. Riots began in Delhi soon afterwards, with a Hindus massacre of Muslims as revenge for Punjab, and once again Gandhi's fast in January 1948 had a temporary impact. This last fast seems to have been directed in part also against Patel's increasingly communal attitudes (the Home Minister had started thinking in terms of a total transfer of population in the Punjab, and was refusing to honour a prior agreement by which India was obliged to give ₹55 crores of pre-Partition Government of India financial assets to Pakistan). 'You are not the Sardar I once knew,' Gandhi is said to have remarked during the fast. On 27 January 1948 the man whom a generation of Muslims had been taught to hate as the most dangerous Hindu leader was invited by them to speak from the platform of a religious shrine near in Delhi. Three days later the Mahatma was dead, murdered by a Hindu fanatic, Nathuram Godse, as a climax to a conspiracy hatched by a Poona Brahman group originally inspired by V.D. Savarkar—a conspiracy which, despite ample warnings, the police of Bombay and Delhi had done nothing to foil.

Intensely moving and heroic, the Gandhian way in 1946-47 was no more than an isolated personal effort with a local and often rather short-lived impact. It is futile and dangerous to speculate about what might have been, but one might still argue that the only real alternative lay along the path of united militant mass struggle against imperialism and its Indian allies— the one thing which, as we have repeatedly seen, the British really dreaded. Despite the obvious distruption caused by the riots, this possibility was by no means entirely blocked even in the winter of 1946-47. Five months after the August riots, the students of Calcutta were again on the streets on 21 January 1947 in 'Hands off Vietnam' demonstrations against the use of Dum Dum airport by French planes, and all communal divisions seemed forgotten in the absolutely united and ultimately victorious 85-day tram strike under Communist leadership which began the same day, followed soon afterward by port employees and Howrah engineering workers. January and February in fact saw a new strike wave, with 100,000 out in Kanpur textiles, a threat of a coal stoppage, and strikes in Coimbatore, Karachi and elsewhere due 'largely to Communist agitation'. (Wavell, quoting Labour Minister Jagjivan Ram, 14 January 1947, *Viceroy's Journal,* p. 410) 'There are strikes everywhere.... everybody wants higher wages and less work', Birla complained to Gandhi's secretary Pyarelal on 18 January (G.D. Birla, *Bapu,* Volume, p. 434). The strikes, however, were all on purely economic demands; what remained lacking was a sufficiently influential and determined political leadership.

The new development in 1946-47 was an upsurge in the countryside in several regions, most notably Bengal, parts of Kerala, and Telengana in Hyderabad state. Everywhere the Communist-led Kisan Sabha was moving towards more militant forms of action, and reaching out below the level of the revenue-or rent-paying landholding peasantry towards share-croppers, landless labourers, and tribals.

From 1945, Communist cadres like Shamrao and Godavari Parulekar had started living among the wretchedly exploited and backward Warli tribals of Umbargaon and Dahanu *talukas* of Thana district near Bombay. They organized a series of successful movements against forest-contractors, merchant-moneylenders and outside landlords on issues like debt-slavery, *veth* or vethi (forced labour), and low wages for harvesting and cutting trees and grass.

Tebhaga

In September 1946, the Bengal Provincial Kisan Sabha gave a call to implement through mass struggle the Floud Commission recommendation of *tebhaga*: two-thirds of the crop, instead of half or even less, for the sharecropper (*bargadar, bhagchasi,* or *adhyar*) working on land rented from *jotedars*. Communist cadres, including many urban student militants, went out into the countryside to organize *bargadars,* who had become a major and growing section of the rural population as poor peasants lost land through depression and famine and were pushed down to the level of share-croppers—they numbered 60% of villagers in some pockets which became *tebhaga* strongholds. The movement caught on suddenly from harvest-time in November, with the central slogan of *nij-khamare dhan tolo*: sharecroppers taking paddy to their own threshing floor and not to the *jotedar's* house as before, so as to enforce *tebhaga*. North Bengal became the storm-centre, particularly Thakurgaon sub-division of Dinajpur and adjoining areas of Jalpaiguri, Rangpur and Malda. *Tebhaga* pockets also developed in Mymensingh (Kishoreganj), Midnapur (Mahisadal, Sutahata and Nandigram) and 24 Parganas (Kakdwip), while the Hajongs in north Mymensingh who had won a reduction in their *tanka* (produce rent) in 1937–38 now demanded its conversion into cash so as to gain from higher prices. The North Bengal base was principally among Rajbansis, a lowly caste of tribal origin, mostly *adhyar* and poor peasant, but also including some big *jotedars,* among whom organization along class lines had already undercut a previous Sanskritizing movement claiming Kshatriya status (the Communist Rupnarayan Roy had won the Dinajpur seat in 1946, defeating both Congress and a Kshatrya Samiti candidate). Muslims did participate in considerable numbers in the *tebhaga* bases, despite Calcutta and Noakhali, producing leaders like Haji Muhammed Danesh, Niamat Ali, and even some *maulvis* who quoted the *Koran* to condemn *jotedar* oppression. But throughout south east Bengal, significantly and understandably enough, remained untouched, including the old Kisan Sabha stronghold of Tippera. Jotedar and (increasingly) police violence was sought to be countered by volunteers with *lathis*— 'Dumb through past centuries...it is inspiring to see him (the *bargadar)* marching across a field with his fellows, each man shouldering a lathi like a rifle, with a red flag at the head of the procession.' (*Statesman,* 19 March 1947, quoted in Sunil Sen, *Agrarian Struggle in Bengal 1946–47* p. 38)

But *lathis* are not rifles, and when the League ministry balanced its sop of a *bargadar* bill (not made into law before 1950, and even then seldom implemented) with intensified repression from February 1947, the movement faced a crisis which proved fatal. 20 Santals were killed near Balurghat in a clash with the police, and Sunil Sen lists 49 peasant martyrs in all. Some peasant militants now wanted arms, but the Communists did not have them and in any case had not really envisaged an all-out armed struggle. Socially, too, limitations were emerging: tribal elements pressed for greater militancy (including some tea-garden coolies in the Duars region of Jalpaiguri), but middle and poor peasant support declined, while in north Bengal towns the professional groups which were the mainstay of the national movement were extremely hostile (many had land, usually cultivated by *bargadars*). The Communists planned a general strike on 28 March, but meanwhile the Hindu Mahasabha campaign for Bengal partition was gaining strength, and renewed riots in Calcutta from 27 March ended all prospects of sympathetic actions in urban areas.

Punnapra-Vayalar

In the Shertalai-Alleppey-Ambalapuzha area of N.W. Travancore State, the Communists by 1946 had built up a very powerful base among coir-factory workers, fishermen, toddy-tappers, and agricultural labourers (employed by the big *jenmis* or landlords of the nearby Kuttanad region). The close proximity of smalltown industries with agricultural occupations made the formula of worker-peasant alliance more of a reality here than in most areas, and trade unions had become powerful enough to control recruitment in coir factories, establish informal but very popular arbitration courts, and even win (after a strike in July 1946) the right to run their own ration shops. Meanwhile an explosive political situation was created by the coincidence of acute food scarcity with the plan announced in January 1946 by Dewan C.P. Ramaswami Iyer of an 'American-model' constitution with assemblies elected by universal suffrage but an executive controlled by a Dewan appointed by the Maharaja. The ambitious Dewan was clearly working for an independent Travancore under his own control when the British left, and would in fact announce this as his intention in June 1947. While the State Congress temporized, with some leaders like Pattom Thanu Pillai apparently not averse to a compromise with Ramaswami Iyer, the Communists launched a massive campaign with the slogan *'Amerikkan modal—Arabyan katalil'* ('throw the American model into the Arabian sea'). From September 1946, the State Government began an all-out campaign against the Communists and trade unions of the Alleppey region, with police camps, mass arrests, and brutal torture in jails. In self-defence much more than out of any plan for insurrection, camps were set up where persecuted workers took shelter, protected by volunteers who were given some elementary military training. A political general strike began in the Alleppey-Shertalai area from 22 October, and a partially-successful attack was made two days later on Punnapra police camp four miles south of Alleppey, with volunteers armed with wooden spears crawling forward despite intense firing to engage the police in hand-to-hand combat. Nine rifles were captured here, but apparently no use could be found for them. Martial law was proclaimed on 25 October, and on the 27th the volunteer head-quarters at Vayalar (near Shertalai), was stormed by the army after a veritable blood-bath. Conservative estimates speak of about 800 killed in this brief but very bloody Punnapra-Vayalar rising. The massacre prevented any alliance between the totally discredited Dewan and the Congress, though the latter was careful next year to bring about the integration of Travancore with India through pressure tactics rather than any uninhibited mass struggle—tactics which succeeded because Ramaswami Iyer realized that the alternative to peaceful surrender might well be a violent revolution. In this sense it was Punnapra-Vayalar which really brought about the integration of Travancore into India, blocking the road towards Balkanization. For the Communists, despite great suffering and an immediate setback, Punnapra-Vayalar meant all the prestige of heroic martyrdom, and its symbolic value is indicated by Communist ministers in Kerala, since 1957, making it a point to visit the two villages before taking office. (K.C. George, *Immortal Punnapra-Vayalar,* New Delhi, 1975; Robin Jeffrey's article in *Congress and the Raj*).

Telengana

Where *tebhaga* and Punnapra-Vayalar had gone to the brink of armed struggle, but failed to cross it, Telengana between July 1946 and October 1951 saw the biggest peasant guerrilla war so far of modern Indian history, affecting at its height about 3000 villages spread over 16,000 square miles and with a population of three million. Hyderabad under the Asafjahi Nizams was marked by a combination of religious-linguistic domination (by a small Urdu-speaking Muslim elite over predominantly-Hindu Telegu, Marathi and Kannada language-groups), total absence of political and civil liberties, and the grossest forms of feudal exploitation particularly in the Telengana region, where Muslim and high-caste Hindu *deshmukhs* (revenue-collectors-turned-landlords) and *jagirdars* extorted *vetti* or forced labour and payments in kind from lower caste and tribal peasants and debt-slaves. Landgrabbing by the *doras* ('masters'—the usual term for landlord), had worsened peasant conditions from the Depression days. Unlike *tebhaga* and to a much greater extent than in Travancore, the Communist-led agrarian revolt thus retained, till the entry of the Indian army in September 1948, the broader dimensions of a national-liberation struggle against the Nizam and his Razakar bands, though a limiting factor was the aloofness or hostility of the urban Muslim population, including even a substantial section of the working-class. Another decisive advantage was the slack manner in which the Arms Act had been enforced in the state, in very sharp contrast to British India: 'Large numbers of country-guns—muzzle-loaders—were available and were in common use.' Till September 1948, funds for buying arms could be collected more or less openly in the neighbouring Andhra districts of Madras, since everyone—including the Congress—wanted to resist the Razakars and block the Nizam's bid to set up an independent Muslim-dominated state-Sundarayya recalls ₹20,000 being raised in three days from Vijayawada alone. (P. Sundarayya, *Telengana People's Struggle and Its Lessons,* Calcutta 1972, pp. 2, 7–9, 40).

The Communists during the war years had built up a very strong base in Telengana villages, working through the Andhra Mahasabha and leading numerous local struggles on issues like wartime exactions, rationing abuses, excessive rents, and *vethi*. The beginning of the uprising is traditionally dated from 4 July 1946, when thugs employed by the *deshmukh* of Visunur (one of the biggest and most oppressive of Telengana landlords, with 40,000 acres) in Jangaon *taluka* of Nalgonda murdered a village militant, Doddi Komaryya, who had been trying to defend a poor washer-woman's mite of land. The initial centres of resistance were in Jangaon, Suryapet and Huzurnagar *talukas* of Nalgonda, but the movement soon spread into the neighbouring districts of Warangal and Khammam. Peasants organized into village *sangams* began by using lathis, slings with stones, and chilli powder. Faced with brutal repression, proper armed guerrilla squads began to be constituted from early 1947, with bands going upto 100 to 120 per squad for a brief while, and including at its height 10,000 village defence volunteers and 2000 regular squad members. Between August 1947 and September 1948, the struggle attained its greatest intensity and strength, with Communists making skilful use of and radicalizing the anti-Nizam slogans of the State Congress leaders (who operated mostly from Indian territory, unlike the Communist guerrillas): thus a call for resignation of revenue officials was converted into a campaign to destroy revenue and rent records. On the eve of the police action of September 1948, the Communists were recognized even by their enemies as *cheekati doralu* ('kings of the night') of much of the Telengana countryside. In villages controlled by the guerrillas, *vetti* and bonded labour disappeared, agricultural wages were raised (despite opposition from otherwise sympathetic rich peasants), unjustly seized land was returned to their previous peasant holders, and steps were taken to redistribute waste lands as well as land above a ceiling of 100 acres dry and 10 acres wet (a fairly high level, fixed in order not to alienate better-off peasants, but still much lower than the later Congress government ceiling). Sundarayya, a leading figure in the armed struggle, has given a vivid and moving picture of life in the liberated areas; measures to improve irrigation and fight cholera, the amicable settlement of many peasant and family disputes, some improvements in the status of women, a decline in untouchability and superstitions, and the use of folk songs and plays to preach revolutionary values.

The situation changed quickly after September 1948, and indeed the police action was probably undertaken in large part as a move to halt the Communist advance, for otherwise New Delhi and particularly Patel had seemed quite willing to strike a deal with the Nizam—'I wondered why the Government of India was disproportionately lenient to the Nizam', comments the State Congress leader Swami Ramananda Tirtha (*Memoirs of Hyderabad Freedom Struggle*, p. 190). The rout of the Razakars gave a lot of arms to the guerrillas, but now they had to face the much better equipped and disciplined regular Indian army, while the slogan of overthrowing the government of newly-independent India naturally had very much less appeal than the earlier anti-Nizam struggle. It might have been wiser, Communists later reflected, to have confined the armed struggle after 1948 to more limited aims of agrarian reform alone and so retained the possibility of a negotiated settlement at some stage; some, like Ravi Narayan Reddi, have even argued that continuing the guerrilla struggle itself had been a mistake once the Indian army had marched in. (Sundarayya, pp. 121–2, 135: Ravi Narayan Reddi, *Heroic Telengana—Reminiscences and Experiences,* New Delhi 1973, p. 60) The Communists now quickly lost the active support of better-off peasants, and energetic and often very ruthless military action drove them out of the settled plains of Nalgonda, Warangal and Khammam into the deep forests of the Nallamallai hills across the Krishna to the south and the Godavari region to the north-east. Here they established some new bases among Chenchu and Koya tribals, whom they rescued from the oppression of forest officials and trader-moneylenders; but by 1950–1, guerrilla action had degenerated into occasional individual sorties and murders, sharp internal political differences had emerged, and sheer survival had become the overriding problem. It is interesting that the last stand of the Telengana guerrillas was in the Godavari forest zone—where Alluri Sitarama Raju had fought a generation earlier.

Even after defeat, the Communists retained enormous support for some years, winning every Assembly seat from Nalgonda and Warangal in 1952 and returning Ravi Narayan Reddi to Parliament by a majority bigger than Nehru's. The positive achievements, direct or indirect, of the Telengana struggle were not inconsiderable. Peasant guerrillas, more than any other factor, brought down the autocratic-feudal regime of India's biggest princely state, frustrating the compromise bid of the November 1947 stand-still agreement made by Patel and V.P. Menon. The destruction of Hyderabad state also cleared the way for the formation of Andhra Pradesh on linguistic lines a few years later, thus realizing another old aim of the national movement in this region. The peasants did win some enduring gains: *vetti* could not be restored, not all the redistributed land was lost, the Congress regime had to abolish *jagirdari* (though with ample compensation) in 1949 and impose at least a theoretical ceiling, and it is significant that Vinoba Bhave's Bhoodan movement began precisely in Nalgonda. It is true that partial gains tended to make the better-off Andhra peasants politically conservative from the mid-1950's—but then that is a problem faced by many peasant revolutionary movements.

1947: FREEDOM AND PARTITION

The socially radical movements of which Telengana was the climax never coalesced into an organized and effective countrywide political alternative. The fear they undoubtedly inspired, however, helped to bring about the final compromise by which a 'peaceful' transfer of power was purchased at the cost of Partition and a communal holocaust. V.P. Menon, the senior bureaucrat who was to play a key role in 1947–48 as confidante of Patel and trusted advisor of Wavell and later of Mountbatten, reported to the Viceroy in the wake of the early-1947 strike wave 'that Congress leaders were losing popularity...there were serious internal troubles in Congress and great fear of the Left Wing; and that the danger of labour difficulties was acute'. A week later, Wavell's *Journal* recorded a conversation with Patel 'about the danger of the Communists. I got the impression he would like to declare the Party illegal'—a desire which the Home Minister would fulfil within a few months of independence, in March 1948. (*Viceroy's Journal*, entries for 9 and 15 January 1947, pp. 408, 411). The British Government was also quick to come forward with a dramatic gesture when in February 1947 League refusal to join the Constituent Assembly and cooperate in Cabinet functioning led to a major political crisis, with the Congress demanding resignation of the League ministers and threatening to withdraw its own nominees from the Interim Government if its demands were not met. This was the immediate context of Attlee's famous speech in the Commons on 20 February 1947, fixing June 1948 as a dead-line for transfer of power. Even if Indian politicians had not agreed by that date on a constitution, the British would relinquish power 'whether as a whole to some form of Central Government for British India, or in some areas to the existing provincial Governments, or in such other way as may seem most reasonable and in the best interests of the Indian people'. British powers and obligations *vis-a-vis* princely states would also end with transfer of power, but these would not be transferred to any successor government in British India. The hint of partition and possibly even Balkanization into numerous states was very clear, but the bait of complete transfer of power by a definite and fairly early date proved too tempting to be refused—particularly as the only real alternative for the Congress was to plunge into another mass confrontation, difficult in the context of communal riots and very dangerous socially in view of what appeared to be a growing Left menace. The British Prime Minister's statement also announced the replacement of Wavell by Mountbatten.

The Mountbatten Plan

Something like a cult has developed around Mountbatten, most obviously in Collins and Lapierre's journalistic best-seller *Freedom At Midnight* (1976) but also in some British and even Indian circles, depicting him as super-statesman-cum-Prince Charming who solved the sub-continent's problems in record time through a combination of military forthrightness, sheer personality, and tact. There is enormous exaggeration here. If Mountbatten proved more decisive and quick in taking decisions than previous Viceroys like Wavell, this was because he had been informally given much greater powers to decide things on the spot by the British Government than his predecessors. Behind this again lay the firm decision to quit at the earliest, since the only real alternative, as Cripps made clear during the Commons debate on Attlee's statement, was to go in for total repression and be prepared to station large numbers of British troops in India for years—to which 'it is certain that the people of this country (Britain)—short as we are of manpower, as we all know—would not have consented', and which 'would be politically impracticable, from both a national and an international point of view, and would arouse the most bitter animosity of all parties in India against us' ('quoted in V.P. Menon, *Transfer of Power in India*, p. 346). Wavell in the final draft of his 'breakdown plan' in September 1946 had already suggested total withdrawal by 31 March 1948 (*Viceroy's Journal*, p. 344). The formula of freedom-with-Partition was coming to be widely accepted well before Mountbatten took over charge. The one major innovation—immediate transfer of power on the basis of grant of Dominion Status (with a right of secession), thus obviating the need to wait for agreement in the Constituent Assembly on new political structures—was suggested not by Mountbatten, but by V.P. Menon to the Secretary of State in January 1947. Patel, significantly enough, had privately agreed with this idea, even though formally it meant a retreat from the Lahore resolution of 1929, since Dominion Status would ensure a peaceful and very quick transfer of power, win for India influential friends in Britain, and allow for some continuity in the bureaucracy and army. (Menon, pp. 363–4) Mountbatten was responsible to a considerable extent for the break-neck speed at which the whole process of transfer was carried out, but this left many anomalies in arranging Partition details, and totally failed to prevent the Punjab massacre. On the whole one tends to agree with Penderel Moon's statement that Mountbatten's claim 'to great merit for the manner of our departure from Indian rings somewhat hollow. (*Divide and Quit,* p. 283)

After a rapid series of 133 interviews with political leaders between 24 March and 6 May, Mountbatten decided that the Cabinet Mission framework had become untenable, and formulated an alternative with the appropriate code-name Plan Balkan. This envisaged transfer of power to separate provinces (or to confederations, if formed before the transfer), with the Bengal and Punjab assemblies being given the options to vote for partition of their provinces; the various units thus formed, along with princely states rendered independent by the lapse of paramountcy, would then have the choice of joining India, Pakistan, or remaining separate. The plan was quickly abandoned, however, when Nehru reacted violently against it after Mountbatten informed him about it privately in Simla on 10 May, and the V.P. Menon-Patel suggestion of transfer to two central governments, India and Pakistan, on the basis of grant of Dominion Status was taken up instead. Accepted by Congress, League, and Sikh leaders on 2 June and announced the next day, this became the basis of the India Independence Act which was ratified by British Parliament and Crown on 18 July and implemented on 15 August. Mountbatten himself, as well as his admirers have been full of praise for the decision, on an 'absolute hunch', of showing the first plan privately to Nehru beforehand. The historically much more significant point surely is that Nehru's opposition was sufficient to make Mountbatten abandon a plan on which British officials had been working for several weeks—once again revealing the potential strength of the Congress position, which its leaders repeatedly, failed to use due to their desire for a quick and peaceful accession to power. It should be added that while Nehru was certainly correct in scenting in the fragmentation proposal an imperialist design to build up in India a number of small client states and so create something like a Northern Ireland problem, the alternative that was adopted also blocked some interesting non-communal regional possibilities. In Bengal, where many in the League were not too eager to be ruled from distant Punjab, Suhrawardy and Abul Hashem had come forward with a plan for a united, independent Bengal, which a few Congress leaders like Sarat Bose seemed prepared to consider (despite the bitter opposition of Hindu communalist opinion to what would have to be a Muslim-majority state). In the N.W.F.P., demands were being raised for a free Pathan state, and the local Congress leadership under Abdul Ghaffar Khan felt that only such a slogan could counter the League bid to capture the province for Pakistan, for anti-Muslim riots in Hindu majority provinces had weakened the old sense of identification with Indian nationalism. The 3 June plan halted these developments by compelling provincial assemblies to choose between the two dominions, India and Pakistan, alone. It is difficult to avoid the conclusion that the Congress leadership in 1947 let down very badly indeed the Pathans who had supported the national movement so consistently from the late-1920s. Though the existing N.W.F.P. assembly had a Congress majority and had voted in favour of joining the Constituent Assembly, a plebiscite was still forced on the province on the question of choice between joining India or Pakistan. The Congress High Command protested, but did not make it a breaking point (as Nehru had successfully done on Plan Balkan); nor did it insist either on a decision by universal franchise, or on inclusion in the choice before voters of the independent Pakhtoonistan option. The N.W.F.P. Congress eventually decided to boycott the plebiscite in protest—and N.W.F.P. went to Pakistan by a vote of 50.99% of the total, very limited electorate of 572,798 (i.e., by the decision of just 9.52% of the total population of the province). The Frontier Gandhi would later declare with justice that he and his movement had been 'thrown to the wolves' by the Congress leadership.

Integration of States

With the impending lapse of paramountcy, the question of the future of the princely states became a vital one. The more ambitious rulers or their *dewans* (like Hyderabad, Bhopal or Travancore) were dreaming of an independence which would keep them as autocratic as before, and such hopes received considerable encouragement from the Government of India's Political Department under Conrad Corfield till Mountbatten enforced a more realistic policy. Meanwhile a new upsurge of the states peoples' movement had begun in 1946–47, demanding everywhere political rights and elective representation in the Constituent Assembly, and containing in some places considerable socially-radical possibilities—as we have already seen in the cases of Travancore or Hyderabad. The Congress criticized the Cabinet Mission plan for not providing for elected members from states. Nehru presided over the Udaipur and Gwalior session of the All India States Peoples' Conference (December 1945 and April 1947), and declared at Gwalior that states refusing to join the Constituent Assembly would be treated as hostile. But verbal threats and speeches apart, the Congress leadership—or more precisely, Sardar Patel, who took charge of the new States (in place of the Political) Department in July 1947, together with V.P. Menon who became secretary—tackled the situation in what had become the standard practice of the party: using popular movements as a lever to extort concessions from princes while simultaneously restraining them (or even using force to suppress them once the prince had been brought to heel, as in Hyderabad). The pattern had already been indicated in Kashmir in 1946. When Sheikh Abdulla was arrested on 20 May while leading the National Conference's 'Quit Kashmir' movement against the very unpopular and despotic Hindu Maharaja of a Muslim-majority state, Nehru initially rushed to the Kashmir leader's support and was even briefly arrested on 20 June for defying a ban on his entry into the state. Patel assured Wavell, however, that Nehru had gone again this advice (Wavell's interview with Patel, 27 June 1946, Mansergh, Vol. VII, pp. 1068–9), and very soon began negotiation with Kashmir's prime minister, Kak, which culminated in the Maharaja's accession to India after raiders from Pakistan invaded the state in October 1947. 'This alters the whole outlook for the States', the Nawab of Bhopal declared on hearing of the appointments of Patel and Menon to head the new States Department, and on 5 July 1947 Patel assured the princes: 'The Congress are no enemies of the Princely Order, but, on the other hand, wish them and the people under their aegis all prosperity, contentment and happiness'. (V.P. Menon, *The Story of the Integration of Indian States,* p. 96)

The incorporation of Indian states took place in two phases, with a skilful combination of baits and threats of mass pressure in both. By 15 August 1947, all states except Kashmir, Junagadh and Hyderabad had agreed to sign an Instrument of Accession with India (or, in a few cases like Bahawalpur, with Pakistan) acknowledging central authority over the three areas of defence, external affairs, and communications. The princes agreed to this fairly easily, for so far they were 'surrendering' only what they had never had (the three functions had been part of the para mountcy of the Crown), and there was no change as yet in internal political structures. The much more difficult process of 'integration' of states with neighbouring provinces or into new units like Kathiawar Union, Vindhya and Madhya Pradesh, Rajasthan or Himachal Pradesh, along with internal constitutional changes in states which for some years retained their old boundaries (Hyderabad, Mysore, Travancore-Cochin), was also accomplished within the remarkably short period of little more than a year. Here the principal bait offered was that of very generous privy purses, while some princes were also made into Governors or Rajpramukhs. The rapid unification of India is certainly Sardar Patel's greatest achievement, but we must not forget the considerable role played here, too, by the existence or at least the potential presence of mass pressures. Thus the eastern States Union formed by recalcitrant princes crumbled in December 1947 in the face of powerful Praja Mandal (as well as some tribal) agitations in Orissa states like Nilgiri, Dhenkanal and Talcher. Junagadh in Kathiawad whose Muslim ruler tried to join Pakistan was brought to heel by a combination of popular agitation with Indian police action. The Congress, exceptionally strong in Mysore since the late 1930s, launched a fairly uninhibited 'Mysore Chalo' agitation on its own in September 1947 which forced substantial political changes in a democratic direction by 12 October. V.P. Menon persuaded the Travancore Dewan C.P. Ramaswami Iyer to give up his dream of continued personal power through the 'American Model' by pointing to the 'Communist menace' (Ibid., p. 111), while the Telengana armed struggle weakened the Nizam and also provided one important reason for military intervention.... Our first task should be to round up the Razakars.... Our next, not in point of importance but because everything could not be attempted simultaneously, was to contain and root out the Communists'. (V.P. Menon, recalling his conversation with Military Governor J.N. Chaudhuri, Ibid., p. 362)

The last two and a half months of British rule saw the working-out of the details of the Mountbatten Plan at remarkable speed, for the political leaders of Bengal Hindus and Punjab Hindus and Sikhs had now become more fervent advocates of partition than the League itself—'with a quite unprecedented unanimity all set forth together on a path leading straight to mass slaughter'. (Penderel Moon, p. 70) As expected, the minority members of the Bengal and Punjab assemblies, who had been given the right to meet separately, voted for partition; the Sind assembly opted for Pakistan; and the League won the plebiscite ordered (again on the existing, limited, franchise) in the Muslim-majority Sylhet district of Assam. Boundary lines were drawn, again at terrific speed and often ignoring local details, by two commissions, both headed by a British lawyer (Radcliffe) who knew next to nothing about Indian conditions or geography. The attempt to combine communal with some economic and strategic considerations caused a number of anomalies: Muslims resented the loss of Gurdaspur in Punjab and of Murshidabad and Nadia (as well as Calcutta) in Bengal; Hindus and Sikhs that of Lahore and the Canal colonies, of Khulna and Chittagong Hill Tracts. But protests remained half-hearted, for nothing was being allowed to stand in the way of the headlong rush of Congress and League leaders towards power. Mountbatten graciously agreed to the Congress request to act as Governor-General of the new Indian Dominion; he was prevented from assuming the same office in Pakistan, too, only by Jinnah's desire to take it up himself.

The Fifteenth of August

So Independence came to the sub-continent, and to many it must have seemed a sorry thing if compared to the generous dreams of the freedom-fighters. For far too many Muslims in India and Hindus in Pakistan, freedom-with-Partition meant or came to mean over the years a cruel choice between threat of sudden violence and squeezing of employment and economic opportunities, or a forcible tearing-out of age-old roots to join the stream of refugees—all the manifold human tragedies so movingly portrayed in Balraj Sahni's last film *Garam Hawa*. At another, not entirely unrelated level, the economic and social contradictions that had provided the deeper roots of popular anti-imperialism had not been resolved, for the privileged groups in town and country had been able to successfully detach attainment of political independence from radical social change. The British had gone, but the bureaucracy and police they had built up continued with little change, and could prove as oppressive and ruthless as before (or even more perhaps at times). The Mahatma's isolation and agony during the last months of his life were not due to communal riots alone. On the eve of his murder, he had warned that the country still had to 'attain social, moral and economic independence in terms of its 700,000 villages', that Congress had 'created rotten boroughs leading to corruption and…institutions, popular and democratic only in name', and that consequently the Congress as a political party should be dissolved and replaced by a Lok Sevak Sangh of genuinely dedicated, self-sacrificing constructive village workers. (N.K. Bose, *My Days with Gandhi,* Calcutta 1953, pp. 305, 307) For many committed Leftists, such independence seemed little better than a mockery: 'The battleships (of the RIN) lie motionless in harbour, disarmed by treachery; in Noakhali, Bihar and Garmukteswar, Hindus and Muslims find unity only after death'; and 'the passions of youth have become the lust of aging men'—a savage, but not entirely unjust, comment on the transformation of patriots into power-hungry politicians. (Samar Sen, in the last two poems he has written)

Yet the millions who rejoiced throughout the sub-continent, thrilled to Nehru's midnight speech on India's 'tryst with destiny', and made of 15 August an unforgettable experience even for someone who was then only a child, had not been entirely deluded. The Communists in 1948–51 learnt to their cost that the slogan *Yeh Azadi Jhuta Hai* ('this freedom is a farce') cut little ice. Indian freedom was the beginning of a process of decolonization which has proved irresistible, at least so far as political independence is concerned. Far from becoming a puppet of Britain or the U.S.A., India under Nehru did gradually develop an independent foreign policy, based on the then-novel concept of non-alignment and friendship with socialist countries and the emerging Third World. A broadly democratic constitution was promulgated in January 1950—despite many limitations, a big advance on British Indian institutions which had avoided universal suffrage till the very end. Princes and *zamindars* were gradually eased out, land ceilings imposed (though seldom implemented), the old ideal of linguistic reorganization of states was achieved in 1956, basic industries were built up through planned development of a public sector, and food production increased considerably in sharp contrast to the near-stagnation of the first half of the century. None of this happened automatically due to August 1947, for much of it was only realized through bitter popular struggles—yet the winning of political independence has surely been an essential prerequisite. The contradictions remain, however, perhaps more glaring than ever before, and rooted in the choice of a broadly capitalist path of development—a path determined by the dominant pattern of our freedom movement, over which the bourgeoisie was able to establish and retain its general leadership.

The six decades of India's history that we have surveyed thus find meaning and relevance if considered as a complex process of change through struggle which is still far from complete. Perhaps the reflections of a British socialist writer on history and its contradictions can serve as an appropriate epitaph:

'...pondered how men fight and lose the battle, and the thing that they fought for comes about in spite of their defeat, and when it comes turns out not to be what they meant, and other men have to fight for what they meant under another name.' (William Morris, *A Dream of John Ball,* 1887)

FURTHER READINGS LIST

CHAPTER 1

The N.A.I. and the N.M.M.L. now have between them the private papers of most Viceroys and Secretaries of State in microfilms. For the papers of Governors and lower-level officials, however, the, researcher still has to go to the I.O.L. (London) or the Cambridge South Asia Study Centre. The N.A.I. holdings of the Government of India files are in some ways superior to those of the I.O.L.; a useful guide here is Low, Iltis and Wainwright, *Government Archives in South Asia* (Cambridge, 1969). The N.M.M.L. has built up a magnificent collection on 20th Century Indian history, including private papers of Indian politicians and businessmen, the All-India Congress Committee files, documents of the States People's Movement and labour and *kisan* organizations, recorded interviews of political activists, and microfilms of unpublished theses. Contemporary pamphlets lie scattered in many libraries, and proscribed publications may be read at the N.A.I., I.O.L. and the British Museum. Newspaper preservation leaves much to be desired, though there are valuable collections at the National Library (Calcutta), N.M.M.L., I.O.L. and the British Museum.

Excerpts from contemporary documents, mainly official, may be read in C. H. Philips (ed.), *Evolution of India and Pakistan 1858–1947* (London, 1962); see also B. L. Grover (ed.), *A Documentary Study of British Policy towards Indian Nationalism* (Delhi, 1967), from which I have taken the quotations from Dufferin and Reay. Constitutional documents are easily available, in A. C. Banerji (ed.), *Indian Constitutional Documents 1757–1947,* 4 vols. (Calcutta, 1961), and Gwyer and Appadorai (ed.) *Speeches and Documents on the Indian Constitution,* 2 vols. (London, 1957). The more advanced student will find fascinating material on the last years of British rule in the official papers printed in N. Mansergh (ed.), *Transfer of Power 1942–47* (Nine volumes published so far, London, 1970 onwards). The Indian Council of Historical Research has planned two multi-volume series of documents, taken more from non-official sources, on the national movement and on the last decade of British rule *(Towards Freedom* project) but these are still at the preparatory stage.

The recent spurt in research has rendered largely out-of-date old textbooks and surveys like P. Spear, *Oxford History of India* (New Delhi, 1974), P. Sitaramayya, *History of the Indian National Congress,* 2 vols. (Bombay, 1946–47) or R. C. Mazumdar (ed.) *British Paramountcy and Indian Renaissance* (Bombay, 1974) and *Struggle for Freedom* (Bombay, 1969). A similar comment has to be made about the two general histories of the national movement, written from sharply opposed points of view; Tarachand, *History of the Freedom Movement in India,* 4 vols. (Delhi, 1961–72) and R.C. Mazumdar, *History of Freedom Movement,* 3 vols. (Calcutta, 1962–63). Bipan Chandra, *Modern India* (New Delhi, 1971), though written for schools, is a valuable introduction. R. P. Dutt, *India Today* (Bombay, 1947; revised edn, Calcutta, 1970) and D. R. Gadgil, *Industrial Evolution of India in Recent Times* (Bombay, 1944) remain useful as general surveys of economic developments. M. N. Srinivas, *Social Change in Modern India* (California, 1966) provides an introduction to relevant sociological concepts.

Official attitudes are surveyed on the basis of private papers in S. Gopal, *British Policy in India 1858–1905* (Cambridge, 1965), while Hutchins, *Illusion of Permaence* (Princeton, 1967), has many illuminating insights. Among the numerous studies of individual Viceroys, mention may be made of Ronaldshay, *Life of Lord Curzon,* Vol. II (London, 1928); M. N. Das, *India under Minto and Morley* (London, 1964); S. Gopal, *Viceroyalty of Lord Irwin* (Oxford, 1957); and the recent study of Chelmsford by P. Robb, *The Government of India and Reform Policies Towards Politics and the Constitution 1916–21*, London, 1976). R. Coupland's old study of constitutional developments, *Constitutional Problem in India* (London, 1944), is still useful in its own limited field.

The official edition of the *Collected Works* of Gandhi (New Delhi, 1958, onwards) now runs into 70 volumes, while the *Selected Works* of Jawaharlal Nehru (New Delhi, 1972 onwards) have gone up to 13 volumes so far. Many Indian leaders have left autobiographies: Surendranath Banerji, *A Nation in Making* (Calcutta, 1925, 1963); Bepin Chandra Pal, *Memories of My Life and Times* (2nd edn., Calcutta, 1973); Lajpat Rai, *Autobiographical Writings* (ed. V. C. Joshi, Delhi, 1965); M. K. Gandhi, *Story of My Experiments with Truth* (First English edn., Ahmedabad, 1927); J. Nehru, *An Autobiography* (London, 1936); Subhas Bose, *The Indian Struggle* (Calcutta, 1935, 1964); Maulana Azad, *India Wins Freedom* (Bombay, 1959), and Rajendra Prasad, *An Autobiography* (Bombay, 1957). The massive biographical literature includes S. Wolpert, *Tilak and Gokhale* (California, 1962); B. R. Nanda, *Gokhale, The Indian Moderates and the British Raj* (Delhi, 1977); Tendulkar's 8 volumes biography of Gandhi, *The Mahatma* (Delhi, 1960–63); Pyarelal's works on Gandhi's first and last phase (Ahmedabad,

1956–58); M. Brecher, *Nehru: A Political Biography* (London, 1959) and S. Gopal, *Jawaharlal Nehru,* Vol. I (London, 1976).

John Strachey, *India* (London, 1888), V. Chirol, *Indian Unrest* (London, 1910), and Verney Lovett, *A History of the Indian Nationalist Movement* (London, 1920, 1968) make interesting reading as typifying unabashed imperialist historiography. A number of State Governments after 1947 commissioned official histories of the freedom movement for their own regions; these at times contain useful source-materials, particularly Government of Bombay, *Source-materials for a History of the Freedom Movement in India,* Vols. I, II (Bombay, 1959) and M. Venkatarangiyya, *Freedom Struggle in Andhra Pradesh,* 3 vols. (Hyderabad, 1965). The first generation of Marxian work on modern Indian history is represented, apart from R. P. Dutt, by M. N. Roy, *India in Transition* (1922; new edn., Bombay, 1971) A. R. Desai, *Social Background of Indian Nationalism,* (Bombay, 1959 and Balabushevich and Dyakov (ed.), *A Contemporary History of India* (New Delhi, 1964). Soviet historians have also published a volume on Tilak: Reisner and Goldberg (eds.), *Tilak and the Struggle for Indian Freedom,* (New Delhi, 1966) and several books on modern economic history, V. Pavlov, *Indian Capitalist Class* (New Delhi, 1964); A. Levkovski, *Capitalism in India,* (New Delhi, 1966).

For interpretations on nationalism in terms of regional elites, see Anil Seal, *The Emergence of Indian Nationalism: Competition and Collaboration in the Later 19th Century* (Cambridge, 1968); J. H. Broomfield, *Elite Conflict in a Plural Society–20th Century Bengal* (Berkeley, 1968); and Judith Brown, *Gandhi's Rise to Power—Indian Politics 1915–1922* (Cambridge, 1972), Brown's second book, *Gandhi and Civil Disobedience; The Mahatma in Indian Politics 1928–34* (Cambridge, 1977), tries to combine, rather uneasily, the early and the revised 'Cambridge' approach. The revised version, emphasizing locality and faction, was announced in Gallagher, Johnson, Seal (eds.), *Locality, Province and Nation* (Cambridge, 1973), and developed in Gordon Johnson, *Provincial Politics and Indian Nationalism: Bombay and the Indian National Congress 1880–1915* (Cambridge, 1973); F. Robinson, *Separatism among Indian Muslims: The Politics of the United Provinces Muslims, 1860–1923* (Cambridge, 1974); C. J. Baker and D. A. Washbrook, *South India 1880–1940* (Delhi, 1975); C. A. Bayly, *Local Roots of Indian Politics—Allahabad 1880–1920* (Oxford, 1975); D. A. Washbrook, *The Emergence of Provincial Politics: Madras Presidency 1870–1920* (Cambridge, 1976); and C.J. Baker, *The Politics of South India, 1920–1927* (Cambridge, 1976). The recently published Gallagher memorial number of *Modern Asian Studies,* Baker, Johnson, Seal, (eds.) *Power, Profit and Politics: Essays on Imperialism, Nationalism and Change in 20th Century India,* (Cambridge,

1981) seems to indicate yet another shift, with political analysis in terms of factions largely abandoned, except in Seal's two articles, in favour of economic history.

D. A. Low has edited two important collections of essays, *Soundings in Modern South Asian History* (California, 1968) and *Congress and the Raj: Facets of the Indian Struggle 1917–47* (London, 1977); while Ravinder Kumar (ed.), *Essays on Gandhian Politics: The Rowlatt Satyagraha of 1919* (Oxford, 1971) is another major product of scholarship based on Canberra. Robin Jeffrey (ed.), *People, Princes and Paramount Power: Society and Politics in the Indian Princely States* (Delhi, 1978), James Manor, *Political Change in an Indian State: Mysore 1917–55* (Delhi, 1977) and Byorn Hettne, *Political Economy of Indirect Rule: Mysore 1881–1947* (London, 1977) venture into so far largely neglected terrain. Recent studies of Imperial policy-making include R. J. Moore, *Crisis of Indian Unity 1917–40* (Oxford, 1974) and P. S. Gupta, *Imperialism and British Labour* (London, 1975). Among American scholars, special mention has to be made of J. R. McLane's excellent study, *Indian Nationalism and the Early Congress* (Princeton, 1977). W. Hauser's thesis on the Bihar Provincial Kisan Sabha remains unpublished, but is available in microfilm at the Nehru Museum. Peter Hardy's *The Muslims of British India* (Cambridge, 1972) is a valuable introduction to the problems of Indian Muslims; see also Zia-ul-Hasan Faruqi, *The Deoband School and the Demand for Pakistan* (Asia, 1963) and Aziz Ahmed, *Islamic Modernism in India and Pakistan 1857–1964* (London, 1967). More recent publications include Rafiuddin Ahmad's interesting attempt at a 'history from below' of rural Islam, *The Bengal Muslims 1871–1906: A Quest for Identity* (Delhi, 1981), and two studies of the post-First World War period, Mushirul Hasan's *Nationalism and Communal Politics in India, 1916–1928* (Delhi, 1979) and D. Page, *Prelude to Partition: All-India Muslim Politics, 1921–32* (Delhi, 1981).

Bipan Chandra's *Rise and Growth of Economic Nationalism in India: Economic Policies of Indian National Leadership 1881–1915* (New Delhi, 1966) and *Nationalism and Colonialism in Modern India* (New Delhi, 1979) represent a strand in recent Indian Marxist history-writing which is very sympathetic towards nationalist leaders. Regional studies written from within a broadly Marxian framework include Sumit Sarkar, *Swadeshi Movement in Bengal 1903–08* (New Delhi, 1973); Amalendu Guha, *Planter Raj to Swaraj: Freedom Struggle and Electoral Politics in Assam 1826–1947* (New Delhi, 1977); Majid Siddiqi, *Agrarian Unrest in North India-United Provinces 1918–22* (New Delhi, 1978); and Gyanendra Pandey, *The Ascendancy of the Congress in Uttar Pradesh 1926–34—A Study in Imperfect Mobilization* (Delhi, 1978). I have used David Hardiman's important Sussex thesis,

Peasant Agitations in Kheda District, Gujarat, 1917–34, available in typescript at the Nehru Museum; since this book went to press, Hardiman has published a revised version as *Peasant Nationalists of Gujarat: Kheda District, 1917–1934* (Delhi, 1981). Stephen Henringham's thesis, *Protest and Control in North Bihar, India, 1917–42* (Australian National University, 1978) is also available in microfilm at the N.M.M.L., and has now been published as *Peasant Movements in Colonial India: North Bihar 1917–1942* (Canberra, 1982). Hitesh Sanyal's as yet incomplete work on rural Gandhians in South-West Bengal is so far available only in a number of papers in Bengali (*Anya Artha*, 1974–75 and *Chaturango* 1976–77). A major contribution to the emerging trend of 'history from below', which came out after this book went to press, is Ranajit Guha, (ed.), *Subaltarn Studies I: Writings on South Asian History and Society* (Delhi, 1982).

C. H. Heimsath's *Indian Nationalism and Hindu Social Reform* (Princeton, 1964) offers a convenient summary of its rather limited theme. A more important recent study is Kenneth Jones, *Arya Dharma: Hindu Consciousness in 19th Century Punjab* (California, 1976). For British educational policy and its impact, see Aparna Basu, *The Growth of Education and Political Development in India 1898–1920* (Delhi, 1974). Out of the vast and growing literature on caste movements, mention ha' to be made of Rudolph and Rudolph, *Vie Modernity of Tradition* (Chicago, 1967); R. L. Hardgrave, *The Nadars of Tamilnadu* (California, 1969); Robin Jeffrey, *Decline of Nayar Predominance—Society and Politics in Travancore 1847–1908* (Delhi, 1976); E. F. Irshchik, *Politics and Social Conflict in South India: The Non-Brahman Movement and Tamil Separatism 1916–29* (California, 1959); Rajni Kothari (ed.), *Caste in Indian Politics* (Bombay, 1970); and Gail Omvedt, *Cultural Revolt in a Colonial Society: The Non-Brahman Movement in Western India (1873–1930)* (Bombay, 1976). Eric Stokes, *Peasants and the Raj* (Cambridge, 1978), and the collection edited by A. R. Desai, *Peasant Struggles in India* (Delhi, 1979) may serve as introductions to the rapidly developing field of peasant studies.

R. C. Dutt's *Economic History of India in the Victorian Age* (London, 1904; reptd. Delhi, 1960), is still often useful, while D. H. Buchanan, *The Development of Capitalistic Enterprise in India* (New York, 1934) was a pioneering study. For agrarian history, Daniel and Alice Thorner's *Land and Labour in India* (Bombay, 1962) offers a stimulating introduction, D. Rothermund's *Government, Landlord and Peasant in India—Agrarian Relations under British Rule 1865–1935* (Wiesbaden, 1978) conveniently summarizes official policy, while more advanced students will find fascinating statistical material in D. Narain, *The Impact of Price Movements in Areas under Selected Crops in India 1900–1939* (Cambridge, 1963) and G. Blyn,

Agricultural Trends in India, 1891–1947: Output, Availability and Productivity (Philadelphia, 1966). Amiya K. Bagchi's *Private Investment in India 1900–1939* (Cambridge, 1972) represented a major breakthrough and is essential reading for twentieth century Indian economic history.

Among journals, the most useful for the period covered in this volume are *Indian Economic and Social History Review, Indian History Review, Economic and Political Weekly, Journal of Asian History,* and *Modern Asian Studies*.

CHAPTER 2

The evolution of British India administrative structure and policies in the late 19th Century may be studied chronologically in S. Gopal, *British Policy in India, 1858-1905* (Cambridge, 1965). Hiralal Singh, *Problems and Policies of the British in India, 1885–1898* (Bombay, 1963) is a useful survey of policies connected with Indianization of services, Council reform, the Army, and the Congress. Anil Seal, *Emergence of Indian Nationalism,* Ch. IV, attempts an interesting comparison between Lytton, Ripon and Dufferin; R. J. Moore, *Liberalism and Indian Politics 1872–1922* (London, 1966) outlines some of the inter-connections between British and Indian politics; see also B. L. Grover, *A Documentary Study of British Policy towards Indian Nationalism* (Delhi, 1965). Indian finances have been best analysed in S. Bhattacharji, *Financial Foundations of the British Raj* (Simla, 1971). Connections between administrative pressures and certain types of Indian politics are explored in C. A. Bayly, *Local Roots of Indian Politics,* Chs. IV-V, and D. A. Washbrook, *Emergence of Provincial Politics,* Ch. II. Interesting data regarding the beginnings of communal separatism in local government is presented by N. Gerald Barrier, 'The Punjab Government and Communal Politics, 1870–1908', *Journal of Asian Studies* (May 1968). Amiya Bagchi, *Private Investment in India, 1909–1939,* is fundamental reading for the economic dimensions of racism. For Indian political reactions, a valuable indicator is the voluminous Dinshaw Wacha-Dadabhai Naoroji correspondence, part of which has been published in R. P. Patwardhan (ed.). *Dadabhai Naoroji Correspondence,* Vol. II (Calcutta, 1977).

ii

The standard nationalist attack on British Indian economic policies was developed in Dadabhai Naoroji, *Poverty and Un-British Ride in India* (London, 1901); R. C. Dutt, *Economic History of India,* 2 vols. (London,

(1901, 1903); and W. Digby, *'Prosperous' British India* (London, 1901). The early critics of this approach included L. C. A. Knowles, *Economic Development of the British Overseas Empire* (London, 1928) and V. Anstey, *Economic Development of India* (Third edn. London, 1949). Bipan Chandra's *Rise and Growth of Economic Nationalism in India* is a most detailed and sympathetic survey of nationalist economic ideas; see also, for the drain and related themes, B. N. Ganguli, *Dadabhai Naoroji and the Drain Theory* (Bombay, 1965); J. McLane, *The Drain of Wealth and Indian Nationalism at the turn of the century*, from which I have taken the statistics on p. 25 in T. Raychaudhuri (ed.), *Contributions to Indian Economic History*, Vol. II (Delhi, 1963); and, for a revisionist view, K. N. Choudhuri, *India's International Economy in the 19th Century: An Historical Survey, MAS* (1968). The deindustrialization debate was revived in Morris, Raychaudhuri, Chandra, Matsui, 'Indian Economy in the 19th Century—A Symposium', reprint from *IESHR* (1968). More substantial contributions include D. and A. Thorner, 'Deindustrialisation in India 1881–1931 in Land and Labour in India' and A. K. Bagchi, 'Deindustrialisation in Gangetic Bihar 1809–1901', in B. De, et al. (ed.), *Essays in Honour of S. C. Sarkar* (New Delhi, 1976). For an up-to-date survey of the broad structure of ndo-British economic relations, see A. K. Bagchi, 'Foreign Capital and Economic Development of India', in Gough and Sharma (eds.). *Imperialism and Revolution in South Asia* (New York, 1973), while S. B. Saul, *Studies in British Overseas Trade* 1870–1914 (Liverpool, 1960) provides valuable data on India's role in solving British balance of payments problems.

Space permits only very selective references to the vast and growing literature on agrarian history. For Bengal, the numerous articles of B. B. Chaudhuri, particularly 'Agrarian Economy and Agrarian Relations in Bengal', in N. K. Sinha (ed.) *History of Bengal 1757–1905*, (Calcutta, 1967), 'Growth of Commercial Agriculture', *IESHR* (1970), 'Land Market in Eastern India', *IESHR*, (1975), and 'Process of Depeasantisation in Bengal and Bihar', *IHR* (1975), also Asok Sen and Partha Chatterji's articles in B. De (ed.), *Perspectives in Social Sciences*, Vol. II (Calcutta, 1982). For South India, see A. Sarada Raju, *Economic Conditions in Madras Presidency 1900–1950* (Madras, 1941) from which I have taken the comment of the Coimbatore peasant; N. Mukherji's article in Frykenburg (ed.), *Land Control and Social Structure in Indian History* (London, 1969); Dharma Kumar, *Land and Caste in South India: Agricultural Labour in Madras Presidency during the 19th Century* (Cambridge, 1965), and D. A. Washbrook, *Emergence of Provincial Politics*, Ch. 3. For U.P., see Bernard Cohn's valuable study of Benares, *Structural Change in Indian Rural Society*, in Frykenburg, *Land Control and Social Structure;* Eric Stokes, *Peasants and the Raj;*

Elizabeth Whitcombe, *Agrarian Conditions in Northern India, Vol. I: United Provinces under British Rule 1860–1900* (New Delhi, 1971); and T. R. Metcalfe, *Landlords and the British Raj: Northern India in the 19th Century* (Delhi, 1979). For Bombay Presidency, see Ravinder Kumar, 'Rise of Rich Peasants in Western India', in D. A. Low, *Soundings in Modern South Asian History.* Case studies of the specifics of commercialization include S. Mukherji 'Imperialism in Action through a Mercantilist Function', in *Essays in Honour of S. C. Sarkar,* and Shahid Amin, 'Peasants and Capitalists in Northern India: Kisans in the Cane Commodity Circuit in Gorakhpur in the 1930s', *Journal of Peasant Studies* (April, 1981). Blyn's findings have been conveniently summarized in D. and A. Thorner, *Land and Labour in India,* Ch. VII, while the possible deficiencies in the agricultural statistics used by Blyn have been analysed in Clive Dewey, 'Patwari and Chaukidar: Subordinate Officials and the Reliability of India's Agricultural Statistics' in Dewey and Hopkins (eds.), *The Imperial Impact* (London, 1978). Jan Breman, *Patronage and Exploitation: Changing Agrarian Relations, in South Gujarat, India* (California, 1974), makes fascinating reading on the problem of agricultural labourers. Advanced students should look up the 'mode of production debate', mainly in the paper of *EPW,* turning around the characterization of modern Indian agrarian relations as feudal, capitalist, or connected with a distinctive 'colonial' mode. Hamza Alavi, 'India and the Colonial Mode of Production', with its references, offers a summary of the earlier phases of this debate, in Miliband and Saville, *The Socialist Register* (London 1975); see also Utsa Patnaik, 'Class Differentiation within the Peasantry: An Approach to Analysis of Indian Agriculture', *(EPW,* 25 September, 1976) and Jairas Banaji, 'Capitalist Domination and the Small Peasantry: Deccan Districts in the late 19th Century', *(EPW* Special No., August, 1977).

On the closely-related problem of the nature of peasant differentiation and its political implications, see Hamza Alavi, 'Peasants and Revolution' in *Socialist Register,* (London, 1965) and N. Charlesworth's recent article, 'The "Middle Peasant Thesis" and the Roots of Rural Agitation in India, 1914–47', *Journal of Peasant Studies,* (April 1980). D. A. Washbrook's recent paper, 'Law, State and Society in Colonial India' in Baker, Johnson, Seal (eds.), *Power, Profit and Politics* raises a number of interesting theoretical issues.

On government economic policies, see S. Bhattacharji, 'Laissez-faire in India', *IESHR* (1965) and A. K. Bagchi, *Private Investment,* Ch. II. For British investments in India, see Arun Bose, 'Foreign Capital,' in V. B. Singh (ed.), *Economic History of India 1957–1956* (Bombay, 1965); M. Kidron, *Foreign Investments in India* (London, 1965); and Bagchi, *Private Investment,* Ch. VI. Bagchi's is also the best analysis of the differential growth of Indian capitalism and its roots in the colonial impact. For an alternative view, see M. O. Morris's review article of Bagchi, *Private Investment* in *MAS*, 1974. Specific studies of business communities include Amalendu Guha on Parsis (*EPW,* 29.8.1970 and 28.11.1970); K. Gillion, *Ahmedabad: A Study in India's Urban History* (California, 1968); T. A. Timberg, *The Marwaris* (Delhi, 1978), along with his articles on the same subject in *IESHR*, 1971, 1973; N. K. Sinha, *Economic History af Bengal*, Vol. III (Calcutta, 1970): C. P. Simmons, *Indigenous Enterprise in the Indian Coal-Mining Industry c. 1835–1939); IESHR* (1976); as well as two works by Soviet scholars, V. Pavlov, *Indian Capitalist Class* (New Delhi, 1964) and A. Levkovski; *Capitalism in India* (New Delhi, 1966). The economic history of labour is in its infancy, but see M. D. Morris, *Emergence of an Industrial Labour Force in India* (California, 1965), and Lalita Chakravarty, 'Emergence of an Industrial Labour Force in a Dual Economy—British India 1880–1920', (*IESHR*, 1978). The standard work on population remains K. Davis, *Population of India and Pakistan* (Princeton, 1951). D. and A. Thorner. *Land and Labour,* Ch. VII, is a critical survey of early national income estimates; the most systematic study so far is S. Sivasubramanian, *National Income of India, 1900–01 to 1946–47* (Mimeographed, Delhi University, 1965).

CHAPTER 3

Kathleen Gough attempted a typology of rural rebellions in 'Indian Peasant Uprisings', (*EPW* Special Number, August 1974); this has been reprinted in A.R. Desai (ed.), *Peasant Struggles in India* (Bombay, 1979), a useful, if uneven, collection. For tribal movements, see K. S. Singh, 'Colonial Transformation of the Tribal Society in Middle India', *Proceedings of the Indian History Congress,* (1977); Stephen Fuchs, *Rebellious Prophets: A Study of Messianic Movements in Indian Religions* (Bombay, 1965); and K. S. Singh, *Dust Storm and Hanging Mist: A Study of Birsa Munda and his movement in Chota Nagpur, (1874–1911* (Calcutta, 1966). David Arnold has recently written three papers on forms of rural and urban protest: 'Dacoity and Rural Crime in Madras 1860–1940', *Journal of Peasant Studies,* (January 1979); 'Looting, Grain Riots and Government Policy in South India', 1918, *(Past and Present,* August, 1979); and 'Industrial Violence in Colonial India', *Comparative Studies in Society and History,* (April, 1980). Arnold's 'Rebellious Hillman: the Gudem-Ramga Risings 1839–1924', in *Subaltarn Studies I,* came out after this book went to press. For a comparative analysis of social banditry and millenarianism as two forms of 'primitive rebellion', see the standard works of E. Hobsbawm, *Primitive Rebels* (Manchester, 1959) and *Bandits* (London, 1972), as well as P. Worseley, *The Trumpet Shall Sound* (London, 1970).

Phadke's autobiography may be read in Government of Bombay, *Source-Materials for a History of Freedom Movement in India,* Vol. I, 1818–85. For the Moplahs, I have used W. Logan, *Manual of Malabar District* (Madras, 1960), D. N. Dhanagare, 'Agrarian Conflict, Religion and Politics: The Moplah Rebellions in Malabar in the 19th and early 20th Century, (*Past and Present,* February, 1977), and–the best analysis so far—Conrad Wood's article cited in the text. See also Stephen F. Dale, *Islamic Society on the South Asian Frontier: The Mappilas of Malabar, 1498–1922* (Oxford, 1980), Ch. V–VII., for an account tracing the roots of Moplah militancy back to the 16th Century struggle against the Portuguese, and emphasising ideological rather than agrarian dimensions. The Deccan riots are studied from two different points of view in I. J. Catanach, 'Agrarian Disturbances in 19th Century India', (*IESHR,* 1966) and N. Charlesworth, 'Myth of the Deccan Riots of 1875', (*MAS,* 1972). On Pabna and other Bengal movements, see K. K. Sengupta, *Pabna Disturbances and the Politics of Rent 1873–85* (New Delhi, 1974) and B. B. Choudhury, 'Agrarian Economy and Agrarian Relations in Bengal, 1859–1885,' in N. K. Sinha (ed.), *History of Bengal 1757–1905* (Calcutta, 1967). The Assam *raijmal* are discussed in A. Guha, *Planter Raj to Swaraj,* (New Delhi, 1977); Deccan no-revenue in the 1890s in R. I. Cashman, *The Myth of the Lokmanya: Tilak and Mass Politics in Maharashtra* (California, 1975) and J. R. McLane, *Indian Nationalism and the Early Congress,* Ch. 8 (Princeton, 1977).

For an introduction to the vast sociological literature on caste and village organization, see M. N. Srinivas, *Social Change in Modern India* (California, 1966); McKim Marriott (ed.), *Village India: Studies in the Little Community* (Chicago, 1955) which contains B. Cohn's article on Jaunpur and Srinivas on Rampura; D. G. Mandelbawm, *Society in India,* 2 vols. (California, 1970); L. Dumont, *Homo Hierarchicus* (London, 1972); T. O. Beidelman, *A Comparative Analysis of the Jajmani System* (New York, 1959); H. Sanyal, 'Social Mobility in Bengal: Its Sources and Constraints', *IHR* (July 1975); F. G. Bailey's two Orissa village studies, *Caste and the Economic Frontier* (Manchester, 1957) and *Tribe, Caste and Nation* (Bombay, 1960); Andre Beteille, *Caste, Class and Power* (Brekeley, 1965), and M. N. Srinivas, *The Remembered Village* (Delhi, 1976). For specific modern caste movements, see Rudolph and Rudolph, *Modernity of Tradition* (Chicago, 1967), R. L. Hardgrave, *The Nadars of Tamilnad* (California, 1969); E. F. Irshchik,' *Politics and Social Conflict in South India: The Non-Brahman Movement and Tamil Separatism 1916–29* (California, 1969); Eleanor Zelliot, 'Learning the Use of Political Means: The Mahars of Maharashtra', in R. Kothari (ed.), *Caste in Indian Politics* (New Delhi, 1970) and Gail Omvedt, *Cultural Revolt in Colonial Society: The Non-Brahman Movement in Western India 1873–1930* (Bombay, 1976).

Alternative interpretations of early labour consciousness have been put forward in Dipesh Chakrabarty, 'Communal Riots and Labour: Bengal's Jute Millhands in the 1980s', Centre for Studies in Social Sciences (Calcutta, Occasional Paper No. 11, 1976) and Ranajit Dasgupta, 'Material Conditions and Behavioural Aspects of Calcutta Working Class, 1875–99', (Ibid., No. 22, 1979); See also Dipesh Chakrabarty, 'Sasipada Banerjee: A Study in the Nature of the First Contact of the Bengali Bhadralok with the Working Classes of Bengal' (Ibid., No. 4, 1975). Essential background reading on such themes are E. P. Thompson, *Making of the English Working Class* (London, 1963); J. Foster, *Class Struggle and the Industrial Revolution* (London, 1974); and G. Rude, *The Crowd in History* (New York, 1964). On the traditionalism of Indian business groups, see T. A. Timberg, *The Mar-waris* and H. Spodek, 'Traditional Culture and Entrepreneurship: A Case-Study of Ahmedabad', (*EPW,* Review of Management, February, 1969).

ii

On the size and social roots of the new intelligentsia, see B. McCully, *English Education and the Origins of Indian Nationalism* (New York, 1940); A. Seal, *Emergence,* Chs. I–III; and J. McLane, *Early Congress,* Introduction and Chs. II, VI, VII. Regional details on the same theme may be found in R. Suntha-ralingam, *Politics and Nationalist Awakening in South India 1852–91* (Arizona, 1974); D. Washbrook, *Provincial Politics;* Gordon Johnson, *Madras Presidency;* R. Cashman, *Myth of the Lokamanya;* C. Dobbin, *Urban Leadership in Western India: Politics and Communities in Bombay City 1840–85* (London, 1972) J. Masselos, *Towards Nationalism: Public Institutions and Urban Politics in 19th Century* (Bombay, 1974); *Dadabhai Naoroji Correspondence,* and C. Bayly, *Local Roots.*

For late-19th Century Hindu reform and revival, see C. Heimsath, *Hindu Social Reform;* B. B. Majumdar, *History of Indian Social and Political Ideas—From Rammohun to Dayananda* (Calcutta, 1967); Bepin Pal, *Memories.* Asok Sen, *Iswarchandra Vidyasagar and His Elusive Milestones* (Calcutta, 1977); G. Forbes, *Positivism in Bengal* (Calcutta, 1975); C. Dobbin, *Urban Leadership,* and J. Masselos, *Towards Nationalism;* B. B. Mazumdar, *Militant Nationalism in India and Its Socio-Religious Background 1897–1917* (Calcutta, 1966)—from which I have taken the extracts of Vivekananda; T. V. Parvate, *M. G. Ranade—A Biography* (Bombay, 1963); Kenneth Jones, *Arya Dharma,* and Lajpat Rai, *Autobiographical Writings,* V. C. Joshi, [ed.] (Delhi, 1965). On trends within Indian Islam, W.W. Hunter's *Indian Musalmans* (Calcutta, 1871) has been influential but misleading; see A. Seal, *Emergence,* Ch. VII; P. Hardy, *Muslims;* F. G. R. Robinson,

Separation; Shan Mohammad (ed.), *Writings and Speeches of Sir Sayid Ahmad Khan* (Bombay, 1972); Aziz Ahmad, *Islamic Modernism;* Z. H. Faruqi, *Deoband School;* Nikki Keddie, *Sayyid Jamal al Din al Alghani* (Calcutta, 1973). Since this book went to press, Rafiuddin Ahmed has published a valuable study of popular Muslim attitudes in Bengal based on a mass of vernacular tracts, *The Bengal Muslims, 1871–1906: A Quest for Identity,* (Delhi, 1981). The best accounts so far of cow-protection riots is J. McLane, *Early Congress,* Chs. IX–X and Gyan Pandey, 'Rallying Round the Cow; Sectarian Strife in the Bhojpur Region, C. 1881–1917', Centre for Studies in Social Sciences (Calcutta, Occasional Paper No. 39, 1981).

Barun De, 'Brajendranath De and John Beames: 'A Study in the Reactions of Patriotism and Paternalism in the ICS' (*Bengal,-Past and Present,* 1962), is a case-study of racism and early patriotic sentiments within the civil service. The flavour of early middle-class nationalism can be appreciated only through literature in the various regional languages; see particularly *Bankim-Rachanavali,* 2 Vols. (Calcutta, 1965, 1970); *Miscellaneous Writings of M. G. Ranade* (Bombay, 1915); M. L. Apte, 'Lokahitavadi and V. K. Chiplunkar: Spokesman of Change in 19th Century Maharashtra' (*MAS,* 1973); Irshchik, *Tamil Separatism,* Ch. 8; Madan Gopal, *Bharatendu Harishchandra* (New Delhi, 1971) Suidhir Chandra, 'Communal Consciousness in Late 19th Century Hindi Literature', in Mushirul Hasan (ed.), *Communal and Pan-Islamic Trends in Colonial India* (*Delhi,* 1981), and for the Urdu-Hindi controversy, Robinson, Separatism, Ch. I–IV and Paul R. Brass, *Language, Religion and Politics m North India* (Cambridge, 1979). References to studies of nationalistic economic theory have been given in the Further Readings for Ch. II.

The most detailed analysis of pre-Congress political associations ard the formation of the Congress is S. R. Mehrotra, *The Emergence of the Indian National Congress* (Delhi, 1971), which is more comprehensive than Anil Seal's better-known book; see also B. B. Mazumdar, *Indian Political Associations and Reform of Legislature 1818–1917,* (Calcutta, 1965) and J. C. Bagal, *History of the Indian Association* (Calcutta, 1953). For the Moderate Congress by far the best account is J. R. McLane, *Early Congress:* Annie Besant, *How India Wrought for Freedom* (Adyar, 1915), is a convenient summary of Congress sessions and resolutions; the proceedings are now being reprinted in A. M. Zaidi, *Encyclopaedia of the Indian National Congress,* 10 vols. (New Delhi, 1976–80). See also C. A Bayly, *Local Roots;* D. A. Wash-brook, *Madras Presidency;* Gordon Johnson, *Provincial Politics;* *Dadabhai Naoroji Correspondence;* Wolpert, *Tilak;* Cashman, *Myth of Lokamanya;* B. R. Nanda, *Gokhale* (Delhi, 1977); Government of Bombay, *Source-Materials of History of Freedom Movement in India,* Vol. II.

(Bombay, 1958) and Surendranath Banerji's and Bepin Pal's autobiographies. For the origins of Extremism, H. and U. Mukherji, *Sri Aurobindo's Political Thought* (Calcutta, 1958) reprint 'New Lamps for Old' series from *Indu Prakash;* see also B. B. Mazumdar, *Militant Nationalism in India,* and *Congress and Congressmen in the Pre-Gandhian Era,* (Calcutta, 1967); A. Tripathi, *The Extremist Challenge* (Calcutta, 1967); and S. Sarkar, *The Swadeshi Movement in Bengal 1903–1908* (New Delhi, 1973).

CHAPTER 4

For Curzon's policies, see A. Lovat Fraser, *India Under Curzon and After* (London, 1911); Ronaldshay, *Life of Lord Curzon,* Vol. II (London, 1928); J. McLane, *Early Congress* I, and S. Gopal, *British Policy in India 1858–1905.* The background to the Partition of Bengal is described in S. Sarkar, *Swadeshi Movement,* Ch. I.

ii

The discussion on the *Swadeshi* movement in Bengal is essentially a summary of my *Swadeshi Movement in Bengal,* plus some material from pamphlet which I saw later in India Office Library, London. See also A. Tripathi, *Extremist Challenge,* J. H. Broomfield, *Elite Conflict in a Plural Society: Twentieth-Century Bengal* (Berkeley, 1968), Rajat Roy, *Social Conflict ard Political Unrest in Bengal 1S75–1917* (unpublished thesis, Cambridge University); H. and U. Mukerji. *Origins of the National Education Movement* (Calcutta, 1957), R. P. Cronin. *British Policy and Administration in Bengal: Partition and the New Province of Eastern Bengal and Assam 1905–12* (Calcutta, 1977), and Rafiuddin Ahmed, *The Bengal Muslims 1871–1906—A Quest for Identity.* For *Swadeshi* ideological trends, essential reading includes the reprints of contemporary articles in Bepinchandra Pal, *Swadeshi and Swaraj* (Calcutta, 1954), Aurobindo Ghosh, *Doctrine of Passive Resistance* Pondicherry, 1948), H. and U. Mukherji (ed.), *Sri Aurobindo and the New Thought in Indian Politics* (Calcutta, 1964), which consists of extracts from the *Bande Mataram,* and *Rabindra Rachanabali,* particularly Vols. III, IV, VI, VIII, X and XII (Calcutta, various dates). On revolutionary terrorism, (Calcutta, 1918) and J. C. Ker, *Political Trouble in India 1907–1917* (Calcutta, 1917). The orthodox viewpoint of the revolutionaries was presented in N. Guha, *Banglay Biplab-bad* (Calcutta, 1923, 1954), while Hemchandra Kanungo's *Banglay Biplab-Prachesta* (Calcutta, 1928) is a fascinating and heretical critique. See also Bhupan Dutt, *Bharater Dwitiya Swadhinata-Sangram* (Calcutta, 1926, 1949).

iii

Bayly, *Local Roots,* and Robinson, *Separatism,* provide useful data on U.P. politics after 1905. For Gujarat, see A. Bhat, 'Caste and political mobilization in a Gujarat district' in Rajni Kothari (ed.), *Caste in Indian Politics.* On Punjab Extremism, the best accounts so far are by N. G. Barrier, 'The Punjab Disturbances of 1907: the Response of the British Government in India to Agrarian Unrest' (*MAS,* 1907), and 'The Arya Samaj and Congress Politics in Punjab;' 1894–1908 (*Journal of Asian Studies* 1967); Lajpat Rai, *Autobiographical Writings,* is essential and fascinating reading. On Madras, there is little secondary work apart from Washbrook, *Madras Presidency,* Ch. V, which is quite inadequate so far as political movements are concerned; I have used also K. V. Narayana Rao, *The Emergence of Andhra Pradesh* (Bombay, 1973), and P. R. Rao, *History of Modern Andhra* (New-Delhi, 1978). For Tilak and Maharashtra, see Wolpert; Cashman; Gordon Johnson; D. V. Athalye, *Life of Lakamanya Tilak* (Poona, 1921); G. P. Pradhan and A. K. Bhagwat, *Lokamanya Tilak* (Bombay, 1959); and Reisnar and Goldberg (ed.), *Tilak and the Struggle for Indian Freedom* (New Delhi, 1966). *Source-Materials for a History of the Freedom Movements,* Vol. II contains important data on Tilak's activities and the Bombay strike. For the Tuticorin and Bombay strikes, 1 have also used archival material, particularly *Home Political* A June 1908 n. 95 and *Home Political* A December 1908 n. 149–169. On the politics of annual Congress sessions and the Surat split, see Wolpert; Tripathi; and D. Argov. *Moderates and Extremists in the Indian Nationalist Movement* (Bombay, 1967).

iv

The early availability of the Morley-Minto correspondence has produced a rather tedious literature, relevant for the study of British policy: Viscount Morley, *Recollections* (London, 1917); Lady Mary Minto, *India, Minto and Morley 1905–10* (London, 1934); and more recently, M. N. Das, *India under Morley and Minto: Politics behind Revolution, Repression and Reforms* 'London, 1964); S. R. Wasti, *Lord Minto and the Indian Nationalist Movement* (Oxford. 1964); and S. A. Wolpert, *Morley and India 1906–10* (California, 1967). The shift in the policy towards the native states is analysed by D. A. Low, 'Laissez-faire and Traditional Rulership in Princely India' in R. Jeffrey (ed.), *People, Princes and Paramount Power.* For the early history of the Muslim League, see Das, Wasti, Tripathi and particularly Robinson, Chs. IV, V; and M. Rahman, *From Consultation to Confrontation: A Study of the Muslim League in British Indian Politics 1906–12* (London, 1978).

For revolutionary terrorism in this period, see Indulal Yajnik, *Shyamaji Krihnavarama—Life and Times of an Indian Revolutionary* (Bombay, 1950); J. C. Ker, *Political Trouble;* A. C. Bose, *Indian Revolutionaries Abroad 1905-22 in the background of international developments* (Patna, 1971); E. C. Brown, *Har Dayal: Hindu Revolutionary and Rationalist* (Delhi, 1975); Randhir Singh, *The Ghadr Heroes* (Bombay, 1945) and Sohan Singh Josh, *Hindustan Ghadr Party: A Short History* (New Delhi, 1977).

v

The *Sedition Committee Report,* J. C. Ker, A. C. Bose, Randhir Singh and Sohan Singh Josh may be consulted for the war-time activities of the revolutionaries; see also Uma Mukherji, *Two Great Indian Revolutionaries* (Calcutta, 1966) and Bhupen Dutt, *Aprakashito Rajnaitik Itihas* (Calcutta, 1953). Robinson and Bayly are useful for League and Congress politics leading up to the Lucknow pact. On the Home Rule Leagues, the best account is H. F. Owen, 'Towards Nation-wide Agitation and Organisation—The Home Rule Leagues, 1915-1918', in D. A. Low (ed.), *Soundings in Modern South Asian History.* H. F. Owen's massive thesis on the same period, *Leadership of the Indian National Movement 1914-20,* is available in microfilm at the N.M.M.L. For Tilak's activities during the war, see Cashman, *Myth of Lokamanya,* and *B. G. Tilak: His Writings and Speeches* (Madras; n.d.).

vi

For tribal movements, see E. Clement Smith, 'The Bastar Rebellion, 1910', *Man in India,* Rebellion Number, December 1945); Stephen Fuchs, *Rebellious Prophets* (for the Tana Bhagat); and Gautam Bhadra, 'The Kuki (?) Uprising 1917-19): Its Causes and Nature, (*Man in India,* (March, 1975). The account of the Khond and Bhil movements is based on my own archival research. On Bijolia see Ram Pande, *Agrarian Movements in Rajasthan* (Delhi, n.d.), by no means satisfactory but the only published account so far. There are numbers of recent accounts of Champaran and its background: J. Pouchepadass, 'Local leaders and the intelligentsia in the Champaran Satyagraha (1917): a study in peasant mobilization' (*Contributions to Indian Sociology* (No. 8, 1978); S. Henningham, 'Social Setting of the Champaran Satyagraha: The Challenge to an Alien Elite' (*IESHR,* 1976); G. Mishra, *Agrarian Problems of Permanent Settlement—A Case-Study of Champaran* (New Delhi, 1974); and S. K. Mittal, *Peasant Uprisings and Mahatma Gandhi in North Bihar* (Meerut, 1978). For Kheda, see D. Hardiman, *Peasant*

Nationalists of Gujarat, Ch. 5 and, for Bardoli, Anil Bhatt's article in R. Kothari, *Caste in Indian Politics.*

The East Bengal Praja movement is the subject of an unpublished thesis by Jatindra Nath De, *History of the Krishak Praja Party in Bengal, 1928–47* (Delhi University, 1978). The Shahabad riots have been studied in Peter Robb, Officials and Non-Officials as Leaders in Popular Agitations: Shahabad 1917 and other 'Conspiracies' in B. N. Pandey, (ed.), *Leadership in South Asia* (New Delhi, 1977). and more recently by Gyan Pandey, 'Sectarian Strife' in R. Guha (ed.), *Subaltern Studies I.* For the Calcutta riots of 1918, see J. H. Broomfield, 'The Forgotten Majority: The Bengal Muslims', September 1918, in D. A. Low (ed.), *Soundings in Modern South Asian History.* On caste movements, apart from Rudolph and Rudolph, Hardgrave, Irshchik, and Omvedt cited in Further Readings to Ch. III, see James Manor, *Political Change in an Indian State: Mysore 1917–55* (Delhi, 1977); Robin Jerffey, *The Decline of Nayar Dominance: Society and Politics in Travancore, 1847–1908* (New Delhi, 1976); D. A. Washbrook, 'Development of Caste Organization in South India' 1880–1925 in C. J. Baker and D. A. Washbrook, *South India Political Institutions and Political Change* and D. A. Arnold, R. Jeffrey, J. Manor, 'Caste Associations in South India—A Comparative Analysis' (*JESHR* 1976). For the Andhra Movement, see P. R. Rao, K. V. Narayan Rao and C. R. Das's Bhowanipur speech in Rajen and B. K. Sen, *Deshabandhu Chittaranjan Das: Brief Survey of Life and Work* (Calcutta, 1928). For Premchand, I have used Madan Gopal, *Munshi Premchand: A Literary Biography* (Bombay, 1944).

CHAPTER 5

From 1919 onwards, the *Indian Annual Register* published annually from Calcutta provides a handy guide to political developments for advanced students and a useful starting-point for research.

i

For the Montford Reforms and their background, see R. Coupland, *Constitutional Problems in India,* Ch. V–VI; S. R. Mehrotra, 'The Politics behind the Montagu Declaration of 1917 in C. H. Philips (ed.), *Politics and Society in India* (London, 1963); and P. G., Robb, *The Government of India and Reform: Policies towards Politics and the Constitution 1916–21,* (London, 1976). The revised 'Cambridge' view of the link between constitutional changes and nationalism is stated in Anil Seal, 'Imperialism and Nationalism in India' in Gallagher, Johnson, Seal (ed.), *Locality, Province and Nation* (Cambridge, 1973), and developed in Washbrook, *Madras Presidency,* Baker. *Politics,* and Bayly, *Local Roots.*

On the economic impact of the First World War, see Balabushevich and Dyakov, *Contemporary History,* Ch. I; A. K. Bagchi, *Private Investment, passim;* S. G. Panandikar, *Some Aspects of the Economic Consequences of the War for India* (Bombay, 1921); and, for regional details, A. D. D. Gordon, *Businessmen and Politics: Rising Nationalism and a Modernizing Economy in Bombay, 1918–1933 (Delhi,* 1978), Ch. I–II, Judith Brown, *Gandhi's Rise to Power: Indian Politics, 1915–22,* Ch. III; D. Hardiman, *Peasant Agitations,* Ch. VI; M. H. Siddiqi, *Agrarian Unrest in North India: United Provinces 1918–1922* (New Delhi, 1978), Ch. II, and C. J. Baker, *The Politics of South India,* Ch. 1. For the labour awakening; see R. Kumar, 'Bombay Textile Strike, 1919' *(IESHR* 1971) and K. Murugesan and C. S. Subramanyam, *Singaravelu—First Communist in South India* (New Delhi, 1975) and for food riots, Rajat Roy, *Social Conflict,* and D. Arnold, 'Looting, Grain Riots and Government Policy in South India, 1918' *(Past and Present,* August 1979).

ii

For the early career of Gandhi, see M. K. Gandhi, *Story of My Experiments with Truth* (Ahmedabad, 1927, 1940); D. G. Tendulkar, *Mahatma,* Vol. I, 1869, 1920 (Bombay, 1960); Judith Brown, *Gandhi's Rise to Power;* Gandhi, 'Hind Swaraj' in *Collected Works,* Vol. X; and for a brief exposition of Gandhian philosophy, J. Bondurant, *Conquest of Violence* (Bombay, 1959). On early Gandhian movements, see also for Champaran, J. Pouchepadass, *Local Leaders,* G. Mishra, *Agrarian Problems,* S. Henningham, *Social Setting,* and B. B. Mishra, (ed.), *Select Documents on Gandhiji's Movement in Champaran 1917–18* (Patna 1973); for Kheda, Hardiman, *Peasant Agitations,* Ch. VI and *Peasant Nationalists,* Ch. V; and for Ahmedabad, Erik Ericson, *Gandhi's Truth,* Part 3 (London, 1970). The classic study of the role of rumour in peasant upheavals is G. Lefebvre, *The Great Fear of 1789* (London, 1973).

iii

The basic sources for the Rowlatt upheaval, the *Hunter Commission Report* (March 1920) and the *Congress Punjab Inquiry Committee Report* (February 1920) are now readily available in *Punjab Disturbances 1919–20,* Vols. I and II (Delhi 1976). See also V. N. Dutt (ed.), *New Light on the Punjab Disturbances,* the once confidential Intelligence Branch's Survey, P. C. Bamford, *Histories of the Non-Cooperation and Khilafat Movements* (Delhi, 1925, reptd., Delhi,

1974); Judith Brown, *Gandhi's Rise to Power;* Ch. V; and, above all, the valuable collection of micro studies in R. Kumar (ed.), *Etsays on Gandhian Politics; The Rowlatt Satyagraha of 1919* (Oxford, 1971)—particularly the articles of H. F. Owen on organizational preparations, R. Kumar on Lahore, D. W. Ferrell on Delhi, K. L. Gillion on Gujarat, J. Masselos on Bombay City, and D. E. U. Baker on the Central Provinces and Berar.

iv

For political developments from mid-1919 to the Nagpur Congress, see D. G. Tendulkar, *Mahatma,* Vols. I and II; Bamford, *Histories;* Judith Brown, *Gandhi's Rise to Power;* Chs. 6–8; Richard Gordon, Non-Cooperation and Council Entry, 1919 to 1920 (in *Locality, Province and Nation);* F. Robinson, *Separatism,* Chs. 7–9; Mushirul Hasan, *Nationalism and Communal Politics in India* (Delhi, 1979), Chs. IV–V; and A. C. Niemijer, *The Khilafat Movement in India* (The Hague, 1972). On the labour movement, see R. K. Das, *Factory Labour in India* Berlin, 1923); Sukomal Sen, *Working Class of India; History of Emergence and Movement* (Calcutta, 1977); G. Adhikari (ed.), *Documents of the History of the Communist Party of India,* Vol. I, *1917–22* (Delhi, 1971); C. Sehanovis, *Rus Biplab o Prabasi Bharatiya Biblabi* (Calcutta, 1973); Murugesan and Subramanyam, *Singaravelu: List of Labour Unions and Associations in Bengal 1920, 1921 and 1922* (Government of Bengal); and Vinay Behl, 'Tata Iron and Steel Company ke Sramik Andolan, 1920–28', *Anya Artha* (1975). Labour history unfortunately is still in its infancy in our country. For *kisan* movements, see Bam Pande, *Rajasthan;* Stephen Henningham, 'Agrarian Relations in North Bihar: Peasant Protest and the Darbhanga Raj, 1919–20' (*IESHR,* 1979) M. H. Siddiqi, *Agrarian Unrest,* Chs. 3–4; Gyan Pandey, 'Peasant Revolt and Indian Nationalism: The Peasant Movement in Awadh, 1919, 1922', in Guha, *Studies I;* and Kapil Kumar, *Peasant Movements in Oudh, 1918–22* (unpublished thesis, Meerut University, 1980).

v

For all-India studies on the Non-Cooperation and Khilafat upsurge of 1921–22, see Bamford, *Histories;* Tendulkar, *Mahatma,* Vol. II; Judith Brown, *Gandhi's Rise to Power,* Ch. 9, Krishna Das, *Seven Months with Mahatma Gandhi* (Calcutta, 1928); Jawaharlal Nehru, *An Autobiography:* Gopal Krishna, 'Development of the Indian National Congress as a Mass Organization', (*Journal of Asian Studies,* May 1966); *Indian Annual Register,* 1921–1922–as well as of course Gandhi's own writings, mostly in *Young India,* reprinted in his *Collected Works*. A. D. D. Gordon, *Businessmen and Politics*, Ch. 5, and Sabyasachi Bhattacharya, *Cotton Mills and Spinning Wheels—Swadeshi in the Non-Cooperation Era* (*EPW,* November, 1976) provide important material on the role of business groups. The secondary works I have used for regional data include Mohinder Singh, *Akali Movement* (Delhi, 1978) for the Punjab; Ram Pande, *Rajasthan* and Rajat Roy, 'Mewar: The Breakdown of the Princely Order' in R. Jeffrey, *People, Princes and Paramount Power,* for Rajasthan; D. Hardiman 'Peasant Nationalists', Ch. 7, and his 'Crisis of the Lesser Patidars: Peasant Agitations in Kheda District, Gujarat 1917–24' in D. A. Low (ed.), *Congress and the Raj* for Gujarat; R. Kumar, 'From Swaraj to Purna Swaraj: Nationalist Politics in the City of Bombay, 1920–32' in D. A. Low, *ibid.,* for Bombay; C. J. Baker, 'Non-Cooperation in Souih India' in Baker and Washbrook, *South India,* D. A. Arnold, *Congress in Tamilnad: Nationalist Politics in South India, 1919–37* (Delhi, 1977) and M. Venkatarangaiya, *Freedom Struggle in Andhra Pradesh,* Vol. III (Hyderabad, 1965) for Tamilnadu and Andhra; Dhanagare and Conrad Wood's already cited articles on the Moplahs, together with R. L. Hardgrave, 'The Mapilla Rebellion, 1921', (*MAS,* 1977), K. N. Pannikar, 'Peasant Revolts in Malabar in 19th and 20th Centuries', in A. R. Desai, *Peasant Struggles,* and Stephen F. Dale, *Islamic Society on the South Asian Frontier,* Ch. VII; A. Guha, *Planter Raj to Swaraj,* for Assam; Rajat Roy's unpublished thesis, his 'Masses in Politics—Non-Cooperation in Bengal 1920–22' (*IESHR,* 1974); Broomfield, *Elite Conflict,* L. A. Gordon, *Bengal: The Nationalist Movement 1876–1940* (Delhi, 1974) and Hitesh Sanyal's already cited articles for Bengal; K.K. Datta, *History of Freedom Movement in Bihar,* Vol. I (Patna, 1957), Ch. 8 and Stephen Henningham's unpublished thesis, *Protest and Control in North Bihar, Inaia, 1907–42* (Australian National University, 1978—available in N.M.M.L. microfishe), Ch. II, for Bihar; and M. H. Siddiqi, *Agrarian Unrest,* Kapil Kumar, *Peasant Movement;* S. K. Mittal and Kapil Kumar, 'Baba Ram Shandra and Peasant Upsurge in Oudh 1920–21' (*Social Scientist,* June 1978) and Gyan Pandey, *Ascendancy,* for United Provinces. Part of this section is also based on my own research using Government of India *Home Political* and Government of Bengal, *Political Confidential* files, together with the *Reading Collection* (*MSS Eur E 238-IOL*).

vi

The major political developments of 1922–27 may be traced from Tendulkar *Mahatma* Vol. II, and the *Indian Annual Register* for the relevant years. For the Gandhian *satyagrahas* and constructive work, see D. Hardiman's thesis, Ch. 7–8; D. Hardiman, *Baroda: The Structure of a 'Progressive State',* and

R. Jeffrey, 'Travancore: Status, Class and the Growth of Radical Politics 1860–1940' in Jeffery (ed.) *People, Princes and Paramount Power;* Hitesh Sanyal's articles; and G. Pandey *Ascendancy* Ch. 3. Rajat Roy's unpublished thesis and Bimalananda Samal's Bengali reminiscences about his father (*Swadhinatar Phanki,* Calcutta, 1967) are useful for Swarajist politics in Bengal; see also G. Pandey for U. P. and D. E. U. Baker, *Changing Political Leadership in an Indian Province: The Central Provinces and Berar, 1919–39* (Delhi, 1980) for that rather neglected region. For the growth of communalism, see G. Pandey, *Ascendancy* Ch. 5; Mushirul Hasan, *Communal Politics,* Chs. 6, 7. Richard Gordon, 'Hindu Mahasabha and the Indian National Congress, 1915–1926' (*MAS* 1975), and K. Macpherson, *The Muslim Microcosm: Calcutta 1918–35* (Wiesbaden, 1974).

vii

For the sharpening of political and economic resentment against imperial policies, see R. J. Moore, *Crisis of Indian Unity 1917–40* (Oxford, 1974); F. Moraes, *Sir Purshotamdas Thakurdas* (Bombay, 1957); and Basudev Chatterji, *Lancashire Cotton Trade and British Policy in India 1919–39* (unpublished thesis, Cambridge, 1978). Venkatarangiyya, *Andhra Pradesh* gives fascinating extracts from Madras Government archives; I have also used some Home Political files for reconstructing the rebellion on Sitarma Raju. Ram Pande and Rajat Roy's articles on Mewar have been used again for Rajasthan peasants. For Bengal Swarajist attitudes on agrarian issues, see Partha Chatterji, 'Agrarian Relations and Politics in Bengal: Some Considerations on the Making of the Tenancy Act Amendment 1928' Occasional Paper No. 30, Centre for Studies in Social Sciences, (Calcutta, 1980). B. Stoddart, 'The Structure of Congress Politics in Coastal Andhra 1925–37', in D. A. Low (ed.) *Congress and the Raj,* provides valuable data on Andhra. On caste movements, apart from Irschik, *Non-Brahman Movement,* and Omvedt, *Cultural Revolt,* see Hetukar Jha, 'The Lower Caste Peasants and Upper Caste Zamindars in Bihar, 1921–25' (*IESHR,* 1977); D. Keer, *Dr Ambedkar: Life and Mission* (Bombay, 1954). Eleanor Zelliot, 'The Leadership of Baba Saheb Ambedkar' and C. J. Baker, 'Leading up to Periyar: The Early Career of E. V. Ramaswami Naicker', both in B. N. Pandey, (ed.) *Leadership in South Asia* (Delhi, 1977); R. Jeffery, *Travancore,* and Murugesan and Subramanyam, *Singaravelu.* For labour, see Sukomal Sen, *Working Class,* Vinay Behl, *Sramik Andolan,* Basudev Chatterji's thesis, R. Chandavarkar, 'Workers' Politics and the Mill Districts in Bombay between the Wars' in Baker, Johnson and Seal, (eds.) *Power, Profit and Politics.* R. Newman's *Workers and Unions in Bombay 1918–1929* (Canberra, 1981) became available after this book had gone to press. On Communists, see G. Adhikari, *Documents,* Vols. I–III, C. Kaye, *Communism in India 1919–24* (reptd. ed., S. Roy, Calcutta, 1971), and D. Petrie, *Communism in India 1924–27* (reptd. ed., M. Saha, Calcutta, 1972). For terrorists, see *Terrorism in India 1917–36* (reptd. Delhi, 1974). On the shift in Jawaharlal Nehru's thinking, see S. Gopal, *Jawaharlal Nehru,* Vol. I.

CHAPTER 6

For economic developments, see Bipan Chandra, 'Colonialism and Modernization', in his *Nationalism and Colonialism in Modern India* (Delhi, 1979); C. J. Baker, *Politics,* Ch. III as well as his 'Colonial Rule and the Internal Economy in Twentieth Century Madras', in *Power, Profit and Politics,* Amiya Bagchi, *Private Investment* and Rajat Ray, *Industrialization in India: Growth and Conflict in the Private Corporate Sector 1914–47* (Delhi, 1979), *passim.* The best study of Indo-British economic relations in this period is Basudev Chatterji, *Lancashire Cotton Trade,* that of Indian business attitudes, Claude Markovits, *Indian Business and Nationalist Politics from 1931 to 1939;* both are due for publication in the near future. Basudev Chatterji lias recently published part of his data in 'Business and Politics in the 1930s: Lancashire and Making of the Indo-British Trade Agreement, 1939 in *Power, Profit and Politics.* I am deeply grateful to Basudev Chatterji and Claude Markovits for permitting me to use some of their findings in my Chs. VI and VII. For an alternative view, which sees India acquiring virtual economic independence already from the 1920s, see I. A. Drummond, *British Economic Policy and Empire, 1919–39* (London, 1972), C. Dewey, 'End of Imperialism of Free Trade: Eclipse of Lancashire Lobby and Concession of Fiscal Autonomy to India', in Dewey and Hopkins, (ed.) *Imperial Impact: Studies in the Economic History of Africa and India* (London, 1978), and B. R. Tomlinson, *Political Economy of the Raj, 1914–47* (London, 1979).

ii

For general accounts of 1928–29, see S. Gopal, *Jawaharlal Nehru* (Vol. I). D. G. Tendulkar, *Mahatma,* Vol. II. Judith Brown, *Gandhi and Civil Disobedience,* Ch. 1–2. The *Indian Annual Register* proved most useful for this and subsequent sections in Chs. 6 and 7. British policy is competently surveyed in R. J. Moore, *Crisis of Indian Unity.* On the Nehru Report negotiations, see also Uma Kaura, *Muslims and Indian Nationalism* (Delhi, 1977), C. Khaliquzzaman, *Pathway,* and P. Hardy, *Muslims of British India.* For princely states, R. L. Handa, *History of Freedom Movement in Princely States* (New Delhi, 1968), and R. J. Moore, *Crisis of Indian Unity*. For youth movements, see Gopal, *Nehru;* J. Nehru, *An Autobiography,* and his *Selected Works,* Vol. IV; and Subhas Bose, *The Indian Struggle,* (Calcutta, 1935, 1964). On the revival of revolutionary terrorism, and new trends within it see *Terrorism in India, 1917–36* (Government of India. *1917–36.* reptd. Delhi, 1974). Bipan Chandra, 'Ideological Development of Revolutionary Terrorists in Northern India in the 1920s, in his *Nationalism and Colonialism* and Bhagat Singh, *Why I Am An Atheist* (reptd. Delhi 1979). On labour and the Communists, see Petrie, *Communism;* Williamson, *India and Communism 1928–35* (in Hallet Collection, I.O.L.). Sukomal Sen, *Working Class,* Murugesan and Subramanyam, Singaravelu, Gautam Chattopadhyay, *Communism and Bengal's Freedom Movement, Volume I, 1917–29* (New Delhi, 1970), Sarkar, *National Movement and Popular Protest in Bengal, 1928–34* (unpublished thesis, Delhi University, 1981), Subodh Roy (ed), *Communism in India—Unpublished Documents 1925–34* (Calcutta, 1972). Vinay Behl, *Sramik Andolan* and G. Omvedt, *Cultural Revolt.* Ch. 13 (which summarizes the findings of R. Newman, *Labour Organization in Bombay Cotton Mills 1919–29,* an unpublished Sussex thesis which I have not been able to see). My account of agrarian issues and *kisan* movements is based on Partha Chatterji, *Agrarian Relations.* T. Sarkar, *Popular Protest,* Azim Husain, *Fazl-i-Husain* (London, 1946). Ramesh Walia, *Praja Mandal Movement in East Punjab States* (Patiala, 1972), W. Hauser, *Bihar Provincial Kisan Sabha, 1929–42* (unpublished thesis, Chicago, 1961, *N.M.M.L.* microfilm): B. Stoddart in Low (ed.), *Congress and the Raj,* Mahadev Desai, *Story of Bardoli* (Ahmedabad, 1929); and Ghanshyam Shah, 'Traditional Society and Political Mobilization: The Experience of Bardoli Satyagraha 1920–28', *Contributions of Indian Sociology,* No. 8, 1974.

The section on Simon boycott and labour upsurge is based on considerable part also on my own research, using the Annual Reports of the Indian National Congress, Indian Chamber of Commerce, and Bombay Millowners' Association; the Home Political and A.I.C.C. files and the private papers of Irwin, Birkenhead and Sykes at I.O.L. of Benthall at Cambridge, and of Thakurdas and Jayakar at the N.M.M.L. and the N.A.I.

iii

Studies of the first Civil Disobedience movement at the all-India level include Tendulkar, *The Mahatma,* Vol. III; S. Gopal, *Jawaharlal Nehru,* Ch. 9; Judith Brown, *Gandhi and Civil Disobedience;* and S. Sarkar, 'The Logic of Gandhian Nationalism: Civil Disobedience and the Gandhi-Irwin Pact, 1930–31', *Indian Historical Review,* July 1976). Gandhi, *Collected Works,*

Vol. 34–35, and Nehru, *Selected Works,* Vol. IV, include much valuable material. See also S. A. Kochanek, *Business and Politics in India* (California, 1974); and G. D. Birla, *The Path to Prosperity* (Allahabad 1950) and *In the Shadow of the Mahatma* (Bombay, 1953) for business attitudes; *Terrorism in India* for the last wave of revolutionary terrorism; S. Sarkar, 'Primitive Rebellion and Modern Nationalism: A Note on Forest Satyagraha in the Non-Cooperation and Civil Disobedience Movements', in K. N. Panikkar (ed), *National and Left Movements in India* (Delhi, 1980); R. J. Moore, *Crisis of Indian Unity,* for British policies.

D. A. Low, (ed.) *Congress and the Raj,* is a collection of valuable regior al surveys; see particularly the articles of D. Hardiman on Gujarat, R. Kumar on Bombay city, B, Stoddart on coastal Andhra, G. Pandey on U.P., D. E. U. Baker on C.P., D. Arnold on Tamilnadu, and G. McDonald on Bihar, an of them focussed partly or sometimes mainly on Civil Disobedience. G. Pandey, *Ascendancy* is the best full-length study of a region available so far for the Civil Disobedience years. See also A. D. D. Gordon, *Businessmen and Politics; D.* Hardiman, *Peasant Nationalists,* Ch. 9; G. Omvedt, *Cultural Revolt;* G. S. Hallappa, *History of Freedom Movement in Kamataka* (Bangalore, 1964); Venkatarangaiyya, *Andhra Pradesh;* C. J. Baker, *Politics,* T. V. Krishnan *Kerala's First Communist: Life of 'Sakha' Krishna Pillai* (New Delhi); D. Arnold, *Congress in Tamilnad,* D. Baker, 'Forest Satyagraha in the Central Provinces'. N. M. M. L. seminar (December 1980); A Guha, *Planter Raj to Swaraj;* J. Gallagher, Congress in Decline: Bengal 1930–39' in *Locality, Province and Nation;* T. Sarkar, 'The First Phase of Civil Disobedience in Bengal 1930–1' *(Indian Historical Review,* July 1977) and *Communal Riots in Bengal 1930–1,* in M. Hasan, (ed.), *Communal and Pan-Islamic Trends in Colonial India,* Delhi, 1981 as well as her unpublished thesis, already cited; R. Walia, *Piara Mandal;* W. Hauser, *Kisan Sabha,* K. K. Datta, *History of the Freedom Movement in Bihar,* Vol. II (Patna, 1957); S. Henningham, *Protest and Control in North Bihar,* Ch. 3; A. K. Gupta, *North-West Frontier Province Legislature and the Freedom Struggle* (New Delhi, 1976); and D. G. Tendulkar, *Abdul Ghaffar Khan* (Bombay, 1967). Original sources used for this section include Home Political and AICC files, the Annual Reports of the Indian Chamber of Commerce and Bombay Millowners' Association and the private papers of Irwin, Sykes, R. E. Hawkins, Benthall, Thakurdas and Walchand Hirachand.

iv

For general accounts of the Truce months, see S. Gopal, *Nehru,* Ch. 9; J. Nehru, *An Autobiography;* Judith Brown, *Civil Disobedience,* and Tendulkar,

Vol. III. Regional details may be sought in D. Hardiman's thesis, already cited; G. Pandey, Ascendancy; B. Stoddart in *Congress and the Raj;* P. N. Bazaz, *History of the Struggle for Freedom in Kashmir* (New Delhi, 1954); W. Hauser, *Kisan Sabha;* T. Krishnan, *Kerala's First Communist;* A. K. Gopalan, *In the Cause of the People* (Madras, 1976); T. Ramakrishna, 'Kisan Movement in Andhra 1918–38, in *Proceedings of Seminar on Socialism in India* (*N.M.M.L.* mimeograph, 1970). For official policies, see R. J. Moore, *Crisis of Indian Unity;* Basudev Chatterji, *Business and Politics;* C. A. Low, 'Civil Martial Law: the Government of India and the Civil Disobedience Movements, 1930–34' in Low, (ed) *Congress and the Raj;* and P. S. Gupta, *Imperialism and British Labour* Ch. 7, 8. The original sources mentioned in the previous section have also been used, along with the *Report of the Karachi Congress* and the *Indian Annual Register.*

V

Many of the references for the first Civil Disobedience Movement are helpful also for 1932–33, particularly *Congress and the Raj,* J. Brown, G. Pandey, T. Sarkar, G. S. Halappa, C. J. Baker, and D. Arnold; see also G. H. Khan, *Freedom Movement in Kashmir 1931–40* (New Delhi, 1980) and H. Kruger, (ed.) *K. M. Ashraf* (*Delhi,* 1969). I have also drawn considerably on AICC and Home Political files and the private papers of Templewood (Hoare), Sykes, Hawkins and Thakurdas. For business realignments, the best accounts are by Basudev Chatterji and Claude Markovits; I have used also Kochanek, *Business;* G D. Birla, *In The Shadow of the Mahatma,* and the Jayakar and Thakurdas papers. There has been little research so far on Gandhi's Harijan campaign: but see Tendulkar, Vol. III; D. Keer, *Ambedkar,* Murugesan and Subramanyam, *Singaravelu;* C. J. Baker, 'Leading up to Periyar' and Eleanor Zelliot, 'The Leadership of Babasaheb Ambedkar in B N. Pandey (ed.), *Leadership in South Asia;* and R. Jeffrey in *People, Princes and Paramount Power.* For conflicting 'Right' and 'Left' political trends, see Gopal; Nehru's *Autobiography* and *Selected Works;* Tendulkar, Vol III; B. R. Tomlinson, *Indian National Congress and the Raj 1929–42;* Hauser, *Kisan Sabha;* N. G. Ranga, *Revolutionary Peasants* (Delhi, 1949); C. Revri, *Indian Trade Union Movement* (Delhi, 1972); E. M. S. Namboodiripad, *How I Became A Communist* (Trivandrum, 1976), A. K. Gopalan, *In the Cause of the People;* and Subodh Ray, *Communism in India.* The most detailed study of the C.S.P. so far is T. A. Rusch, *The Role of the Congress Socialist Party in the Indian National Congress* (Unpublished thesis, N.M.M.L., microfilm). D. M. Laushey, *Bengal Terrorism and the Marxist Left* (Calcutta, 1975), is a disappointing treatment of an important subject.

For the 1935 Act, see Coupland, *Constitutional Problems;* Gwyer and Appadorai, *Speeches and Documents;* R. J. Moore, *Crisis of Indian Unity* and B. R. Tomlinson, *Indian National Congress and the Raj, 1929–42* (London, 1976). S. Gopal gives a good summary of the main political developments, and Jawaharlal Nehru, *A Bunch of Old Letters* (Bombay, 1958) includes some illuminating correspondence of the mid and late-1930s. The *Indian Annual Register* is surprisingly informative, even about *kisan* movements; see also W. Hauser, *Kisan Sabha,* and the issues of the *Congress Socialist* (available at *N.M.M.L.).* For princely states, see R. L. Handa, R. Walia, and the *Indian Annual Register.* On Left trends in literature, see D. Anjanayulu, 'Impact of Socialist Ideology on Telegu Literature between the Wars;' Kaa Naa Subramanyam, 'Socialism in Tamil Letters', 1919–39; P. Padhye, 'Impact of Socialism on Marathi Literature'; and S. S. Chauhan, 'Impact of Socialist Ideology on Hindi Literature' 1918–39—all in *Socialism in India* (*N.M.M.L.*) mimeograph, 1970); Madan Gopal, *Munshi Premchand—A Literary Biography* (Bombay, 1964); Sudhir Chandra, 'The Ideal and the Real in Premchand' (N.M.M.L. seminar paper, 1980); and Ralph Russell, 'Leadership in the All-India Progressive Writers Movement', in B. N. Pandey, (ed.), *Leadership in South Asia* (New Delhi, 1977). For alignments within the Congress, and business attitudes, see Bipan Chandra, 'Jawaharlal Nehru and the Capitalist Class 1936', in his *Nationalism and Colonialism;* Claude Markovits, *Indian Business,* while the Thakurdass papers are particularly illuminating on the latter theme.

CHAPTER 7

There has been surprisingly little detailed research so far on the Congress ministries. For generals accounts, see Coupland, *Constitutional Problems;* B. R. Tomlinson, *Indian National Congress and the Raj 1929–42;* and the *Indian Annual Register,* supplemented by S. Gopal, Nehru, and J. Nehru, *A Bunch of Old Letters.* G. McDonald's article on Bihar in Low, (ed.) *Congress and the Raj,* A. Guha, *Planter Raj;* A. K. Gupta, *North West Frontier Province;* and C. E. U. Baker; *Changing Political Leadership in An Indian Province: The Central Provinces and Bihar 1919–39* (New Delhi, 1980) provide some essential regional details. On communal relations, see Uma Kaura, *Muslims;* C. Khaliquzzaman, *Pathway;* C. Baxter, *The Jana Sangh* (Pennsylvania, 1969); Rajat Roy, *Urban Roots of Indian Nationalism—Pressure Groups and Conflict of Interests in Calcutta City Politics 1875–1939* (Delhi, 1979); M. A. H. Ispahani, *Qaid-e-Azam Jinnah as I knew him* (Karachi, 1966); Abul Mansur Ahmed, *Amar Dekha Rajnitir Panchash Bachhar* (Dacca, 1970), and Shila Sen, *Muslim Politics in Bengal*

1937–47 (New Delhi, 1976). On business attitudes and relations with the Congress, the best work is C. Markovits, *Indian Business,* and 'Indian Business and the Congress Provincial Governments 1937–39' in *Power, Profit and Politics;* see also B. Chatterji, *Business and Politics;* and, for a different emphasis, Rajat Roy, *Industrialization in India,* and A. Mukherjee, 'Indian Capitalist Class and Congress on National Planning and Public Sector 1930–47', in K. N. Panikkar, (ed.) *National and Left Movements in India* (New Delhi, 1980). For *kisan* movements, the *Indian Annual Register* is very useful; see also W. Hauser, and S. Henningham, for Bihar, and T. Ramakrishna, for Andhra. Of the considerable literature on states people's agitations, the main references are R. L. Handa, *Princely States;* R. Walia, Praja Mandal; T. V. Krishna's life of P. Krishna Pillai A. K. Gopalan, *In the Cause of the People;* Swami Ramananda Tirtha, *Memoirs of Hyderabad Freedom Struggle* (Bombay, 1967); Ravi Narayan Reddi, *Heroic Telengana: Reminiscences and Experiences* (New Delhi, 1973); James Manor, *Political Change in an Indian State—Mysore 1917–55* (Delhi, 1977); H. Mahtab, *et. al., History of Freedom Movement in Orissa,* Vol. IV (Cuttack, 1959); R. Jeffrey's article on Travancore in Low, (ed.) *Congress and the Raj;* and J. R. Wood, 'Indian Nationalism in the Princely Context: The Rajkot Satyagraha of 1938–39' in R. Jeffrey, (ed.) *People, Princes and Paramount Power.* For the Tripuri split, see S. Gopal, and Nehru's *Bunch of Old Letters.*

ii

On British policy during 1939–42, see Coupland, *Constitutional Problems;* B. C. Tomlinson. *Indian National Congress* R. J., Moore, 'British Policy and the Indian Problem, 1936–40', in C. H. Philips and M. D. Wainwright, (ed.) *The Partition of India: Politics and Perspectives* (London, 1970); R. J. Moore, *Churchill, Cripps and India 1939–45* (Oxford, 1979); and N. Mansergh, (ed.) *Transfer of Power,* Vol. I. The development of the Pakistan demand may be studied in Uma Kaura, *Muslims;* C. Khaliquzzaman, *Pathway;* V. P. Menon, *Transfer of Power in India* (1950); and Z. H. Zaidi, 'Aspects of the Development of Muslim League policy, 1937–47', in Philips and Wainwright, *Partition.* For nationalist and Left politics, see S. Gopal, *Nehru;* B. R. Tomlinson, *Indian National Congress;* J. Manor, *Mysore,* A. K. Gopalan, *in the Cause of the People;* T. V. Krishnan, *Krishna Pillai;* G. Chattopadhyay, *Swadhinata-Sangrame-Banglar Chatra-Samaj* (Calcutta, 1980); and Sunil Sen, *Agrarian Struggle in Bengal, 1946–47* (New Delhi, 1972). For economic developments, see Wadia and Merchant, *Our Economic Problem* (6th edn. Bombay, 1959).

iii

There has been relatively little detailed work so far on the Quit India Movement. General studies include Amba Prasad, *Indian Revolt of 1942* (Delhi, 1958); L. Hutchins, *Spontaneous Revolution* (Delhi, 1971); Y. B. Mathur, *Quit India Movement* (Delhi, 1979); and, in some ways more useful though obviously partisan, Govind Sahai, *42 Rebellion* (Delhi, 1947). Certain types of official documentation (including excerpts from seized illegal literature) are easily available: see Mansergh, Vols. II and III; *Indian Annual Register*, July–December, 1942 (this includes Tottenham's *Congress Responsibility for the Disturbances*); and P.N. Chopra, (ed.), *Quit India Movement: British Secret Reports* (Faridabad, 1976). For regional data, see Max Harcourt, 'Kisan Populism and revolution in rural India: the 1942 disturbances in Bihar and east UP', in Low, (ed.), *Congress and the Raj;* R. H. Niblett's fascinating *Congress Rebellion in Azamgarh, August-September 1942* (Allahabad, 1957) S. Henningham, *Peasant Movements*, Ch. VII; H. Mahatab, *History of Freedom Movement in Orissa*, Vol. IV: Satish Samanta, *et al.,* *August-Revolution and Two Years National Government in Midnapar* (Calcutta, 1946); and the excellent recent paper by Gail Omvedt, 'The Satara Parallel Government, 1942–47' (N.M.M.L. seminar, December, 1980).

For developments during the closing years of the war, see Mansergh, Vols. III–V; Wavell, *The Viceroy's Journal* (Oxford, 1973); V. P. Menon, *Transfer of Power;* Wadia and Merchant, *Our Economic Problem;* A. K. Sen, 'Famine Mortality: A Study of the Bengal Famine of 1943', in Hobsbawm, *et al,, Peasants in History,* (Delhi, 1980); D. D. Kosambi, 'The Bourgeoisie comes of age in India' (*Science and Society* 1946), reptd. in *Exasperating Essays,* Poona, n.d.; Rajat Roy, *Industrialization in India;* M. Kidron, *Foreign Investments in India* (London, 1965); A. Mukherji, *Indian Capitalist Class;* M. A. H. Ispahani, *Jinnah;* Hugh Toye, *77ie Springing Tiger* (London, 1959); G. Adhikari, *Pakistan and National Unity* (Bombay, 1942); and A. Johnson, *Another's Harvest* (Bombay, 1946).

CHAPTER 8

The large number of secondary works on 1945–47, overwhelmingly focused on top-level negotiations, include V. P. Menon, *Transfer of Power,* perhaps the most convenient summary; V. P. Menon, *Story of Integration of Indian States* (Bombay, 1956); A. Campbell Johnson, *Mission with Mountbatten* (London, 1951); H. V. Hodson, The *Great Divide* (London, 1969); Penderel Moon, *Divide and Quit* (London, 1961), a moving account of the Punjab riots; Maulana Azad, *India Wins Freedom* (Bombay, 1959); Pyarelal, *Mahatma: The Last Phase,* 2 vols. (Ahmedabad, 1956–58); M. Brecher, *Nehru* and S. Gopal, *Nehru;* C. Khaliquzzaman, *Pathway;* Sudhir Ghosh, *Gandhi's Emissary* (London, 1967); N. K.. Bose, *My Days with Gandhi* (Calcutta 1953) as well as Collins and Lapierre's journalistic best-seller, *Freedom At Midnight* (Delhi, 1976). Popular movements, in sharp contrast, have attracted little scholarly attention so far. Accounts by participants include *The RIN Strike* (by a group of victimized ratings, New Delhi, 1954; reptd?. New Delhi 1981); Sunil Sen, *Agrarian Struggle in Bengal* 1946–47 (New Delhi, 1972); P. Sundarayya, *Telengana People's Struggle and Its Lessons* (Calcutta, 1972); Ravi Narayan Reddi, *Heroic Telengana—Reminiscences and Experiences* (New Delhi, 1973); S. V. Parulekar, 'Liberation Movement among Varlis', in A. R. Desai (ed.), *Peasant Struggles in India* (Bombay, 1979); and K. C. George, *Immortal Punnapra-Vayalar* (New Delhi, 1975). See also G. Chattopadhyay, 'The Almost Revolution', in *Essays in Honour of S. C. Sarkar* (New Delhi, 1976); D. H. Dhanagare, 'Social Origins of Peasant Insurrection in Telengana, (*Contributions to Indian Sociology,* 1974), reptd. in A. R. Desai, *Peasant Struggles* and R. Jeffrey, 'A Sanctified Label—Congress in Travancore Politics, 1938-48', in D. A. Low, (ed.), *Congress and the Raj.* P. C. Joshi's *For the Final Bid For Power* (Bombay, 1945) is useful for understanding Communist tactics during these years.

It will be clear from the text that my account is heavily based on published first-hand sources: Mansergh, *Transfer of Power,* Vols. VI–VIII, above all; also Wavell, *The Viceroy's Journal* [(ed.) Moon Oxford, 1973]; Durga Das's multi-volume edition of *Sardar Patel's Correspondence, 1945–50* (Ahmedabad, 1971); Manibehn Patel and G. M. Nandurkar, *Sardar's Letters—Mostly Unknown,* Vol. IV (Ahmedabad, 1977); and G. D. Birla, *Bapu: A Unique Association—Correspondence, 1940–47* (Bombay, 1977). I have also used Home Political (Internal) and A.I.C.C. files. See also my 'Popular Movements, National Leadership, and the Coming of Freedom with Partition', 1945–47 (*N.M.M.L. seminar,* December, 1980; reprinted, *EPW Annual Number,* 1982).

INDEX

A

Afghanistan, British policy towards, 13–14
Age of Consent Act of 1891, 61
agricultural production, 31–32
al-Din al-Afghani, Jamal, 67
Aligarh Anglo-Muhammadan Oriental College, 66
Aligarh movement, 65–67
All-India Movement, 176–78
All-India States People's Conference, 313
All India Students Federation, 293
anti-autocratic and anti-feudal agitations, 272
anti-Brahrnanical movements, 48–49
anti-feudal peasant movement, 173
anti-*mahajan* riots, 271
anti-*sowkar* Deccan riots, 43
army, 14–15
Aryan tradition, 62
Arya Samaj, 63–65
Assam: Forest Laws and grazing restrictions, 16
Assam tea plantations, 20
Azad Hind Government, 350–51

B

Bagchi, Amiya, 20–21, 26, 32, 34
Banerji, Sasipada, 52
Banerji, Surendranath, 57
Banga Lakshmi Cotton Mills, 100
banking and industrial management, modern methods of, 32–34
Bank of India, 34
Baring, Evelyn, 1
Bengal: Calcutta industrial area, 36; colonies of educated Bengalis, 56–57; revolutionary terrorism, 124–26
Bengali intelligentsia: aloofness from business, 58; *bhadralok,* 57–58; commercial elite, 59; Hindu reform and revival, 60–65; labour riots and, 53; Western-educated groups, 59
Besant, Annie, 129
bhadralok, 33
Bhandarkar, R. G., 61
Bharat Dharma Mahamandal, 65
Bhattacharji, Sabyasachi, 15
Bombay Millowners' Association, 60
Bombay Presidency Association, 60
Bonnarji, W. C., 18
Bose, Subhas Chandra, 217
British capital investment in India, 33
British Chamber of Commerce, Rangoon, 14
British Government in India (1885–1905): agricultural production, 31–32; army, 14–15; capitalist development, 33–36; capitalist production relations, 32–33; colonial economy, 21–22; commercialization of agriculture, 27–28; deindustrialization, 25–26; developments after 1858, 11; drain of wealth, 22–25; encouragement of divisions within Indian elite-groups, 18–19; financial and administrative strains, 15–17; foreign policy, 13–14; imperial and local Legislative Councils, 11; local self-government and council reform, 17–18; military policy, 14; modern methods of banking and industrial management, 32–33; structure and policies, 11; structure of land relations, 29–31; Tories *vs* Liberals, 12–13; Viceregal periods, 11–13; White racism, 19–21
British India: Macaulay's vision of an English-educated intelligentsia, 1; privileges of the Europeans, 1
British Indian finance capitalism, 24
British-owned Exchange Banks, 23

British party divisions, 12–13
Burma, annexation of, 12, 14
Burma, Chettiar traders and moneylenders in, 35
business groups and upper classes, 54–56; 1928 and 1929, 240–42; Bengali Marwaris, 54–55; Gujarati Vanias, 54; 'native' princes and *zamindars,* 55–56; Parsis of Bombay, 54

C

Calcutta Hindu College, 57
Calcutta jute mill riots, 52–54
capitalist development, 33–36
capitalist industrialization, 36
capitalist production relations, 32–33
caste consciousness, 47–50
caste mobility, 47–50
caste movements, 135–39, 208–10
caste solidarity, 47
Chand, Lala Lal, 64
Chandavarkar, N. C., 61
Chauri Chaura incident, 193–95
Chotanagpur Tenancy Act of 1908, 41
Civil Disobedience Movement, 177, 195; Borsad *satyagraha,* 196–97; business realignments, 279–81; in Chittagong, Peshawar and Sholapur, 246–48; constructive work in villages and, 197–99; Council politics, 283–84; Harijan campaign, 281–83; Left alternative, 284–88; Nagpur Flag *satyagraha,* 196–97; official attitudes, 273–75; phases of, 248–54; and *Purna Swaraj,* 242–44; regional variations, 255–64; repression and resistance, 275–79; salt satyagraha, 244–46; Vaikom *satyagraha,* 196–97
civil disturbances, 37
colonial economy, 21–22; banks, export-import firms and managing agency houses, 21; Industrial Revolution, 21; 'mercantilist' phase, 21
commercial elite, 59
commercialization of agriculture, 27–28; tensions within tribal society, 38
communal consciousness, 50–52; Ganapati festival, Maharashtrian, 52; rioting over cow-slaughter, 51–52

communalism, 134–35, 201–4
Communism, emergence of, 212–15; labour upsurge and, 232–36; 'People's War' line, 351–53
constitutional reform, 18
Coral Cotton Mills, 112
cotton excise duty, 79, 85, 99, 212
cotton import duties, 144
cotton trade, 13, 16, 21–22, 25–26, 28–29, 32, 35, 45, 52, 60, 148–52, 178–79, 190, 205, 222, 239
Council Bills, 23
Council politics, 383–84
cow-protection society, 52
cow-slaughter, rioting over, 51–52, 68
Cripps Mission, 329–32
Curzon, Lord, 20–21

D

Deccan Agriculturists' Relief Act of 1879, 44
Deccan Education Society, 69
Deccan famine of 1876–77, 41
Deccan riots, 43–44
deindustrialization, 25–26
Delhi Pact, 268, 270
Deoband Dar-ul-Ulum, 65
depression years, impact on India, 222–25
drain of wealth, 22–25, 73–75; economic and social consequences of World War, 146–54
Dufferin, Lord, 12–14
Durand agreement, 13
Dutt, Guru, 64

E

East India Company, 11, 22
educated natives in Madras, 57
Elgin, Lord, 12
elite-groups, 57, 59
English educated 'middle-class' groups, 12
English-educated professional groups, 2
English education, 56
exports from India, 22–23, 27
extremism (1905–1908), 107–18; in Bombay Presidency, 108–9; impact on the United Provinces, 108; in Madras Presidency, 111–13; in Maharashtra, 113–16; in Punjab, 109–11
Ezhavas of Kerala, 48

INDEX | 421

F

Factory Act, 114
Factory Acts of 1881 and 1891, 52
Faizpur Session, 294–95
Famine Code, 46
fanaticism, 42–43
Floud Commission, 376
foreign policy, 13–14

G

Ganapati festival, Maharashtrian, 52
Gandhi, Mahatma, 374–76; Champaran indigo cultivators, Ahmedabad textile workers, and Kheda peasants, influence on, 158–61; ideology and methods, 154–57; Khilafat movement and, 168–71; reforms, 306; role of rumour, 157–58
Gandhi-Irwin Pact, 219, 266–67, 269
Gangohi, Rashid Ahmed, 65
gantidars, 58
Ghosh, Lalmohan, 18
Gladstone, William Ewart, 13
Gokhale, G. K., 18
Gosh, Rash-behari, 46
Government of India Act, 1935, 288–90
Government of India Act of 1919, 145
Grievances Enquiry Commisson, 272

H

handicrafts trade, 25
Harijan campaign, 281–83
Hindu and Muslim 'communalism,' 50–52
Hindu Defence Fund, 64
Hindu-Muslim elite conflict, 70
Hindu-Muslim tensions, 18–19
Hindu-Muslim unity of 1919–22, 195
Hindu reform and revival, 60–65; Age of Consent issue, 61; Arya Samaj, 63–64; in Bengal, 62–63; in Maharashtra, 63; principles of *brahmacharya* and Vedic training, 64; proposals against child-marriage, 61; in Punjab, 64; secular movements, 65; Theosophical movement, 62; widow remarriage, 61
Hindu Social Reform Association, 61
Hindustan Socialist Republican Army (H.S.R.A.), 230–31

Home Charges, 15, 22–24
Home Rule agitation, 144
Hunter Commission, 58

I

Ilbert Bill, 12, 19
Imperial Councils, 18
imperialism, 36
Imperial Legislative Council, 46
Indian Banking Enquiry Committee Report (1929–30), 240
Indian Civil Service, 1
Indian Councils Act of 1861, 11
Indian Councils Act of 1909, 122
Indian Home Rule Society, 124
Indian independence and partition: Cabinet Mission, 367–70; elections (1945–46), 365–66; I.N.A. trials, 358–63; integration of states, 385–87; Mountbatten Plan, 383–85; post-war negotiations, 355–57; radical movements, 376–82; R.I.N. mutiny, 363–65; Simla Conference, 357–58
Indian intelligentsia, 35
Indian National Congress, 1; bureaucracy and, 301–2; capitalists and, 306–9; communal problem, 302–6; Congress leadership, 75–76; Congress ministries (1937–39), 299–301; consolidation of a Rightwing within, 295–98; extermism and factionalism, 82–86; Khilafat movement and, 168–71; *kisans* and, 310–13; labour and, 309–10; left ideology and, 316–18; objectives and methods, 76–79; phases of politics, 79–81; split among members, 116–18; trends within (1941–42), 325–28; Tripuri session, 318–21
Indian National Evolution, 12
Indian nationalism, 50–52
indigenous textile production, 26
intelligentsia: Congress leadership and, 75–76; against drain of wealth, 73–75; Hindu reform and revival, 60–65; leftism in literature, 293–94; patriotism, expression of, 70–73; social roots of, 56–60; upper-class Muslims, 65–70
12Irish Home Rule
Irish Home Rule movements, 129

Islam, trends in, 65–70
Islamization, 67
Iyer, Muthusamy, 19

J

Jadav, Bhaskarrao, 49
jajmani system, 25–26
Jinnah, M. A., 349
Jorhat Sarvajanik Sabha, 46
jotedars, 30

K

Karachi session, 267–68
Khan, Sir Sayyid Ahmed, 65
Kherwar or Sapha Har movement of the 1870s, 39
Khilafat movement, 68
khoti rights, 59
khuntkatti land system, 40
kisan movements, 175–76, 290–93
Kisan Sabha movement, 272
Kshatriyas, 48
Kurmi-Kshatriya Sabha, 175

L

labour migration, 36
labour movement, 173, 210–12, 225–29, 290–93; Communism and, 232–36
labour riots, 52–54; in Bombay Mills, 52; Calcutta jute mill riots, 52–54
landlord rights, 42; Moplah outbreaks, 42–43
land relations, structure of, 29–31
land tax, 16
Lansdowne, Lord, 12
Legislative Council reforms, 17
Legislative Councils, 11
Lord Cross Bill, 13
Lord Cross' Indian Councils Act of 1892, 17
Lord Stanley's Act, 11
Lucknow Pact, 129
Lucknow Session, 294–95
Lytton, Lord, 12

M

Macaulay's Minutes, 1
Madras: Forest Laws and grazing restrictions, 16; land revenue, 16

mahajans, 27
Mahars of Maharashtra, 48
Mahdi movement, 1885–86, 14
Malaviya, Madan Mohan, 60
Mallaya, Korra, 39
martial races, 48
Marwari expansion, 35
mass politics, emergence of, 143–46
Mazumdar, Ambikacharan, 12
Mehta, Pherozeshah, 18, 128
'middle-class' nationalism, 51–52
millenarianism, 39
moneymarket, organized, 34
Montagu-Chelmsford reforms, 143–46
Moplahs of Malabar, revolt of, 42–43
Moral and Material Progress Reports, 11
Morley and Minto reforms, 118–20
Morris, D. Morris, 25
Mountbatten Plan, 383–85
Muhsin al-Mulk, 66
Muslim intellectuals, 65
Muslim League: advance of, 349–50; and Pakistan movement, 323–26
Muslim tyranny, 65

N

Nagri Pracharini Sabha, 108
Nagri resolution (1900), 108
Naikda forest tribe, agitation of, 39
Namboodripad, E.M.S., 48
Nanawtawi, Muhammad Qasim, 65
Naoroji, Dadabhai, 12
'national bourgeois' development, 55
national movements, 2–3
Nehru, Jawaharlal, 217
Non-Cooperation Movement, 171–72; 1922–27, 204–6; response of different social groups, 178–81; varied dimensions and contradictions of, 181–93
no-revenue movements, 45–47

O

occupancy *raiyats,* legal rights of, 45–46
October Revolution, 126

P

Pallis of northern Tamilnadu, 48
Paramhansa, Ramakrishna, 62

Patidar Yuvak Mandal, 109
Patidar Yuvak Mandel, 134
patriotic literature, 70–73
patriotism, expression of intelligentsia, 70–73
peasant uprisings, 37, 206–8; in Bardoli, 236–40; Calcutta, Noakhali, Bihar, Punjab, 370–74; caste organizations, 48; Gandhi's intervention, 133; in Mewar, 133; in Motihari-Bettiahi region, 134; Telengana peasant armed revolt in Hyderabad, 355
Permanent Settlement, 16, 29, 33
Permanent Settlement Bengal, 58
Phadke, Vasudeo Balvant, 41–42, 46
Phule, Jyotiba, 49
political awakening (1927–1937), 219–21
Poona intelligentsia, 59
Poona Pact, 281
Poona Sarvajanik Sabha, 46
Progressive Writers' Association, 293
pro-landlord modifications, 12
Provincial and Supreme Councils, 1
public administration in Guntur, 16–17
Punjab National Bank, 34
Punnapra-Vayalar movement, 378–79

Q

Quit India Movement: aftermath of, 345–46; all-India pattern, 337–39; regional variations, 341–45; roots of rebellion, 332–36; social groups participating, 339–41

R

racial discrimination, 20
Rahman, Abdur, 13
Rai, Lala Lajpat, 64
raijmels, organization of, 45
railway construction, 27
railway investments, 33
raiyatwari system, 29–30, 34
Raj, Lala Hans, 64
Rajahmundri Social Reform Association, 61
Rajguru, 267
Ram, Lala Munshi, 64
Ram, Lekh, 64
Ramakrishna Mission, 62

Ranade, M. G., 60–61, 71
regional literature and nationalism, 70–73
remittance of profits on British capital, 25
'reserved' forests, 38
revitalization movement, 39
revivalism, 65
revolutionary terrorism, 124–26, 215–17
rioting over cow-slaughter, 51–52
Ripon, Lord, 12
Roberts, Lord, 13, 15
Round Table Conference, 264–66
Rowlatt Act and *satyagraha,* 162–68

S

sabha courts, 68
Salisbury, Tory, 12
samitis, 97–99, 103–4
Sanskritization, 47–50
Santhal rebellion (1855), 39
Sanyal, Sachindranath, 108
Saraswati, Dayanand, 63
Satyashodhak movement, 49
Scientific Society, 66
Secretary of State, 11, 23
Shanans, 48
Simla Deputation, 120–24
Simon Commission, 195, 217, 219, 225–29, 264, 288
Singh, Bhagat, 267
Siva-Narayana sect, 48
Smuts' Indian Relief Act of June 1914, 158
social history (1885–1905): caste consciousness, 47–50; communal consciousness, 50–52; Deccan riots, 43–44; labour riots, 52–54; no-revenue movements, 45–47; Pabna agitation, 44–45; rising of Vasudeo Balvant Phadke, 41–42; tribal movements, 38–41; turbulent history of the Moplahs of Malabar, 42–43
social history (1905–1917): administrative reforms, 88–90; extremism (1905–1908), 107–18; foreign policy, 87–88; Lord Curzon's administration, 87–96; Morley and Minto reforms, 118–20; nationalist intelligentsia *vs* Lord Curzon, 90–91; partition of Bengal, 91–96; revolutionary terrorism, 124–26;

Simla Deputation and Muslim League, 120–24; Swadeshi Movement in Bengal (1905–1908), 96–107
states peoples movements, 313–16
Sterling Bills, 23
Strachey, Sir John, 2, 14, 23
Sukhdev, 267
Surendranath, 18
Swadeshi Movement in Bengal (1905–1908), 96–107; boycott and *Swadeshi* mood, 99–100; Hindu-Muslim relations, 104–5; labour unrest, 101–2; national education efforts, 101; *samitis* or 'national volunteer' movement, 103–4; terrorism, 106–7; trends, 97–99
Swarajist politics, 199–201

T

Tamil literature, 72–73
Tangals of Mambram, 42
taxation, 16
Tebhaga movement, 376–78
Telang, K. T., 61
Telengana movement, 379–82
tenancy bills, 12
tenant rights campaigns, 44–45
terrorism, 106–7; revolutionary, 124–26, 215–17
textile firms, 35
Theosophical movement, 62
Thibaw, King, 14
Thorner, Daniel, 25
Tilak, Balgangadhar, 18, 49, 52, 59, 61, 113–16
Tories *vs* Liberals, 12–14
tribal movements, 38–41, 206–8; Khond rebellion, 132; by Koli group, 42; Naikda forest tribe, agitation of, 39; Nallamalai hills of Cuddapah and Nellore, 131–32; rebellion in 1879–80, 39; Santhal rebellion (1855), 39; 'Tana Bhagat' movement, 132; *Ulgulan* (Great Tumult) of Birsa Munda, 40–41

U

Upper Burma, annexation of, 12
Urdu-Devanagri controversy, 68

V

Vanniya Kula Kshatriya, 48
Viceroy, 11
Vidyasagar, Iswarchandra, 60
Vivekananda, Swami, 62–63

W

Wacha, Dinshaw, 12, 60
Western-educated groups, 59
white 'collective monopoly,' 34
White racism, 19–21
widow remarriage, 61
World War and Indian politics: British policies in India, 329; caste movements, 135–39; communalism, 134–35; economic and social consequences of, 146–54, 328, 346–49; Home Rule agitation, 129–31; joint platform of Moderates, Extremists, and the 'Young Party,' 128–29; peasant uprisings, 133–34; regional sentiments along linguistic lines, 139–41; revolutionary activities, 126–28; second, 321–22; tribal movements, 131–32

Y

'Young Bombay' intellectuals, 60
youth movements, 229–30

Z

Zakaria, Haji Nur Muhammad, 54
zamindari patronage, 55–56
zamindari system, 17, 27, 29, 31, 34, 37, 271; abolition of, 3; Kisan Sabha movement against, 271; Moplah outbreaks against, 42–43; Pabna movement against, 44–45
zamindars, 68, 174
zamindars intelligentsia, 58